## LIST OF PREDEFINED IDENTIFIERS

| | |
|---|---|
| Abs | Pack |
| Arctan | Page |
| Boolean | Pred |
| Char | Put |
| Chr | Read |
| Cos | Readln |
| Dispose | Real |
| Eof | ReSet |
| Eoln | ReWrite |
| Exp | Round |
| False | Sin |
| Get | Sqr |
| Input | Sqrt |
| Integer | Succ |
| Ln | Text |
| MaxInt | True |
| New | Trunc |
| Odd | Unpack |
| Ord | Write |
| Output | Writeln |

# PASCAL: PROBLEM SOLVING AND STRUCTURED PROGRAM DESIGN

# PASCAL: PROBLEM SOLVING AND STRUCTURED PROGRAM DESIGN

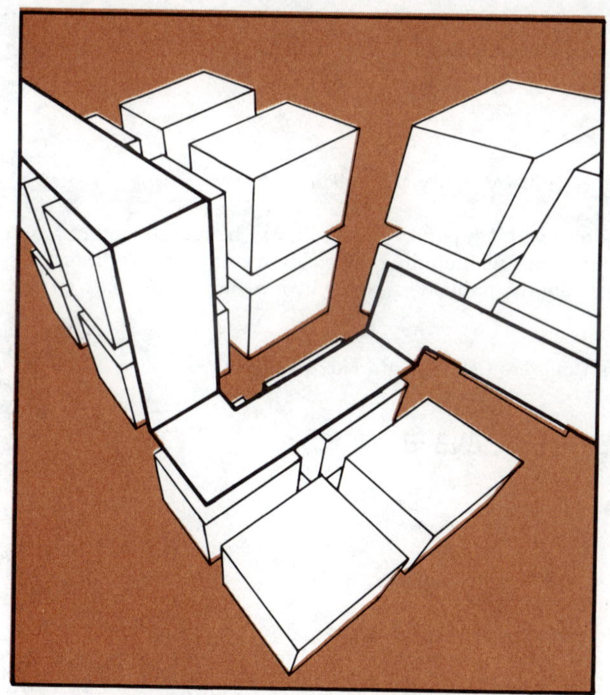

Henry M. Walker

Grinnell College, Grinnell, Iowa

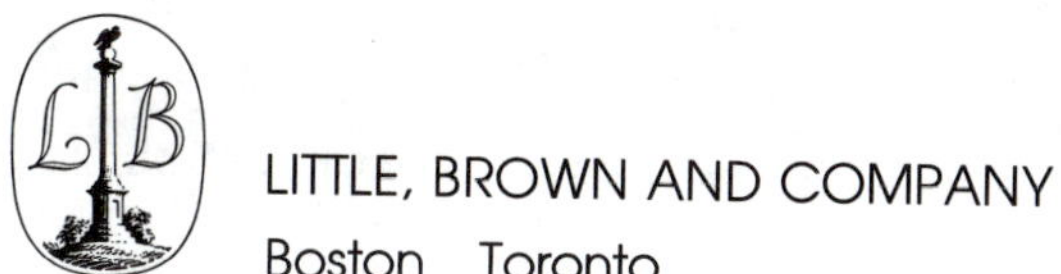

LITTLE, BROWN AND COMPANY
Boston Toronto

**Library of Congress Cataloging-in-Publication Data**

Walker, Henry M., 1947–
Pascal : problem solving and structured program design.

(Little, Brown computer science series)
Includes index.
1. PASCAL (Computer program language) 2. Structured programming. I. Title. II. Series.
QA76.73.P2W35 1986 005.13′3 86-20914
ISBN 0-316-91848-2



Library of Congress Catalog Card No. 86–20914

ISBN 0-316-91848-2

9 8 7 6 5 4 3 2 1

MV

Published simultaneously in Canada
by Little, Brown & Company (Canada) Limited

Printed in the United States of America

*Disclaimer of Liabilities:* Due care has been exercised in the preparation of this book to ensure its effectiveness. The author and publisher make no warranty, expressed or implied, with respect to the programs or other contents of this book. In no event will the author or publisher be liable for direct, indirect, incidental, or consequential damages in connection with or arising from the furnishing, performance, or use of this book.

**Acknowledgments**

Syntax diagrams in Appendix A reproduced from OH! PASCAL by Doug Cooper and Michael Clancy, by permission of Doug Cooper and W.W. Norton & Company, Inc. Copyright © 1982 by W.W. Norton & Company, Inc.

To my parents, Alice K. and Benjamin M. Walker

# PREFACE

At an elementary level, computer programming provides a vehicle by which people give instructions to a computer. By following these instructions, the computer can store, retrieve, and manipulate data in ways that can help people solve many kinds of problems.

Computer programming, when examined more thoroughly, is only part of an extensive process that starts with the initial analysis of problems and continues through stages of problem solving. Computers can be valuable in helping people attain needed solutions to these problems. In this broad context, however, programming is just one important part of the general work of problem solving that also includes such topics as

- Problem solving methodology
- Algorithm design and analysis
- Data structures
- Computer organizations and systems
- Applications

*Pascal: Problem Solving and Structured Program Design* describes computer programming at both of these levels. At the elementary level, the book covers the syntax and semantics of the full ANSI Standard Pascal programming language, and shows how parts of this language can be put together to form working programs. Further, this presentation places this programming material within the more general framework of computer science, which addresses the entire problem solving process. With this orientation, this book is designed to prepare readers for subsequent work in computing.

## Main Features

The presentation in this Pascal programming text includes many features designed to aid in the learning process.

- *Problem solving orientation and methodology*

  Structured problem solving and top-down, modular design are emphasized. Most examples begin with a statement of a problem, followed by an analysis of the problem and an appropriate outline for solution. Thus, structured software appears as a natural consequence of good analysis rather than as a pedagogical nicety.

- *Tie between problem solving methodology and program structure*

  With this orientation toward problem solving, Pascal is viewed as a programming language which encourages good problem solving techniques and which is sufficiently rich to provide exposure to appropriate control structures and data types that are seen in many modern languages.

- *Motivation of topics from applications*

  The role of computers in solving problems is stressed, and various techniques and language constructs are introduced as a means of finding solutions to given problems.

- *Early treatment of procedures and functions*

  Simple procedures and functions are introduced very early (in Chapters 3 and 4) to emphasize top-down design and modular program structure. Thus, from an early stage, students can incorporate modularization, using procedures and functions, as a natural part of their approach to problem solving.

- *Spiral approach*

  Many topics in computing and computer science can be viewed from several levels of complexity and sophistication. For example, procedures and functions can be considered without parameters; with simple use of value or reference parameters; or with full consideration of side-effects, aliases, and multiple declarations. In such cases, this text often divides these topics into several pieces and then covers the pieces in separate chapters. Thus, beginning students can write simple algorithms and programs using some of the easier aspects of a subject. Then, as they gain experience, they are prepared for more advanced techniques.

- *Presentation via examples*

  Algorithms and language constructs often are introduced via frequent annotated examples. Readers can see how features of Pascal can be used as well as what the syntax and semantics are. Further, the many Pascal programs can serve as models for beginners starting to write their own programs.

- *Data structures introduced at several levels, from simple data types to abstract data structures*

  Data types and structures are introduced at various levels. At the beginning the text considers only a few simple data types, so that the variety of data available does not diffuse the focus on other programming constructs (procedures, functions, loops, conditional statements). Then additional simple data types are introduced. Next, data are grouped in records and sets. Finally, linked lists and trees are presented to introduce the general concept of abstract data structures, with objects and operations.

- *Discussion of trees and recursion*

  The text ties together many programming techniques and concepts by introducing both the concept of trees and the technique of recursion in Chapter 16. With this discussion of trees, students see a major application of pointers beyond simple linked lists, and they can begin to see how general data structures can be defined. Then, these tree structures provide a natural framework for discussing the important and powerful technique of recursion.

- *Material covered consistent with recommended introductory sequences*

  Our coverage of material is consistent with several recommendations for introductory courses or course sequences in computer science. In particular, the text covers

  1. all topics included by the ACM Curriculum Committee Task Force for course CS1.[1]
  2. all topics suggested by the IEEE Computer Society for course SE-1.[2]
  3. all topics for the CS1 course described in the Model Curriculum for Liberal Arts Colleges developed in workshops sponsored by the Alfred P. Sloan Foundation.[3]
  4. all required topics suggested by the Elementary and Secondary Schools Subcommittee for an introductory one-year sequence entitled Introduction to Computer Science I.[4]

---

[1]ACM Curriculum Committee Task Force for CS1, "Recommended Curriculum for CS1, 1984," *Communications of the Association for Computing Machinery*, Vol. 27, No. 10, October 1984, pp. 998–1001.

[2]IEEE Computer Society, "A Curriculum in Computer Science and Engineering," *IEEE Computer Society Education Committee Report* (Rev. 1), November 1976.

[3]Norman E. Gibbs and Allen B. Tucker, "A Model Curriculum for a Liberal Arts Degree in Computer Science," *Communications of the Association for Computing Machinery*, Vol. 29, No. 3, March 1986, pp. 202–210.

[4]Elementary and Secondary Schools Subcommittee of the Association for Computing Machinery, *Computer Science for Secondary Schools: Course Content*, Draft dated July 1984, and subsequent drafts.

- *Wide variety of applications illustrated*

  The text includes varied applications, including a large number of both numeric and nonnumeric problems. Examples introduce many of these applications, and problems indicate many possible extensions and additional uses.

- *Adherence to ANSI Standard Pascal*

  Except where specifically noted, all sample Pascal programs in the text conform to the ANSI Standard Pascal Programming Language. All programs also have been compiled and run, generating the output shown in the text.

  In the few cases where the ANSI Standard is not followed, extensions to Pascal are included to illustrate more general computing concepts. For example, separate compilation is mentioned because this topic is important in many large-scale software applications.

- *Concise chapter reviews*

  Each chapter ends with a list of key words, phrases, and concepts; a list of Pascal statements covered in the chapter; and a Chapter Summary.

- *Many diverse problems*

  Each chapter contains a substantial number of exercises, covering a wide range of difficulty.

- *Workbook available*

  A workbook, with chapter reviews, additional examples, and short-answer questions, is available to help guide students through this book.

## Prerequisites

The text is largely self-contained, and minimal background is assumed. In particular, no prior computing experience is assumed. Of course, some of the beginning stages of programming may proceed faster if the reader has worked with computers in some way. Such background is not necessary, however.

Also, this text assumes that the reader is comfortable only with mathematics through algebra, although, in a few cases, some analysis of algorithms does require minimal acquaintance with logarithms. Beyond this minimal level the text is structured so that no special mathematics background is required to read it. In a few cases, exercises suggest applications in other areas, such as chemistry or mathematics, and these problems may require some additional experience. Such problems are always clearly marked, though, and may be safely skipped.

## Acknowledgments

The development of this book has been greatly aided by the contributions of many people, and the author would like to express his deep thanks to all those who helped. First, the author wishes to thank Lee Ripley, formerly of Little, Brown, who was invaluable in the initial development of the manuscript itself. The author also thanks Little, Brown's Computer Science Editor, Tom Casson, for his help in resolving various issues in the development and production of this book.

Many parts of this text have benefited greatly from the helpful comments and reviews of many people. In particular, the author wants to thank Derald Boline, Shawnee Mission East High School; Steven Bruell, University of Minnesota; Henry Etlinger, Rochester Institute of Technology; Robert Fischer, De Paul University; Wayne Gibson, Santa Ana College; James Gips, Boston College; Peter Henderson, SUNY, Stony Brook; Joseph Kent, University of Richmond; Harry Lewis, Harvard University; David Rine, Western Illinois and George Mason Universities; Robert Streett, Boston University; Patrick Wheatley, California Polytechnic State University; Lawrence Wright, Williams College; Marvin Zelkowitz, University of Maryland. I also want to thank David Rine for his contributions to the workbook developed in conjunction with this book.

In addition, the author wants to thank these people who contributed exercises: Arnold Adelberg, Charles Duke, Eugene Herman, Thomas Moberg, and John Stone from Grinnell College; and John Vogel.

The author also has received great encouragement and support from Grinnell College, and special thanks are due Dean Catherine Frazer for her active interest in this project and for her allocation of part of a special grant to Grinnell College from the Exxon Educational Foundation for the preparation of this manuscript. In addition, I want to express my thanks to Ms. Betty Deminoff for her expert typing and editing of drafts of the manuscript.

I am deeply grateful to my family, my wife Terry and my daughters Donna and Barbara, for encouraging me throughout the development of this book and for tolerating my moods during the writing and revision. Their understanding and support were essential to the entire project.

Finally, I want to thank my parents, Alice K. and Benjamin M. Walker, for their loving support and encouragement throughout my life. They helped me grow in many ways, and my development has depended greatly upon their guidance and concern. The background they gave me has been essential in completing a project of this type, and it is to them that this book is dedicated.

# BRIEF CONTENTS

# CONTENTS

# PASCAL:
# PROBLEM SOLVING AND STRUCTURED PROGRAM DESIGN

# CHAPTER 1

# PROBLEM SOLVING AND PROGRAMMING

Over the past several years, we have seen a dramatic rise in the widespread popularity of computers, and many applications have been affected by computing in major ways. Perhaps one of the most basic reasons for this growth depends on the help that computers can give people in answering questions that could not be answered as quickly or as completely without the use of these sophisticated machines. When computers are used as tools to help solve problems, people still must take an active role in analyzing the problem, formulating a plan of attack, and instructing a computer what steps to follow. Computers can be extremely valuable aids in many ways, but computers depend on people to specify how a solution to a problem can be obtained.

This text focuses much of its attention on one part of the problem solving effort, namely programming, which is the process of instructing a computer what steps to follow. However, throughout programming, we need to recognize that problem solving requires other activities as well. Therefore, we begin our study of programming by reviewing the entire problem solving process.

## SECTION 1.1 THE PROCESS OF PROBLEM SOLVING

When we discuss problem solving, we mean the process of finding answers to questions. The actual process of finding answers frequently depends, however, upon the nature of the questions themselves. For example, some problems may involve ideas that we understand well and that we can apply easily. In solving these problems, we may be able to derive a solution easily and quickly, without resorting to careful analysis or research. We may even be able to write down an answer with little thought at all. However, when problems become more involved and when computers are used as tools in the solution, we may need to be more methodical in our attempts to find solutions. For these harder problems, we will find it useful to identify some major steps that apply in a large number of situations. Our main points are illustrated in Figure 1–1.

1. In problem solving, we often begin with an **initial statement of the problem** that is quite general and vague. For example, I may decide to fix my stereo when I notice that something is missing in the sound of records being played.
2. Once we have this general topic, we must sharpen our problem so that we know precisely what we are assuming and what we are looking for (our results). In the stereo example, a more precise statement of the problem might be: No sound comes out of the left speaker when I play records. What needs to be fixed? This formulation of a problem in precise terms is often called the **specification of requirements.**
3. For nontrivial problems, we then need to develop a **general design or plan** to attack the problem. In working with the stereo system, I might approach the problem by trying to identify the component (turntable, amplifier, speaker, connecting wires) where the sound is lost.
4. Once we have developed our general design, we know what approach to take, but not how each part of the plan is to be carried out efficiently. The next step includes developing one or more techniques or **algorithms** to accomplish the individual steps in the general design. To fix the stereo, I must check an owner's manual to determine specific ways of testing the turntable or amplifier. I must also decide which specific connecting wires need testing. I need to specify tests for checking each part of the system. This step is sometimes called a **detailed design or plan.** We will discuss algorithm development more in the next section and again in later sections of the book.
5. Once our detailed design is complete, we must describe our algorithm to the computer in a detailed, step-by-step way, so that the computer can follow these required steps to obtain the solution. In this description, we need to write instructions in a language that a computer can interpret. This writing of computer instructions is called **programming** or **coding,** and the resulting algorithmic description for the computer is called a **computer program.**

FIGURE 1–1 • **Process of Problem Solving Using Computers**

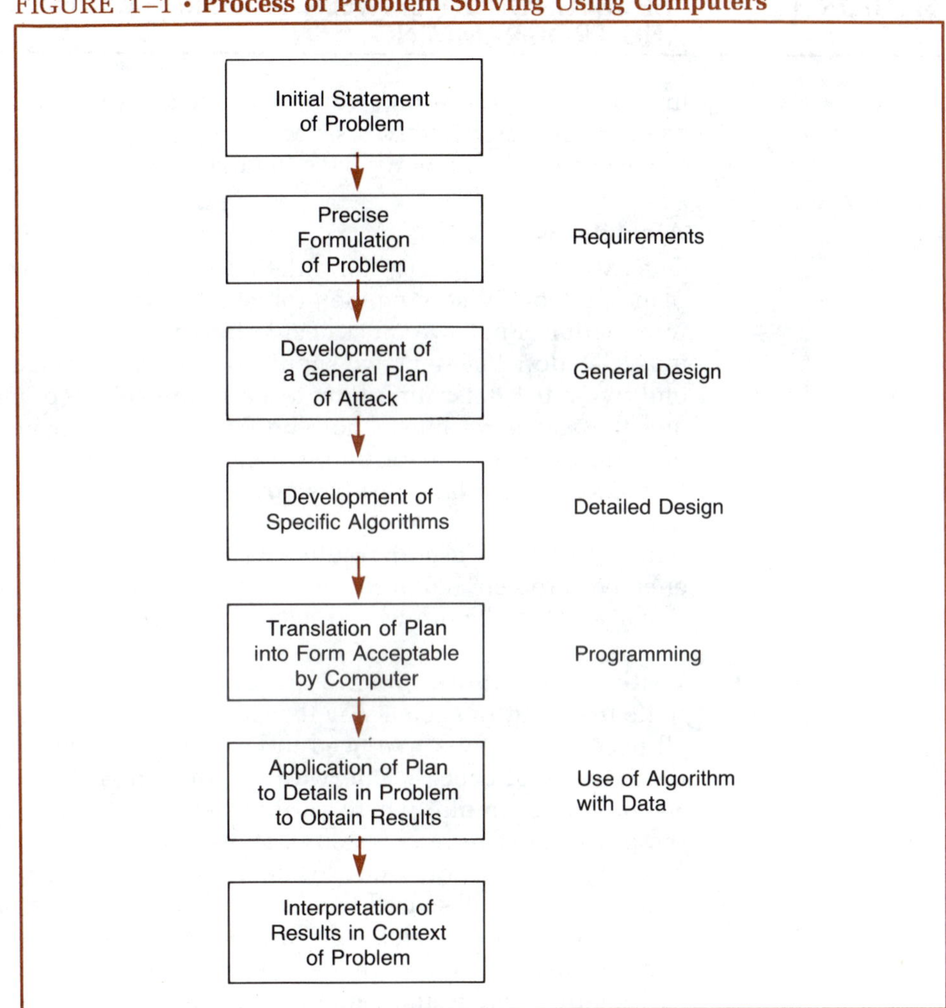


6. Once our detailed design is complete, we must apply our algorithms to the data. I might follow through the checklist and tests for the stereo and find that some connections have become loose.
7. Finally, we need to interpret our results in the context of the problem. Once I have identified a problem with wire connections, I can infer that these connections were the likely cause of the trouble and proceed to fix the stereo.

Of course, the steps in this process may be followed in a systematic manner, or various parts of these steps may be combined. When we analyze many types of problems, however, we see that these steps normally occur.

## SECTION 1.2 THE DISTINCTION BETWEEN ALGORITHM DESIGN AND PROGRAMMING

In the previous section, we noted that the first step in problem solving using a computer involves several major steps. In this section, we emphasize some distinctions we have made in this process.

### Algorithms

Once we have a precise formulation of a problem, we need to develop a plan of attack for solving the problem. Typically, this requires two types of information. First, we must decide how to structure our attack; that is, we must decide what steps we should follow to have a successful attack. Second, we must determine how to perform each step. Once we have identified the steps, we must know how to carry them out. In the process, we have developed an algorithm, which is a logical series of steps we can follow to solve a problem. At this point in our problem solving, we often have not used a computer at all; we are simply trying to describe a solution that will help us get useful results. As we will see throughout this book, in effective problem solving, we will need to develop and understand effective algorithms before we can use the computer in useful ways.

**Writing Algorithms.** As we are developing our algorithms, we need to write them out in such a way that we can see both their basic structure and all necessary details. We need to keep track of the overall ideas as well as the individual pieces. One way of doing this is with flowcharts. Figure 1–1 is one example, where various steps in the algorithm are stated and the progression from one step to another is illustrated by arrows. For complex algorithms, however, flowcharts can be hard to follow. The overall structure can be obscured by a mass of arrows and major steps can become confused with minor details. Flowcharts do not encourage careful structuring of steps, and so flowcharts will not be used much in this text.

Another way to indicate the structure of various steps is to use an outline form, where the major steps are shown at one level and the details are shown to be subsidiary. In contrast to flowcharting, we will see that outlining does work quite well with complex problems. The major headings remain unchanged as more details are added. In this book, therefore, we will concentrate on the use of outlines to develop algorithms to solve problems. Our motivation for learning about computers is our hope that computers can help us in problem solving, and we will see that algorithms written in outline form can be used effectively with computers.

### Programming

Once algorithms have been written out, we know what work needs to be done if we are to solve a problem. Our next step is to write our algorithm in sufficient detail and in an appropriate language so that a computer can follow the necessary steps. This is the concept of a **computer program.** A computer program is a detailed, step-by-step set of instructions for performing a task, written in a language that a computer can interpret.

When writing a program, we must realize that the computer will not make inferences about steps that have been omitted or about the order of steps. We must tell the machine what steps to perform in what order, for a machine will do only what we tell it to do.

Computers can follow instructions very quickly and accurately, but they do not analyze instructions; they perform incorrect operations if we tell them to do so. They make no judgments about what we really mean, if we do not write out our intentions explicitly. They cannot fill in missing steps. They will not correct us if we tell them to perform operations in an incorrect order. They must be given instructions in a carefully defined format. The omission of even a single semicolon may prevent a computer from processing a program.

That machines will only follow our instructions may be quite different from the image of computers in movies or science fiction stories. Computers are often portrayed as having great intellectual powers capable of making incredible inferences at lightning speed. In reality, computers can help us use our algorithms very effectively, but we must tell computers what to do, with great care and precision.

Programming, then, is the process of instructing the computer what to do. However, all programming depends on the earlier step of algorithm design, where we determine how our solution should proceed. Thus, as we are learning to program, we also need to pay attention to approaches for developing algorithms. For this reason, in this text, we regularly outline algorithms as part of the problem solving process. Programming then follows as a natural next step.

## SECTION 1.3 USING PROGRAMS TO SOLVE PROBLEMS

We have noted that we must write algorithms in language that computers can interpret if we wish to use computers as a tool in the problem solving process. In this section we will look at this computer language somewhat more carefully and consider some characteristics of the machines we are likely to encounter. In many respects, these details of programming language and hardware are only tangential to the problem solving process, just as setting margins and inserting paper in an electric typewriter are tangential to writing a paper. Thus we will outline only the major points in the process; we will not worry at this point about many subtleties. We do need to have some general overview of the process, however, if we are to understand how we can use computers easily and effectively.

## Software Environment

A computer itself is essentially a mass of electrical switching circuits, so our instructions must ultimately take the form of information about circuits. We might write "0" for a circuit where no current flows or where a low voltage is detected and "1" for a circuit where current flows or where a high voltage is found. In this code, instructions must end up in a form such as "01101011," which indicates something about how the computer circuitry is to behave.

**Computer Languages.** In early machines all instructions were written in the 01 form, and algorithms were translated into appropriate sequences of 0s and 1s, called **machine language.** Even today all instructions must end up in this form before a computer can follow them. Different machines may use different sequences of 0s and 1s to represent an instruction, but each machine does have its own machine language. While this form of language may be essential for machines, we can see that it is not a form that people normally find comfortable or natural.

People like to think more abstractly. Over the years, therefore, a variety of other languages have been developed for computers, and these languages allow us to specify our instructions in a more natural way than is possible with machine language. These people-oriented languages are called **high-level languages,** and programming in them is a two-step operation. First, we write instructions in an appropriate high-level language; then, the program must be translated to machine language for the computer to follow (see Figure 1–2).

**Translation to Machine Language.** Fortunately, the second step of translation can be done by a computer itself, as long as we have written the program in an appropriate format, following appropriate rules of grammar for that language. This translation can be done in two ways. The whole program may be translated to machine language at one time, before the machine tries to follow the instructions. In this case we say the program is **compiled,** and the translator is called a **compiler.** The second approach is for the instructions to be translated one at a time, with the machine following one instruction before it translates the next. Here we say our language is **interpreted,** and the translator is called an **interpreter.** In either case, instructions in a relatively natural language are translated to machine language, and the computer follows the machine-language versions of the program.

Throughout this text we will have to be aware of both parts of writing programs. We will concentrate on writing instructions in high-level languages, but we will have to be aware of translation. If mistakes are made in writing a program, translation may be impossible; we will identify some errors that are frequently made. Other errors may translate into valid machine-language programs, but produce errors or omissions in logic. We will see some helpful ways to find and correct these errors as well.

FIGURE 1–2 • **Steps for Programming in High-Level Languages**

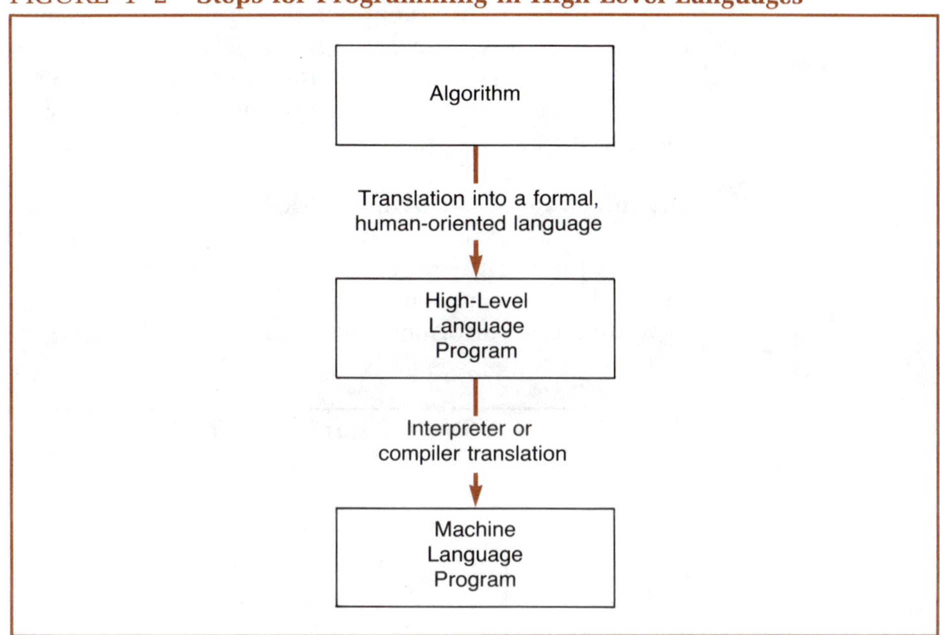


Language compilers and interpreters are often part of a general collection of tools that can help us write, modify, test, and run programs. This general set of tools comprises a **software environment,** and frequently this environment includes capabilities for editing and monitoring programs, as well as translating and running them.

**Pascal.** In this text we will concentrate on one high-level language, called **Pascal,** because this language contains features common to many languages and because this language is particularly well suited to problem solving. Pascal is new enough (it was first introduced about 1970) that it reflects much of what was learned from earlier languages, but Pascal is old enough to be commonly available. In 1982 a National Standard Pascal was adopted by the American National Standards Institute,[1] and so the Pascal found on one machine will usually run on other machines as well. Some versions of Pascal have some extra features, but most versions contain the same fundamental features.

---

[1] *IEEE Standard Pascal Computer Programming Language,* approved September 17, 1981, IEEE Standards Board; approved December 16, 1982, American National Standards Institute. Sponsored jointly by the IEEE Pascal Standards Committee of the IEEE Computer Society and ANSI/X359 of the American National Standards Committee X3. Published by the Institute of Electrical and Electronic Engineers, New York, 1983.

## Hardware Environment

The software environment must be built for particular machinery. Each machine has its own machine language and its own special capabilities, although some features are common to most computers. In programming, we must consider the **hardware environment** as well as the software environment (see Figure 1–3).

**Organization of Hardware.** Most computers are organized in much the same way, although details may differ dramatically. The heart of the computer is the **central processing unit (CPU),** which controls all the functioning of the machine. The CPU determines what instructions are performed, how they are performed, what data are to be used, and where the results

FIGURE 1–3 • **A Typical Hardware Configuration**

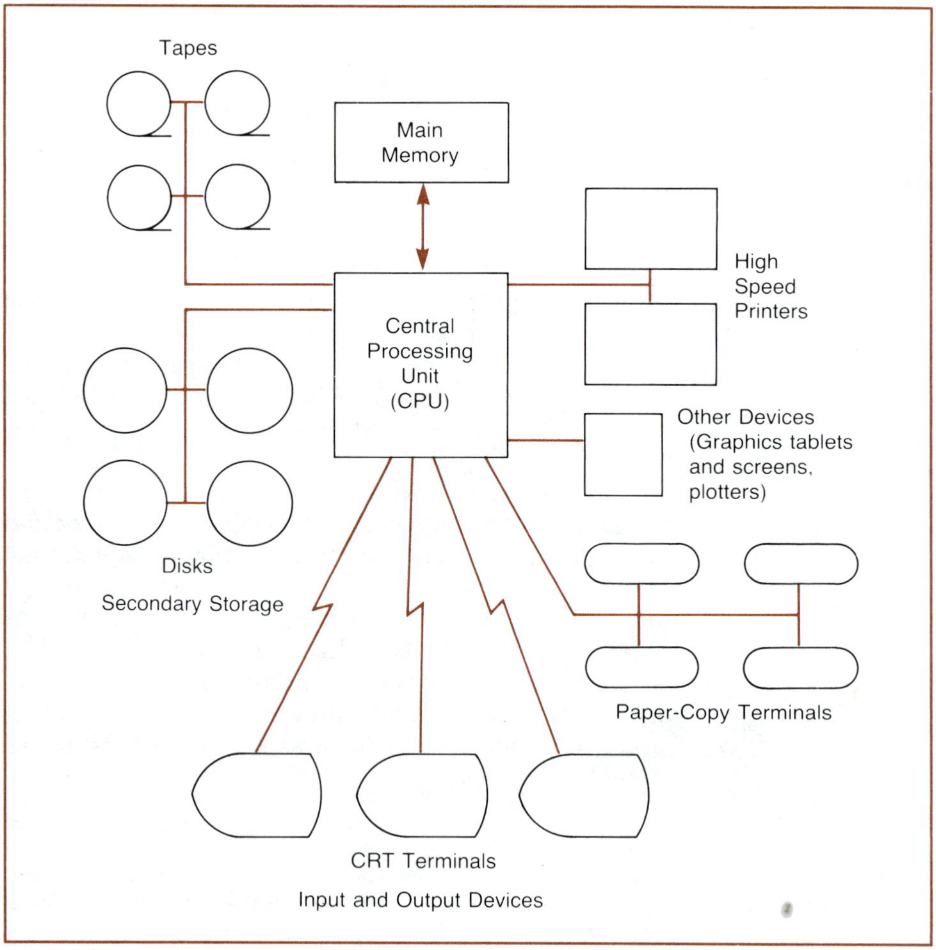

are to be put. The CPU acts as the manager of the computer, and all other work in the computer is done on command from the CPU.

Connected closely with the CPU itself is the **main memory** of the computer. In most cases, main memory is located physically close to the CPU, often in the same cabinet, and data can move between main memory and the CPU very rapidly. During processing, information is normally stored in main memory, where it can be used quickly and easily.

Most of the other machinery in a computer is designed either to store information or to move information in and out of the CPU and main memory. This equipment, such as keyboards, printers, terminals, and storage devices, is sometimes called the **peripheral equipment** or the **peripherals,** and is often physically distinct from the CPU and main memory, with wires or cables running from one cabinet to the next.

Long-term or **secondary storage** comes in several forms, with the most common being **disks** and **tapes.** Disks have two basic forms: hard disks and floppy disks. Both types of disks look much like phonograph records, and an "arm" moves to the correct band or cylinder to store or retrieve information. Tapes follow the same principle for computers as for audio; information is stored as magnetic impulses and these impulses are read as the tape moves over sensors or heads. Both disks and tapes have the capacity to store large amounts of data, but in each case some mechanical activity is needed to retrieve the data. Thus, disks and tapes require more time to process information than the electronic main memory, but they can store much more information.

**Input and output devices** also come in several forms. Some devices, such as **high-speed printers,** are designed to print data rapidly, but they are unable to move data into the CPU. Other devices, called **terminals,** allow data to flow both to and from the CPU. Most terminals have keyboards on which users type information to the CPU, while information coming back is either printed on paper or displayed on a **cathode-ray tube (CRT),** which looks like a television screen. On occasions, other approaches are used for moving information in and out of the CPU. Paper cards and paper tape can be punched, with the position of the holes indicating the data. In recent years, however, cards and paper tape have become completely out of date, and magnetic tape is used instead.

In many cases, programming may not require extensive knowledge of these various units, but some applications will require planning what information will be stored where, at what time. Thus a basic understanding of the various pieces of hardware is needed for effective use of a computer.

**Running a Program.** As an example of how these processes work, this outline shows what happens when we run a simple program:

1. From a terminal, we type our program into the CPU.
2. The CPU may store the program in main memory or on a disk.

3. When we want to compile the program to get machine language instructions, we tell the CPU to use a compiler (which is usually stored on a disk). The CPU follows the directions from the compiler to get the machine instructions needed.
4. The machine instructions are stored in main memory or on a disk.
5. The CPU runs the program, following the machine language instructions.
6. If needed, data for analysis are typed into the CPU from a terminal.
7. The CPU prints the results at a terminal.

Throughout this process, the CPU controls all activities, going to the terminal (for the program or data), main memory (for storing the program and the corresponding machine language instructions), and secondary storage (for the compiler) as needed.

## SECTION 1.4 THE ROLE OF CAREFUL METHODOLOGY

### A Top-Down Methodology

At this point it is useful to formulate a general strategy for approaching problems. To begin, we make two observations: First, short, easy problems often require less time and effort than hard problems. Second, we are less likely to make mistakes if the answers are short and straightforward. While these observations may not seem profound, they do suggest a general approach to solving difficult problems. The idea, simply, is to reduce complicated problems to a series of simple ones that we can solve without trouble. This approach, called a **top-down methodology** for problem solving, starts with the major pieces and gets down to the details later.

To be more specific, when we have a hard problem, we will divide it into small, (usually) easier subproblems. When necessary, we will subdivide these smaller problems. At the end of the dividing process, we will have a collection of relatively simple tasks to accomplish, and we can hope to have little difficulty solving these easy pieces.

You will note that this is precisely the process followed in writing an outline, so it is an approach with which we are somewhat familiar. Begin with the major steps or tasks and divide them into smaller, more manageable pieces.

This same approach is seen in the organization of books or large papers. The entire book discusses a subject (e.g., Pascal: Problem Solving and Structured Program Design), but that subject is too big to work with all at once. Thus the book is divided into chapters (e.g., Chapter 1, Problem Solving and Programming), so the author can focus on one part of the topic at a time. The one topic may be too large to be manageable, so the chapter is divided into sections (e.g., Section 4, The Role of Careful Methodology). If the sections are still too big, they can be broken down (e.g., an example about book organization). If the outline is carefully structured, the author will find that each paragraph and sentence contributes to the overall book, and the text has a coherent style and content.

Throughout this text, we will emphasize a structured methodology that will allow us to solve complex problems. We will normally outline solutions before writing programs, and we will structure our algorithms carefully. In some cases, this careful approach may seem unnecessarily formal for the problem at hand. If you can become comfortable with the style of structuring problems and working from general steps to details, however, you will be ready to attack complex problems later on.

## SUMMARY

1. The problem solving process frequently involves the following major steps:
   a. Initial statement of problem
   b. Precise formulation of problem—**requirements**
   c. Development of a plan of attack—**general design**
   d. Determination of an efficient **algorithm** to perform each task in the general design—**detailed design**
   e. Translation of algorithm into a language that a computer can interpret—**programming** or **coding**
   f. Use of algorithm with data from problem—algorithm **execution**
   g. **Interpretation** of results
2. When a computer processes data following an algorithm, the computer requires that instructions be coded in a **machine language,** which can be awkward for people. **High-level languages,** such as Pascal, have emerged to help people communicate with computers. People translate algorithms into high-level language programs, and computers themselves translate **(compile** or **interpret)** the programs into machine language.

## EXERCISES

1.1 Write a careful definition of each of the key terms for this chapter.

1.2 The organization of this chapter illustrates the top-down methodology. The major problem solving steps are shown in Section 1.1 and expanded in later sections.

Outline this chapter, with the major problem solving steps as the main headings. Identify major themes in the sections as secondary headings. Subdivide headings as needed, and organize details under the appropriate headings.

1.3 Review the flow of information for running a small program (Section

1.3). At each step, identify what the CPU is doing, where it is getting information, and where it is sending the results of that step.

**1.4** For each of the following situations, develop a detailed algorithm for performing the desired task.

**a.** Filling your car's gas tank and checking the oil.

**b.** Obtaining money from an automatic teller banking machine.

**c.** Making a cup of coffee. (*Caution:* In this problem you must decide what type of coffee and what type of coffeemaker you will use!)

**d.** Paying a baby sitter for hours worked. The sitter receives $1.25 an hour from 6:00 AM to 9:00 PM, $1.00 an hour between 9:00 PM and midnight, and $1.50 an hour for time in the early morning, before 6:00 AM. (This pay scale reflects the family's schedule; the kids go to bed at 9:00 PM. The pay scale also acknowledges that the sitter has early-morning classes, which make late nights difficult.)

**1.5** Consider the following three approaches for finding a word in a dictionary.

*Approach A*

- *Step 1.* Look at the first word in the dictionary. Compare this first word with your word. If they match, you have found your word and you may stop.
- *Step 2.* Look at the second word in the dictionary. Compare this word with your word. If they match, you have found your word and you may stop.
- *Subsequent steps.* Continue looking at successive words and comparing until you have found your word or until you run out of words in the dictionary.

*Approach B*

- *Step 1.* Look at the first letter of your word. Use the tabs in the dictionary to turn to the page where words beginning with that letter start (i.e., turn to the beginning of the As, or Bs, . . . ).
- *Step 2.* Proceed word by word as in Approach A.

*Approach C*

- *Step 1.* Turn to the middle page of the dictionary. Using the key words at the top of the page, see if your word is before that page, on that page, or after that page. If your word is on that page, proceed with the last step below. Otherwise, you have found which half of the book your word is on; continue with the next step.
- *Step 2.* Divide your half of the dictionary in half again. (You are now determining which quarter of the book your word is in.) See if your word is in the first part, on that page, or in the last part.
- *Next Steps.* Continue dividing parts of the dictionary in half until you find the page your word is on.
- *Final Step.* When you find the correct page, go through the words one at a time (as in Approach A) until you find your word.

Each of these approaches will allow you to find your word in the dictionary. Informally analyze each approach. Describe which approach you like best. Is there a fourth approach that you like better than any of these? If so, describe it.

## KEY TERMS, PHRASES, AND CONCEPTS

| | |
|---|---|
| Algorithm | Interpreter |
| Algorithm Execution | Machine Language |
| Cathode-Ray Tube (CRT) | Main Memory |
| Central Processing Unit (CPU) | Pascal |
| Coding | Peripherals |
| Compiler | Printer |
| Computer Program | Programming |
| Design | Requirements |
| Detailed Design | Secondary Storage |
| Disk | Software Environment |
| Hardware Environment | Specifications |
| High-Level Language | Tape |
| General Design | Terminals |
| Input and Output Devices | Top-Down Methodology |

# CHAPTER 2

# THE FIRST STEPS WITH SIMPLE EXAMPLES

In Chapter 1 we observed that a major reason for the widespread use of computers was their capacity to help people solve problems. In this chapter we consider some simple problems, and we will see how to use the computer to help us find the answers.

Throughout the chapter, our applications will be quite elementary; we will use the computer as little more than a simple electronic calculator. This will allow us to become comfortable with much of the form, or syntax, of computer programs written in Pascal. At first the details of format may appear a bit overwhelming, as many pieces must fit together to get a complete program. One analogy would be learning to drive a car. If you know how to drive, you may remember that learning to drive involved many details, including steering, signaling, shifting, braking, and accelerating. Certain specialized maneuvers, such as parking or starting on a hill, had to be mastered. When you were learning to drive you had to think carefully about each detail, and it took time before you could perform the common maneuvers smoothly. After some practice, however, these details became automatic, and you can now concentrate more on general traffic patterns, nearby drivers, etc.

Your experience in programming will be similar. After the first few programs, you can expect many of the beginning details to become familiar and automatic. Eventually, in later chapters, you will be able to look at more complicated problems without being sidetracked by details of form.

## SECTION 2.1 EXAMPLE: COMPUTING UNIT PRICING

We begin by considering a simple problem.

**PROBLEM 2.1**

In a store, we want to compute the unit cost for a package. Write a program that will compute the cost per ounce for a particular package.

### Solution to Problem 2.1

To compute unit cost, we will need to know the size of each package and its cost. For convenience, we decide to measure size in ounces (rather than in pounds, grams, or some other weight). Cost can be in dollars.

Our solution can have the following steps.

### Outline for Problem 2.1

**I.** Determine size and cost of the package
- **A.** Determine size (in ounces)
- **B.** Determine cost (in dollars)

**II.** Compute cost per ounce
The appropriate formula will be

$$\text{cost per ounce} = \text{cost/size.}$$

**III.** Write down cost per ounce as the final answer

From this outline we can now write a Pascal program that will perform these steps.

```
Program UnitPricing (Output);
```

This Pascal 'Program' is called by the name 'UnitPricing' and this program will print some 'Output'.

```
{This program computes cost per ounce,
given cost and number of ounces.}
```

We describe in words what the program does, as an integral part of the program.

```
Var Ounces, Cost, CostPerOunce: Real;
```

In this program, we will use variables called 'Ounces', 'Cost', and 'CostPerOunce'.

```
Begin                                                    Our computations start here.

    {I.  Determine size and cost of the package}         We include our outline in our
         {Determine size (in ounces)}                    program as well.

         Ounces := 16.0;                                 This size was picked arbitrarily.

         {Determine cost (in dollars)}

         Cost := 1.25;                                   This cost was also picked at
                                                         random.
    {II. Compute Cost Per Ounce}

         CostPerOunce := Cost / Ounces;                  This is the formula we noted in
                                                         our outline.

    {III.Write down the cost per ounce as the final answer}

         Writeln(CostPerOunce)

End.                                                     Our program "End's" here with a
                                                         period.
```

This Pascal program, as written, is complete and ready to be typed into a computer. When our typing is complete, we can tell the machine to compile the program (translate it to machine language) and run it (follow the instructions).

After running the program, the computer prints

```
7.812500E-02
```

This output is the same as $7.812500 \times 10^{-2}$ or 0.078125.

In this particular program, we compute the cost per ounce for a 16 ounce package costing $1.25. We could compute the unit price for a package of a different size or cost by changing the appropriate lines in our program. Once these changes were made, the revised program would be recompiled and run to yield the new unit price.

From this example, we see that Pascal programs can be written in a form that is easy to read and allows us to follow our outline solution very closely. The program includes all the steps we want performed, and these steps are placed in the correct order for solving our problem.

## SECTION 2.2 ELEMENTS OF A SIMPLE PROGRAM

The program in Section 2.1 illustrates many of the pieces that make up a Pascal program. In this section we will consider these pieces in some detail.

We will identify three general types of statements:

- Statements that tell the computer about the structure of the program.
- Statements that tell the computer about the work that must be performed at each step.
- Statements that act as notes for ourselves in reading the program and are ignored by the computer.

For each type of statement we will need to distinguish among three topics:

- **Syntax**—the format required for a Pascal program (the "grammar" of the language)
- **Semantics**—the meaning of the statements
- Relationship to solving problems

For convenience, we will refer to the following stripped-down version of the unit-pricing program. We have added line numbers at the left margin for ease of reference. They are *not* part of the program.

```
Reference
  Line
 Number             Actual Pascal Program
-------      ---------------------------------------

    1        Program UnitPricing (Output);
    2        {This program computes cost per ounce,
    3        given cost and number of ounces.}
    4        Var Ounces, Cost, CostPerOunce: Real;
    5        Begin
    6            Ounces := 16.0;
    7            Cost := 1.25;
    8            CostPerOunce := Cost / Ounces;
    9            Writeln(CostPerOunce)
   10        End.
```

This illustration contains the following pieces, which are found in typical Pascal programs:

program heading (line 1)

comments (lines 2–3)

declarations (line 4)

statements (lines 5–10)

In considering each of these pieces, we will see that the program heading and the declarations indicate structure, the statements indicate specific tasks to be done, and comments act as notes for ourselves. We also will see how various pieces and statements can be formatted so we can read a program easily, making a clear division between one part of a program and the next.

We will now look at the syntax and semantics of each of these pieces in some detail.

## Program Heading

Every Pascal program begins with a formal heading, just as every book begins with its title and author on a title page. In the unit-pricing program, the heading was

```
Program UnitPricing (Output);
```

This heading has three parts:

- *Program* announces the start of a program.
- The name, *UnitPricing*, we wish to give our program. The program name can help keep track of what the program is about, so we have chosen a one-word name that suggests the purpose of the program.
- A list in parentheses that tells the computer something about how data will move into the CPU and how data will move out of the CPU. We want to print results at a terminal, so we have used the word *Output* on this list. We will consider other possibilities later.

The semicolon at the end of the line separates the program heading from the rest of the program.

To summarize, a Pascal program begins with a program heading, which has the syntax (or form):

```
Program ProgramName (Output);
```

where *ProgramName* is a descriptive name of our choosing and *(Output)* indicates that we will print data at a terminal.

## Comments

We may want to remind ourselves, throughout a program, what we are doing or what algorithm we plan to follow. We can make notes to ourselves within a program to aid our memory as we read the code. Such notes are called **comments,** and we can insert comments anywhere in a program by enclosing them in braces { }. In the example, lines 2 and 3 form a comment, since line 2 begins with { and line 3 ends with }.

NOTE: The symbols (* and *) are allowed as alternates for { and }, respectively, in the Pascal Standard. These alternatives are useful if the braces are not available on your terminal.

When we type comments into a program, they appear in the program listings, so we will have the benefit of our notes as we read the code. Comments are ignored by the computer, however, when the program is compiled.

The program in Section 2.1 has comments inserted throughout the program. Comments can start or stop anywhere in a line, regardless of what other material is to appear. Whenever we write comments, the computer will type the text with the program, but the computer will not try to interpret the comment. The comment is for our use, not the computer's. It is good practice to place a comment at the start of each program to describe what task the program performs.

## Declarations

After the program heading (and usually some comments), we list the variables that are used in the program. Here we need to consider both what variable names can be used and how to tell the computer about these names.

**Identifiers.** In computer science, these names are called **identifiers,** and the example includes several different identifiers. We have already mentioned the identifiers *Program* and *Output*. Other identifiers or names in the program include *Ounces, Cost, CostPerOunce, Writeln, Begin, End,* and *Var*.

More generally, in Pascal identifiers can be any meaningful sequence of letters and digits, provided the first character is a letter. (Most compilers do have a practical limit on the length of identifiers, but that limit may be fairly large.) Spaces are not allowed, but we can use capitalization to "separate" words. The following identifiers are allowed:

```
Me2
ThisIsAVariable
FourScoreAnd7YearsAgo
```

These identifiers are *not* allowed:

| | |
|---|---|
| 2BeOrNot2Be | (starts with a number) |
| WOW!!! | (! is not a letter or number) |
| Gee Wiz | (contains a space) |

**Specifying Identifiers.** Now that we know what identifiers are, we need to see how we can tell a computer about them in Pascal. In some cases this is easy, because the names have special meanings in Pascal. For example, the identifier *Program* is used for a special purpose at the beginning of our program, and this identifier may not be used in any other way. Such an identifier is called a **reserved word.** The Pascal language dictates how the identifier will be used, and that use is incorporated into the compiler. (All Pascal reserved words are listed in the front cover of this text for easy reference.)

A few other identifiers have been **predefined** in Pascal, and a compiler will recognize these terms automatically. For example, a compiler interprets the identifier *Output* in a program header to mean that the program will transmit data to a terminal. (The inside front cover also contains a list of predefined identifiers.) Later we will see that we can change the meanings of predefined identifiers, but in practice we can think of reserved words and predefined identifiers in much the same way.

Beyond these few identifiers that are already known to a compiler before we start, we need to tell the computer what identifiers we plan to use as variables, and we need to say what types of values they will have. In our illustration we mention the variables *Ounces*, *Cost*, and *CostPerOunce*, and we indicate that they will contain **real** numbers. (We will see a variable type **integer** later in this chapter, and we will encounter other types in later chapters.) In specifying these identifiers to the computer, we say that we are **declaring** our variables.

The syntax for this declaration of variables is shown in our sample program, where we have

```
Var Ounces, Cost, CostPerOunce: Real;
```

Here we used the reserved word *Var* to begin our declarations. Then we listed the identifiers we will use. Finally, after a colon, we indicate these variables will have *Real* values.

A more extended syntax is possible if we want to declare a larger number of variables. After the keyword *Var* we can list the identifiers and their type (*Real*) on several lines. In the illustration we could replace line 4 with

```
Var Ounces: Real;
    Cost: Real;
    CostPerOunce: Real;
```

or

```
Var Ounces, Cost: Real;
    CostPerOunce: Real;
```

In each case, we have mentioned the names of all of our variables, and we have indicated that all of these will represent *Real* numbers.

NOTE: Most of the program so far has been quite formal in specifying structure. We have had to worry about syntax (form), but this form has not really helped us solve our problem very much. In time, you will find this initial work does help clarify your thinking, and you will not mind the formalism.

### Statements

Once the Program Heading and the Declarations have set up the program, we are ready to tell the computer the steps involved in the algorithm.

The steps themselves (lines 5–10) start with the word *Begin* (line 5) and finish with the word *End* (line 10); the statements between *Begin* and *End* tell the machine what to do and in what order. These statements are sometimes called a **Begin–End Block.**

**Assignments and Arithmetic.** In the lines

```
Ounces := 16.0;
Cost := 1.25;
CostPerOunce := Cost/Ounces;
```

we are computing values for the variables. First we assign the value 16.0 to the variable *ounces*, and then we assign the value 1.25 to the variable *cost*. These values are then used to compute a value for the variable *CostPerOunce*. In these lines the symbols := are used to denote the **assignment** of values to variables; the computer finds the value on the right side of the := and gives that value to the variable on the left.

Just as the division operator (/) is shown in the illustration, other arithmetic operations may be performed, using +, −, and * for addition, subtraction, and multiplication, respectively. Several operations may be put together on one line, and parentheses may be used to group terms as in arithmetic.

Pascal performs arithmetic operations in the same order as is done in algebra. That is, expressions within parentheses are done first. Multiplication and division are performed before addition or subtraction. We say that multiplication and division have **higher precedence** than addition or subtraction. If multiplications and divisions or additions and subtractions are mixed, then operations are performed from left to right. We say multiplication and division have the **same precedence.** Similarly, addition and subtraction have the same precedence. These rules are summarized in Figure 2–1, and examples follow in Table 2–1 (see page 22).

Note, however, that the computer will not perform algebraic steps with equations, so line 8 is not the same as

```
Cost := CostPerOunce * Ounces;
```

We must be sure that all quantities on the right of an assignment statement have been given values by previous Pascal statements and that the correct variable is on the left.

**Printing.** After values have been computed and assigned, we can ask the computer to print the results. In line 9 we have asked the computer to write the value of *CostPerOunce*. If we wanted *Ounces* and *Cost* printed as well, we could replace line 9 with

```
Writeln (Ounces, Cost, CostPerOunce);
```

and the output of the program would be:

```
1.6000000E+01    1.2500000E+00    7.812500E-02
```

The values of the three variables are printed in the order specified.

The word *Writeln* instructs the computer to print something, and the variables in parentheses indicate what is to be printed. When several variables are listed, these variables are separated by commas.

FIGURE 2–1 • **Summary of Rules for Evaluating Arithmetic Expressions**

1. Compute within parentheses first.
2. Perform operations of higher precedence before operations of lower precedence.
3. When several operations of the same precedence appear, work left to right.

**TABLE 2–1 • Examples**

| Expression | Result | Comment |
|---|---|---|
| 7.0*(5.0 − 2.0) | 21.0 | Subtraction, in parentheses, done first. |
| 7.0*5.0 − 2.0 | 33.0 | With no parentheses, multiplication has higher precedence and so is done before subtraction. |
| 30.0/3.0 * 5.0 | 50.0 | Since division and multiplication have equal precedence, evaluation proceeds from left to right. 30.0/3.0 is computed first; the result, 10.0, is then multiplied by 5.0. |

In the next section we will see how to modify this statement to make the output easier to read. For now, the main point is that we can determine the results of computation by the statement *Writeln*.

**Formatting and Punctuation.** As a final element of Pascal syntax, we need to consider how Pascal programs can be formatted, and we need to consider two types of punctuation: the semicolon and the period.

Pascal allows programs to be typed in a rather free format. We may not leave spaces within words (within *CostPerOunce* for example), but we may leave as many spaces between words as we wish. We may even start new words or symbols on new lines, and we may indent as much as we wish. For example, the statement

```
CostPerOunce := Cost/Ounces
```

could be written on several lines

```
CostPerOunce
                :=
                    Cost
                        /
                          Ounces
```

Several statements could also be written on one line, such as

```
Ounces := 16.0; Cost := 1.25;
```

This example also illustrates the need in Pascal for separating one statement from another. The **semicolon** is used to separate any two Pascal statements. Using this convention, we can type programs so they are easy to read. We do not have to cram formulas onto a single line. The semicolon tells the computer when one statement is done and the next is about to start. (If we omit the semicolon, the compiler will not be able to tell where one statement ends and the next begins, and the program will not run.)

Note, however, that since *Begin* and *End* are markers for the ends of the program statements, we do not need a semicolon after *Begin* or before *End*. We do not need to separate the Pascal statements from these markers.

One last element of syntax on this illustration concerns the **period.** Every Pascal program must end with a period. In writing English, we customarily conclude a simple sentence with a period, and Pascal works the same way. (Unlike English, we are not allowed to use marks such as ? or ! in place of the period in Pascal!)

We have now covered many of the basic details of Pascal syntax and semantics, and you can now write many simple Pascal programs. In the next sections we will look at several more examples where Pascal programs can help solve simple problems.

## SECTION 2.3 ANOTHER EXAMPLE: COMPUTING SALES TAX AND TOTAL COST

In Section 2.1 we saw an example of a Pascal program that helped us with a problem of Unit Pricing, and in Section 2.2 we used this example to identify the basic parts of a Pascal program. Now we are ready for another example, and we will see how some modifications can make the final results easier to read.

**PROBLEM 2.3**

Sales tax is to be computed for a particular item. Write a program that will compute the amount of tax and the total purchase price, given the cost of the item and the tax rate.

Our solution to this problem follows a form similar to the solution of Problem 2.1.

### Outline for Problem 2.3

**I.** Determine item cost and tax rate
  **A.** Determine cost (in dollars)
  **B.** Determine tax rate
**II.** Compute tax and total purchase price
  **A.** The appropriate formula for tax will be

$$\text{tax} = \text{cost} * \text{tax rate}$$

**B.** The appropriate formula for total price will be

total price = cost + tax

**III.** Write tax and total purchase price as the final answers.

From this outline we can write a Pascal program, following the format we have discussed in Section 2.2. In the problem we have arbitrarily picked the cost of the item to be $25.99 and the tax rate to be 0.07 (7%).

```
Program TaxComputation {Version 1} (Output);

{This program computes the tax and total cost of an item,
 given the original cost of the item and the tax rate}

Var Cost, TaxRate: Real;          {The Givens in our problem}
    Tax, TotalCost: Real;         {Our Desired Results}

Begin

    {Determine Item Cost and Tax Rate}
    Cost := 25.99;
    TaxRate := 0.07;

    {Compute Tax and Total Purchase Price}
    Tax := Cost * TaxRate;
    TotalCost := Cost + Tax;

    {Write out the desired results}
    Writeln (Tax, TotalCost)

End .
```

When this program is run, the computer prints

```
1.819300E+00    2.780930E+01
```

We can interpret these numbers by shifting the decimal point appropriately. (Recall that the E+01 indicates we should multiply 2.780930 by $10^1$ to get 27.80930; the E stands for the exponent or power of 10.)

Strictly speaking, the program solves the problem, but the output of the program is not ideal for several reasons. We have to interpret the numbers by shifting a decimal point. We have to remember that 1.819300E+00 is the tax and 2.780930E+01 is the total cost. We have to remember what the initial values were for item cost and the tax rate.

We therefore modify the output so we will be able to interpret the results more easily. Consider the following revised program. For convenience, we have added a variable *PerCentTax*, which is the tax rate in percent. The last parts of several *Writeln* statements specify output formatting, which we will describe shortly.

```
Program TaxComputation {Version 2} (Output);

{This program computes the tax and total cost of an item,
 given the original cost of the item and the tax rate}

Var Cost, TaxRate: Real;          {The Givens in our problem}
    PerCentTax: Real;             {The Tax in Percent}
    Tax, TotalCost: Real;         {Our Desired Results}

Begin

    {Determine Item Cost and Tax Rate}
    Cost := 25.99;
    TaxRate := 0.07;
    PerCentTax := TaxRate * 100.0;

    {Compute Tax and Total Purchase Price}
    Tax := Cost * TaxRate;
    TotalCost := Cost + Tax;

    {Write out the desired results}
    Writeln ('This program computes the tax and total cost of an item.');
    Writeln ('Cost of item = $', Cost:6:2);
    Writeln ('Tax Rate =', PerCentTax:4:1, ' %');
    Writeln ('For this purchase, the tax is $', Tax:5:2);
    Writeln ('and the total cost is $', TotalCost:6:2, ' .')

End .
```

When this revised program is run, the output is

```
This program computes the tax and total cost of an item.
Cost of item = $ 25.99
Tax Rate = 7.0 %
For this purchase, the tax is $ 1.82
and the total cost is $ 27.81 .
```

This output is much easier to interpret than the output of the first program. All of the objections raised earlier in this section are resolved.

If we look at how we achieved this better output, we see that our improvements fall into two categories, printing text labels and formatting numbers.

## Labeling Output

The example illustrates that we can print text in output by placing the text in single quotes within a *Writeln* statement. Any text placed in single quotes is printed exactly as it is written. All spaces and punctuation marks are printed in the format that we specify, with one exception. If you want a single quote mark printed, you must use two symbols '', for otherwise the single quote would be interpreted as the end of the text. Thus the contraction 'Don't' must be typed 'Don''t'. In all other respects, however, the computer will print text exactly as you type it.

### Formatted Output

The example also illustrates how to format real numbers, but we first must consider the form that real numbers have. Real numbers are positive and negative numbers with decimal points, such as 3.1415927 or −12345.67, and these numbers have two characteristics. First, they require a certain number of spaces to print (e.g., both 3.1415927 and −12345.67 require nine symbols). In addition, they contain a certain number of digits to the right of the decimal place. Thus, to format real numbers, we need to specify the total width for the number and a number of digits to the right of the decimal point. In the example, this format is specified by placing both formatting items after the variable. Thus,

```
Tax:5:2
```

specifies that we want to allow five spaces (including the decimal point) for printing the value for *Tax*, and we want the number rounded to two decimal places.

In the example, Tax:5:2 left five spaces for the number, even though the number required less space than five characters. Since 1.82 only required four spaces, the first of the five characters was left blank. In general, if the number does not require all of the space allocated, the first spaces will be left blank; the number is right-justified in the space specified.

On the other hand, if a number requires more space to the left of the decimal point than allocated, then Pascal adds space to the width. Thus, if *Tax* were 135.79 and the format remained Tax:5:2, an extra character would be added to the overall width of the number: 135 requires three characters; the decimal point . requires one character; and we specified two decimal places in our format. The number printed, 135.79, requires six characters total. Further examples are found in Table 2–2, where ____ indicates that space is left in the output.

### Formatting Hints

We have seen several ways to add text to output and to format numbers. Now we can discuss some general guidelines for putting these pieces together.

Perhaps the most basic principle is that output should be readable. A user of the program should be able to understand easily what is printed. This implies that enough space should be left on the page so various results can be distinguished. It may even be worthwhile to leave some blank lines between various parts of the output. To leave a blank line insert a *Writeln* followed by a semicolon. This will print out simply as a blank line. To skip several blank lines, just repeat this *Writeln;* statement for each line.

**TABLE 2–2 • Formatting Real Numbers**

| Number to be printed | Format specified | Actual output* | Comments |
|---|---|---|---|
| 123.46 | 7:2 | _ 123.46 | Number right-justified |
| 123.46 | 7:1 | __123.5 | Number rounded to one decimal place and right justified |
| 123.42 | 7:1 | __123.4 | Number rounded to one decimal place and right justified |
| 123.5 | 6:2 | 123.50 | Two decimal places printed |
| 123.46 | 3:2 | 123.46 | Extra space allocated, as number requires six characters |
| 123.46 | 3:1 | 123.5 | Number rounded, extra space allocated |

*__ indicates space left in the actual output.

Numbers should be identified so anyone reading the output will know what each number represents. For example, our previous output included

Cost of item = $25.99

We can follow many approaches to identify results, and any approach that yields readable output can be acceptable. Here we will mention two common approaches, which are summarized in Table 2–3.

**Approach 1: Placing Results Within Text.** In the revised program to compute tax and total cost we included the results of computations within some text. The output included several sentences. In this particular program we knew how large our various numbers would be, so we could allocate exactly the right amount of space for each number. In this situation, we could determine the appropriate formatting information while we were writing the program. (A tax of $10 seemed unlikely, so we only needed to allow 1 digit to the left of the decimal point when printing this computed tax.) We did have to print a space before the final period, so the number $27.81 would not be crammed next to the period at the end of the sentence. However, all of the information was known ahead of time, and we could specify our formats without great difficulty.

Even if we do not know what output to expect, we still must specify formats. In this situation it is best to decide upon the approximate number of decimal places and then to underestimate the total number of spaces required. For example, we might specify *Tax:1:2*. Here, we know that 1

**TABLE 2–3 • Formatting Guidelines**

1. Output should be readable.
   a. Leave enough space.
   b. Do not cram.
   c. Label numbers.
2. When numbers appear within text:
   a. specify the appropriate number of decimal places;
   b. underestimate total width;
   c. leave spaces in text both before and after numbers.
3. When numbers appear in a table:
   a. specify titles for the table;
   b. be sure enough room is left for each number.

space is not enough (we need a leading digit, a decimal point, and two decimal places, for a minimum of four spaces). But we also know that Pascal will add spaces as they are needed. The *Tax:1:2* format will allow the computer to print the tax correctly, but we will not have any extra spaces printed at the start of the number. If we specified *Tax:10:2*, we would have plenty of room for our tax of 1.82, but there would be six blank spaces between the $ we printed and the number. *Tax:1:2* gives us adequate space without leaving unnecessary gaps.

To conclude Approach 1, when we print results within some text, we must decide upon the number of decimal places we want printed. To avoid large gaps in the text, guesses about the total width of numbers should be too small rather than too large.

**Approach 2: Placing Results in Tables.** A second way to print output in a readable form is to place results in tables. For example, consider the following version of the tax program:

```
Program TaxComputation {Version 3} (Output);

{This program computes the tax and total cost of an item,
 given the original cost of the item and the tax rate.
 The results are printed in a table.}

Var Cost, TaxRate: Real;         {The Givens in our problem}
    Tax, TotalCost: Real;        {Our Desired Results}

Begin

    {Determine Item Cost and Tax Rate}
    Cost := 25.99;
    TaxRate := 0.07;

    {Compute Tax and Total Purchase Price}
    Tax := Cost * TaxRate;
    TotalCost := Cost + Tax;
```

```
    {Write out the desired results}
    Writeln ('This program computes the tax and total cost of an item');
    Writeln ('when the tax rate is ', TaxRate*100.0:4:2, '% .');
    Writeln ;    {skip line}
    Writeln ('                    Amount');
    Writeln ('                   (Dollars)');
    Writeln ;   {skip line}
    Writeln ('Cost of Item:', Cost:10:2);
    Writeln (' Tax on Item:', Tax:10:2);
    Writeln ('  Total Cost:', TotalCost:10:2)
End .
```

When this program is run, the output is

```
This program computes the tax and total cost of an item
when the tax rate is 7.00% .

                  Amount
                 (Dollars)

Cost of Item:      25.99
 Tax on Item:       1.82
  Total Cost:      27.81
```

All dollar amounts are shown in a column that is clearly labeled and easy to read.

In printing such a table, we must allocate enough room for each number so that the columns of the table are properly aligned. Any guessing about the size of numbers should be on the large size. We must allow enough room so that the machine will not add more spaces and ruin the alignment of the columns.

Next, we note that the table is easier to read if we insert blank lines to set the table off from other parts of the output. (In some instances, we may want to leave spaces within a table as well to aid readability.)

## Some Programming Aids

There are some further techniques that can help when we place numbers within text or when we format tables. We may need to print long lines of text or numbers, and we may find it difficult to fit this text in a *Writeln* statement comfortably. Here we may proceed in either of two ways.

1. We may divide the text into a few lines within the *Writeln*. For example, the line

```
Writeln ('This program computes the tax and total cost of an item,')
```

may be written on two or more lines of a Pascal program:

```
Writeln ('This program computes the tax and ',
         'total cost of an item,')
```

Here we broke the long text into two smaller pieces and told the computer to print the first piece and then the second. Each piece was placed in quotes, and the pieces were separated by a comma. Notice that we still included the space after "and " so the pieces would fit together correctly.

2. We may use a variant of *Writeln* for the first parts of the line. For example, the above line may be printed

```
Write ('This program computes the tax and ');
Writeln ('total cost of an item,')
```

Here the *Write* statement works much the same way as *Writeln*, except that the machine does not go on to a new line after the output is printed. (The *ln* of *Writeln* means "line.") Instead, the next output will start where the *Write* finished.

Further, to divide an output line into several pieces, we may follow the form

```
Write (_ _ _ _);
Write (_ _ _ _);
Write (_ _ _ _);
   .        .
   .        .
   .        .
Write (_ _ _ _);
Writeln (_ _ _ _);
```

All of the material specified will be printed on the same line, with one *Write* starting on the line where the previous one finished. At the end of the line *Writeln* prints its text (if any) and moves on to the start of the next line.

Thus when we have long lines of text or numbers, we can divide the lines into short pieces, as different pieces in the same *Write* or *Writeln*, or in a sequence of *Write* and *Writeln* statements.

Another technique that can simplify programs is also illustrated in the last example. We wanted to print the tax rate in percent, so we needed to compute TaxRate * 100.0 . In Version 2 of the program, we did this as a separate step:

```
PerCentTax := TaxRate * 100.0
```

Then we printed *PerCentTax*. The computation was not needed for the problem, only for the output.

In Version 3 of the program we included the computation in the *Writeln* statement itself, and we wrote

```
Writeln ('when the tax rate is ', TaxRate * 100.0:4:2, '% .')
```

In this line the first text was printed, and then *TaxRate * 100.0* was computed and formatted. Finally, the last text, '% .', was printed. In the revised program the percentage of tax is relegated to an expression in the output where it logically belongs in the problem.

With these observations and techniques using *Write* and *Writeln* statements, we are now able to print our results in any form that is helpful for our problem. We have sufficient flexibility in designing output to meet the needs of any problem. In the next section we will see how to run programs with different sets of data for input.

## SECTION 2.4 LABELED INPUT

We have seen how to write simple programs, and we have learned how to format output so we can interpret the results easily. In this section we will see how to use the same program to help solve several related questions.

Consider the following example.

**PROBLEM 2.4**

Write a program that converts yards, feet, and inches to meters.

Once again, the solution follows a familiar form:

### Outline for Problem 2.4

**I.** Determine values for yards, feet, and inches.

**II.** Compute meters.

From a handbook we find:

1 inch = 0.0254001 meters

1 foot = 0.304801 meters

1 yard = 0.914403 meters

**III.** Print results

From this outline we develop the following program:

```
Program YardsToMeters {Version 1} (Output);
{This program converts Yards, Feet, and Inches to Meters.}

Var Yards, Feet, Inches:Real;             {The Givens}
    Meters: Real;                         {The Desired Result}

Begin
    {Determine values for Yards, Feet, and Inches}
    Yards  := 4.0;
    Feet   := 2.0;
    Inches := 7.0;

    {Compute the corresponding number of meters}
    Meters := 0.914403*Yards + 0.304801*Feet
              + 0.0254001*Inches;
```

```
    {Print the results in a short table}
    Writeln ('Yards    Feet  Inches    =    Meters');        {Write heading}
    Write (Yards:5:2, Feet:8:2, Inches:8:2);                  {Write givens}
    Writeln (Meters:13:2)                                     {Complete output line}

End.
```

When we run the program, we get

```
Yards    Feet  Inches    =    Meters
 4.00    2.00    7.00           4.45
```

(Note how we divided the last output line into pieces. Then we used *Write* to print the first three pieces and *Writeln* for the last piece.)

This program works well for the particular data we used, namely 4.0 yards, 2.0 feet, 7.0 inches. Whenever we want to run other data, we must change the appropriate line(s) in the program and recompile and run the program. Instead we might prefer to write the program so we can type our data at a terminal when the program is run. This suggests the following revised program, where we have added *Input* to our program heading.

```
Program YardsToMeters {Version 2} (Input, Output);
{This program converts Yards, Feet, and Inches to Meters.}

Var Yards, Feet, Inches:Real;              {The Givens}
    Meters: Real;                          {The Desired Result}

Begin
    Writeln ('This program converts yards, feet, and inches to meters.');

    {Determine values for Yards, Feet, and Inches}
    Writeln ('Enter values for yards, feet, and inches');
    Readln (Yards, Feet, Inches);          {Type values at our terminal}

    {Compute the corresponding number of meters}
    Meters := 0.914403*Yards + 0.304801*Feet
              + 0.0254001*Inches;

    {Print the results in a short table}
    Writeln ('Yards    Feet  Inches    =    Meters');        {Write heading}
    Write (Yards:5:2, Feet:8:2, Inches:8:2);                  {Write givens}
    Writeln (Meters:13:2)                                     {Complete output line}

End.
```

When this program is run, the computer begins

```
This program converts yards, feet, and inches to meters.
Enter values for yards, feet, and inches
```

The computer then waits for us to type in our data.

```
Readln (Yards, Feet, Inches);
```

specifies that we will enter values for these variables (in the order specified and separated by spaces) when the program is run. If we type

```
4.0 2.0 7.0
```

then the computer has the needed values, so it continues and prints

```
Yards  Feet  Inches = Meters
 4.00  2.00    7.00     4.45
```

Thus this revised program performs the same computations as the first version when we enter the same numbers. If we run the program again, we can enter new data without retyping any part of the program. We just need to type our new values in place of 4.0, 2.0, and 7.0. As before, we need to leave one or more spaces between numbers.

*Some cautions:* Inserting *Readln* statements can greatly increase the flexibility of programs, but they do require the person running the program to enter appropriate values. Whenever we use *Readln,* therefore, we must be sure to tell the user what is expected. In the revised program, this is done in two ways:

- The first *Writeln* in the program tells the user what the program does. The user learns the context of the program.
- The second *Writeln* gives the user specific instructions. The statement

  ```
  Writeln ('Enter values for yards, feet, and inches');
  ```

  tells the user that three numbers are needed. The user knows what these values represent and in what order to type them.

Without these two *Writeln* statements, a user could still run the program. However, when the computer encountered the *Readln,* the machine would wait for the required values. No messages would be printed, and the user could wait for a long time for something to happen. Even if a user realizes that some information is needed, the user may not know how much data are required or in what order the values should be typed. (Should we type "inches" first or "yards"?). Therefore, it is essential to prompt the user whenever information must be entered from the keyboard.

## Programming Aids

We have the same flexibility in reading data that we noted earlier for writing. In particular, a *Read* statement is a variant of *Readln* that allows us to obtain a value from a terminal without moving to a new line. Thus

```
Readln (Yards, Feet, Inches);
```

is equivalent to

```
Read (Yards);
Read (Feet);
Readln (Inches);
```

In either case we could type

```
4.0 2.0 7.0
```

to represent 4.0 yards, 2.0 feet, 7.0 inches.

Alternatively, we could type

```
4.0 2.0
7.0
```

on two lines if we wanted more room for our numbers.

On the other hand, the statements

```
Readln (Yards);
Readln (Feet);
Readln (Inches);
```

would require us to type our numbers on three separate lines:

```
4.0
2.0
7.0
```

If we typed the numbers on the same line,

```
4.0 2.0 7.0
```

the *Readln (Yards)* would set *Yards* to 4.0, but the remaining numbers would be skipped. The *ln* indicates we must move to the next line. Thus the machine would still need values for *Feet* and *Inches*, and we would have to enter these values on two succeeding lines. This capacity to skip lines can be convenient, but it can also be a source of errors if we are not careful.

We can gain still more flexibility in labeling data and entering numbers if we combine *Write*, *Writeln*, *Read*, and *Readln* in various patterns. For example, we might want to prompt the user for each number on a separate line. In this case we might replace

```
Writeln ('Enter Yards, Feet, and Inches');
Readln (Yards, Feet, Inches);
```

with the lines

```
Write ('Enter Yards:   ');
Readln (Yards);
Write ('Enter Feet:   ');
Readln (Feet);
```

```
Write ('Enter Inches:   ');
Readln (Inches);
```

When we run this revised program and enter the data 4.0, 2.0, 7.0, we see the following:

```
Enter Yards:   4.0
Enter Feet:   2.0
Enter Inches:   7.0
```

The computer pauses on each line after printing the text so the user can type the data. The *Write* does not move the machine to the next line, so we are able to type our information on the same line as the prompt. The *Readln* with one variable tells the computer we plan to type only one number; other information we might add to the line should be skipped.

By carefully choosing which combination of *Read–Readln* and *Write–Writeln* statements we use, we can tailor our input and output to fit most problems. Users can be prompted at appropriate places, and both input and output can be readable. We should include planning for this user contact as part of our problem solving activities.

## SECTION 2.5 INTEGER DATA TYPE

So far, all of our examples have included computations with real numbers. In Pascal, real numbers must have decimal points and at least one digit before and after the decimal point. Thus the real number 3 must be written 3.0 or 3.00, rather than just 3., and the real number ½ must be written 0.5 or 0.50, rather than just .5. Such numbers arise in many settings, and we should recognize their importance.

Many problems, however, require other types of data. In this section we consider numbers that are whole numbers or integers. In Pascal, **integers** are numbers that are written without decimal points—such as 0, 3, and −37—and we must be careful to distinguish these numbers from reals. In fact, computers store real numbers and integers in different ways, so that the numbers 3 and 3.0 are treated differently.

To begin we consider a simple division problem.

**PROBLEM 2.5A** Compute the quotient and remainder when one integer is divided by another.

### Outline of Problem 2.5A

**I.** Determine the dividend and divisor.
**II.** Compute the quotient and remainder.
**III.** Print and label all results.

This outline leads to the following program:

```
Program IntegerDivision (Output);
{This Program computes the quotient and remainder when one
 integer is divided by another.}

Var Divisor, Dividend: Integer;
    Quotient, Remainder: Integer;
Begin

    {Determine values for dividend and divisor}
    Dividend := 13;
    Divisor := 5;

    {Compute quotient and remainder}
    Quotient := Dividend Div Divisor;
    Remainder := Dividend Mod Divisor;

    {Print out all numbers in the problem}
    Writeln ('When ', Dividend:1, ' is divided by ', Divisor:1, ' ,');
    Writeln ('the quotient is ', Quotient:1,
             ' and the remainder is ', Remainder:1, ' .')

End.
```

When this program is run, we get the following output.

```
When 13 is divided by 5 ,
the quotient is 2 and the remainder is 3 .
```

This program illustrates several characteristics of integers in Pascal. Integers are numbers without decimal points, and integer data are considered distinct from real data. The variables are declared in the program to be *Integer*, not *Real* as in the past.

When we print integers, we have to specify the number of spaces needed for the number, but we do *not* indicate a number of decimal places. As with real numbers, the total width may be larger than required, in which case the number is right justified. If the width is set too small, extra space is allocated as required. In the program we allowed one space for each number. This was adequate for *Division, Quotient,* and *Remainder,* and each number was printed in the space provided. However, *Dividend* required two spaces, so an extra space was added over the specifications.

When we divide one integer by another, we might mean any of three operations. In Pascal, each of these operations has a distinct symbol, as noted in the following chart:

| Operation | Symbol | Example |
| --- | --- | --- |
| Integer Quotient | Div | 22 Div 7 = 3 |
| | | 20 Div 4 = 5 |
| Remainder | Mod | 22 Mod 7 = 1 |
| | | 20 Mod 4 = 0 |
| Real Quotient | / | 13 /6 = 2.1666 . . . |
| | | 1 /4 = 0.25 |

These three forms of division are illustrated further in the next program.

```
Program IntegerDivision (Input, Output);
{This Program illustrates the three types of integer division}

Var Divisor, Dividend: Integer;
    Quotient, Remainder: Integer;
    RealQuotient: Real;

Begin
    {Determine dividend and divisor}
    Write ('Enter Dividend: ');
    Readln (Dividend);
    Write ('Enter Divisor: ');
    Readln (Divisor);

    {Perform various divisions}
    Quotient := Dividend Div Divisor;
    Remainder := Dividend Mod Divisor;
    RealQuotient := Dividend / Divisor;

    {Print results in a table}
    Writeln {Skip Line} ;
    Writeln ('                      Integer               Real');
    Writeln ('Dividend  Divisor    Quotient  Remainder Quotient');
    Writeln ('                       (Div)     (Mod)     ( / )');
    Writeln (Dividend: 5, Divisor: 10, Quotient: 10,
             Remainder: 10, RealQuotient: 12:3)
End.
```

When we use 13 for our dividend and 5 for our divisor, the program produces the following output:

```
Enter Dividend: 13
Enter Divisor: 5

                          Integer                  Real
Dividend    Divisor      Quotient   Remainder Quotient
                           (Div)      (Mod)      ( / )
   13          5             2          3        2.600
```

We see that Pascal allows us to decide just what type of division we want to perform between two integers. The arithmetic operations of addition, subtraction, and multiplication do not require us to choose the type of operation intended; and these operations are denoted +, −, *, respectively, just as for arithmetic with real numbers.

## Conversion Between Integer and Real Types

Although these arithmetic operations may seem the same for integers and real numbers, we need to emphasize that Pascal treats these types of numbers differently, and we cannot interchange the two types directly. The different types are stored in different ways, and we must consciously change a number from one form to the other.

Conversion from integer to real is straightforward—just add a decimal point and zeros. For example, the integers 17 and −325 convert to the reals 17.0 and −325.0, respectively. With this ease of conversion, Pascal allows us to mix integers and reals in the same arithmetic expression, and in each case the integer is converted to a real number before the operation is applied. For example, in computing 17.3 + 14, the 14 is changed to 14.0, then 17.3 and 14.0 are added, to get 31.3. When such conversions are needed, the resulting values are always real.

On the other hand, we have to be careful in converting reals to integers. We would normally want to convert the real 14.3 to the integer 14. However, the conversion of 14.9 is less clear. The number is not as big as 15, so we might want to forget the .9. Still, 14.9 is closer to 15 than to 14, so we might want to convert 14.9 to 15. In Pascal, therefore, conversion from reals to integers is not automatic; we must specify which of two conversions to apply:

*Round (14.9)* rounds 14.9 to 15

*Trunc (14.9)* truncates the .9 to 14.

In general, to convert a real number to an integer, we apply *Round ( )* to round the number and *Trunc ( )* to discard values to the right of the decimal point. Some examples are listed in Table 2–4.

**Example: Making Change.** We conclude this section by looking at an example that puts together some of the features of integers and reals in a practical setting.

**TABLE 2–4 • Examples**

| Number | Round(Number) | Trunc(Number) |
|---|---|---|
| 17.35 | 17 | 17 |
| 16.89 | 17 | 16 |
| 0.99999999 | 1 | 0 |

**PROBLEM 2.5B**

In a store, a customer is to receive change for a purchase. Write a program that reads the amount of change and determines the number of $10 bills, $5 bills, $1 bills, and the amount in coins that should be paid back to the customer.

Our outline here is a bit more complex than we have encountered in previous problems.

### Outline for Problem 2.5B

**I.** Determine amount of change.
**II.** Compute the amount to be given in bills.
Look at the dollar amount, ignoring the cents.
**III.** Compute the amount to be paid in coins.
Subtract the dollar amount paid from the total amount of the change.
**IV.** Compute the number of $10 bills.
The number of $10 bills is the integer quotient when the amount in bills is divided by 10.
**V.** Compute the number of $5 bills.
**A.** The amount in bills left to return is the remainder after paying out the $10 bills.
**B.** When the amount is divided by $5, the integer quotient gives the number of $5 bills.
**VI.** Compute the number of $1 bills.
The amount of bills left after paying out $5 bills must be paid in $1 bills.
**VII.** Print amount to be paid in coins.

This outline yields the following program:

```
Program MakingChange (Input, Output);
{This program reads the change due a customer and determines
 number of $10, $5, and $1 bills and the total amount of coins
 that the customer should receive.}

Var TotalChange: Real;
    Bills, Tens, Fives, Ones: Integer;
    BillsAfter10s: Integer;
    Coins: Real;
```

```
Begin

    {Determine amount of change}
    Writeln ('This program makes change for a customer.');
    Write ('Please enter the amount of change due:  ');
    Readln (TotalChange);

    {Compute the Number of bills}
    Bills := Trunc(TotalChange);

    {Compute the Amount to be Paid in Coin}
    Coins := TotalChange - Bills;

    {Compute the Number of Ten Dollar Bills}
    Tens := Bills Div 10;
    Writeln ('Ten dollar bills required:   ', Tens:1);

    {Compute the Number of Five Dollar Bills}
    BillsAfter10s := Bills Mod 10;
    Fives := BillsAfter10s Div 5;
    Writeln ('Five dollar bills requried:  ', Fives:1);

    {Compute the Number of One Dollar Bills}
    Ones := BillsAfter10s Mod 5;
    Writeln ('One dollar bills required:   ', Ones:1);

    {Print Change in Coins}
    Writeln ('Change in coins required:  $ ', Coins:1:2)

End.
```

When this program is run using 17.85 as the change due, we get:

```
This program makes change for a customer.
Please enter the amount of change due:  17.85
Ten dollar bills required:   1
Five dollar bills requried:  1
One dollar bills required:   2
Change in coins required:  $ 0.85
```

This program uses the *Trunc* function, as well as the *Div* and *Mod* operations. You should check that each function and operation performs the task required in the outline.

In this program you might also note that several statements can be combined for brevity. For example, the computation of the amount to be paid in five-dollar bills could be written

Fives : = (Bills Mod 10) Div 5;

The resulting code is shorter, but harder to check with the outline.

## SECTION 2.6 CONSTANTS

In our work so far, we have used real numbers and integers, we have seen how to compute and print values from expressions, and we have seen how to assign those values to variables. In using these variables we may expect the values of the variables to change. For example, when we read a value, we do not know what number will be typed until the program is actually run, and different values may be entered if the program is run several times. Some values, however, will remain the same every time the program is run. These objects are **constants,** and we may want to think of these items differently from the variables we have encountered up to now. For example, consider the following problem.

## PROBLEM 2.6

Compute the volume and the surface area of a sphere, given its radius.

### Outline for Problem 2.6

**I.** Determine the radius.

**II.** Compute the volume and surface area from a handbook.
From a handbook, we find

$$\text{volume} = 4/3\ \pi\ r^3$$

and

$$\text{surface area} = 4\ \pi\ r^2,$$

where *r* is the radius and $\pi$ is the familiar 3.1415926535. . .

**III.** Print the results.

In these formulas, we may expect the radius under consideration to change from one run to the next, but we know $\pi$ will always be 3.1415926535. . . . Thus, when we write the program, we declare *Pi* to be a *Constant* rather than a *Variable*:

```
Program Spheres (Input, Output);
{This Program computes the volume and surface area of a sphere,
 given the radius of the sphere}

Const Pi = 3.1415926535;           {Pi is the constant 3.1415926535}

Var Radius, Volume, Area: Real;

Begin

    {Determine Radius}
    Writeln ('This program computes a sphere''s volume and surface area.');
    Write ('Enter radius:  ');
    Readln(Radius);
```

```
    {Compute Volume and Area}
    Volume := 4.0/3.0 * Pi * Radius * Radius * Radius;
    Area := 4.0 * Pi * Radius * Radius;

    {Print Results}
    Writeln ('When the radius of a sphere is ', Radius:1:2, ' ,');
    Writeln ('then the volume is ', Volume:1:2,
             ' and the surface area is ', Area:1:2)
End.
```

When this program is run, we get

```
This program computes a sphere's volume and surface area.
Enter radius:  2.0
When the radius of a sphere is 2.00 ,
then the volume is 33.51 and the surface area is 50.27
```

In this program, *Pi* is declared at the beginning of the code to be the constant 3.1415926535. Then we use this number in the rest of the program. The resulting program is clear to read, since we can use *Pi* in all the formulas instead of the long, cumbersome decimal that it represents.

### MaxInt

There is a special constant that is always defined in Pascal, although its value depends on the particular machine. The constant *MaxInt* is **machine-defined** to be the largest integer allowed on that machine. Pascal requires that all values in the range from −*MaxInt* to *MaxInt* (inclusive) are valid for integers. The following program will allow you to determine how large integers can be on your computer:

```
Program FindMaximumInteger (Output);
{This program prints the maximum integer allowed on this machine.}

Begin
   Writeln ('The maximum integer allowed on this machine is ', MaxInt:1)
End.
```

On some machines you may be able to use a few integers that are beyond this range. (On a PDP-11/70, *MaxInt* is 32767, but the smallest allowed integer is −32768.) You can only depend, however, on integers from −*MaxInt* to *MaxInt* in your programs!

On most machines the limitation on the range of integers is quite severe, and this is one reason why real numbers are used in many applications. The range for real numbers is always considerably larger than for integers, although reals have other limitations, which are based on the ways numbers are stored inside a machine.

We have now seen how to write sample Pascal programs, and we have seen that constants can help us clarify some of the values in our programs. We will see other uses for constants in later chapters. In the next section we pause to note other ways we can make our programs readable and easy to understand.

## SECTION 2.7 STYLE

When we consider the elements of style in the programs we have seen so far, we can distinguish the following categories:

**Comments.** We have already seen in Section 2.2 that comments can be placed anywhere in a program. Further, all of our sample programs share several characteristics. At the very beginning of each program, we have stated what task the program performs and recorded special features of the algorithms and any limitations that the program might have. Throughout each program we noted in comments the major points of the problem outline, so that any reader will know what each part of the program is supposed to do. Special comments guide us through specific parts of the code. For example, we often identified givens and desired results.

Since comments are so important in describing algorithms, we must be sure to write enough of them. On the other hand, we should not write an essay for each line of a program.

**Indenting and spacing.** We can also aid the readability of a program by clear formatting of the program. We can use indenting and spacing to show the program's structure. We can skip a space after each logical unit of the program, to separate one piece of code from the next. We can indent consistently following the structure of the code. For example:

- In our declarations we did not indent the word *Var*, but we did indent all declarations in subsequent lines.
- In the statement block, we did not indent the initial *Begin* or the final *End*, but we did indent all statements within the block.
- Whenever a statement continued on more than one line, we indented the second and subsequent lines to show that these lines were logically part of the first one.

If we follow consistent patterns of indenting and spacing, and if we allow enough white space to separate pieces of code, then the visual appearance of a program will indicate its structure, and we will be able to read the code easily and quickly.

**Descriptive names.** In our programs, we carefully used descriptive names for all variables and constants. Of course, we could use short abbreviations, such as *Y* for yards and *F* for feet. As we need more names, however, these abbreviations become hard to remember. For example, we could use the following variables in the program for making change (Section 2.5):

*CO* for TotalChange
*C1* for Coins
*BO* for Bills
*B1* for BillsAfter10s

These variable names will work, but as programs get longer, we will find it hard to keep track of which name represents what quantity. On the other hand, extremely long variable names also invite misspelling and can be cumbersome.

**Constants.** Similarly, the use of Constants can help us simplify our code by allowing us to replace a long decimal with a descriptive name.

**Input and output.** Sections 2.3 and 2.4 showed how to read and write information in whatever format we desired. In writing programs this means that we should choose a format that will be easy to use and understand. In those sections we noted this formatting could be guided by several principles.

- All results should be identified, so we know what each item is supposed to represent. Placing items within text or in tables often helps identify results.
- Users should be prompted when input is expected. Users must know what information is desired and how that information should be ordered.
- Sufficient space should be allowed between parts of the output, so the results are not jumbled together and hard to read. Inserting blank lines can help separate one set of results from the next.

Each of these elements of style can help us read and understand our programs. In many cases, just reading our code will help us detect and correct errors we might have made. Other times, we will have to rely upon testing to detect errors, and then we will need to read the program to find where and how the error occurred.

Now that we can write programs clearly, we are ready to begin running them.

## SECTION 2.8 PROGRAM CORRECTNESS AND TESTING

We have seen how to create simple programs that are well structured and easy to read. We cannot be sure, though, that these programs help solve our problems until we know that what we have written works correctly. In this section, we will identify a few ways to check programs.

When we try to compile a program, the compiler may report some errors in syntax or semantics. For example, we may have misspelled an identifier, left out a semicolon between statements, or omitted a right brace at the end of a comment. In these cases, we are told we have made a mistake, but we have to reread the program carefully to find the error. For example, a misspelled identifier in a declaration may only be caught later by the compiler, when we try to use the identifier.

Once errors in syntax and semantics are corrected, the program will compile, and we will have a machine language program to run. Then we are ready to test the program to be sure it works the way we intend. We might begin by running the program with several pieces of data where we know the correct results. If the program works correctly on data that we know or where the answers are obvious, then we may have some confidence that the program will also work correctly on other data.

On the other hand, if the program does not produce correct results with test data, then we need to go through the code line by line to find the mistake. We might find that we mistyped a number or copied a formula incorrectly. In other cases, we might find that the logic in the solution outline was incorrect, and we need to revise our approach to the problem.

As you gain experience in programming, you will find you can recognize and correct errors reported by the compiler more easily and quickly than when you began. In subsequent chapters, you will also see many techniques that can help in writing programs that perform as intended. You will also find, however, that you can never assume a program is working correctly unless you check it carefully. Running code with a variety of test cases is one excellent way to do this checking.

## SUMMARY

1. Pascal programs have the following form:
   - **Program Header**
   - **Comments**
   - **Program Block**
     - **Declarations**
     - **Statements**

2. All programs begin with the **header**

   Program ProgramName (Input, Output)

   *Input* may be omitted if the program will only write results and not read data.
3. You can write **comments** to help you understand your programs. Such notes are placed in braces { }.
4. In Pascal, the compiler must be able to recognize all names, or **identifiers,** that you use in a program. Some identifiers are already known to the compiler, including **reserved words** and **predefined identifiers.** You must **declare** all other identifiers, and you must specify whether each variable represents **Integer** or **Real** data.
5. After the declarations, indicate the steps the machine is to follow, in a **statement block.** Start with *Begin* and conclude with *End*. The steps may include
   - *Input of data.* Use *Read* or *Readln* when you want to type data into the computer from a keyboard.
   - *Arithmetic operations.* Use the arithmetic operations +, −, *, / for real or integer data. Use *Mod* and *Div* for integers.
   - *Conversion of types.* Conversion from integer to real is done automatically. Conversion from real to integer can be done in either of two ways, and you must specify the appropriate function, *Round* or *Trunc*.
   - *Assignments.* Once values have been computed, these values can be assigned to identifiers, using :=.

| KEY TERMS, PHRASES, AND CONCEPTS | | ELEMENTS OF PASCAL SYNTAX | |
|---|---|---|---|
| Arithmetic Operators and Operator Procedure | Printing Numbers and Text | Arithmetic operations: +, −, *, / , *Div*, *Mod* | Quotes ' ' for text |
| Assignments | Program Heading | *Begin* | *Read* |
| Begin–End Block | Program Readability and Style | Comments { } | *Readln* |
| Comments | Real Number | *Const* | *Real* |
| Constants | Reserved Words | *End* | *Round* |
| Declarations | Semantics | Identifier | Semicolon ; |
| Formatting Programs and Output | Statements | *Input* | *Trunc* |
| Identifiers | Syntax | *Integer* | *Var* |
| Input of Data | Testing | *MaxInt* | *Write* |
| Integers | Type | *Output* | *Writeln* |
| Output | Type Conversion | *Program* | |
| Precedence | Variables | | |
| Predefined Identifier | | | |

- *Output*. Use *Write* or *Writeln* to print numbers or text. With some care, you can identify all results clearly and prompt the user when input is required.

6. Write programs in a style and format that allow you and others to understand them easily and clearly. When writing programs you should make effective use of comments, indenting and spacing, descriptive names, constants, and input and output.
7. After a program is written, **test** it to be sure that it works as intended.

## EXERCISES

**2.1** Rewrite the Unit Pricing program in Section 2.1 so the output is nicely labeled and formatted.

**2.2** Rewrite the Unit Pricing program further so that the cost and the size of the item are entered from the keyboard.

**2.3** Section 2.7 lists several features of good programming style. Find a sample program in this chapter to illustrate each feature.

**2.4** Section 2.8 suggests selecting test data where the answers are already known or obvious. Determine a good set of test data for checking each of the following programs:

a. The Sales Tax program (Section 2.3)
b. The Change-Making program (Section 2.5)
c. The Sphere program (Section 2.6)

**2.5** When shopping for pizza, we can find the best buy by determining the relative cost of each size. Assuming pizzas all have the same thickness, write a program that reads the cost of a pizza and its diameter (in inches) and computes the cost per square inch of pizza.

**2.6** In the previous problem, suppose that pizzas can have different thicknesses (e.g., deep-dish and thin crust). Modify your program to include the thickness of the pizza as well as the cost and diameter in determining the cost per unit volume of the pizza.

**2.7** As a pizza restaurant owner, you have determined that you can sell your 6-inch pizza for $3.50 to make a reasonable profit and still stay competitive. If your 10-inch, 12-inch, and 14-inch pizzas all have the same thickness, how much should you charge for these sizes?

HINT: Compare the areas of the pizzas.

**2.8** In the previous problem, you computed the costs of pizzas based on a thin-crust, 6-inch pizza. Suppose that your price for a deep-dish 6-inch pizza should be $4.50. Write a program that computes the appropriate prices for 6-inch, 10-inch, 12-inch, and 14-inch pizzas for both deep-dish and thin crust styles. Use the relative areas of the pizzas to determine price, and print your results in a table.

**2.9** Write a program that computes the molecular weight of a hydrocarbon molecule, given the number of atoms of carbon, oxygen, and hydrogen. From a handbook, we find

| Atom | Atomic Weight |
|---|---|
| Carbon | 12.011 |
| Hydrogen | 1.0079 |
| Oxygen | 15.9994 |

**2.10** *Making Change, Expanded.* Modify the change-making problem of Section 2.5 so that it reads the amount of change a customer is to receive and then determines the number of bills, quarters, dimes, nickels, and pennies to be paid back to the customer.

**2.11** A family wants to determine the cost and the efficiency of its car during a trip. Write a program that computes miles per gallon and cents per mile, given total cost, distance, and fuel consumption on the trip.

**2.12** Write a program to compute a person's weight in grams, given weight in pounds (1 pound avoirdupois = approximately 473.59 grams).

**2.13** A common algorithm for finding the distance between you and a flash of lightning goes like this: When you see the lightning flash, count the seconds before you hear the thunder. If you divide this time by 5, you will have the approximate number of miles between you and the lightning.

This algorithm is based on the fact that sound normally travels about 1100 feet per second. In comparison, light's velocity is almost instantaneous; it takes virtually no time for the light to go from the lightning flash to where you are standing. Thus, the time you count before hearing the thunder gives a good measurement of the time it takes for sound to travel from the lightning to you.

Write a program that will compute the distance in feet and in miles from you to the lightning, given the time delay in seconds before you hear the thunder.

**2.14** Write a program that reads a volume in quarts and computes the corresponding volume in liters (1 liter = 1.056710 quarts).

**2.15** Write a program that converts temperature in Fahrenheit to Centigrade and Kelvin.

NOTE: Centigrade = 5/9 (Fahrenheit − 32);
Kelvin = Centigrade + 273.

# CHAPTER 3

# STRUCTURE IN PROBLEM SOLVING: INTRODUCTION TO FUNCTIONS

In Chapter 2 we saw how to write simple programs to help solve fairly straightforward problems. In this chapter we return to our problem solving theme, describing a more complete methodology for finding solutions. We will consider a general approach to problem solving. Then we will discuss the first of two major applications of this general approach by considering the concept of *functions*. Chapter 4 will expand this notion of functions to a more general setting, using the Pascal concept of *procedures*.

## SECTION 3.1 PROBLEM SOLVING METHODOLOGY

In Chapter 1 we identified the following basic steps in the problem solving process:

- initial statement of the problem
- precise formulation of the problem—requirements
- development of a general plan of attack—general design
- development of efficient algorithms—detailed design

- application of the plan to the details of the problem—algorithm execution
- interpretation of results

We also discussed one approach for designing algorithms, a **top-down methodology.** In this section we will look at this approach and a second approach in some detail, and we will identify a general-purpose problem solving strategy.

In the precise formulation of a problem, we identify what we are given and determine what results we want. Algorithms then specify the means for getting from our givens to our desired results.

Sometimes we can see immediately how to proceed to get results, but in complex problems the path may not be so obvious. It is worthwhile to analyze why this path may be difficult to find. Although each problem has its own characteristics, the difficulties often fit into one or more categories:

solutions that involve many steps

problems that involve many details

problems that involve some complicated steps

If we analyze these difficulties further, we see that much of the trouble reduces to a fundamental human limitation: Our minds can only keep track of a certain amount of information at a time. We try to focus our attention on the problem at hand, but when the problem gets too big, we cannot keep all parts of the problem in mind at the same time.

For example, if a solution requires many steps, we may be able to keep the basic steps in mind, but we may not be able to look at the overall outline of steps while we figure out the details of each step. Similarly, if a problem contains many details, we may find it hard to remember all of these details at once.

## Motivation for a Top-Down Strategy

Once we have made these observations about our own limitations, we can also see how to resolve some of the difficulties. First, we need to organize our work so we do not have to remember everything at once. Second, we need to be able to distinguish between the basic steps and the details of those steps. Sometimes we must worry about details, but we must also be able to step back from the details to see the general task that motivates the details. If we can apply these two principles, then we can avoid being overwhelmed by the complexity or the size of a problem.

When faced with a complex problem, we can begin a solution by identifying the major steps needed to perform the task. Once we know that the major steps fit together logically to give a solution to a problem, we can decide how to do each step in turn.

For example, consider the solution to the Making Change problem in

Section 2.5. The original problem was to determine the number of $10 bills, $5 bills, $1 bills, and coins that are needed to make change for a customer. When considering this problem, we analyzed how we actually make change. Once we knew the amount to be paid, we first counted out tens, then fives, then ones, and finally the amount in coins as needed. This analysis suggested the following initial outline:

*Initial Outline for Making Change*

**I.** Determine the amount of change.
**II.** Compute the amount to be paid in bills.
**III.** Compute the amount to be paid in coins.
**IV.** Compute the number of $10 bills.
**V.** Compute the number of $5 bills.
**VI.** Compute the number of $1 bills.
**VII.** Print the amount paid in coins.

This initial outline does not contain any details concerning how the various computations might be made. Rather, this outline covers the main steps needed in a solution. Further, when you read this outline you can see that the problem will be solved if you can do each of these steps. The outline is short enough to keep track of what you are doing, and you can see that these basic steps will fit together correctly. Once you have this initial outline, you can focus your attention on each step individually. For example, in Step IV you only have to determine how to compute the number of $10 bills required, and you can assume that Steps I, II, and III have been performed. Thus your work in Step IV is reduced to finding the number of tens required, given the amount to be paid in bills.

The point is that once an initial outline is developed at a general level, you can look at each step in the outline as a simpler, smaller problem. Then you can focus your attention on each smaller problem in turn, without being distracted by the magnitude of the entire problem. In the example, Step IV presents a relatively simple task to handle, to compute the number of $10 bills required given the total amount to be paid in bills.

While this task may not be trivial, it is certainly much easier than the initial problem. In Section 2.5 we came up with the idea of dividing the amount to be paid in bills by 10 and taking the integer quotient. There might be other approaches that work as well. If you do find several solutions, you will have to pick a method that seems best.

This approach of dividing a major problem into steps has a second advantage as well, which is also illustrated in the Making Change problem. The solution of one of the smaller pieces (e.g., Step IV) may suggest similar approaches for solving some of the other pieces (e.g., Steps V and VI). Thus, when we look at the detailed outline in Section 2.5, we find that several of our steps follow the same idea of integer division. (We will expand on this observation shortly.)

This approach to problem solving has the further advantage that once the initial outline is established, you can apply the entire approach to any or all of the steps in turn. If one of the steps still seems quite complicated, you can treat that step as a new problem and find a general outline to finish that task. As a result, one step may contain several headings under it. This process can then continue until the pieces are sufficiently small to work out in detail.

### Top-Down Methodology

This general approach is called a top-down methodology, and it will be our major problem solving approach throughout this text. To summarize the strategy we can identify the following features:

1. Start by outlining a solution at a general or abstract level.
2. Consider each step of the outline separately.
3. If necessary, outline specific steps, so some headings are subdivided into subheadings.
4. At each stage in the process, start at a general level and work toward more detailed levels.

### Bottom-Up Methodology

Instead of the top-down approach, you might analyze various details and then identify several places where you need to perform the same tasks. For example, in the Making Change problem, we followed the same general approach in computing the number of $10 bills, $5 bills, and $1 bills.

This task identification is called a **bottom-up methodology,** for it generalizes from details and moves toward an overall structure. Note that this bottom-up approach is philosophically opposed to a top-down methodology, where you work from a general outline down to the details.

### A Revised Top-Down Strategy

After considering these two strategies, it is apparent that the top-down methodology more effectively allows us to focus attention on a few pieces at a time, so we will always begin working top-down with an initial outline, refining the outline and adding subheadings as appropriate. In analyzing one part of the outline, however, we may also look at other parts to see if there are several places where we want to do the same work. If so, we will determine the details of that task just once, note the details outside the outline, and refer to that common task from the several places.

For example, in designing a wagon, we would start from the general concept of "wagon." Then, once we decide that the wagon must be supported in four places, we will not try to invent the wheel four times!

## SECTION 3.2 STANDARD FUNCTIONS

The previous section developed a revised top-down strategy for solving complex problems. In this section we will see how we can apply this strategy in a rather elementary setting. The following sections will expand upon this simple application.

Already in problem solving, we have needed to perform certain operations beyond the simple arithmetic computations of addition, subtraction, multiplication, and division. For example, in Chapter 2, we needed to convert real numbers to integers, and we used *Trunc* and *Round* in various expressions for this conversion. In Pascal, *Trunc* and *Round* are two examples of the more general concept of a function, which allows us to compute various values effectively within a program. In using these functions, we can perform some of the details of a solution to a problem without losing track of the main steps of our solution outline.

A complete list of the standard numeric functions available in Pascal is given in Table 3–1. When any of these functions are used, a value is computed for the function, and this value is substituted for the function in the arithmetic expression. In the following problem, we see how these functions might be used.

**TABLE 3–1 • Standard Arithmetic Functions**

| Function Code | Meaning | Examples |
|---|---|---|
| Abs(x) | Compute the absolute value of x.<br>If x is real, then Abs(x) is real.<br>If x is an integer, then Abs(x) is also an integer. | 3.2 = Abs(3.2)<br>5.1 = Abs(−5.1)<br>0.0 = Abs(0.0)<br>3 = Abs(3)<br>2 = Abs(−2) |
| Sqr(x) | Compute the square of x.<br>As with Abs(x), Sqr(x) will be the same type (real or integer) as x. | 1.44 = Sqr(1.2)<br>9.61 = Sqr(−3.1)<br>0 = Sqr(0)<br>64 = Sqr(8) |
| Sqrt(x) | Compute the nonnegative square root of x.<br>x must be a nonnegative number, although x may be either real or integer.<br>Sqrt(x) is always real.<br>(If x < 0, then Sqrt(x) produces an error.) | 2.0 = Sqrt(4.0)<br>1.414. . . = Sqrt(2.0)<br>0 = Sqrt(0.0)<br>ERROR = Sqrt(−103) |

**TABLE 3–1 • Standard Arithmetic Functions (continued)**

| Function Code | Meaning | Examples |
|---|---|---|
| | Logarithms and Exponentials[1] | |
| Exp(x) | Compute $e^x$, i.e., raise the number e to the exponent x. x may be real or integer, but Exp(x) is always of real type. | 1.0 = Exp(0)<br>2.718. . . = Exp(1) |
| Ln(x) | Compute the natural logarithm of x; $\log_e x$ x must be a positive number, although x may be either real or integer. Ln(x) is always real (If $x \leq 0$, then Ln(x) produces an error.) | 0.0 = Ln(1.0)<br>1.0 = Ln(2.718) |
| | Trigonometry[2, 3] | |
| Sin(x) | Compute the sine of x. x may be real or integer. Sin(x) is always real. | 0.0 = Sin(0.0)<br>1.0 = Sin(Pi/2.0) |
| Cos(x) | Compute the cosine of x. x may be real or integer. Cos(x) is always real. | 1.0 = Cos(1.0)<br>0.0 = Cos(Pi/2.0) |
| Arctan(x) | Compute the principal value of the arctangent of x. x may be real or integer. Arctan(x) is always real. | 0.78 ≈ Arctan(1)<br>(Recall 0.78 ≈ Pi/4.0) |

[1]e is the base of the natural logarithms, e ~ 2.718281828459. . . .
[2]A knowledge of trigonometry is not required for this text, although some exercises do use this background. These problems will be marked specifically, and they may be skipped without loss of continuity.
[3]All angles are measured in radians. In the examples in this section, assume Pi is the constant 3.14159265. To convert from degrees to radians, use the formula

$$\text{radians} = \frac{\text{Pi}}{180}\text{ degrees}$$

**PROBLEM 3.2**

Each fall, you need to clean the gutters on your house, and you need a ladder to get to the roof. You can measure the length of the ladder, and you can estimate the height of the house.

FIGURE 3–1 • **A Ladder from the Ground to the Top of a House**

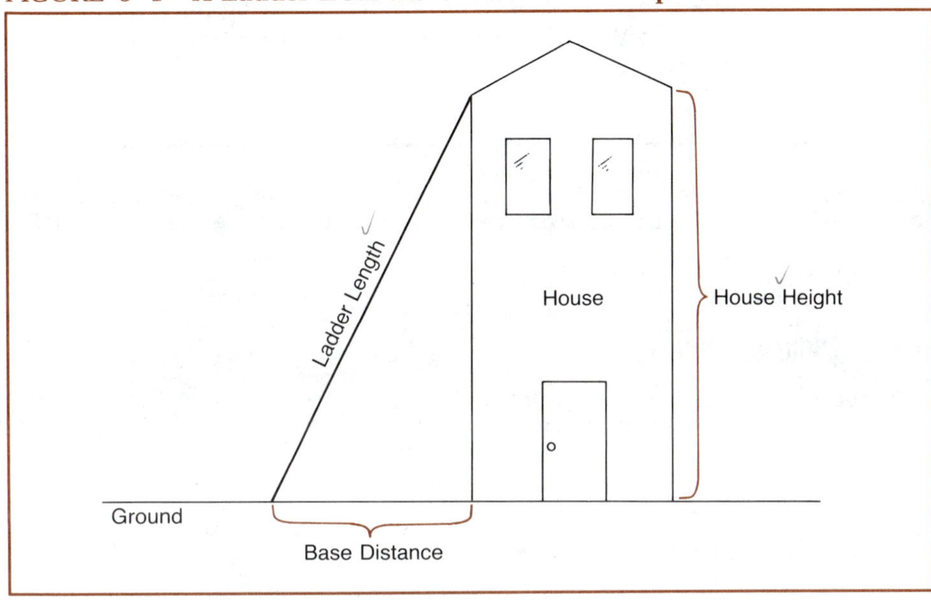


Compute the distance that the base of the ladder should be from the house so that the top of the ladder will reach the roof (see Figure 3–1).

## Solution for Problem 3.2

We know the length and the height in our figure, and we want to find the base distance for the ladder. We assume here that this information was measured correctly and that it will be entered into the computer correctly. In a later chapter, we will see how this entry might be controlled. Using the Pythagorean theorem, which relates these quantities, we find

$$(\text{Length})^2 = (\text{Base})^2 + (\text{Height})^2.$$

With this equation, we can outline the solution.

## Outline for Problem 3.2

**I.** Determine house height and ladder length.

**II.** Compute the base distance for the ladder.
The correct formula is

$$\text{Base} = \sqrt{(\text{Length})^2 - (\text{Height})^2}$$

**III.** Print results.

## Discussion of Problem 3.2

While this outline follows the same general form as many earlier outlines, we cannot compute the required square root with the simple arithmetic operations from Chapter 2. From Table 3–1, however, we see that Pascal can compute square roots using a function called *Sqrt*. We can compute a square root of a number x by writing *Sqrt(x)*.

With the *Sqrt* function, we are ready to write a program for Problem 3.2.

```
Program Ladder (Input, Output);
{This program computes the distance required between the base of a ladder
 and a house, if the top of the ladder is to reach the roof of a house.}

Var Height, Base, Length: Real;
    BaseSquared: Real;

Begin {Main}

    {Determine Length and Height}
    Writeln ('This program determines the distance between the base of a');
    Writeln ('ladder and a house, so the ladder reaches a house''s roof.');
    Write ('Please enter the length of the ladder: ');
    Readln (Length);
    Write ('Please enter the height (in feet) of the house: ');
    Readln (Height);

    {Compute the length of the ladder}
    BaseSquared := Length*Length - Height*Height;
    Base := Sqrt(BaseSquared);

    {Print Results}
    Writeln;
    Writeln ('Position the base of the ladder ', Base:1:1,
             ' feet from the house.')

End {Main} .
```

When this program is run with a house height of 18 feet and a ladder length of 20 feet, we will have the following interaction with the computer.

```
This program determines the distance between the base of a
ladder and a house, so the ladder reaches a house's roof.
Please enter the length of the ladder: 20
Please enter the height (in feet) of the house: 18

Position the base of the ladder 8.7 feet from the house.
```

This program first computes the square of the desired base distance, then it applies the *Sqrt* function to obtain the desired base distance. The computations proceed as in earlier problems, except that we have used *Sqrt* to compute the needed square root, with this statement:

Base := Sqrt (BaseSquared)

*BaseSquared* is the appropriate distance squared, and we apply the square root function *Sqrt* to the value.

In fact, we could do all of the computation in one line, without reference to the intermediate value *BaseSquared*. In this version, we would replace the two lines in the computation section with

Base := Sqrt (Length*Length − Base*Base)

The value

Length*Length − Base*Base

is computed first, then the square root of the quantity is determined. The computer works first with the expression inside parentheses and then applies *Sqrt*.

Pascal also has a squaring function, *Sqr* (see Table 3–1). The solution could therefore take the following form:

```
Program Ladder {Revised} (Input, Output);
{This program computes the distance required between the base of a ladder
 and a house, if the top of the ladder is to reach the roof of a house.}

Var Height, Base, Length: Real;

Begin {Main}

    {Determine Length and Height}
    Writeln ('This program determines the distance between the base of a');
    Writeln ('ladder and a house, so the ladder reaches a house''s roof.');
    Write ('Please enter the length of the ladder: ');
    Readln (Length);
    Write ('Please enter the height (in feet) of the house: ');
    Readln (Height);

    {Compute the length of the ladder}
    Base := Sqrt( Sqr(Length) - Sqr(Height) );

    {Print Results}
    Writeln;
    Writeln ('Position the base of the ladder ', Base:1:1,
             ' feet from the house.')

End {Main} .
```

In this program the computation of *Base* is reduced to one line, as before, and the *Sqr* function is used twice—*Sqr(Length)* computes *Length*Length; Sqr(Height)* computes *Height*Height*. In computing the value of this expression, the computer again starts inside the parentheses. First, *Sqr(Length)* and *Sqr(Height)* are computed. Then, these values are added. Finally, the *Sqrt* function is applied to the sum.

You can use any of the standard arithmetic functions in Pascal programs, in the same way that you use the other operations of arithmetic, such as addition and subtraction. These functions are easy to use, and they expand the range of computations you can do.

Finally, note that these functions do not require understanding any details about performing the computations. For example, you need not know how square roots are computed. The details of computation are hidden within the functions themselves, and you can ignore the details when you use the functions. This use of functions is completely consistent with the problem solving methodology discussed earlier. You can think of these functions as performing common tasks, and you can distinguish between the steps of the outline and the technical details of various tasks.

## SECTION 3.3 EXAMPLE OF A USER-DEFINED FUNCTION

Section 3.1 developed a revised top-down strategy for solving complex problems, where a problem is divided into pieces and each of these pieces is then considered separately. We also saw that we can identify common tasks that we can use when several parts of a solution outline require the same work. Next, Section 3.2 presented several functions that were useful in performing some of the detailed steps required in the solution of a problem. In using these functions, the details of individual steps did not detract from the overall flow of a solution.

In this section, we combine the revised top-down strategy with the idea of functions by considering an example where we define our own functions to compute some results needed in a solution outline.

### PROBLEM 3.3

Suppose you deposit a specific amount of money in a bank account at a given rate of interest. Determine how the money in the account would grow over a year if the interest is compounded annually, semiannually, quarterly, monthly, and daily. With these computations, you will be able to conclude which compounding gives the best return on your money.

### Discussion of Problem 3.3

From handbooks or texts you can find the following formula:

$$\text{Balance} = \text{Principal}\ (1 + \text{rate/frequency})^{\text{frequency}}$$

where

*Balance* is the amount in the account at the end of the year,

*Principal* is the amount deposited at the start of the year,

*rate* is the annual interest rate,

*frequency* is the number of times interest is compounded during the year.

### Restatement of Problem 3.3

With this formula and jargon, we can restate our problem as follows: Given the Principal and rate for a bank account, compute the Balance in the account for frequency = 1, 2, 4, 12, 365.

When we consider this revised problem statement, we observe that we want to use the same formula in several computations. This suggests that we can consider the balance formula as a common task for use in several places in our program. Also, for readability we decide to format our results in a table. This analysis leads to the following.

### Outline for Problem 3.3

Common Task: Compute the Balance using the formula

$$\text{Balance} = \text{Principal}\ (1 + \text{rate/frequency})^{\text{frequency}}$$

**I.** Determine Principal and interest rate.
**II.** Print headings for table.
**III.** Compute the Balance for frequency = 1
**IV.** Compute the Balance for frequency = 2
**V.** Compute the Balance for frequency = 4
**VI.** Compute the Balance for frequency = 12
**VII.** Compute the Balance for frequency = 365

When we try to translate this outline into a Pascal program, we make two observations. First, Steps III through VII all use the common task that we identified at the start of the outline. We are not particularly interested in the formula for computation; we want to focus on the *Balance* itself. Therefore, we would like to write a program in a way that focuses on the *Balance* for the given *Principal, rate,* and *frequency.*

Second, the formula requires taking the quantity (1 + *rate/frequency*) to the power *frequency*. We do not care about the details of the computation, but we do need to compute with this exponent. Unfortunately, Pascal does not allow us to perform this exponentiation directly. Instead, to compute $r^s$ in Pascal, we need to write the expression *exp(s*ln(r))*, which uses the two Pascal functions *exp* and *ln*.

In the problem at hand, the formula is tangential to our focus on bank interest, so we can write a program where the formulas for computing balances and powers are removed from the main steps of the outline, as in the following program.

```
Program BankInterest {Version 1} (Input, Output);
{This program computes one's bank balance after one year.}

Var Principal: Real;
    Interest: Real;

Function Powers (Base, Exponent: Real): Real;
{This function raises Base to the power Exponent.}
    Begin
        Powers := Exp(Exponent * Ln(Base))
    End {Powers} ;

Function Balance (Prin, Rate, Freq: Real): Real;
{This function computes the Balance in a bank account,
 given the Principal, annual interest Rate,
 and the Frequency of compounding.}
    Begin
        Balance := Prin * Powers (1 + Rate/Freq, Freq)
    End {Balance} ;

Begin {Main Program}

    {Determine Principal and Interest}
    Writeln ('Computation of Bank Balances');
    Writeln;
    Write ('Enter Principal and Interest Rate:  ');
    Readln (Principal, Interest);

    {Print Headings for the Output}
    Writeln;
    Writeln (' Number of');
    Writeln ('Compounding');
    Writeln ('  Periods      Balance');

    {Compute and Print the Balances}
    Writeln (  1:6, Balance(Principal, Interest,  1.0):15:2);
    Writeln (  2:6, Balance(Principal, Interest,  2.0):15:2);
    Writeln (  4:6, Balance(Principal, Interest,  4.0):15:2);
    Writeln ( 12:6, Balance(Principal, Interest, 12.0):15:2);
    Writeln (365:6, Balance(Principal, Interest,365.0):15:2);

End {Main Program}.
```

Before we look at how this program works, note the output when we specify a *Principal* of $1500 at an annual interest *rate* of 8 percent:

```
Computation of Bank Balances

Enter Principal and Interest Rate:  1500.0  0.08
```

```
 Number of
Compounding
  Periods       Balance
     1          1620.00
     2          1622.40
     4          1623.65
    12          1624.50
   365          1624.98
```

Now we are ready to trace the execution of this program. An overview of the steps that are followed in running this program is shown in Figure 3–2. The program starts with the *Begin* of the Main Program. After printing some text the computer reads values for *Principal* and for *Interest*. This completes Step I of the outline.

The next three lines print the headings for the table, completing Step II. So far, we are proceeding straight through the program.

In Step III the execution becomes more involved. The first line reads

```
Writeln (1:6, Balance(Principal, Interest, 1.0):15:2);
```

This tells the computer to print two numbers in specified formats. The computer will write the numbers one at a time. First the computer prints the number 1, allowing six spaces. Then the computer must print *Balance*. It proceeds in several steps. For this example we will use *Principal* = 1500 and *Interest* = 0.08.

*Step 1:* Function *Balance* is called.

```
        { Function Balance (Prin, Rate, Freq: Real): Real;
Program {
        { Writeln (1:6, Balance (Principal, Interest, 1.0):15:2);
                                    1500.      .08
```

The values for *Prin*, *Rate*, and *Freq* in the function are supplied in the *Writeln* statement:

The value (1500.0) for *Principal* will be used for *Prin* on the function;
the value (0.08) for *Interest* will be used for *Rate* in the function;
The number 1.0 will be used for *Freq* in the function.

*Step 2:* Computation within function *Balance* begins.

```
        {                   1500.  .08    1.0
        { Function Balance (Prin, Rate, Freq: Real): Real;
        { Begin
        {                 1500.               1.08      1.0
Program {    Balance := Prin*Powers(1 + Rate/Freq, Freq)
        {
        {
        {                           1500       .08
        { Writeln (1:6, Balance (Principal, Interest, 1.0):15:2);
```

FIGURE 3–2 • **Schematic Diagram for the Execution of the Bank Interest Program**

Since we have values for *Prin*, *Rate*, and *Freq*, computation begins with 1 + *Rate/Freq*. From earlier data, we have

$$1 + \text{Rate/Freq} = 1 + 0.08/1.0 = 1.08$$

Before the program can go on, however, it must evaluate *Powers*.

*Step 3:* Function *Powers* is called.

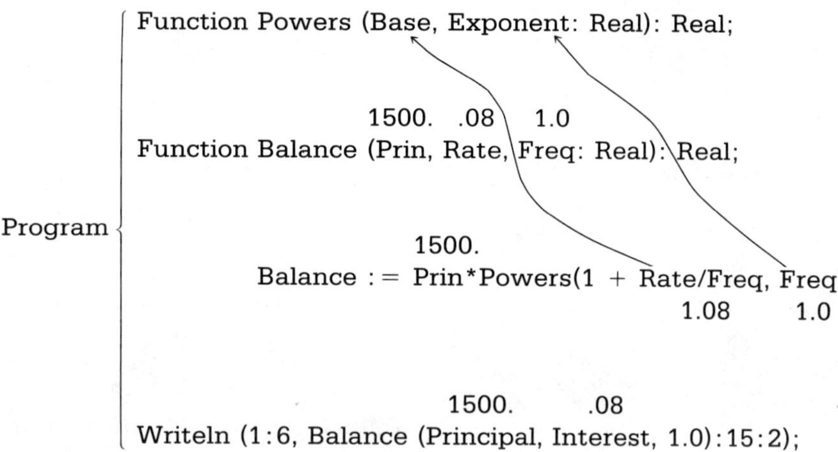


As at the start of the *Balance* function, function *Powers* requires two starting values, *Base* and *Exponent*. These two values are determined by the call in the *Balance* function.

The value 1 + *Rate/Freq* (1.08) will be used for *Base;*
the value *Freq* (1.0) will be used for *Exponent*.

*Step 4:* Computation within function *Powers* begins.

```
                           1.08      1.0
         Function Powers (Base, Exponent: Real): Real;
                                     1.0        1.08
               Powers := Exp (Exponent*Ln(Base))
                         _________________________
                                 1.08

Program                    1500.  .08   1.0
         Function Balance (Prin, Rate, Freq: Real): Real;
                              1500.              1.08     1.0
               Balance := Prin*Powers (1 + Rate/Freq, Freq)


                                 1500.     .08
         Writeln (1:6, Balance (Principal, Interest, 1.0):15:2);
```

The values for *Base* and *Exponent* are used in the Standard Pascal Functions *Ln* and *Exp* to give a value (1.08) for *Powers*. Note that the value is a real number, which agrees with the declaration

```
Function Powers (. . .): Real;
```

*Step 5:* Function *Powers* concludes.

When we reach the *End* of the *Powers* function, the computed value for *Powers* is returned to *Balance*, where it was requested.

```
                  1.08    1.08       1.0
         Function Powers (Base, Exponent: Real): Real;


                               1500.  .08    1.0
         Function Balance (Prin, Rate, Freq: Real): Real;
Program

                           1500.                      1.08      1.0
                Balance := Prin*Powers (1 + Rate/Freq, Freq)


                                  1500.       .08
         Writeln (1:6, Balance (Principal, Interest, 1.0):15:2);
```

Then function *Powers* disappears, as it is no longer needed, and the computer goes back to function *Balance* to continue the computations.

```
                               1500.  .08    1.0
         Function Balance (Prin, Rate, Freq: Real): Real;

Program                    1500.  1.08          1.08        1.0
                Balance := Prin*Powers (1 + Rate/Freq, Freq)

                                 1500.       .08
         Writeln(1:6, Balance (Principal, Interest, 1.0):15:2);
```

*Step 6:* Computation within function *Balance* resumes.

```
                               1500.  .08    1.0
         Function Balance (Prin, Rate, Freq: Real): Real;

                           1500.  1.08          1.08        1.0
Program         Balance := Prin*Powers (1 + Rate/Freq, Freq)
                ____________________________________________
                                   1620.00

                                  1500.       .08
         Writeln (1:6, Balance (Principal, Interest, 1.0):15:2);
```

From function *Powers* the computer has a value (1.08), which can be substituted for Powers (1 + Rate/Freq) in the line

```
Balance := Prin * Powers(1 + Rate/Freq, Freq)
```

Now the computer can complete the computation to obtain a value (1620.00) for *Balance*. Again, note that *Balance* is a real number, which agrees with the function declaration:

```
Function Balance (. . .): Real;
```

*Step 7:* Function *Balance* concludes.

After computing *Balance*, the function *Ends*. As with *Powers*, two actions occur at this point. The computed *Balance* is returned to the Main Program from the function *Balance*.

```
         1620.00 1500.  .08    1.0
        Function Balance (Prin, Rate, Freq: Real): Real;
Program
                                1500.      .08
        Writeln (1:6, Balance (Principal, Interest. 1.0):15:2);
```

Function *Balance* then disappears and the computer goes back to the Main Program.

```
                   1620.00    1500.       .08
Program  Writeln (1:6, Balance (Principal, Interest, 1.0):15:2);
```

## Conclusion of the Writeln Statement

The Main Program has a value for *Balance*, so the computer can print that value in the format designated (:15:2). The computer prints 1620.00 to complete this line of the Main Program.

## Execution of Subsequent Lines

Once the first *Writeln* statement is finished, the computer moves on to subsequent *Writeln* statements. For each *Writeln* statement, the computer repeats the steps just described, using new values for *Freq* as specified. In each case the computer prints the resulting balance and goes on to the next statement.

The output shows that daily compounding gives a little more money in the account at the end of the year, but that amount is not much more than the other compounding possibilities.

## Overview and Summary of the Example

With this explanation of the details of the program's execution, we return to our outline and major motivation in writing this program. Our outline states that we want to use the same formula to determine various bank balances. Our focus is on the balances, and we use the same formula as a common task in each case. Therefore, we write our main program to emphasize each *Balance* and the values *(Principal, Interest, Frequency)* that it depends upon. The details of the formula are isolated in a function that is separate from the main steps in our outline.

Looking at the *Balance* formula itself, we need to compute various powers. Again, the details of computing the powers are tangential to our interest in the *Balance* formula, so we have moved those details to a function *Powers*.

For *Balance* and for *Powers*, we need to compute a value, and we want to separate the computational details from the main point of our work. We can use functions for these details, and the separation can be reflected in the Pascal code.

## SECTION 3.4 ELEMENTS OF DEFINING SIMPLE FUNCTIONS

Section 3.3 presented some illustrations of functions defined by the programmer. We gave a function some values at the start, then let the function perform a computation, and finally concluded with a specific value. In this section we look at these functions more formally.

In Pascal, we begin a program with a heading and then a listing of the pieces we will use (constants, variables, and functions). Then we use these pieces in the main program, between the reserved words *Begin* and *End*. This same structure is repeated when we look at the form for defining functions, as was illustrated by our example from the previous section:

```
Function Balance (Prin, Rate, Freq: Real): Real;
    Begin
          Balance := Prin*Powers(1 + Rate/Freq, Freq)
    End
```

We now comment on each part of a function in more detail.

### Function Name

Functions always start with the reserved word *Function*, followed by an identifier we wish to use to refer to our function.

### Parameter List

Next, in parentheses, we list the values we will need for computation, and we give those values names. In the example, we needed three real numbers to begin the computation—*Prin*, *Rate*, and *Freq*. This list of variables, or **formal parameters**, declares some of the identifiers to be used within the function. The example also shows that when the function is called in a program, initial values are assigned to the formal parameters.

In the declaration and initialization you must be consistent in the order of parameters, because the computer matches up formal parameters with values, or **actual parameters**, each time the function is used. From the example, the function declaration begins

```
Function Balance (Prin, Rate, Freq: Real)
```

and the function is used with the statement

```
Balance (Principal, Interest, 1.0)
```

Here *Prin, Rate,* and *Freq* are the formal parameters, referred to within the function itself. *Principal, Interest,* and 1.0 are the actual parameters, used to initialize the formal parameters. It is important to note the order used to specify the parameters. The first formal parameter, *Prin,* is given the value of the first actual parameter, *Principal,* in the function call. Similarly, the second formal parameter, *Rate,* is given the value from the second actual parameter, *Interest.* Finally, the third elements on each list, *Freq* and 1.0, are matched. Be sure to list the formal parameters in the same order that you write the actual parameters. If you change the order of elements in a formal parameter list, you must be sure to change the order of the actual parameters as well. If you list formal parameters in a different order from the actual parameters, computations will be based on inappropriate data and will give erroneous results.

The formal parameter list at the start of the function specifies the type of each of the formal parameters. *Prin, Rate,* and *Freq* were declared to be real. As with other variables discussed in earlier chapters, parameters may be declared individually or in groups. All of the following parameter lists are equivalent:

```
(Prin, Rate, Freq: Real)
(Prin: Real; Rate: Real; Freq: Real)
(Prin, Rate: Real; Freq: Real)
(Prin: Real; Rate, Freq: Real)
```

In each case, the formal parameters have the same type (real) and are listed in the same order. In contrast, the parameter list

```
(Prin, Freq: Real; Rate: Real)
```

is not equivalent to those above, since the parameters appear in a different order.

In summary, the parameter list in a function declaration serves three purposes: It specifies the names of the formal parameters to be used in a function; it specifies the order of the parameters; and it specifies the type—real or integer—of the parameters. Each time that the function is used, we must be sure that the actual parameters have the same order and type specified in the function's parameter list.

## Function Type

After the parameter list, we specify the type of value—real or integer—that the function computes. In the example, we specify that the final *Balance* would be a real number.

## Function Block

Once the parameters have been defined, we can proceed with actual computations. Here the syntax has a form that is similar to the main program itself. The work starts with *Begin* and concludes with *End;* . Between these keywords, statements are specified, separated by semicolons. In writing these statements, we have considerable flexibility in writing out the details of our function. However, we must be aware that our motivation for using functions is to compute a specific result that can be used later. Therefore, at some point in our function, we must assign the function a value. For example, in our illustrations in this section we have written

```
Balance := Prin*Powers(1 + Rate/Freq, Freq)
```

In each case, we performed some computations and stored a result under the function name *Balance* for use when the function finishes.

In a function block we can use formal parameters in computations, and we must assign a value to the function name before the function is done. Until you have more background, however, you should not use the function name within the function itself as part of the computations on the right side of the assignment statements.

This completes our description of the pieces that make up a function. In the next section, we consider an example involving new variables that may defined within a function itself.

## SECTION 3.5 SCOPE AND LOCAL AND GLOBAL VARIABLES

In the previous sections, we saw how to write functions that compute results based upon initial parameters. To begin this section, we consider a new example where the computations are somewhat more involved than we have encountered earlier in this chapter.

## PROBLEM 3.5 Determining Loan Payments

In investigating the possibility of taking a loan from a bank, we want to determine the amount of the monthly payment, given the interest rate of the loan. Write a program that computes the amount of these payments, if the loan is to be paid off in 3, 5, 10, 15, or 20 years.

### Discussion of Problem 3.5

The following formula may be found in various textbooks and handbooks:

$$\text{Payment} = \text{Amount}\,\frac{\text{MRate}}{1 - (1 + \text{MRate})^{-\text{Months}}}$$

where

*Payment* is the monthly payment,

*Amount* is the initial amount of the loan,

*MRate* is the monthly interest rate (that is, the annual interest rate divided by 12), and

*Months* is the number of months over which the loan is to be paid off.

In applying the formula, our solution parallels the Monthly Interest Problem of Section 3.3, although the computations involve several steps. Once again, the formula may be regarded as a common task that is required several times, and for readability we organize the output in the form of a table.

### Outline for Problem 3.5

Common Task: Compute the Monthly Payment, given the amount of the loan and the annual interest rate.

**A.** Compute number of months:

$$\text{Months} := 12 * \text{years}.$$

**B.** Compute monthly interest rate:

$$\text{MRate} := \text{annual interest rate} / 12.$$

**C.** Compute the monthly payment:

$$\text{Payment} = \text{Amount} \frac{\text{MRate}}{1 - (1 + \text{MRate})^{-\text{Months}}}.$$

**I.** Determine the amount of loan and annual interest rate.
**II.** Print headings for table.
**III.** Compute the monthly payment for 3 years.
**IV.** Compute the monthly payment for 5 years.
**V.** Compute the monthly payment for 10 years.
**VI.** Compute the monthly payment for 15 years.
**VII.** Compute the monthly payment for 20 years.

When we translate this outline into a Pascal program, we use one function to perform the details of the payment computation and another function to compute the power in the formula. Further, since these computations involve several steps, we define some new variables within the functions to aid our work.

---

```
Program MonthlyPayment (Input, Output);
{This program computes the monthly payment required for a bank loan,
 given the size of the loan and the annual interest rate.}

Const ThreeYear = 3;
      FiveYear  = 5;
      TenYear   = 10;
      FifteenYr= 15;
      TwentyYr = 20;

Var Amount: Real;           {Initial amount of loan}
    AnnRate: Real;          {Annual interest rate}
```

```
Function Powers (Base, Exponent: Real): Real;
{This function raises Base to the power Exponent.}
    Var Product: Real;
    Begin
        Product := Exponent * Ln(Base);
        Powers := Exp(Product)
    End {Powers} ;

Function Payment (Amt, ARate: Real; Years: Integer): Real;
{This function computes the monthly loan payment, given the
 amount (AMT) of the loan and the annual interest rate (ARate)
 and the length of the loan in years.}
    Const MonthsPerYear = 12.0;

    Var Months: Real;        {Length of the loan in months}
        MRate: Real;         {Monthly interest rate}
        Denominator: Real; {Part of the required formula}
    Begin
        Months := Years * MonthsPerYear;
        MRate := ARate / MonthsPerYear;
        Denominator := 1.0 - Powers (1.0 + MRate, -Months);
        Payment := Amt * MRate / Denominator
    End {Payment} ;

Begin {Main Program}

    {Determine Loan Amount and Annual Rate}
    Writeln ('Computation of Monthly Payments');
    Writeln;
    Write ('Enter Amount of Loan and Annual Interest Rate:  ');
    Readln (Amount, AnnRate);

    {Print Headings for the Output}
    Writeln;
    Writeln (' Number of');
    Writeln ('   Years      Monthly Payment');

    {Compute and Print the Loan Payments}
    Writeln (ThreeYear:6, Payment(Amount, AnnRate, ThreeYear):15:2);
    Writeln ( FiveYear:6, Payment(Amount, AnnRate, FiveYear):15:2);
    Writeln (  TenYear:6, Payment(Amount, AnnRate, TenYear):15:2);
    Writeln (FifteenYr:6, Payment(Amount, AnnRate, FifteenYr):15:2);
    Writeln ( TwentyYr:6, Payment(Amount, AnnRate, TwentyYr):15:2)

End {Main Program}.
```

When this function is run for a car loan of $5000.00 at a rate of 9.5%, we get the following output:

```
Computation of Monthly Payments

Enter Amount of Loan and Annual Interest Rate:  5000.00 0.095
```

```
Number of
  Years      Monthly Payment
    3          160.16
    5          105.01
   10           64.70
   15           52.21
   20           46.61
```

Once again the main program is structured according to our outline, with function *Payment* performing the details of the monthly payment computation. This program, however, also contains some new aspects of variables and functions, and we need to look at these points in more detail.

## Constants and Variables

In the *Monthly Payment* program, we declared

```
Const ThreeYear =  3;
      FiveYear =   5;
      TenYear =   10;
      FifteenYr = 15;
      TwentyYr =  20;
Var Amount: Real;
    AnnRate: Real;
```

at the start of our program. Then we used these constants and variables as parameters in our functions. Here, we have declared *ThreeYear*, *FiveYear*, *TenYear*, *FifteenYr*, and *TwentyYr* in the main program, and we say that these are **global constants.** Similarly, we declared the variables *Amount* and *AnnRate* in the main program, and these are called **global variables.** These global identifiers are declared at the start of a program, and they can be used anywhere within the program.

In contrast, in function *Payment*, we declared a new constant, called *MonthsPerYear*, which is called a **local constant,** and we declared new variables, called *Months*, *MRate*, and *Denominator*, which are called **local variables.** Local identifiers are declared at the start of a function, and they can be used only within that function. For example, we compute values for these variables within function *Payment*, but we do not use them elsewhere. Similarly in function *Powers*, we declared a local variable *Product*, which we use only in that function.

In each of these cases, local variables allow us to perform computations within a function, but these variables cannot be used outside of the function. For example, if we tried to write the values of *Months*, *MRate*, or *Denominator* in the main program, our program would not compile. The main program knows nothing of the variable *Months*.

### Scope

This distinction between local and global variables is very important, and we must be sure we understand where various constants and variables can be used. We say that the **scope** of global variables is the entire program, and the **scope** of a local variable is the function where it is declared. Scope is the part of a program where an identifier is defined and can be used. As we gain experience with functions, we will find that we will want to use local constants and variables whenever possible, and we will avoid globals whenever possible. (In Chapter 9, we will discuss ways to eliminate virtually all global variables.) For now, we will use global variables as necessary, but we will be careful to use local variables whenever we can restrict our work with a variable to be within a single function.

Visually, we can picture scope through the use of a set of nested boxes (see Figure 3–3). The program **MonthlyPayment** is a large box containing the constants *ThreeYear, FiveYear, TenYear, FifteenYr,* and *TwentyYr;* the variables *Amount* and *AnnRate;* and two functions. Each function has its own smaller box, and all details of that function are hidden in its box.

When we are at any point in a box, we can look out of the box, and we can look within the box. For example, when working within any function, we can look out and use the global constants and variables. However, we cannot look inside other boxes to use variables that might be there. (Here, it might be useful to think of the box walls as one-way mirrors; we can look out but not in.)

Global variables appear outside of all functions, and we can see them from anywhere inside the program. For example, if we declared the constant *MonthsPerYear* in the main program instead of in the function *Payment,* we could use that constant within either of the functions *(Powers* or *Payment)* or anywhere in the main program.

Local variables, on the other hand, appear inside smaller boxes. For example, *Months, MRate,* and *Denominator* appear in the *Payment* box. Thus, we can see (or use) these variables within the *Payment* function but not outside that function. We cannot see them from the main program or from function *Powers.*

We now have seen many of the important aspects of functions and variables. We have distinguished between local and global variables and have examined the scope of these variables. In the next section, we discuss some elements of style that can help us in using functions effectively and easily.

## SECTION 3.6 STYLE

In this chapter, we have refined our approach to problem solving. We start by dividing our solution into steps, and we subdivide each step as needed. Then, when we find a task that is required in several places, we consider

FIGURE 3–3 • **Levels of Declarations for the Monthly Payment Program**

MonthlyPayment Program

| ThreeYear | 3 |
|---|---|
| FiveYear | 5 |
| TenYear | 10 |
| FifteenYr | 15 |
| TwentyYr | 20 |
| Amount | |
| AnnRate | |

Function Powers (Base, Exponent)

| Product | |
|---|---|

Fuction Payment (Amt, ARate, Years)

| MonthsPerYear | 12.0 |
|---|---|
| Months | |
| MRate | |
| Denominator | |

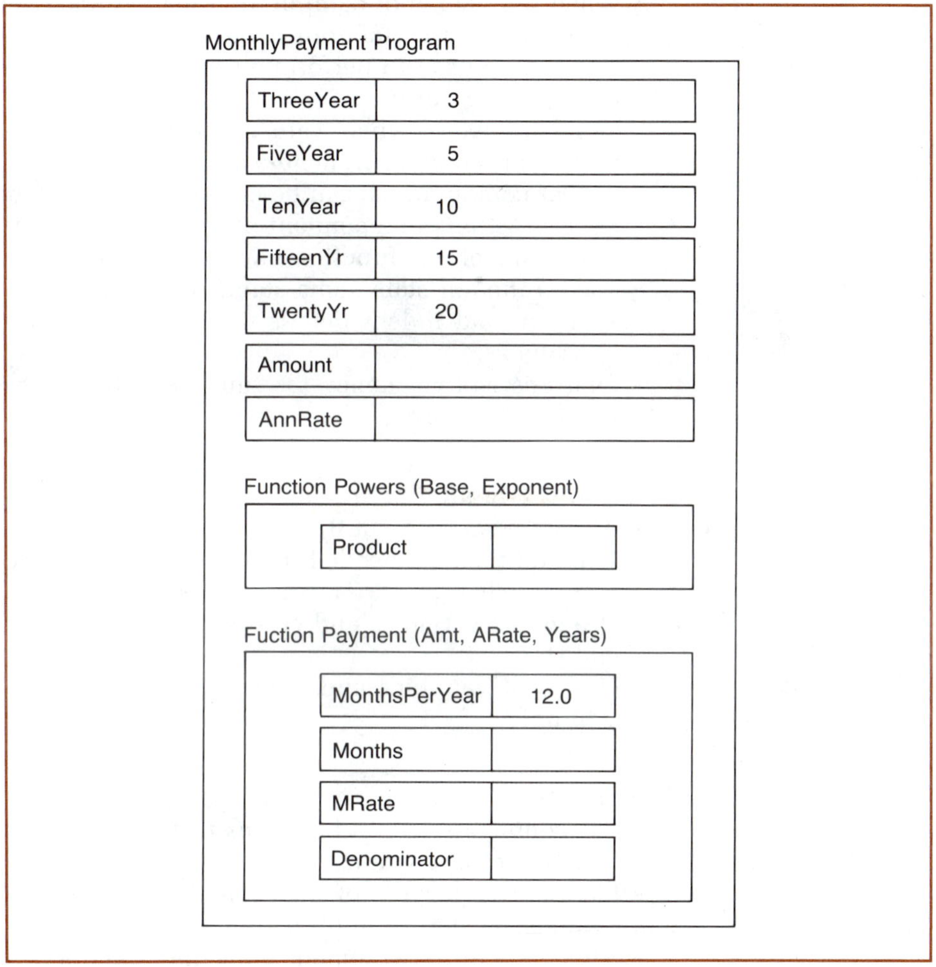

that step separately. This common task is defined outside of our outline, but we refer to it at each appropriate point in our outline.

When we move from the outline to a Pascal program, we can retain the same features of structure. Each separate computation or common task can be written separately as a function. This allows us to apply to programs the same principles of organization that we discussed for outlines.

To be more concrete, our remarks on problem solving suggest the following principles of program style. On this practical level, we will want our programs to be written in a format that further emphasizes the parallelism between solution outlines and programs.

### Functions

- When the details of computation may detract from the general flow of the program, use functions to compute a single result. A function therefore can be used to perform a separate computation or a common task in a solution outline.
- Use parameters when values are needed to start the computations within a function. Parameters allow data to be transmitted to functions, so that computations can be based on the appropriate values.
- Keep functions independent of each other as much as possible, so that the details of one function have little or no impact on other functions.
- Make function statements stand out as major steps in the program or solution, and indent details, including local declarations and *Begin–End* blocks.
- Pick descriptive names for functions that suggest the work that the functions perform.

### Local and Global Variables

- At each step of an outline, distinguish between data needed within a step and the data needed in other steps. Then, declare variables on the basis of what data are needed where.
- Use global variables and constants only when data are needed in several steps.
- Use local variables and constants when data are needed within one step only.

### Comments

- Use comments within functions just as you use them for clarifying the structure of a program.
- Identify the purpose of each function by stating this purpose in a comment at the start of the function.
- Align this initial comment with the *Function* statement; the comment should not be indented. (See programs throughout the chapter as examples.)
- Clarify where each function ends by placing the function's name in a comment after the function's *End* statement.

When we follow these general guidelines in the writing and formatting of our programs, we will find that the style of our programs follows our solution outline very closely. Our program appears as a carefully written, well-organized outline. The general structure of our program stands out clearly, and the details are contained within appropriate steps.

## SUMMARY

1. In an expanded problem solving strategy, we begin with a **top-down** analysis of our problem, dividing our solution into several major steps and subdividing these steps as necessary. However, when we identify the same task in several places, we consider that common task separately. A common task is defined outside of our outline, and we then refer to that task within our outline as needed. This identification of common tasks may be found in a **bottom-up** analysis, and we must be careful not to let the common tasks obscure our overall approach to solving the problem.
2. **Functions** allow us to organize our programs following the steps of our outline. We define a function to compute a single result in our outline.
3. The **Pascal Library** contains functions that we may need for some computations. We can use these basic functions when our work requires some simple algebra or computations with logarithms, exponents, or trigonometry.
4. When we need to define our own function, we declare it, stating the computations it will perform and specifying a final value for the function to return.
5. We can use **parameters** to supply initial values to functions to start the computations. In declaring functions, we specify **formal parameters** that will be used within the functions. Then we state **actual parameters** each time the function is used.
6. Each function can reference **global variables** and **constants** that are needed throughout the problem. Within each function, we also may declare **local variables** and **constants** for the specific details of the step itself. Local variables help us separate the details of one procedure from

| KEY TERMS, PHRASES, AND CONCEPTS | | ELEMENTS OF PASCAL SYNTAX | |
|---|---|---|---|
| Bottom-Up Methodology | Parameters | *Function* | *Ln* |
| Functions | Actual Parameters | Functions | *Round* |
| Calls | Formal Parameters | *Abs* | *Sin* |
| Declarations | Parameter List | *Arctan* | *Sqr* |
| Execution | Pascal Library | *Cos* | *Sqrt* |
| Global Variables | Scope of Constants, Functions, and Variables | *Exp* | *Trunc* |
| Local Variables | Top-down Methodology | | |
| Main Program | | | |

those in other functions. Whenever possible, we should use local identifiers, so our functions can remain as independent as possible.

7. With some care in writing and formatting our programs, the programs can become an extension of our solution outline. Our program has the same structure as our solution, and programming can help us organize and clarify our thoughts in the problem solving process.

## EXERCISES

**3.1** Write a program to input a number and print that number with its square root and cube root.

**3.2** *Purchasing a Ladder.* A ladder will be used to reach the roof of a garage, and the ladder must extend over some bushes next to the garage. For safety, the ladder must extend beyond the roof by more than one foot. Also, in practice, ladders are available only in certain sizes. Find the length of the ladder you should purchase if

a. ladders are available in any whole-foot length;

b. (more challenging) ladders only come in lengths divisible by 2 (e.g., 10 feet, 12 feet, 14 feet)

**3.3** *Quart to Liter Conversion.* From a handbook, we find that 1 quart = 1.056710 liters. Write a program that prints a table of quart and liter equivalents, including appropriate entries for 1, 2, 4, 6, and 8 quarts. In your program, use a function to compute the number of liters for a given number of quarts.

**3.4** *Slope of a Line.* Write a function that computes the slope of a line between two points, where the x and y coordinates of the points are specified as function parameters. Use the function in a program that has the coordinates of two points as parameters and that returns the slope of the line containing those points.

As part of your testing, see what your program does when the line is vertical, but do not try to correct your program to handle this special case.

**3.5** *Equation of a Line.* Expand the previous problem to compute the equation of the line passing through two points.

**3.6** *Composition of a Function.* Write a program that contains two functions $f(x)$ and $g(x)$. For various values of x, compute $f(x)$, $g(x)$, $f(g(x))$, and $g(f(x))$. Run the program several times using different functions of your own choosing for $f(x)$ and $g(x)$. Compare (by hand) the values of $f(g(x))$ and $g(f(x))$.

**3.7** *Sphere Volume and Area.*

a. Rewrite the *Spheres* program of Section 2.6, so that the computations of volume and surface area are performed in separate functions.

**b.** Extend your program from part (a) so that the program prints a table, giving the volume and surface area for spheres of radius 1, 1.5, 2.0, 3.0, and 6.0.

**3.8** *Logarithms.*

**a.** Write a program that reads positive numbers $a$ and $b$ and prints $\log_b a$.

**b.** Write a program that reads a positive number $a$ and computes the common logarithm of $a$.

*Hint:* A basic formula of logarithms is

$$\log_b a = \frac{\ln(a)}{\ln(b)}.$$

**3.9** *Other Trigonometric Functions.* Write a program that reads the measure of an angle in radians and computes the sine, cosine, tangent, cotangent, secant, and cosecant of that angle. (Hint: Since all trigonometric functions can be defined in terms of sine and cosine, the exercise can be done using the two standard Pascal functions *Sin* and *Cos*.)

**3.10** *Radian Measure.*

**a.** Write a program that reads the measure of an angle in degrees and uses a function *Rad* to find the size of the angle in radians.

**b.** Define functions *DegSin* and *DegCos* with an angle in degrees as formal parameter and that use the *Rad* function from part (a) and the standard *Sin* and *Cos* functions to compute the sine and the cosine of the angle, respectively.

**c.** Use your functions in a program that reads the measure of an angle in degrees and prints the sine and cosine of that angle.

(The conversion between degrees and radians is given in a note to Table 3–1.)

radian = $\frac{Pi}{180}$ · degrees

# CHAPTER 4

# SIMPLE PROCEDURES AND PARAMETERS

In Chapter 3, we refined our approach to problem solving, and we divided our overall solution into small pieces. Then, we saw how to use functions to incorporate this strategy into our programs when we needed to compute a particular value during one step of our solution outline.

In this chapter, we extend the notion of a function to the more general situation when one step of an outline may involve several computations or smaller steps. In particular, we study the general notion of *procedures*, which allow us to separate the final results of a step from the details of computation. We will see that procedures are motivated by the same philosophy and top-down problem solving strategy that we followed in using functions, although procedures may be useful in a wider variety of situations.

Lastly, as an extension of our discussion of functions, we will see how we use parameters not only to pass values into functions and procedures but also to get new values returned.

## SECTION 4.1 EXAMPLES OF SIMPLE PROCEDURES

The previous chapter developed a revised top-down strategy for solving complex problems and introduced functions to compute particular results.

In this section, we will see how we can follow this strategy more generally in our programs.

First, we consider the following.

**PROBLEM 4.1A** Write a program that prints a Tic-Tac-Toe board. More precisely, write a program that generates the following output:

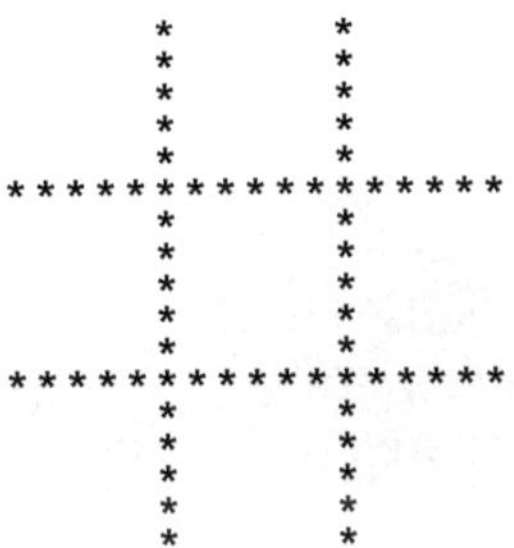

Our first approach to the problem might be to draw the two vertical lines and then the two horizontal lines, for that is how we might proceed if we drew such a board on paper. Few computer terminals and printers, however, can move paper backward or back up on a line. Our approach must therefore proceed from one line to the next down the paper.

With this in mind, we might divide the problem into five basic steps:

**I.** Print the upper part of the vertical lines (the top five lines).
**II.** Print a horizontal line.
**III.** Print the middle part of the vertical lines.
**IV.** Print a horizontal line.
**V.** Print the bottom part of the vertical lines.

This outline includes all parts of the desired output, so we can be confident that this general outline will solve the problem.

We can now consider the details of each step in turn. First, we consider Step I, print the upper part of the vertical lines:

```
Writeln ('          *     *');
Writeln ('          *     *');
Writeln ('          *     *');
Writeln ('          *     *');
Writeln ('          *     *')
```

Next, we look at Step II, print a horizontal line. Again, the desired output is clearly specified in the problem, and can be accomplished by the following Pascal statement:

```
Writeln ('     *****************')
```

Considering Step III, the desired output is exactly the same as for Step I. Skipping ahead, Steps I, III, and V all call for the same output. We have found a common task, which we might call *PrintVertical*. This task consists of the five *Write* statements for Step I and solves three parts of the outline.

Similarly, considering Step IV we need the same work as for Step II. Thus we have identified another common task, which we might call *PrintHorizontal*.

Our outline now reduces to the following abbreviated steps:

**I.** *PrintVertical*
**II.** *PrintHorizontal*
**III.** *PrintVertical*
**IV.** *PrintHorizontal*
**V.** *PrintVertical*

We need to write out the details for the tasks PrintVertical and PrintHorizontal, but once those details are given, we have solved the problem, as in the following program, where such tasks are called **procedures.**

```
Program TicTacToe {Version 1} (Output);
{This program prints a Tic Tac Toe board.}

Procedure PrintVertical;
{This procedure prints part of the vertical lines on the board.}

    Begin
        Writeln('          *      *');
        Writeln('          *      *');
        Writeln('          *      *');
        Writeln('          *      *');
        Writeln('          *      *')
    End {PrintVertical} ;

Procedure PrintHorizontal;
{This procedure prints a horizontal line for the board.}

    Begin
        Writeln('     *****************')
    End {PrintHorizontal} ;

Begin {Main Program}

    PrintVertical;
    PrintHorizontal;
    PrintVertical;
    PrintHorizontal;
    PrintVertical;

End {Main Program} .
```

In this program two tasks, Procedure *PrintVertical* and Procedure *PrintHorizontal*, are defined first (where variables and functions have been declared in earlier programs). In the last few lines the program uses those procedures (or tasks), following the outline. Pascal allows us to define separate procedures or tasks; once those procedures are specified we can use them anywhere in a program.

When the program runs, the machine starts with the *Begin* of the Main Program. The first instruction is *PrintVertical*, so the machine jumps to this procedure to *Write* the lines specified. Here we say that the Main Program **calls** procedure *PrintVertical*. When those lines are printed, *PrintVertical* is done, so the machine returns to the Main Program.

Since the first *PrintVertical* is done, the machine moves to the next task, *PrintHorizontal*. With this procedure call, the machine again must jump to procedure *PrintHorizontal* to perform this step. In *PrintHorizontal* the machine *Writes* the appropriate line. When this is completed, *PrintHorizontal* is done, and the machine returns to the Main Program. *PrintVertical* comes next, so the machine jumps again to perform this procedure, and the machine returns when that procedure concludes.

The Main Program guides the computer through the main steps of the program, and the machine jumps to the procedures whenever it needs to see the details of a step.

To continue this example, we might break *PrintVertical* into five smaller steps, where each step is to print the single line

```
      *     *
```

In the next program, this common work is contained in a procedure *PrintDots*, and we call this *PrintDots* procedure from inside the *PrintVertical* procedure as needed.

```
Program TicTacToe {Version 2} (Output);
{This program prints a Tic Tac Toe board.}

Procedure PrintDots;
{This procedure prints the dots for the vertical line.}

   Begin {PrintDots}
      Writeln('            *     *')
   End {PrintDots} ;

Procedure PrintVertical;
{This procedure prints part of the vertical lines on the board.}

   Begin {PrintVertical}

      PrintDots;
      PrintDots;
      PrintDots;
      PrintDots;
      PrintDots

   End {PrintVertical} ;
```

```
Procedure PrintHorizontal;
{This procedure prints a horizontal line for the board.}

    Begin
        Writeln('      ******************')
    End {PrintHorizontal} ;

Begin {Main}

    PrintVertical;
    PrintHorizontal;
    PrintVertical;
    PrintHorizontal;
    PrintVertical;

End {Main} .
```

---

Again, the procedures *PrintVertical* and *PrintHorizontal* are defined before they are used in the main program. Within *PrintVertical*, however, we have used procedure *PrintDots* to perform a subtask. That task is defined before *PrintVertical*, and after it is defined, it can be used as required in *PrintVertical*.

To conclude this example, note that in this revised form we have isolated the details of printing in two lines (one in *PrintDots* and one in *PrintHorizontal*). This isolation has the added advantage that we can modify the program very easily to accommodate changes in the problem. For example, consider the following revision.

**PROBLEM 4.1B** Write a program that generates the following output:

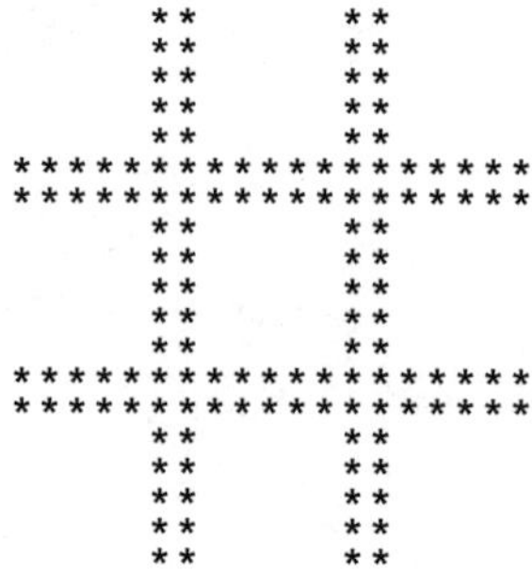

The problem is closely related to the original problem, and we can use the same basic outline for a solution; we only have to change the lines of the Tic-Tac-Toe board to double thickness. The new program is:

```
Program TicTacToe {Version 3} (Output);
{This program prints a Tic Tac Toe board.}
{The lines of this Board are all double thickness.}

Procedure PrintDots;
{This procedure prints the dots for the vertical line.}

    Begin {PrintDots}
        Writeln('          **     **')
    End {PrintDots} ;

Procedure PrintVertical;
{This procedure prints part of the vertical lines on the board.}

    Begin {PrintVertical}

        PrintDots;
        PrintDots;
        PrintDots;
        PrintDots;
        PrintDots

    End {PrintVertical} ;

Procedure PrintHorizontal;
{This procedure prints a horizontal line for the board.}

    Begin
        Writeln('     ********************');
        Writeln('     ********************')
    End {PrintHorizontal} ;

Begin {Main}

    PrintVertical;
    PrintHorizontal;
    PrintVertical;
    PrintHorizontal;
    PrintVertical;

End {Main} .
```

As with our use of functions, procedures allow our program structure to parallel our solution outline. Pascal allows us to incorporate our revised top-down approach to problem solving into our Pascal program. The overall problem can be divided into major steps, and we can use functions and procedures to handle the steps. These functions and procedures allow us to separate the details of a step from the overall outline of our solution. When the same task must be done in several places, our program can use the same function or procedure each time. When tasks are independent, we can define distinct functions or procedures. Thus, Pascal programming can be an extension of our problem solving methodology; we do not need to change our perspective when we move from algorithm design to programming.

### Elements of Defining Simple Procedures

These examples illustrate the general form for defining and using procedures, and we find that this general form for procedures is very similar to the form we have used for functions and entire programs.

A procedure starts out with a formal declaration or heading

    Procedure Name

where the *Name* indicates how we will refer to this procedure later. Following this heading, the procedure may contain constant or variable declarations, just as we have seen for functions and entire programs. (We will see an example of these local declarations in the next section.) Then, the procedure concludes with a statement block which starts with the reserved word *Begin* and concludes with *End*, where the details of the procedure can be given.

We will have more to say about the details involved in the declaration and use of procedures, but first we consider some more examples.

## SECTION 4.2 EXAMPLE USING SEVERAL PROCEDURES

In Section 1, we used procedures to perform some of the details of the solution outline, but these steps did not involve any computations. In this section, we will use **parameters** with procedures just as we did with functions in the previous chapter to allow procedures to compute values based on initial values. We extend this idea of procedures with parameters further in the next section.

To begin, consider the following example.

**PROBLEM 4.2**

A florist wants to price flowers to reflect two distinct costs:

- Each flower costs a certain amount to grow.
- A clerk must serve each customer.

The florist notes that the time spent by the clerk does not depend upon the number of flowers purchased. For example, the clerk spends the same amount of time showing flowers, offering suggestions, wrapping flowers, and handling money whether one flower or one dozen flowers are purchased.

The florist decides upon a pricing structure in which a price is fixed as the Base Price of a flower. This Base Price reflects the cost to grow the flower, with appropriate profit. (The Base Price may vary with the type of flower.) A service charge is fixed to cover the clerk's time. Once the Base Price and the Service Charge are known, the customer is charged the Base Price for each flower, and the Service Charge is added at the end. Stated as a formula, if $n$ flowers are purchased, then

$$\text{Customer Charge} = n*(\text{Base Price}) + \text{Service Charge}$$

Recently the florist determined the following price schedule:

Base Price of Roses: $2.00

Base Price of Carnations: $.75

Base Price of Mums: $1.00

Service Charge: $.50

Write a program to complete the following chart showing flower charges:

| Flower | Single | Half Dozen | Dozen |
|---|---|---|---|
| Roses | | | |
| Carnations | | | |
| Mums | | | |

In analyzing this program, we will concentrate on the table we need to complete.

### Outline for Problem 4.2

**I.** Print titles at top of table.
**II.** Compute and print charges for Roses.
**III.** Compute and print charges for Carnations.
**IV.** Compute and print charges for Mums.

Each of Steps II, III, and IV involves the same work:

**A.** Print name of flower.
**B.** Determine Base Price.
**C.** Compute and print cost for single flower:

Cost = Base + Service Charge

**D.** Compute and print cost for a half-dozen flowers:

Cost = 6*Base + Service Charge

**E.** Compute and print cost for a dozen flowers:

Cost = 12*Base + Service Charge

In translating this outline into a Pascal program, we use a procedure to perform this common task, with our computations depending upon the base price of a flower. This leads to the following program.

```
Program Florist (Output);
{This program prints the cost of various types of flowers,
 using a base cost per flower and a service charge.}

Const Service = 0.50;
```

```
Procedure PrintHeadings;
{This procedure prints the headings for the price table.}
    Begin
        Writeln ('Table of charges for various quantities of flowers.');
        Writeln;
        Writeln ('                    Flower Charges');
        Writeln ('   Flower     Single   Half Dozen    Dozen')
    End {PrintHeadings} ;

Procedure ComputeCharges (Base: Real);
{This program computes the flower charges and prints those charges
 in the table.}
    Var Single, Half, Dozen: Real;
    Begin
        Single := Base + Service;
        Half := 6.0*Base + Service;
        Dozen := 12.0*Base + Service;
        Write (Single:7:2);
        Write (Half:12:2);
        Writeln(Dozen:11:2)
    End {ComputeCharges} ;

Procedure Roses;
{This procedure computes and prints the charges for roses.}
    Begin
        Write ('    Roses   ');
        ComputeCharges (2.00)
    End {Roses} ;

Procedure Carnations;
{This procedure computes and prints the charges for carnations.}
    Begin
        Write (' Carnations ');
        ComputeCharges (0.75)

    End {Carnations} ;

Procedure Mums;
{This procedure computes and prints the charges for mums.}
    Begin
        Write ('    Mums    ');
        ComputeCharges (1.00)
    End {Mums} ;

Begin {Main}

    PrintHeadings;
    Roses;
    Carnations;
    Mums

End {Main} .
```

Once again, our main program is structured according to our outline, with separate procedures *PrintHeadings, Roses, Carnations,* and *Mums* for each outline step. In addition, we have a separate procedure for our common task of computing and printing prices on the basis of the Base Price and Service Charge. Further, in performing these computations, the Base Price is specified as a parameter for the *ComputeCharges* procedure. Then in the program, we call *ComputeCharges* for each type of flower, specifying the appropriate value for this Base. In addition, since the Service Charge is constant throughout the program, we declare this constant globally and then use this constant in *ComputeCharges* as needed.

This program illustrates many important features of procedures, parameters, and local variables. As with functions, we can use procedures to perform individual steps in an outline, we can pass values into the procedures using parameters, and we can define local variables to aid with the work within the procedures. These capabilities allow us to use procedures whenever one part of an outline requires several steps, and our programs can then follow the same structure developed in a solution outline.

## SECTION 4.3 VALUE AND REFERENCE PARAMETERS

Up to this point, we have been able to pass information into functions and procedures using parameters, and we could base our computations in the functions on these initial values. In some cases, however, we want procedures to return values as well, and in these situations, we need to use a different type of parameter. Such a situation is illustrated in the following problem.

## PROBLEM 4.3 Applying Paint

Many latex wall paints specify that one gallon of paint will cover about 400 square feet. Varnishes and stains specify one gallon for 500 square feet.

Write a program that reads the dimensions (length and height) of a wall and computes the number of gallons of paint and of varnish needed for the wall.

### Solution for Problem 4.3

In this problem, we can proceed using steps which are similar to several of our earlier problems.

### Outline for Problem 4.3

**I.** Determine Length and Height of Wall

**II.** Compute Gallons Needed

- **A.** Determine Area of Wall
- **B.** Compute Gallons of Paint

Paint Gallons = Area / 400

**C.** Compute Gallons of Varnish

Varnish Gallons = Area / 500

**III.** Print Results

### Discussion of Problem 4.3

When we program using this outline, we may try to structure our code by using a separate procedure or function for each of the three major steps. However, in both Steps I and II, our computations require us to obtain more than one value; Step I needs two values, and Step II computes three values. Thus, in this program, functions are not adequate for performing each major step. Instead, we use procedures with a new type of parameter that allows appropriate values to be returned when the procedures finish. This gives rise to the following program.

```
Program Paint (Input, Output);
{This program computes the amount of paint needed to cover a wall.}

Var Length, Height: Real;
    GalPaint, GalVarnish: Real;

Procedure FindDimensions (Var Length, Height: Real);
{This procedures computes the dimensions of the wall}
    Begin
        Write ('Please enter the length of the wall: ');
        Readln (Length);
        Write ('Please enter the height of the wall: ');
        Readln (Height)
    End {FindDimensions} ;

Procedure Compute (Length, Height: Real; Var Paint, Varnish: Real);
{This procedures computes the area of the wall and the amount of
 paint and varnish needed to cover this area}
    Const PaintSqFeet = 400.0;    {Number of square feet covered by}
          VarnishSqFeet = 500.0;  {a gallon of paint or varnish}
    Var Area: Real;
    Begin
        Area := Length * Height;
        Paint := Area / PaintSqFeet;
        Varnish := Area / VarnishSqFeet
    End {Compute} ;

Procedure Print (Length, Height, Paint, Varnish: Real);
{This procedure prints the results of the computation}
    Begin
        Writeln;
        Writeln ('For a wall measuring ', Length:1:1, ' by ',
                 Height:1:1, ',');
        Writeln ('we need ', Paint:1:2, ' gallons of paint, or ',
                 Varnish:1:2, ' gallons of varnish.')
    End {Print} ;
```

```
Begin {Main}
    Writeln ('This program computes the amount of paint and varnish');
    Writeln ('needed to paint a wall.');
    FindDimensions (Length, Height);
    Compute (Length, Height, GalPaint, GalVarnish);
    Print (Length, Height, GalPaint, GalVarnish)
End {Main} .
```

When this program is run using the dimensions for a rather large living room, we get the following.

```
This program computes the amount of paint and varnish
needed to paint a wall.
Please enter the length of the wall: 25
Please enter the height of the wall: 9

For a wall measuring 25.0 by 9.0,
we need 0.56 gallons of paint, or 0.45 gallons of varnish.
```

This program provides another example of the type of parameters used in the previous sections, and the program also illustrates a second type of parameter. In particular, in the Print procedure, we use values that have been computed earlier in our program, and we use parameters as before. The declaration:

Procedure Print (Length, Height, Paint, Varnish: Real);

indicates that we must supply four values to the Print procedure. Here, we specify four parameters, called **value parameters**, and Procedure Print uses the values specified in its work.

In contrast, in the FindDimensions procedure, we need to return values from the procedure to the main program. In order to return these values, we add the keyword *Var* to our declaration:

Procedure FindDimensions (Var Length, Height: Real);

The addition of this *Var* keyword allows this procedure to return values to the calling program, and these parameters are called **reference parameters.**

Finally, in the Compute procedure, we need to use both types of parameters. We begin with values for length and height, and we use value parameters (without the *Var*) for these parameters. Then, we want to compute values for the amount of paint and varnish, and we want these values returned so we can use them later. Thus, we use reference parameters (with the *Var*) for these values.

To summarize: When we want to start computations within a procedure or a function but we do not want revised values when the procedure or function is done, we use value parameters, and we omit *Var* in our procedure declarations. However, when we want parameters to have new or revised values after a procedure or function is completed, we use reference parameters, and we precede them with the keyword *Var* in our procedure declarations.

## SECTION 4.4 STYLE

Throughout our discussion of functions and procedures, we have focused upon the use of these Pascal features in programming a step in our solution to a problem. Functions and procedures allow us to separate major steps from details and to handle common tasks efficiently. This use of functions and procedures allows our programs to retain the same features of structure found in a solution outline to a program, as shown in Figure 4–1. This figure also shows that with appropriate formatting, we can reinforce this parallelism between solution outlines and programs. In particular, Figure 4–1 illustrates how our programs can appear as extended solution outlines. For example, indenting and formatting of functions and procedures can

FIGURE 4–1 • **Program Form Parallels Outline Form**

```
                               Program
                               Var {global variables}
Common Task A                  Procedure TaskA
                                   Var {local variables}
                                   Begin
                                   .
                                   .
                                   .
                                   End;
Common Task B                  Procedure TaskB
                                   Var {local variables}
                                   Begin
                                   .
                                   .
                                   .
                                   End
        .                      .
        .                      .
        .                      .
I. Step I                      {StepI}
   A. Subdivision 1            Procedure StepI
                                   Var {local variables}
                                   Procedure SubI
                                       Var {local variables}
                                       Begin
                                       .
                                       .
                                       .
                                       End
```

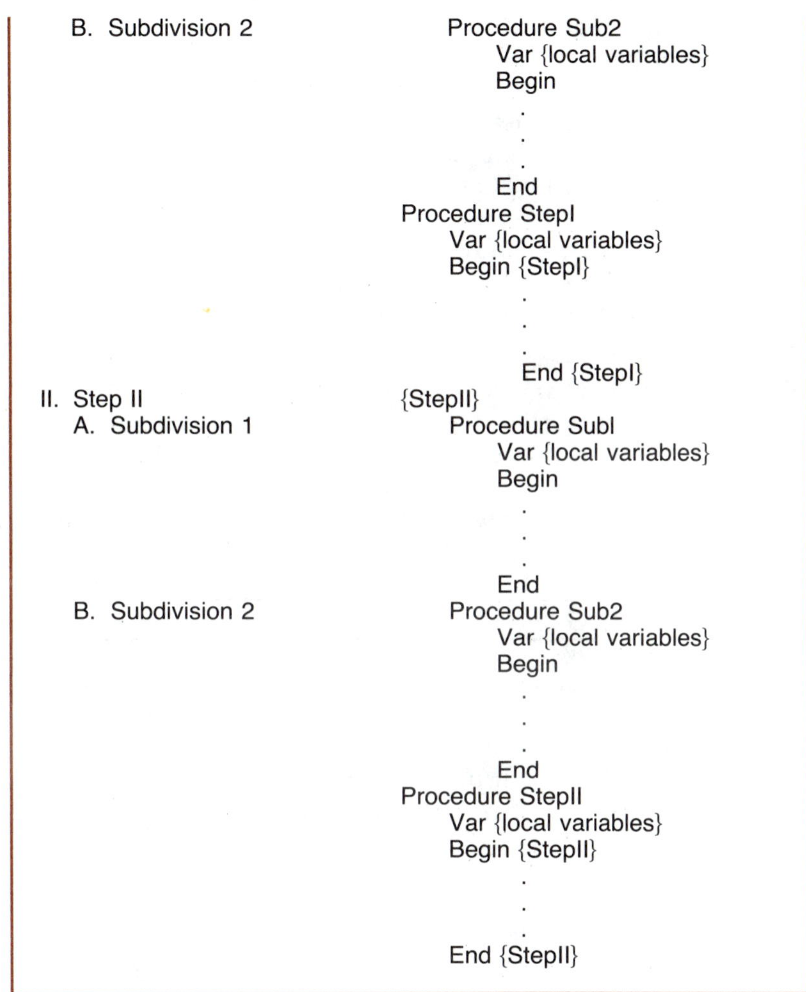

```
   B. Subdivision 2               Procedure Sub2
                                      Var {local variables}
                                      Begin
                                        .
                                        .
                                        .
                                      End
                                Procedure StepI
                                    Var {local variables}
                                    Begin {StepI}
                                        .
                                        .
                                        .
                                        End {StepI}
II. Step II                     {StepII}
   A. Subdivision 1                 Procedure SubI
                                      Var {local variables}
                                      Begin
                                        .
                                        .
                                        .
                                      End
   B. Subdivision 2                 Procedure Sub2
                                      Var {local variables}
                                      Begin
                                        .
                                        .
                                        .
                                      End
                                Procedure StepII
                                    Var {local variables}
                                    Begin {StepII}
                                        .
                                        .
                                        .
                                    End {StepII}
```

reflect the structure of the solution outline. Each program in this chapter illustrates how to indicate program structure by program format. For example, indenting indicates where various variables are defined. Local variables are known only within functions, and indenting the declaration of these variables within a function illustrates this. On the other hand, the procedure name and the parameter list are links between the procedure and the Main Program, so these aspects of the function are not indented.

## Choosing Local and Global Variables and Parameters

The solution outline can help us decide when to use local variables, global variables, and parameters in functions or procedures: we can see how each value fits into the general solution. When a computation and result are needed only within one step of the outline, then the corresponding function or procedure should use local variables. The variables are logically meaningful only within the function or procedure, and the program should reflect this.

When we need initial values to start a step, then parameters are appropriate. Parameters form a convenient link between the Main Program and a function. When the computations require continuity through several steps, we maintain that continuity through the use of parameters. We can use either value or reference parameters to bring values into functions or procedures. In contrast, we must use reference parameters when procedures or functions will return new or revised values to those parameters.

Here are some general guidelines:

- Use local variables, rather than global ones, whenever possible in functions and procedures.
- Use parameters to link the Main Program with a function and to highlight the key initial values for a function.
- Try to minimize the use of global variables, so that functions and procedures can remain independent of each other as much as possible.

## SECTION 4.5 TESTING

Dividing a program into separate procedures and functions not only allows us to read and understand our programs better, it also helps us check that our programs and solutions are correct.

Since each function or procedure should be largely self-contained, we can test each piece separately before we put the pieces together. For example, the Bank Interest program in Section 3.3 used

Function Powers (Base, Exponent)

to compute $Base^{Exponent}$. Once we have written this function, we can check that it does the appropriate computation, using a simple program:

```
Program TestPowers (Output);
{This program tests the function Powers.}

Function Powers (Base, Exponent: Real): Real;
{This function raises Base to the power Exponent.}
    Begin
        Powers := Exp(Exponent * Ln(Base))
    End;

Begin {Main}

    Writeln (Powers(2.0, 0.0));
    Writeln (Powers(1.0, 9.0));
    Writeln (Powers(3.0, 2.0));
    Writeln (Powers(2.0, 3.0))

End {Main} .
```

This program does not solve the Bank Interest problem, but it does test *Powers* in several easy cases. In particular, the program computes $2^0$, $1^9$, $3^2$, and $2^3$. When running this test program yields the desired results, we can be fairly confident that function *Powers* works correctly.

testing

We can follow this same approach whenever we have functions or procedures in a program. We can test each piece of the program and can correct errors until we are reasonably sure that each piece works as we expect. Then, when we put the pieces together in the final solution to a problem, we should expect that most bugs have been found. There may be some troubles with the functions and procedures interacting in unexpected ways, so we still need to test the final program. If we keep the steps independent, however, potential interaction problems will be minimized.

In later chapters we will see that **modular testing,** where each procedure and function is tested separately, is particularly helpful when programs are fairly long. A long program contains many steps, and it is easy to make a simple mistake in one of the steps. If an error can be isolated in a small procedure, it often can be found and corrected without much difficulty. Testing each procedure and function allows us to perform this error isolation before we must contend with the whole program.

## SECTION 4.6 COMPILING AND LINKING

In this chapter we have seen how to use procedures as well as functions to perform specific tasks. With this background, we will look a little more closely at the process that builds complete machine-language programs from Pascal programs. This process actually proceeds in two steps (see Figure 4–2).

As noted in Chapter 1, whenever we write a Pascal program, we must use a compiler to translate the program to machine language. Programs nor-

FIGURE 4–2 • **The Compiling and Linking Process**

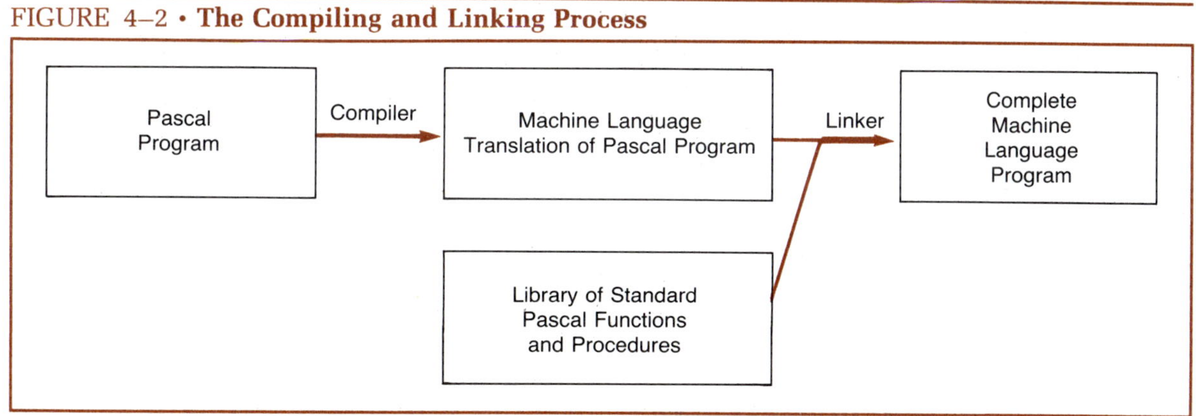

mally use some standard Pascal functions and procedures, however. Some programs, for example, use *Sqr*, *Ln*, and *Exp*, and almost all programs use the procedures *Write*, *Writeln*, *Read*, and *Readln*. Before a program can run, the various parts of these functions and procedures must be added to the code.

This addition of standard functions and procedures is done in a second step by a **linker.** The machine instructions for standard tasks are normally stored in a Pascal library on a disk that is accessible to programmers. After the compiler has generated machine code for a Pascal program, the linker adds the appropriate machine instructions from a Pascal library and links the two parts together into a complete machine language program.

Later, in Chapter 9, we will see that some compilers and linkers even allow us to write our own procedures in separate pieces. With this capability we can compile various parts of a program at different times and then link the pieces together.

On some computers, the linker is called automatically after the compiler is used, and you may never be aware that linking and compiling involve two separate steps. On other machines you must run the compiler and the linker with two distinct commands.

Whichever way you produce complete machine language programs, you will use functions and procedures throughout your work. You can write your own functions and procedures to accomplish special tasks that arise in particular problems, and you can rely upon a Pascal library for tasks, such as *Read* and *Write*, that arise in many problems.

## SUMMARY

1. **Procedures** allow us to organize programs following the steps of an outline to a solution. We define a procedure to perform each step and task in the outline. When steps are split into pieces, we define several small procedures to be used by large ones.
2. Procedures may be declared and used in much the same way as functions stating the necessary parameters and defining the steps it will perform.

| KEY TERMS, PHRASES, AND CONCEPTS | | ELEMENTS OF PASCAL SYNTAX |
|---|---|---|
| Compiler<br>Linker<br>Modular Testing<br>Parameters<br>  Reference<br>  Value | Procedures<br>  Procedure Declaration<br>  Procedure Block<br>  Procedure Parameters | *Procedure* parameters with and without *Var* |

3. Once the procedure is defined we can use it whenever it is appropriate. In this way, the details of computation are separated from the main idea of the program.
4. With both functions and procedures, we can start our work with certain values; that is, we can specify **parameters** that we need to get going. Here, we define functions and procedures with formal parameters, and we state the actual parameters each time the functions or procedures are used. Parameters form a link between the main program and a function or procedure, and this link can take on two forms. **Value parameters** allow us to pass values into a function or procedure, while **reference parameters** allow new or revised values to be returned. Finally, global variables extend throughout the entire program and local variables are restricted to one specific function or procedure.
5. In previous chapters, we used some standard Pascal procedures such as *Readln* and *Writeln*. These procedures and other standard functions must be added to our compiled program. Thus, after we **compile** a Pascal program, we **link** our code with the required instructions in the Pascal library to obtain a complete machine language program.

## EXERCISES

**4.1** Consider the following Pascal program:

```
Program Problem1 (Input, Output);

Var First, Second: Integer;

Procedure EnterData (Var One, Two: Integer);
    Begin
        Write ('Enter First Integer: ');
        Readln (One);
        Write ('Enter Second Integer: ');
        Readln (Two)
    End {EnterData} ;

Procedure PrintHeadings;
    Begin
        Writeln;
        Writeln ('                            Integer                Real');
        Writeln ('Dividend  Divisor  Quotient  Remainder Quotient');
        Writeln ('                             (Div)      (Mod)       ( / )')
    End {PrintHeadings} ;

Procedure IntegerDivision (Dividend, Divisor: Integer);
    Var Quotient, Remainder: Integer;
        RealQuotient: Real;
```

```
    Begin {IntegerDivision}
        Quotient := Dividend Div Divisor;
        Remainder := Dividend Mod Divisor;
        RealQuotient := Dividend / Divisor;
        Writeln (Dividend: 5, Divisor: 10, Quotient: 10,
                 Remainder: 10, RealQuotient: 12:3)
    End {IntegerDivision} ;

Begin {Main}
    EnterData (First, Second);
    PrintHeadings;
    IntegerDivision (First, Second);
    IntegerDivision (Second, First)
End {Main} .
```

Suppose the user enters the numbers 15 and 4 (in that order) in response to the prompt. Write, in the appropriate format, what is printed by this program.

**4.2** The preceding Pascal program has three independent procedures. We can picture the declaration block as follows:

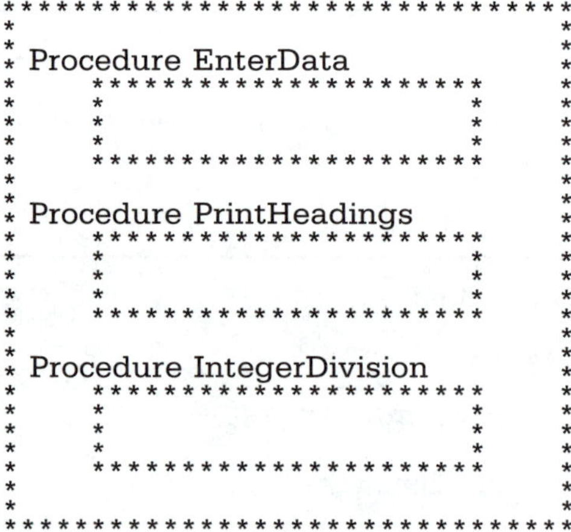


Write a program to print this geometric figure. In your solution, identify the different parts of the pattern, and organize the parts into appropriate procedures.

**4.3** Modify your program from the previous problem so that all "lines" are made up of double asterisks (**). (If your solution to the previous problem was carefully organized and structured, then this change will require only minor modifications to your program.)

**4.4** In the program in Problem 4.1, we note that a semicolon was not needed before the *Ends* of any of the procedures. A semicolon is required after these *End* statements, however. Please explain why the semicolons are required one place but not another.

NOTE: In Pascal, it is possible to define a "null" or "blank" statement, where no action of any sort is performed. With this information, explain why two semicolons (;;) may appear next to each other in a Pascal program. Also, explain why we could place a semicolon before the *End* statements in the program in Problem 4.1, and the resulting program would still be valid.

**4.5** Write a program to print the following geometric pattern:

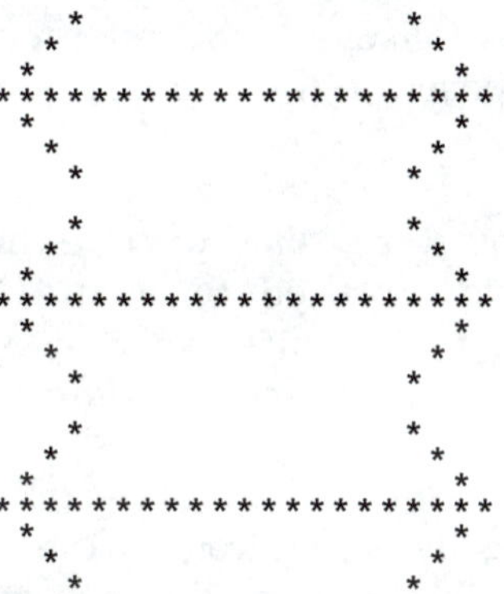

In your solution to the problem, identify different parts of the pattern, and write a procedure for each part.

**4.6** Modify your program from Exercise 4.5 to make the arrows double thickness. The arrows in the revision should appear as follows:

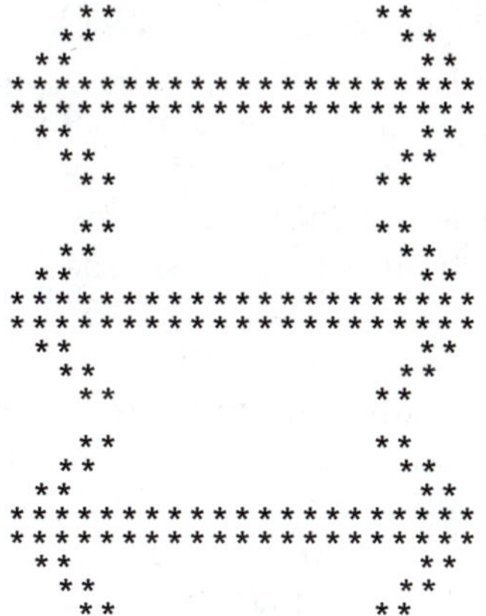

**4.7** The lyrics of many familiar songs have the following organization:

- Verse 1
- Chorus
- Verse 2
- Chorus
- Verse 3
- Chorus
- etc.

Several verses are sung, with a chorus or refrain repeated after each verse. (Sometimes this chorus is sung before the first verse as well.)

Pick a song that has this form, and write a program to print the lyrics. In your program, use a procedure to write each separate verse, and use another procedure to print the chorus.

**4.8** *Reference Parameters and Functions.* A common programming guideline states that reference parameters normally should not be used with functions. Discuss why reference parameters might be philosophically opposed to the concept of a function which returns a single value.

**4.9** *Read and Write Parameters.*

**a.** Suppose you were asked to code the familiar "Read" procedure in Pascal. In your procedure, would you use value or reference parameters? Explain your answer.

**b.** Answer the same question if you were coding the "Write" procedure.

**4.10 a.** Modify the paint program of Section 4.3 so that it will compute the number of gallons required for the job, where any quantity over 0.1 gallons is rounded up to the next whole gallon.

**b.** Modify the paint program further so that it will compute the total cost of the paint required, given the price per gallon. Use procedures with appropriate parameters for each step in your program.

**4.11** (This problem revises the pizza program from Problem 8 of Chapter 2.) As a pizza restaurant owner you have determined that you can sell your 6-inch thin-crust pizza for $3.50 to make a reasonable profit and still stay competitive. You have also decided that the appropriate price for a 6-inch deep-dish pizza is $4.50.

Write a program that computes the appropriate prices for 6-inch, 10-inch, 12-inch, and 14-inch pizzas for both deep-dish and thin-crust styles. Use relative areas of the pizza to determine price, and print your results in a table.

In your program, define a procedure *SetPrice* that has the 6-inch price as a formal parameter and computes and prints a line of the table based on that price.

**4.12** *Metric Conversion.* Write a program that inputs a distance in meters and converts the distance to yards, feet, and inches. For example, given a distance of 2.5 meters, your program should print the conclusion

```
2.5 meters = 2 yards, 2 feet, 2.3 inches
```

In your program, write separate procedures for data entry, data conversion, and printing.

NOTE: The appropriate conversion factors are

1 yard = 0.914403 meters

1 foot = 0.304801 meters

1 inch = 0.0254001 meters

**4.13** The Bird Call Travel Agency has negotiated special rates for vacations in Phlatt Cliffs, Po-Dunque, and East Overshoot. In cooperation with Buzzard Airlines and Exotic Hotels, Inc., the full adult costs for a seven-day vacation are:

| | Air Travel (Round Trip) | Hotel Room (Full Week) |
|---|---|---|
| East Overshoot | $450 | $300 |
| Phlatt Cliffs | $550 | $400 |
| Po-Dunque | $600 | $200 |

When a family travels together, the following discounts are available:

*Hotel Room*
A second adult pays 60% of the room cost.
Children stay in the room free.

*Air Travel*
Each adult pays full fare.
Each child pays 50% of the adult rate.

Write a program that computes the cost of travel plus lodging for a single adult and for a family of two, three, and four people (two adults plus zero, one, and two children).

Print the results in this table:

| | Number of people | | | |
|---|---|---|---|---|
| | 1 | 2 | 3 | 4 |
| East Overshoot | | | | |
| Phlatt Cliffs | | | | |
| Po-Dunque | | | | |

**4.14** An avid gardener regularly prepares stewed tomatoes for freezing, using tomatoes, peppers, and various herbs and spices from the garden. Over the past several years, the gardener has found that a pint of stewed tomatoes requires between five and seven tomatoes, depending upon their size.

Write a program that computes the number of pints that the gardener can expect from 50, 100, and 150 tomatoes, assuming that five, six, or seven tomatoes are needed for each pint. The output of the program should be in the form of the following table:

| Number of | Pints Produced | | |
|---|---|---|---|
| Tomatoes | Minimum | Middle | Maximum |
| 50 | | | |
| 100 | | | |
| 150 | | | |

Use a procedure to print the headings and another procedure to perform the actual computations.

**4.15** An engineer uses a micrometer to measure the diameter of ball bearings that are used in a particular machine. The micrometer can measure accurately to three decimal places, so all readings are correct within 0.0005 cm. When four bearings of one size are measured, the diameters are found to be 0.491 cm, 0.498 cm, 0.506 cm, and 0.512 cm. Compute the volume of each of these bearings, using the actual measurements. Also compute the volume taking into account the possible errors in each reading. Express your results in a table of the form

| Measured Radius | Minimum Volume | Measured Volume | Maximum Volume |
|---|---|---|---|

Use procedures to structure your program clearly.

**4.16** A person wishes to drive to a conference 500 miles away, and the individual wants to determine how the car's miles-per-gallon performance will affect the trip. The car's gas tank holds 18 gallons, and the individual fills the tank just before leaving town. Assuming gas costs $1.40 per gallon, write a program to fill in the following table for the round trip to the conference and back.

| Miles per Gallon | Cost of Gas on Trip | Number of Refueling Stops | Gas Left at Destination |
|---|---|---|---|
| 18 | | | |
| 21 | | | |
| 24 | | | |
| 27 | | | |
| 32 | | | |
| 36 | | | |

Use procedures to help structure your program.

# CHAPTER 5

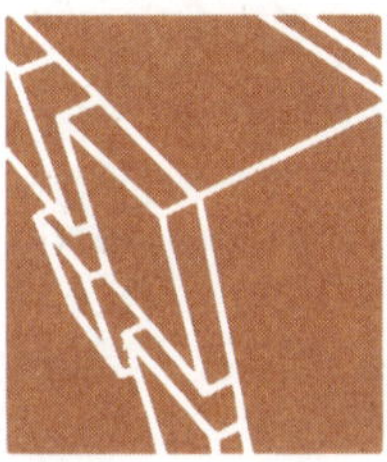

# SIMPLE LOOPS: THE FOR–DO STATEMENT

In our work up to now, we used the computer to calculate various values. When we considered a problem, we divided the problem into steps, identified appropriate formulae to help with these steps, and translated the formulae into Pascal. In this process we typed various declarations, and we wrote a line of Pascal code for each value we needed. With all of this effort in developing a Pascal program, you may have felt that the computer was little if any help in problem solving. We used the computer as a simple calculator, but instead of pushing buttons on a calculator we had to write, compile, and link a Pascal program, and we still had to enter the data. In these applications a calculator would have been quicker and equally useful.

In this chapter we describe some ways that computers can go beyond a calculator to reduce the work of solving problems. In particular, once we set up a process, we can ask the computer to repeat that process many times. This repetition of work is the notion of a **loop,** and we will see that a loop can be a great aid in solving problems. In this chapter we will consider one basic approach to loops. In Chapter 7 we will look at two other approaches.

## SECTION 5.1 EXAMPLE: CHART OF SECONDS PER MILE VERSUS MPH

We introduce our discussion of loops with an example.

### PROBLEM 5.1

When driving along an Interstate Highway, we know that if we travel 60 miles per hour (MPH), then we will travel one mile in one minute. To see how long it will take to travel a mile at different speeds we can construct a chart:

| Seconds Per Mile | Miles Per Hour |
|---|---|
| 55 | . |
| . | . |
| . | . |
| . | . |
| 60 | 60 |
| . | . |
| . | . |
| . | . |
| 75 | . |

With such a chart we can check that our car speedometer is working properly by timing our travel between two mile markers.

Print a chart relating seconds per mile (SPM) with miles per hour (MPH), where SPM ranges between 55 and 75.

### Discussion of Problem 5.1

In attacking this problem, it is clear that we need to perform the same conversion from SPM to MPH many times. Thus computations can proceed in two major steps: Determine how to convert SPM to MPH; tell the computer to repeat these computations for SPM between 55 and 75.

To convert SPM to MPH we will need the formulae

time(hours) = time(seconds)/(60*60)
rate(MPH) = 1 mile / time(hours)

### Outline for Problem 5.1

**I.** Print headings for the chart.
**II.** Repeat the following steps for time(seconds) = 55, 56, . . . , 75.

**A.** Compute time(hours)

time(hours) = time(seconds)/3600.0

**B.** Compute MPH

MPH = 1 mile/time(hours)

**C.** Print time(seconds) and MPH

The following program demonstrates that this outline can be translated into Pascal quite easily. In this program, note that steps A, B, and C of Part II are put together by placing these Pascal statements between the keywords *Begin* and *End*.

```
Program MPHChart (Output);
{This program prints a chart of Seconds Per Mile
 versus Miles Per Hour.}

Var Seconds: Integer;
    Hours, MPH: Real;

Begin
    Writeln('A Chart of Seconds Per Mile Versus Miles Per Hour');
    Writeln;    {Skip Line}

    {Print Headings}
    Writeln('  Seconds       Miles');
    Writeln(' Per Mile     Per Hour');

    {Repeat Computations}
    For Seconds := 55 To 75
        Do Begin
            Hours := Seconds / 3600.0;
            MPH := 1.0 / Hours;
            Writeln (Seconds:6, MPH:14:1)
        End {For}

End {Main} .
```

When this program is run, we get the following output:

```
A Chart of Seconds Per Mile Versus Miles Per Hour

  Seconds       Miles
 Per Mile     Per Hour
     55         65.5
     56         64.3
     57         63.2
     58         62.1
     59         61.0
     60         60.0
     61         59.0
     62         58.1
     63         57.1
     64         56.3
     65         55.4
```

```
66          54.5
67          53.7
68          52.9
69          52.2
70          51.4
71          50.7
72          50.0
73          49.3
74          48.6
75          48.0
```

This example shows that Pascal allows us to repeat computations quite easily. Once we decide what we want done, we can ask the computer to repeat the steps many times. In this program we used a *For–Do statement* to ask the computer to repeat the steps. More generally, when we want the computer to repeat some statements several times, we need a **loop structure** or a **loop** in the program to instruct the computer what to repeat and how often these steps are to be repeated.

### Syntax and Semantics of the For–Do Loop

The only new element in this program is the For–Do statement itself. A common syntax for this For–Do loop was illustrated in the MPH Chart program:

*For* ControlVariable *:=* InitialValue *To* FinalValue *Do* Statement

In the example, we have the following correspondences.

```
ControlVariable    Seconds
InitialValue       55
FinalValue         75
Statement          Begin
                       Hours := Seconds/3600.0;
                       MPH := 1.0/Hours;
                       Writeln (Seconds:6, MPH:14:1)
                   End;
```

The **Control Variable** must be an integer variable, and the **Initial Value** and the **Final Value** must be integers. Real numbers are not allowed. (We will see other possible data types that can be used as control variables in Chapter 11.) The statement is repeated for *ControlVariable* = *InitialValue*, *InitialValue* + 1, *InitialValue* + 2,. . ., *FinalValue*.

In this syntax, we note that only one statement will be repeated. For example, if you write

```
For Number := 1 to 3
        Do Writeln('Going');
        Writeln('Gone');
```

the output will be

Going
Going
Going
Gone

Only the first *Writeln ('Going')* is repeated.

## SECTION 5.2 ELEMENTS OF A LOOP

In this section we will look at the process of **iteration** or **repetition** more carefully. We will begin by identifying the elements typically found in a loop, then we look at the Pascal syntax for the *For–Do* loop from Section 5.1. With this background we can trace the computer's execution of the program in Section 5.1.

### Anatomy of a Loop

Programs that contain loops, such as the example in Section 5.1, have four major elements:

**Initialization** (optional): Before a loop begins, we may need some statements to get started. In the example, we printed a title for the table before the loop began. Titles should be printed only once, at the top of the table, so we need a *Writeln* statement before any other work is done. The printing of the titles cannot be part of the loop itself, for we do not want to repeat the titles many times.

**Repetitive statement:** We need a statement that instructs the computer to repeat some work. In the example the *For–Do* statement specified that something should be done several times.

**Loop block:** We must specify what statements are to be repeated. In the example we repeated the computation of hours, the computation of MPH, and some printing.

**Conclusion** (optional): Just as we may need to perform some work before a loop begins, once a loop is over other tasks may be needed. In the example the program stopped after the loop, so this step was omitted. We might have repeated the printing of titles, however, or we might have written some concluding notes. If any output was needed after the table, we would need some concluding statements after the loop.

In applying this general loop structure to a *For–Do* loop structure, we see that the *For–Do* statement itself includes an initialization, since the control variable is given an initial value. The *For–Do* statement is the repetitive statement that tells the computer to repeat something, and the statement following the *Do* is the loop block that is repeated.

A loop block may contain any single statement, such as a *Read* or *Write*, a procedure call, or a function. Just one statement can be repeated,

however. When we want more than one operation performed, we have some choices. In the example in Section 5.1 we placed multiple statements inside a *Begin–End* block. In this situation, the several statements are considered part of one compound statement, and the entire compound statement is repeated. We could also place several operations in a separate procedure and call that procedure in the *For–Do* statement, as in the following program:

```
Program MPHChart {With a Procedure} (Output);
{This program prints a chart of Seconds Per Mile
 versus Miles Per Hour.}

Var Seconds: Integer;

Procedure ComputeAndPrintMPH (TimeInSeconds:Integer);
    {This procedure computes and prints MPH.}
    Var Hours, MPH: Real;
    Begin
        Hours := TimeInSeconds / 3600.0;
        MPH := 1.0 / Hours;
        Writeln (TimeInSeconds:6, MPH:14:1)
    End {ComputeAndPrintMPH} ;

Begin
    Writeln('A Chart of Seconds Per Mile Versus Miles Per Hour');
    Writeln;    {Skip Line}

    {Print Headings}
    Writeln('  Seconds       Miles');
    Writeln(' Per Mile     Per Hour');

    {Repeat Computations}
    For Seconds := 55 To 75
        Do ComputeAndPrintMPH(Seconds)

End {Main} .
```

Here all computations and printing are done in procedure *ComputeAndPrintMPH*, and the *For–Do* only specifies that this procedure should be repeated. We do not need a *Begin–End* statement after the *For–Do* in this case, as only one statement is needed to call a procedure.

In each of these examples, one statement (a compound *Begin–End* or a procedure) is repeated several times. We now trace the execution of a loop, so we are sure we know how the computer performs its work.

## Tracing a Loop

We consider the loop from the example in Section 5.1:

```
For Seconds := 55 to 75
     Do Begin
            Hours := Seconds/3600.0;
            MPH := 1.0/Hours;
            Writeln(Seconds, MPH)
     End;
```

When the computer begins this section of code, several events occur.
*Step 1:*

- The computer sets

  Seconds := 55

- This value is immediately checked against the final value (75).
- Since *Seconds* is no bigger than 75 (the final value), the computer performs the steps in the *Begin–End* block:
  *Hours* becomes 55/3600.0, or 0.01528;
  *MPH* becomes 1.0/0.01528, or 65.5;
  *Seconds* and *MPH* (55 and 65.5) are printed.
- Since it has reached the *End* statement for 55 seconds, the machine goes back to the beginning of the segment of code (back to the *For*).

*Step 2:*

- The computer goes on to the next value for *Seconds*, 56.
- Since *Seconds* is no bigger than 75, the computer performs the steps in the *Begin–End* block:
  *Hours* becomes 56/3600.0, or 0.01556;
  *MPH* becomes 1.0/0.01556, or 64.3;
  the values for *Seconds* and *MPH* (56 and 64.3) are printed.
- The work is done for 56 seconds, so the machine goes back to the beginning of the segment of code.

**Successive Steps.** The same process continues for 57 seconds, 58 seconds, etc., up to 75 seconds:
*Step 21:*

- The computer goes on to the next value for *Seconds*, 75.
- Since *Seconds* is no bigger than 75, the computer performs the steps in the *Begin–End* block:
  *Hours* becomes 0.02083;
  *MPH* becomes 1.0/0.02083, or 48.0;
  the values for *Seconds* and *MPH* (75 and 48.0) are printed.
- The work is done for 75 seconds, so the machine goes back to the beginning of the segment of code.

*Step 22:*

- The computer recognizes that the last value for seconds, 75, is the final value designated in the *For* statement. All computations specified in the loop have been done, and the loop is completed. The computer moves to any concluding statements that may follow the *For–Do* and its *Begin–End* block.

This tracing illustrates how the computer methodically repeats the statements specified in the loop block. The control variable, *Seconds*, takes on succeeding values from the initial value (55) to the final value (75). Once the computer finishes with the final value, the loop is over and the computer moves on to any subsequent code in the program.

## Variables and Assignments

Tracing the program also illustrates that variables may change value during the course of a program. To understand this process more clearly, we will now consider how variables are given values in a computer.

We can envision the main memory of a computer as a collection of storage locations, in much the same way as a post office contains a number of post-office boxes. When we declare a variable in a program, one of these locations is reserved for that variable. Thus when we declared, in the original *MPH Chart* program,

```
Var Seconds: Integer;
    Hours, MPH: Real;
```

we reserved three "mailboxes" for the three variables *Seconds, Hours,* and *MPH* (see Figure 5–1). In the language of computer science, we even talk

FIGURE 5–1 • **Variables Seconds, Hours, and MPH in Main Memory**

| | |
|---|---|
| Seconds | |
| Hours | |
| MPH | |
| | |
| | |

of the **address** corresponding to a variable. Whenever we assign a value to a variable, the computer stores the value at that variable's address. Whenever we use a value in a computation, the computer looks up the value in the corresponding location.

For example, consider the loop

```
For Seconds := 55 to 75
         Do Begin
               Hours := Seconds/3600.0;
               MPH := 1.0/Hours;
               Write (Seconds, MPH)
         End
```

At the start there are no values stored in *Seconds, Hours,* or *MPH,* so main memory looks much like Figure 5–1. When the *For–Do* statement starts, the initial value 55 is placed in the *Seconds* mailbox (see Figure 5–2a). Next, values are computed for *Hours* (0.01528) and then for *MPH* (65.5). These values are stored in main memory and are found when the computer must print out numbers for *Seconds* and *MPH* (Figure 5–2b).

When the loop starts over again, *Seconds* is changed to 56 (Figure 5–2c). Note that while Seconds has a revised value, the computer has not yet changed *Hours* or *MPH*. Only when the loop block is done the second time do the values for *Hours* and *MPH* get updated.

From this discussion, you may note that the assignment statement has a different interpretation from that of an equal sign (=) in algebra. In particular, if we write

```
Hours := Seconds/3600.0;
```

the machine goes to its memory and finds the value in the location for *Seconds*. This value is divided by 3600.0 and the result is stored in the location for *Hours*. The computer does nothing with the location *Hours* until after the computation is completed (see Figure 5–3).

FIGURE 5–2 • **Assigning Values to Locations in Main Memory**

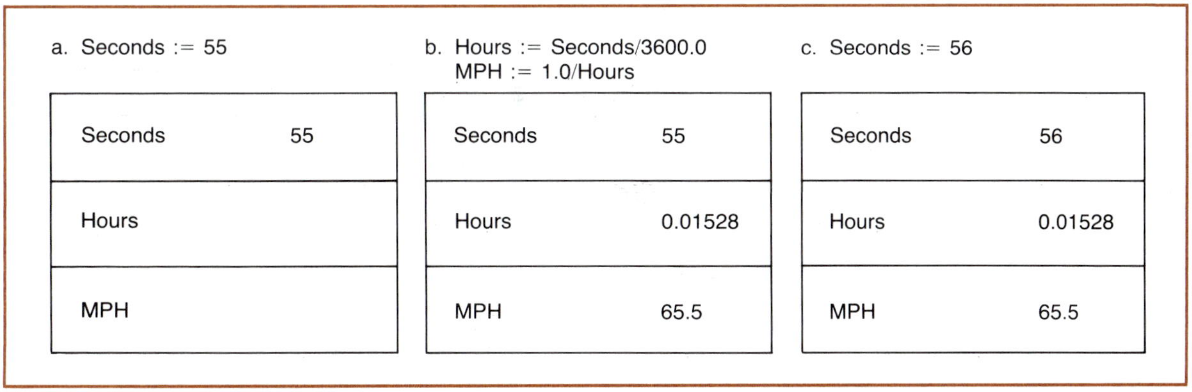

a. Seconds := 55

| Seconds | 55 |
|---|---|
| Hours | |
| MPH | |

b. Hours := Seconds/3600.0
MPH := 1.0/Hours

| Seconds | 55 |
|---|---|
| Hours | 0.01528 |
| MPH | 65.5 |

c. Seconds := 56

| Seconds | 56 |
|---|---|
| Hours | 0.01528 |
| MPH | 65.5 |

FIGURE 5–3 • **Performing Hours := Seconds/3600.0**

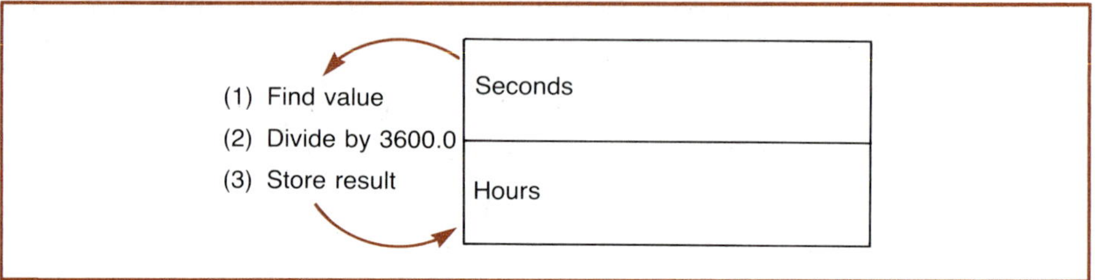


This same sequence can be used to explain the statement

```
Sum := Sum + 3.0
```

Certainly, this is not valid mathematically, but it makes sense to the computer (see Figure 5–4). The machine finds the old value of *Sum*, adds 3.0, and stores the new value in location *Sum* (destroying the previous value).

In the next section we will use this type of statement effectively in several applications. First, we need a few more observations to complete our formal discussion of syntax and semantics.

## Alternate Syntax: DownTo

We consider how we might proceed with the following revision of Problem 5.1:

**PROBLEM 5.2**

Print a chart relating seconds per mile to miles per hour, where seconds per mile = 75, 74, 73, . . . , 55.

This problem is very similar to the earlier one, except that we want the chart to start at 75 rather than 55. The solution outline can have the same form as the outline for Problem 5.1, but we must be a little careful in using the *For–Do* construction. If we write

```
For Seconds := 75 To 55
        Do . . .
```

FIGURE 5–4 • **Performing Sum := Sum + 3.0**

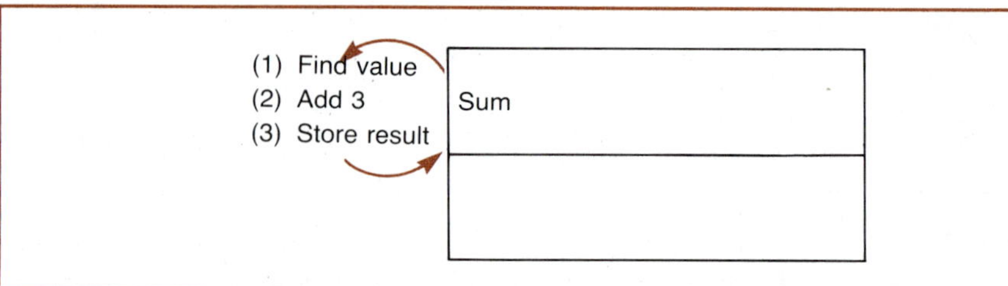

nothing will be printed in the loop! The difficulty is that when we start with 75 seconds we are already bigger than the final value of 55. The machine skips the loop block completely.

To solve this difficulty, we replace the word *To* with *DownTo:*

```
Program MPHChart {Using 'DownTo'} (Output);
{This program prints a chart of Seconds Per Mile
 versus Miles Per Hour.}

Var Seconds: Integer;
    Hours, MPH: Real;

Begin
    Writeln('A Chart of Seconds Per Mile Versus Miles Per Hour');
    Writeln;     {Skip Line}

    {Print Headings}
    Writeln('  Seconds        Miles');
    Writeln(' Per Mile      Per Hour');

    {Repeat Computations}
    For Seconds := 75 DownTo 55
        Do Begin
            Hours := Seconds / 3600.0;
            MPH := 1.0 / Hours;
            Writeln (Seconds:6, MPH:14:1)
        End {For}

End {Main} .
```

The program works the same as the earlier ones, but the chart starts with 75 seconds rather than 55. When we want a control variable to take on ascending values, we use *To* in the *For* statement. If we want the control variable to descend, we use *DownTo.* With either form we instruct the computer to repeat a task as the control variable progresses through a range of values.

## SECTION 5.3 EXAMPLE: AVERAGING NUMBERS

We now consider one more example, which will illustrate several additional techniques that can be very helpful in using loops.

**PROBLEM 5.3** Find the average of the numbers $(0.5)^2$, $1^2$, $(1.5)^2$, $2^2$,. . ., $(9.5)^2$, $(10).^2$

### Discussion of Problem 5.3

To solve this problem we must address two more basic problems, how to compute an average and how to compute the squares of 0.5, 1.0,. . ., 10.0.

**Averages.** Recall that the average of the $n$ numbers $a_1$, $a_2$,. . ., $a_n$ is

$$\text{average} = (a_1 + a_2 +. . .+ a_n)/n.$$

To decide how to do this computation, we consider how we might proceed without the help of a computer.

We would start with *a Sum = 0.0* and then add succeeding numbers one at a time until all of the numbers were included. To write it more formally,

**A.** Start with the initial

*Sum* := 0.0

**B.** Repeat the following for $j$ = 1, 2, 3, 4,. . ., $n$

Add the number $a_j$.
*Sum* := *Sum* + $a_j$.

(In the last step, recall that we are taking the "old" sum and adding $a_j$; the result is the "new" sum.)

**Computing Squares.** Next we need to determine how to get the computer to compute the squares we need. We proceed in two steps. First we identify a pattern for going from one number to the next; the numbers start with 0.5 and move up 0.5 at a time. Next we apply the *Sqr* function to each number in turn.

## Outline for Problem 5.3

**I.** Set up starting values:
  Number := 0.0;
  Sum := 0.0;
**II.** Repeat for 20 terms:
  Number := Number + 0.5;
  Square := Sqr(Number);
  Sum := Sum + Square;
**III.** Compute *Average.*
**IV.** Print results.

Here we use two variables to keep track of the terms to be averaged. *Number* starts at 0.0 and grows by 0.5 each time through the loop, so it takes on the values 0.5, 1.0,. . ., 10.0. *Square* is $Number^2$, so *Square* takes on the values $(0.5)^2$, $(1.0)^2$,. . ., $(10.0),^2$ which we want to sum and average. The outline has been followed in the following program. In this program, Steps I and II require more than a single line of code, so we perform these steps in separate procedures.

```
Program Average20Squares (Output);
{This program averages the squares of 0.5, 1, 1.5, ... , 9.5, 10}

Var Number. Real; {next number in the series}
    Sum, Average: Real;

Procedure Initialize (Var Number, Sum: Real);
{This procedure sets values to 0.0}
    Begin
        Number := 0.0;
        Sum := 0.0
    End {Initialize} ;

Procedure ComputeSum (Var Number, Sum: Real);
{This procedure computes desired sum for 20 terms}
    Var j: Integer;   {Control variable to count terms processed}
        Square: Real; {Square term to be added}
    Begin
        For j := 1 to 20
          Do Begin
            Number := Number + 0.5;
            Square := Sqr(Number);
            Sum := Sum + Square
          End
    End {Compute} ;

Begin {Main}
    Writeln ('This program averages the squares of');
    Writeln ('   0.5, 1, 1.5, 2, ... , 9.5, 10 .');

    Initialize (Number, Sum);

    ComputeSum (Number, Sum);

    {Compute the average}
    Average := Sum / 20.0;

    {Print results}
    Writeln ('The average of these numbers is ', Average:1:2, ' .')
End {Main} .
```

The program does not ask for any user input; it just prints:

```
This program averages the squares of
   0.5, 1, 1.5, 2, ... , 9.5, 10 .
The average of these numbers is 35.87 .
```

This program illustrates the parts of a loop:

1. Initialization

    Number := 0.0;
    Sum := 0.0;

**2.** Repetitive statement

```
For J := 1 to 20 Do
```

**3.** Loop block

```
Number := Number + 0.5;
Square := Sqr(Number);
Sum := Sum + Square;
```

**4.** Conclusion

```
Average := Sum/20.0
```

## SECTION 5.4 STYLE

There are several important stylistic principles for programs that use loops. Of course, the principles of structure and form discussed in earlier chapters still apply, so you might want to review the earlier sections on style. Here we will focus on some additional points that deal specifically with loops.

As with other programming constructions, the format of a loop should reflect the structure of the outline. An outline would use the form

**1.** Repeat the following steps for a range of values
  **a.**
  **b.**
  **c.**

When writing loops in programs, we use a similar form:

```
For                    For
    Do                     Do Begin



                           End
```

In each case the *For* statement is aligned with other major headings, and the *Do* phrase is indented. When several statements are included between *Do Begin* and *End*, each is indented further. The statements are enclosed by the *Do Begin* and *End* and the starting and stopping points have the same level of indentation.

The steps performed within the loop should be clearly designated; the loop should be clean and easy to read, so the overall structure of the loop is clear. If the steps within a loop involve many details, we code the steps as separate procedures.

In a *For–Do* loop, we use the control variable to methodically step through a designated range of variables. For example, we write

```
For Index := 3 to 9
   Do
```

to repeat a task for Index = 3, 4, 5, 6, 7, 8, 9. Be careful not to change the control variable within the loop, as in

```
For Index := 3 to 9
   Do Begin
         Write (Index);
         Index := Index + 1            {NO!!!}
   End;
```

Here changing Index interferes with the meaning of the *For–Do* loop. Changing control variables within a loop is illegal in Pascal. The compiler may generate an error message if you attempt such a change.

The control variable should be considered local to the loop. One step in the outline tells us to repeat a task, and the repetition is restricted to that one basic step. We should not declare control variables globally, unless the loop is in the Main Program itself, and we may not use the control variable in computations after the loop until it is assigned a new value. In fact, in Pascal, a Control Variable must be declared as local to the procedure or function where the loop is defined (see Figure 5–5).

After a *For* loop, a control variable logically can have at least two distinct values. For example, when the loop

```
For Index := 3 to 9
   Do
```

is finished, we can argue that the *Index* now has achieved its final value of 9 or that it has finished all processing with the value of 9 and has gone up to the next value of 10. Further, when we look at specific implementations of Pascal for different machines, we can find examples where *Index* has each of these values when the loop is over. For this reason, *in Pascal, the value of a control variable is undefined after a loop is completed.* On individual machines, a control variable may have some particular value, but

FIGURE 5–5 • **Declaration of a Control Variable**

```
Program Fig5Dash5 (. . .);
Procedure A;
    Var Index:  Integer;
    Begin
        For Index :=   3 to 9
            Do ---
    End {A} ;
Begin   {Main}
End  {Main}  .
```

*Correct*
Index declared in the procedure that contains the loop.

```
Program Fig5Dash5 (. . .);
Var Index:  Integer;
Procedure A;
    Begin
        For Index :=   3 to 9
            Do---
    End {A} ;
Begin   {Main}
End  {Main}  .
```

*Wrong*
Index is declared outside the procedure that contains the loop.

this value depends upon the way that Pascal is implemented on that machine. We cannot depend on that value for later processing.

In general, these principles all follow from the philosophy of structuring solutions to the problems. Loops may arise as major steps, and they may contain several smaller tasks. When we outline solutions, we naturally incorporate these structures in our writing. Our programs need to follow a similar form.

## SECTION 5.5 EXAMPLE: PRINTING TIC-TAC-TOE BOARDS, REVISITED

To further clarify the concept of loops, we return to our Tic-Tac-Toe problem of Section 4.1, where we wanted to print a simple board for a Tic-Tac-Toe game. In the present section, we consider the following extension of that problem.

### PROBLEM 5.5

Write a program that prints a Tic-Tac-Toe board, where the user specifies the size of each square. More precisely, the user should be asked to enter a number N, and then the program should print a board so that each square is N characters wide. For example, if the user specifies that N = 3, then the program should type:

```
   *   *
   *   *
   *   *
***********
   *   *
   *   *
   *   *
***********
   *   *
   *   *
   *   *
```

### Discussion of Problem 5.5

When we discussed this problem in Section 3.2, we derived the following basic outline.

**I.** Print the upper part of the vertical lines.
**II.** Print a horizontal line.
**III.** Print the middle part of the vertical lines.
**IV.** Print a horizontal line.
**V.** Print the bottom part of the vertical lines.

In programming from this outline, we found that Steps I, III, and V all required a common task which we declared as a procedure *PrintVertical*. Similarly, we used a procedure *PrintHorizontal* for Steps II and IV.

Next, we realized that in writing the vertical lines for one space, we could print a single line pattern

```
*   *
```

on each line. Thus, we defined a procedure *PrintDots* to print the individual lines within the *PrintVertical* task.

In the present problem, we can follow the same basic approach, but here we need to take the size of each square into account. For example, within the *PrintVertical* procedure, we must repeat *PrintDots* *N* times, so that the vertical line for a square is long enough. Similarly, within *PrintDots*, we must print *N* spaces for the first, middle, and last square on each line. To accomplish this, we use a *For* loop to count the number of spaces or *'s that we are printing. Then, after we print one entire line, we need to move to a new line with a *Writeln* statement. For each part of the pattern on our game board, we use a loop to repeat a process the correct number of times. The result is the following program.

```
Program TicTacToe {Version 2} (Input, Output);
{This program prints a Tic-Tac-Toe board of the specified size}

Var SquareSize: Integer;

Procedure EnterSize (Var Size: Integer);
{This procedure reads the size desired for a single square}
    Begin
        Write ('Please enter the size of a square on the board: ');
        Readln (Size)
    End {EnterSize} ;

Procedure PrintDots (Size: Integer);
{This procedure prints the dots for one of the vertical lines}
    Var SpaceCounter: Integer;
    Begin
        {Space over and print first '*'}
        For SpaceCounter := 1 To Size
            Do Write (' ');
        Write ('*');

        {Space over and print second '*'}
        For SpaceCounter := 1 To Size
            Do Write (' ');
        Writeln ('*');
    End {PrintDots} ;

Procedure PrintVertical (Size: Integer);
{This procedure prints part of the vertical lines on the board}
    Var LineNumber: Integer;
    Begin
        For LineNumber := 1 To Size
            Do PrintDots(Size)
    End {PrintVertical} ;
```

```
Procedure PrintHorizontal (Size: Integer);
{This procedure prints a horizontal line for the board}
    Var Counter: Integer;
    Begin
        {Since one square has the given Size, three squares
         require 3*Size '*'s.  In addition, we must add two
         characters for the two vertical lines.}

        For Counter := 1 To 3*Size+2
            Do Write ('*');
        Writeln
    End {PrintHorizontal} ;

Begin {Main}
    Writeln ('This program prints a Tic-Tac-Toe board');
    EnterSize (SquareSize);

    Writeln;
    PrintVertical (SquareSize);
    PrintHorizontal (SquareSize);
    PrintVertical (SquareSize);
    PrintHorizontal (SquareSize);
    PrintVertical (SquareSize)

End {Main} .
```

When this program is run with three spaces specified, then the output looks like the example at the beginning of this section. In developing this program, we follow the same basic steps that we identified in Section 3.2 for a somewhat simpler problem. However, here, within each step, we need to repeat a sequence of events a prescribed number of times. Therefore, in this program, we use For loops to count the number of times that we are repeating an action.

## SECTION 5.6 NESTED LOOPS

Once you understand the idea of repeating some work several times, it is natural to consider situations where repeated work itself includes a loop. This situation, where one loop is inside another one, is called a **nested loop.** In this section we will look at a problem that involves nested loops.

## PROBLEM 5.6 Car Loan Payment Tables

If you are planning to buy a car, you want to know what your monthly payments would be on a loan, which you expect to pay off over five years.

Determine the monthly payments for loans of $5000, $6000, $7000,. . ., $15,000 at annual interest rates of 9%, 10%, 11%,. . ., 15%.

### Discussion of Problem 5.6

The results will be most helpful if we plan to produce a table of the following type:

| Loan Amount | Annual Interest Rates 9% | 10% | 11% | 12% | 13% | 14% | 15% |
|---|---|---|---|---|---|---|---|
| $5000 | | | | | | | |
| $6000 | | | | | | | |
| $7000 | | | | | | | |
| . | | | | | | | |
| . | | | | | | | |
| . | | | | | | | |

The key task will be to print one line of the table. On each line we print the loan amount, then we repeat the same calculation for each interest rate. Thus, for one line, we have the following outline:

**A.** Print loan amount.
**B.** Repeat for rates 9%, 10%,. . ., 15%.
  **1.** Compute monthly payment.
  **2.** Print payment.
**C.** Move to next line.

From a handbook, here is the formula for computing the monthly payment:

$$\text{Payment} = \text{Loan} * \text{i}/[1-(1+\text{i})^{-\text{n}}],$$

where $n$ = number of months of loan (60 months, or 5 years), and $i$ = monthly interest rate (annual rate/12). Once you know how to compute one line, you can repeat the process for each loan amount. This suggests the following outline:

### Outline for Problem 5.6

**I.** Print table headings.
**II.** Print payments for loans of $5000, $6000,. . ., $15000.
  **A.** Print loan amount.
  **B.** Repeat for rates 9%, 10%,. . ., 15%.
    **1.** Compute monthly payment.
    **2.** Print payment.
  **C.** Move to next line.

When we translate this outline into a Pascal program, we use functions to compute the messy payment formula. In addition, as each major step of the outline requires several lines of code, we write procedures for each of these major steps. Otherwise, the program follows the outline very closely:

```
Program LoanPayments (Output);
{This program computes the monthly payments needed to pay off
 various loans at various interest rates over 5 years.}

Function Powers (Base, Exponent: Real). Real;
{Function raises the base to the given exponent.}
    Begin
        Powers := exp(Exponent * Ln(Base))
    End {Powers} ;

Function MonthlyPayment (Loan, Rate: Real): Real;
{Function computes the monthly payment for a loan at the given
 monthly rate to be paid in 5 years (60 months).}
    Var Top, Bottom: Real;
    Begin
        Top := Loan * Rate;
        Bottom := 1 - Powers(1+Rate, -60.0);
        MonthlyPayment := Top / Bottom
    End {MonthlyPayment} ;

Procedure PrintHeadings;
{This procedure prints the headings for the table of payments.}
    Begin
        Writeln ('Computation of monthly payments for various 5-year loans');
        Writeln;
        Writeln (' Loan                          Annual Interest Rates');
        Writeln ('Amount    9%      10%      11%',
                 '      12%      13%      14%      15%');
    End {PrintHeadings} ;

Procedure PrintPayments;
{This procedure prints payments for loans of 5000, 6000, 7000, ..., 15000}
    Var Loan: Real;
        Thousand: Integer; {Loan amounts in thousands}
        AnnRate: Integer;  {annual interest rate}
        MonRate: Real;     {monthly interest rate}
        Payment: Real;
    Begin
        For Thousand := 5 To 15
          Do Begin
            {Print loan amount}
            Loan := 1000.0 * Thousand;
            Write (Loan:5:0);

            {Repeat for each rate}
            For AnnRate := 9 to 15
              Do Begin
                MonRate := AnnRate / 1200.0;
                Payment := MonthlyPayment(Loan, MonRate);
                Write (Payment:8:2)
              End {AnnRate};

            {Move to next line}
            Writeln
          End {Thousand}

    End {PrintPayments} ;
```

```
Begin {Main}
    PrintHeadings;
    PrintPayments
End {Main} .
```

Notice how the indenting in this program clarifies the nested loops. When the program is run, we get

Computation of monthly payments for various 5-year loans

| Loan | | | Annual | Interest | Rates | | |
|---|---|---|---|---|---|---|---|
| Amount | 9% | 10% | 11% | 12% | 13% | 14% | 15% |
| 5000 | 103.79 | 106.23 | 108.71 | 111.22 | 113.76 | 116.34 | 118.95 |
| 6000 | 124.55 | 127.48 | 130.45 | 133.47 | 136.52 | 139.61 | 142.74 |
| 7000 | 145.31 | 148.73 | 152.20 | 155.71 | 159.27 | 162.88 | 166.53 |
| 8000 | 166.07 | 169.98 | 173.94 | 177.96 | 182.02 | 186.15 | 190.32 |
| 9000 | 186.82 | 191.22 | 195.68 | 200.20 | 204.78 | 209.41 | 214.11 |
| 10000 | 207.58 | 212.47 | 217.42 | 222.44 | 227.53 | 232.68 | 237.90 |
| 11000 | 228.34 | 233.72 | 239.16 | 244.69 | 250.28 | 255.95 | 261.69 |
| 12000 | 249.10 | 254.96 | 260.91 | 266.93 | 273.04 | 279.22 | 285.48 |
| 13000 | 269.86 | 276.21 | 282.65 | 289.18 | 295.79 | 302.49 | 309.27 |
| 14000 | 290.62 | 297.46 | 304.39 | 311.42 | 318.54 | 325.76 | 333.06 |
| 15000 | 311.37 | 318.70 | 326.13 | 333.67 | 341.29 | 349.02 | 356.85 |

This example illustrates one general situation that arises when a problem contains several distinct variables, each varying over a range of values. The result is a table. To create this table, we first considered what we needed to do for a single row or a particular loan amount. For a particular loan, we needed to compute payments at various interest rates, and we used a loop to make these various payment computations. For this loop, we had an initialization *Write(Loan)*, a repetitive statement *For AnnRate*, a loop block, and a conclusion *Writeln*.

When we had identified what we needed to do for a given loan amount, we repeated that computation for the various loan amounts. As a result, we had one large loop (for loan amounts) which contained a smaller loop (for various interest rates); the loop for interest rates was nested inside the loop for loan amounts.

## SECTION 5.7 TESTING AND DEBUGGING

In earlier chapters, our programs followed simple formulae and the amount of computation performed was rather small. Such programs were fairly easy to check. We had little difficulty following the formulae, and we could easily test that the programs produced correct results. The task of checking programs that contain loops can be harder. The computer may be performing many more computations, and it may be impractical for us to do the same work. Similarly, once we discover that a program produces incorrect results, we may have a hard time locating the errors, or **bugs.**

In this section we will begin a discussion of ways to test programs and find bugs when we use loops. We will review some ways of selecting good test data for checking programs; then we will identify places in loops where errors are frequently made. Finally, we will mention some techniques for locating specific errors. This discussion will allow us to get started testing and correcting many programs that contain loops. After we have some experience (by Section 7.5), we will consider a few additional ideas for testing and debugging.

## Choosing Test Cases

Back in Chapter 2 we tested programs by running them with data where we knew the answer ahead of time. When the programs worked correctly on the test cases, we felt fairly confident that the programs would work on other cases as well.

This idea still applies, but we need to select test cases carefully. It would be best to avoid long, involved computations, even if the computer will perform the work. We may be able to identify special cases where we know an answer without doing all the steps. For example, if we want to compute the average of several numbers, we know the average is a "middle" value. Thus, we could pick data where this "middle" can be determined at a glance:

The average of 2, 2, 2, 2, 2 is clearly 2.

The average of 1 and 2 is clearly 1.5.

The average of 9, 10, 12, 13 is 11.

In such special cases, we use our general knowledge (of averages) to select test cases with known answers. We do not need to repeat the work of the program to find our results for our tests.

## Finding Errors

After a program is run with test data, you may know that the program contains an error, or bug. The next task is to find and correct the error, often called **debugging.** We will now consider a few ways to find errors.

**Common Errors.** While errors can occur in many places, you often can find an error quickly if you check the places where troubles most frequently arise. These common errors in writing loops are summarized in Table 5–1; you might start your debugging work by reading the code to try to correct these potential errors.

**TABLE 5–1 • Common Errors in Writing Loops**

| Error | Description |
|---|---|
| Initialization | First datum often either omitted completely or counted twice. |
| Moving from case to case | One variable often not updated or changed incorrectly. |
| Ending at the right time | Steps in a loop may be done one time too many or one time too few. |
| Putting too much or too little in the loop | Part of the initialization or conclusion of a loop may be inside the loop itself. For example, a sum may be reset to 0.0 each time in a loop. |
| Changing the control variable | If you change the control variable in a loop, you lose track of how many repetitions have occurred. |

**Tracing Execution.** A second important technique is to trace through the program with test data, printing out what the computer is doing at each step. Two tracing techniques are helpful. You can go through the program step by step, using notepaper to keep track of each variable and computation; you "play computer," following each instruction in the program.

You could also insert *Write* statements at various places in the program, to see what the computer has done. For example, you could write out the values of variables at the beginning or end of each procedure and before and after loops. In this technique you let the computer perform the computations, but you monitor the program as the work proceeds. Placing *Write* statements in a loop often helps identify errors in initialization, conclusion, and moving from case to case in a loop.

Frequently you can combine these two techniques effectively. First you might insert a few *Write* statements to determine what section of code the bug is in. If the program has correct values before a piece of code and incorrect values after, then there must be an error in that piece. Once you have narrowed down the location of the bug, you can trace the program yourself, on paper, to find the error.

When the bugs are found and corrected, remove the extra *Write* statements after rechecking the program with the test cases. While you are becoming proficient in the tracing process, you may find some suggestions helpful:

- When you insert *Write* statements, it is helpful to print where the statements are. Then, when the program is run, you know what statement produced what output.

- Extra *Write* statements should be identified in some way in the program listing, so they can be found quickly and removed easily after the program is corrected.
- When tracing through a program, be sure you keep track of enough information. When inserting *Write* statements, print enough data to trace through the next part of the program if necessary.

A sample of a *Write* statement inserted for debugging is shown in Figure 5–6.

**Loop Invariants.** When developing loops, you may find it helpful to write out explicitly what you need to be true each time you start the loop. For example, our program to average the numbers $(0.5)^2, \ldots, (10.0)^2$ contained the statements

```
Number := 0.0;
Sum := 0.0;
For J := 1 to 20
      Do Begin
            Number := Number +0.5;
            Square := Sqr(Number);
            Sum := Sum + Square
      End;
```

Here, each time the loop repeats, we can check that *Number* is the last value processed and *Sum* equals the sum of the squares from 0.5 up to *Number*. These two conditions are called **loop invariants** in this program; we need them to be true each time we start or finish our loop.

Once you have identified loop invariants, you can check that initialization and updating of variables keeps the statements true. If they are not true, you can check the list of common errors to see if you have forgotten to update a variable appropriately, or if initialization allows the loop to start correctly the first time. To trace a program's execution, you can insert *Write* statements at the beginning of a loop to see if the loop invariants

FIGURE 5–6 • **Inserting a Write Statement for Debugging**

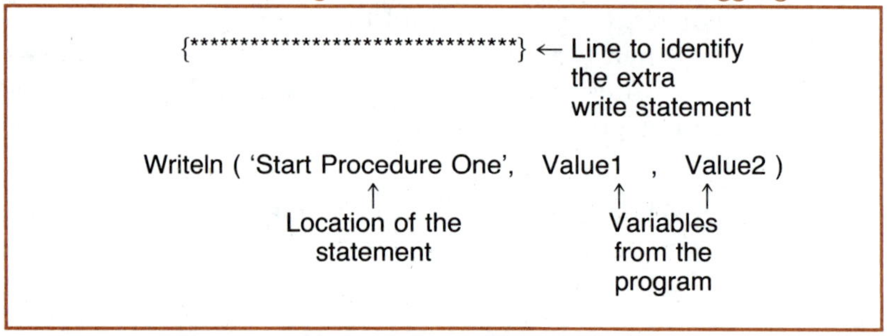

```
{*********************************} ← Line to identify
                                      the extra
                                      write statement

Writeln ( 'Start Procedure One',  Value1  ,  Value2 )
                ↑                    ↑          ↑
          Location of the          Variables
            statement              from the
                                   program
```

really do hold each time the loop begins. In many cases, once you write out explicitly what the loop invariants should be, you can locate and correct errors quite effectively.

## SUMMARY

1. A **loop** is a repetitive structure that allows you to repeat steps several times. This process of **repetition,** or **iteration,** has the following basic steps:

   I. **Initialization:** Before the loop begins, you may need to get ready for the loop.

   II. Loop itself

      A. **Repetitive statement:** A statement that tells the computer to repeat something.

      B. **Loop block:** Specifies what statements must be repeated.

   III. **Conclusion:** After the loop is over, you may have some final work to do.

2. This chapter presents two forms for repetitive statements:

   *For* ControlVariable := InitialValue *To* FinalValue *Do* LoopBlock

   and

   *For* ControlVariable := InitialValue *DownTo* FinalValue
   *Do* LoopBlock

   The loop block can be either a single Pascal statement or a **Begin–End block.**

3. Within the loop itself, you may need to start the loop each time with certain conditions being true. You need to update variables at the end of the loop for the **loop invariants** to be true when you start the next

| KEY TERMS, PHRASES, AND CONCEPTS | | ELEMENTS OF PASCAL SYNTAX |
|---|---|---|
| Address | Iteration | *Begin–End Block* |
| Bug | Loop | *For–To–Do* |
| Conclusion of a Loop | Loop Block | *For–DownTo–Do* |
| Control Variable | Loop Invariants | |
| Debugging | Nested Loops | |
| Initial Value | Repetition | |
| Final Value | Repetitive Statement | |
| Initialization of a Loop | Tracing Program Execution | |

iteration of the loop. The loop block often contains two parts: Perform work for this iteration; get ready for next iteration.

4. When you test a program, you may need to **trace** through the code to determine what the computer is doing. You can review what the computer has done by inserting extra *Write* statements, and you can follow the instructions yourself using pencil and paper to keep track of your work.
5. Finally, this chapter includes many applications. Some applications involve simple loops. In other cases, you need **nested loops,** with one loop inside another.

## EXERCISES

**5.1** *Converting Quarts to Liters.* Write a program that shows the conversion of quarts to liters, for quarts in the range 1, 2, 3,. . ., 20. Label the columns of the table "Quarts" and "Liters."

NOTE: 1 liter = 1.056710 quarts.

**5.2** *Temperature Conversion.* Write a program to produce a table of Fahrenheit temperatures with corresponding centigrade and absolute (Kelvin) temperatures. The Fahrenheit temperatures in the table should include 0, 1, 2,. . ., 212. Label the columns of the table "Fahrenheit," "Centigrade," and "Kelvin." The appropriate conversion formulae are:

$$\text{Centigrade} = 5/9(\text{Fahrenheit} - 32)$$
$$\text{Kelvin} = \text{Centigrade} + 212$$

**5.3** *Sum of Cubes.* For $n = 1, 2, 3,\ldots, 50$, compute both $n^3$ and the sum

$$1^3 + 2^3 + 3^3 + \cdots + (n - 1)^3 + n^3.$$

Print the results in a table with headings "N," "N Cubed," and "Sum."

**5.4** *Table of Roots and Powers.* Write a program to print a table where each row contains a number N with its square, square root, cube, and cube root. The table should cover numbers N = 1, 2, 3,. . ., 50. Label each of the columns in the table appropriately.

**5.5** *Approximating $\pi$.* It can be shown that $\pi$ can be approximated by any of the following series:

a. $\pi/4 = 1 - 1/3 + 1/5 - 1/7 + \cdots$

b. $\pi^2/6 = 1 + 1/2^2 + 1/3^2 + 1/4^2 + \cdots$

c. $\pi^2/12 = 1 - 1/2^2 + 1/3^2 - 1/4^2 + \cdots$

d. $\pi^2/8 = 1 + 1/3^2 + 1/5^2 + 1/7^2 + \cdots$

e. $\pi^2/24 = 1/2^2 + 1/4^2 + 1/6^2 + 1/8^2 + \cdots$

To use any of these series to approximate $\pi$, first compute the first $n$

terms of the right side to get an approximate value for the series, then solve for $\pi$ using the approximate value for the series.

For example, using the first 20 terms from formula d, $\pi^2/8$ is approximately 1.2212. Thus $\pi^2$ is about 8 * 1.2212, and $\pi$ is about Sqrt(8 * 1.2212) = (3.125).

*Problems a through e.* Use the above series to approximate $\pi$; try 10, 20, 30, and 40 terms.

**5.6** *Tic-Tac-Toe Outline.* Section 5.5 develops a program to print a Tic-Tac-Toe board with squares of a specified size, and the general organization of the program follows the outline developed in Section 4.1. Expand the outline of Section 4.1 to include the loops that are needed in this revised problem.

**5.7** *Converting Quarts and Gallons to Liters.* Print a table that shows the conversion of quarts and gallons to liters. In the table, use the format

| | Quarts | | | |
|---|---|---|---|---|
| Gallons | 0 | 1 | 2 | 3 |
| 0 | | | | |
| 1 | | | | |
| 2 | | | | |
| 3 | | | | |
| . | | | | |
| . | | | | |
| . | | | | |
| 10 | | | | |

NOTE: one liter = 1.056710 quarts.

**5.8** *Converting Feet and Inches to Centimeters.* Print a table that shows the conversion of feet and inches to centimeters. In the table, use the headings

| | Inches | | | | | |
|---|---|---|---|---|---|---|
| Feet | 0 | 1 | 2 | 3 | . . . | 12 |
| 0 | | | | | | |
| 1 | | | | | | |
| 2 | | | | | | |
| 3 | | | | | | |
| 4 | | | | | | |
| 5 | | | | | | |

NOTE: one inch = 2.54 centimeters.

**5.9** *Extended Chart for Seconds Per Mile Versus Miles Per Hour.* Write an extended table relating seconds per mile to miles per hour, where seconds per mile covers the range 30, 31, 32,. . ., 129. The output should be in the form of a compact chart:

```
Seconds
Per Mile                          Units
--------    -----------------------------------------------
  Tens       0    1    2    3    4    5    6    7    8    9
   3 --                                .
   4 --                                .
   5 --                                .
   6 --  - - - - - - - - - - - - - - - .
   7 --
   8 --
   9 --
  10 --
  11 --
  12 --
```

The chart illustrates how to look up 65 seconds per mile. Move down the left column to find the 6 in 65, then move across the row to find the column labeled 5.

**5.10** *Mortgage Payments (1).* Given the length of a mortgage (read from the terminal), determine the monthly payments on mortgages of 15,000, 20,000,. . ., 80,000 at annual interest rates of 7%, 8%, 9%,. . ., 15%. Display the results in a chart:

```
Mortgage                    Annual Interest Rate
Amount      7    8    9    10    11    12    13    14    15
--------   ------------------------------------------------

15000
20000
25000
  .
  .
  .
80000
```

**5.11** *Mortgage Payments (2).* Given an annual interest rate (read from the terminal), determine the monthly payments on mortgages of 15,000, 20,000, 25,000, 30,000,. . ., 80,000 for periods of 15 years, 20 years, 25 years, 30 years, and 35 years.

Display the results in a chart:

```
Annual Interest Rate: ____

Mortgage    Length of Mortgage in Years
Amount      15    20    25    30    35
--------   ----------------------------

15000
20000
25000
```

30000
35000
.
.
.
80000

**5.12** *Mortgage Payments (3).* Investigate the monthly payments on mortgages of 15,000, 20,000, 25,000, . . . , 80,000 at annual interest rates of 7%, 8%, 9%, . . . , 15% over periods of 15 years, 20 years, 25 years, 30 years, and 35 years. Display your results in a series of charts, where each chart has the form shown in the previous problem.

**5.13** *Windchill Temperature.* In cold weather the windchill temperature is used to indicate the effect of the wind and temperature on cooling the body. Suppose the wind is measured at *W* miles per hour, and suppose the thermometer shows a temperature of *F* degrees Fahrenheit. The approximate windchill temperature is given by the formula

$$T = 1.05 + 0.93T - 3.65W + 3.62\sqrt{W} + 0.103T\sqrt{W} + 0.0439W^2.$$

Compute the windchill temperature for temperatures of 10°, 9°, 8°, . . . , −30° Fahrenheit and for winds 0, 5, 10, . . . , 40 MPH. Display the results in a table labeled as follows:

| | Wind Speed | | | | | | | | |
|---|---|---|---|---|---|---|---|---|---|
| Temperature | 0 | 5 | 10 | 15 | 20 | 25 | 30 | 35 | 40 |
| 10 | | | | | | | | | |
| 9 | | | | | | | | | |
| 8 | | | | | | | | | |
| . | | | | | | | | | |
| . | | | | | | | | | |
| . | | | | | | | | | |

NOTE: In practice, the windchill temperatures reported by the weather bureau are modified from a formula such as the one above. We therefore cannot expect a formula to give exact windchill temperatures.

**5.14** *Table of Natural Logarithms.* Ln(x) can be shown to be closely approximated by the formula

$$2[y + y^3/3 + y^5/5 + \cdots + y^{2n-1}/(2n - 1)],$$

where $y = (x-1)/(x+1)$, and where *n* is sufficiently large. Use this formula to compute ln(x) for $x = 1, 1.1, 1.2, \ldots, 4$ with $n = 8$, and compare the results with the Pascal *Ln* function. Display the output in the form

| X | Computed Ln(x) | Pascal Ln(x) |
|---|---|---|
| 1.0 | 0.000 | 0.000 |
| 1.1 | | |
| 1.2 | | |
| . | | |
| . | | |
| . | | |

*Programming Notes:*

Use a function *MyLn(x)* to compute the value from the above formula. (In the function, declare *n* to be the constant 8.)

In this problem you must use multiplication to compute powers of *y*. You may not use the *Powers* function discussed in Section 4.2.

In practice, the Pascal *Ln(x)* function uses formulae similar to this to compute natural logarithms. Other such formulae are used for *Exp(x)*, *Sin(x)*, *Cos(x)*, etc.

**5.15** Write a table that contains the values of $n$, $n^2$, $\log_2(n)$, $n*\log_2(n)$, and $10n*\log_2(n)$ for $n = 2, 4, 8, 16, 32, \ldots, 16384$. Display your computations in a table with the appropriate headings.

NOTE: When we analyze various algorithms in later chapters, you will find numbers such as these will tell you the amount of work required for *n* pieces of data. Thus comparisons of this type can help you pick the best algorithms to solve certain problems.

**5.16** What are the loop invariants in the programs in Sections 5.1, 5.3, and 5.5?

# CHAPTER 6

# CONDITIONAL STATEMENTS AND BOOLEAN DATA TYPE

In our work up to this point, we have always followed the same steps every time we ran a program. *For–Do* statements allow us to repeat some steps, but even then we always repeat exactly the same statements.

In this chapter we address problems where some steps apply in certain circumstances and other steps apply in other cases. Much of this work depends upon expressions that are true or false. Such expressions are called **conditional** or **Boolean expressions,** and we will introduce a new **Boolean data type** for these values. With this new material you will be able to write programs where the solutions involve dividing problems up into different cases, with different work required for each case.

## SECTION 6.1 EXAMPLE: COMPUTING THE COST OF A TELEPHONE CALL

We begin with a rather simple problem, where one step of the solution must be performed only in some circumstances. Later we will add some details to make the problem somewhat more complex. Then we will want to divide the solution into separate cases and handle each case separately.

## PROBLEM 6.1A

Compute the cost of a daytime telephone call from Grinnell, Iowa, to Chicago, Illinois.

### Discussion of Problem 6.1A

The telephone company has supplied the following daytime rate schedule for station-to-station calls (basic rate): first minute \$0.58; each additional minute \$0.39. Thus, the cost of a five-minute call would be computed as follows:

| | |
|---|---|
| First minute | \$0.58 |
| 4 minutes at \$0.39 | \$1.56 |
| Total cost | \$2.14 |

Further, in computing costs, times are always rounded up, so that a call lasting 4 minutes, 10 seconds is rounded up to count as a five-minute call. This computation suggests the following steps:

1. The first minute (or less) of the call is \$0.58.
2. If the call lasts over one minute, then \$0.39 is added for each minute beyond the first.

We now can outline the solution.

I. Determine the length (in minutes) of the call.
II. Charge for the first minute: *Cost* := *\$0.58*.
III. Charge for any time beyond the first minute.
If the call lasts over one minute, then \$0.39 is added for each minute beyond the first.
IV. Print results.

In Pascal we can code this outline as follows:

```
Program TelephoneCall {Version 1} (Input, Output);
{This program computes the cost of a daytime telephone call
 from Grinnell, Iowa (Where?) to Chicago, Illinois}

Const FirstMinute = 0.58;
      AdditMinute = 0.39;

Var Length: Integer;      {The length of the call in minutes}
    Cost: Real;           {the cost of the call in dollars}

Begin
    Writeln ('This program computes the cost of a daytime telephone call');

    {Determine data about the call}
    Write ('Please enter the length of the call in minutes: ');
    Readln (Length);

    {Charge for the first minute}
    Cost := FirstMinute;
```

```
    {Charge for any time beyond the first minute}
    If Length > 1
        Then Cost := Cost + AdditMinute * (Length-1);

    {Print results}
    Writeln ('The cost of the call was $', Cost:1:2)

End {Main} .
```

When this program is run for a three-minute call, the following appears:

```
This program computes the cost of a daytime telephone call
Please enter the length of the call in minutes: 3
The cost of the call was $1.36
```

### Describing and Handling Two Distinct Possibilities

One new feature appears for Step III of the outline, to charge for time beyond the first minute. In this step there are two distinct possibilities; the call may last more than one minute, or the call may last one minute or less. In the first case we have extra work to do, but the second case does not require further computations.

This situation prompts the use of an *If–Then* statement:

```
If Length > 1
    Then Cost := Cost + AdditMinute*(Length – 1)
```

When the computer executes this command, the machine first looks at the condition *Length > 1*. In the test run, where *Length* is 3, this condition is true, so the computer performs the *Then* part of the statement. If *Length* is 1, however, the condition *Length > 1* is false and the *Then* statement is skipped by the computer.

This program illustrates two important points. When solving problems, we may want to divide a solution into cases. An *If–Then* statement allows us to perform work for a specified case. This work is omitted if the condition specified is not met.

This capability of performing operations for particular cases also allows us to look at a more general problem:

**PROBLEM 6.1B** Compute the cost of a telephone call from Grinnell, Iowa, to Chicago, Illinois.

### Discussion of Problem 6.1B

Complete telephone rate information for this call is given in the following chart.

| | |
|---|---|
| Basic rate: | $0.58 for the first minute<br>$0.39 for each additional minute |
| Evening rate:<br>(5 PM to 11 PM) | discount of 40% from the basic rate<br>(charge is 60% of thc basic rate) |
| Night rate:<br>(11 PM to 8 AM) | discount of 60% from the basic rate<br>(charge is 40% of the basic rate) |

If a five-minute call is made at 9:30 in the morning, the cost of the call would be $2.14, as we computed earlier. If a five-minute call begins at 4:00 AM, however, the cost of the call is 40% of $2.14, or $0.86.

Note that the rate charged for the call depends only on the time the call begins. A five-minute call starting at 7:58 AM would all be charged at the night rate ($0.86), and a five-minute call starting at 4:58 PM would all be charged at the basic rate ($2.14).

With this rate schedule, we need two more pieces of data to compute the cost of a call from Grinnell to Chicago, the length of the call (in minutes) and the hour when the call started. To avoid ambiguity in distinguishing between AM and PM, we might use a 24-hour clock; 2 PM would be written 14:00.

### Outline for Problem 6.1B

**I.** Determine data about the call:
- **A.** *Length* (in minutes) of the call.
- **B.** *Hour* when call started.

**II.** Use *Length* to compute the basic *Cost*.

**III.** Use *Hour* to determine the appropriate discount (if any).
- **A.** If *Hour* is between 5 PM (17:00) and 11 PM (23:00), *Cost* is 60% of the basic *Cost*.
- **B.** If *Hour* is before 8 AM or after 11 PM (23:00), *Cost* is 40% of the basic *Cost*.

**IV.** Print results.

This outline yields the following program:

```
Program TelephoneCall {Version 2} (Input, Output);
{This program computes the cost of a telephone call
 from Grinnell, Iowa (Where?) to Chicago, Illinois}

Const FirstMinute = 0.58;
      AdditMinute = 0.39;

Var Length: Integer;     {the length of the call in minutes}
    Hour: Integer;       {the hour when the call began}
    Cost: Real;          {the cost of the call in dollars}
```

```
Begin
    Writeln ('This program computes the cost of a daytime telephone call');

    {Determine data about the call}
    Write ('Please enter the length of the call in minutes: ');
    Readln (Length);
    Write ('Enter the hour when the call started: ');
    Readln (Hour);

    {Compute the cost of the call}
    If Length = 1
        Then Cost := FirstMinute     {Call lasts one minute}
        Else Cost := FirstMinute + AdditMinute * (Length-1);

    {Compute discount, if any}
    If (Hour >= 17) And (Hour < 23)  {Evening Rate Applies}
        Then Cost := 0.60 * Cost;
    If (Hour < 8) or (Hour >= 23)    {Night Rate Applies}
        Then Cost := 0.40 * Cost;


    {Print results}
    Writeln ('The cost of the call was $', Cost:1:2)

End {Main} .
```

This program illustrates two additional points about programming for distinct cases. First, to compute the basic cost, we observe that the problem has only two distinct cases (Case A, one minute; Case B, longer). In the program we wrote

```
If Length = 1
    Then Cost := FirstMinute
    Else Cost := FirstMinute + AdditMinute*(Length - 1)
```

When the computer executes this statement, it first determines whether the call lasted one minute. If this condition is true (Case A), the *Then* clause is executed. If the condition is false (Case B), the *Else* clause is performed. Again, the work of the computer depends upon the initial condition.

Second, this program illustrates that the condition for a discount can be split into pieces, and these pieces can be put together with *And* and *Or*. In Pascal we cannot make two comparisons at once, so 17 <= *Hour* < 23 is beyond the capabilities of the machine. Such expressions can be split up into pieces, however, so that only two items are being compared in each piece. (Hour is compared to 17 in one piece and to 23 in another.) In Pascal, a variety of comparisons are possible. The complete list of comparison operators is listed in Table 6–1.

We now look at *If* statements more carefully.

**TABLE 6–1 • Logical Operators Between Numbers**

| | |
|---|---|
| < | less than |
| <= | less than or equal to |
| = | equal to |
| > | greater than |
| >= | greater than or equal to |
| <> | not equal |

## SECTION 6.2 ELEMENTS OF CONDITIONAL EXECUTION

Section 6.1 illustrated the two basic forms of the conditional *If* statement:

*Form 1*

```
If Condition
        Then Statement
```

*Form 2*

```
If Condition
        Then Statement 1
        Else Statement 2
```

NOTE: In the second form, the *If–Then–Else* is considered all one statement, so no semicolon is used after Statement 1.

In either form, *Condition* is an expression that has a true-or-false value. *Statement, Statement 1,* and *Statement 2* are any single Pascal statements or compound *Begin–End* blocks.

When the computer encounters an *If* statement, it first evaluates the condition to see if that condition is true or false. In either form, if the condition is true the computer executes the *Then* clause, performing the work specified in the statement or statements. When this work is finished, the computer moves to the next command after the *If* statement. (If there is an *Else* clause, it is skipped.)

If the condition is false, the *Then* clause is skipped. The computer goes on to the next statement following the *If,* or executes the *Else* clause if it is there. These patterns of execution are illustrated in the following examples:

```
If Rain > 0
   Then Writeln('It is Raining');
Writeln ('Tomorrow may be nice')
```

```
If Rain > 0
   Then Writeln('It is Raining')
   Else Writeln ('No Rain Today');
Writeln ('Tomorrow may be nice')
```

In either example, if the code is run with *Rain* having the value 1, the result would be

```
It is Raining
Tomorrow may be nice
```

In each case, the condition *Rain* > *0* is true (1 is greater than 0), and the *Then* clause applies. After the *Then* clause is executed, the computer goes to the *Writeln* statement after the *If*. The *Else* clause in the second example is not executed for this value of *Rain*. The examples give different output, however, if the code is run with *Rain* set to 0. The first example prints only one line:

```
Tomorrow may be nice
```

The second example prints two lines:

```
No Rain Today
Tomorrow may be nice
```

The condition *Rain* > *0* is false, so the *Then* clause is skipped. In the first example the computer goes on to the next statement, which is a *Writeln*. In the second example the false condition causes the *Else* clause to be executed. When the *Else* clause is finished, the computer continues with the next statement, the last *Writeln*.

To summarize, in a conditional statement, the condition is first evaluated. If the condition is true, the *Then* clause is executed. If the condition is false, an *Else* clause is executed, if such a clause exists. These three steps complete the execution of the *If* statement. When the *If* statement is done, the computer goes on to whatever statement comes next.

## Compound Statements Within an *If* Statement

In either form of conditional statement, we can ask the computer to perform multiple steps as part of a *Then* or *Else* clause by using a *Begin–End* block for the statement. For example, in the first program to compute telephone charges, we might print out a message if the length of the call exceeded one minute. The revised statement might be

```
If Length > 1
   Then Begin
         Writeln ('Call took over one minute');
         Cost := Cost + AdditMinute*(Length - 1)
         End;
```

Two tasks would be done if we talked for more than one minute. First a message would be written. Second, the cost for the additional time would be computed. We can also have multiple statements in the *If–Then–Else* form of conditional statement, using a *Begin–End* block in either or both of the *Then* and *Else* clauses. For example, we could write

```
If Length = 1
   Then Cost := FirstMinute
   Else Begin
         Writeln ('You talk too much');
         Cost := FirstMinute + AdditMinute*(Length - 1)
         End;
```

This points out a general concept: A *Begin–End* block can be used anywhere in a Pascal program where a single statement is used. Whenever a *Begin–End* block is used, the block is considered to be a single entity. The statements within the block can be considered pieces of one big step.

We use *Begin–End* blocks with *For–Do* statements and with *If* statements when we want several pieces of work done as part of a single step. We can also use a *Begin–End* block to clarify how various pieces fit together, such as when we put *If* statements together.

## Nested *If* Statements

Many times, we will want to consider several distinct cases. For example, in the Telephone Call Problem 6.1B, we can distinguish three cases:

| | |
|---|---|
| Basic rate | Calls originating between 8 and 17 o'clock |
| Evening rate | Calls starting after 17 o'clock, but before 23 o'clock |
| Night rate | Calls starting after 23 o'clock or before 8 o'clock |

These cases are mutually exclusive; if one rate applies, then the other rates do not apply. If the *Hour* of the call implies the basic rate, there is no reason to check further to see if we should use an evening or night rate. We include these observations in the following revised outline, which also tells how to print the rate used in the computation.

### Revised Outline for Problem 6.1B

**I.** Determine data about the call:
- **A.** *Length* (in minutes) of the call.
- **B.** *Hour* when call started.

**II.** Compute the *Cost* of the call.
- **A.** Determine whether basic rate applies ($8 \leq Hour \leq 17$).
- **B.** If so,
  - **1.** Make appropriate computations using basic rate.
  - **2.** Print that basic rate is used.
- **C.** If not, determine whether the evening rate applies ($17 < Hour \leq 23$).
  - **1.** If the evening rate applies,
    - **a.** Make appropriate computations using the evening rate.
    - **b.** Print that evening rate is used.
  - **2.** If the evening rate does not apply, then we must use the night rate. (We have already checked for basic and evening rates, and these rates do not apply. The only other possibility is the night rate.)
    - **a.** Make appropriate computations using the night rate.
    - **b.** Print that night rate is used.

**III.** Print Results.

From this outline we write the following program. As in our previous programs, we use procedures here for Steps I and II which involve several lines of code.

```
Program TelephoneCall {Version 3} (Input, Output);
{This program computes the cost of a telephone call
 from Grinnell, Iowa (Where?) to Chicago, Illinois}

Const FirstMinute = 0.58;
      AdditMinute = 0.39;

Var Length: Integer;     {the length of the call in minutes}
    Hour: Integer;       {the hour when the call began}
    Cost: Real;          {the cost of the call in dollars}

Procedure DetermineCallData (Var Length, Hour: Integer);
{This procedure reads the necessary data about the call}
    Begin
        Write ('Please enter the length of the call in minutes: ');
        Readln (Length);
        Write ('Enter the hour when the call started: ');
        Readln (Hour)
    End {DetermineCallData} ;

Function BasicRate (Length: Integer; First, Additional: Real): Real;
{This function computes the basic rate for the call}
    Begin
    If Length = 1
        Then BasicRate := First      {Call lasts one minute}
        Else BasicRate := First + Additional * (Length-1)
    End {BasicRate} ;

Procedure ComputeCost (Length, Hour: Integer; Var Cost: Real);
{This procedure computes the cost of the call, using the appropriate rate}
    Begin
        If (8 <= Hour) And (Hour < 17)
          Then Begin
              Writeln ('Basic Rate Applies');
              Cost := BasicRate (Length, FirstMinute, AdditMinute);
          End
          Else Begin
            If (Hour >= 17) And (Hour < 23)
                Then Begin
                    Writeln ('Evening Rate Applies');
                    Cost := 0.60 * BasicRate (Length, FirstMinute, AdditMinute)
                End
                Else Begin
                    Writeln ('Night Rate applies');
                    Cost := 0.40 * BasicRate (Length, FirstMinute, AdditMinute)
                End
          End {Else}
    End {ComputeCost} ;

Begin
    Writeln ('This program computes the cost of a daytime telephone call');

    DetermineCallData (Length, Hour);

    ComputeCost (Length, Hour, Cost);

    {Print results}
    Writeln ('The cost of the call was $', Cost:1:2)

End {Main} .
```

This program uses a second *If* statement within the *Else* clause of the first *If*. The program does not explicitly test that the night rate applies, because that rate can be inferred if the other rates do not apply. Read this code carefully to be sure you understand the program logic.

The first *Begin–End* block is not actually needed in the *Else* clause. An *If* statement is a single Pascal statement, so an *If* could be used directly in a *Then* or *Else* clause. The computation for this program could also be written as follows:

```
{Compute the cost, using the appropriate rate}
If (8 <= Hour) And (Hour < 17)
   Then Cost := BasicRate                    {Basic Rate Applies}
   Else If (Hour >= 17) And (Hour < 23)
        Then Cost := 0.6*BasicRate           {Evening Rate Applies}
        Else Cost := 0.4*BasicRate           {Night Rate Applies}
```

Here the *Begin–End* is not needed, but can make the program clearer.

## Common Errors

We conclude this section on the elements of the *If* statement by noting four common errors.

1. Ambiguity can arise when we combine *If–Then* statements with *If–Then–Else* statements. In particular, the code *If–Then–If–Then–Else* has two reasonable interpretations, as suggested by indenting:

```
If A > 0
    Then If B > 0
         Then Writeln('One')
         Else Writeln('Two')
If A > 0
    Then If B > 0
         Then Writeln('One')
    Else Writeln('Two')
```

The issue here is whether *Else Writeln ('Two')* goes with the first *If (A > 0)* or with the second *If (B > 0)*. In computer science, different languages address this difficulty in various ways. In Pascal the *Else* always goes with the most recent *If–Then* (the first interpretation). If we want to use the second interpretation, we must put the *If B > 0* statement inside a *Begin–End* block. It is good practice to use *Begin–End* blocks for clarity even when they are not needed technically.

2. There is a tendency to forget the *Begin–End* in a *Then* or *Else* clause when we want several steps done. For example, we may write

```
If Length = 1
    Then
         Writeln ('One Minute Call');
         Cost := FirstMinute
    Else  Cost := FirstMinute + AdditMinute*(Length-1);
```

Here we omitted the *Begin–End,* and *Else* is separated from the *If–Then.* In this situation, the compiler frequently will not be able to tell where the *Else* belongs, and the program would not compile.

A similar, but more subtle error occurs when we forget the *Begin–End* in an *Else* clause or in a *Then* with no following *Else.* For example, we may write

```
If Length = 1
     Then Cost := FirstMinute
     Else Cost := FirstMinute + AdditMinute*(Length-1);
          Writeln ('You talk too much');
```

Here we indented the *Writeln* to be part of the *If–Then–Else.* As written, however, the *Writeln* is a separate statement, and the message is always printed. The program contains a logical error, but the syntax is correct; the program will compile, but will not give the expected results.

3. The third common error is the addition of a semicolon immediately after the word *Then.* For example, consider the statement

```
If Length > 1 Then ;
     Cost := Cost + AdditMinute * (Length - 1)
```

Here the semicolon separates the *If–Then* statement from the computation of *Cost,* and the *Then* clause contains a null statement. Thus, the cost computation is always performed because it is not part of the *Then* clause of the *If* statement.

4. A similar error is the insertion of a semicolon before an *Else* clause. Philosophically, the *If–Then–Else* is all part of one statement. There is a strong tendency, however, to type a semicolon after the *Then* clause. When a semicolon is included there, the *Else* is separated from the *If–Then* and the program normally will not compile.

## SECTION 6.3 EVALUATING A LOGICAL STATEMENT

In Sections 6.1 and 6.2 we saw how to use conditional statements to solve problems. Before looking at further examples, you must be sure you know how to write conditions effectively.

### Logical Operators

Every conditional expression ends with a value of True or False, and it often begins with some numbers to compare. When comparing two numbers, we can use any of the operators <, <=, =, >, >=, <> (see Table 6–1). We could write

```
x < y       (x is less than y)
6 <> x      (6 is not equal to x)
5.0 >= y    (5.0 is greater than or equal to y)
```

In each case the expression is true or false, depending upon the values of x and y. For example, if x = 2 and y = 5, then all three expressions would be true, but if x = 6 and y = 5.5, then each statement is false. In these comparisons the numbers can be real or integer, and we can mix these two types in our expressions.

We can put comparisons together with the operators *Not*, *And*, and *Or*, which have the following meanings: Suppose E, $E_1$, and $E_2$ are expressions that have values of True or False:

| | |
|---|---|
| *Not* E | true if E is false<br>false if E is true |
| $E_1$ *And* $E_2$ | true if both $E_1$ and $E_2$ are true<br>false if either $E_1$ or $E_2$ is false (or if both are false) |
| $E_1$ Or $E_2$ | true if either $E_1$ or $E_2$ is true (or if both are true)<br>false if both $E_1$ and $E_2$ are false |

*Examples*

| Expression | Value | Comment |
|---|---|---|
| *Not* (3 < 4) | False | (3 < 4) is true, so *Not* (3 < 4) is false. |
| (3 < 4) Or (4 < 3) | True | (3 < 4) is true, so the result is true. The value of (4 < 3) does not matter. |
| (3 < 4) Or (4 < 5) | True | (3 < 4) is true, so the result is true. The value of (4 < 5) does not matter. |
| (3 > 4) Or (4 > 5) | False | Both (3 > 4) and (4 > 5) are false, so the result is false. |
| (3 < 4) *And* (4 < 3) | False | (4 < 3) is false, so the result is false. The value of (3 < 4) does not matter. |
| (3 < 4) *And* (4 < 5) | True | Both parts of the expression are true. |
| (3 > 4) *And* (4 > 5) | False | (3 > 4) is false, so the result is false. The value of (4 > 5) does not matter. |

### Putting Operators Together: Parentheses and Operator Precedence

We can put the logical operators together in many ways, and we can even mix logical and arithmetic operators. As with arithmetic expressions, however, we must be careful that our expressions will be evaluated as we intend. Table 6–2 shows the precedence of the various operators. When an expression uses several operators of the same precedence, execution proceeds from left to right.

The expression *3*5 < 20* is a valid expression with value True. From

**TABLE 6–2 • Precedence of Operators**

| | |
|---|---|
| *First Precedence* | *Not* |
| *Second Precedence* | * / *Div Mod And* |
| *Third Precedence* | + – *Or* |
| *Fourth Precedence* | = <> < > <= >= |

the table, * has higher precedence than <, so the multiplication 3*5 is done first, and we have 15 < 20; the < operator is applied, and the result is True.

The expression *3 < 4 And 4 < 5* is not valid. *And* has higher precedence than <, so the computer will first try to evaluate *4 And 4*. *And* can only be applied to true and false values, not to numbers, so *4 And 4* cannot be evaluated and the expression *3 < 4 And 4 < 5* is invalid. If our intention was to apply the *And* to (3 < 4) and (4 < 5), then we must add parentheses to our expression, to get *(3 < 4) And (4 < 5)*.

This example illustrates a general situation in Pascal. Whenever logical expressions involving <, <=, >, >=, =, <> are put together with *Not*, *And*, or *Or*, we must use parentheses to form expressions. We may elect to add parentheses to other expressions, for clarity, but we have no choice when using *Not*, *And*, or *Or* with operators of lower precedence.

As a final example, we consider

(3 > 4) And (5 = 5) Or (6 = 6)

The parentheses make this a valid expression. From Table 6–2, *And* has higher precedence than *Or*, so the computer will apply *And* first. The expression is evaluated as if parentheses were added as follows:

((3 > 4) And (5 = 5)) Or (6 = 6)

If we wanted *Or* to be applied before *And*, we would need to place parentheses differently:

(3 > 4) And ((5 = 5) Or (6 = 6))

The original expression is true, but this revised statement is false.

These examples suggest several general principles. While we can put logical and arithmetic operators and terms together in a wide variety of ways, we must be careful to apply arithmetic operations to numbers and logical operations to Boolean (true–false) values.

Precedence rules govern what operations will be performed in which order; we can add parentheses to alter this order. We will often add parentheses to help us understand what we have written, even if parentheses are not strictly needed. The addition of parentheses can help avoid mistakes in writing long or complex expressions.

## SECTION 6.4 EXAMPLE: DRAWING A CIRCLE

Conditional statements can be helpful in solving a wide variety of problems. Section 6.1 illustrated an application where a problem could be divided naturally into cases. In this section, we will "draw" a geometric shape.

## PROBLEM 6.4 Drawing a Circle

We wish to print the approximate shape of a circle at our terminal by reading a radius $R$ and then printing a pattern of asterisks, *, in the shape of a circle of the given radius.

### Discussion of Problem 6.4

From geometry, we know that the points in a circle satisfy the equation:

$$x^2 + y^2 \leq R^2$$

For this problem, we should look at a variety of values for x and for $y$ and then print * at the appropriate places.

In working at a terminal, we need to make this printing systematic. Therefore, we will think about both x and $y$ values over the range $-R$ to $R$, with the x-coordinate moving horizontally across a line and with the $y$-coordinate moving vertically from line to line. Further, as we proceed across a line, we will need to look at each point and decide if the point is in the circle or not. If so, we should print * at that point. On the other hand, if the point is not on the circle, then we do not want anything appearing at the terminal at that point. One way to guarantee that nothing appears at our terminal at a given point is to print a space at that location. This discussion suggests the following outline.

### Outline for Problem 6.4:

**I.** Determine the radius $R$ for the circle.

**II.** Repeat for $y$-coordinates from $-R$ to $R$. Print the line corresponding to this $y$-coordinate.

- **A.** Repeat for x-coordinates from $-R$ to $R$.
  - **1.** Consider the point $(x, y)$.
  - **2.** If the point is in the circle,
    print *.
  - **3.** If the point is not in the circle,
    print a space.
- **B.** Move to a new line.

This outline forms the basis for the following program.

```
Program Circle (Input, Output);
{This program prints a circle of a specified radius.}

Var Radius: Integer;
```

```
Procedure EnterData (Var R: Integer);
{This procedure reads the value of the radius}
    Begin
        Write ('Enter radius of desired circle: ');
        Readln (R)
    End {EnterData} ;

Procedure PrintCircle (R: Integer);
{This procedure prints the circle of radius R at the terminal}
    Var X, Y: Integer;
    Begin
        {Skip lines}
        Writeln;
        Writeln;

        {Draw Circle}
        For Y := -R To R
          Do Begin
            For X := -R to R
              Do If (Sqr(X) + Sqr(Y)) <= Sqr(R)
                   Then Write ('*')
                   Else Write (' ');
            Writeln
            End
    End {PrintCircle} ;

Begin {Main}

    Writeln ('This program prints an outline of a circle at the terminal.');

    EnterData (Radius);
    PrintCircle (Radius)

End {Main} .
```

When this program is run for a circle of radius 4, we get the following result. In this output, we note that characters within a line are closer together than characters on successive lines. Thus, the "circle" that we see looks more like an oval.

```
This program prints an outline of a circle at the terminal.
Enter radius of desired circle: 4
```

```
    *
  *****
 *******
 *******
*********
 *******
 *******
  *****
    *
```

This program illustrates the use of the *If–Then–Else* statement, where we need one action performed in some cases and another action in other cases. Further, the program illustrates that when we use either *For* or *If* statements, a single statement can follow a *Do, Then,* or *Else*. However, when we want two or more statements as part of a *Do, Then,* or *Else*, we need to use a *Begin–End* block to enclose these statements.

## SECTION 6.5 BOOLEAN DATA TYPE

In each of the previous examples in this chapter we used a conditional statement (*If* statement) to determine which case we should execute at a particular point. In these examples we evaluated a true-or-false expression and acted accordingly. Sometimes, however, we may want to evaluate a conditional expression at one time and then act upon the result later. In this case we must store a True or False value for later reference.

In other cases the details of a Boolean expression may be complicated while the idea is simple. We may want to separate the complex details from the use of the idea, so we may want to use a function as we did in Chapter 3. These considerations require another type of data, **Boolean Data Type.** Boolean data type allows us to work with True and False values, just as real and integer data types allow us to consider numbers.

In this section we will discuss this new data type and consider some examples. We begin with a particularly simple problem.

### PROBLEM 6.5

Read two numbers, divide the smaller into the bigger to find the quotient and remainder, and print which number is bigger.

The following outline may be inelegant, but the solution is correct and elementary.

### Outline for Problem 6.5

**I.** Determine Two Numbers, *A* and *B*.
**II.** Decide whether *A* is bigger.
**III.** Compute quotient.
  **A.** If *A* is bigger, compute *A Div B*.
  **B.** If *B* is bigger, compute *B Div A*.
**IV.** Compute remainder.
  **A.** If *A* is bigger, compute *A Mod B*.
  **B.** If *B* is bigger, compute *B Mod A*.
**V.** Print which is larger.
  **A.** If *A* is bigger, print *A*.
  **B.** If *B* is bigger, print *B*.

To program from this outline we must decide, in Step II, whether *A* is bigger than *B* and use the conclusion in Steps III, IV, and V. In this process, we must record the result of Step II for future use. Since the result of Step II is a true or false value, we use a Boolean variable *AIsBigger*, which will have values *True* or *False*.

```
Program Bigger (Input, Output);
{This program prints a quotient and remainder when the smaller
 of two numbers is divided into the larger.}

Var A, B: Integer;    {Our two  given numbers}
    Quotient, Remainder: Integer; {results of division}
    AIsBigger: Boolean;   {True if A > B}

Begin
    Writeln('This program divides a smaller number into a larger one');
    Writeln('to get a quotient and a remainder');

    {Determine two numbers, A and B}
    Write('Enter two numbers: ');
    Readln (A, B);

    {Decide if A is bigger}
    AIsBigger := (A > B);

    {Compute quotient}
    If AIsBigger
        Then Quotient := A Div B
        Else Quotient := B Div A;
    Writeln (Quotient:1, ' is the quotient');

    {Compute remainder}
    If AIsBigger
        Then Remainder := A Mod B
        Else Remainder := B Mod A;
    Writeln (Remainder:1, ' is the remainder');

    {Print which is bigger}
    If AIsBigger
        Then Writeln(A:1, ' is the larger number')
        Else Writeln(B:1, ' is the larger number')

 End {Main} .
```

If we run this program with the numbers 4, 13, we get the following:

```
This program divides a smaller number into a larger one
to get a quotient and a remainder
Enter two numbers: 4 13
3 is the quotient
1 is the remainder
13 is the larger number
```

The same output results if we reverse the numbers, typing 13 4.

This example illustrates the following points about Boolean data type: To assign *True* or *False* values to a variable we first must declare the variable to be of type *Boolean*. In the declarations we wrote

```
AIsBigger: Boolean;
```

The form of declaration is the same as for numbers; we just replace "Real" or "Integer" with the word "Boolean."

Once a variable is declared to be Boolean, we can use it to record the results of Boolean expressions. We wrote

```
AIsBigger := (A > B);
```

Here the expression *(A > B)* has a true-or-false value, depending upon the values of *A* and *B*. This value is stored in the Boolean variable specified.

We can use Boolean variables in conditional statements. Recall that the *If* statement has the form

```
If Condition
        Then Statement 1
        Else Statement 2
```

Here *Condition* is an expression that is true or false. Since the value is recorded in a Boolean variable, it makes sense to use the variable as the *Condition* in the *If* statement. In the example,

```
If AIsBigger
        Then Quotient := A Div B
        Else Quotient := B Div A;
```

we compute *A Div B* if *AIsBigger* is *True*, and we compute *B Div A* if *AIsBigger* is *False*.

We can use Boolean data in much the same way that we use numbers. The values of the data are *True* or *False*, and we can work with this data in any context where true or false makes sense.

We can use Boolean variables within other Boolean expressions. For example, we could write

```
Var A, B: Integer;
    AIsBigger, BIsBigger, NotEqual: Boolean;
    AIsBigger := (A > B);
    BIsBigger := (B > A);
    NotEqual := AIsBigger Or BIsBigger
```

This segment of code also illustrates a second way that Boolean variables can be useful. If we need to evaluate a complex Boolean expression, Boolean variables allow us to break the expression into pieces. We do not have to write out the whole expression at once.

Pascal contains Boolean constants *True* and *False*, so we can initialize Boolean variables. For example, we could write

```
Fun := True;
  .
  .
  .
If (Rain > 0) Or (Homework > 0)
      Then Fun := False;
```

We can write out the value of a Boolean variable. We could say

```
Write (AIsBigger);
```

The result would be the word *True* or the word *False*. To format the *True* or *False* value, we specify the number of spaces that should be used in the printing. If we write

```
AIsBigger := True;
Write (AIsBigger :10);
```

we would see ten spaces allocated for the word *True*. As this word only requires four spaces, the first six spaces would be left blank. On the other hand, if we write

```
AIsBigger := True;
Write (AIsBigger :1);
```

then only the initial "T" will be printed. The word is truncated after the number of characters specified. You should note that this formatting is different from writing numbers, where spaces are added automatically if more room is needed.

While we can write Boolean values, Pascal does not allow us to read them. We cannot write

```
Read(YesOrNo)
```

where *YesOrNo* is a Boolean variable.

We can compare Boolean values with the logical operators $<$, $<=$, $>$, $>=$, $=$, $<>$. If we write $E = F$, we mean both $E$ and $F$ are true or both are false, as we might expect. Pascal also uses the convention that *False* is less than *True*. Thus $E < F$ is true only if $E$ is *False* and $F$ is *True*.

Pascal contains standard Boolean functions, just as it contains various numerical functions such as *Sqrt* and *Round*. One of the Boolean functions is *Odd*. For the integer x, *Odd(x)* is true if x is odd and false if x is even. Thus *Odd(x)* gives the same value as the Boolean expression

$$((x \text{ Mod } 2) = 1)$$

Finally, as with variables, we can define Boolean functions and Boolean parameters by using the word "Boolean" instead of "Integer" or "Real."

## SECTION 6.6 EXAMPLE: SCORING A BOWLING GAME

In this section we consider a somewhat complex problem that will tie the topics of conditional statements and Boolean data type from this chapter with the topics of procedures and loops from previous chapters.

### PROBLEM 6.6

Write a program to score a bowling game.

*Review of Scoring in Bowling:* A game of bowling is divided into ten frames. In each frame each bowler is allowed to throw two balls at ten pins in an attempt to knock them down. Roughly speaking, the score is the total number of pins knocked down over the course of ten frames. If a player knocks down five pins on the first ball and three pins on the second, the score for the frame is eight pins. If this pattern of knocking down eight pins is repeated in each of the ten frames, the score for the game would be 80.

This simple idea is complicated, however, by two basic "bonus" opportunities. If you knock down all ten pins on the first ball, you have rolled a "strike." In this case, you count those ten pins for that frame, plus what you roll on the next two balls. The pins knocked down in those next two balls are counted both in the frame when a strike was rolled and in their own frame(s).

If you take two balls to knock down all ten pins in a frame, you have rolled a "spare" (i.e., you do not get all ten on the first ball, but the second ball gets all the pins missed on the first ball). In this case, the score is ten plus the pins you roll on the next ball.

To clarify these scoring rules look at four short examples, illustrated in Figure 6–1. In Example 6–1a the bowler knocked down 8 pins (7 on the first ball, 1 on the second). Since all 10 pins were not knocked down, this is called an "open frame," and there are no bonus points. The score for the frame is 8.

In Example 6–1b the bowler got a strike (shown by the "X" in the small box) in Frame 1 and then 8 (7 on the first ball, 1 on the second) in Frame 2. In Frame 1 the bowler scores 10 plus the score on the next two balls (7 + 1), for a total of 18. The balls from Frame 2 are added without bonus for Frame 2, so the score after two frames is 26.

Example 6–1c is similar to Example 6–1b, except the bowler got a spare in Frame 1 instead of a strike. Only the first ball (7 pins) in Frame 2 is added as a bonus.

Example 6–1d shows the special case of strikes in successive frames. Here, as a bonus for the first strike, you count the next two balls (10 from Frame 2, 7 on first ball of Frame 3 for a total of 27). You get 18 more in Frame 2, as in Example 6–1b, for a total of 45 through two frames. Frame 3 gives 8 additional pins, as in Example 6–1a.

Finally, if you get a spare or a strike on the tenth frame, entitling you to count your pins on the next one or two rolls, you are allowed the appropriate extra rolls to knock down bonus pins.

FIGURE 6–1 • **Sample Bowling Games**

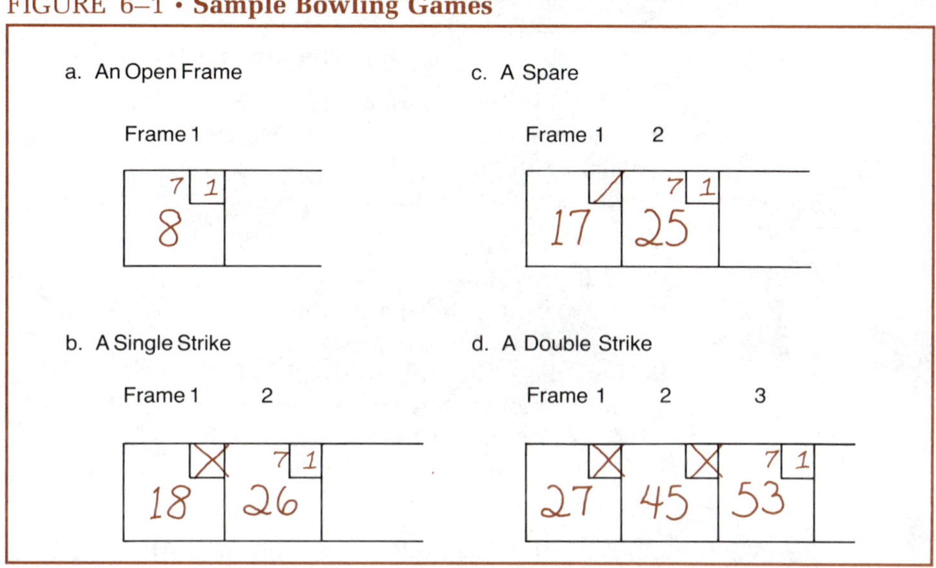


## Discussion of Problem 6.6

To attack this problem, we try to find a pattern that we you can apply frame by frame.

## General Design for Problem 6.6

**I.** Initialize conditions before the game.
  **A.** Score starts at 0.
**II.** Repeat scoring for ten frames.
  **A.** Roll first ball.
  **B.** Score first ball.
  **C.** If first ball not a strike,
    **1.** Roll second ball.
    **2.** Score second ball.
**III.** Roll extra balls for tenth frame if necessary.
**IV.** Print final score.

This general outline gives the main steps to follow, but we still need to determine the details of the scoring. There are three special conditions: *Double strike*–strikes in the previous two frames; *Strike*–a strike in the previous frame (this includes the possibility of a double strike); *Spare*–a spare in the previous frame. These conditions call for the following outline for scoring a particular frame:

**A.** First ball in a frame:
  **1.** Count the pins knocked down.
  **2.** If on a strike or spare, count the pins for the previous frame.
  **3.** If on a double strike count the pins for the last two frames.

**B.** Second ball in a frame (if needed):
  **1.** Count the pins.
  **2.** If on a strike, count the pins for the previous frame.

To include these details of scoring in the general outline, two additions are necessary. First, at the start of the game we note there are no spares, strikes, or double strikes. Next we consider how to go from one frame to the next, under the following rules:

**A.** Ten pins on first ball:
  **1.** If previous frame is a strike, then we have a double strike. Otherwise, we do not have a double strike.
  **2.** We now have a strike and not a spare.

**B.** Less than ten pins on the first ball:
  **1.** We cannot have a strike or double strike.
  **2.** We must roll the second ball.
  **3.** If sum of pins on two balls is ten, then we have a spare. Otherwise, we do not have a spare.

With this discussion, we can fill in the outline for scoring a bowling game.

### Detailed Algorithm for Problem 6.6

**I.** Initialize conditions before the game.
  **A.** Score starts at 0.
  **B.** We have not rolled spares, strikes, or double strikes.

**II.** Repeat scoring for ten frames:
  **A.** Roll first ball.
  **B.** Score first ball:
    **1.** Count the pins.
    **2.** If on a strike or spare, count the pins for the previous frame.
    **3.** If on a double strike, count the pins for the last two frames.
  **C.** If the first ball is not a strike:
    **1.** Roll second ball.
    **2.** Score second ball:
      **a.** Count the pins.
      **b.** If on a strike, count the pins for the previous frame.
  **D.** Prepare for next frame.
    **1.** Ten pins on first ball:
      **a.** If previous frame is a strike, then we have a double strike. Otherwise, we do not have a double strike.
      **b.** Regardless of past history, we now have a strike, not a spare.
    **2.** Less than ten pins on the first ball:
      **a.** We consider our score on both balls.
      If sum of pins on two balls is 10, then we have a spare.
      Otherwise, we do not have a spare.
      **b.** We cannot have a strike or double strike.

**III.** Roll extra balls for tenth frame if necessary.

**A.** If on a strike, roll ball.
  **1.** Count pins.
  **2.** If on double strike, count pins for ninth frame.
**B.** If on a strike or spare, roll ball.
  **1.** Count pins.

**IV.** Print final score.

Writing a program from this extended outline, we find that the algorithm is quite detailed at several places, so we will use procedures for many of the more involved steps. Also, to keep track of the conditions *DoubleStrike*, *Strike*, and *Spare*, we use Boolean variables. When we need these values for scoring, we can use the variables as parameters in procedures.

---

```
Program BowlingScore (Input, Output);
{This program scores a bowling game}

Var First, Second: Integer; {pins knocked down on first
                             or second ball in a frame}
    Score: Integer;  {Our current score in the game}
    Frame: Integer;  {Control variable to determine current frame}
    Double, Strike, Spare: Boolean;  {Results of previous frames}

Procedure Initialize;
{Procedure to initial conditions before game}
    Begin
        Score := 0;
        Double := False;
        Strike := False;
        Spare := False
    End {Initialize} ;

Procedure ScoreFirstBall (Mark, Double: Boolean);
{Procedure tallies score after first ball.}
{Procedure checks if there is a double strike and
 if there was a mark (spare or strike) in the previous frame}
    Begin
        Score := Score + First;
        If Mark
            Then Score := Score + First;
        If Double
            Then Score := Score + First
    End {ScoreFirstBall} ;

Procedure ScoreSecondBall (Strike: Boolean);
{Procedure tallies score after second ball.}
{Procedure checks if ;there is a strike in the previous frame}
    Begin
        Score := Score + Second;
        If Strike
            Then Score := Score + Second
    End {ScoreSecondBall} ;
```

```
Procedure PrepareNextFrame;
{Procedure updates Double, Strike, and Spare for the next frame}
    Begin
        If (First = 10)

          Then Begin
            {We now have a double if we had a strike before}
            Double := Strike;
            {We have a strike, not a spare}
            Strike := True;
            Spare := False
            End {Strike}

          Else Begin {Consider second ball}
            {We cannot have a strike or a double}
            Strike := False;
            Double := False;
            {If sum of balls is 10 then we have a spare}
            Spare := (First+Second = 10)
            End {Second ball}

    End {PrepareNextFrame} ;

Procedure ExtraRoll (Strike, Double: Boolean);
{Procedure rolls the extra balls needed to finish 10th frame}
    Begin
        If Strike

          Then Begin
            {Roll Ball}
            Write ('Enter first extra ball: ');
            Readln (First);

            {Count Pins}
            Score := Score + First;

            If Double
                Then Score := Score + First
            End {First strike ball} ;

        {Roll last ball}
        Write ('Enter last extra ball: ');
        Read (Second);

        {Count pins}
        Score := Score + Second
    End {ExtraRoll} ;

Begin {Main}
    Initialize; {conditions before game}

    {repeat scoring for 10 frames}
    For Frame := 1 to 10
      Do Begin

        {Roll First Ball}
        Write ('Frame ', Frame:1,':  Enter first ball count: ');
        Readln (First);
```

```
      ScoreFirstBall (Strike Or Spare, Double);

      If (First <> 10)
        Then Begin
          {Roll Second Ball}
          Write ('Enter second ball: ');
          Readln (Second);

          ScoreSecondBall (Strike)
        End;

      PrepareNextFrame

   End; {Frame}

  {Roll extra balls for 10th frame if necessary}
  If Strike Or Spare
      Then ExtraRoll (Strike, Double);

  {Print final score}
  Writeln ('The Final score of the game is ', Score:1)

End {Main} .
```

Running this program with the scores from a good game, we get the following output:

```
Frame 1:  Enter first ball count: 10
Frame 2:  Enter first ball count: 7
Enter second ball: 3
Frame 3:  Enter first ball count: 8
Enter second ball: 1
Frame 4:  Enter first ball count: 10
Frame 5:  Enter first ball count: 10
Frame 6:  Enter first ball count: 10
Frame 7:  Enter first ball count: 6
Enter second ball: 4
Frame 8:  Enter first ball count: 7
Enter second ball: 2
Frame 9:  Enter first ball count: 9
Enter second ball: 1
Frame 10:  Enter first ball count: 10
Enter first extra ball: 6
Enter last extra ball: 3
The Final score of the game is 188
```

This program illustrates several points.

*Problem Solving:* In solving this problem, we started with an initial, general outline, which described the main steps required for a solution, then we added detail to some steps to concentrate on specific parts of the problem. We did not have to consider the problem as a whole. Thus we followed the top-down methodology discussed early in this book (Chapters 1 and 3).

*Procedures:* While the outline contained various steps involving considerable detail, the program retained the same concise form of the initial, general outline. Procedures allowed us to separate the details of these steps from the main tasks of the program.

*Boolean Data Type:* We used Boolean variables to record the results (strike, double strike, spare) of one frame for scoring in subsequent frames. The Boolean variables were used as parameters in the procedures for scoring and in conditions for *If* statements. When assigning values to Boolean variables, we used the constants *True* and *False*, and we also evaluated appropriate logical expressions.

## SECTION 6.7 STYLE

The last section illustrated several ways to use Boolean variables and conditional statements with procedures and loops to solve problems. We will now consider several elements of style that can help in writing clear, easy-to-read, correct programs.

### Formatting and Structure

In previous sections we have seen that it is easier to understand how various parts of a program fit together if the form of the program reflects the structure of the outline. To apply this idea to *If* statements, we must indent *Then* and *Else* clauses further than the *If*, since the execution of the *Then* or *Else* depends upon the *If* condition. When we use a *Begin–End* to include several statements within a *Then* or *Else* clause, these statements are all dependent upon the *Then* or *Else* and should be indented further. For example, we might write

```
If Rain
    Then Begin
          Writeln ('Sky is cloudy');
          Writeln ('Tennis match is canceled')
          End
```

The *Then* is indented beyond the *If*, and the *Writeln* statements within the *Begin–End* are indented beyond the *Then*. (We must be careful however not to indent so far that we reach the right margin!)

Within a *Begin–End* block, we should use procedures or functions if necessary, so that details of a *Then* or *Else* clause do not overwhelm the basic structure for the conditional statement. We always use procedures or functions when details are complex.

## Elegance and Simplicity in Programs

Whenever we try to solve problems, we should look for ways to simplify our work. Of course, simple, elegant answers do not always exist, but it is astonishing how often a complex solution indicates that we have overlooked something in our analysis. *When we find ourselves bogged down in a mass of details we should spend some time trying to find an easier way.* We should be willing to search for an elegant solution, particularly when our first effort is messy. Moreover, we should actively seek opportunities to simplify and clarify our work.

## Simplification Opportunities

The above comments on simplicity and elegance apply to all phases of the problem solving process. Here, we identify four ways to simplify Boolean expressions and conditional statements, namely negation and double negation, DeMorgan's laws, turning conditions around, and omitting redundant or impossible conditions. In the following discussion, we will consider simplifications that are possible in each of these areas, and we will examine some elementary examples. The main points of this discussion are outlined in Tables 6–3 and 6–4.

**Negation and Double Negation.** The *Not* operator has many useful applications, but we should always ask whether a *Not* expression can be rewritten in a more elementary way. For example, when we apply *Not* to a simple comparison, we often can rewrite the condition without the *Not* by changing the comparison. For example *Not (A > B)* means "A should not be greater than B." Another way to express this relationship is "A is less than or equal to B," i.e., *(A <= B)*. Similarly, *Not (A = B)* is equivalent to *(A <> B)*.

Similarly, the double negation *Not(Not(E))* is equivalent to *E* itself. (If *E* is true, *Not(E)* is false, so *Not(Not(E))* is true again.) Whenever we find a double negative, we can remove both *Not* operators.

**TABLE 6–3 • Simplification Opportunities for Boolean Expressions**

1. *Not* applied to a simple comparison
   Simplification: Turn comparison around
2. Double Negation *Not(Not(E))*
   Simplification: Omit both *Not* operators to get just *E*
3. DeMorgan's laws:
   *(Not E) Or (Not F) = Not (E And F)*
   *(Not E) And (Not F) = Not (E Or F)*

**TABLE 6–4 • Simplification Opportunities for Conditional Statements**

1. Turn conditional statements around:

```
If Condition
        Then Statement 1
        Else Statement 2
```

   is equivalent to

```
If Not Condition
        Then Statement 2
        Else Statement 1
```

2. Omitting redundant or impossible conditions:

```
If E1
  Then Begin
     If E2
        Then —
  End
```

   Check whether the result of test $E_2$ can be inferred from test $E_1$.

**DeMorgan's Laws.** Two relationships can help when an expression involves *Not* in conjunction with *And* or *Or*. If *E* and *F* are two Boolean expressions, the following formulae are called **DeMorgan's Laws:**

```
(Not E) Or (Not F) = Not(E And F)
(Not E) And (Not F) = Not(E Or F)
```

Both of these formulae can be proven rigorously, but we omit the proofs here. (The interested reader should consult a book on logic.) Instead, consider two examples that illustrate how these laws can help simplify expressions, particularly when used in conjunction with the simplifications of negation and double negation.

```
Not((A > 1) And (B <= 3))
            = (Not(A > 1)) Or (Not(B <= 3))    DeMorgan's laws
            = (A <= 1) Or (B > 3))             Simplification of negatives
 Not((A > 1) Or Not(B <= 3))
        = (Not(A > 1)) And (Not(Not(B <=3)))   DeMorgan's laws
        = (A <= 1) And (B <= 3)                Simplification of negative
                                               and double negative
```

In each case, we can replace the initial expression by an equivalent one which is shorter and clearer.

**Turning Conditions Around.** When we use Boolean expressions in *If* statements, we often can simplify our code significantly by turning the condition around. For example, consider

```
If ((x < -1) Or (x > -1)) And ((x < 2) Or (x > 2))
   Then Write ('Neither -1 or 2')
   Else Write ('-1 or 2')
```

If we analyze this condition, we find that the statement is true for any value of x except −1 and 2. If we turn the statement around, we can replace a complex condition with

```
If (x = -1) Or (x = 2)
   Then Write ('-1 or 2')
   Else Write ('Neither -1 or 2')
```

**Omitting Redundant or Impossible Conditions.** When we put various conditions together, some conditions become redundant or impossible, and these can be omitted. For example, consider the code

```
If A > 1
   Then Begin
          If    A > 0
                Then Write ('A is big enough')
          End
```

Here, the test *A > 0* is redundant. We can only execute the statement *If A > 0* when the test *A >1* is true. If *A* is greater than 1, however, *A* must be greater than 0. This compound statement is logically equivalent to the simpler

```
If A > 1
          Then Write ('A is big enough')
```

All of these simplifications are possible fairly frequently in practice, and each can help us write much cleaner, easier-to-read code. If we combine these simplifications with the guidelines for good formatting and structure, our programs will be relatively easy to test, correct, and modify.

## SECTION 6.8 TESTING

Typically, we use conditional statements when we have divided a solution into various cases. In testing programs that handle these cases, we can be guided by two basic ideas. First, we check that the results for each case are correct. Then we must be sure the program shifts from one case to the next at the appropriate time. These goals are met by two guidelines for choosing test data, **every-path testing** and **boundary value testing**.

## Every-Path Testing

We should test all possible ways that a program might be executed. For example, to test

```
If A > 0
  Then Statement 1
  Else Statement 2
```

we should pick data where $A > 0$ and where $A <= 0$. With these two test cases, we can check that both Statement 1 and Statement 2 are correct.

The same idea applies when we put several conditions together. To test

```
If A > 0
  Then If B > 0
         Then Statement 1
         Else Statement 2
  Else Statement 3
```

we should choose data where (1) $A > 0$ and $B > 0$, (2) $A > 0$ and $B <= 0$, and (3) $A < 0$. Only with these three sets of test data can we check all three statements in the program.

Similarily, we need to check the various possibilities when one *If* statement follows another. For example, consider

```
If A > 0
  Then Statement 1
  Else Statement 2 ;
If B > 0
  Then Statement 3
  Else Statement 4
```

Here we should check four cases: (1) $A > 0$, $B > 0$; (2) $A > 0$, $B <= 0$; (3) $A <= 0$, $B > 0$; (4) $A <= 0$, $B <= 0$. All these data sets are needed to test that both Statement 3 and Statement 4 work correctly after either Statement 1 or Statement 2.

Putting these ideas together for the Bowling Score program from Section 6.6, we must check games that contain open frames, as well as spares, strikes, double strikes, and sequences of these possibilities. For example, we might check what happens when a spare or open frame follows a strike or a double strike.

## Boundary Value Testing

While every-path testing demonstrates that our work is correct for each case, we must also check that each case is performed at the correct time. To test this, we select data at the boundary of each case. For example, in the telephone call program in Section 6.1, rates change at 8 AM, 5 PM, and 11 PM. To test this program, we should check the times 7:59 and 8:00, 17:00 and 17:01, 23:00 and 23:01 to see that the correct rates are used when the time periods change.

Similarly, to test the Bowling Score program, we should check the results when we knock down nine pins instead of ten. We must be sure that a frame that is "close" to a spare or a strike is not scored as a spare or strike.

### Testing and Modularity

When programs are long and complex, there may be very large numbers of possible paths and boundary values. It may not be practical to test all these cases. In such situations, testing will probably be incomplete, but we can still find most bugs if we divide large programs into several procedures and then test the individual procedures.

Procedures can be short enough to test the appropriate paths and boundary values for these pieces. Then, when we know the pieces are correct, we can select some representative sets of data to see if the pieces fit together in an appropriate way. This selective testing may fail to find some subtle interactions among procedures, but we should find many of the bugs that might exist.

In practice, we are likely to find occasional errors in large programs, even if these programs have been used for many years. We may try a new path in the program, or the data may land on a new boundary between cases. These cases always allow the chance for a new error to be discovered. After a point, such bugs are relatively rare when we use a program normally, but such errors can arise when complete testing is impractical. Testing of individual pieces can help reduce the number of remaining bugs, but more persistent bugs may remain.

## SUMMARY

1. **Conditional Statements** allow you to break your work into pieces to be handled separately. These statements come in two forms:

   *If* Condition<br>
     *Then* Statement

   *If* Condition<br>
       *Then* Statement 1<br>
       *Else* Statement 2

   Here the Condition is a **Boolean expression** that has a *True* or *False* value, and each Statement is a single Pascal statement or a *Begin–End* block.
2. You can form Boolean expressions by comparing various items with the Boolean operators <, <=, >, >=, =, and <>, and you can put these comparisons together using the operators *And*, *Not*, and *Or*. When you form such expressions, **precedence rules** determine the order in which the operators will be applied. Use parentheses if you wish to use operators in another order.
3. **Boolean variables and functions** may be declared and used when you

need to consider the values *True* and *False*. These variables and functions may be used in logical expressions and in the conditions of *If* statements. You may Write (but not Read) the values of such variables.

4. Boolean variables can be helpful when you compute a *True* or *False* value at one place in a program and use it later on, and to divide a complex Boolean expression into simple pieces.
5. Boolean functions help separate the technical details of a condition from the idea of the test.
6. In writing Boolean expressions, you may be able to simplify your work by eliminating **negation** and **double negation,** by applying **DeMorgan's laws,** by **turning conditions around,** and by **omitting redundant or impossible conditions.**
7. Apply the principles of **every-path testing** and **boundary value testing** to help determine if a program works correctly.

## EXERCISES

**6.1** Assume *A*, *B*, *C*, and *D* are integer variables; assume *E*, *F*, and *G* are Boolean variables, and suppose the variables have been given the following values:

| | |
|---|---|
| *A* := 1 | *E* := *True* |
| *B* := 2 | *F* := *False* |
| *C* := 3 | *G* := *True* |
| *D* := 6 | |

Determine which of the following expressions make sense, and evaluate those that have logical values.

a. *Not A >= B*

b. *A*B < C − D*

c. *A = B Or E*

| KEY TERMS, PHRASES, AND CONCEPTS | | ELEMENTS OF PASCAL SYNTAX | |
|---|---|---|---|
| Boolean Data Type | *If–Then* | *Boolean* | Logical Operators: |
| Expressions | *If–Then–Else* | *Else* | <, <=, >, >=, =, <> |
| Functions | DeMorgan's Laws | *False* | *And, Not, Or* |
| Parameters | Double Negation | *If* | *Then* |
| Variables | Elegance and Simplicity | | *True* |
| Boundary Value Testing | Every-Path Testing | | |
| Conditional Statements | Logical Operators and Precedence | | |
| | Negation | | |

**d.** $F = (\text{Not } E \text{ And } G)$
**e.** $(A < B)$ *And* $(C > D)$
**f.** *Not* $(E >= F)$
**g.** $(A >= B)$ *Or* $(C <= D)$
**h.** *Not* $(F <> E)$ *And* $(B*C = D)$
**i.** *E And* $(A = B)$ *Or F*
**j.** *Not E And Not F Or Not F*

**6.2** Simplify the following Boolean expressions. ($A$, $B$, $C$, $D$ are integer variables; $E$, $F$, $G$ are Boolean variables.)
**a.** *Not* $(A >= C)$
**b.** *Not (Not E And Not F)*
**c.** $(A <= C)$ *And* $(A >= C)$
**d.** *Not* $((A < B)$ *Or* $(C < B))$
**e.** *Not* $((A < B)$ *And Not* $(C < B))$
**f.** Not E and Not G Or E

**6.3** Simplify the following pieces of code. ($A$, $B$, $C$ are integer variables, and $S$, $T$, $U$ are procedures.)

**a.**
```
If A >= 3
    Then If A >= 4
        Then S
```
**b.**
```
If A < C
    Then If (A = B) And (B > C)
        Then S
        Else T
```
**c.**
```
If A < 2 And C > 1
    Then If B < 2 and A > 1
        Then S
        Else T
```
**d.**
```
If A < 2
    Then Begin
        If B < 3
            Then S
            Else T
        End
    Else Begin
        If B >= 3
            Then T
            Else S
        End
```

**6.4** *Quadratic Formula.* Find all real solutions of the quadratic equation

$$ax^2 + bx + c = 0.$$

Use the discriminant, $b^2 - 4ac$, to compute and print the number of real solutions as well as the values for the existing real solutions. Your work should allow for the case where $a = 0$.

**6.5** *Windchill Danger.* In the problems for Chapter 5, we stated that the windchill Temperature $T$ may be approximated from the Fahrenheit temperature $F$ and the wind speed $W$ by the formula

$$T = 1.05 + 0.93F - 3.65W + 3.62\sqrt{W} + 0.103F\sqrt{W} + 0.0439W^2$$

Windchill temperatures are rated in the following categories (for covered skin):

| | |
|---|---|
| Little danger of freezing | Above 0°F |
| Moderate danger of freezing | 0°F to −30°F |
| Extreme danger of freezing | Below −30°F |

Write a program that reads the current Fahrenheit temperature and wind speed (in MPH) and prints the appropriate windchill danger category.

**6.6** Write a program that reads three numbers and prints out the smallest of the numbers.

**6.7** Write a program that reads an integer $N$ followed by $N$ numbers, and then computes and prints the largest of these numbers. (You should not assume that the numbers will be entered in order.)

**6.8** *Wind Strength.* Table 6–5 gives the terms used by the U.S. Weather Service to describe winds of various strengths. Write a program that reads the speed of the wind (in MPH) and then prints the corresponding descriptive term.

**6.9** *Integer Factoring*

**a.** Write a program that will compute all factors of a given positive integer.

NOTE: $N$ is divisible by $I$ if the remainder after dividing $N$ by $I$ is 0.

**b.** An integer is *prime* if its only factors are 1 and itself. Modify the program in part (a) so that after the factors are printed the program states whether or not the given integer is prime.

**TABLE 6–5 • Wind Speed Terms Used by the U.S. Weather Service**

| Velocity (MPH) | Term |
|---|---|
| Less than 1 | Calm |
| 1–7 | Light |
| 8–12 | Gentle |
| 13–18 | Moderate |
| 19–24 | Fresh |
| 25–38 | Strong |
| 39–54 | Gale |
| 55–75 | Whole gale |
| Above 75 | Hurricane |

**6.10** *Paying a Baby Sitter*. A baby sitter charges $1.50 per hour until 9:00 PM (while the kids are still up) and $1.00 per hour thereafter (when the kids are in bed).

Write a program that reads the sitter's starting time in hours and minutes and the ending time in hours and minutes and then computes the sitter's fee. Assume all times are between 6:00 PM and 6:00 AM. (*Optimal Simplification*: Assume all times are between 6:00 PM and 12:00 midnight.)

[This problem was initially suggested by John Vogel.]

**6.11** *Tax Computation*. Table 6–6 presents the 1984 Tax Rate Schedule for single taxpayers of the federal income tax. The following example shows how this table is read:

If my taxable income is $12,000, I find the line where $12,000 falls in the table, over $10,800 but not over $12,900. From the next two columns, my tax is $1203 plus 18% of the amount over $10,800,

$$\$1203 + 0.18(\$12000 - \$10800), \text{ or } \$1419.$$

Write a program that reads taxable income and computes the taxpayer's tax.

**TABLE 6–6 • 1984 Tax Rate Schedule for Single Taxpayers**

Taxable Income is:

| Over | But not over | Tax is | Of the amount over |
|---|---|---|---|
| $0 | $2,300 | —$0— | |
| 2,300 | 3,400 | 11% | $ 2,300 |
| 3,400 | 4,400 | 121 + 12% | 3,400 |
| 4,400 | 6,500 | 241 + 14% | 4,400 |
| 6,500 | 8,500 | 535 + 15% | 6,500 |
| 8,500 | 10,800 | 835 + 16% | 8,500 |
| 10,800 | 12,900 | 1,203 + 18% | 10,800 |
| 12,900 | 15,000 | 1,581 + 20% | 12,900 |
| 15,000 | 18,200 | 2,001 + 23% | 15,000 |
| 18,200 | 23,500 | 2,737 + 26% | 18,200 |
| 23,500 | 28,800 | 4,115 + 30% | 23,500 |
| 28,800 | 34,100 | 5,705 + 34% | 28,800 |
| 34,100 | 41,500 | 7,507 + 38% | 34,100 |
| 41,500 | 55,300 | 10,319 + 42% | 41,500 |
| 55,300 | 81,800 | 16,115 + 48% | 55,300 |
| 81,800 | ——— | 28,835 + 50% | 81,800 |

Source: 1984 Form 1040 Federal Income Tax Forms and Instructions, page 33. (U.S. Government Printing Office 1984 – 423–003 23–188–5979)

**6.12** *Unusual Canceling.* The fraction $^{64}/_{16}$ has the unusual property that its reduced value of 4 may be obtained by "canceling" the 6 in the numerator with that in the denominator. Write a program to find the other fractions whose numerators and denominators are two-digit numbers and whose values remain unchanged after "canceling."

NOTE: Suppose $ab$ is the two-digit number $n$ (e.g., if $n = 64$, then $a = 6$, $b = 4$). Then we have

$$n = 10a + b$$
$$a = n \textit{ Div } 10$$
$$b = n \textit{ Mod } 10.$$

**6.13** *Details in Then or Else Clauses.* Section 6.7 suggests using procedures and functions when details of *Then* and *Else* clauses are complex. This principle becomes particularly clear when we see a program with all details included in *Then* and *Else* clauses.

Rewrite the Bowling Score program from Section 6.6 without using any procedures or functions. Compare your program with the program in Section 6.6 for readability.

# CHAPTER 7

# CONDITIONAL LOOPS

In Chapter 5 we saw one way to tell the computer to repeat some operations a specific number of times. Since then, we have used these loops in several applications to tackle problems that would otherwise be quite tedious. In each application we specified the number of iterations for the loop when we started.

In many applications, however, we do not know the appropriate number of repetitions until we solve the problem. In this chapter we will consider two new types of loops, where the number of iterations is not fixed from the start, and we will apply these new loop structures to several applications. In addition, we will look more carefully at program correctness, expanding the concept of loop invariants, mentioned briefly in Section 5.8.

## SECTION 7.1 EXAMPLE: CREDIT BALANCE PAYMENTS

To introduce the new repetitive statements of this chapter, we begin with a brief review of the basic parts of any loop, and we consider an example that illustrates a *While–Do* loop, which is one of the new repetitive statements.

## Basic Loop Components

The loops used in previous chapters have the following fundamental components:

1. *Initialization* to set up the work before the loop begins.
2. *Repetition* of a certain number of steps within the loop.
3. *Exit condition* to indicate when the loop is to stop.

For example, in the *For–Do* loop

```
For I := 1 to 10
     Do Writeln (I);
```

the initialization sets *I* equal to 1, the *Writeln* is in the repetition component, and the limit of 10 implies an exit condition.

In the following problem we will need a somewhat different type of exit condition.

## PROBLEM 7.1 Credit-Balance Payments

You have charged the cost of an item on your credit card, planning to make fixed monthly payments to pay for the purchase. Compute the monthly balance of the credit account for the life of the loan. Compute the final payment and the total interest paid.

### Discussion of Problem 7.1

Each month of the loan, the account will see activity of two types: Interest will be charged at the start of each month, and a payment will be made sometime during the month.

Monthly payments will continue until the loan is paid off. We will have to pay the full payment until the last month, when we will pay a (perhaps smaller) amount that just covers the final balance plus the appropriate interest. In this situation, we do not know how many times the loop should continue. Instead, each time we must test a condition such as:

```
Payment <= Balance + Interest
```

To be more precise, in our outline, we keep track of the following items:

*Cost* = cost of item purchased

*Rate* = monthly interest rate

*Payment* = normal monthly payment

*Balance* = balance in the account at the start of a month, before interest has been added

*Interest* = interest for a given month

*TInterest* = total interest accumulated to the current time

*Month* = Number of months the loan has run so far

### Outline for Problem 7.1

**I.** Determine *Cost, Rate, Payment.*
**II.** Print table headings.
**III.** Set up account for first month:
*Month* := 1
*Balance* := *Cost*
*Interest* := *Balance***Rate*
*TInterest* := *Interest*
**IV.** Continue normal monthly payments as long as *Payment* does not exceed *Balance* plus *Interest*:
**A.** Add *Interest* and deduct *Payment* activity for the month:
*Balance* := *Balance* + *Interest* − *Payment*.
**B.** Print results.
**C.** Set up for the next month:
**1.** Compute *Interest* to start the next month:
*Interest* := *Balance***Rate*.
**2.** Update total interest for the next month:
*TInterest* := *TInterest* + *Interest*.
**3.** Update *Month*:
*Month* := *Month* + 1.
**V.** Make final payment:
*Payment* := *Balance* + *Interest*

In the following, we use a repetitive statement in Procedure *ProcessNormalMonth* that allows us to write out the more involved Exit Condition in Step IV.

```
Program CreditBalancePayments (Input, Output);
{This program follows the balance of a charge account
 month by month as monthly payments are made.}

Var Cost: Real;              {Cost of item purchased}
    Rate: Real;              {Monthly interest rate}
    Payment: Real;           {Normal monthly payment}
    Balance: Real;           {Account balance at start of month,
                              before interest has been added}
    Interest: Real;          {Interest for month}
    TInterest: Real;         {Total accumulated interest}
    Month: Integer;          {Month number}

Procedure SetUpCharge (Var Cost, Rate, Payment: Real);
{This procedure determines Cost, Rate, Payment}
    Begin
        Write ('Enter cost of item purchased: ');
        Readln (Cost);
        Write ('Enter monthly interest rate: ');
        Readln (Rate);
        Write ('Enter normal monthly payment: ');
        Readln (Payment);
    End {SetUpCharges} ;
```

```
Procedure PrintHeadings;
{This procedure prints the headings for the payment table}
    Begin
        Writeln;
        Writeln ('       Month''s   Total');
        Writeln ('Month Interest  Interest    Balance');
        Writeln (0:3, Cost:32:2);
    End {PrintHeadings} ;

Procedure SetUpFirstMonth (Cost: Real; Var Month: Integer;
                           Var Balance, Interest, TInterest: Real);
{This procedure sets up the account for the first month}
    Begin
        Month := 1;
        Balance := Cost;
        Interest := Balance * Rate;
        TInterest := Interest;
    End {FirstMonth} ;

Procedure ProcessNormalMonth (Cost, Payment: Real; Var Month: Integer;
                              Var  Balance, Interest, TInterest: Real);
{This procedure continues normal monthly payments while appropriate}
    Begin
        While (Payment <= Balance + Interest)
          Do Begin
            Balance := Balance + Interest - Payment;
            Writeln (Month:3, Interest:10:2, TInterest:10:2, Balance:12:2);
            Interest := Balance * Rate;
            TInterest := TInterest + Interest;
            Month := Month + 1
          End;
    End {ProcessNormalMonth} ;

Procedure FinalPayment (Balance, Interest, TInterest: Real; Var Payment: Real);
{This procedure makes the final payment}
    Begin
        Payment := Balance + Interest;
        Writeln;
        Writeln ('Interest for final payment is ', Interest:1:2);
        Writeln ('The final payment is ', Payment:1:2);
        Writeln ('The total interest charged was ', TInterest:1:2)
    End {FinalPayment} ;

Begin {Main}
    Writeln ('This program follows the balance of a charge account.');

    SetUpCharge (Cost, Rate, Payment);
    PrintHeadings;
    SetUpFirstMonth (Cost, Month, Balance, Interest, TInterest);
    ProcessNormalMonth(Cost, Payment, Month, Balance, Interest, TInterest);
    FinalPayment (Balance, Interest, TInterest, Payment)

End {Main} .
```

When we run this program for a charge of $1000 at a monthly interest rate of 1 percent and a normal monthly payment of $100, we get the following output:

```
This program follows the balance of a charge account.
Enter cost of item purchased: 1000.00
Enter monthly interest rate: 0.01
Enter normal monthly payment: 100.00

      Month's    Total
Month Interest  Interest    Balance
  0                         1000.00
  1    10.00     10.00       910.00
  2     9.10     19.10       819.10
  3     8.19     27.29       727.29
  4     7.27     34.56       634.56
  5     6.35     40.91       540.91
  6     5.41     46.32       446.32
  7     4.46     50.78       350.78
  8     3.51     54.29       254.29
  9     2.54     56.83       156.83
 10     1.57     58.40        58.40

Interest for final payment is 0.58
The final payment is 58.98
The total interest charged was 58.98
```

When the program is run with a charge of $50 at a monthly interest rate of 1 percent and a normal monthly payment of $100, we get this output:

```
This program follows the balance of a charge account.
Enter cost of item purchased: 50.00
Enter monthly interest rate: 0.01
Enter normal monthly payment: 100.00

      Month's    Total
Month Interest  Interest    Balance
  0                           50.00

Interest for final payment is 0.50
The final payment is 50.50
The total interest charged was 0.50
```

In this case, the loop was never executed, as the normal monthly payment exceeds the amount due, $50.50.

This program illustrates several important points. In Pascal, we can repeat a sequence of steps in several different ways. Here, we used a

*While–Do* loop instead of the *For–Do* construction we saw earlier. When we use the *While–Do* construction, we can place statements we want repeated in a *Begin–End* block following the *Do* statement, just as we might in a *For–Do* loop.

A *While–Do* has no control variable, and so no variables are updated automatically; we must write out all operations explicitly. We must also specify when the loop is to continue. Here, we said the loop was to continue as long as

```
Payment <= Balance + Interest
```

The *While–Do* construction allows us considerable flexibility in writing loops; we do not need to know our results when we start. In the next section, we look at the details of these conditional loops more closely.

## SECTION 7.2 ELEMENTS OF CONDITIONAL STATEMENTS

In this section, we discuss the syntax and semantics for two forms of repetitive statements, the *While–Do* construction, which we saw in the previous section, and a *Repeat–Until* construction. Each of these new forms allows us to specify exit conditions explicitly, although these statements work in slightly different ways. With these forms we will have considerable flexibility in specifying loops.

### Syntax and Semantics of While–Do Statements

As the program in Section 7.1 illustrates, the *While–Do* statement has the following syntax.

```
While Condition
    Do Statement
```

Here the "Condition" is a Boolean statement and the "Statement" is a single Pascal statement (which may be a *Begin–End* block).

This syntax is interpreted as follows: The "Condition" is evaluated. If the "Condition" is true, the loop continues. If the "Condition" is false, the loop stops. As long as the loop is continuing, the "Statement" is executed. With this form, we see that

- initialization must be done before the *While* statement;
- the "Condition" implies the exit condition; and
- the "Statement" forms the body for the repetition.

Figure 7–1 shows these elements for the Credit-Balance Payments program of Section 7.1. For brevity, we omit those parts of the program that are not strictly related to the loop.

Before looking at the next type of repetitive statement, we need to note

FIGURE 7–1 • **Loop Elements for the Credit-Balance Program Using the While–Do Construction**

```
Program CreditBalancePayments (Input, Output);

Begin
    Month := 1;                          ⎫
    Balance := Cost;                     ⎬ Initialization
    Interest := Balance * Rate;          ⎪
    TInterest := Interest;               ⎭

    While (Payment <= Balance + Interest)} Exit Condition

      Do Begin                                          ⎫
        Balance := Balance + Interest - Payment;        ⎪
        Writeln (Month, Interest, TInterest, Balance);  ⎬ Repetition
        Interest := Balance * Rate;                     ⎪
        TInterest := TInterest + Interest;              ⎪
        Month := Month + 1                              ⎪
      End;                                              ⎭

End {CreditBalancePayments} .
```

two other important points about the *While–Do* construction. First, the "Statement" is not executed until the "Condition" is evaluated. Our Exit Condition is evaluated at the very beginning of our loop, so we must initialize all variables needed in the condition before the loop starts. In addition, if our Condition is False, then our Statement will not be executed at all. Thus, it is possible for this loop to be skipped entirely in the program.

## Syntax and Semantics of Repeat–Until Statements

Next, we turn to the final form of repetitive statement, called the *Repeat–Until* construction. This statement has many of the characteristics of the *While–Do* loop, but we will see that there are also some important differences. This statement has the following syntax.

*Repeat*
    Statements
*Until* Condition

Here, "Statements" may include any number of Pascal statements (separated by semicolons), and "Condition" is a Boolean condition.

The semantics of this statement are similar to that of the *While–Do*, but the order of events is different. In particular, with the *Repeat–Do* statement, the "Statements" are executed once, and the "Condition" is then evaluated. If the "Condition" is true, the loop stops. If the "Condition" is false, then we go back to the beginning of the loop and repeat this process. Thus, in the *Repeat–Until* construction, we see that

- initialization normally precedes the *Repeat;*
- the specified "Statements" form the body of the repetition; and
- the "Condition" gives our exit condition.

As a specific example, we translate the loop from Section 7.1 into this alternate form (see Figure 7–2).

The main ideas of the loop are the same in both constructions, but there are a few differences. With the *Repeat–Until* loop our Exit Condition is evaluated at the end of the loop. (This implies that some variables used in this condition need not be initialized before the loop, as long as they are given values within the loop itself.) The condition for the *Repeat* is reversed from that for the *While*. The *While* continues while the "Condition" is true and the *Repeat* keeps going while the "Condition" is false. We can place as many "statements" as we wish between the *Repeat* and *Until;* we do not need to use a *Begin–End* block for multiple statements within the loop.

Because the "Condition" is at the bottom of the *Repeat* loop, we see that the body of the loop will always be executed once before "Condition" is tested. The "Statements" will always be followed the first time through, even if the "Condition" is true initially.

FIGURE 7–2 • **Loop Elements for the Credit-Balance Program Using the Repeat–Until Construction**

```
Program CreditBalancePayments (Input, Output);

Begin
    Month := 1;                         }
    Balance := Cost;                    }
    Interest := Balance * Rate;         } Initialization
    TInterest := Interest;              }

    Repeat

        Balance := Balance + Interest - Payment;           }
        Writeln (Month, Interest, TInterest, Balance);     } Repetition
        Interest := Balance * Rate;                        }
        TInterest := TInterest + Interest;                 }
        Month := Month + 1                                 }

    Until (Payment > Balance + Interest)} Exit Condition

End {CreditBalancePayments} .
```

## SECTION 7.3 EXAMPLE: FINDING AN ODD NUMBER

In Section 7.1, we saw an example where we needed to use the *While–Do* construction. Before we try to compare the details of the various types of loops, we consider a problem that illustrates the use of the *Repeat–Until* construction.

## PROBLEM 7.3

Read a sequence of integers from the terminal and count when the first odd number appears.

### Discussion of Problem 7.3

In this problem, we can identify many of the same parts of a loop that we have just reviewed. In particular, before we start the loop, our initialization must set the count of integers to 0. Then, within the loop we need a statement that reads successive numbers and increases our count by one until we read an odd number. This suggests the following outline.

### Outline for Problem 7.3

**I.** Initialization.
  **A.** Set count to 0.
**II.** Continue until the number read is odd.
  **A.** Increase the count by 1.
  **B.** Read the next number.
**III.** Print the first odd number and the total count of numbers read.

When we program from this outline, we use a *Repeat–Until* loop for two reasons. First, we decided that our loop should continue until a certain type of number was found. This is the principle behind the *Repeat* construction.

Second, we will always need to read at least one number, since we must read a number before we can check if our number is odd. The execution of a loop at least once is required by the *Repeat* construction but not with the *While* form.

Once we decide to use the *Repeat–Until* loop for Step II, we have the following program.

```
Program FindFirstOdd (Input, Output);
{This program reads numbers from the terminal until an odd number
 is found.}

Var Number: Integer;
    Count: Integer;

Begin
    Writeln ('This program reads numbers until an odd number is found.');
    Writeln ('Please enter your numbers:');
```

```
    {Initialization}
    Count := 0;

    {Read successive numbers}
    Repeat
        Read (Number);
        Count := Count + 1
    Until Odd(Number) ;

    {Print conclusions}
    Writeln ('The first odd number entered was ', Number:1, ' .');
    Writeln ('This was Item number ', Count:1, ' that was entered.')

End {FindFirstOdd} .
```

In this program, we place the steps that repeat within a *Repeat–Until* loop. The loop continues until the specified condition becomes true. When we run this program for a particular sequence of numbers, we get the following output.

```
This program reads numbers until an odd number is found.
Please enter your numbers:
2 4 6 7
The first odd number entered was 7 .
This was Item number 4 that was entered.
```

This example illustrates how we can use the *Repeat–Until* loop effectively in our programming. It also demonstrates the advantage of testing a condition at the end of a loop in some cases.

## SECTION 7.4 CHOOSING AMONG *FOR, REPEAT,* AND *WHILE*

We have seen the three major constructions available for looping in Pascal, namely:

*For–Do*

*While–Do*

*Repeat–Until*

In this section we will discuss how to choose the right construction for a particular situation. Figure 7–3 summarizes the discussion.

FIGURE 7–3 • **Choosing Among *For, Repeat,* and *While***

*Definite repetition* (number of iterations known)
*For–Do*
Control variable counts iterations.

*Conditional repetition* (number of iterations not known)
*While–Do*
Test at top of loop.
Loop may never be performed.
Continue looping while condition true.
Stop looping when condition false.
*Repeat–Until*
Test at bottom of loop.
Loop is always performed at least once.
Continue looping while condition false.
Stop looping when condition true.

## Definite Repetition

The problems in Chapters 5 and 6 required repetition of work a specified number of times. We knew how many iterations we would need in a loop before we started. For example, in our Circle Drawing program in Chapter 6, we knew that we wanted to consider values from $-R$ to $R$. In such situations the *For–Do* loop applies, since the control variable counts the number of iterations exactly.

## Conditional Repetition

This chapter has studied problems where the number of iterations is not known ahead of time. Here we must evaluate a condition each time and decide whether to continue on the basis of that condition. For conditional repetition we have two possible constructions, *Repeat–Until* and *While–Do*. These statements have the following major features:

*While–Do* tests a condition at the beginning of the loop; the loop is executed only if the condition is true. If the condition is false initially, then the loop is never executed at all. Looping continues as long as the condition is true and stops when the condition is false.

*Repeat–Until* tests a condition at the bottom of the loop; the loop continues only if the condition is false. The loop is executed once before the condition is ever checked. Looping continues as long as the condition is false and stops when the condition is true.

The major difference between these two constructions is in when the condition is evaluated. The *While* loop may never be executed; the *Repeat* loop is always performed at least once. The examples in Sections 7.1 and 7.3 show how to exploit this difference effectively in certain problems.

In the Credit-Balance Payment problem, we needed to allow the possibility that the normal payment would be too much. The *While* loop tested this condition *before* making a normal payment. A *Repeat* loop would have required at least one normal payment, because we would check the balance only *after* making a normal payment.

In contrast, in our program for finding an odd number, we had to read at least one number before we could stop. Thus, we used the *Repeat* statement so we could be sure that we had read the first number. Similarly, to compute an average, we must process at least one number before work can stop, and we would use a *Repeat* statement to guarantee this initial processing. From this discussion we derive the following major guideline for choosing between *While* and *Repeat*.

### Major Guideline for Conditional Repetition

- Choose *While* when you need a test at the top of the loop.
- Choose *Repeat* when you want to delay the test to the bottom of the loop.

In any problem, first determine whether the steps in the loop must be carried out at least once, or if there are cases when you definitely want to skip those steps. By applying the answers to these questions to the above guideline, you often can choose the correct construction.

In cases where the answers to the questions are less clear, however, the solution may not depend on whether the loop is executed once, and you may have trouble applying this guideline. In these cases, write out the loop using each construction and compare the resulting code.

The following additional guidelines may help you choose.

When problems can be solved using either the *While* or the *Repeat* construction, one solution may be much cleaner and more elegant than the other. For example, in one looping form you find special cases arise that do not occur in the other form. *When you can find solutions using both While and Repeat, choose the cleaner, more elegant program.*

When you write an outline, ask how you are thinking of the loop.

- Do you want to continue until something happens (e.g., until a loan is paid off), or
- Do you want to continue while something holds true (e.g., while you need to make your full monthly payment)?

Philosophically, the *Repeat* applies when you answer yes to the first question, and the *While* applies when you answer yes to the second. *Thus your thinking about the nature of the loop can suggest which construction to use.*

In practice, these guidelines almost always suggest how to program a loop. As you write programs, the choice of *For* loops may be relatively clear, but you may have to work harder to choose between *While* and *Repeat*. The above guidelines can help while you get the practice you need to make this choice more comfortably.

## SECTION 7.5 PROGRAM STYLE AND CORRECTNESS

We have seen how to write various types of loops, and we have some guidelines for choosing among Pascal's three loop constructions. Now we turn our attention to program correctness.

Chapter 5 discussed several important and relevant topics, including indenting and formatting, local declaration of variables, choosing test cases, tracing program execution, and common errors. These comments apply generally to all types of loops. In this section we will expand briefly on the topic of indenting and formatting for the *Repeat* and *While* constructions. Good program structure remains a vital part of program correctness, but we will not repeat the other topics here.

Then we expand the concept of loop invariants, mentioned briefly in Chapter 5. This latter topic is becoming recognized as a particularly important one in the area of program correctness, so we will consider loop invariants at some length.

### Indenting and Formatting

Throughout our discussion of programming, we have stressed that the form of a program should reflect its structure. Our basic principle has been to indent when one piece of code depends upon another. Applying this principle to the new loop constructions of this chapter, we can identify the words *Repeat–Until* and *While–Do* as major headings, and we can consider the details of a loop as being dependent upon these headings. These considerations suggest the following basic forms:

```
Repeat                          While Condition
     Statement 1;                    Do Statement;
     Statement 2;
     .
     .
     .
     Statement n
Until Condition ;
```

In each case the main repetitive statement stands out, and the details of the loop are shown as being dependent. As in the past, if we replace the statement of the *While* loop with a *Begin–End* block, we should indent the individual parts of the block further.

### Loop Invariants

We now turn to a second topic that can be helpful in developing correct programs—loop invariants. In Chapter 5 we said that a **loop invariant** is a condition that is expected to be true at the beginning or at the end of a loop. Each time the loop is repeated, that same condition must be valid.

More generally, we can speak of an **assertion** in a program. An assertion is a condition that must be true at a given point in a program. Comparing the definitions of assertions and loop invariants, we see that an assertion located at the start or the end of a loop is a loop invariant.

To see how assertions and loop invariants can be of help in writing correct programs, consider an example.

## PROBLEM 7.5

Given a list of numbers, find their mean (or arithmetic average), and the maximum and minimum values.

### Discussion of Problem 7.5

In attacking this problem we analyze how we might proceed without the help of a computer. Since we discussed computing means in Section 5.3, we will focus here on finding maximum and minimum values.

**Computing Maximums.** To find a maximum by hand (without a machine), we might scan down the list, looking for bigger and bigger numbers. More formally, we might proceed as follows:

1. We start with the first number. So far, that is the maximum (and the minimum, too).
2. We look at the second number. If the second number is bigger than the first, we have a new maximum.
3. We look at the third number. If the third number is bigger than the previous maximum, we have a new maximum.

The same process continues down the list of numbers. A similar process would work for computing the minimum.

**Determining Loop Invariants.** We want to process other numbers on the list one by one, following the patterns we have identified for computing means, maximums, and minimums. After we have processed any of the numbers, we will want the following:

*Maximum* = maximum value read thus far

*Minimum* = minimum value read thus far

*Sum* = sum of numbers read thus far

*N* = number of items read thus far

These invariants will guide us in writing a loop in the outline. Two more topics need discussion before we write out all the steps, namely initialization and the exit condition.

**Initialization.** Applying the loop invariants after the first item on the list is processed, we have the following:

*Maximum* = first number

*Minimum* = first number

*Sum* = first number

N = 1

One clear way to accomplish this initialization is to read and process the first item on the list separately.

**Exit Condition.** The problem does not specify how many items appear on the list. It would be good to be able to run the program with a variety of sets of data, and not to have to count the items before we enter data. Thus, we must have some flexible way to decide when to stop processing numbers. One very useful approach is to place some special value at the end of the list of numbers. We would keep reading until we read this special value. (The special value is not processed; it just marks the end of the list.) In programming we call this special value (or values) a **sentinel**.

For example, we might put the number −9999 at the end of the list, or we might decide the list will contain only positive numbers and read until we find the value 0 (or maybe a negative number). In these cases, −9999 and 0 would be sentinels. With a sentinel marking the end of the list, the exit condition from a loop is a test for the sentinel value. Of course, we must be sure the sentinel is not included in the data processing itself (the sentinel should not be included in the computation of an average, a maximum, or a minimum).

With these comments, we can suggest an outline for solving the problem. Since we must check the sentinel before processing, we have restated the loop invariants slightly.

## Outline for Problem 7.5

**I.** Read and process first item on the list:
- **A.** Read item.
- **B.** Initialize *Minimum*, *Maximum*, *Sum* to the item.
- **C.** Set N = 1.

**II.** Read next item.

**III.** Continue processing as long as the last item read is not the sentinel:

Loop Invariants at Top of Loop:

*Maximum* = maximum value read prior to this latest value.
*Minimum* = minimum value read prior to this latest value.
*Sum* = sum of numbers read prior to this latest value.
N = number of items read prior to this latest value.

Steps:

Update *Maximum* and *Minimum*, if needed.
Update *Sum*.
Update N.
Read next item.

**IV.** Compute *Average*.

**V.** Print results.

Using the value 31416.0 as the sentinel, this outline yields the following program. Note that the sentinel is declared as a constant within the program.

```
Program FindMaxAndMin (Input, Output);
{This program computes the mean, maximum, and minimum
 for a list of numbers.}

Const Sentinel = 31416.0;

Var Number: Integer;              {number of items read}
    Sum: Real;                    {sum of items read}
    Maximum, Minimum: Real;       {extremes of items read}
    Average: Real;                {average of items}

Procedure FirstRead (Var Sum, Max, Min: Real; Var N: Integer);
{This procedure reads and processes first item on list}
    Var Item: Real;
    Begin
        Writeln ('Enter numbers; finish by typing ', Sentinel:1:1);
        Read (Item);
        Sum := Item;
        Max := Item;
        Min := Item;
        N := 1
    End {FirstRead} ;

Procedure ProcessRemainder (Var Sum, Max, Min: Real; Var N: Integer);
{This procedure reads and processes the second and subsequent input items.}
    Var Item: Real;
    Begin
        {Read next item}
        Read (Item);

        {Process items until sentinel is read}

        While (Item <> Sentinel)
          Do Begin
            If Item > Max
                Then Max := Item;
            If Item < Min
                Then Min := Item;
            Sum := Sum + Item;
            N := N + 1;
            Read (Item)
          End {Processing of items} ;
    End {ProcessRemainder} ;

Procedure PrintResults (Var Avg, Max, Min: Real);
{This procedure prints the average, maximum, and minimum data values}
    Begin
        Writeln ('The average of the items on the list is ', Avg:1:2);
        Writeln ('The largest number is ', Max:1:2);
        Writeln ('The smallest number is ', Min:1:2);
    End {PrintResults} ;
```

```
Begin {Main}
    Writeln ('Computation of mean, maximum, and minimum ',
             'for a list of numbers');

    FirstRead (Sum, Maximum, Minimum, Number);
    ProcessRemainder (Sum, Maximum, Minimum, Number);
    Average := Sum / Number;
    PrintResults (Average, Maximum, Minimum)
End {Main} .
```

Study Step III to be sure you know why we used a *While* loop. You should also check that the loop invariants are valid. When we run this program for the list 7.0, 5.0, 1.0, 11.0, 9.0, 3.0, we have the following interaction. Note that the sentinel value, 31416.0, is entered after the last item.

```
Computation of mean, maximum, and minimum for a list of numbers
Enter numbers; finish by typing 31416.0
7.0
5.0
1.0
11.0
9.0
3.0
31416.0
The average of the items on the list is 6.00
The largest number is 11.00
The smallest number is 1.00
```

### Practical Uses of Assertions and Loop Invariants

This discussion demonstrates that loop invariants can help in writing correct programs, in several ways. They encourage precision in stating assumptions. By writing down what you expect, you can see ambiguities and contradictions. For example, you can check that the meanings of variables have not changed from one part of a program to another.

Loop invariants can also help you examine various parts of a program carefully. Loop invariants located at the beginning of a loop can help you check initialization and repetitive statements. With care you can also check exit conditions and any concluding statements.

When loop invariants or assertions include Boolean expressions, you can evaluate these expressions within a program. Thus, a program can monitor itself for errors. For example, after computing new maximums and minimums in a loop, you could check that the maximum was never smaller than the minimum with the statement

```
If (Minimum > Maximum)
   Then Writeln('Invalid Minimum or Maximum');
```

As software quality becomes more and more important to computer users, loop invariants and assertions are being incorporated into programming languages.

Loop invariants and assertions may be used to prove that a program is correct, just as axioms are used to prove theorems in geometry.

Assertions can help you check various parts of a program carefully, and spot places where your thinking may be fuzzy or contradictory. Specifying and checking loop invariants and assertions can also complement your use of test data in finding bugs and reducing errors.

## SECTION 7.6 EXAMPLE: FINDING WHERE GRAPHS CROSS AN AXIS

To conclude this chapter, we consider one more problem that draws on the notion of loop invariants to develop a solution. This problem will also show another application for conditional loops.

### PROBLEM 7.6 Approximating Roots

Given a function $y = f(x)$, find a root of $f$. In other words, find a number $x_0$, where $f(x_0) = 0$. (This is the place where the graph of the function crosses the x axis. See Figure 7–4.)

This is such a common problem in all sciences, engineering, and mathematics that many approaches have been developed. Here we will consider a simple method that works in a very wide range of cases.

**Bisection Method for Approximating Roots.** We will assume that we know (or can find) values $a$ and $b$ ($a < b$) so that $f(a)$ and $f(b)$ have opposite signs. As long as $f$ is continuous (i.e., has no jumps), then $f$ must have

FIGURE 7–4 • **The Root of a Function**

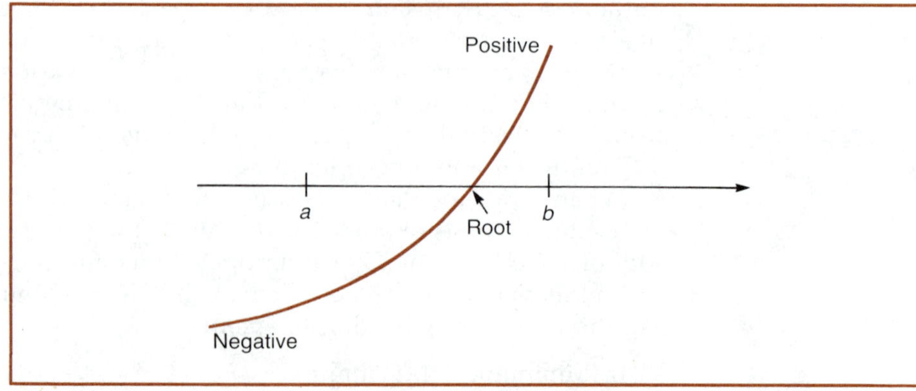

FIGURE 7–5 • **Cases for the Bisection Method**

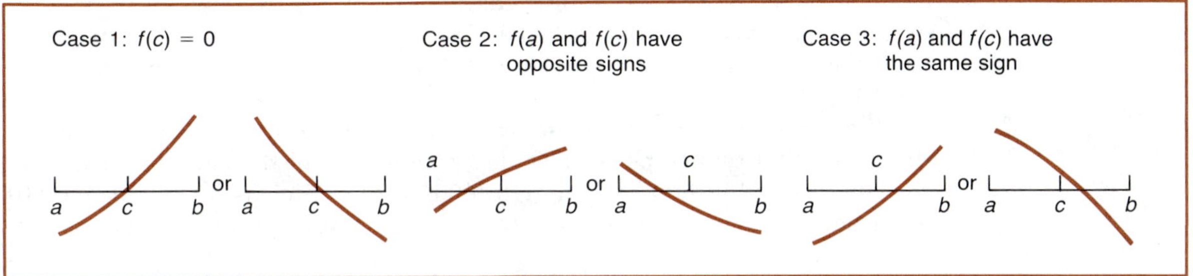


a root in the interval $[a,b]$. (In Figure 7–4, $f(a)$ is negative and $f(b)$ is positive.) In this situation, we can get better and better approximations to the root.

We begin with two observations: Since the root lies between $a$ and $b$, one approximation for the root is the midpoint $c$ of the interval $[a,b]$, where $c = (a + b)/2$. Second, if $[a,b]$ is a small interval, then $c$ would be a good approximation. In particular, if $[a,b]$ has length $L$, then $c$ must be within $L/2$ of the actual root.

From the cases in Figure 7–5 we can see how to use the midpoint $c$ to narrow down the interval where the root lies. There are three possibilities. If $f(c) = 0$, we have found a root. If $f(a)$ and $f(c)$ have opposite signs, a root must be in $[a,c]$. If $f(a)$ and $f(c)$ have the same sign, then $f(c)$ and $f(b)$ must have opposite signs, and a root must be in $[c,b]$.

In the first case, we can stop. Otherwise we cut the interval containing a root in half, from $[a,b]$ to either $[a,c]$ or $[c,b]$. We can then repeat this

FIGURE 7–6 • **Approximating $\sqrt{2}$**

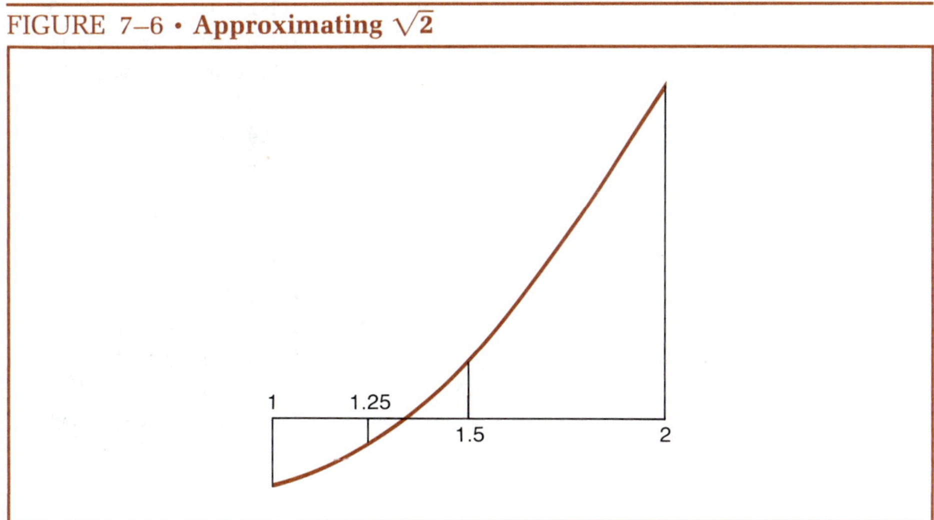

process until either we have found the root or the interval is small enough to ensure we have a good approximation.

*Example:* $\sqrt{2}$ is a root of $f(x) = x^2 - 2$. Here we find $\sqrt{2}$ to two decimal places (error $< 0.005$), so the final interval must have a length $< 0.01$.

We know $1 < \sqrt{2} < 2$, so we begin with $[a,b] = [1,2]$. Figure 7–6 shows the first two steps, and Table 7–1 gives all of the calculations.

The last subinterval has length 0.0078125, which is less than the 0.01 required. Thus the midpoint 1.4180 of this last subinterval

$$[1.40625, 1.421875]$$

is within 0.005 of the desired root. We use 1.4180 as our approximation of $\sqrt{2}$. (Note: This agrees with the true value of $\sqrt{2}$, 1.41431, to two decimal places.)

In the following outline we have included appropriate loop invariants.

**TABLE 7–1 • The Bisection Method Used to Find the Root of *Sqr(x)* − 2**

| Step | Interval | Midpoint | Function Values | Roots Lie in This Subinterval |
|---|---|---|---|---|
| 1 | [1.0000, 2.0000] | 1.5000 | f(1.0000) = −1.0000<br>f(1.5000) = 0.2500<br>f(2.0000) = 2.0000 | [1.0000, 1.5000] |
| 2 | [1.0000, 1.5000] | 1.2500 | f(1.0000) = −1.0000<br>f(1.2500) = −0.4375<br>f(1.5000) = 0.2500 | [1.2500, 1.5000] |
| 3 | [1.2500, 1.5000] | 1.3750 | f(1.2500) = −0.4375<br>f(1.3750) = −0.1094<br>f(1.5000) = 0.2500 | [1.3750, 1.5000] |
| 4 | [1.3750, 1.5000] | 1.4375 | f(1.3750) = −0.1094<br>f(1.4375) = 0.0664<br>f(1.5000) = 0.2500 | [1.3750, 1.4375] |
| 5 | [1.3750, 1.4375] | 1.4063 | f(1.3750) = −0.1094<br>f(1.4063) = −0.0225<br>f(1.4375) = 0.0664 | [1.4063, 1.4375] |
| 6 | [1.4063, 1.4375] | 1.4219 | f(1.4063) = −0.0225<br>f(1.4219) = 0.0217<br>f(1.4375) = 0.0664 | [1.4063, 1.4219] |
| 7 | [1.4063, 1.4219] | 1.4141 | f(1.4063) = −0.0225<br>f(1.4141) = −0.0004<br>f(1.4219) = 0.0217 | [1.4141, 1.4219] |

An approximate root is 1.4180

## Outline for Problem 7.6

**I.** Initialization:
  **A.** Determine $a$,$b$, and maximum error allowed.
  **B.** Note root not yet found.

**II.** Continue as long as root not found and length of interval [$a$,$b$] exceeds twice the allowed error:
  *Loop Invariants*
    $f(a)$ and $f(b)$ have opposite signs
    Desired root lies in interval [$a$,$b$]
  *Steps*
    Compute midpoint:
      $c = (a + b)/2$.
    If $f(c) = 0$, then root has been found.
    Otherwise,
      if $f(a)$ and $f(c)$ have opposite signs,
        then root is in [$a$,$c$];
        else root is in [$c$,$b$].

**III.** Print approximation to root:
  If root found, then $c$ is root.
  Otherwise midpoint of [$a$,$b$] is an approximate root.

In programming from this outline, note that $f(a)$ and $f(c)$ have opposite signs if their product is negative. In the following program we have chosen $f(x) = x^2 - 2$ as the function.

---

```
Program BisectionMethod (Input, Output);
{This program uses the Bisection Method to compute the
 root of the function f(x) in the interval [a,b], with
 an error not exceeding a given tolerance.}

Var a, b: Real;           {interval for the root}
    c: Real;              {midpoint of the interval}
    TwiceError: Real;     {Twice the prescribed tolerance}
    Found: Boolean;       {specifies if actual root found}

Function f(x: Real): Real;
{This is the function under consideration}
    Begin
        f := Sqr(x) - 2.0
    End {f} ;

Procedure Initialize (Var a, b, TwiceError: Real; Var Found: Boolean);
{This procedure initializes variables for the Bisection Method.}
    Var Error: Real;          {prescribed tolerance}
    Begin
        Write ('Enter the endpoints of the interval containing the root: ');
        Readln (a, b);
        Write ('Enter maximum error allowed: ');
```

```
        Readln (error);
        TwiceError := 2.0 * Error;
        {Note that root has not yet been found}
        Found := False;
    End {Initialize} ;

Procedure FindRoot (Var a, b, c, TwiceError: Real; Var Found: Boolean);
{This procedure continues while root not found and length of
 interval [a,b] too big}
    Begin
        While (Not Found) and (Abs(b-a))>= TwiceError)
          Do Begin

            {Compute midpoint}
            c := (a + b)/2.0;

            {Check function}
            If f(c) = 0.0
                Then Found := True
                Else Begin
                    {check signs of f(a) and f(c)}
                    If (f(a)*f(c) < 0.0)
                        Then b := c                 {root in [a,c]}
                        Else a := c                 {root in [c,b]}
                    End

          End {While} ;
    End {FindRoot} ;

Procedure PrintResults (a, b, c: Real; Found: Boolean);
{This procedure prints the root or its approximation.}
    Begin
        If Found
            Then Writeln ('The exact root is ', c:1:4)
            Else Writeln ('An approximate root is ', (a+b)/2.0 :1:4)
    End {PrintResults} ;

Begin {Main}
    Writeln ('The Bisection Method is used to find the root of a function');

    Initialize (a, b, TwiceError, Found);
    FindRoot (a, b, c, TwiceError, Found);
    PrintResults (a, b, c, Found)
End {Main} .
```

When we run this program with $a = 1$, $b = 2$, and error $= 0.005$, as in the example, we get the following output:

```
The Bisection Method is used to find the root of a function
Enter the endpoints of the interval containing the root: 1 2
Enter maximum error allowed: 0.005
An approximate root is 1.4180
```

Table 7–1 shows each step in this loop.

This program combines conditional loops and loop invariants, as suggested in this chapter, with Boolean variables and conditional statements, from Chapter 6. The loop invariants make the program easy to check. The conditional loop depends on a two-part Boolean expression.

This practical problem arises in many applications and uses many of the concepts and constructions developed thus far. The final result is a relatively short, but somewhat sophisticated solution to the problem.

## SUMMARY

1. This chapter introduced the *While–Do* construction and the *Repeat–Until* construction for writing loops and compared them with the *For–Do* loop introduced in Chapter 5.
2. Initialization, repetition, and exit conditions are specified in any loop.
3. *For–Do* gives **definite repetition;** you must know the number of iterations before you start a loop.
4. *Repeat* and *While* specify **conditional repetitions;** you do not know the number of iterations when you start. *Repeat* or *While* specifies an **exit condition** that determines when the loop continues and when it terminates. *While* tests the exit condition at the top of the loop; *Repeat* tests the exit condition at the bottom of the loop.
5. **Assertions** and **loop invariants** can help in developing a solution to a problem and in specifying what conditions should be true at various places in a program.

## EXERCISES

**7.1** **a.** Rewrite the Odd Number program of Section 7.3, using a *While–Do* construction instead of the *Repeat–Until*.

**b.** Compare your program with the program in the text.

| KEY TERMS, PHRASES, AND CONCEPTS | | ELEMENTS OF PASCAL SYNTAX | |
|---|---|---|---|
| Assertions | Loop Invariants | *Do* | *Until* |
| Conditional Repetition | Placing of Exit Condition | *Repeat* | *While* |
| Definite Repetition | Test at Bottom of Loop | | |
| Exit Condition | Test at Top of Loop | | |
| Initialization | Sentinel | | |

**7.2** *Rewriting the* For *in Pascal.* Rewrite the Pascal construction

For I: = A to B
    Do Statement

**a.** into a loop using the *While* construction.
**b.** into a loop using the *Repeat* construction.
*Caution:* What happens in Pascal if $A > B$?
NOTE: In either part (a) or (b), feel free to use an *If* statement when you need to.

**7.3** *Proving Program Correctness.* Consider the Credit-Balance Payment program from Section 7.1.
**a.** Develop loop invariants for *Month, Balance, Interest,* and *TInterest* at the beginning of each month.
**b.** Use your assertions in part (a) to argue the validity of the program in Section 7.1.

**7.4** *While Loops Versus Repeat Loops.* Figures 7–1 and 7–2 both address the Credit-Balance Payment problem of Section 7.1, and Figure 7–2 was developed as a translation of a *While–Do* loop into a *Repeat–Until* loop. However, the results of the program in Figure 7–2 will not always be the same as the results of the program in Figure 7–1.
**a.** Determine when the program segments will produce different answers.
**b.** Modify the program segment in Figure 7–2 so that the revised code will produce the same results as in Figure 7–1. (You may need to add an *If–Then* statement in your work.)

**7.5** *Assertions—Finding Errors.* Consider the following program that claims to solve the Credit-Balance Payment problem from Section 7.1. (The program is simplified from several attempts made by students in various programming classes.)

```
Program CreditBalancePayments (Input, Output);
{This program follows the balance of a charge account
 month by month as monthly payments are made.}

Var Cost: Real;              {Cost of item purchased}
    Rate: Real;              {Monthly interest rate}
    Payment: Real;           {Normal monthly payment}
    Balance: Real;           {Account balance at start of month,
                              before interest has been added}
    Interest: Real;          {Interest for month}
    TInterest: Real;         {Total accumulated interest}
    Month: Integer;          {Month number}

Begin {Main}
    Writeln ('This program follows the balance of a charge account.');
```

```
    {Determine Cost, Rate, Payment}
    Write ('Enter cost of item purchased: ');
    Readln (Cost);
    Write ('Enter monthly interest rate: ');
    Readln (Rate);
    Write ('Enter normal monthly payment: ');
    Readln (Payment);

    {Print table headings}
    Writeln;
    Writeln ('        Month''s   Total');
    Writeln ('Month Interest  Interest    Balance');
    Writeln (0:3, Cost:32:2);

    {Set up account for first month}
    Month := 0;
    Balance := Cost;
    Interest := 0.0;
    TInterest := 0.0;

    {Continue normal monthly payments while appropriate}
    While (Payment < Balance)
      Do Begin
        Month := Month + 1;
        Interest := Balance * Rate;
        TInterest := TInterest + Interest;
        Balance := Balance + Interest - Payment;
        Writeln (Month:3, Interest:10:2, TInterest:10:2, Balance:12:2);
      End;

    {Make Final Payment}
    Interest := Balance * Rate;
    TInterest := Interest + TInterest;
    Payment := Balance + Interest;
    Writeln;
    Writeln ('Interest for final payment is ', Interest:1:2);
    Writeln ('The final payment is ', Payment:1:2);
    Writeln ('The total interest charged was ', TInterest:1:2)

End {Main} .
```

a. Following the example in Section 7.5 as a model, write out some possible assertions and loop invariants for this program.

b. Use your assertions from part (a) to find an error in this program.

If you run this program with the test cases from Section 7.1, the program output is exactly the same as the output shown for the correct program. Thus, the error is subtle. The precision of your loop invariants should be helpful in finding the bug.

(HINT: You might try the test case *Cost* = 1037.50, *Rate* = 0.01, *Payment* = 100.00.)

**7.6** $N^{th}$ *Roots*. Write a program that computes the $N^{th}$ root of the positive number $R$ to three decimal places, using the Bisection Method from Section 7.6.

Read the values of N and R and check your program using the *Powers* function of Section 4.2. $\sqrt[N]{R}$ is a root of $f(x) = x^N - R$.

**7.7** *Syracuse Numbers.* Consider the following iteration procedure, applied to a positive integer $n_0$ to generate a sequence $n_0, n_1, n_2, n_3, \ldots$ Once the integer $n_j$ is known, the next integer $n_{j+1}$ is computed by the rules

$$\begin{aligned}(1)\ n_{j+1} &= n_j/2 &&\text{if } n_j \text{ is even;}\\ (2)\ n_{j+1} &= 3n_j + 1 &&\text{if } n_j \text{ is odd.}\end{aligned}$$

We call the original number $n_0$ *Syracuse* if the number 1 appears in the sequence $n_0, n_1, n_2, n_3, \ldots$

*Example:* The number 5 is Syracuse, because if the iteration begins with $n_0 = 5$, the sequence is 5, 16, 8, 2, 1,. . . .

Write a program to show that all integers between 1 and 2000 inclusive are Syracuse.

[This problem was suggested by Professor Arnold Adelberg.]

**7.8** *Insipid Integers.* Consider an iteration procedure that begins with a positive integer $n_0$ and generates a sequence by the rule

$$n_{j+1} = \text{sum of the squares of the digits of } n_j.$$

*Remarks*

**1.** If any term in the sequence equals 1, then all successive terms are 1.

**2.** If any term in the sequence equals 58, then the sequence cycles:

. . ., 58, 89, 145, 42, 20, 4, 16, 37, 58, 89,. . .

**3.** It is known that either Condition 1 or 2 must occur.

*Definition*

An integer $n_0$ is called *insipid* if Condition 1 occurs.

Find all integers between 1 and 99 that are insipid.

NOTE: It is interesting to investigate what patterns occur if the integers are represented in a number base other than base 10.

[This problem was suggested by Professor Arnold Adelberg.]

**7.9** *Finding Prime Numbers.* A prime number is a positive integer greater than 1 that is divisible only by itself and 1. Thus, 2, 3, and 5 are prime integers, while 6 is not (6 is also divisible by 2 and 3).

Write a Boolean function *Prime(N)* that returns *True* if N is a prime number and *False* otherwise.

Use the function *Prime* to write out the first 100 primes.

**7.10** *Doubling Your Bank Balance.* Suppose you deposit a certain amount of money in a savings account at a specified annual interest rate, compounded monthly. Follow the balance in the account month by month until the balance doubles. Compute the balance, monthly interest, and total interest each month until the new balance is at least twice the initial balance.

# CHAPTER 8

# SUBSCRIPTING AND ARRAYS

All of our applications up to this point have had the common feature that little information was needed at any particular time. We have specified separate variable names for each item, and we have needed only a fairly small number of such variables.

In this chapter we will consider problems that require keeping track of more pieces of information, which would make it cumbersome to write out separate variables for each piece of data. Instead, we can use one name to refer to several items, and this collection of data items is called an **array.** We can distinguish among various items in an array by giving each piece of data separate labels, called **subscripts.**

## SECTION 8.1 EXAMPLE: PRINTING DATA IN VARIOUS ORDERS

To motivate our work in this chapter, we begin with two closely related problems.

### PROBLEM 8.1

Read 25 integers and then print them out as follows:

**a.** Print the numbers in reverse order.
**b.** Print all of the odd integers and then print all of the even integers.

### Discussion of Problem 8.1

Each part of this problem requires storing some of the numbers as they are read. For part (a), you cannot start printing anything until all 25 numbers are read, because the last number read will be the first number printed. For part (b), you cannot print any even integers until all of the numbers are read, since you will not know when the odd integers are finished printing until all of the numbers have been read. To solve these problems, therefore, you will need to store all 25 numbers.

### Outline for Problem 8.1

**I.** Read all 25 numbers.
**II.** Print the 25 numbers in reverse order:
  **A.** Print the last number.
  **B.** Print the next-to-last number.
  Etc.
**III.** Print the odd integers and then the even ones:
  **A.** Print the odd integers:
    **1.** Check each number to see if it is odd.
    **2.** Print each odd number.
  **B.** Print the even integers:
    **1.** Check each number to see if it is even.
    **2.** Print each even number.

### Further Discussion of Problem 8.1

As you program from this outline, you might choose a separate name for each number; for example, you might pick names *A, B, C,. . ., Y*. However, if you use this approach, your reading would be

```
Read (A);
Read (B);
Read (C);
etc.
```

Even if you try to condense these *Read* statements, reading 25 numbers will be quite tedious. Writing the numbers in reverse order would be equally tedious. For Step III A you would have to test each number separately, using Pascal's *Odd* function. This part of our program might begin

```
If Odd (A)
    Then Write (A:5);
```

Similar coding would be repeated for each of the other variables. When the odd numbers were printed, you would have to repeat a similar process to print the even numbers. The resulting code would be long, tedious, and error prone.

The problem becomes much simpler if you call the numbers $Item_1$, $Item_2$, $Item_3$,. . ., $Item_{25}$. Each number is an "Item," and you can distinguish among the items with subscripts, as you may have seen in algebra.

Look at the reading step again with this notation:

Read ($Item_1$);
Read ($Item_2$);
Read ($Item_3$);

.
.
.

Read ($Item_{25}$);

While this coding looks just as tedious as *Read(A); Read(B); . . .*, there is a pattern here, reading successive *Items*. In fact, this code can be abbreviated:

Read ($Item_i$);

for $i$ = 1, 2,. . ., 25. Since subscripts are difficult to type on a computer terminal, we place them in square brackets [ ]. In Pascal, a subscripted variable such as *Item* is called an **array.**

Repetition over a sequence of values for $i$ suggests a *For* loop, where we replace the long sequence of *Read* statements with

```
For I := 1 to 25
    Do Read (Item [I]);
```

This simple statement reads all 25 values.

A similar approach works for printing out the values. To print

Write ($Item_{25}$)
Write ($Item_{24}$)

.
.
.

the pattern is

Write ($Item_i$:5)

where $i$ = 25, 24,. . .1. We can program this with the statement

```
For I := 25 DownTo 1
    Do Write (Item[I]:5);
```

We can also use loops and subscripts to solve the odd–even part of the problem, as in the following program:

```
Program ChangeOrder (Input, Output);
{This program reads a sequence of 25 integers and prints
 the sequence in two ways:
    1.  the sequence is printed in reverse order
    2.  the odd integers are printed first followed
        by the even integers in the sequence}
```

```
Const NumberOfItems = 25;      {the problem specifies 25 items}

Var I: Integer;                {we use I as a subscript}
    Item: Array[1..NumberOfItems] of Integer; {integers in sequence}

Begin
    Writeln ('A sequence of integers is printed in various ways.');

    {Read all items in the sequence}
    Writeln('Enter sequence of ', NumberOfItems:1, ' integers:');
    For I := 1 to NumberOfItems
        Do Read(Item[I]);

    {Print integers in reverse order}
    Writeln;
    Writeln('Sequence in reverse order');
    For I := NumberOfItems Downto 1
        Do Write(Item[I]:5);

    {Print the odd integers in the sequence}
    Writeln;
    Writeln;
    Writeln('Sequence with odd integers followed by even ones');
    For I := 1 To NumberOfItems
        Do If Odd(Item[I])
            Then Write(Item[I]:5);

    {Print the even integers in the sequence}
    For I := 1 to NumberOfItems
        Do If (Not Odd(Item[I]))
            Then Write(Item[I]:5)

End {Main} .
```

Running this program with a sequence of integers picked at random, we get

```
A sequence of integers is printed in various ways.
Enter sequence of 25 integers:
3 8 11 15 19 21 23 1 18 17 16 12 7 4 2
25 22 20 10 9 6 5 13 24 14

Sequence in reverse order
   14   24   13    5    6    9   10   20   22   25    2    4    7   12   16
   17   18    1   23   21   19   15   11    8    3

Sequence with odd integers followed by even ones
    3   11   15   19   21   23    1   17    7   25    9    5   13    8   18
   16   12    4    2   22   20   10    6   24   14
```

This program illustrates several important features about the use of subscripts in Pascal programs. Declarations with subscripts are somewhat modified. First, we state explicitly that the variable *Item* will be subscripted, and then we state what range of subscripts might be possible; here the subscripts are in the range from 1 to the constant *NumberOfItems* (25). Next, we state what type of information is being stored in the array; here the subscripted variables are integers. Finally, after the array is declared, we place the subscripts in square brackets.

Let us look at the use of subscripted variables more closely.

## SECTION 8.2 ELEMENTS OF ARRAYS

In this section we will discuss with some care the syntax and semantics of arrays. The discussion divides naturally into three pieces: array declarations, storage of arrays in main memory, and use of arrays in programs.

### Array Declarations

To use a subscripted variable, the declarations must include four features: the name of the subscripted variable; the specification that the variable will be an array; the range for the subscripts; the type of data to be stored in the subscripted variable. The formal syntax for this array declaration is illustrated by the example in Section 8.1:

```
Var; Item: Array [1 . . 25] of Integer;
```

We start an array declaration with an identifier (e.g., *Item*), which will be the name of the array. After a colon and the reserved word *Array*, we write the range for the subscripts in *square* brackets [ ]. In specifying this range, we list the lowest possible subscript and the highest possible subscript, and we place 2 periods between them. In the example above, the subscripts ranged from 1 to 25, so we wrote [1 . . 25]. Finally, after the reserved word *of*, we indicate what type of data will be stored within the array; in the example, the array data were of type *Integer*.

We can store any type of information, integer, real, or Boolean, in an array. For example, we might record whether the integers in the array *Item* were positive, by declaring

```
Var Positive: Array [1 . . 25] of Boolean;
```

*Positive*[1] might be true if $Item_1$ is positive and false otherwise. This array would store Boolean values (*True* or *False*) rather than integers. In other cases we might want an array of real numbers.

However, each array can store only one type of data. If $Item_1$ is to be an *Integer*, then $Item_2$ through $Item_n$ must be integers, not reals or Booleans.

Turning to our subscripts, we have noted that the array declaration must specify the range for the subscripts: the range [1 . . 25] indicates that all the subscripts will be between 1 and 25, inclusive. In Pascal we have considerable flexibility in giving this range, as shown in Table 8–1.

From this discussion of syntax and semantics, we can see what types of arrays are possible and what subscript restrictions we have. Next, we will see that we can understand these declarations better if we consider how our declared arrays are stored in main memory.

### Storage of Arrays in Main Memory

One of the major purposes of array declarations is to allow the computer to allocate appropriate space for the data when you run a program. For example, if you have declared

```
Var Item: Array [1. .10] of Integer;
```

the computer must allocate enough space for the variable *Item* to store 10 integers. In main memory, an integer takes up a certain amount of space, and this declaration reserves the space for 10 integers (see Figure 8–1). Within this block of space, the first integer will hold the value of $Item_1$, the second integer is for $Item_2$, etc.

On the other hand, if you write

```
Var Item: Array [1. .10] of Real;
```

**TABLE 8–1 • Specifying Ranges in Array Declarations**

| Rule or Principle | Example | Comment |
|---|---|---|
| Not all subscripts specified must be used | For range [−10. .50] you may use only 1,2,3,. . .,25 | You may declare ranges larger than needed |
| Subscripts used must be in range specified | For range [−10. .50] you may not use 57 as a subscript | You may not declare ranges smaller than needed |
| Constants can be used in range declarations | We used [1. .*NumberOfItems*] in the declaration of *Item* in the previous section | Constants allow easy modification of code for other sizes of data |
| Range declarations may not include variables or expressions | The following are invalid: [7/7. .30–5] [1. .N] | The second example assumes *N* is a variable |
| Ranges may include Booleans or integers, but not real numbers | [Boolean] is valid [1.0. .2.0] is invalid | |

[false. . true]

you would again reserve enough space for 10 distinct numbers, but you must store real numbers rather than integers. Real numbers require a different amount of space from that for integer values, so an array of integers is physically different from an array of reals (see Figure 8–1). Boolean variables have still different space requirements.

An array declaration tells the computer two major pieces of information about an array. First, the range of subscripts allows the computer to determine how many spaces must be allocated (it specifies the number of boxes in the array). Second, the array type tells the computer how much space is required for each value (the size of each box).

This notion of storage allocation may clarify the variety of options noted in Table 8–1. You can use Boolean or integer subscripts, because the computer can determine how many subscripts are possible. Two Boolean subscripts, *True* and *False*, can be used. Also, you can use integer ranges

[−27. .−3] or [−12. .12] or [0. .24].

Thus, you are free to choose any range of Boolean or integer subscripts that makes sense in a problem. (However, you cannot use real subscripts, since a range of real numbers would require too much space.)

## Use of Arrays in Programs

Once storage space in main memory is allocated on the basis of the information in the array declaration, you can use the array in a program in ei-

FIGURE 8–1 • **Storage Allocation for Array Declarations**

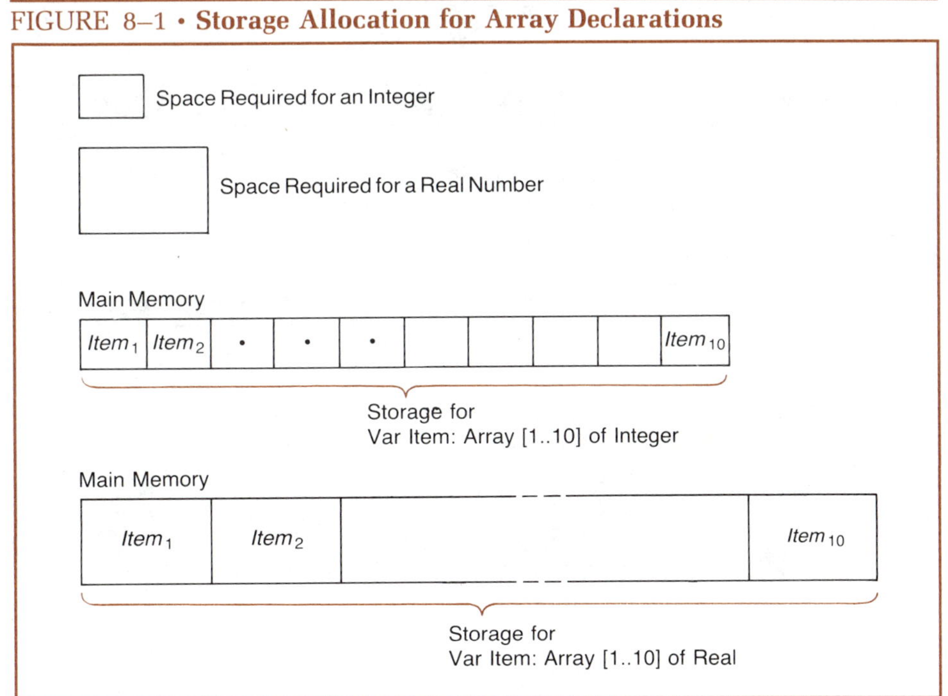

ther of two ways. You may work with the elements of an array one at a time, or you may consider the entire array as a whole.

**Individual Array Elements.** In Section 8.1 we referred to a specific item in an array by putting a subscript in brackets. In working with array elements, however, we must be careful to distinguish between the value of a subscript and an item stored within the array. For example, 1 might be a subscript, while *Item* [1] refers to the value stored in the first location of the array *Item*.

**Arrays as a Whole.** In some situations, Pascal also allows us to consider an entire array as a complete unit. For example, in Section 8.4 we will see that Pascal allows us to copy whole arrays. We will also use entire arrays as parameters in functions and procedures. In these cases, we will think of an array as a single entity (containing several parts), and we will work with that entire collection of data.

In many cases, however, we cannot use an entire array, for various philosophical or technical reasons. For example, consider the arrays in Figure 8–2, where it is not clear whether the expression *Item* < *Stuff* is true or false. Similarly, we cannot perform arithmetic operations, such as addition or multiplication, on arrays, and we cannot read or write an entire array in Pascal.

Thus, while Pascal does allow use of entire arrays for assignments and parameters, we cannot directly use an entire array in other contexts. These restrictions do not apply to the elements of arrays, since those elements are just numbers or Boolean values.

## SECTION 8.3 EXAMPLE: SEQUENTIAL (LINEAR) SEARCH

A very common task in many computer applications involves searching a set of data to find a particular item. In this section we will consider a sim-

FIGURE 8–2 • **Comparison of Arrays Is Not Allowed**

| Item | Stuff |
|---|---|
| 3 | 5 |
| 7 | −3 |
| −1 | 4 |
| 2 | 5 |

ple variation of this problem and an elementary algorithm to solve it. A second algorithm, which can be much more efficient in certain cases, is presented in Section 8.5.

**PROBLEM 8.3** Given an array filled with data, suppose we are given a particular item of information. Determine whether the particular item is in the array.

### Discussion of Problem 8.3

To determine whether a particular item is in an array, you could simply look at each element in the array until either you find the desired element or you run out of items in the array. This elementary approach suggests the following outline:

### Outline for Problem 8.3

**I.** Read the data:
  **A.** Determine item of interest
  **B.** Determine array of data
**II.** Search through successive array elements until the desired item is found or until you run out of elements.
**III.** Print results of the search.

NOTES: (1) You can search through successive elements by changing the subscripts. For example, to consider $Element_1$, $Element_2$, $Element_3$,. . ., check $Element_J$, starting $J$ at 1 and increasing $J$ by 1.

(2) After you finish the search, you must see why you stopped: You might have found the desired item, or you might have run out of array elements. You must distinguish between these two cases.

This outline suggests the following program, which is designed for arrays of 10 elements. The details of reading data are in procedure *ReadData*. The search algorithm is in a separate Boolean function, which returns *True* if the element is found and *False* otherwise.

```
Program LinearSearch (Input, Output);
{This program determines if a particular Item is included
 in a specified array of data.}

Const Max = 10;          {Our array contains this many numbers}

Var Item: Integer;       {The desired element}
    Element: Array [1..Max] of Integer;    {Our array of numbers}

Procedure ReadData (Var Number: Integer);
    {This procedure reads the appropriate data from the terminal}
    Var I: Integer;     {Array subscript for reading}

    Begin
        {Determine Particular Item of Interest}
        Write ('Enter Desired Number: ');
        Readln (Number);
```

```
        {Determine Element of Data}
        Writeln ('Enter the ', Max:1, ' array elements.');
        For I := 1 to Max
            Do Read(Element[I]);

    End {ReadData} ;

Function ItemFound (Number: Integer): Boolean;
{This function searches for the Item in the Array}
    Var J: Integer;    {Array subscript for search}

    Begin
        {Set up for search}
        J := 0;

        {Search through Array}
        Repeat
            J := J + 1
        Until ((Number = Element[J]) Or (J = Max));

        {Determine if Number found at end of search}
        ItemFound := (Number = Element[J])

    End {ItemFound} ;

Begin {Main}
    Writeln ('An array of data is searched for a particular item.');

    ReadData (Item);

    {Search for Item and Print Results}
    If ItemFound (Item)
        Then Writeln (Item:1, ' was found in the array.')
        Else Writeln (Item:1, ' was not found in the array.')

End {Main} .
```

Two sample runs of this program are shown below:

```
First Trial Run

An array of data is searched for a particular item.
Enter particular item: 7
Enter the 10 array elements.
3 1 4 7 5 9 2 6 3 8
7 was found in the array.

Second Trial Run

An array of data is searched for a particular item.
Enter particular item: 13
Enter the 10 array elements.
3 1 4 7 5 9 2 6 3 8
13 was not found in the array.
```

This program illustrates three additional points. First, we can perform the same process with several values in an array by changing a subscript in a loop. Second, we can use a constant to specify the size of an array and then write all other work in terms of that constant. (We used the constant *Max* in this program.) Thus, we can adapt the programs to different amounts of data with only minor changes in the code. Third, in this problem we have followed a basic algorithm called a **sequential** or **linear search,** which starts with the first element in our array and continues element by element through our array.

### Evaluation of Efficiency of a Linear Search

Now that we have seen one method for finding a particular item in an array, let us analyze how much work the algorithm requires. In general, we consider an array of $n$ elements (in the example, $n = 10$).

In the example, the search stopped once we found the desired item. Sometimes, the item is near the beginning of the array; other times it is near the end. On the average, we might expect to examine about half of the array elements to find the desired item. The times when we find the item early will be balanced by other times when the item occurs late in the array.

On the average, then, if we find the desired item, we will need about $n/2$ checks or comparisons. On the other hand, if the desired item is not in the array, we must check all of the array elements. We will not know the item is missing until the entire array has been examined; we will need $n$ checks or comparisons to conclude the desired item is not present.

This is our first illustration of an analysis of the time and effort required to perform a specified task. The analysis tells us, for example, that if we have an array of 1000 elements ($n = 1000$), then we would have to perform an average of 500 comparisons ($n/2 = 500$) to find a particular item in the array. If we want to look up items frequently, then this same amount of work would be required each time.

In this text, we will see other algorithms, and we will be able to analyze them as well. Our results will suggest how to choose among various algorithms to use the best algorithm for a particular application.

## SECTION 8.4 TYPE STATEMENTS

In previous chapters, we have seen how to define our own constants, variables, procedures, and functions. We have discussed real, integer, and Boolean data, and we have seen how to put this data together in an array. In this section we will introduce defining our own types, and we will see some applications of type declarations when using arrays. We will expand considerably upon this discussion in Chapter 11.

We begin with an example. We have rewritten the Linear Search program from the previous section, declaring a new type of data, *ArrayOfData*, and using our array *Element* as a parameter in the *ItemFound* function. The revised program produces the same output as the original version.

```
Program LinearSearch {With new array type} (Input, Output);
{This program determines if a particular Item
 is present in a specified array of data.}

Const Max = 10;      {Array contains this many elements}

Type ArrayOfData = Array [1..Max] of Integer;  {The type of array}

Var Item: Integer;            {The desired element}
    Element: ArrayOfData;   {The Array of elements}

Procedure ReadData (Var Number: Integer; Var Info: ArrayOfData);
{This Procedure reads the appropriate data from the terminal}
    Var I: Integer;  {Array subscript for reading}

    Begin
        {Determine Particular Item of Interest}
        Write ('Enter Desired Number: ');
        Readln (Number);

        {Determine Array of Data}
        Writeln ('Enter the ', Max:1, ' array elements.');
        For I := 1 to Max
            Do Read(Info[I]);

    End {ReadData} ;

Function ItemFound(Number: Integer; Info: ArrayOfData): Boolean;
{This function searches for the Item in the array}
    Var J: Integer;   {Array subscript for search}


    Begin
        {Set up for search}
        J := 0;

        {Search through array}
        Repeat
            J := J + 1
        Until ((Number = Info[J]) Or (J = Max));

        {Determine if Item found at end of search}
        ItemFound := (Number = Info[J])

    End {ItemFound} ;

Begin {Main}
    Writeln ('A collection of data is searched for a particular item.');

    ReadData (Item, Element);
```

```
    {Search for Item and Print Results}
    If ItemFound (Item, Element)
       Then Writeln (Item:1, ' was found in the array.')
       Else Writeln (Item:1, ' was not found in the array.')

End {Main} .
```

In this program, we declared

Type ArrayOfData = Array [1. .Max] of Integer;

You can use a type *ArrayOfData* as well as the types *Real, Integer, Boolean*. *ArrayOfData* designates an array with a particular range of subscripts.

Once we defined the type, we declared

Var Element: ArrayOfData;

The variable *Element* has the new type *ArrayOfData*, which we have just described.

So far, the declaration of *Element* seems equivalent to the more familiar declaration

Var Element: Array [1. .Max] of Integer;

The new type, however, also allows us to declare the formal parameter in procedure *ReadData* and in the *ItemFound* function:

Procedure ReadData (Var Number: Integer; Var Info: ArrayOfData);

and

Function ItemFound (Number: Integer; Info: ArrayOfData): Boolean;

The formal parameter *Info* has the same type as the global variable *Element*, so we can use *Element* as an actual parameter in the main program. Declaring the new type *ArrayOfData* enabled us to use the array *Element* as a parameter both in procedure *ReadData* and in the function *ItemFound*.

### Agreement of Formal and Actual Parameter Types

When we discussed parameters for functions and procedures, we distinguished between formal parameters and actual parameters, and we said that the declaration of a function specifies the type of parameter for the function. Actual parameters must have the same type as the formal parameters. In Pascal, this notion of the same type is interpreted very strictly. In particular, we must have names for all formal parameters, and the type names for formal and actual parameters must agree.

In the revised Linear Search program we declared a new type, *ArrayOfData*, and both the formal paramenter *Info* and the actual parameter *Element* for function *ItemFound* had this type. Pascal would not allow declaring *Info* and *Element* separately as

```
Array [1. .Max] of Integer
```

Thus when we want to use arrays as parameters in Pascal, we must declare an appropriate type first in a *Type* statement. Then, we can use that type to declare formal parameters and appropriate variables. This use of a *Type* statement guarantees that formal parameters and actual parameters actually have the same type, since the type names are identical.

## Type Statements for Assignments

The philosophy of the same type also applies to the transfer of data from one array to another. If you declare

```
Var Stuff, Item: Array [1. .4] of Integer;
```

Then you may write

```
Stuff := Item;
```

Here *Stuff* and *Item* are arrays of the same type, and you can transfer data from one array to the other. The line

```
Stuff := Item;
```

is equivalent to

```
Stuff[1] := Item[1];
Stuff[2] := Item[2];
Stuff[3] := Item[3];
Stuff[4] := Item[4];
```

More generally, Pascal allows the transfer of data from one variable to another whenever the variables have the same type. Here Pascal again interprets the word "same" very strictly. The assignment

```
A := B;
```

is only valid when *A* and *B* are declared in the same declaration statement or when their type has the same identifier as a name. To declare *A* and *B* in different lines or in different procedures, we must use the *Type* statement to give the variables the same type. Thus, we could write

```
Type  Data = Array [-2. .6] of Integer;
Var   A: Data;
      B: Data;
        .
        .
        .
      A:= B;
```

since *A* and *B* are explicitly the same type.

### Summary

This discussion of Pascal types and *Type* statements raises four major points.

1. Pascal allows us to define data types, using *Type* statements.
2. Pascal has a very strict interpretation of types. It does not analyze different declarations to determine whether two variables have the same type. We must be explicit if we want two variables to have the same type.
3. *Type* statements allow us to specify arrays as parameters in functions and procedures; formal parameters and actual parameters can be declared to be the same type, through *Type* statements.
4. When variables have the same type, we can transfer data from one to the other with the simple assignment statement $A := B$.

We will now look at some more examples that use arrays to solve common problems.

## SECTION 8.5 EXAMPLE: BINARY SEARCH

Section 8.3 presented one approach to searching an array for a particular item. This section presents a much more efficient approach for an array that has already been sorted (i.e., placed in ascending or descending order).

We begin with an array of data $a_1, \ldots, a_n$, and we want to find a particular item $P$. Whereas, in the Linear Search, we potentially had to look at the entire array $a_1, \ldots, a_n$, in a Binary Search we can eliminate much of the data without having to look at them directly. In particular, the Binary Search allows us to divide the amount of data under consideration in half each time.

To understand how this is done, consider how you might look up a name in a telephone book. To begin, open the telephone book to the middle. If you are lucky, you will see the name on the page in front of you. Even if you are unlucky, however, you can tell which half of the book contains the name you want.

Once you know which half the name is in, turn to the middle of that half. Again, you might be lucky and find the name immediately. Otherwise, you can restrict your attention to just the part where the name must be (now just one-quarter of the original book).

Continue looking at the middle page of the section remaining and dividing that section in halves until you find the name or until you run out of pages to look at.

**Algorithm Design.** When we write this approach as a formal algorithm, we must keep track of four things in the general step: the first element, $a_F$, in a short array; the last element, $a_L$; the middle element, $a_M$; and the desired element, $P$.

**Outline for Binary Search.** With this notation we have the following outline.

**I.** Read the data:
- **A.** $P$.
- **B.** The array of data $a_1, \ldots, a_N$.

**II.** Binary search:
- **A.** Initialize search:
  - $F := 1$
  - $L := N$
- **B.** Repeat until $P$ is found or there are no elements left to consider:
  - **1.** Find the middle element: $M := (F+L)/2$.
  - **2.** Check $P$ and $a_M$:
    - If $P = a_M$, then element found.
    - If $P < a_M$, then $L := M - 1$.
    - If $P > a_M$, then $F := M + 1$.
- **C.** Determine whether the element is found.

**III.** Print results.

This outline yields the following program, which produces the same output as the Linear Search program from Section 8.3.

---

```
Program BinarySearch (Input, Output);
{This program determines if a particular Item is present
 in a specified array of data.}

Const Max = 10;         {Our array contains this many elements}

Type ArrayOfData = Array [1..Max] Of Integer;

Var Item: Integer;            {The desired element}
    Element: ArrayOfData ;    {Our array of elements}

Procedure ReadData (Var Number: Integer; Var Info: ArrayOfData);
{This procedure reads the appropriate data from the terminal}
    Var I: Integer;     {Array subscript for reading}

    Begin
        {Determine Particular Item of Interest}
        Write ('Enter Desired Number: ');
        Readln (Number);

        {Determine Array of Data}
        Writeln ('Enter the ', Max:1, ' array elements.');
        For I := 1 To Max
            Do Read(Info[I])

   End {Read Data} ;
```

```
Function ItemFound (Number: Integer; Info: ArrayOfData): Boolean;
{This function searches for the Item in the array}
    Var First, Last: Integer;  {Binary Search of
                                  Info[First] to Info[Last]}

        Middle: Integer;  {the middle of our array}

    Begin
        {Initialize Search}
        First := 1;
        Last := Max;

        {Perform search}
        Repeat
            Middle := (First + Last) Div 2;
            If Number < Info[Middle]
                Then Last := Middle - 1
                Else First := Middle + 1;
        Until (Number = Info[Middle]) Or (Last < First) ;

        {Determine if item found}
        ItemFound := (Number = Info[Middle])

    End {ItemFound} ;

Begin {Main}
    Writeln ('A collection of data is searched for a particular item.');

    ReadData (Item, Element);

    {Search for Item and Print Results}
    If ItemFound (Item, Element)
        Then Writeln (Item:1, ' was found in the array')
        Else Writeln (Item:1, ' was not found in the array')

End {Main} .
```

**Evaluation of Efficiency.** This algorithm works very efficiently, because inferences can be made about the array after each comparison. In particular, it halves the number of array elements considered in each iteration. For example, if you start with $N$ elements, then after one step, the number of remaining elements is $N/2$. After two steps, the number of remaining elements is $N/4$.

In general, after $m$ steps, the number of elements left to check is $N/2^m$. You can continue this process until you either find the element or run out of elements. If you are lucky, you might find the element very quickly, so you might stop very soon. Even if you are unlucky, however, you will run out of elements quite fast.

In particular, you can stop when the number of elements left to check is less than 1. You can stop by $m$ steps

if

$$N/2^m < 1,$$

or

$$N < 2^m,$$

or

$$\log_2 N < m,$$

or

$$1 + \log_2 N \leq m$$

Thus, for an array of N elements, the Binary Search will finish in no more than $1 + \log_2 N$ steps. By the nature of logarithms, this analysis shows that if you double the size of the array, you only add one iteration to the loop. Other comparisons are shown in Table 8–2.

### Choosing Between Linear and Binary Search Algorithms

Our analysis and Table 8–2 show that if you have sorted data, then the Binary Search is vastly superior to the Linear Search. Thus, you should choose the Binary Search whenever a problem involves sorted data.

In addition, the Binary Search should be used whenever you will need to search the same data many times. In this situation, the time spent ordering the data is offset by the gain in each Binary Search. We will see one way to sort data in the next section.

This general "divide and conquer" approach applies to many other applications as well. For example, this same idea formed the basis of the Bisection Method in Section 7.6.

On the other hand, if the data are not sorted, and if you do not need to search the data very often, then a Linear Search is the preferred algorithm.

**TABLE 8–2 • Steps Required for Two Searching Methods, Based on $n$ Elements of Data**

| | Linear Search | | Binary Search |
|---|---|---|---|
| n | Average number of Steps (n/2) | Maximum Number of Steps n | $1 + \log_2 n$ |
| 100 | 50 | 100 | 8 |
| 1000 | 500 | 1000 | 11 |
| 10000 | 5000 | 10000 | 14 |

In this situation, the time required to sort data is not balanced by the faster Binary Search.

This Binary Search example also shows that an effective way to improve a program may well be to change the algorithm. Sometimes, you can polish the code to make it run more efficiently. When you need dramatic improvements, however, you may need a different approach to the problem altogether.

## SECTION 8.6 EXAMPLE: MAINTAINING LINEAR STRUCTURES

In previous examples, we first entered data and then worked with them. In this section we will see how to edit data. Then we will apply these ideas to develop a sorting algorithm.

### PROBLEM 8.6 Simple Editing

Write a procedure that starts with some elements in an array and then allows you to edit the data. You must be able to insert new items and delete existing ones.

#### Discussion of Problem 8.6

In the past, we have always used a constant *Max* to specify the maximum number of elements to be stored in an array, and we always used this full number. Here, we want to allow additions and deletions to the elements, so we need two changes. We must allow more space than we might need initially, so we have room for additions, and we must keep track of the exact number of elements present at any time. In the program, therefore, we need to set *Max* larger than in the past, and we need a distinct variable *Number* to record the current number of data items.

Suppose an array is declared

```
Var A: Array[1. .Max] of Integer;
```

and suppose we have already entered some data, so *Number* > 0. When we add a piece of data *P*, we must increment *Number* by 1. (Of course, if this new *Number* is bigger than *Max*, then we cannot store any more data and must stop.)

With *Number* increased, we next need to decide where to place the new piece of data *P*. If the array is not sorted, then we can place *P* at the end of the array,

```
A[Number] := P;
```

However, if the array is sorted and we want to keep it sorted, then we must proceed in two steps (see Figure 8–3): slide values bigger than *P* down in the array to make room for *P*, then insert *P* in the vacant space.

FIGURE 8–3 • **Insertion in a Sorted Array**

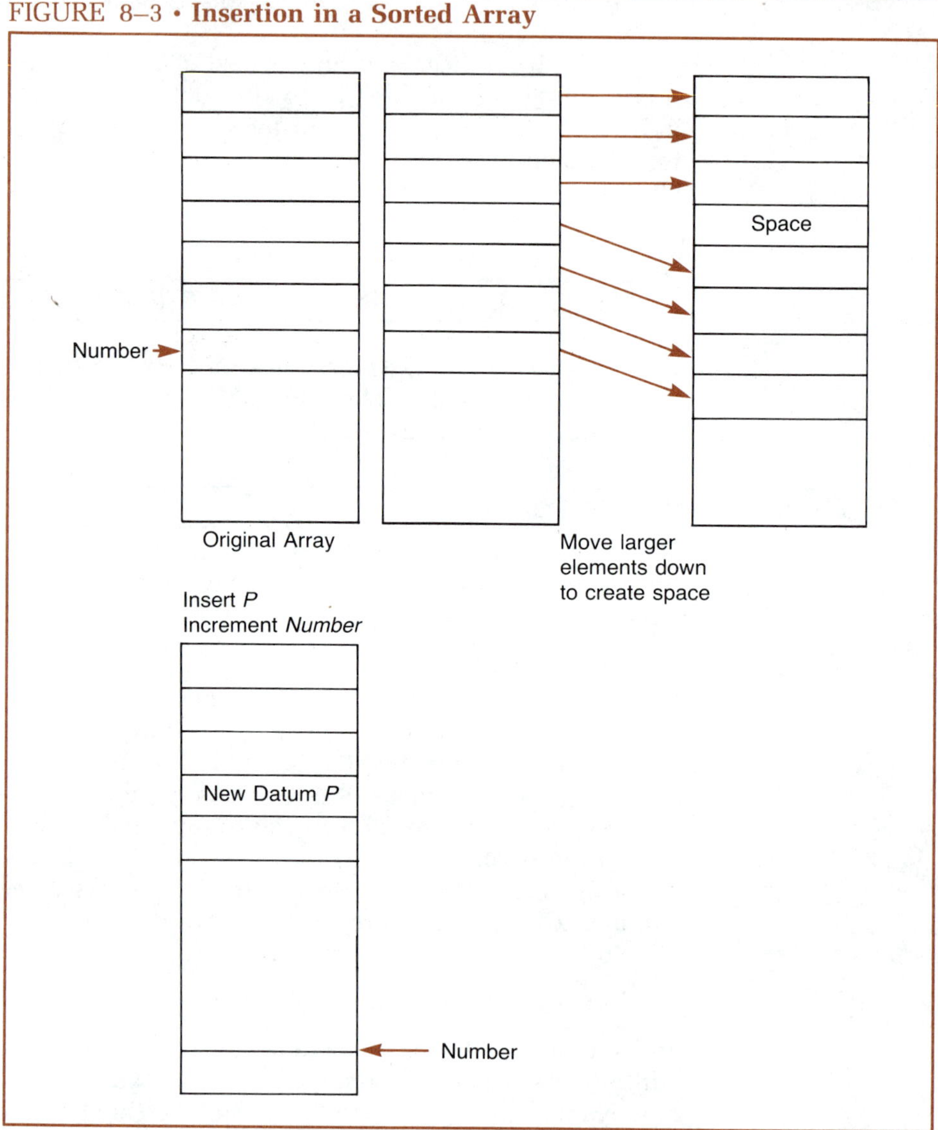


**Outline for Insertion.** One way to perform this insertion task is outlined below.

**I.** Check that there is room for another item in the array.
**II.** Use binary search to find where the new item should go.
**III.** Slide elements beyond this point down.
**IV.** Insert the item and increment *Number*.

This suggests the following segment of code:

```
{Procedure Insert and Function ItemLocation assume that
    Max   is declared as a constant,
    Data  is declared as a type of data, such as integer or real,
    ArrayOfData is declared as "Array [1..Max] of Data"}

Function ItemLocation (Item: Data; Number: Integer;
                       Info: ArrayOfData): Integer;
{This function searches for the Item in the Array}
    Var First, Last: Integer;  {Binary Search of Info[First] to Info[Last]}
            Middle: Integer;   {the middle of our array}

    Begin
        If Item > Info[Number]
            Then ItemLocation := Number + 1
            Else Begin {Binary Search}
                {Initialize Search}
                First := 1;
                Last := Number;

                {Perform search}
                Repeat
                    Middle := (First + Last) Div 2;
                    If Item < Info[Middle]
                        Then Last := Middle - 1
                        Else First := Middle + 1;
                Until (Item = Info[Middle]) Or (Last < First) ;

                {Record where Item should be}
                If Item <= Info[Middle]
                    Then ItemLocation := Middle
                    Else ItemLocation := Middle + 1
            End {Binary Search}

    End {ItemLocation} ;

Procedure Insert (Item: Data; Var Number: Integer; Var Element: ArrayOfData);
{This procedure inserts the specified Item from the Array}
    Var ItemIndex: Integer;    {Location of Item on Array}
        Index: Integer;        {Array subscript}

    Begin
      {Check if there is room in the array}
      If Number = Max
        Then Writeln ('Array is Full - Insertion is impossible')
        Else Begin
            {Find Where New Item Should Go}
            ItemIndex := ItemLocation (Item, Number, Element);

            {Slide Subsequent Elements Down}
            For Index := Number DownTo ItemIndex
                Do Element[Index+1] := Element[Index];

            {Insert Item}
            Element[ItemIndex] := Item;
            Number := Number + 1
            End {Insertion of Item}

    End {Insert} ;
```

This coding uses the efficient binary search to locate where the new element should go, so it allows us to insert new data efficiently.

**Deletion of Items.** To delete elements, the process is reversed:

**I.** Locate the element in the array to be deleted.
(If the item is not found, print an error message.)
**II.** Move subsequent elements down to close up "space" left by deleted element.
**III.** Decrement *Number* by 1.

When we write the corresponding procedure for deletion, we use the same *ItemLocation* function we used for insertion. We omit the listing of this *ItemLocation* function in the following deletion procedure.

```
{This procedure assumes the following declarations:
      Max    is declared as a constant,
      Data   is declared as a type of data, such as real or integer,
      ArrayOfData is declared as "Array [1..Max] of Data" }

Procedure Delete (Item: Data; Var Number: Integer; Var Element: ArrayOfData);
{This procedure deletes the specified Item from the Array}
    Var ItemIndex: Integer;    {Location of Item in Array}
        Index: Integer;        {Array subscript}

    Begin
        {Locate Item in Array - Using Binary Search}
        ItemIndex := ItemLocation (Item, Number, Element);

        {Check if element found}
        If (Element[ItemIndex] <> Item)
            Then Writeln ('Item not in array - deletion impossible')
            Else Begin
                {Shift subsequent elements down}
                For Index := ItemIndex To Number-1
                    Do Element[Index] := Element[Index+1];

                {Decrement Number by 1}
                Number := Number - 1

                End {Deletion of Item Completed}
    End {Delete} ;
```

With these pieces, we can present an outline for the entire editing process:

### Outline for Problem 8.6

**I.** Enter initial data:
  **A.** *Number* of items in array initially.

**B.** Initial *Items:*
   **1.** Read each *Item*.
   **2.** Place *Items* in array so result is ordered.

**II.** Edit data:
Repeat as long as insertions or deletions are required:
**A.** If insertion is desired, follow insertion outline.
**B.** If deletion is desired, follow deletion outline.

**III.** Print final array.

We leave the complete editing program based on this outline as an exercise and turn to another use of the insertion process.

### Insertion Sort

We can incorporate the insertion process into a sorting algorithm very easily for two arrays. We start with array *A* and end with array *B*, which contains the values from *A*, in order.

**Outline for Two-Array Insertion Sort.** The approach is very simple; start with elements *A*[1], . . ., *A*[*N*].

**I.** Put first element into array *B*, using the insertion algorithm. *Number* = 1 in array *B*, and *B*[1] := *A*[1].

**II.** Repeat for element *A*[2], *A*[3], . . ., *A*[*N*] (i.e., repeat for *I* := 2, 3, . . ., *N*):
**A.** Insert item *A*[*I*] into array *B* and increment *Number*.

This outline yields the following procedure:

```
Procedure InsertionSort (A: ArrayOfData; Var B: ArrayOfData);
{This procedure moves the elements of data from Array A
 to a sorted array B using an Insertion Sort}
    Var NumberInserted: Integer;    {Number of items inserted}
        I: Integer;             {Array subscript for insertion}

    Procedure Insert (Item: Data; Var Number: Integer; Var B: ArrayOfData);
    {This procedure inserts the specified Item into B}
        Var ItemIndex: Integer;     {Location of item on B}
            Index: Integer;         {Array subscript}

        Function ItemLocation (Item: Data; Number: Integer;
                               B: ArrayOfData): Integer;
        {This function searches for the Item on the B}
            Var First, Last: Integer;  {Binary Search of B[First] to B[Last]}
                Middle: Integer;  {the middle of our array}

            Begin
                If Item > B[Number]
                    Then ItemLocation := Number + 1
                    Else Begin {Binary Search}
                        {Initialize Search}
                        First := 1;
                        Last := Number;
```

```
                    {Perform search}
                    Repeat
                        Middle := (First + Last) Div 2;
                        If Item < B[Middle]
                            Then Last := Middle - 1
                            Else First := Middle + 1;
                    Until (Item = B[Middle]) Or (Last < First) ;

                    {Record where Item should be}
                    If (Item <= B[Middle])
                        Then ItemLocation := Middle
                        Else ItemLocation := Middle + 1
                End {Binary Search}

            End {ItemLocation} ;

        Begin
            {Find Where New Item Should Go}
            ItemIndex := ItemLocation (Item, Number, B);

            {Slide Subsequent Elements Down}
            For Index := Number DownTo ItemIndex
                Do B[Index+1] := B[Index];

            {Insert Item}
            B[ItemIndex] := Item;
            Number := Number + 1

        End {Insert} ;

    Begin {InsertionSort}
        {Insert First Element Into B}
        NumberInserted := 1;
        B[1] := A[1];

        {Insert subsequent elements}
        For I := 2 To Max
            Do Insert(A[I], NumberInserted, B)

    End {InsertionSort} ;
```

**Outline for One-Array Insertion Sort.** In each insertion step we add the element $A[I]$ into the array $B[1], \ldots, B[I-1]$ to get a new array $B[1], \ldots, B[I]$. If we store the value of $A[I]$ first, however, we do not actually need the array $B$ at all. The revised outline is as follows.

**I.** First element begins in place.
**II.** Repeat for $I := 2, \ldots, N$:
- **A.** Store value of $A[I]$:
  $Value := A[I]$
- **B.** Insert $Value$ into array $A[1], \ldots, A[I-1]$.

The revision of the two-array procedure to use just one array is left as an exercise.

### Observation for Problem Solving

In these examples, you can see illustrations of another general problem solving principle: Once you solve one problem (e.g., Binary Search or editing an array), you may find a similar idea applies elsewhere (e.g., inserting an element or sorting). If you have written a program with distinct procedures for solving one problem, you may be able to use the same procedures to solve other problems as well.

## SECTION 8.7 EXAMPLE: WAREHOUSE INVENTORY

In the previous sections, we used single subscripts to distinguish among various pieces of data. In this section, we consider a problem where a single subscript is not adequate for us to outline solutions easily.

**PROBLEM 8.7**

A manufacturer requires eight types of parts, which are stored in five warehouses. Table 8–3 shows the cost of each part and the inventory level of the various parts in the different warehouses.

**a.** Compute the total number of parts and the total cost of these parts in each warehouse.
**b.** Compute the total number of each type of part.

### Discussion of Problem 8.7

Table 8–3 contains two types of information, cost data and inventory levels. The table associates cost information with each type of part and organizes the inventory data in tabular form. Thus, to solve the problem, we want to think of cost data as depending upon part number, and we want to maintain the tabular form for inventory data.

To notate this data, we can use a single subscript for cost. $Cost_1$, $Cost_2$, . . ., $Cost_8$ can represent the costs of various parts, and we might use an array *Cost* to store the information. Considering the inventory ta-

**TABLE 8–3 • Warehouse Inventory**

| Part number | Part cost | Warehouse 1 | 2 | 3 | 4 | 5 |
|---|---|---|---|---|---|---|
| 1 | $1.25 | 3 | 1 | 4 | 1 | 5 |
| 2 | $3.37 | 9 | 2 | 6 | 5 | 3 |
| 3 | $0.79 | 5 | 8 | 9 | 7 | 9 |
| 4 | $4.73 | 3 | 2 | 3 | 8 | 4 |
| 5 | $1.97 | 6 | 2 | 6 | 4 | 3 |
| 6 | $0.67 | 3 | 8 | 3 | 2 | 7 |
| 7 | $2.29 | 9 | 5 | 0 | 2 | 8 |
| 8 | $3.85 | 8 | 4 | 1 | 9 | 7 |

ble, however, we need to know both the part number and the warehouse. We might notate this data with two subscripts, in the general form $Inventory_{Part,\ Warehouse}$ for the inventory of the particular part in the specified warehouse.

This representation of data allows us to work with our table directly. We can use this tabular form to guide our solution to the problem. In particular, we can find the total number of parts in a warehouse [part (a) of the problem] by adding down each column in the table. We can find the total number of each type of part [part (b)] by adding across each row. Here is the outline for this problem:

### Outline for Problem 8.7

**I.** Enter table information:
- **A.** Part costs.
- **B.** Inventory levels:
  - **1.** Read a row of inventories at a time, for the warehouse levels of a given part.

**II.** Compute totals for each warehouse:
- **A.** Print headings for warehouse totals.
- **B.** Repeat the following for each warehouse:
  - **1.** Totals start at 0:
    Number of parts := 0.
    Cost of parts := 0.
  - **2.** Add down the column for the warehouse for each type of part:
    - **a.** Add part inventory.
    - **b.** Add cost of part.
  - **3.** Print totals for each warehouse.

**III.** Compute totals for each part:
Repeat the following for each part:
- **A.** Totals start at 0:
  Part inventory := 0.
- **B.** Add across the row for the part.
  For each warehouse:
  - **1.** Add part inventory.
- **C.** Print total part inventory.

The addition process is similar to work we have done previously. It starts with *Sum* := 0, then we add successive numbers (down a column or across a row). A new feature is the use of two subscripts for referencing the inventory. The following program illustrates how to include double subscripts in Pascal code. Again, we use type statements so that we can specify that the procedure parameters are tables.

```
Program Inventory {Version 1} (Input, Output);
{This program reads part-warehouse information and
 computes and prints various totals.}
```

```
Const MaxPart = 8;      {Number of types of parts}
      MaxWare = 5;      {Number of warehouses}

Type CostArray = Array[1..MaxPart] of Real;
     Table = Array[1..MaxPart, 1..MaxWare] Of Integer;

Var Price: CostArray;
    InventoryLevel: Table;

Procedure EnterData (Var Cost: CostArray; Var Inventory: Table);
{Procedure to enter Part Costs and Inventory Levels}

    Var Part, Warehouse: Integer;  {Control Variables}

    Begin
        {Read Cost Information}
        Writeln ('Enter the cost of each type of part');
        For Part := 1 To MaxPart
          Do Begin
            Write ('Cost of Part Type ', Part:1, ': ');
            Readln (Cost[Part])
          End;

        {Read Inventory Levels one row at a time}
        For Part := 1 To MaxPart
          Do Begin
            Writeln ('Enter inventory levels for part type ',
                Part:1, ' for the ', MaxWare:1, ' warehouses');
            For Warehouse := 1 To MaxWare
                Do Read(Inventory[Part, Warehouse])
          End
    End {EnterData} ;

Procedure ComputeWarehouseTotals (Cost: CostArray; Inventory: Table);
{Procedure to compute number of parts in each warehouse and the
 total cost of those parts}

    Var Part, Warehouse: Integer;  {Control Variables}
        Number: Integer;    {Total number of parts for given warehouse}
        PCost: Real;        {Total cost of parts for warehouse}

    Begin
        {Print Warehouse Headings}
        Writeln;
        Writeln ('Warehouse Totals');
        Writeln;
        Writeln ('             Number     Cost');
        Writeln ('              of         of');
        Writeln ('Warehouse     Parts    Parts');
        Writeln;

        For Warehouse := 1 To MaxWare
          Do Begin

            {Totals start at 0}
            Number := 0;
            PCost := 0.0;
```

```
            {Add down columns of the table}
            For Part := 1 To MaxPart
              Do Begin
                Number := Number + Inventory[Part, Warehouse];
                PCost := PCost + Inventory[Part,Warehouse] * Cost[Part]
              End;

            {Print warehouse totals}
            Writeln (Warehouse:5, Number:11, PCost:11:2)

          End {Warehouse computation}

    End {ComputeWarehouseTotals} ;

Procedure ComputePartTotals (Inventory: Table);
{Procedure to compute to total number of each type of part}

    Var Part, Warehouse: Integer;  {Control Variables}
        Total: Integer;    {Total number of parts of given type}

    Begin
        Writeln;
        Writeln ('Part Totals');
        Writeln;

        For Part := 1 To MaxPart
          Do Begin
            Total := 0;

            {Add part inventories accross a row}
            For Warehouse := 1 To MaxWare
                Do Total := Total + Inventory[Part, Warehouse];

            {Print total}
            Writeln ('There are ', Total:1, ' parts of type ',
                Part:1, '.')

          End {Part computation}

    End {ComputePartTotals} ;

Begin {Main}
    Writeln ('This program computes various part-warehouse totals.');

    EnterData (Price, InventoryLevel);

    ComputeWarehouseTotals (Price, InventoryLevel);

    ComputePartTotals (InventoryLevel)

End {Main} .
```

When this program is run using the data from Table 8–3, we get the following results:

```
This program computes various part-warehouse totals.
Enter the cost of each type of part
Cost of Part Type 1: 1.25
Cost of Part Type 2: 3.37
Cost of Part Type 3: 0.79
Cost of Part Type 4: 4.73
Cost of Part Type 5: 1.97
Cost of Part Type 6: 0.67
Cost of Part Type 7: 2.29
Cost of Part Type 8: 3.85
Enter inventory levels for part type 1 for the 5 warehouses
3 1 4 1 5
Enter inventory levels for part type 2 for the 5 warehouses
9 2 6 5 3
Enter inventory levels for part type 3 for the 5 warehouses
5 8 9 7 9
Enter inventory levels for part type 4 for the 5 warehouses
3 2 3 8 4
Enter inventory levels for part type 5 for the 5 warehouses
6 2 6 4 3
Enter inventory levels for part type 6 for the 5 warehouses
3 8 3 2 7
Enter inventory levels for part type 7 for the 5 warehouses
9 5 0 2 8
Enter inventory levels for part type 8 for the 5 warehouses
8 4 1 9 7

Warehouse Totals

              Number      Cost
                of          of
Warehouse     Parts      Parts

    1          46       117.46
    2          32        59.92
    3          32        64.20
    4          38       109.92
    5          46        98.26

Part Totals

There are 14 parts of type 1.
There are 25 parts of type 2.
There are 38 parts of type 3.
There are 20 parts of type 4.
There are 21 parts of type 5.
There are 23 parts of type 6.
There are 24 parts of type 7.
There are 29 parts of type 8.
```

## SECTION 8.8 ELEMENTS OF ARRAYS (MULTIPLE SUBSCRIPTS)

With the inventory example in the previous section, we are ready to consider the use of two or more subscripts in Pascal more closely.

### Two Subscripts

The previous section illustrates one way that Pascal allows us to use multiple subscripts in programs. In the program, we declared

```
Var Inventory: Array[1. .MaxPart, 1. .MaxWare] of Integer;
```

Then we could refer to a particular entry in the table by writing *Inventory* [*7, 3*] or *Inventory* [*Part, Warehouse*].

More generally, we can declare an array

*Var* Name: *Array* [$Range_1$,$Range_2$] *of* DataType;

where *Name* is the variable name (or identifier) for the array; $Range_1$ specifies the possible values for the first subscript; $Range_2$ specifies the possible values for the second subscript; and *DataType* specifies the type of data stored in the array. In the example, we had the correspondences:

*Inventory—Name*
1. .*MaxPart—*$Range_1$
1. .*MaxWare—*$Range_2$
*Integer—DataType*

To refer to an item in the array, then, we specify the identifier *Name*, and we give the specific values for the subscripts in square brackets [ ]. Once we declare an array, we can solve problems by working with this table. This use of a table motivated the program in the previous section.

### Many Subscripts

In other problems, we may want more than two subscripts. For example, for weather forecasting we may want to record the temperature at various places on the earth and at various heights above the earth. Thus, we may want a temperature with subscripts for latitude, longitude, and height. If we measure latitude and longitude in tens of degrees and height in thousands of feet above the earth, then we might declare

```
Var Temp: Array[0. .18, 0. .36, 0. .10] of Real;
```

We can refer to the temperature at latitude 20°, longitude 50°, height 10,000 feet by *Temp*[*2, 5, 10*].

In fact, Pascal allows us to use as many subscripts as we wish in arrays. In this general setting, declarations have the form

*Var* Name: *Array* [$Range_1$,. . ., $Range_n$] *of* DataType;

In this declaration, we specify the name of the array and the subscripts allowed. For each subscript we state the type of subscript (e.g., integer, Boolean) and the range of values (e.g., 0. .10, *False*. .*True*). We also specify the DataType being stored in the array (e.g., real temperature values). When we want to use the data, we can refer to particular items by specifying the array name and the appropriate subscript values.

While Pascal does not limit the number of subscripts available, in practice, particular compilers may have some limitations. Most compilers will allow several subscripts (up to 6 or 7), but they may not be able to work with more levels of subscripts. (We may have trouble with that many subscripts as well!)

## Two Views

At this point in our discussion of subscripting, we have implicitly assumed one of two views of data. We can think of data as a whole (e.g., the entire table of inventories or an entire set of temperature readings), or we can focus on one particular piece of data (e.g., *Inventory*[7,3] or *Temp*[2,5,3]). Section 8.4 illustrated how a *Type* statement can support a view of data as a whole, defining a new type that is an entire array. We can then work with that array as a single entity when making assignments and when passing parameters.

Similar comments apply to using tables; we can use a *Type* statement to define a table as a separate entity. Thus, in the inventory program in Section 8.7, we wrote

```
Type Table = Array[1. .MaxPart, 1. .MaxWare] of Integer;
Var Inventory: Table;
```

Here, we view our table of inventories as a single object, and we can work with the entire table. If we also declared

```
Var NewItems: Table;
```

we could set one table equal to the other by writing

```
NewItems := Inventory
```

Similarly, we could use a table as a parameter for procedures and functions.

## More Views of Data

This two-level view of arrays (entire array and specific array elements) often is quite adequate for many applications, particularly when you only want one subscript. We may find, however, that some intermediate views can also be helpful when considering tables (or several subscripts.) For example, in the inventory problem we may want to focus on the rows of the table, or on the columns.

In Pascal, the *Type* statement allows us to work with some of these intermediate views. For example, when we viewed the table of inventories as a whole, we wrote

```
Type Table = Array[1. .MaxPart, 1. .MaxWare] of Integer;
Var Inventory: Table;
```

Alternately, we could think of the table as being made up of rows, with one row for each type of part. In this case, we could write

```
Type PartTotals = Array[1. .MaxWare] of Integer;
     Table = Array[1. .MaxPart] of PartTotals;
Var  Inventory: Table;
```

Here, we have the same choices for arrays with several subscripts that we had in the previous chapter, for arrays with one subscript. We can work with any array as a complete collection of data, and we can reference individual items. For example, after writing

```
NewItems := Inventory
```

we can print a specific item in the table, such as

```
Writeln (NewItems[7, 3]);
```

With these declarations we could also consider the inventory levels for Part 1 or Part 2. When we focus on the inventory for a specific part, we use one row of the table. With this view of our data, we could write *Inventory* [1] to stand for the entire row for PartType 1. *Inventory* [1] represents the row:

3 1 4 1 5

Thus, *Inventory* [1] is an array with five elements. More precisely, *Inventory* [1] has the data type *PartTotals*, which we declared as

```
PartTotals = Array[1. .MaxWare] of Integer;
```

Within this row, we can ask about the third piece of data (the inventory for Warehouse 3). To be more precise, we ask about element [3] in *Inventory* [1], and we write *Inventory* [1] [3]. Alternatively, Pascal allows us to simplify the notation, omitting the middle brackets, so we can write this as *Inventory* [1, 3].

With these declarations, then, we can view our data in three ways:

*Inventory* represents the entire table.

*Inventory*[7] represents the seventh row of the table.

*Inventory*[7, 3] or *Inventory*[7][3] represents the element in the third column of row seven.

As an illustration of these views of our data, we have rewritten the inventory program with these alternate declarations of Type *Table* and Array *Inventory*. In the first part of the program, we still enter the data with two subscripts, just as we did earlier. In Step II, to work with columns, we can still proceed by referring to each item in a given column. In Step III, however, we use a row as a separate entity, and we pass each row of the table to a procedure to compute and print the totals.

```
Program Inventory {Version 2} (Input, Output);
{This program reads part-warehouse information and
 computes and prints various totals.}

Const MaxPart = 8;      {Number of types of parts}
      MaxWare = 5;      {Number of warehouses}

Type CostArray = Array [1..MaxPart] of Real;
     PartTotals = Array[1..MaxWare] Of Integer;
     Table = Array [1..MaxPart] Of PartTotals;

Var Price: CostArray;
    InventoryLevel: Table;

Procedure EnterData (Var Cost: CostArray; Var Inventory: Table);
{Procedure to enter Part Costs and Inventory Levels}

    Var Part, Warehouse: Integer;  {Control Variables}

    Begin
        {Read Cost Information}
        Writeln ('Enter the cost of each type of part');
        For Part := 1 To MaxPart
          Do Begin
            Write ('Cost of Part Type ', Part:1, ': ');
            Readln (Cost[Part])
          End;

        {Read Inventory Levels one row at a time}
        For Part := 1 To MaxPart
          Do Begin
            Writeln ('Enter inventory levels for part type ',
                Part:1, ' for the ', MaxWare:1, ' warehouses');
            For Warehouse := 1 To MaxWare
                Do Read(Inventory[Part, Warehouse])
          End
    End {EnterData} ;

Procedure ComputeWarehouseTotals (Cost: CostArray; Inventory: Table);
{Procedure to compute number of parts in each warehouse and the
 total cost of those parts}

    Var Part, Warehouse: Integer;  {Control Variables}
        Number: Integer;    {Total number of parts for given warehouse}
        PCost: Real;        {Total cost of parts for warehouse}

    Begin
        {Print Warehouse Headings}
        Writeln;
        Writeln ('Warehouse Totals');
        Writeln;
        Writeln ('              Number     Cost');
        Writeln ('                of        of');
        Writeln ('Warehouse     Parts     Parts');
        Writeln;
```

```
        For Warehouse := 1 To MaxWare
          Do Begin

            {Totals start at 0}
            Number := 0;
            PCost := 0.0;

            {Add down columns of the table}
            For Part := 1 To MaxPart
              Do Begin
                Number := Number + Inventory[Part, Warehouse];
                PCost := PCost + Inventory[Part,Warehouse] * Cost[Part]
              End;

            {Print warehouse totals}
            Writeln (Warehouse:5, Number:11, PCost:11:2)

          End {Warehouse computation}

    End {ComputeWarehouseTotals} ;

Procedure TypeTotal (Row: PartTotals; PartNumber: Integer);
{This procedure computes the total number of parts,
 given the inventory levels in each warehouse.}

    Var Warehouse: Integer;   {Control Variable for Warehouse}
        Total: Integer;       {Part total for the given type}

    Begin
       Total := 0;

        {Add part inventories accross a row}
        For Warehouse := 1 To MaxWare
            Do Total := Total + Row[Warehouse];

        {Print total}
        Writeln ('There are ', Total:1, ' parts of type ',
            PartNumber:1, '.')

    End {TypeTotal} ;

Procedure ComputePartTotals (Inventory: Table);
{Procedure to compute to total number of each type of part}

    Var Part: Integer;     {Control Variable for Part Type}

    Begin
        Writeln;
        Writeln ('Part Totals');
        Writeln;

        For Part := 1 To MaxPart
          Do TypeTotal(Inventory[Part], Part)

    End {ComputePartTotals} ;
```

```
Begin {Main}
    Writeln ('This program computes various part-warehouse totals.');

    EnterData (Price, InventoryLevel);

    ComputeWarehouseTotals (Price, InventoryLevel);

    ComputePartTotals (InventoryLevel)

End {Main} .
```

This program follows the same outline as the example in Section 8.7 and produces identical output, but it illustrates how to work with rows of a table, as well as with individual elements.

We can make one additional observation. Pascal allowed us to define a row *PartTotals* and then put these rows together to get an entire table. Once we work with rows, however, we have no mechanism to work with columns at the same time. Pascal does not allow us to consider both rows and columns of the same table in a program. If we decide *Inventory*[2] will represent a row of the table, we cannot decide that this symbol will also represent a column later on.

In the next section we will look at another example involving several subscripts.

## SECTION 8.9 EXAMPLE: STORING GAME BOARDS AND MAPS

Multiple subscripting can be useful in a great many applications. In this section, we consider an example of storing data on game boards or maps. To be concrete, we focus on the game of Tic-Tac-Toe.

## PROBLEM 8.9 Tic-Tac-Toe

Two people play Tic-Tac-Toe, alternately writing Xs and Os on a game board. Write a program that reads successive moves, prints out the board after each move, and stops either when one player wins or when all squares are filled.

### Discussion of Problem 8.9

When we picture a Tic-Tac-Toe board (Figure 8–4), we can identify three rows and three columns. Thus, we can consider the board as a 3-by-3 table or array. The upper right square would be in Row 1, Column 3, and we might refer to the element *Board*[1, 3].

For each square we can identify three possible situations: The square could be blank; the square could contain an X; or the square could contain

FIGURE 8–4 • **A Tic-Tac-Toe Board with Labeled Rows and Columns**

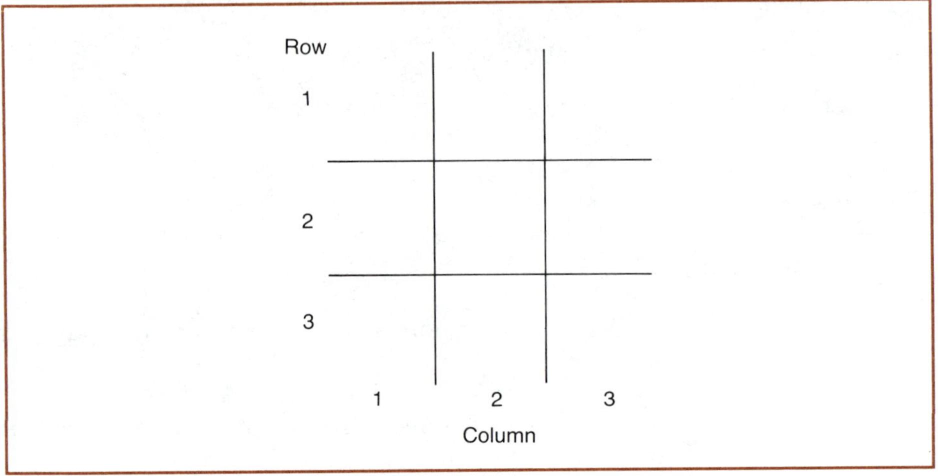


an O. For convenience, we will code these choices as integer constants as follows:

| *Square* | *Code* |
|---|---|
| X | −1 |
| blank | 0 |
| O | 1 |

A game is won when there are all Xs or all Os in a row, in a column, or on a diagonal. With our coding, this says that a game is won when the sum of the entries in a row, a column, or a diagonal is +3 or −3. Thus, after each play, we could find the sum of each row, each column and each diagonal. If any of these sums is +3 or −3, then the game is over.

To check for a win after each move, we can reduce our work considerably by some additional analysis. When we write an X or an O, we will change only the row and the column that contain this move. Other rows and columns are not affected.

We can check if the move is on a diagonal by carefully analyzing the square (see Figure 8–5). Row = Column means the square is on the diagonal moving down to the right. Row + Column = 4 means the square is on the diagonal moving up to the right.

Finally, note that after nine moves the game must be done, since the board contains only nine squares.

## Outline for Problem 8.9

**I.** Initialize board:
- **A.** All squares are blank.
- **B.** Number of moves is 0.
- **C.** Neither side has won.
- **D.** X will play first.

FIGURE 8–5 • **A Tic-Tac-Toe Board with Diagonals Analyzed**

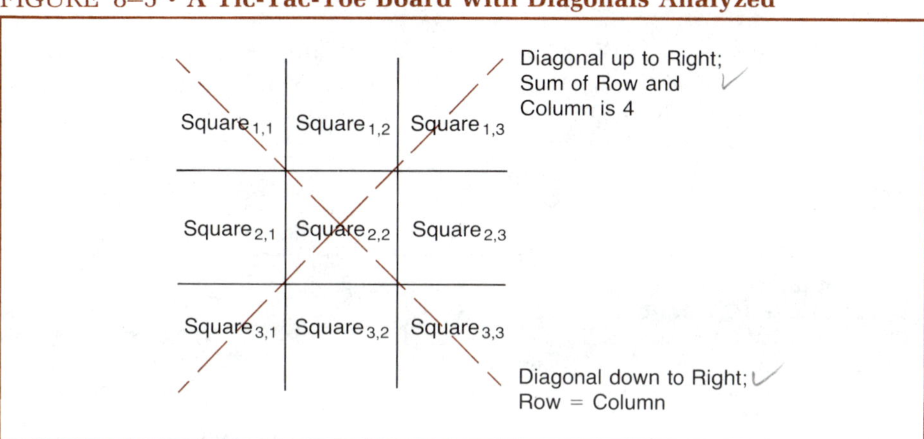


**II.** Repeat the following for each move until one side wins or until all nine squares are filled:
- **A.** Read move (row and column).
  1. Increase number of moves by one.
  2. Check move is legal (check that row and column are on board; check that square was blank).
  3. Record move.
- **B.** Print revised board:
  1. Print board, one row at a time.
  2. Print dashes between rows.
- **C.** Check if game is won.
- **D.** Other player will move next.

**III.** Record outcome of game:
Either X wins, O wins, or there is a draw.

## Checking User Input

Before we write the program based on this outline, we note a special feature in reading data, which we have not seen before. In reading a move, we can check the input to see if the move is legal. In particular, we can check that the row is 1, 2, or 3; the column is 1, 2, or 3; and the square chosen is blank. If any of these conditions is violated, then the information entered cannot be correct, and we can ask the user to correct the data.

This is a specific example of a general principle, which we can incorporate into many programs. When we ask a user to enter data, we should try to determine if the data are reasonable. Unreasonable data may indicate a typographical error. When requesting data, we should allow for the possibility of error, and we should plan how the program will respond to incorrect information.

In the present program, we ask the user to retype data that are obviously wrong. In other programs, we might allow the user to modify all or part of the data before continuing, or we might require the user to run the program all over again.

We now write the program based on the outline. Note how it tests data for a legal move. Note also that it uses a Boolean variable *PlayerXMoves* to indicate if X moves next or not.

```
Program PlayTicTacToe (Input, Output);
{This program reads moves in Tic-Tac-Toe,
 prints out the board after each move, and
 stops when either one player wins or
       when all squares are filled.}

Const X = -1;          {our code for the play "X"}
      O = 1;           {our code for the play "O"}
      Blank = 0;       {our code for a blank square}

Type RowOfBoard = Array [1..3] Of Integer;
    GameBoard = Array[1..3] Of RowOfBoard;

Var Board: GameBoard;             {the game board}
    XWins, OWins: Boolean;        {Record of the winner}
    PlayerXMoves: Boolean;        {True if "X" moves next}
    Moves: Integer;               {Number of moves in the game}

Procedure InitializeBoard (Var Board: GameBoard; Var Moves: Integer;
                          Var XWins, OWins, XMoves: Boolean);
{This procedure sets up the board and initializes variables}
    Var Row, Col: Integer;
    Begin
        {Each square is blank}
        For Row := 1 to 3
            Do For Col := 1 to 3
                Do Board[Row, Col] := Blank;

        {No moves so far}
        Moves := 0;

        {Neither side has won}
        XWins := False;
        OWins := False;

        {"X" will play first}
        XMoves := True;

    End {InitializeBoard} ;

Procedure ReadMove (Var Moves, Row, Col: Integer; XMoves: Boolean;
                   Var Board: GameBoard);
{This procedure reads a legal move from the terminal}
    Var Legal: Boolean;
```

```
    Begin
        Moves := Moves + 1;
        If XMoves
            Then Writeln ('X moves next')
            Else Writeln ('O moves next');
        Writeln ('Enter row and column for move ', Moves:1);

        {Read until a legal move is entered}
        Repeat
            Read (Row, Col);

            {Determine if move is legal}
            Legal := (1 <= Row) And (Row <= 3) And
                     (1 <= Col) And (Col <= 3);
            If Legal
                Then Legal := (Board[Row, Col] = Blank);
            If Not Legal
                Then Writeln ('Move is not valid,',
                              ' please re-enter row and column')
        Until Legal;

        {Record move}
        If XMoves
            Then Board[Row, Col] := X
            Else Board[Row, Col] := O

    End {ReadMove} ;

Procedure PrintSquare (Square:Integer);
{Procedure prints the given square of the board}
    Begin
        If Square = X
            Then Write ('  X  ');
        If Square = O
            Then Write ('  O  ');
        If Square = Blank
            Then Write ('     ')
    End {PrintSquare} ;

Procedure PrintRow (Row: RowOfBoard);
{Procedure prints the specified row of the board}

    Begin {PrintRow}
        Writeln ('     ¦     ¦');

        {Print each square in the row}
        PrintSquare (Row[1]);
        Write ('¦');
        PrintSquare(Row[2]);
        Write ('¦');
        PrintSquare(Row[3]);
        Writeln;

        Writeln ('     ¦     ¦');
    End {PrintRow} ;
```

```
Procedure PrintBoard (Moves: Integer; Board: GameBoard);
{Procedure prints the Tic-Tac-Toe Board}

    Begin {PrintBoard}
        Writeln;
        Writeln ('Board position after move', Moves:2);
        Writeln;

       PrintRow(Board[1]);
       Writeln ('-----+-----+-----');
       PrintRow(Board[2]);
       Writeln ('-----+-----+-----');
       PrintRow(Board[3]);

       Writeln
    End {PrintBoard} ;

Procedure Check (Code: Integer; Var XWins, OWins: Boolean);
{Procedure checks if Code gives a win for X or for O}
    Begin
       If Code = -3
           Then XWins := True;
       If Code = 3
           Then OWins := True
    End {CheckForWin} ;

Procedure CheckForWin (Var XWins, YWins: Boolean; Board: GameBoard;
                       NRow, NCol: Integer);
{This procedure checks to see if the latest move has causes
 either player X or player O to win}
    Begin {CheckForWin}
        {Check row for possible win}
        Check(Board[NRow,1] + Board[NRow,2] + Board[NRow,3], XWins, OWins);

        {Check column for possible win}
        Check(Board[1,NCol] + Board[2,NCol] + Board[3,NCol], XWins, OWins);

        {Check diagonals, if appropriate}
        If NRow = NCol
            Then Check(Board[1,1] + Board[2,2] + Board[3,3], XWins, OWins);
        If (NRow + NCol = 4)
            Then Check(Board[1,3] + Board[2,2] + Board[3,1], XWins, OWins)
    End {CheckForWin} ;

Procedure PlayGame (Var Board: GameBoard; Var Moves: Integer;
                    Var XWins, OWins, PlayerXMoves: Boolean);

{This procedure plays Tic-Tac-Toe, reading successive moves
 from the terminal}
    Var NewRow, NewCol: Integer;  {The square for the new move}


    Begin {Playgame}
        Repeat
            ReadMove (Moves, NewRow, NewCol, PlayerXMoves, Board);
            PrintBoard (Moves, Board);
            CheckForWin (Xwins, OWins, Board, NewRow, NewCol);
```

```
            {Note other player moves next}
            PlayerXMoves := Not PlayerXMoves
        Until XWins Or OWins Or (Moves = 9)
    End {PlayGame} ;

Procedure CheckGameOutcome (XWins, OWins: Boolean);
{This procedure prints the final outcome of the game}
    Begin
        If XWins
            Then Writeln('"X" has won the game');
        If OWins
            Then Writeln('"O" has won the game');
        If Not(XWins or OWins)
            Then Writeln('The game ends in a draw')
    End {CheckGameOutcome} ;

Begin {Main}
    Writeln ('This program records the moves in a game of Tic-Tac-Toe');
    InitializeBoard (Board, Moves, XWins, OWins, PlayerXMoves);
    PlayGame (Board, Moves, XWins, OWins, PlayerXMoves);
    CheckGameOutcome (XWins, OWins)
End {Main} .
```

Note how the various parts of the outline are coded concisely as procedures, and how the program is divided into simple, modular procedures. While this program is somewhat long, each module is very easy to check; this program ran correctly the first time it was compiled!

A sample game is shown below:

```
This program records the moves in a game of Tic-Tac-Toe
X moves next
Enter row and column for move 1
1 1

Board position after move 1

     |     |
  X  |     |
     |     |
-----+-----+-----
     |     |
     |     |
     |     |
-----+-----+-----
     |     |
     |     |
     |     |

O moves next
Enter row and column for move 2
2 1
```

```
Board position after move 2
```

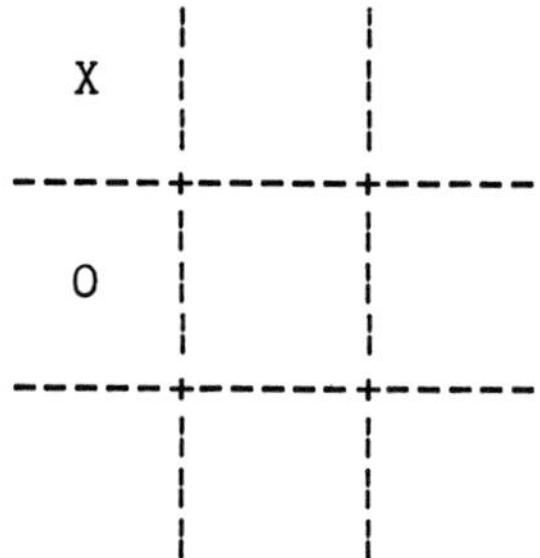

```
X moves next
Enter row and column for move 3
2 2

Board position after move 3
```

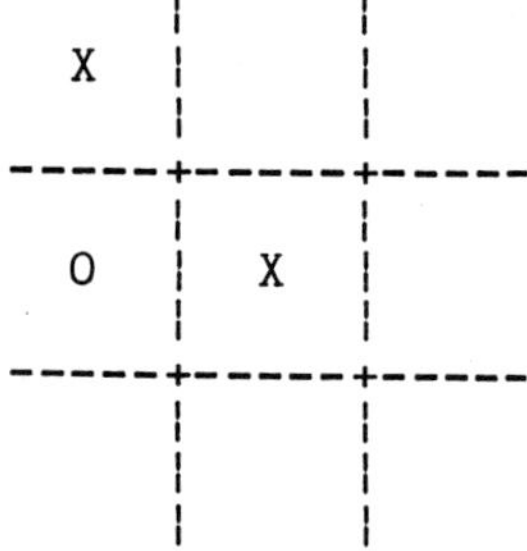

```
O moves next
Enter row and column for move 4
3 3

Board position after move 4
```

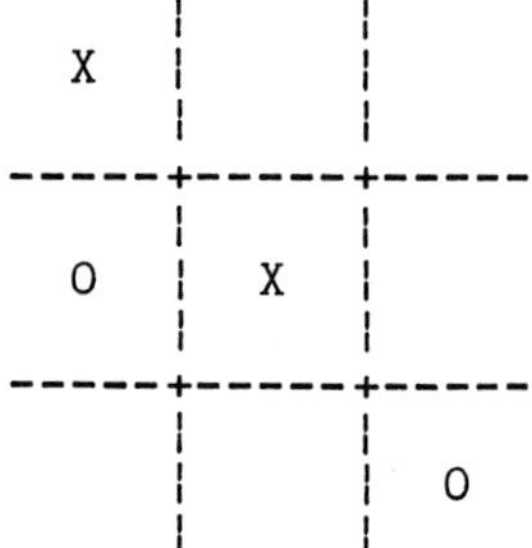

```
X moves next
Enter row and column for move 5
1 3
```

```
Board position after move 5

     |     |
  X  |     |  X
     |     |
-----+-----+-----
     |     |
  O  |  X  |
     |     |
-----+-----+-----
     |     |
     |     |  O
     |     |

O moves next
Enter row and column for move 6
3 1

Board position after move 6
```

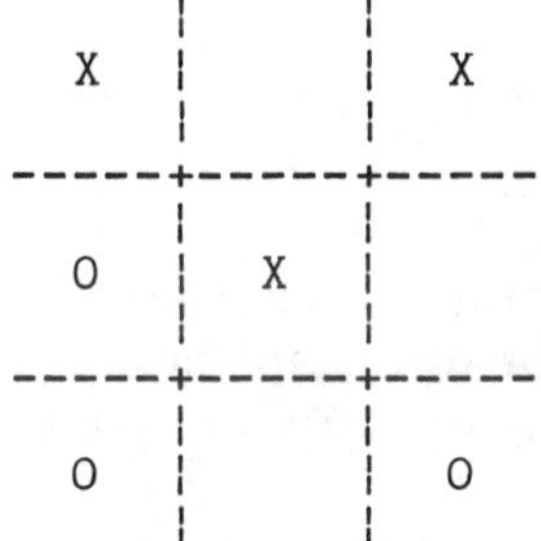

```
X moves next
Enter row and column for move 7
1 1
Move is not valid, please re-enter row and column
1 2

Board position after move 7

     |     |
  X  |  X  |  X
     |     |
-----+-----+-----
     |     |
  O  |  X  |
     |     |
-----+-----+-----
     |     |
  O  |     |  O
     |     |

"X" has won the game
```

This Tic-Tac-Toe problem shows how to use an array with two subscripts to record information about a game board. A similar approach could be used to record information on a map, where *Map[Lat, Long]* represents the elevation (or temperature, or rainfall, etc.) at the given latitude and longitude.

## SUMMARY

1. **Arrays** allow you to use subscripts to help solve problems that require you to keep track of many pieces of data at once.
2. To use subscripted variables, declare the name of the array, the type of subscript and the range of values allowed, and the type of data stored in the array. With this declaration the computer can allocate the appropriate storage space in main memory to store the data.
3. Once arrays are declared, you can work with them on several levels, including
   a. individual array elements, e. g., *Table* [7, 3].
   b. entire arrays as whole, e. g., *BoxScores* := *Table*.
   c. parts of arrays, e. g., row 7 of Table by writing *Table*[7].
4. Arrays may be used in two ways: Individual elements in the array may be referenced by placing the appropriate subscript in square brackets [ ]. The entire array may be considered as a single entity for assignments and for parameter passage.
5. You can define your own type of data with a ***Type* statement.** Use a *Type* statement to declare several variables or parameters to have the same type.

| KEY TERMS, PHRASES, AND CONCEPTS | | ELEMENTS OF PASCAL SYNTAX | |
|---|---|---|---|
| Array<br>  Declarations<br>  As Parameter<br>  Use for Data<br>    Storage and<br>    Retrieval<br>Array Manipulation<br>  Data Deletion<br>  Data Insertion<br>Checking User Input<br>Data in Tabular Form | Insertion Sort<br>Searching Algorithms<br>  Binary<br>  Linear (or Sequential)<br>Subscript<br>  Multiple Subscripts<br>  Single Subscripts<br>Type Specification<br>User Defined Types | *Array* [. . .] *of Type*<br>Subscript [ ] | User Defined *Type*<br>*Type* |

6. Several common applications of arrays with single subscripts include **searching** through an array of data to find a particular item and **sorting** a set of data to put the data in order. Particular algorithms introduced include a **Linear** or **Sequential Search,** a **Binary Search,** and the **Insertion Sort.**
7. Several common applications of arrays with more than one subscript include recording inventory of warehouses, positions on a game board, and features on a map.
8. Once you have developed an algorithm to perform a task, you can analyze the algorithm to evaluate its **efficiency.**

## EXERCISES

**8.1** *Modified Linear Search.* Modify the Linear Search program of Section 8.3 so that the computer prints where the item is in the array in the case that the element is found.
(*Hint:* Determine the array subscript where the item is located.)

**8.2** The Linear Search program of Section 8.3 is written assuming that the data are not ordered.

a. How could the program be improved if the data can be assumed to be sorted?

b. Analyze the efficiency of your improved linear search, determining (on the average) how many steps or comparisons are needed to find an element in the array and how many steps are needed to conclude an element is not present.

(*Hint:* For a sorted array, we do not always have to search to the end of an array.)

**8.3** The Binary-Search Insert procedure of Section 8.6 fails if the array contains no elements (i. e. *Number* = 0), since in the initial test

```
Item > Element[Number]
```

the subscript of *Element* is not between 1 and Max. Correct this insert procedure to allow for this special case.

**8.4** Throughout Section 8.6, a *Type* statement is used to specify the form of data under consideration in our array. Discuss why you think this approach is used.

**8.5** *One Array Insertion Sort.* Modify the Insertion Sort program in Section 8.6 so that only one array is used.

**8.6** *Counting Repetitions.* Write a program that reads 20 integers into an array and then prints the distinct integers together with the number of times each integer appears. For example, if the initial data were

3, 1, 4, 1, 5, 9, 2, 6, 5, 3, 5, 8, 9, 7, 9, 3, 2, 3, 8, 4

then the output might be

| Element | Number of Occurrences |
|---|---|
| 0 | 0 |
| 1 | 2 |
| 2 | 2 |
| 3 | 4 |
| 4 | 2 |
| 5 | 3 |
| 6 | 1 |
| 7 | 1 |
| 8 | 2 |
| 9 | 3 |

**8.7** *Comparing Linear and Binary Searches.* Write a program that uses both Linear and Binary Searches to find elements in an array of data. Have your program count the number of iterations required to find the desired item or to conclude the element is missing.

Use an initialization procedure to establish the original array. Run your program on sorted data containing at least 100 items (e.g., *For I* := 1 *To N Do A*[*I*] := 2*I). Choose a variety of items to search for.

Compare your results (by hand).

**8.8** *Sieve of Eratosthenes.* In ancient Greece, Eratosthenes gave the following algorithm for determining all prime numbers up to a specified number *M*:

**I.** Write down the numbers 2, 3, . . ., *M*.
**II.** Cross out numbers as follows:
  **A.** Keep 2, but cross out all multiples of 2 (i.e., cross out 4, 6, 8 . . .).
  **B.** Keep 3, but cross out all multiples of 3 (i.e., 6, 9, . . .)
  NOTE: While 6 is crossed out twice, it only matters that it has been crossed out. We will attach no significance to the number of times the 6 is crossed out.
  **C.** Since 4 is already crossed out, go on to the next number that is not crossed out (i.e., 5). Keep 5, but cross out all multiples of 5 (i.e., 10, 15, . . .).

*General Step.* In general, suppose you have just processed the number *P*. Go on to the next number that is not crossed out—*Q*.
Keep *Q*, but cross out all multiples of *Q*.
After you have finished all the crossing out, the numbers remaining are primes.

This method is called the **Sieve Method of Eratosthenes.** Write a program to implement this method, where *M* is a constant defined in the program. Run your program for *M* = 100 and *M* = 500.

*Programming Hints.* Use an array

```
Var Keep: Array [2. .M] of Boolean
```

to record which elements are still kept and which are crossed out.

Begin with each *Keep[I] set equal to True.* When you cross out the number *I*, set *Keep[I]* to *False.*

**8.9** *Tabulating Polynomial Functions.* Polynomial functions are often written in the form

$$p(x) = a_n x^n + a_{n-1} x^{n-1} + \cdots + a_2 x^2 + a_1 x + a_0.$$

Write a program that reads the coefficients $a_n, a_{n-1}, \ldots, a_2, a_1, a_0$ and then uses these coefficients to compute $p(x)$ for $x = 0, 0.5, 1, 1.5, 2.0, \ldots, 10$.

NOTE: One efficient way to compute $p(x)$ without using powers is to use algebra to rewrite the polynomial. Here are two examples of the general technique:

$$\begin{aligned} 2x^3 - 3x^2 + 5x - 6 &= x(2x^2 - 3x + 5) - 6 \\ &= x[x(2x - 3) + 5] - 6. \end{aligned}$$

$$\begin{aligned} a_4x^4 + a_3x^3 + a_2x^2 + a_1x + a_0 &= x(a_4x^3 + a_3x^2 + a_2x + a_1) + a_0 \\ &= x[x(a_4x^2 + a_3x + a_2) + a_1] + a_0 \\ &= x\{x[x\,(a_4x + a_3) + a_2] + a_1\} \\ &\quad + a_0. \end{aligned}$$

*Optional Problems.* This general factoring approach is called **Horner's method.** This approach is quite efficient for evaluating general polynomials.

**a.** Find the general formula to compute $p(x)$ using this factoring process, and incorporate this approach in your program.

**b.** Determine the number of additions and multiplications required to compute $p(x)$ using Horner's method.

**8.10** *Baseball League Standings.* In a baseball league, we want to record team standings in a table such as that shown below:

| Team | Wins | Losses | Total | Games | Percentage Wins |
|---|---|---|---|---|---|

For simplicity, we will assume teams are numbered 1, 2,. . . .

**a.** Write a program that will read the team number and the number of wins and losses, and then will fill out the table.

**b.** (Optional) Expand the program in part (a) so the ranking of the teams is also computed and printed. Add a column to the table for this ranking.

**c.** (Optional) Modify your program in part (a) so the teams are printed out in the order of their league ranking, with the best team in the league printed first.

*Hint:* For parts (b) and (c) you might want to use a sorting algorithm on the rows of the table, with order determined by percentage wins.

**8.11** *Three-Dimensional Tic-Tac-Toe.* Three-dimensional Tic-Tac-Toe is a generalization of Tic-Tac-Toe to three dimensions. The board consists of four layers, each of which is 4-by-4, and we think of the layers being stacked on top of each other to form a cube (see Figure 8–6).

As in conventional Tic-Tac-Toe, two players alternately play Xs and Os until one player gets four in a row (horizontally on one layer, vertically through all four layers, diagonally on one layer, or diagonally through all four layers). If all squares become filled with no winner, the game ends in a draw.

Write a program generalizing this problem to read successive moves from this three-dimensional game and to stop when one player wins or when all "squares" are filled.

**8.12** *Storing Maps.* Information from a map can be stored in a table by introducing a grid system (e.g., latitude and longitude). For example, Figure 8–7 shows various elevations on an island at each point on a

FIGURE 8–6 • **A Board for Three-Dimensional Tic-Tac-Toe**

Layer 1

Layer 2

Layer 3

Layer 4

Board "Cube"

Layer 1
Layer 2
Layer 3
Layer 4

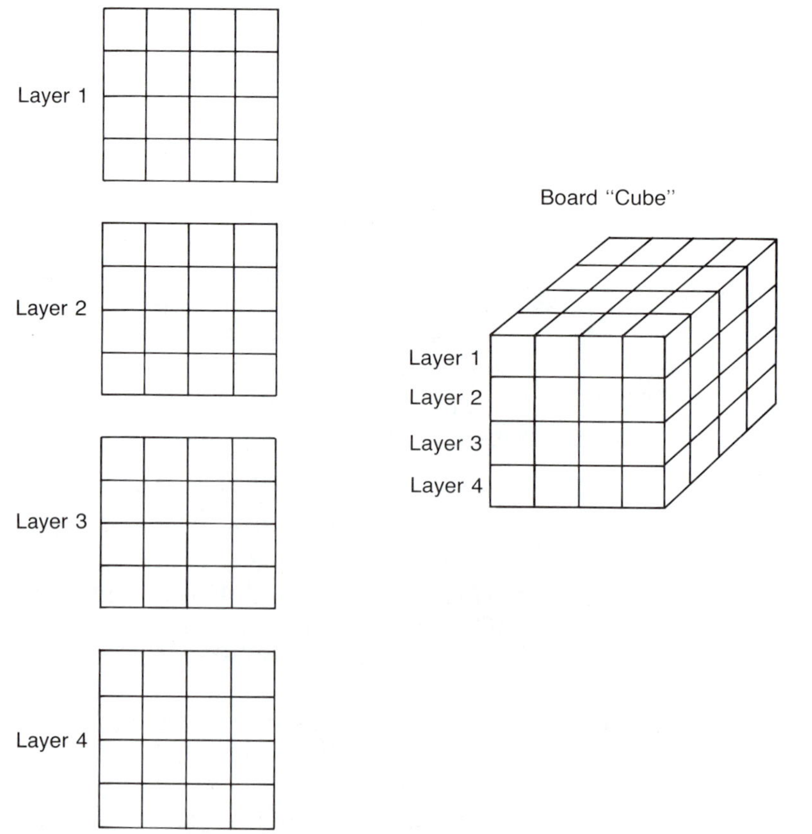

FIGURE 8–7 • **Elevations on an Island (in Feet)**

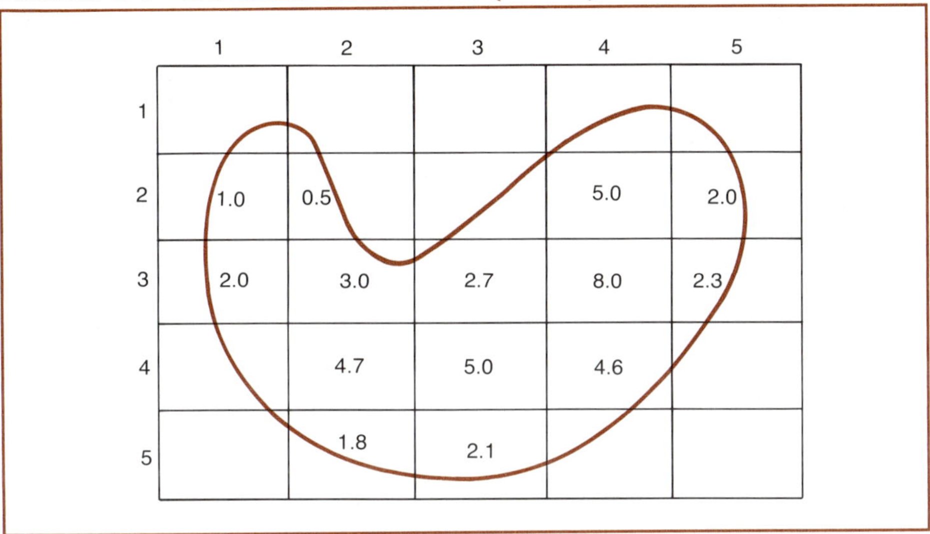


5-by-5 grid. (Places off the island are in the water and so have an elevation of 0 feet above sea level.)

**a.** Write a program that reads this elevation information into an appropriate table.

**b.** Compute the grid coordinates for the highest point on the island.

**c.** Find the average height on the island. (Do not count height 0 in the average, as that height is in the water.)

**d.** Given a point on the island, find the nearest adjacent location on the island of minimum height. [For example, in the figure the lowest spot adjacent location (3,4) is a height of 2.0 feet at location (2,5).]

**8.13** *Play Selection.* In football, a defense often will try to anticipate what play the opposing offense will run next. While this guessing of the next play can involve a very sophisticated analysis of many details, we can suggest some basic ideas here. First, we number each of the plays that the opponent might try. (For example, play 43 might be a run up the middle by the fullback.) Then we review previous games by recording the down, yards to go, and play number for each play. Next we tabulate how many times each play was run in each situation. (For example, we may find that play 43 was tried in 18 of 22 times when it was third down and less than 3 yards to go.) Write a program that

**a.** reads the play selection information for all previous games.

**b.** prints all plays run for each down according to these yards categories:

- less than 3 yards to go

- 3 to 6 yards to go
- 7 to 10 yards to go
- over 10 yards to go

(After each play, write the number of times it was run.)

c. prints the five most common plays for each down and yardage category.

NOTES:

1. Your program should check the data input when possible.
2. Your program should not assume that all categories will be represented in the data. (For example, we may never see a first down with less than 3 yards to go.)

# CHAPTER 9

# PROCEDURES AND FUNCTIONS (REVISITED)

Throughout this book, we solve problems by breaking them down into pieces, and we structure our programs according to these logical pieces using procedures and functions. Further, in declaring procedures, we use reference and value parameters to move information both in and out of those procedures.

In this chapter we re-examine our use of parameters and local and global variables, and we identify a wide variety of situations that can occur. Then, we consider how functions and procedures can be placed inside of each other. With this discussion we will be able to develop guidelines for structuring programs so we can use these capabilities while minimizing the likelihood of introducing errors into our programs.

## SECTION 9.1 VALUE AND REFERENCE PARAMETERS

To begin, we need to look at procedures and function parameters more closely, so we can understand the difference between value parameters and reference parameters more clearly.

### Parameter Passage by Value

When we pass information into procedures or functions using parameters, we normally have declared parameters by specifying indentifiers and their types (omitting an initial keyword *Var*). More formally, this connection between an actual parameter and a formal parameter is called **parameter passage by value** and has the following characteristics.

1. When a procedure or function is called, a new storage location is created for the formal parameter.
2. The value of the actual parameter is copied into this new address.
3. After this copying, the actual parameter and the formal parameter are considered separate, unrelated entities. Either of these can be changed without changing the other.
4. When the procedure or function ends, the storage location for the formal parameter is ignored in future work. Only the actual parameter remains.

With this form of parameter passage, we cannot use these parameters to return new values. In a procedure, formal parameters have their own storage locations, which are unrelated to any global variables. Thus, while we can store values in locations allocated to our formal parameters, all of these values are lost when the procedure finishes.

### Parameter Passage by Reference

In contrast, when we add the keyword *Var* to our parameter declaration, we maintain a tie between the actual and formal parameters, and we can use this **Parameter Passage by Reference** to get data out of a procedure. This parameter passage has the following characteristics.

1. When a procedure or function is called, a new storage location is created for the formal parameter.
2. This new location is used to store the address of the actual parameter.
3. All subsequent uses of the formal parameter then refer back to the address of the actual parameter. Thus, a reference to either the formal or the actual parameter involves the data stored for the actual parameter.
4. When the procedure or function ends, the storage location for the formal parameter is ignored in the future, but any changes in the actual parameter remain.

To clarify the distinction between these two types of parameters further, we consider the following example. (Here, we have added line numbers along the left-hand side for future reference.)

```
 Line
Number    Program Listing

   1      Program Parameter (Output);
   2      {A value is passed into a procedure, but nothing is returned.}
   3
```

```
 4      Var A :Integer;
 5
 6      Procedure InAndOut (Var X: Integer);
 7          Begin
 8              Writeln ('Procedure 1:', A:5, X:5);
 9              X := 18;
10              Writeln ('Procedure 2:', A:5, X:5)
11          End {InOnly} ;
12
13      Begin {Main}
14          Writeln ('    Location      A    X');
15          A := 15;
16          Writeln ('      Main 1:', A:5);
17          InAndOut (A);
18          Writeln ('      Main 2:', A:5)
19      End {Main} .
20
```

When this program is run, we get the following output:

```
   Location     A    X
     Main 1:   15
Procedure 1:   15   15
Procedure 2:   18   18
     Main 2:   18
```

From the output of this program, we see that the addition of the reserved word *Var* before the formal parameter *X* has allowed procedure *InAndOut* to change the value of the actual parameter *A*. Figures 9–1 to 9–4 describe in more detail how this change occurs. The key point here is that in parameter passage by reference, the formal parameter always refers back to the actual parameter, so a change in the formal parameter is reflected by a change in the actual parameter.

In contrast, when we pass parameters by value (leaving out the *Var* reserved word) we get the following output:

```
   Location     A    X
     Main 1:   15
Procedure 1:   15   15
Procedure 2:   15   18
     Main 2:   15
```

Here, the actual parameter is not changed because the values of the actual parameter and formal parameter are kept separate, as shown in Figure 9–5. Then, when the procedure is finished and the storage for *In-*

FIGURE 9–1 • **Schematic of Program Parameter after Executing Line 15**

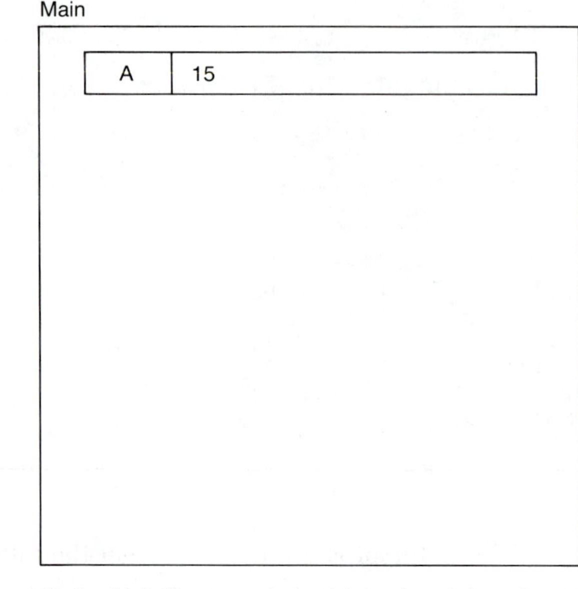


As the Main Program starts, *A* is assigned the value 15 and this value is written.

FIGURE 9–2 • **Schematic of Program Parameter after Procedure InAndOut Is Called**

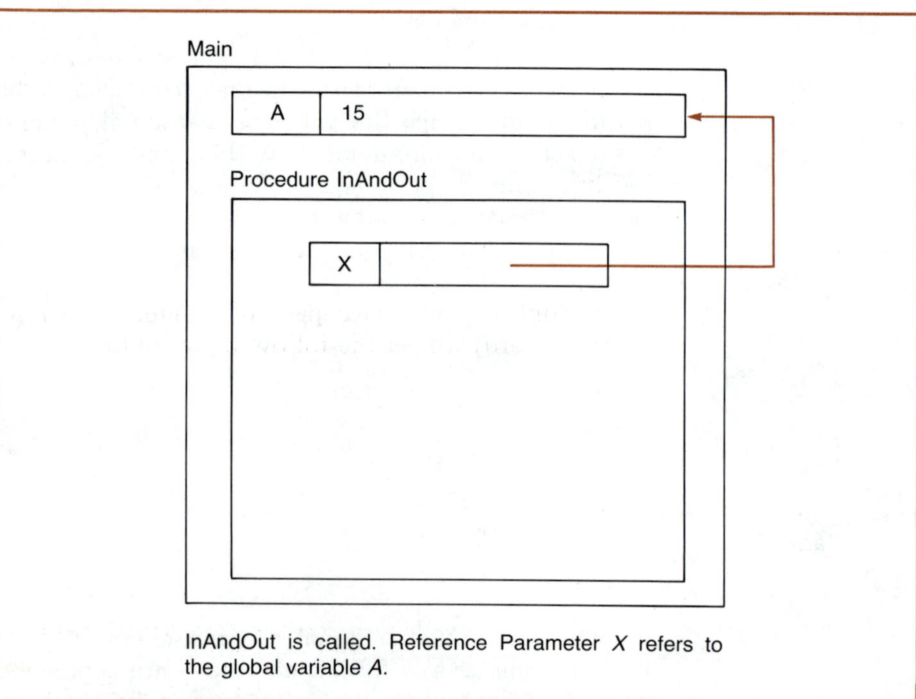


InAndOut is called. Reference Parameter *X* refers to the global variable *A*.

FIGURE 9–3 • **Schematic for Program Parameter after Executing Line 9 (in Procedure InAndOut)**

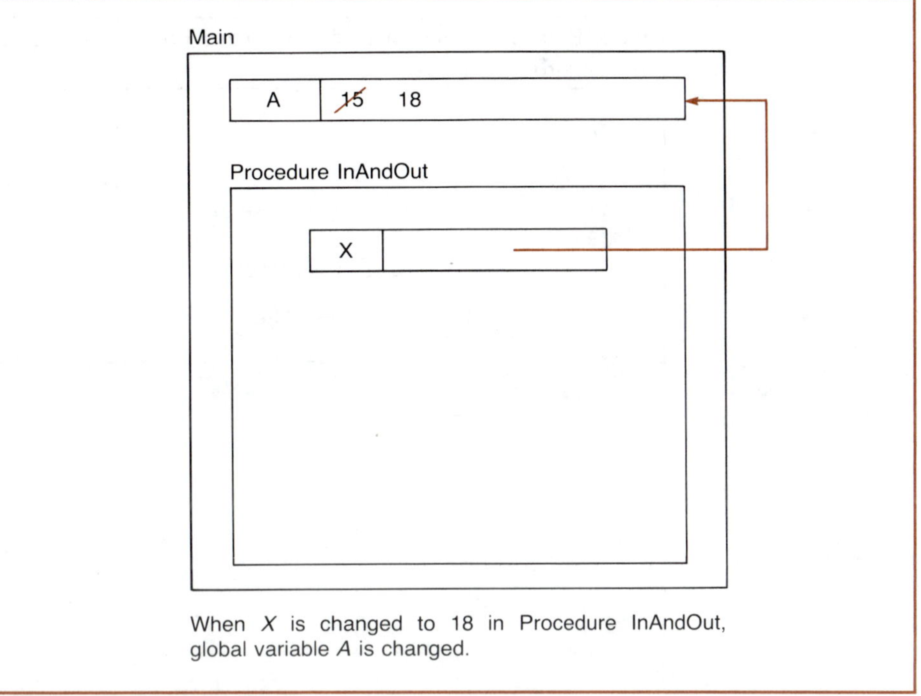


When *X* is changed to 18 in Procedure InAndOut, global variable *A* is changed.

FIGURE 9–4 • **Schematic of Program Parameter after Executing Line 18 in the Main Program**

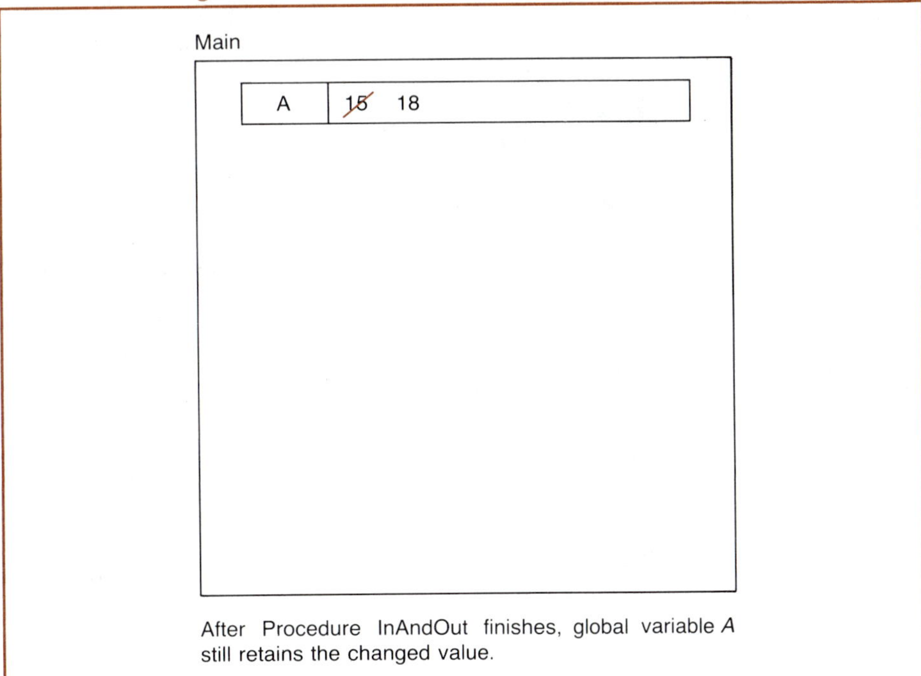


After Procedure InAndOut finishes, global variable *A* still retains the changed value.

FIGURE 9–5 • **Schematic of Program Parameter after Executing Line 9 (in Procedure InAndOut)**

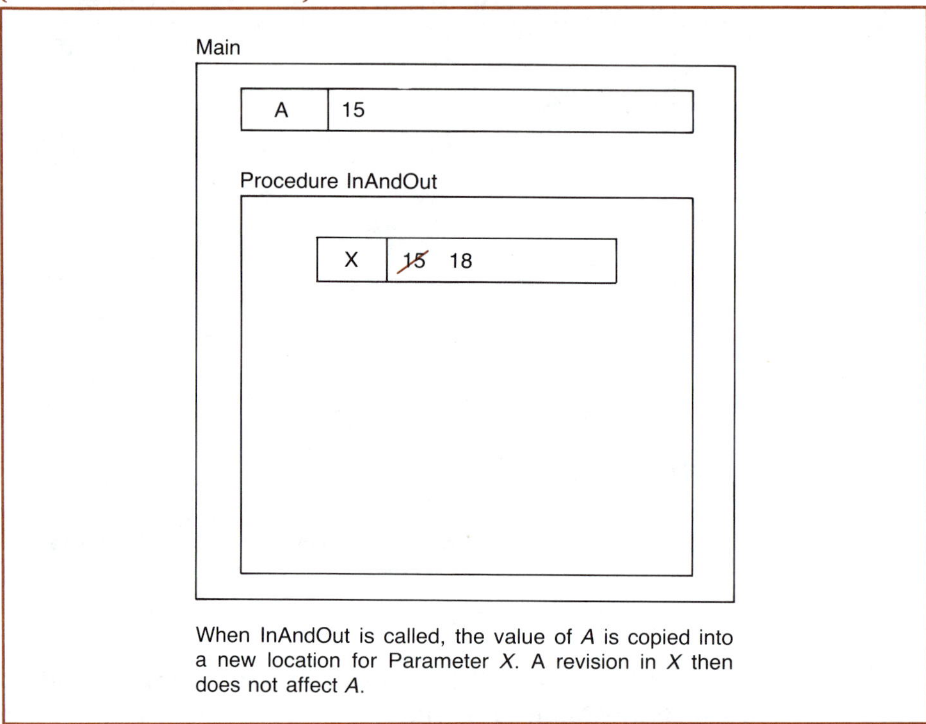


When InAndOut is called, the value of *A* is copied into a new location for Parameter *X*. A revision in *X* then does not affect *A*.

*AndOut* is freed for other use, only the storage for the main program remains. (See Figure 9–1.) *A* retains the value 15.

This example illustrates Pascal's two types of parameter passage very clearly, and we summarize our conclusions in Table 9–1. From this table and our examples in this section, we see that we can use either reference or value parameters when we want to supply procedures with initial values. However, only reference parameters allow procedures to return values.

## SECTION 9.2 SCOPE OF IDENTIFIERS

While parameters are vital to the effective use of procedures and functions, we find that the use of parameters, especially reference parameters, can also involve some subtleties that we may not anticipate. If we are not careful, the interplay between various parameters and local and global variables can cause errors in our programs that can be difficult to locate and correct.

Thus, in this section and the next, we examine some of the interrelationships that can exist among the various types of parameters and vari-

**TABLE 9–1 • Reference and Value Parameters**

| Passage by Reference | Passage by Value |
|---|---|
| 1. A new storage location is reserved for the formal parameter when a function or procedure is called. This location is used to refer to other locations. (addresses) | 1. A new storage location is reserved for the formal parameter when a function or procedure is called. This location is used to store values of the formal parameters. |
| 2. The address of the actual parameter is stored in this new location. | 2. The value of the actual parameter is copied into this new location. |
| 3. Thereafter, the formal parameter refers to the actual parameter. | 3. Thereafter, the formal parameter and actual parameters are considered separately. |
| 4. Any change in either formal or actual parameter changes the other. | 4. A change in either the formal or actual parameter does not change the other. |
| 5. The actual parameter remains changed after a procedure finishes. | 5. The actual parameter cannot be changed by the formal parameter. |

ables. Then, in Section 4, we state some guidelines for using parameters and variables effectively while minimizing the potential for errors. We begin by clarifying which identifier refers to which storage location.

## Multiple Declarations

In the following program, we use the identifier *A* for both a local and a global variable.

```
 Line
Number    Program Listing

   1      Program TwoAs (Output);
   2      {This program uses the identifier A for both a global
   3       and a local variable.}
   4
   5      Var A: Integer;
   6
   7      Procedure P;
   8          Var A: Integer;
   9          Begin
  10              A :=18;
  11              Writeln ('Procedure:', A:5)
  12          End {P} ;
  13
```

```
14      Begin {Main}
15          Writeln (' Location      A');
16          A := 15;
17          Writeln ('   Main 1:', A:5);
18          P;
19          Writeln ('   Main 2:', A:5)
20      End {Main} .
```

When this program is run, we get the following output:

```
 Location     A
   Main 1:   15
Procedure:   18
   Main 2:   15
```

When we analyze this program, we find that the declaration of *A* in our procedure specifies a new variable with a new address. Then, within the procedure all references to the identifier *A* refer to this new storage location. When the procedure finishes, this local variable is no longer defined, and *A* refers to the global variable. The details of this program are shown in Figures 9–6 to 9–8.

FIGURE 9–6 • **Schematic of Program TwoAs after Executing Line 16 in the Main Program**

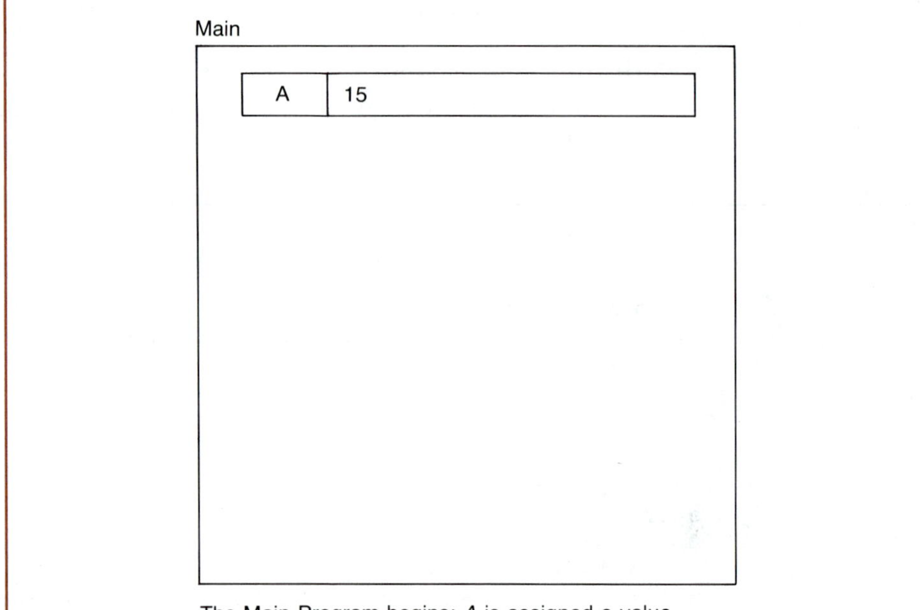


The Main Program begins; *A* is assigned a value.

FIGURE 9–7 • **Schematic of Program TwoAs after Executing Line 10 in Procedure P**

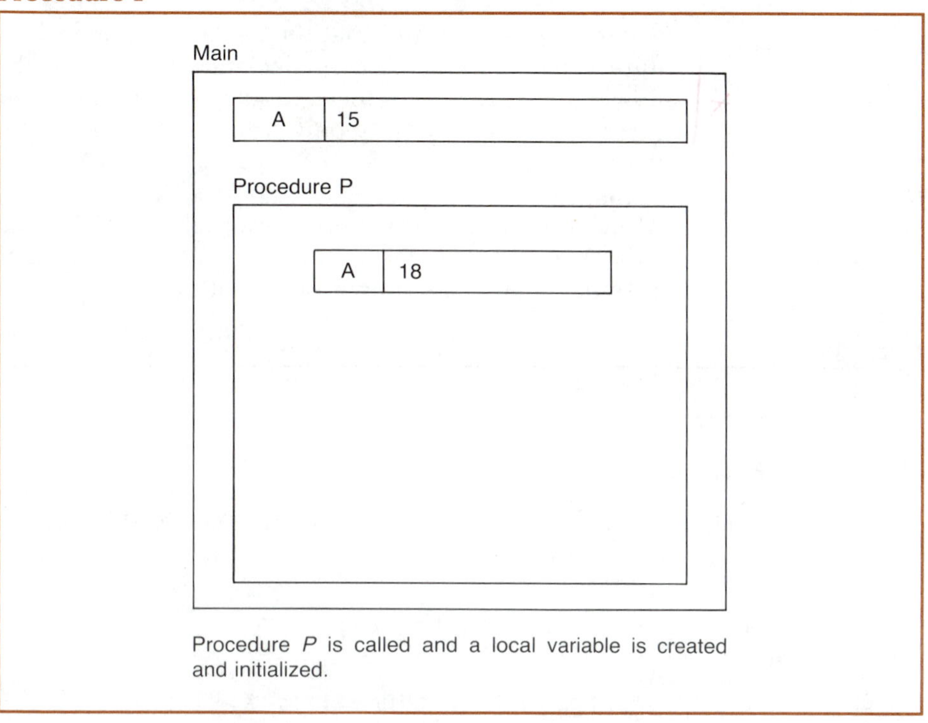


Procedure *P* is called and a local variable is created and initialized.

FIGURE 9–8 • **Schematic of Program TwoAs after Procedure P Returns**

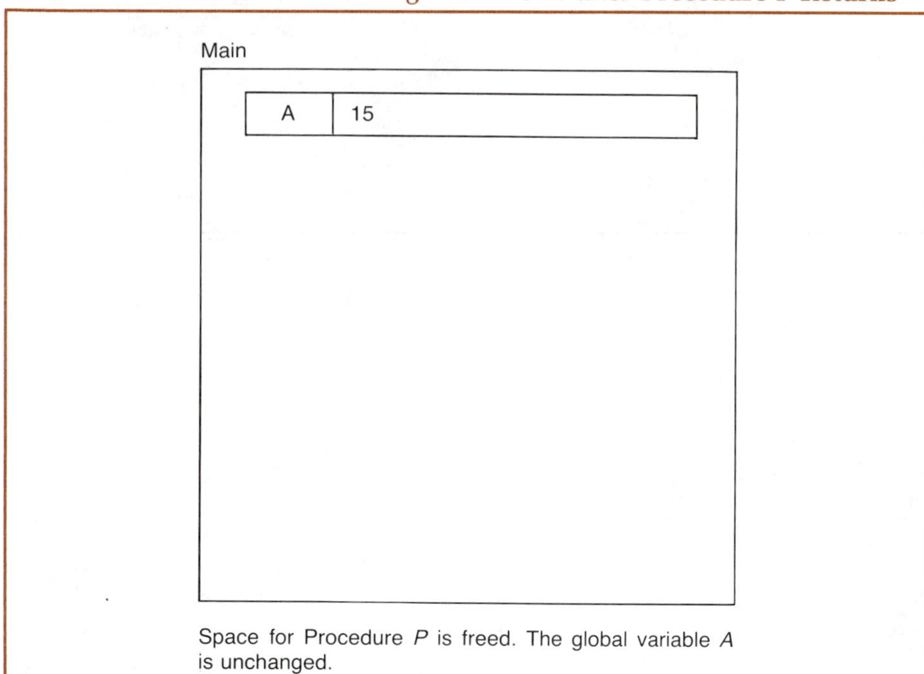


Space for Procedure *P* is freed. The global variable *A* is unchanged.

In general, we find that the declaration of an identifier within a procedure takes precedence over declarations outside the procedure. Inside a procedure or function, local variables or formal parameter names are used first. Global names apply only if these identifiers have not been redefined.

### Aliasing

Although we cannot access these global variables directly, the computer still retains storage space for them. We can access this space using reference parameters, as shown in the following example.

```
 Line
Number    Program Listing

   1      Program AliasA (Output);
   2      {This program uses the identifier A for both a global
   3       and a local variable and a formal parameter X.}
   4
   5      Var A: Integer;
   6
   7      Procedure P(Var X: Integer);
   8         Var A: Integer;
   9         Begin
  10            Writeln ('Procedure 1:', X:10);
  11            A := 13;
  12            X := 25;
  13            Writeln ('Procedure 2:', A:5, X:5)
  14         End {P} ;
  15
  16      Begin {Main}
  17         Writeln ('   Location      A    X');
  18         A := 7;
  19         Writeln ('      Main 1:', A:5);
  20         P(A);
  21         Writeln ('      Main 2:', A:5)
  22      End {Main} .
```

When this program is run, we get the following output:

```
   Location      A    X
      Main 1:    7
Procedure 1:          7
Procedure 2:    13   25
      Main 2:   25
```

Figures 9–9 to 9–12 trace this program in some detail. In this program, the identifier *A* was used as a local and a global variable. In the Procedure *P*, the identifier *A* refers to the local variable, not the global one; however, notice that *X* is used as an alternate name for accessing the global data.

FIGURE 9–9 • **Schematic for Program AliasA after Executing Line 18 in the Main Program**

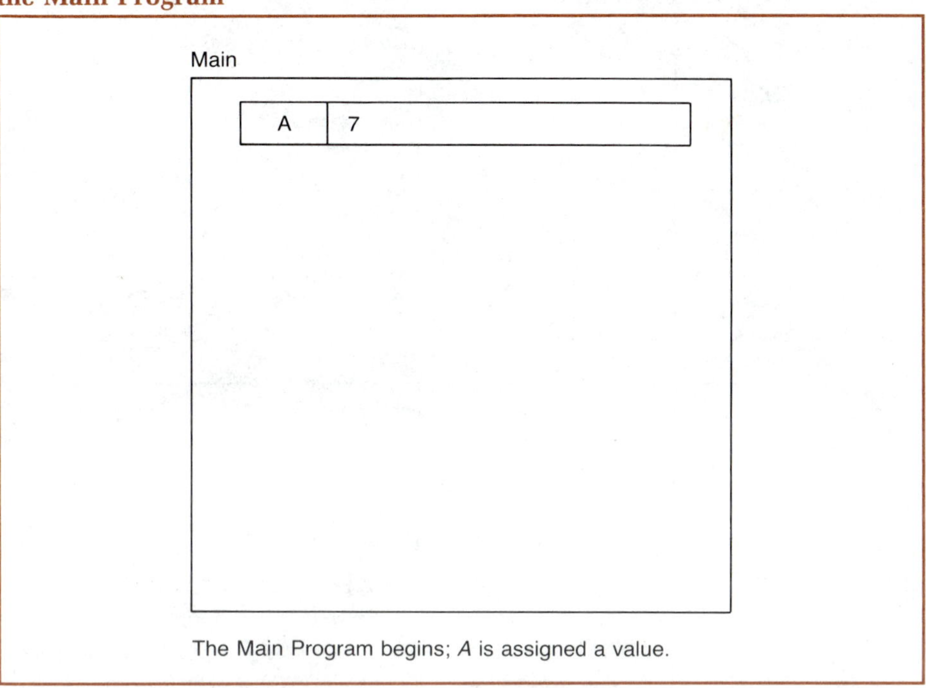


The Main Program begins; *A* is assigned a value.

FIGURE 9–10 • **Schematic of Program AliasA after Calling Procedure P (at Line 9)**

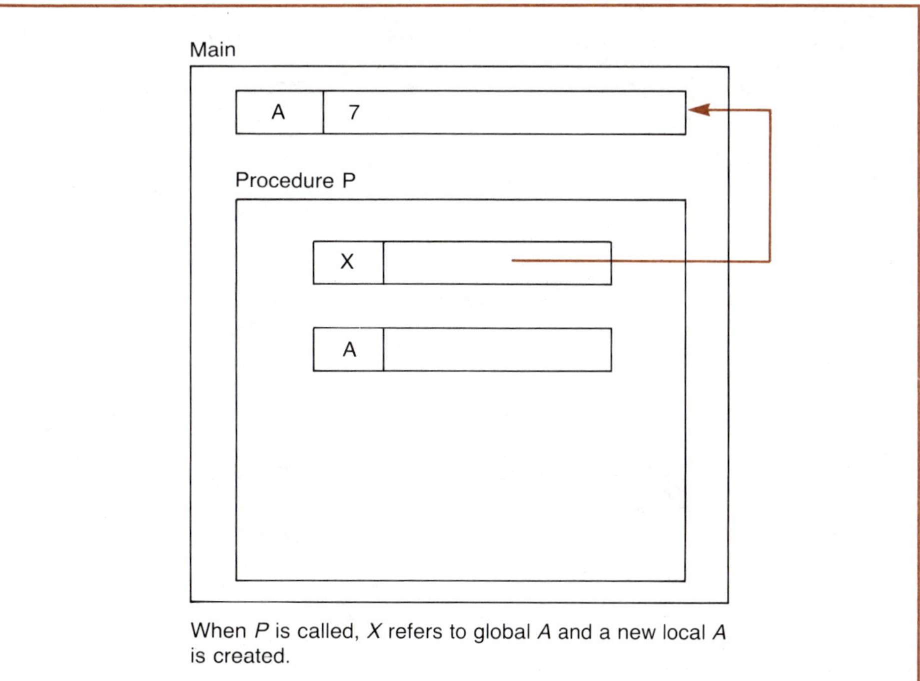


When *P* is called, *X* refers to global *A* and a new local *A* is created.

FIGURE 9–11 • **Schematic of Program AliasA after Executing Line 12 in Procedure P**

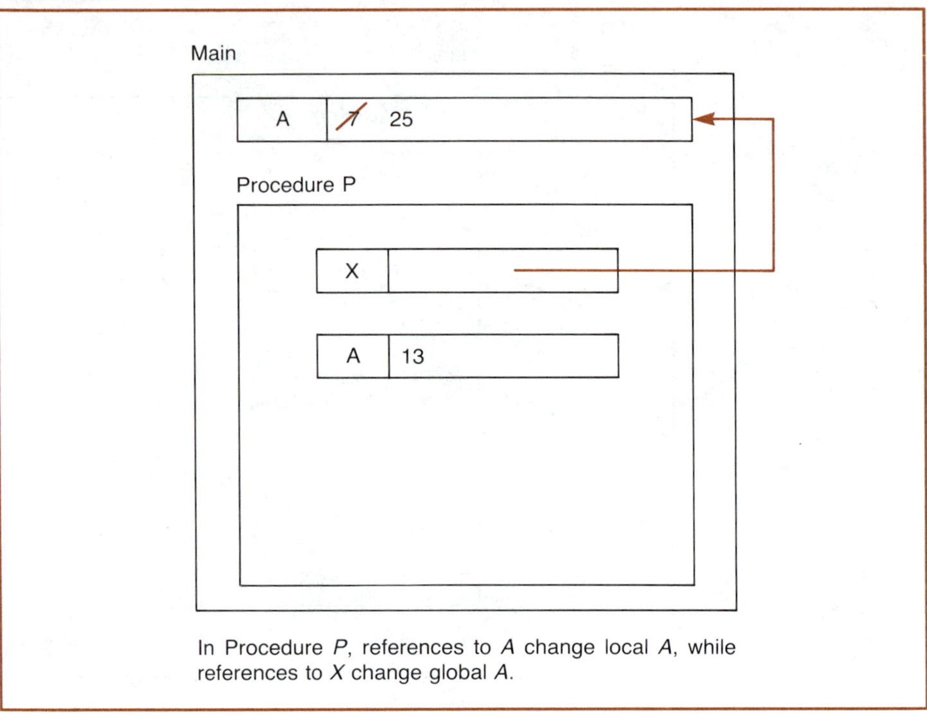


In Procedure *P*, references to *A* change local *A*, while references to *X* change global *A*.

FIGURE 9–12 • **Schematic for Program AliasA after Completing Procedure P (Line 21)**

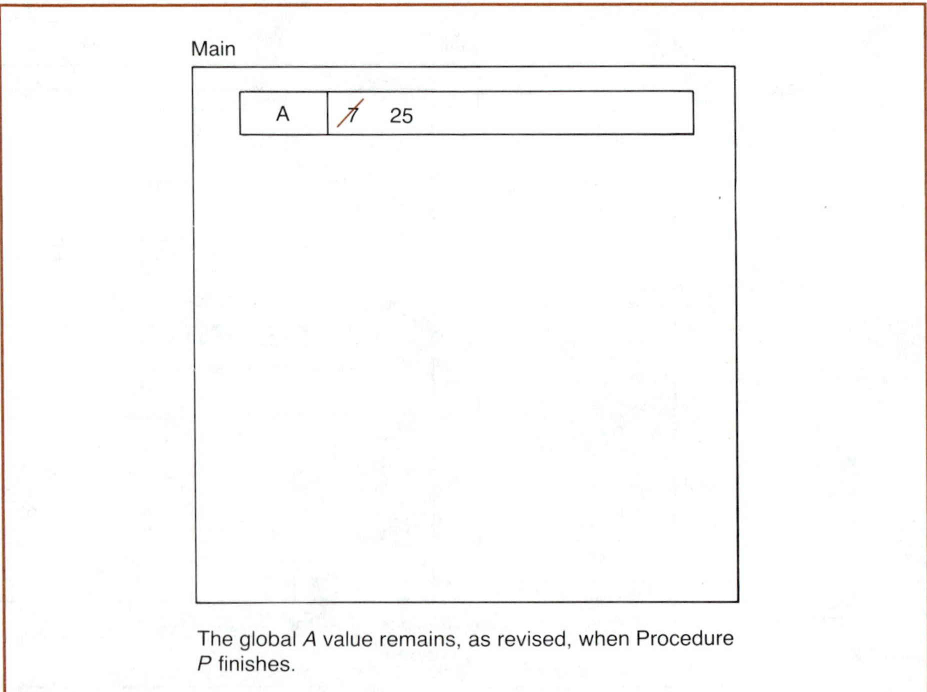


The global *A* value remains, as revised, when Procedure *P* finishes.

Here we say that *X* is an **alias** for the global variable *A*. Both global *A* and formal parameter *X* refer to the same storage location.

## Scope of Identifiers

The **scope of an identifier** is that part of the program where an identifier is defined. In Chapter 3, we noted that global identifiers exist throughout the running of a program, whereas local identifiers (and formal parameters) exist only within the procedures where they are defined. Thus, the scope of global identifiers is the entire program; the scope of local identifiers is limited to specific procedures.

These basic scope rules can be complicated in several ways. For example, the *TwoAs* program shows that identifiers can be **redefined** with procedures. Also, the *AliasA* program shows that a reference parameter allows the same storage location to be specified under a different name, or alias.

In the following example, we combine these ideas of scope, redefinition, and aliasing. Since our discussion applies equally to functions and procedures, we use a function in the following program.

```
 Line
Number    Program Listing

   1      Program AliasAndRedef (Output);
   2      {This program illustrates how the ideas of scope, redefinition,
   3       and aliasing can fit together.}
   4
   5      Var A, B, C, D: Integer;
   6
   7      Function F(A: Integer; Var B: Integer): Integer;
   8          Begin
   9              Writeln ('Function 1:', A:5, B:5, C:5, D:5);
  10              A := -A;
  11              B := B + 4;
  12              C := -C;
  13              D := 10;
  14              F := A + B + C + D;
  15              Writeln ('Function 2:', A:5, B:5, C:5, D:5);
  16          End {F} ;
  17
  18      Begin {Main}
  19          Writeln ('  Location     A    B    C    D');
  20          A := 7;
  21          B := 18;
  22          C := 26;
  23          D := 5;
  24          Writeln ('    Main 1:', A:5, B:5, C:5, D:5);
  25          D := F(C, C);
  26          Writeln ('    Main 2:', A:5, B:5, C:5, D:5)
  27      End {Main} .
```

When this program is run, we get the following output:

```
    Location      A    B    C    D
      Main 1:     7   18   26    5
  Function 1:    26   26   26    5
  Function 2:   -26  -30  -30   10
      Main 2:     7   18  -30  -76
```

To explain this output, we examine the details of program execution in Figures 9–13 to 9–17. In this program, identifiers *A* and *B* were redefined and formal parameter *B* was an alias for global variable *C*. The scope of global variables *A*, *B*, *C*, and *D* included the entire program, although *A* and *B* were not accessible when the function was active. On the other hand, the scope of formal parameters *A* and *B* was limited to the function itself.

Our next example illustrates another subtlety concerning the scope

FIGURE 9–13 • **Schematic for Program AliasAndRedef after Line 23 in the Main Program**

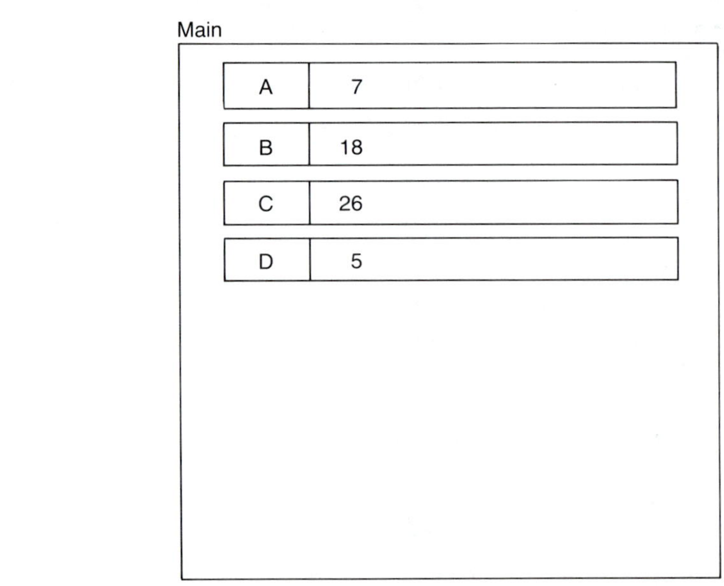


When the Main Program begins, variables *A*, *B*, *C*, and *D* are initialized.

FIGURE 9–14 • **Schematic for Program AliasAndRedef after Calling Function F**

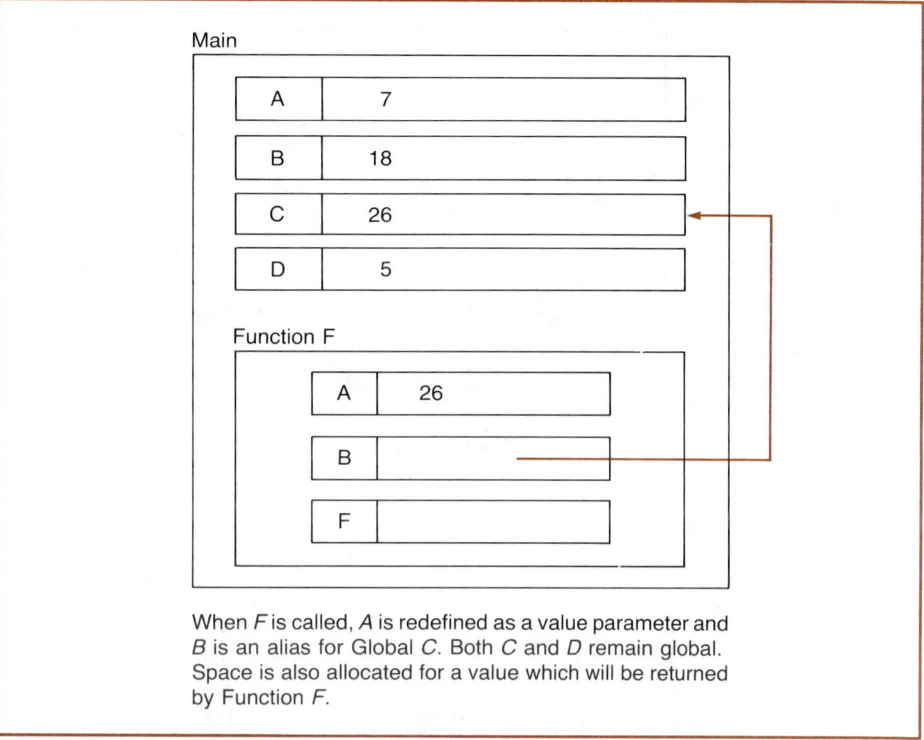


When *F* is called, *A* is redefined as a value parameter and *B* is an alias for Global *C*. Both *C* and *D* remain global. Space is also allocated for a value which will be returned by Function *F*.

FIGURE 9-15 • **Schematic for Program AliasAndRedef after Executing Line 11 in Function F**

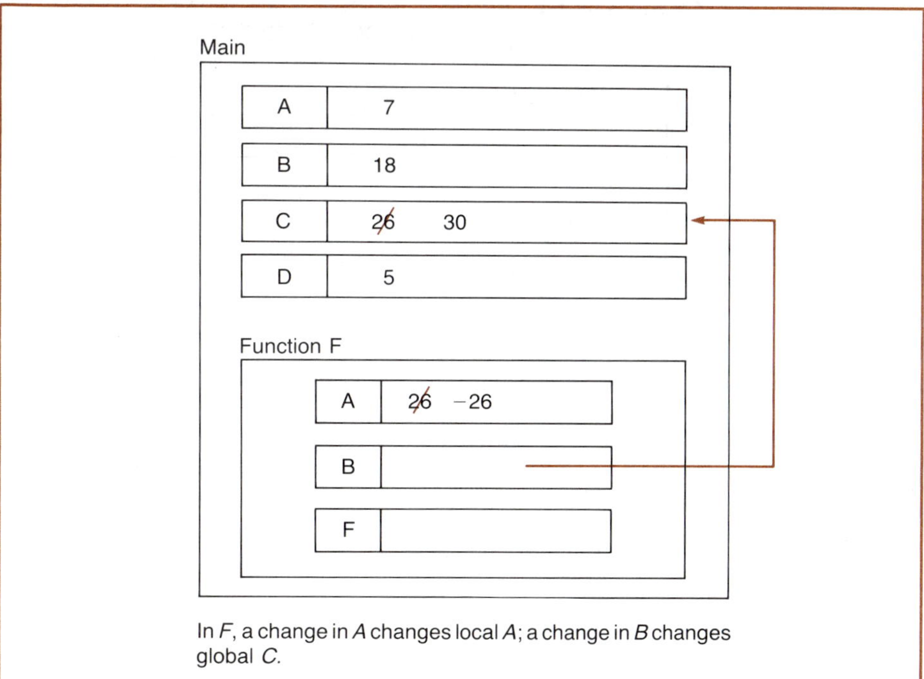


In *F*, a change in *A* changes local *A*; a change in *B* changes global *C*.

FIGURE 9-16 • **Schematic for Program AliasAndRedef after Executing Line 14 in Function F**

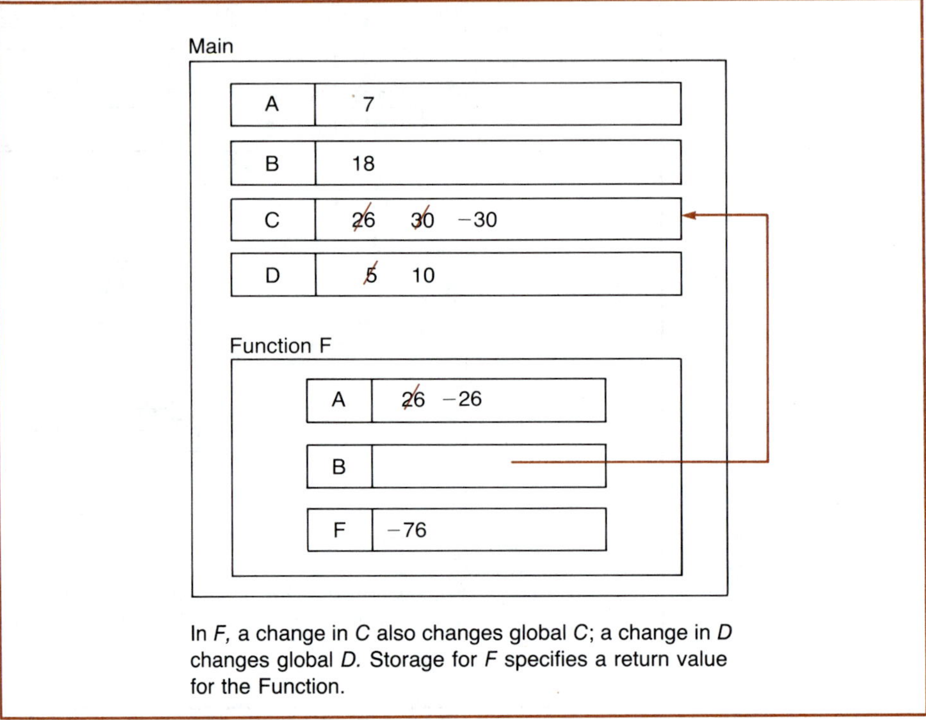


In *F*, a change in *C* also changes global *C*; a change in *D* changes global *D*. Storage for *F* specifies a return value for the Function.

FIGURE 9-17 • **Schematic for Program AliasAndRedef after Line 25 in the Main Program**

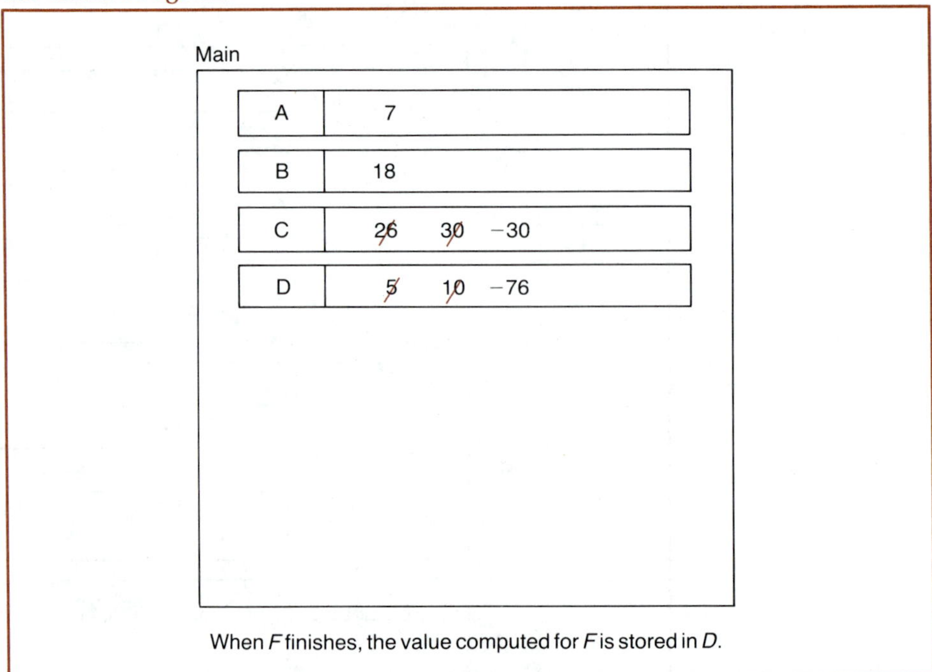


When *F* finishes, the value computed for *F* is stored in *D*.

of identifiers. We will see that identifiers in functions and procedures refer to storage locations as they are declared at the time of compilation.

```
 Line
Number    Program Listing

   1      Program Environment (Output);
   2      {This program illustrates one way that the compiler environment
   3       determines the scope of identifiers.}
   4      Var A: Integer;
   5
   6      Procedure One;← doesn't have any variables.
   7          Begin
   8              Writeln (' One 1:   A = ', A:1);
   9              A := 32;                              global A
  10              Writeln (' One 2:   A = ', A:1)
  11          End {One} ;
  12
  13      Procedure Two;
  14          Var A: Integer;
  15          Begin                              local A of TWO.
  16              A := 13;
  17              Writeln (' Two 1:   A = ', A:1);
  18              One;
  19              Writeln (' Two 2:   A = ', A:1)
  20          End {Two} ;
  21
  22      Begin {Main}
  23          A := 7;
  24          Writeln ('Main 1:   A = ', A:1);
  25          Two;
  26          Writeln ('Main 2:   A = ', A:1)
  27      End {Main} .
```

When this program is run, we get the following output:

```
Main 1:  A = 7
 Two 1:  A = 13
 One 1:  A = 7
 One 2:  A = 32
 Two 2:  A = 13
Main 2:  A = 32
```

When we trace through this program to understand the output, the first part of the program execution in which the Main Program calls Procedure Two is similar to our previous examples. (See Figure 9–18.)

FIGURE 9–18 • **Schematic for Program Environment after Executing Line 17 in Procedure Two**

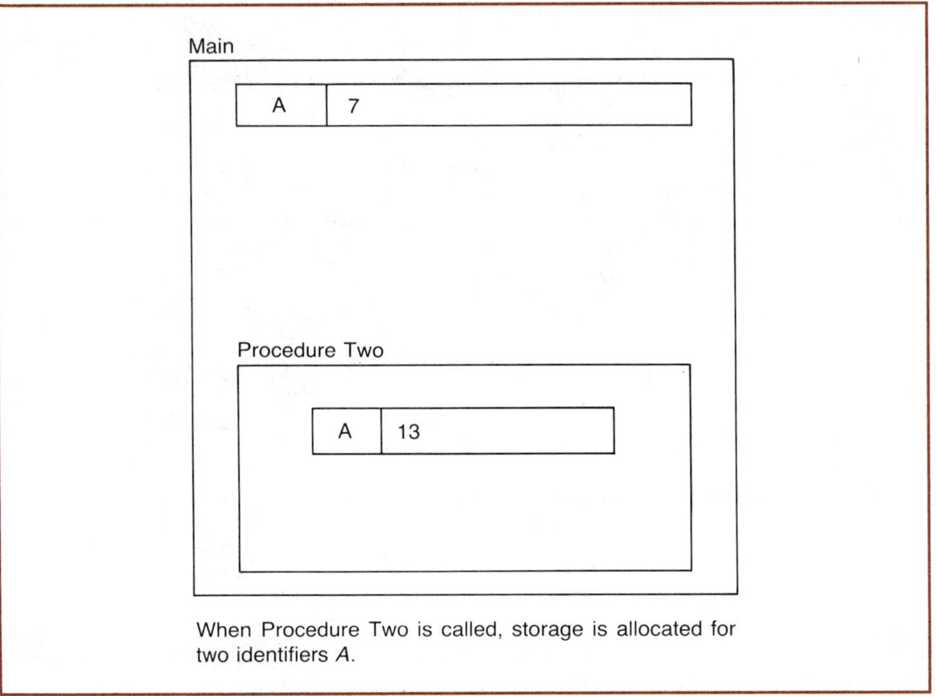


When Procedure Two is called, storage is allocated for two identifiers *A*.

Procedure Two calls Procedure One, and we must determine which variable we mean when we use identifier *A*. Here, we could argue that Procedure One is declared outside of Procedure Two, and with this declaration, One cannot use the local variable *A* declared inside Procedure Two. (See Figure 9–19.)

Alternatively, we could claim that Procedure One is called by Procedure Two, and within Two, local variable *A* has superseded global *A*. (See Figure 9–20.)

In Pascal and several other languages, the first argument is followed, and the global variable *A* is used inside Procedure One. Here, it does not matter that One was called by Two; the local variables of Procedure Two have no effect on Procedure One. Because it is declared separately from Procedure Two, Procedure One will always refer to global variable *A* regardless of where it is called from. (We say the scope of *A* is determined at **compile time** not at **execution time**.)

The rest of the execution of this program is detailed in Figures 9–21 and 9–22.

In this program, identifier *A* was used both as a global and a local variable. The scope of local variable *A* was confined to statements inside Procedure Two, and this local variable became inactive when we called

FIGURE 9–19 • **Schematic for Program Environment after Calling Procedure One (Line 8) Based on Procedure Environment at Time of Compilation**

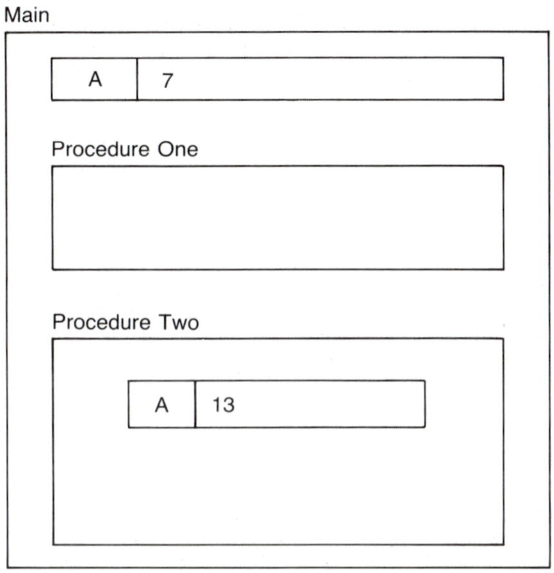

Main

| A | 7 |
|---|---|

Procedure One

Procedure Two

| A | 13 |
|---|---|

In Pascal, Procedure One is declared outside Procedure Two, and One does not have access to local *A* in Two. Rather, *A* in One refers to global *A*.

FIGURE 9–20 • **Schematic for Program Environment after Calling Procedure One (Line 8) Based on Procedure Environment at Run-Time**

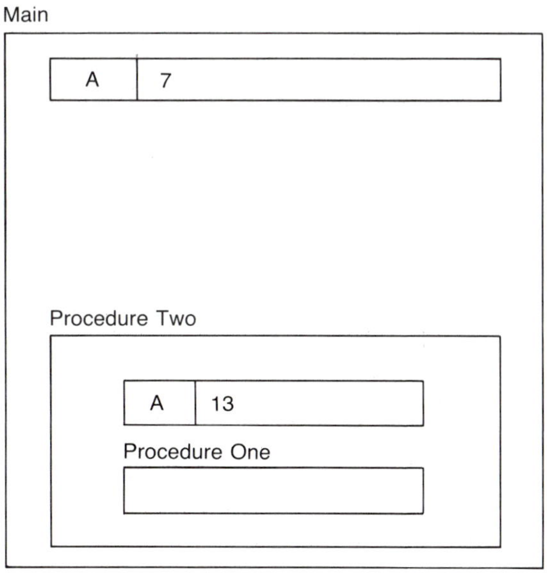

Main

| A | 7 |
|---|---|

Procedure Two

| A | 13 |
|---|---|

Procedure One

At run-time, One is called from inside Procedure Two. (This view is not followed in Pascal.)

FIGURE 9–21 • **Schematic for Program Environment after Executing Line 9 in Procedure One**

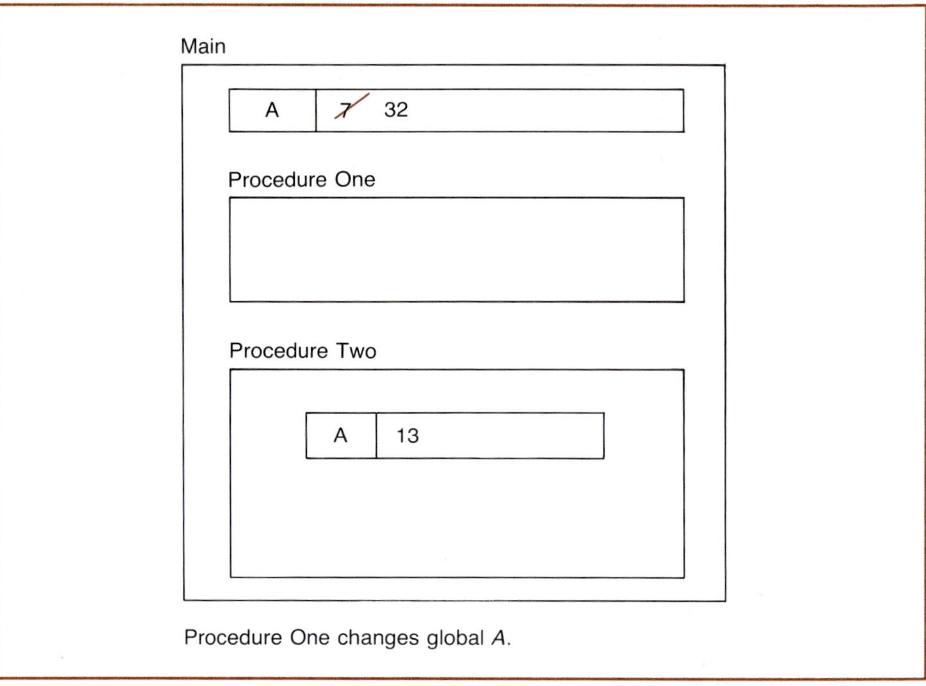


FIGURE 9–22 • **Schematic for Program Environment after Executing Line 19 in Procedure Two**

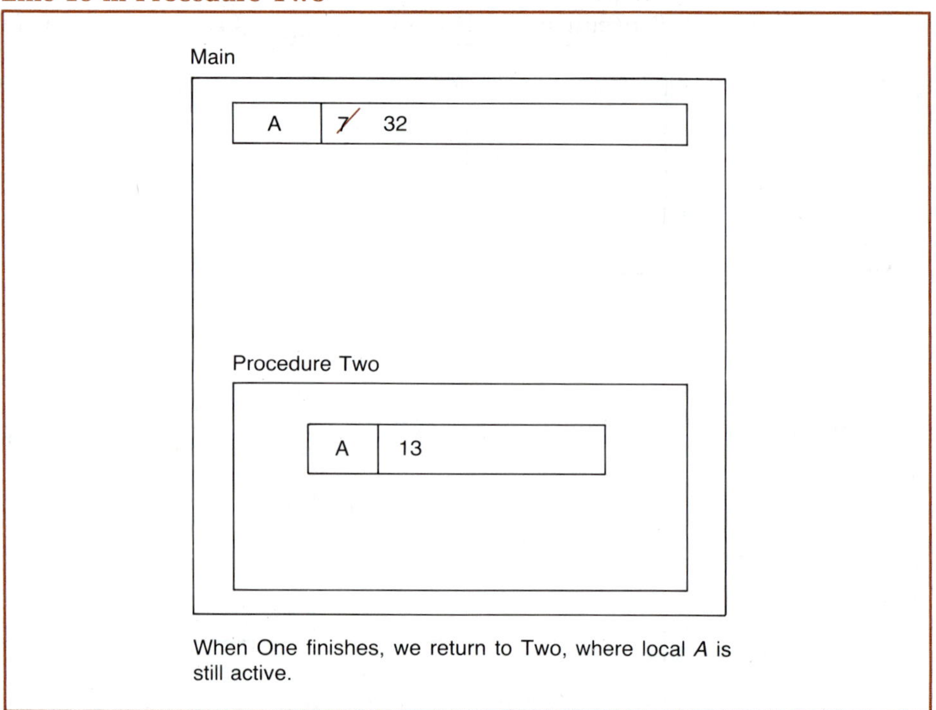

Procedure One which was declared outside Two. The scope of global variable *A* extended to all statements outside of Procedure Two, including the Main Program and Procedure One.

### Nesting of Functions and Procedures

These examples of multiple declarations and aliasing illustrate that we must be careful to distinguish between identifiers declared outside a function or procedure and those declared inside. We must be sure that we know the scope of each of our identifiers so that we refer to the variables we mean when we are writing programs. Beyond these distinctions, Pascal allows us to place functions and procedures inside each other, and we say that functions and procedures are **nested** when one is declared within another. A simple example of nesting procedures is shown below. The example also shows that the same principles of local and global variables apply to nested procedures and functions, and identifiers may be used only within the procedures or functions where they are declared.

NESTING

```
 Line
Number   Program

   1      Program NestedProcedures (Output);
   2      {This program illustrates the nesting of procedures, where one
   3       procedure is declared inside another}
   4
   5      Var A, B, C: Integer;
   6
   7      Procedure One;
   8      {Procedure One is declared inside the program with new, local
   9       variables called A and B.  Within this procedure, identifier C
  10       refers to the global variable.}
  11         Var A, B: Integer;
  12
  13         Procedure Two;
  14         {Procedure Two is declared inside One, with the new local
  15          variable A.  When identifiers B and C are mentioned within this
  16          procedure, the computer first looks at Procedure One, and uses
  17          identifier B which is declared there.  However, C is not
  18          declared in either One or Two, so Two references global C}
  19            Var A: Integer;
  20            Begin {Two}
  21               A := 24;
  22               Writeln ('  Two 1:', A:5, B:5, C:5);
  23               B := 26;
  24               C := 28;
  25               Writeln ('  Two 2:', A:5, B:5, C:5)
  26            End {Two} ;
  27
```

```
28          Begin {One}
29              A := 12;
30              B := 15;
31              Writeln ('   One 1:', A:5, B:5, C:5);
32              Two;
33              Writeln ('   One 2:', A:5, B:5, C:5)
34          End {One} ;
35
36      Begin {Main}
37          Writeln ('Location     A    B    C');
38          A := 3;
39          B := 7;
40          C := 9;
41          Writeln (' Main 1:', A:5, B:5, C:5);
42          One;
43          Writeln (' Main 2:', A:5, B:5, C:5)
44      End {Main} .
```

When this program is run, we get the following output:

```
Location     A    B    C
 Main 1:     3    7    9
  One 1:    12   15    9
  Two 1:    24   15    9
  Two 2:    24   26   28
  One 2:    12   26   28
 Main 2:     3    7   28
```

As we trace through this program, we apply many of the same principles of scope that we have already encountered. In particular, when an identifier is redefined within a procedure, the local variable is used within that procedure, but the global variable remains for reference outside the procedure. In addition, when a nested procedure refers to an identifier, the computer first looks for a variable that is local to that procedure. Then, if none is found, the computer looks at the procedure where the nested procedure is declared. In general, where referring to an identifier within a procedure, the computer works its way outward, from the procedure toward the main program to find which identifier to use. Further details for the execution of this sample program are given in Figures 9–23 to 9–26.

Beyond this relatively simple example, all of the comments about identifier redefinition, aliases, and program environment that we made earlier apply to nested procedures as well. In some cases, nesting procedures can allow us to break large tasks into small procedures contained within larger procedures. Thus, Pascal allows us a great deal of flexibility in structuring our programs. However, this nesting of procedures also allows programs to become quite complex, and we may need to limit the redefinition of identifiers and nesting of procedures and functions to help reduce this complexity.

FIGURE 9-23 • **Schematic for Program NestedProcedures During Line 31 in Procedure One**

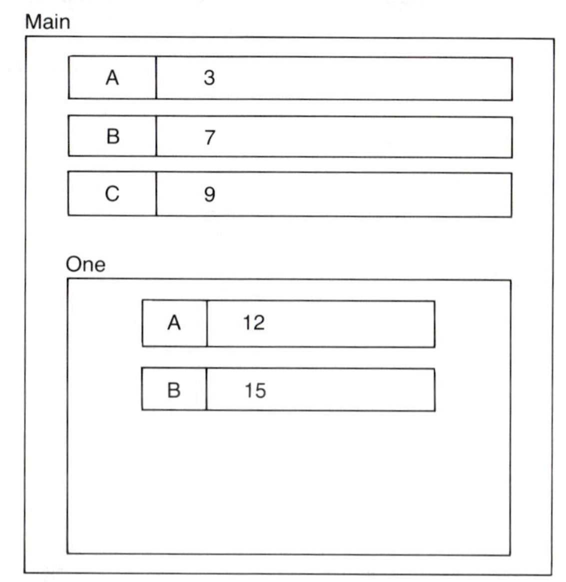


The Main program initializes global variables *A, B,* and *C*. Then the first part of Procedure *One* initializes its local variables.

FIGURE 9-24 • **Schematic for Program NestedProcedures During Line 22 in Procedure Two**

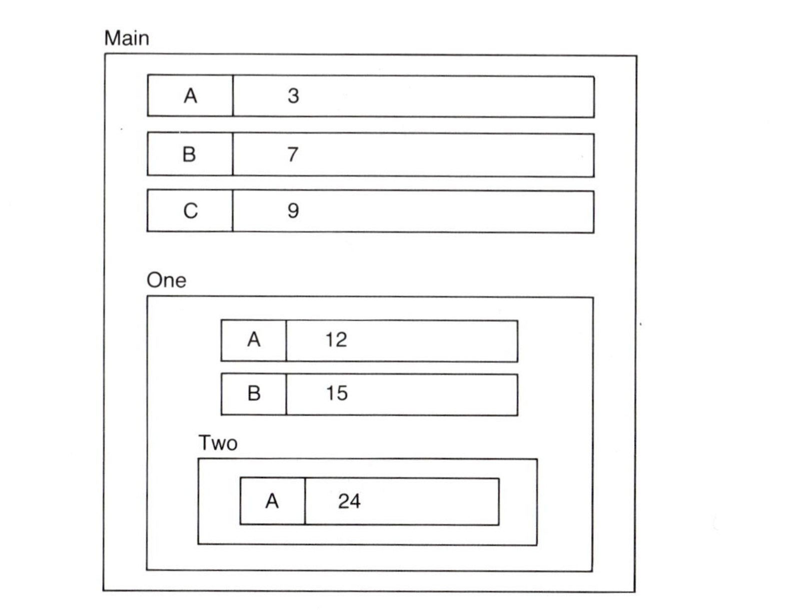


During the first part of Procedure *Two*, a new local variable is created and initialized for this procedure.

FIGURE 9-25 • **Schematic for Program NestedProcedures During Line 25 in Procedure Two**

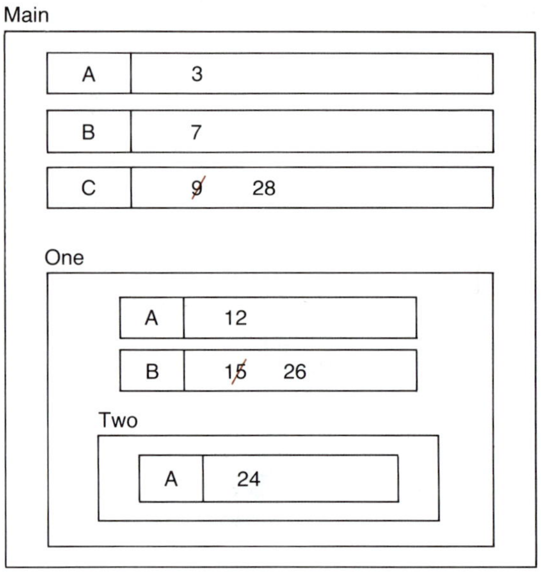

Main

A 3

B 7

C 9 28

One

A 12

B 15 26

Two

A 24

When *Two* refers to variable *B*, we must move outside of Procedure *Two* to Procedure *One* to find a variable. When *Two* refers to variable *C*, we must continue moving outside *Two* and *One* to reach the global variable *C*.

## SECTION 9.3 SIDE EFFECTS

In the previous section, we saw how scope, identifier redefinition, aliases, program environment, and function and procedure nesting can all fit together in a program. In this section, we look at some consequences of these features. We will see that Pascal allows us great flexibility in solving problems, but we will also see that this freedom can get us into trouble.

One type of difficulty is illustrated in the following.

### PROBLEM 9.3

Suppose we measure the time (in seconds) that it takes us to travel one mile. Compute our speed in miles per hour, and compute the number of minutes it takes us to travel 30 miles.

This problem is related to Problem 5.1, and we use some of the ideas from Section 5.1 to develop the following outline.

### Outline for Problem 9.3

**I.** Determine time (seconds).
**II.** Compute MPH.

FIGURE 9-26 • **Schematic for Program NestedProcedures During Line 33 in Procedure One**

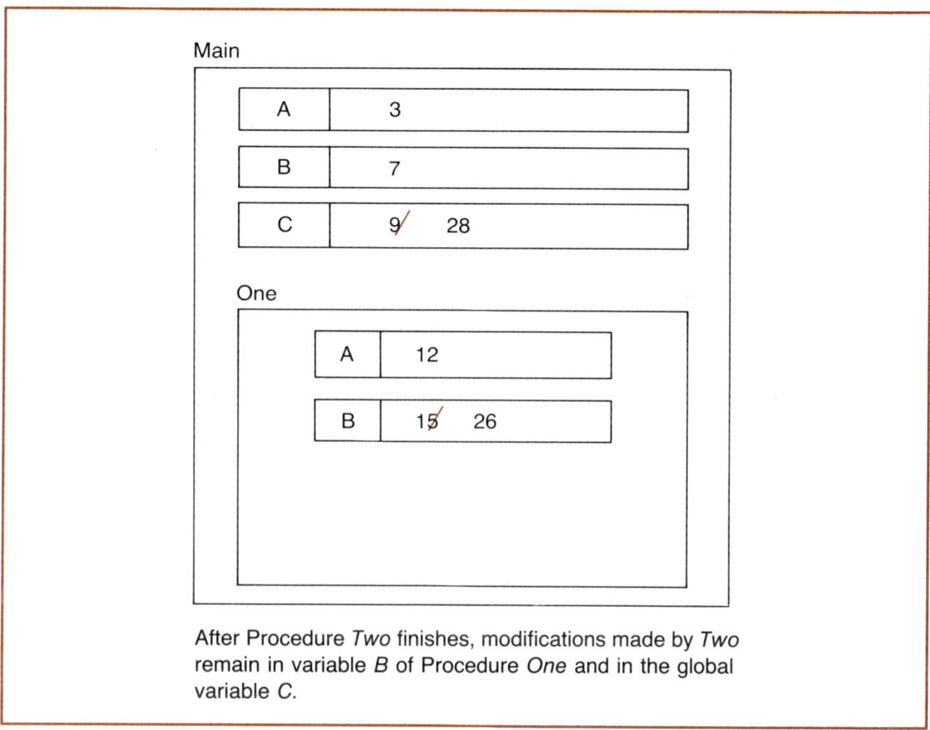


After Procedure *Two* finishes, modifications made by *Two* remain in variable *B* of Procedure *One* and in the global variable *C*.

   **A.** time(hours) := time(seconds)/3600.0
   **B.** MPH := 1.0/time(hours)

**III.** Compute minutes to travel 30 miles.
   **A.** time(seconds) for 30 miles := 30.0 * time(seconds) for 1 mile
   **B.** time(minutes) := time(seconds) for 30 miles / 60.0

**IV.** Print results.

Our outline is correct and straightforward. In our programming, we decide to compute Steps II and III by using functions. This yields the following program, which contains a common error.

```
Program MPHAndTime {Wrong, but good idea} (Input, Output);
{This program computes speed in miles per hour and time in minutes
 for 30 miles, given time in seconds for one mile.}

Var Time: Real;          {Our time in seconds}
    MPH: Real;           {Our speed in miles per hour}
    TimeFor30: Real;     {Our time in minutes for 30 miles}
```

```
Function ComputeMPH (Seconds: Real): Real;
{Compute MPH, given time in "Seconds" for 1 mile}
    Begin
        {Convert time to seconds}
        Time := Seconds / 3600.0;

        {Compute MPH}
        ComputeMPH := 1.0 / Time
    End {ComputeMPH} ;

Function FindMinutes (Seconds: Real): Real;
{Compute time in minutes for 30 miles, given "Seconds" for 1 mile}
    Begin
        {Find time in seconds for 30 miles}
        Time := Seconds * 30.0;

        {Change to minutes}
        FindMinutes := Time / 60.0
    End {FindMinutes} ;

Begin {Main}
    Writeln ('This program computes information about speed and time.');

    {Determine time(seconds)}
    Write ('Enter your time in seconds for 1 mile: ');
    Read (Time);

    {Compute MPH}
    MPH := ComputeMPH (Time);

    {Compute minutes to travel 30 miles}
    TimeFor30 := FindMinutes (Time);

    {Print results}
    Writeln ('When you travel 1 mile in ', Time:1:2, ' Seconds,');
    Writeln ('your speed is ', MPH:1:2, ' miles per hour,');
    Writeln ('and you will travel 30 miles in ', TimeFor30:1:3, ' minutes.')

End {Main} .
```

When we analyze this program, we note that our Main Program follows our outline exactly. We enter *Time* in seconds. Then we use that to compute miles per hour and time in minutes for 30 miles. Finally, we print the results. These steps correspond exactly to our outline.

However, when we look at our functions, we see that we are using this same global *Time* variable for other things. In *Function ComputeMPH* we use *Time* to mean "time in hours," and in *Function FindMinutes* we use *Time* to mean "time in seconds for 30 miles." Thus, in this program, we are using one global variable for three different things.

In each function, we change the value of *Time* for that particular interpretation. Here we say that the global variable *Time* is changed as a **side effect** of the function. *Time* is not a parameter of the function. In fact, in reading the Main Program, we cannot tell that our function has any effect on *Time* whatsoever. We mean to compute *MPH* or TimeFor30 from a *Time*, and we do not expect other changes to be made.

This is an example where a side effect causes errors in our program. In each function, we want to use *Time* for a particular purpose, but that purpose is restricted to the function. There is no reason to depend on a global variable for this detail within the function. Thus, we need to introduce a local *Time* variable in each function to correct this problem due to side effects.

### Side Effects Can Cause Ambiguity

In previous examples, we have seen instances in which side effects cause errors and others in which side effects can clarify our code. In each instance, we could predict what our code would produce, although sometimes the results were incorrect.

The following example illustrates a situation where side effects can produce ambiguous results; we cannot predict what will be printed.

```
Program Ambiguous (Output);
{A program where side effects produce ambigious results.}

Var A, B, X: Integer;

Function F(U: Integer): Integer;
     Begin
          B := 2 * U;
          F := B - 4
     End;
Begin
     Writeln ('  A    B    X');

     A := 3;
     B := 4;
     X := B + F(A);
     Writeln (A:3, B:5, X:5, '   B + F(A)');

     A := 3;
     B := 4;
     X := F(A) + B;
     Writeln (A:3, B:5, X:5, '   F(A) + B')
End.
```

This code could produce any of the following four results, depending on the compiler.

**Compiler 1**

| A | B | X | |
|---|---|---|---|
| 3 | 6 | 8 | B + F(A) |
| 3 | 6 | 8 | F(A) + B |

**Compiler 2**

| A | B | X | |
|---|---|---|---|
| 3 | 6 | 6 | B + F(A) |
| 3 | 6 | 6 | F(A) + B |

**Compiler 3**

| A | B | X | |
|---|---|---|---|
| 3 | 6 | 6 | B + F(A) |
| 3 | 6 | 8 | F(A) + B |

**Compiler 4**

| A | B | X | |
|---|---|---|---|
| 3 | 6 | 8 | B + F(A) |
| 3 | 6 | 6 | F(A) + B |

Let us look at the program with some care. We find that Function $F$ does two things: $B$ is given the value 6 as a side effect, and $F$ is given the value 2.

Now let us consider the two computations of $X$ in the main program:

```
X := B + F(A)
X := F(A) + B
```

In these lines, we know $F$ will have the value 2, but we cannot be sure of the value of $B$. If the initial value of $B$ is used, then $X$ becomes $2 + 4 = 6$. If the later value of B is used, then X becomes $2 + 6 = 8$. Thus, the value of $X$ depends upon whether B is considered before or after the function F(A) is computed. Since the Pascal Standard says that the terms $B$ and $F(A)$ can be evaluated in either order, any of the four results are possible.

From these examples, we see that we must be careful in our procedures and functions to control side effects. Side effects can change global variables unintentionally. We should use parameters to transmit data both to and from procedures and functions. This transmission with parameters is much cleaner and less error-prone than with global variables.

## SECTION 9.4 GUIDELINES ON DECLARING AND USING VARIABLES AND PARAMETERS AND NESTED PROCEDURES AND FUNCTIONS

The previous sections suggest that unanticipated or inadvertent side effects can cause a wide variety of subtle changes and errors, and we need to control such side effects if we are to write correct programs. In this section, we develop some guidelines which will allow us to use various parameters and variables effectively while we control side effects and minimize the chances for errors.

## Global Variables

In the previous sections, a large number of the subtleties we encountered were due to side effects. Procedures and functions used global variables directly rather than referring to them in a more controlled way through appropriate parameters. Further, we might change global variables accidentally if we forget to redeclare identifiers locally within a function or procedure. For example, our Miles Per Hour program in Section 9.3 contained several errors because we omitted the declaration of some local variables.

Unfortunately, whenever we use global variables we always face the possibility that these values will be changed inadvertently by side effects because we omitted a needed declaration in a function or a procedure. Our programs may be syntactically correct, but we risk having procedures interfere with each other because they change global variables.

These observations about side effects and this potential for introducing subtle errors motivates the following major guidelines.

*Guideline 1.* All programs should be written in a way that eliminates all global variables, unless we can identify truly extraordinary arguments otherwise. Most programs we write should have *no* global variables.

The second guideline emphasizes this principle and suggests a way to accomplish this goal in many cases.

*Guideline 2.* To avoid global variables, move global declarations together with the steps of the main program to a separate, independent procedure. Then, allow the main program to call this separate driver procedure, and use parameters to transfer all values between the driver and other functions and procedures in the program.

To clarify this approach further, we rewrite the Miles Per Hour program of Section 9.3 in this style.

```
Program MPHAndTime (Input, Output);
{This program computes speed in miles per hour and time in minutes
 for 30 miles, given time in seconds for one mile.}

{This version uses procedure ControlProcessing to eliminate all
 global variables}

Function ComputeMPH (Seconds: Real): Real;
{Compute MPH, given time in "Seconds" for 1 mile}
    Var Time: Real;
    Begin
        {Convert time to seconds}
        Time := Seconds / 3600.0;

        {Compute MPH}
        ComputeMPH := 1.0 / Time
    End {ComputeMPH} ;
```

```
Function FindMinutes (Seconds: Real): Real;
{Compute time in minutes for 30 miles, given "Seconds" for 1 mile}
    Var Time: Real;
    Begin
        {Find time in seconds for 30 miles}
        Time := Seconds * 30.0;

        {Change to minutes}
        FindMinutes := Time / 60.0
    End {FindMinutes} ;

Procedure ControlProcessing;
{This procedure controls the processing required for the overall problem.}
    Var Time: Real;         {Our time in seconds}
        MPH: Real;          {Our speed in miles per hour}
        TimeFor30: Real;    {Our time in minutes for 30 miles}
    Begin
        {Determine time(seconds)}
        Write ('Enter your time in seconds for 1 mile: ');
        Read (Time);

        {Compute MPH}
        MPH := ComputeMPH (Time);

        {Compute minutes to travel 30 miles}
        TimeFor30 := FindMinutes (Time);

        {Print results}
        Writeln ('When you travel 1 mile in ', Time:1:2, ' Seconds,');
        Writeln ('your speed is ', MPH:1:2, ' miles per hour,');
        Writeln ('and you will travel 30 miles in ',
                 TimeFor30:1:3,' minutes.')
    End {ControlProcessing} ;

Begin {Main}

    Writeln ('This program computes information about speed and time.');
    ControlProcessing

End {Main} .
```

Following Guidelines 1 and 2, we see that this program has no global variables at all. Instead, we define our "globals" in a new *ControlProcessing* procedure, which controls all computations. Our main program is now reduced to printing an initial title and calling Procedure *ControlProcessing*. Then, *ControlProcessing* uses the same functions we used before.

However, here, we are unlikely to change values inadvertently by side effects. With no global variables, we must use parameters to transfer data, so we see explicitly how all information is entering and leaving each function and procedure.

## Value Versus Reference Parameters

Eliminating global variables forces us to use parameters to move data to and from procedures and functions. Thus, our next task is to develop guidelines for choosing the appropriate type of parameters, and these guidelines will depend upon the main distinctions between value and reference parameters from Section 9.1. When we use *value* parameters, the value of the actual parameter is copied into a new location for a formal parameter, and a change in the formal parameter does not change the actual parameter. In contrast, with *reference* parameters, the formal parameter refers to an actual parameter; the copying of values is not needed; and for arrays, only the base address must be transmitted from actual to formal parameters. In addition, a change in formal parameters does change actual parameters.

In reviewing these differences, one consideration needs to be stressed: *Reference parameters can change actual parameters.* This fact has two major implications. First, many of the problems associated with side effects apply to reference parameters. Actual parameters can be changed accidently by procedures and functions when reference parameters are used. Such changes cannot occur with value parameters, so value parameters are safer. Second, when data must be returned by a procedure, value parameters cannot be used. Reference parameters are mandatory when we want to get data from a procedure. These two observations will motivate our guidelines for choosing between value and reference parameters.

However, there is one other important consideration: *Value parameters require values to be copied.* Again, this has two implications. First, for simple data types (Boolean, integer, real), the work required to copy a value is about the same as the work required to set up the reference from the formal parameter to the actual one. Storage requirements are similar as well. Second, for arrays, value passage requires considerably more work and storage. In value passage, a completely new array must be created and all values in the array copied. On the other hand, in reference passage, only a single starting address must be transferred to the formal parameter and stored. With large arrays, this difference can be considerable; value passage requires much more work. Also, depending on the computer, it is possible that the machine will run out of space when it tries to set up another large array.

These comments suggest the following guidelines for choosing between value and reference parameters.

*Guideline 3.* Use reference parameters to return data from procedures.

*Guideline 4.* Use value parameters whenever data need not be returned.

*Exception.* When dealing with a large array, use reference parameters to reduce storage and copying overhead. Be careful not to make inadvertent changes in actual parameters.

Mistakes involving procedures often are caused by the wrong choice of parameter passage. If a procedure or function seems to be working by itself but does not seem to work when it is put in the program, we always should check the choice of parameter passage.

### Use of Function and Procedure Nesting

With these four guidelines, our primary goal is to control the flow of data between procedures and functions as much as possible, so that we do not make inadvertent changes in our values, yielding unexpected results. In stating our final guideline, we want to reduce the complexity of our programs that can result from the nesting of procedures and functions. In particular, when we consider the various difficulties that we have identified for global variables, we find that the same troubles can arise for local variables if we nest procedures and functions inside each other. A nested procedure can refer to variables declared in an outer procedure, just as any procedure can refer to global variables. Therefore, our final guideline restricts the use of function and procedure nesting.

*Guideline* 5. Avoid the nesting of functions and procedures whenever the nested function or procedure computes new values for variables.

A nesting of functions or procedures might be permissible when an inner function involves a single formula to compute a final value or when a procedure prints only headings. However, nesting should usually be avoided so that variables are not changed inadvertently.

With these guidelines, we will be able to organize solutions to complex problems into manageable pieces, and we will be able to control the complexity of our resulting programs. In particular, as we proceed through the rest of the text, we will consistently follow these guidelines, and we will frequently write programs that have no global variables at all and where the nesting of procedures is minimized.

## SECTION 9.5 MODULARITY: INDEPENDENCE OF PROGRAM UNITS

We have now seen all of the fundamental pieces of procedures and functions, and we have stressed ways that we can make these procedures and functions independent. We now look at this work more formally. We also consider some additional techniques that can be helpful in developing algorithms and in writing and testing programs.

### Coupling and Cohesion

Throughout our work, we have followed a basic top-down approach to problem solving—we divide complex problems into small, manageable pieces, and we may identify some tasks that are common to several steps. This approach leads us to an algorithm written in outline form, in which major steps are differentiated from small details. Function and procedures then allow us to structure our code to parallel this outline form.

In our problem analysis, we have tried to keep our steps independent, so these steps do not interfere with each other, and the guidelines from the previous section will help us write procedures and functions so they will be independent. More formally, we can consider the **coupling** of functions and procedures in our programs. Here coupling describes the amount that various procedures and functions depend upon each other, and our principles of independence suggest that we want to minimize coupling in our programming.

In addition, in writing procedures and functions, we write a separate function or procedure for each part of our outline. We should not combine outline steps into a single piece of our program, since our program should retain the same structure and clarity found in our outline. We want the statements within a procedure or function to relate to a single task, and we do not want other tasks disrupting our central focus. In computer science, this relating of the various statements in a procedure or function to a central theme is called **cohesion,** and we should strive to write short, cohesive procedures and functions for each part of our solution outline.

## Specifications with Pre- and Post-Assertions

Once we write our outline for a complex problem, we may find it useful to describe the work of each step formally. In large development projects, different people may be assigned to work on different steps, and the overall job will run correctly only if those steps fit together. In such a situation, the work of each step must be specified very carefully, so there can be no confusion about what each step does.

One way to formalize the work required for a step is through the specification of **pre-assertions** and **post-assertions.** Pre-assertions specify what can be assumed when the step begins; post-assertions specify what must be true when the step ends. For example, consider a step that computes the mean, or average, of a set of numbers

$$a_1, \ldots, a_n.$$

Pre-assertions for the step might be

1. $n$ is an integer.
2. $n \geqslant 1$.
3. $a_1, \ldots, a_n$ are declared as real numbers.
4. $a_1, \ldots, a_n$ have all been given values.

Post-assertions for the step might be

1. *Mean* is the arithmetic average of $a_1, \ldots, a_n$.
2. $n$ and $a_1, \ldots, a_n$ remain unchanged by the step.
3. No global data are accessed within the step.
4. Nothing is read or printed by the step.

When we want to translate this step into a procedure, we also need one additional piece of information, the **calling format,** which is a precise statement of the procedure name, and the number, type, and meaning of parameters. For example, we might specify a calling format

```
Stat(A, N, Mean)
```

where

*Stat* is the procedure name,

*A* is a real array of type *ArrayType*,

*N* is the maximum number of elements in the array, and

*Mean* is a real parameter that returns the value specified in the post-assertions.

Once we know the calling format and the pre- and post-assertions, we can program the procedure without knowing anything more about how the step will be used. For example, we could begin

```
Procedure Stat (A:ArrayType; N:Integer; Var Mean: Real);
```

Next, we could declare any local variables we might need. From the post-assertions, we know what we must compute; that we will not use any *Read* or *Write* statements; and which values we must return when the procedure finishes.

When we use pre- and post-assertions, we should keep in mind two things. First, the pre- and post-assertions do not say how we will do our work in the step; the algorithm is not specified. In fact, we could try several algorithms to see which was most efficient. Second, when we write code on the basis of pre- and post-assertions, we should include these assertions as comments at the beginning of each procedure and function. These comments specify what each piece of code is supposed to do and thus help us understand our program. Also, these comments can help us in testing.

## Testing Procedures with Small Driver Programs

The division of programs into independent pieces with clearly specified pre- and post-assertions has several important consequences for program testing.

When procedures and functions are independent, we can test them individually before we try to put them together. One way to proceed uses a small **driver program** that includes the function or procedure in a context that has just enough variables so we can run our procedure or function with test data. More precisely, a driver program to test a given procedure or function contains global declarations, initialization of required variables to meet all pre-assertions, a procedure or function call, and printing or evaluation of all post-assertions.

For example, if we are writing a complete statistics package that includes data entry, data editing, computation of many statistics, and printing of graphs, we could look at these parts separately. In particular, if we use a Procedure *Stat* to compute means as described earlier in this section, we could write a driver program as follows:

```
Program TestStat(Input, Output);
{Driver to test Stat procedure}

Const N = 6;

Type ArrayType = Array [1..10] of Real;

Var B: ArrayType;
    Mean: Real;
    I: Integer;

Procedure Stat (A:ArrayType; N: Integer; Var Mean: Real);
    {Details of this procedure are given here}

Begin
    {Initialize Variables}
    Writeln ('Enter values');
    For I := 1 To N
        Do Read (B[I]);

    {Test Routine}
    Stat (B, N, Mean);

    {Print Results}
    Writeln ('Array elements:');
    For I := 1 To N
        Do Write (B[I]);
    Writeln;
    Writeln ('Mean =', Mean:5:2)
End {Test} .
```

This program allows us to test Procedure *Stat* easily for a variety of test cases. However, it does not require us to write extensive data entry procedures. We do not have to worry about editing our data nor about drawing graphs. This simple driver program allows us to focus on a single procedure (or group of procedures) rather than the entire complex solution.

## Stubbing

A second aid to testing and debugging independent procedures is the use of **stubbing.** In this approach, we write our main program with all of the outlined steps as procedures or functions. However, the body of these procedures is greatly abbreviated.

For example, if we want to test our statistics package, the controlling procedure might contain the following procedure calls:

```
Begin {Control Processing}
        EnterData(A, N);
        EditData(A, N);
        Stat (A, N, Mean);
```

```
        PrintStatistics(A, N, Mean);
        PrintHistogram(A, N, Mean)
    End {ControlProcessing};
```

This program involves many steps, but we can begin by simplifying several of them. For example, our editing procedure could be the following stub:

```
Procedure EditData(Var A: ArrayType; N: Integer);
    Begin
        Writeln('Data Editing Not Available at this Time!')
    End;
```

When we run our program, we can call *EditData*, and the procedure will tell us that it is being used. We still could test other procedures.

This same approach could apply to our *Stat* procedure, but here our post-assertions require that *Mean* be given a value by the procedure. Thus, our procedure stub might be the following:

```
Procedure Stat(A:ArrayType;N:Integer;Var Mean:Real);
    Begin
        Mean :=3.0
    End;
```

Obviously this stub does not perform the required computations. However, if our short-term goal is to test our data entry and printing routines, then this stub is adequate. Later, when the input and output procedures are completed, we can come back to this computational procedure.

## Debugging Print Procedures

Another aid to testing includes writing special procedures to help in the debugging process. For example, in debugging we often need to print out various values to help us trace the execution of the program. This debugging task is so common that we may decide to write a debugging print procedure that we can call whenever we need to monitor the progress of our program.

A simple way to do this is to declare the following:

```
Procedure PrintValues(B: ArrayType; N: Integer; VarMean: Real);
   Var I: Integer;
   Begin
      Writeln;
      For I := 1 to N
         Do Write(B[I]);
      Writeln;
      Writeln ('Mean =', Mean:5:2)
   End;
```

With this procedure, we simply insert a call to *PrintValues* in our code whenever we want to trace what our program is doing. If we already have a print procedure as part of our problem solution, we can use it without modification. We do not need special formatting for our debugging, so we could use any form we want elsewhere.

In more complex problems, we may want to keep our tracing statements in the code even after we believe we have tested our program fairly well. Long programs often contain subtle bugs that we find only after considerable use. When such bugs arise, we want to follow our program through the special cases without having to add our *Write* statements all over again.

One approach for these long programs involves the addition of a global Boolean constant *Debug*. Our program begins

```
Const Debug = True;
```

and our debugging procedure is

```
Procedure DebuggingPrint ( . . . );
    Begin
        If Debug
            Then Begin
                Writeln . . .
                    .
                    .
                    .
                Writeln . . .
                End
    End
```

With this code, we call *DebuggingPrint* whenever we wish to trace our program. When we test our program, we set global constant *Debug* to *True*, and all the data we need to follow our program are printed. When our testing is done, we edit the program and set *Debug* to *False*, and then recompile. This simple change eliminates all of our extra printing. Then, if we need to trace our code at a later time, we just set *Debug* to *True*. Thus, a simple constant can allow us to include extra printing statements in our code for use in special circumstances.

## Separate Compilation Sometimes Allowed

One final technique that can save considerable time in writing and debugging programs involves the separate compilation of procedures and functions. In Chapter 4, we noted that after we write our Pascal program, two steps are required before we can run it. First, our program must be compiled; Pascal must be translated to machine language. Second, references to functions and procedures must be added at appropriate places in a linking stage.

In some, but not all, Pascal compilers, independent procedures and functions can be compiled separately. Then, when all pieces are compiled, they can be linked together.

When this feature is available, we can save a great deal of time in several ways. To begin, we write and compile procedures and functions separately, and then, we write and compile small drivers for various procedures and functions as separate entities. Next, by linking a driver to its specific procedures and functions, we can test individual parts of our code. Here, as changes are needed, only a single function or procedure must be revised and recompiled. We do not need to recompile other pieces of code. The revised function or procedure is then linked again to the driver. Further, as we add features, individual stubs can be expanded to full working procedures and functions. Again, only the new pieces must be recompiled before linking. In the end, our final program can utilize the separate working pieces without further editing or copying. We just link the various pieces together in the complete main program.

Thus, with the capability of separate compilation, we can take full advantage of the independence of program parts in the ways we have mentioned in this section. Writing, testing, and changing code can be done one piece at a time; we do not have to recompile the entire program just to change one piece. Thus, independence of program units not only helps us in the early stages of problem solving, but also can help us minimize our work in writing, correcting, and compiling our code.

## SUMMARY

1. **Parameter passage** can occur in two ways.
   a. With *value* passage, a new storage location is created for the formal parameter, and the value of the actual parameter is copied to the new location.

### KEY TERMS, PHRASES, AND CONCEPTS

Alias
Ambiguous Evaluation of Code
Cohesion
Coupling
Debugging Print Procedures
Driver Program
Parameter Passage
  by Reference
  by Value
Procedure Specification Calling Format
Post-Assertion
Pre-Assertion
Program Environment
  Defined at Compile Time
  Defined at Execution Time
Redefinition of Identifiers
Scope of Identifiers
Separate Compilation
Side Effect
Stubbing

   b. With *reference* passage, the formal parameter refers to the address of the actual parameter.
2. Various identifiers can be active at different times.
   a. The **scope** of an identifier is the time it is active.
   b. Identifiers can be **redefined.**
   c. A parameter may refer to another variable **(aliasing).**
   d. Scope is based on the program **environment at compile time,** not at **execution time.**
3. Functions and procedures can be **nested** inside each other, but we must be careful not to use this nesting to increase the complexity of our programs.
4. A variable may be changed as a **side effect** of a function or procedure.
5. When writing programs, we should *eliminate global variables.*
6. In developing and testing independent procedures, we may use the following techniques.
   a. procedure specifications with **calling format, pre-assertions,** and **post-assertions**
   b. testing procedures with small **driver programs**
   c. **stubbing**
   d. **debugging print procedures**
   e. **separate compilation** of functions and procedures.

## EXERCISES

**9.1** *Redefinition of Identifiers.* Write a program in which identifier *A* is used in different places as a formal parameter in a function, an actual parameter, a global variable, a local variable, and a procedure name.

**9.2** Describe several ways that the value of a global variable can be changed during a procedure call.

**9.3** *Effect of Parameter Passage.* Write a procedure that returns different results depending upon whether the parameters are passed by value or by reference.

**9.4** *Parameter Passage-1.* What is printed by the following program?

```
Program Passage (Output);
Var w, x, y, z: Integer;

Function F(x: Integer; Var y: Integer): Integer;
    Begin
        x := x - 3;
        y := y + 3;
        w := w Div 2;
        f := w + x + y + z;
        Writeln('F    ', w, x, y, z)
    End {F} ;
```

```
Function G(Var w: Integer): Integer;
    Var x, z: Integer;
    Begin
        x := 2;
        w := 3;
        z := 4;
        z := F(x, w);
        G := w + x + y + z;
        Writeln('G     ', w, x, y, z)
    End {G} ;

Begin {Main}
    x := 1;
    y := 2;
    w := 5;
    z := 3;
    z := F(x, y);
    Writeln('Main1', w, x, y, z);
    z := G(x);
    Writeln('Main2', w, x, y, z)
End {Main}.
```

**9.5** *Parameter Passage-2*. What is printed by the following program?

```
Program MorePassage (Output);
Var A, B, C, D: Integer;

Function F(A: Integer; Var B: Integer): Integer;
    Var C: Integer;

     Begin
        Writeln ('Function 1', A:5, B:5,  D:10);
        C := A + B;
        D := B + C;
        A := C + D;
        B := D + A;
        F := 3*A - 2*B;
        Writeln ('Function 2', A:5, B:5, C:5, D:5)
    End {F} ;

Begin {Main}
    Writeln (' Location     A    B    C    D');
    A := -1;
    B := 2;
    C := -3;
    D := 4;
    Writeln ('    Main 1', A:5, B:5, C:5, D:5);
    D := F(A, B);
    Writeln ('    Main 2', A:5, B:5, C:5, D:5);
    B := F(C, D);
    Writeln ('    Main 2', A:5, B:5, C:5, D:5)
End {Main} .
```

**9.6** *Ambiguity with Parameters.* The following program could print several sets of output. What are they?

```
Program Ambiguous (Output);
Var A, X: Integer;
Function F(Var U: Integer): Integer;
     Begin
          U := 2 * U;
          F := U - 4
     End;
Begin
     Writeln ('  A    X');
     A := 3;
     X := A + F(A);
     Writeln (A:3, X:5);
     A := 3;
     X := F(A) + A;
     Writeln (A:3, X:5)
End.
```

**9.7** *Finding Errors.* The following program was written to find the average of 10 or fewer numbers. Numbers are read until a sentinel value is encountered. Find four of the six errors in the program.

NOTE: The semicolons are correct. The errors are fundamental errors; that is, the program will not compile in its present form and correcting the syntax errors still leaves a program that produces incorrect results. Do not count issues of style; that is, ignore the lack of user prompting and the form of the output.

```
Program Errors (Input, Output);

Const Max = 10;

Type ArrayType = Array[1..Max] of Integer;

Var I, J, Item: Integer;
    B: ArrayType;
    Avg: Integer;

Procedure FindMean (A: ArrayType; N: Integer; Mean: Real);
    Var Sum: Integer;
    Begin
        Sum := 0;
        For I := 1 To Max
            Do Sum := Sum + A(I);
        Mean := Sum / N
    End {FindMean} ;
```

```
Begin {Main}
    {Initialize}
    For I := 1 To Max
        Do B[I] := 0;
    J := 0;

    {Read data}
    Read (Item);
    While (Item <> -3.1416)
      Do Begin
        J := J + 1;
        B[J] := Item;
        Read (Item)
      End;

    {Compute and Print Average}
    FindMean (B, J, Avg) ;
    Writeln (Avg)

End {Main} .
```

**9.8** *Potpourri.* What is printed by the following program?

```
Program Potpourri (Output);
{This program illustrates many ways that identifiers can
 be redefined and changed.}

Var A, B, C: Integer;

Function TwiceSum (Var X, Y: Integer; B: Integer): Integer;
    Var A: Real;
    Procedure Double(Var A: Integer; B: Real);
        Begin
            Writeln ('    Double 1:', A:5, B:6:1, C:4, X:5, Y:5);
            A := 2 * A;
            B := A;
            Writeln ('    Double 2:', A:5, B:6:1, C:4, X:5, Y:5)
        End {Minus} ;
    Begin {TwiceSum}
        A := 2.7;
        Writeln ('  TwiceSum 1:', A:6:1, B:4, C:5, X:5, Y:5);
        C := X + Y;
        X := B + C;
        Double (X, A);
        TwiceSum := X;
        Writeln ('  TwiceSum 2:', A:6:1, B:4, C:5, X:5, Y:5)
    End {TwiceSum} ;
```

```
Procedure PartTwo(X: Integer; Var Y: Integer);
    Var C: Integer;
    Function A: Integer;
        Begin
            Writeln ('Function A 1:', B:10, C:5, X:5, Y:5);
            C := X + Y;
            A := 2 * C;
            Writeln ('Function A 2:', B:10, C:5, X:5, Y:5)
        End {FunctionA} ;
    Begin {PartTwo}
        C := -3;
        Writeln ('    PartTwo 1:', B:10, C:5, X:5, Y:5);
        B := A + TwiceSum(X, Y, B);
        Writeln ('    PartTwo 2:', B:10, C:5, X:5, Y:5)
    End {PartTwo} ;

Begin {Main}
    {Print Headings}
    Writeln ('     Location    A    B    C    X    Y');

    {Initialization}
    A := 1;
    B := 2;
    C := 3;
    Writeln ('      Main 1:', A:5, B:5, C:5);

    {Apply Function TwiceSum}
    C := TwiceSum (A, A, B);
    Writeln ('      Main 2:', A:5, B:5, C:5);

    {Apply Procedure PartTwo}
    PartTwo (A, B);
    Writeln ('      Main 3:', A:5, B:5, C:5)
End {Main} .
```

**9.9** *Test Driver Programs.* Section 8.6 includes an Insertion procedure, a Deletion procedure, and an Insertion Sort procedure. Write driver programs to test these procedures.

# CHAPTER 10

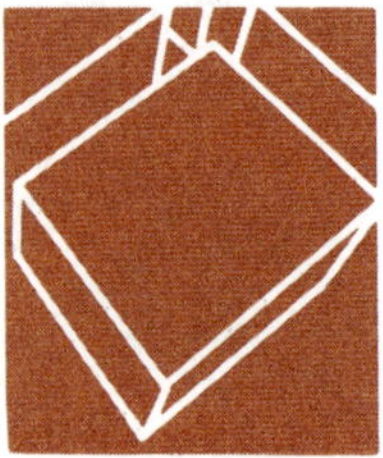

# PROGRAM CORRECTNESS AND ACCURACY

Our work to this point has included a top-down methodology for attacking problems and various programming techniques that allow us to translate our solution outlines into Pascal programs. In this chapter, we consider how we can be sure that our final programs produce correct answers.

To begin, we identify various potential sources of error. Then, we examine what we mean by the correctness of a program, and we discover that we can view correctness at two different levels. Finally, this background allows us to identify strategies to improve the quality of our programs at several stages in the development process.

## SECTION 10.1 POTENTIAL SOURCES OF ERROR

From our programming up to now, we are probably quite familiar with typographical errors, because they are often caught by the compiler when we try to compile our program. However, these errors represent only one of the many places that difficulties can arise. Mistakes can occur in our work before we even start coding. Also, in some situations, "correct" programs may produce unsatisfactory output.

When we think of problem solving as a process that starts with problem design and analysis and ends with the running of a program, we find we might make errors at each stage in this process. When we analyze these errors, we might divide them into the following categories.

- *Logical Errors.* These arise from mistakes, inconsistencies, or omissions in our approach to a problem.
- *Numerical Errors.* Many real numbers cannot be stored exactly in computers. The resulting numerical errors may significantly affect our answers in some cases.
- *Algorithm Selection Errors.* The algorithm we select may not produce answers in a reasonable amount of time, or the answers may not be sufficiently accurate.
- *Coding Errors.* We may make mistakes in translating our detailed algorithm into program code.
- *Data Entry Errors.* Even when a program is correct, we may obtain incorrect results if we have not entered our data correctly.

In the next five sections, we look at each of these types of error in more detail. Then, in the later part of this chapter we will develop strategies to find or avoid these problems early in the problem solving process.

## SECTION 10.2 LOGICAL ERRORS

Logical errors arise from mistakes in our approach to a problem. Of course, people demonstrate considerable creativity in making mistakes, and we cannot possibly describe all ways that people can go wrong. However, we can identify some of the most common errors, including

- incorrect or unstated assumptions;
- faulty algorithm choice or specification;
- omissions; and
- inconsistencies.

### Assumptions

As we work on a problem, we should be aware of the assumptions we are making. For example, we may assume that a user usually will enter all of the required data on one line, or that the data will be in ascending order. Similarly, when we choose an algorithm to perform a particular task, we may assume that certain conditions are true. For example, to use the extremely efficient Binary Search Algorithm, our data must be ordered. Further, when we develop a formula to compute a desired quantity, our work may rest on certain conditions. For example, if we use the following variation of the standard deviation formula

$$\text{Standard Deviation} = [(x_1 - \overline{x})^2 + \ldots + (x_n - \overline{x})^2]/[n - 1]$$

the formula assumes $n > 1$.

In any of these cases, we need to identify what our assumptions are, so we can be sure they are met. For example, we must notify the user if we assume something about the way data will be entered. Similarly, we must decide how to proceed if our data violate the conditions that we need. (How will we deal with standard deviation if $n = 1$?)

In general, we must be sure we know what our assumptions are, so we can take them into account in the problem solving process and so our resulting programs will be correct and accurate.

## Algorithms

When we choose or develop an algorithm to accomplish a task, we obviously want our final algorithm to do the work required. Clearly, our choice of algorithm is correct if the algorithm does the right job, and our choice is wrong otherwise. For example, we would hardly pick an algorithm that scores a bowling game if we want to sort data. Blatant problems in algorithms may be easy to find, but more subtle errors frequently occur that are much harder to locate.

Two examples illustrate ways that trouble can arise if we are not absolutely clear what the algorithm is to do. In the first one, suppose we are to search a list of data for a particular item. Here, we need to know what result we want when the search is complete. Do we want a result "True" or "False" indicating whether the item is found? Or, do we want to know the location on the list where the specified item is located? Similar searching algorithms could address either question, but the details of these two algorithms would be different.

As a second example, suppose we are to insert a new item into our ordered list of data, and we specify a function to locate the place for our insertion. Here, the function might return either the location of the next smaller datum in the list or the location of the next larger datum. If our algorithm returns one of these when we expected the other, our problem solution will be wrong. If our algorithm sometimes returns one of these and sometimes the other, the error in our solution may be quite hard to find.

In a related matter, we must be sure that any loops start and stop correctly. For example, if we want to read data entered from a terminal until we encounter a sentinel value, we must be sure the sentinel is not included in our processing. Similarly, if we want to add

$$(1.0)^2 + (1.5)^2 + \ldots + (9.5)^2 + (10.0)^2$$

we must account for 19 terms. If we miscount these terms, so we have 18 or 20 items instead, our result will be related to the correct answer, but the algorithm will be wrong.

Once we describe carefully what an algorithm is to do, we may be able to check that a particular algorithm works correctly. Errors frequently arise when our algorithm specification is not sufficiently precise. When we are a bit sloppy, our algorithm may look fine, but it may answer a slightly different question than we are asking.

## Omissions

Another common source of trouble is the omission of important considerations. For example, we can ask the following.

*Do all loops stop?* We must check each loop to be sure that the exit condition will eventually be met. For example, in a search, our loop must stop even if an item is not found.

*Are all cases covered?* For example, in tabulating a survey, we must consider the case where no one answers a particular question.

*Do we need a special case for the first or last step in a loop?* We must check whether the processing for the first or last iteration in a loop follows the general pattern. For example, in an Insertion Sort, we do not check the first item against previous ones before inserting it in a list, but we do check subsequent items.

*Will our subscripts always be within proper bounds?* We may need to check subscripts to ensure they will not be too big or too small. For example, we should be sure that there is space to add an item to a list of data stored in an array.

Each of these questions has many implications for problem solving. When we neglect special cases, we may find that our resulting programs work sporadically. Sometimes the programs seem to work fine, but other times they stop abruptly. Such bugs can be hard to locate.

## Inconsistencies

Inconsistencies arise most often in large programs, when we change our perspective from one step to another. Thus, when we look at successive steps in our solution outline, we should ask the following.

*Are we using consistent variable names?* Variable names may be confused in different parts of the program. The use of two names may be interchanged from one procedure to another.

*Are our data types the same?* Data may be considered in tabular form one place in a program but in list form later on. Double subscripting in one procedure will not agree with single subscripting elsewhere.

*Are reference parameters accidentally changed by side effects?* We may use reference parameters by mistake instead of value parameters, or we may inadvertently change reference parameters in a function or procedure.

Problems in these areas may be found in almost every beginning programming class, when reasonably long programs (more than 200 lines) are required. Problems arising from the use of global variables in inconsistent ways are particularly common. Many of these problems are reduced if we write out what each step in our outline is to do, where it is to get its data from, and how it is to return its results. In short, a careful top-down approach to problem solving normally prevents most inconsistencies from occurring. However, shortcuts in this approach regularly yield programs that are hopelessly confused because of the inconsistent use of data types and variables.

## SECTION 10.3 NUMERICAL ERRORS

Computers may not store real numbers exactly, because of various practical limitations on storage. In particular, a computer can store only a certain number of significant digits of a real number, and when real numbers require more than that degree of accuracy, **round-off error** results. The amount of round-off error may vary from one machine to another, but such an error is always potentially present. In contrast, integers are stored exactly, so they need not involve round-off error.

### Decimal-Binary Conversion

Storage of real numbers is further compounded by the way computers are built. In particular, electrical devices depend upon closed and open circuits (current flowing or not), and this circuitry is then used to represent numbers. For example, when writing numbers, a computer might interpret 1 as current flowing or high voltage and 0 as no current flowing or low voltage. Thus, numbers are usually represented using two digits, 0 and 1, rather than in decimal form. The resulting numbers are called **binary numbers** (we omit the details of these numbers in this text). Here, our main concern is that not all decimals translate exactly into a few binary digits.

*Example:* ⅓ does not translate into an exact decimal that can be stored by a computer. If we store 8 significant digits, then ⅓ = 0.33333333. All of the places beyond the eighth are lost.

The same situation arises when various decimal numbers are stored in binary form. For example, 0.1 cannot be stored exactly in a computer in binary form.

This leads to the following basic principle which we must recognize.

*Whenever we work with real numbers in a computer, we cannot assume the numbers are exact; there is always the potential for a numerical error.*

### Consequences of Numerical Errors

This potential for numerical error has several practical consequences in programming. Here, we consider

- writing Boolean expressions;
- writing exit conditions;
- non-associativity;
- promulgation of errors; and
- use of index or control variables.

A few illustrations dramatize these consequences particularly well.

**Boolean Expressions.** Consider the following program:

```
Program LongLoop (Output);

Const Inc = 0.1;         {Increment added each time through loop}
Var Sum: Real;           {The result of our additions}
    Difference: Real;    {Difference between Sum and 1.0}

Begin
    Writeln ('We add 0.1 successively, starting at 0.0 until we reach 1.0');
    Writeln;
    Writeln ('    Sum       Difference from 1.0');

    Sum := 0.0;
    Repeat

        Difference := 1.0 - Sum;
        Writeln (Sum:10:8, Difference:18:10);
        Sum := Sum + Inc

    Until (Sum = 1.0);

    Writeln('Program Done')
End.
```

When we ran this program on one particular machine the output began as follows.

```
We add 0.1 successively, starting at 0.0 until we reach 1.0

    Sum       Difference from 1.0
0.00000000      1.0000000000
0.10000000      0.9000000000
0.20000000      0.8000000000
0.30000000      0.7000000000
0.40000000      0.6000000000
0.50000000      0.5000000000
0.60000000      0.4000000000
0.70000000      0.3000000000
0.80000010      0.1999999000
0.90000010      0.0999999000
1.00000000     -0.0000001192
1.10000000     -0.1000001000
1.20000000     -0.2000002000
1.30000000     -0.3000002000
1.40000000     -0.4000002000
1.50000000     -0.5000002000
1.60000000     -0.6000003000

    .
    .
    .
```

Here, the computer continues to produce output beyond the point we expect. The program starts at 0 and adds 0.1 until we get to 1.0, so we expect our program will stop after 10 iterations.

However, here the 0.1 is not stored exactly. When we add 0.1 several times, this inaccuracy grows and our sum never actually equals 1.0. Our sum does equal 1.0 to six decimal places, but our result contains a small numerical error. *Program Done* is never printed.

This example shows that when we compare real numbers, we may want to allow for possible error. Thus, in this program, instead of continuing until *Sum* = 1.0, we might substitute a test for proximity:

Abs(Sum − 1.0) < 0.001

**Exit Conditions.** A modification of the above program illustrates a related problem with Boolean expressions as exit conditions.

```
Program ShortLoop (Output);

Const Inc = 0.1;          {Increment added each time through loop}
Var Sum: Real;            {The result of our additions}

Begin
    Writeln ('We add 0.1 successively, starting at 0.0 ',
             'while we do not exceed 1.0');
    Writeln;

    Sum :=.0.0;
    While (Sum <= 1.0)
      Do Begin
        Write (Sum:5:1);
        Sum := Sum + Inc
      End;

    Writeln('   Program Done')
End.
```

Here, we want to continue our loop but not exceed 1.0. However, our output appears to skip the final case where *Sum* = 1.0. The actual output is

```
We add 0.1 successively, starting at 0.0 while we do not exceed 1.0

  0.0  0.1  0.2  0.3  0.4  0.5  0.6  0.7  0.8  0.9   Program Done
```

When we look at the output from the previous program, we see the difficulty is that the numerical error gives us results that are slightly too large. In particular, the machine computes 1.000001192 instead of 1.0 during the 10th time through the loop. Thus, while we expected a *Sum* of 1.0 to be printed at the end of our loop, this case was skipped. The loop stopped one iteration before we expected. Here, numerical errors have shortened our loop by one iteration.

This example illustrates the following:

> *We cannot depend upon real variables to count loop iterations; numerical errors may cause steps to be skipped when real variables are incremented and tested in exit conditions.*

This potential for numerical error is precisely the reason why Pascal does not allow real variables as control variables. Some other languages do not have this restriction, but they always have the potential for unexpected results when a particular iteration is skipped. Pascal eliminates this possibility of error in control variables.

**Non-Associativity.** Another consequence of real number storage is that arithmetic no longer follows the familiar rules that we depend upon in much of our traditional thinking about numbers. In particular, *addition is not associative.* In other words, we cannot assume that

$$(a + b) + c = a + (b + c)$$

for all real numbers $a$, $b$, $c$. Instead it may matter if we perform $(a + b)$ or $(b + c)$ first.

As an example, suppose that our computer stores exactly 8 digits of accuracy and suppose that it rounds to those 8 digits after each operation. Now, suppose we add

$$1.0000000 + 0.00000004 + 0.00000004$$

in two ways.

a. If we add the first two numbers, we get

$$\begin{aligned} & 1.0000000 + 0.00000004 \\ &= (1.00000004) \\ &= 1.0000000 \qquad \text{rounding to 8 significant digits (including the 1).} \end{aligned}$$

Thus

$$\begin{aligned} & (1.0000000 + 0.00000004) + 0.00000004 \\ &= (1.0000000) + 0.00000004 \qquad \text{first addition with rounding;} \\ &= 1.0000000 \qquad \text{second addition with rounding.} \end{aligned}$$

b. If we add the second two numbers first, we get

$$0.00000004 + 0.00000004 = 0.00000008$$

and

| | |
|---|---|
| 1.0000000 + (0.00000004 + 0.00000004) | |
| = 1.0000000 + (0.00000008) | first addition; |
| = (1.00000008) | second addition before rounding; |
| = 1.0000001 | second addition after rounding. |

These three numbers demonstrate that the order of addition matters. When we add small numbers to large numbers, the small numbers can be lost completely (as in a. above). On the other hand, if we add small numbers first, the small pieces can accumulate enough to affect the large number (as in b. above).

When we are adding many such numbers, the cumulative effect of these errors can be quite noticeable. For example, consider the following:

**PROBLEM 10.3**

It can be shown that

$$\pi^2 = 6 + 6/2^2 + 6/3^2 + 6/4^2 + \ldots .$$

Use this series to approximate the value of $\pi$.

## Discussion of Problem 10.3

The above formula indicates that we can approximate $\pi^2$ by adding more and more terms of this series. In other words,

$$\pi^2 \approx 6 + 6/2^2 + 6/3^2 + 6/4^2 + \ldots + 6/n^2$$

where $n$ is a large integer.

When we compute the right-hand side of this equation, we will get an approximate value of $\pi^2$. Then by taking the square root, we can approximate $\pi$.

When we look at this series carefully, we see that the terms get smaller continually as the denominators get bigger. Thus, we must be careful when we add up our terms. If we start with the first term 6, we will have our large numbers first, and the small terms will not affect these large results. If we start with the small terms, the small values can accumulate. This difference is illustrated in the following program.

```
Program Series (Output);
{Approximation of Pi}
{Using the series Sqr(Pi) = 6 + 6/Sqr(2) + 6/Sqr(3) + ...}
Var SumUp, SumDown, IReal: Real;
    Index, N: Integer;

Begin {Main}
    {Determine number of terms to be used in the approximation}
    Writeln ('The value of Pi is approximated by using N terms of a series.');
    Write('Enter N: ');
    Readln(N);
```

```
    {Compute terms in ascending order}
    SumUp := 0.0;
    For Index := 1 to N
      Do Begin
        IReal := Index;
        SumUp := SumUp + 6.0/Sqr(IReal)
      End;

    {Compute terms in descending order}
    SumDown := 0.0;
    For Index := N DownTo 1
      Do Begin
        IReal := Index;
        SumDown := SumDown + 6.0/Sqr(Ireal)
      End;

    {Print Results}
    Writeln;
    Writeln(' Number Of        Approximations to Pi');
    Writeln('  Terms    Biggest First    Smallest First');
    Writeln(N:7, Sqrt(SumUp):17:10, Sqrt(SumDown):17:10)
End {Main} .
```

When this program is run for various values of $n$, we get the following output:

```
First Trial Run

The value of Pi is approximated by using N terms of a series.
Enter N: 1000

 Number Of        Approximations to Pi
  Terms    Biggest First    Smallest First
   1000     3.1406390000     3.1406380000


Second Trial Run

The value of Pi is approximated by using N terms of a series.
Enter N: 3000

 Number Of        Approximations to Pi
  Terms    Biggest First    Smallest First
   3000     3.1412800000     3.1412740000


Third Trial Run

The value of Pi is approximated by using N terms of a series.
Enter N: 3543
```

```
 Number Of        Approximations to Pi
   Terms     Biggest First    Smallest First
    3543      3.1413630000     3.1413230000

Fourth Trial Run

The value of Pi is approximated by using N terms of a series.
Enter N: 5000

 Number Of        Approximations to Pi
   Terms     Biggest First    Smallest First
    5000      3.1413630000     3.1414020000

Fifth Trial Run

The value of Pi is approximated by using N terms of a series.
Enter N: 30000

 Number Of        Approximations to Pi
   Terms     Biggest First    Smallest First
   30000      3.1413630000     3.1415610000
```

This output illustrates several important points:

- When we add a series in one order, we can get different results than if we add it in another order.
- When we add terms in descending order, the large terms dominate and small terms can be lost. In this program, when we add the large terms first, our approximation for $\pi$ does not change after $n = 3542$. After this, the additional terms are too small to affect the already large sum.
- When we add terms in ascending order, the small terms can contribute. When we add the small terms first, our approximation for $\pi$ continually improves as we add more terms.

**Propagation of Errors.** The previous example also illustrates that when we put real numbers together, the size of the numerical errors can increase. Each real number may be off by a small amount; when we combine these numbers, we may combine these errors. This error can be particularly significant when we subtract two numbers of about the same size, for then our result depends largely on the least accurate parts of the original numbers.

## SECTION 10.4 CHOICE OF ALGORITHM

Any algorithm that we might select for a program must meet at least two fundamental criteria, namely efficiency and accuracy. The algorithm must be efficient enough to produce results in a reasonable length of time, and the results must be sufficiently accurate to solve the problem. In this section, we look at some practical consequences of each of these criteria.

## Efficiency

Algorithm efficiency can be divided into two fairly obvious parts. First, we must be confident that an algorithm eventually will stop. A program containing an infinite loop cannot be helpful. Second, once we know the algorithm will stop, we can analyze how much time will normally be required for the output.

While these points may seem obvious in considering program efficiency, they do have important practical implications in our design of algorithms. Consider the following:

- Given the possibility of numerical errors discussed in the previous section, Boolean expressions and exit conditions must allow for small differences between real numbers that theoretically should be the same.
- If an algorithm requires a great deal of computer time to produce an answer, we may want to find a better way to proceed. In some cases, we may be able to streamline a given algorithm to make it work more effectively. In other cases, we may have to discard one algorithm completely, and we may need to discover a new approach to the problem. For example, when data are ordered, we changed our approach from the simple Linear Search to develop the substantially better Binary Search.

## Accuracy

In the last section, we saw that arithmetic cannot be assumed to be associative. Thus, when adding many numbers, we should add the smallest ones first. Similarly, we saw round-off error can accumulate; when adding many numbers, our results may include some error even when the results theoretically should be getting very close to the "correct" answers.

Thus, in choosing an algorithm, we must have confidence that our final results will be sufficiently accurate to be helpful. Here, we can distinguish three types of algorithms.

- Some algorithms (e.g., the Bisection Method of Section 7.6) do not tend to accumulate errors. In these algorithms, each step starts fresh, and previous computations are not used again. Thus, in these algorithms, numerical error does not tend to accumulate.
- Other algorithms tend to accumulate round-off error. Any inaccuracy in one step is compounded in the next step. (We will see an example of such an algorithm later in this section.) For these algorithms, we must be aware that numerical errors can accumulate, and we must be careful not to expect too much accuracy in our results.
- Some algorithms may even be self-correcting. In these algorithms, any errors in previous steps tend to be corrected in subsequent steps. (For

example, in finding the solutions of an equation, two common algorithms, called Newton's Method and the Method of False Position, are self-correcting. More details on these algorithms may be found in texts on calculus or numerical methods.)

## Coding Implications

These comments on efficiency and accuracy have several coding implications.

In some programs, we may want to count the number of times that a loop is executed. If the number exceeds a specified limit, we might want to stop the loop as a special case, thereby avoiding the possibility of an infinite loop.

When we are unsure about the efficiency of an algorithm, we may want to write the algorithm as a separate procedure. Then, if the algorithm does not run as efficiently as required, a new algorithm can be substituted in the program by changing only this procedure.

We can code our algorithms to minimize possible numerical errors. For example, we can identify two ways to compute

$$(0.1)^2 + (0.2)^2 + \ldots + (100.0)^2.$$

*Approach 1:*

```
Sum := 0.0;
XValue := 0.1;
While  (XValue <= 100.0)
       Do  Begin
              Sum := Sum + Sqr(XValue);
              XValue := XValue + 0.1
       End;
```

*Approach 2:*

```
Sum := 0.0;
For  I :=  1 to 1000
     Do Begin
          XValue := I/10.0;
          Sum := Sum + Sqr(XValue)
     End;
```

In looking at the first approach, we see two problems. First, our exit condition does not allow for possible error in *XValue*, and we may stop one iteration too soon in our loop. In addition, any inaccuracy in the storage of 0.1 will be compounded as the loop proceeds, since the values of *XValue* depend upon previous values.

In contrast, the second approach does not allow these errors to accumulate. Since our loop depends on an integer control variable, we will continue our loop the correct number of times. Further, *XValue* is recomputed from the exact integer *I* each time in the loop. Previous inaccuracies in *XValue* are not included.

## SECTION 10.5 CODING ERRORS

Once we have chosen our algorithm and outlined our solution, we are ready for coding. Here, we can distinguish two principal types of errors.

- Typographical errors
- Errors in translating from our algorithm or outline to our Pascal program.

### Typographical Errors

As early as Section 2.8, we saw that a compiler will find many typographical errors, since each variable, function, and procedure we use must agree with an identifier we have declared. However, Section 2.8 also noted that some typographical errors cannot be caught by a compiler. For example, a compiler cannot find errors in literal numbers, characters, or Booleans (3.1416 might be written 3.1614). Similarly, the compiler will not detect substitutions of one identifier for another. For example, if both I and J are declared, I might be used for J on a particular line.

The first of these errors can be minimized by the wise use of constants. For example, if we declare

Const Pi = 3.1416

then we only need to check the digits of the constant once. Thereafter, we can refer to it symbolically as *Pi*.

The elimination of the second class of these errors depends upon careful proofreading. We must examine our code in detail to be sure we have typed what we meant. This is a major point where program formatting and style become important. If our code reads naturally, we often can find typographical errors fairly easily. Descriptive identifiers are particularly useful here, for the names tell us what we are doing. For example, we will find it harder to confuse identifiers *Quarts* and *Liters* than the abbreviations *Q* and *L*.

### Translation Errors

Errors also can arise in translating from our algorithms and solution outline into Pascal. One way this might happen is if we implement particular steps incorrectly. Translation errors also may result if our outline is not sufficiently complete so that logical errors may occur as we add the required details to our code.

In each of these areas, careful formatting and the division of our program into procedures and functions can help us check our work. Normally, details are easy to check if they are isolated in short pieces of code. Also, the major flow of our program is clear if details are separated from major steps. In short, programs that are well structured generally are easy to proofread and correct.

### Caution

This discussion of program structure assumes considerable preliminary work in structuring solutions. When this preliminary work is not done, the task of developing algorithms and writing details falls into the coding process. In any approach to problem solving, we must complete all details before we are done. Thus, if we avoid the details at one stage, we must face them later on.

When we consider the programming process, it is easier to correct programs before they are written. Adding details at coding time is a highly error-prone venture. Experience suggests that we take the time to write out our design carefully, before we are committed to particular pieces of code.

## SECTION 10.6 DATA ENTRY ERRORS

In Section 8.9, we noted that even a correct program can produce inappropriate results if the program is given incorrect data. Thus, in planning a program, we should consider the possibility that errors will be found in the program input. These input errors fall into three classes:

input that is impossible;

input that is unlikely, but possible; and

plausible input that is incorrect.

For each of these types of errors, we may need to proceed differently.

### Impossible Input

In some situations, we may be able to determine that a particular input value could not possibly be correct. The following examples illustrate such situations.

In the Tic-Tac-Toe game of Section 8.9, our move must be in row 1, 2, or 3 and in column 1, 2, or 3. Further, we cannot mark a square that has been taken previously. If we try to move into row 5 or if we try to move on an occupied square, our move is invalid.

If we are recording telephone numbers, we know the form of our input should be

(area code)-(exchange)-(number).

Further, we know

the area code contains 3 digits, and the second digit is 0 or 1;

the exchange contains 3 digits and the second digit cannot be a 0 or 1; and

the number contains 4 digits.

Thus, we can conclude that each of the following telephone numbers is invalid.

| | |
|---|---|
| 123-456-7890 | second digit of area code incorrect |
| 312-5555-8901 | wrong number of digits for exchange |
| 312-515-5432 | incorrect second digit of exchange |

Many credit card numbers include digits for checking typing. For example, in a 10-digit number, the 10th digit might be chosen so the sum of the digits is 0 mod 10. Thus,

| | |
|---|---|
| 1234567895 | is possible |
| 0123456789 | is impossible |

In any of these cases, we can state rules that can be used to check if an input value is possible. Then, in programming we can check this, and we can request users to reenter data that are definitely wrong.

This checking is particularly important if we write our programs based on certain assumptions in the data. For example, in the Tic-Tac-Toe program of Section 8.9, we want to write

```
Read (Row, Column)
   .
   .
   .
Board [Row, Column] := X
```

Here, we must know our *Row* and *Column* will have values 1, 2, or 3. Any other values will cause our array subscript to be out of bounds, and our program will terminate prematurely. Thus, in this program, invalid data could halt processing if we do not check each input value first.

## Possible but Unlikely Input

In other applications, we may want a user to double check an input value before we continue. Here, we might expect values of a certain type or range, but we cannot rule out the possibility of other values.

- In a grocery store, we expect most individual items to be between $0.00 and $100.00 (exclusive). Items over $100.00 are very unlikely, although they are possible. (For example, one side of beef from the meat department could exceed this amount.)
- Test scores rarely exceed 100% although extra credit sometimes brings scores over this point.
- Few customers have a birth date before the year 1900, but a few might.

In these cases, we need to scan an input value to see if it is unlikely to be correct, and we may ask the user to verify the correctness of the datum. For example, if a grocery item costs $150.00, we may wonder if the cashier has entered an extra "0," and we may give the cashier an opportunity to correct this value. However, since this value is possible, our program must allow this value to be processed.

### Possible but Incorrect Input

In the previous two cases, we have been able to identify input data that were suspect. Our job of verifying input is much harder if the values seem plausible. For example, if a grocery item costing $3.29 is incorrectly marked as $2.39, we will have difficulty spotting an error. The $2.39 value seems to be a reasonable cost for an item, and we would have no reason to suspect a mistake unless we checked an inventory list or invoice.

In such situations, we may elect several approaches to data entry.

1. We may decide that such errors are too costly or time consuming to find, and we may elect to ignore them.
2. We may supply the user with a printout of all data entered, so the user can check the values manually. (The paper receipt at the grocery store allows this type of checking.)
3. We may add digits to our data, so the data can be checked automatically. For example, after a cost, we may write the sum of the digits (mod 10) and the product of the odd digits (mod 10). Thus, for $3.29

$$\text{sum of digits} = 3 + 2 + 9 = 14$$
$$\text{product of odd digits} = 3 * 9 = 27$$

and 3.29 would be coded

$$3.29 - 4 - 7$$

Such checks do not completely eliminate the possibility of error, but these checks could spot many typographical errors. In general, the field of Coding Theory includes the study of how these check-digits can be added to numbers so that many types of data errors can be identified.

### Implications in Programming

In practice, we may find that we want to combine several types of checks for input data. Some values may be impossible. Other values may be possible, but unlikely. When checking input data, we often write the details of data entry in a separate procedure:

```
Procedure Enter (Var Value: Data)
```

This procedure reads a value, checks it for being impossible or unlikely, asks the user for corrections, if necessary, and returns a "correct" value. All details of data entry are buried inside this procedure, so the rest of the program can rely upon this procedure for obtaining correct values. Checking is not required outside the procedure.

## SECTION 10.7 DEGREES OF PROGRAM CORRECTNESS

Now that we have seen how various types of errors can arise, we can put several of these ideas together in our development of correct programs.

Of course, any program is correct and useful only if it answers the questions that we are asking. Thus, in evaluating a program, we first must specify explicitly what the program is to do. Then the correctness of the program depends upon whether it meets this specification. We cannot discuss the correctness of a program in isolation; we must know what problem we are solving before we can evaluate a program.

### Testing and Correctness

Once we know what a program is supposed to do, we can try to determine if the program performs correctly. Here, we should be careful to distinguish between two categories of statements:

> "This program produces correct answers for all possible values of data."

> "This program *seems* to produce correct answers." (At least, we have not found any instances where incorrect results are obtained.)

The first of these statements asserts that the program is correct, while the second asserts that the program is *likely* to be correct. In the first case, we can rely upon our results, for we know that no bugs are present in our program. In the second case, we know we have not found any bugs, but we cannot rule out the possibility that a subtle error might exist somewhere. Thus, the first statement is much stronger than the second.

To clarify this distinction, we consider the following.

## PROBLEM 10.7 Prime Numbers

A positive integer is *prime* if it is divisible only by 1 and itself. Thus, 2, 3, and 5 are prime, but 6 is not. (6 is divisible by 2 and 3 as well as by 1.)

Write a program that reads a positive integer and determines if the number is prime.

Let us consider the following attempt to solve this program.

```
Program PrimeMaybe (Input, Output);
{This program attempts to determine if a given Number is prime.}
Var Number: Integer;
Begin
    Writeln ('Prime tester');
    Write ('Enter integer to be tested: ');
    Readln (Number);
    If (Number = 2) Or
       ((Number > 1) And ((Number Mod 2) = 1))
        Then Writeln ('The number is prime.')
        Else Writeln ('The number is not prime.')
End .
```

When we run this program for the test cases 1, 2, 3, 4, 5, 6, 7, and 8, we find the program gives correct results. Further, if we try larger numbers such as 28, 29, 30, 31, 101, 102, 103, and 104, the program works correctly. From these tests, we may conclude that our program *seems* to be correct, and we might expect that these sixteen test cases are more than adequate to check our code. However, we cannot conclude that the program works correctly for all possible values, and in fact, the program incorrectly identifies the integer 9 as a prime number. (More generally, the program fails for odd, non-primes larger than 1.)

This example illustrates two important points.

1. When we say a program is correct, we mean that the program will produce correct results for all possible input values.
2. Testing specific values of input cannot prove a program is correct, unless we actually test all possible input values.

When we test a program by using selected data, we may be able to conclude that our program is not correct. Certainly, we know that a bug is present if our answers are wrong. However, correct test runs cannot prove our programs work for all input values unless we have tested all such values. We must be careful not to infer too much from a few test cases. Test cases may give us some confidence about our work, but they do not prove the work.

## Determining Program Correctness

Next, we need to ask how we could conclude that a program is correct. This can be done in two basic ways: exhaustive testing and verification.

**Exhaustive Testing.** In some problems, we can actually test all possible cases. For example, if we want the computer to print the number of days in each month for the year 1986, we can check the output in complete detail. Similarly, if our problem only makes sense for integer values between $-5$ and 10 (inclusive), then we could enter each value and check the results. This approach to proving program correctness is called **exhaustive testing,** and it is feasible only when the number of possible cases in our problem is fairly small.

**Verification.** If the number of data items in our problem is large, exhaustive testing is not feasible, and we must proceed differently. One approach that has sparked a great deal of research in computer science is called **program verification.** Here, the task of the program is specified in precise, formal terms, and a formal proof is constructed to show that the program does the desired task.

For example, when proving results about a procedure or function, we can begin with some pre-assertions which we assume to be true. From these givens, we might prove in a formal way that our post-assertions hold. The approach is similar to the approach used in geometry where axioms (pre-assertions) are assumed to be true and theorems (post-assertions) are then proven. In this process, we may find it convenient to make statements about what happens in the middle of a procedure or function. These intermediate statements are the assertions and loop invariants that we discussed in Sections 5.7 and 7.5.

Throughout this approach, we do not rely on testing to check that a program seems to run correctly. Rather, formal logic is used to make conclusions about a program. Then, whenever we run our program, we know our results will be correct (according to our post-assertions) for any input data meeting our pre-assertions.

## SECTION 10.8 METHODS OF PROGRAM TESTING

In the previous section, we said that exhaustive testing can guarantee that a program is correct, but we noted that such testing is rarely feasible. In this section, we look at how we might select test data when our tests cannot cover all cases. Here, we hope that some carefully selected test runs can help us eliminate many bugs that might be in our code initially. In particular, we can identify two basic approaches for testing.

**Top-Down Testing.** When we have organized our program into modules, we can first test each module separately. Then, when our testing has helped us correct any errors within each module, we can put these pieces together and test that the pieces interact properly.

In this approach, we can use stubbing and small driver programs, which we discussed in Section 9.5. Also, where a compiler allows procedures and functions to be compiled and linked separately, we can save time in correcting individual pieces and in putting them together.

**Bottom-Up Testing.** We can assemble our entire program first and then run tests for the entire code. Here, when a program produces an error for a test, we trace our code line-by-line and module-by-module until we find a bug.

With either of these approaches, we want to select tests to uncover as many bugs as possible. Occasionally, our problem may allow the exhaustive testing that we discussed in the previous section. With such problems, our test data can include all possible cases, and our selection of test cases is straightforward.

When exhaustive testing is not feasible, we must select some sample test data. Here, we can apply the ideas of **every-path testing** and **boundary value testing** from Section 6.8 in two ways: we can focus on our statement of our problem or we can concentrate on our code. This suggests the following possibilities.

*Problem Analysis, Every-Path Testing.* We can identify the various cases that can arise in our problem, and we can test our program with representative data for each case.

*Problem Analysis, Boundary Value Testing.* We can identify the conditions that separate one case from another, and we can check that our program moves from one case to another at the appropriate time.

*Code Analysis, Every-Path Testing.* Within our code, we can try to identify all possible ways that a computer can execute our program, and we can test each of these execution paths.

*Code Analysis, Boundary Value Testing.* We can identify and test that the computer shifts from one execution path to another at the appropriate time.

### Comparison of Top-Down and Bottom-Up Testing

When we apply these guidelines with a Top-Down or Bottom-Up approach to testing, we can make several useful observations. First, when the total number of possible cases in our problem or program is small, then either testing approach can work well. We can manage the various cases without being overwhelmed. On the other hand, when the total number of possible cases is large, we may find that the complete set of cases may not be feasible to check. In this situation, we may need to structure our testing to reduce the number of possibilities. With our top-down testing strategy, such structuring is possible because our modules can be relatively simple. We can try each procedure or function under a variety of situations. Then, in putting the modules together, we can limit our attention to the possible interaction of the modules. We may not have to test how every possibility for one module works with every possibility for another module. Unfortunately, this structuring of our testing is not compatible with the bottom-up testing strategy, and we may not be able to manage a large number of cases with this alternate approach.

While the testing of modules and the review of final results does not eliminate the possibility of error, we can expect that many (if not all) of our bugs have been discovered and corrected.

## SECTION 10.9 WRITING CORRECT SOLUTIONS

The previous section has outlined several techniques that we can use to test whether our programs work correctly. In this section, we observe that these same ideas can be applied fruitfully to the earlier phases of the problem solving process.

We have seen that programming is only one step in a process that begins with specifications, design, and choice of algorithms. Each of these steps builds on our earlier work, so we can expect errors (e.g., omissions, inconsistencies) from one step to be reflected in our subsequent work. If we can correct difficulties before we start to code, we will not have to change our programs to correct such trouble after the programs are written. Programs are easiest to correct before they are written, so we can find it worthwhile to analyze and check each problem solving step before we move to the next one. More specifically, we can analyze each of these steps to see if we can spot errors or potential problems. Table 10–1 lists some questions we should address throughout the problem solving process.

## Walk Throughs

When our problems are relatively simple, we may tend to be somewhat casual about such questions. For example, we may decide just to proofread our specifications or design. On the other hand, complex problems require more care. In such cases, we can formally review our work for various sample data sets to see if our outlines are adequate. Here, our review is called a **walk through,** and we begin with particular data from the problem, checking that our work leads us methodically to a correct result. For example, we may trace our design step-by-step for a given set of data, just as we may trace the execution of our programs when we are testing with test data.

In major software development projects, where problems are complex and several people are involved in the work, special meetings are often scheduled for this testing. **Design reviews** allow many people to check

**TABLE 10–1 • Checklist for the Problem Solving Process**

| | |
|---|---|
| *Specifications* | Are the specifications complete? |
| | Have we omitted any cases? |
| | Have we indicated what is required in each case? |
| | Do the specifications state what is actually meant? |
| | Are the specifications contradictory? |
| | Do some cases overlap? |
| *Design* | Have we broken our problem into logically independent pieces? |
| | Will the pieces fit together to meet the specifications? |
| | Have we left cases out? |
| | Are the cases contradictory? |
| | Have we defined each piece clearly and unambiguously? |
| *Algorithm Selection* | Does each algorithm do the task required? |
| | Have we considered all cases? |
| | Is the algorithm accurate, or could numerical errors reduce the usefulness of our results? |
| | Is the algorithm efficient? |
| | Will the algorithm always finish? |

through the details of the algorithms and design. Before that, software developers meet formally with clients to check that specifications address the desired job.

Throughout this chapter, we have identified various ways that errors can arise and we have seen techniques to help reduce or eliminate errors. When we consider the questions mentioned in this section and the possibilities for testing, we see that our techniques for coding apply equally well to the earlier stages of problem solving. When we apply these techniques, we often can eliminate errors before they require a major revision of much of our work.

## SUMMARY

1. Programs are correct when they produce the results required by a problem.
2. Errors in our final programs may be introduced at any of the stages of the problem solving process, including specifications, design and algorithm selection, and programming.
3. Potential sources for errors include **logical errors,** such as mistaken assumptions, omissions, or inconsistencies; **numerical errors,** which may arise from **round-off error,** real arithmetic, or decimal-binary conversions; **poor selection of algorithms,** since some algorithms may compound error, affecting the **accuracy** of the results, while others may not be **efficient; coding errors,** which arise when we translate our algorithms into programs; **data entry errors,** which may produce undesired results.
4. We may establish program correctness either by **testing** or **verification.**
   a. **Testing** involves the use of test data and may proceed in either a **top-**

### KEY TERMS, PHRASES, AND CONCEPTS

Algorithm
  Accuracy
  Efficiency
Binary Numbers
Design Reviews
Errors
  Coding
  Data Entry
  Logical
  Numerical
    Decimal-Binary
      Conversion
    Finite Storage
      of Reals
    Non-Associativity
    Round-Off
Program Verification
Testing
  Bottom-Up
  Boundary Value
  Every-Path
  Exhaustive
  Top-Down
Walk Throughs

**down** or **bottom-up** manner. Testing can occur at each phase of the problem solving process. Thus, testing can include **walk throughs** for specifications, design, and algorithms as well as the identification of test data for checking programs.

b. **Verification** uses assertions and loop invariants to produce logical proofs that a program performs correctly in all cases.

## EXERCISES

**10.1** *Computing Infinity*. Consider the following program.

```
Program Infinity (Output);
Var Index: Integer;
    OldSum, Sum: Real;

Begin
    Writeln('This program adds 1.0 to a sum until the sum stops changing.');
    Sum := 0.0;
    Repeat
        OldSum := Sum;
        Sum := Sum + 1.0
    Until (Sum = OldSum);
    Writeln ('The sum stopped changing when it reached the value ',
             Sum:1:1, ' .')
End.
```

When this program is run on one particular machine, the output is

```
This program adds 1.0 to a sum until the sum stops changing.
The sum stopped changing when it reached the value 33554430.0 .
```

- Explain this result.
- (Optional) What happens when this program is run on your local system?

**10.2** *Harmonic Series: A Small Infinity*. In mathematics, one can show that the sum

$$1 + \frac{1}{2} + \frac{1}{3} + \frac{1}{4} + \ldots$$

approaches infinity. (This sum is called the *Harmonic Series* and is sometimes said to *diverge*.) From this viewpoint, the following program should never stop.

```
Program HarmonicSeries(Output);
Var Index: Real;
    Sum: Real;
Begin
    Writeln('This program computes the limit ',
            'of the harmonic series.');
    Sum := 0.0;
    Index := 1.0;
    Repeat
        Sum := Sum + 1.0/Index;
        Index := Index + 1
    Until (Sum = Sum + 1.0/Index);
    Writeln ('After ', Index:1:1, ' terms,');
    Writeln ('the harmonic series converges to ', Sum:1:5, ' !')
End.
```

Run this program on a computer and explain what happens.

**10.3** *Convergent Series.*[1] In mathematics, the convergence of series is defined as a limit of partial sums. In particular, we let

$$S_n = \sum_{i=1}^{n} a_i,$$

and then we define

$$\sum_{i=1}^{\infty} a_i = \lim_{n\to\infty} S_n.$$

With this definition, many tests for convergence and divergence are well established. One theorem states,

*Theorem:* If $\sum_{i=1}^{\infty} a_i$ converges, then $\lim_{n\to\infty} a_n = 0$.

However, the Harmonic Series shows that the converse of this theorem is not true.

**a.** Use what you know about numerical errors to prove that the converse is true if the partial sums are evaluated by computer.

**b.** Find a series in which partial sums do converge on your computer but where $\lim_{n\to\infty} a_n \neq 0$.

**10.4** *Comparison of Algorithms.* Consider the following problem.

After a fly settles on a table, a person tries to hit the fly with a flyswatter. In particular, the person starts with the flyswatter 1 yard from the table and the person moves the flyswatter at the rate of 1

[1] This problem requires a knowledge of convergent series. Students without this background should skip this problem.

yard/second. Does the person hit the fly? If so, when? (You may assume the fly remains still and the person has good aim.)

Now consider two solutions.

*Plato's Paradox.* We divide time into various intervals. In the first time interval, the flyswatter moves from 1 yard to ½ yard from the table. In the second interval, the flyswatter moves half the remaining distance, from ½ yard to ¼ yard from the table. In the third interval, the distance is again halved. In subsequent time intervals, this halving of distance continues. With all of these time intervals, the flyswatter never reaches the table.

*Another Approach.* The flyswatter travels 1 yard per second. Thus, in 1 second the flyswatter travels 1 yard. Since this is the distance from the initial position of the flyswatter to the table, the flyswatter must hit the table (and thus the fly) in 1 second.

**a.** Explain the apparent contradictory conclusions of these algorithms.

**b.** Write programs that implement each of these algorithms and compare the output of these programs.

**10.5** *Checking Input Data.* In each of the following, develop appropriate tests to determine if input data are impossible, implausible, or plausible.

**a.** Scholastic Aptitude Scores (SATs) are always between 200 and 800, inclusive.

**b.** Test grades normally range between 0 and 100. However, sometimes up to 20 points of extra credit are possible.

**10.6** *Checking Telephone Numbers.* Write a procedure that will read a telephone number and check that it has the appropriate form:

(area code)-(exchange)-(number).

If a number of the wrong form is entered, the procedure should ask the user to reenter the number.

**10.7** *Checking Input Data—Check Digits.* A particular product code has the form

(number)-(check)

where "number" is a four-digit number, and "check" is a check digit, derived from the number by adding the digits (mod 10). Thus,

1234-0 is a valid number (check = 1 + 2 + 3 + 4, mod 10)
5827-1 is invalid (check should be 2 if number is valid).

Write a procedure that reads a product code and checks that the code is legal. If the code is not legal, the procedure should ask the user to reenter the code.

**10.8** *Checking for Unlikely Input.* In a grocery store, we expect most individual items to be between $0.00 and $100.00 exclusive. Costs below $0.00 or above $300.00 are considered impossible, and costs between $100.00 and $300.00 (inclusive) are considered possible, but unlikely.

a. Write a program that
   - reads the costs of successive items until the sentinel value of $0.00 is read;
   - asks the user to verify possible, but unlikely, values;
   - finds impossible input values and asks the user to reenter these values; and
   - computes the total bill for the grocery items.

b. Modify your program so that all valid grocery costs are recorded and then printed after the bill total. (You may assume no more than 100 items will be purchased at one time.)

**10.9** *Selection of Test Data.* Choose test data for the following:

a. The Baby Sitter Problem (Exercise 6.10.)

b. The Bowling Score Program of Section 6.6.

c. The Credit-Balance Payment Program of Section 7.1.

d. The Insertion Sort Program (Exercise 8.5.)

**10.10** *Social Implications of Program Correctness in Administering Medicines.* In this chapter, we have seen several ways that can help us write correct programs, but we have also noted that these methods can be very hard to apply when dealing with large, complex programs. Certainly, we cannot use exhaustive testing for such programs. Similarly, we may find that it is not feasible even to list all possible cases for processing, so that every-path testing and boundary value testing are not possible or practical. Similar practical difficulties arise in applying the details of program verification to prove program correctness. Thus, we can identify circumstances where we cannot know if programs are correct. This uncertainty about a program's correctness presents many interesting philosophical problems when we try to use computers in various applications.

Consider the use of computers to monitor the condition of patients in hospitals. In some cases, certain changes in a patient's condition may require a very fast response for the life to be saved.

At least two approaches can be developed to meet these conditions.

1. While monitoring a patient, a computer could call hospital personnel whenever a significant change in the patient's condition occurs. The personnel then are responsible for responding in time.
2. To save time and labor, the computer could be allowed to administer needed medicines in response to a change in condition.

This second approach eliminates the possibility that hospital personnel will be delayed, but it relies upon the computer responding correctly in all cases.

**a.** Discuss some implications of the uncertainty of program correctness in this situation.

**b.** (Optional) If either approach is followed, suppose a bug results in the death of a patient. Who do you think should be legally liable, the programmer(s)? the hospital personnel? both? Explain your answer.

# CHAPTER 11

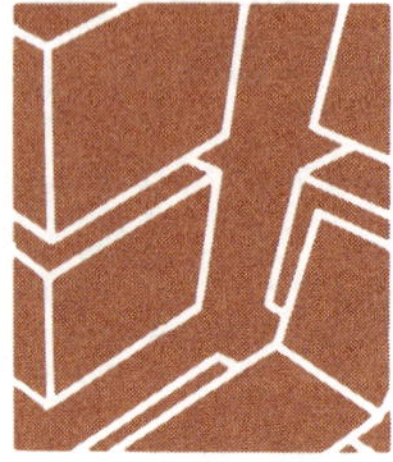

# SOME SIMPLE PROBLEMS INVOLVING CHARACTERS: ADDITIONAL SIMPLE DATA TYPES

Up to this point, we have limited the complexity of our problems by restricting our attention to applications that involve numbers. In this chapter, we shift our focus to applications that involve nonnumeric information, such as alphabetical data. For example, we will see how we can process data typed at a terminal by dealing with one character at a time. We also will see how we can introduce our own simple data types, so our work can closely reflect the problems we are solving.

## SECTION 11.1 CHARACTERS

We introduce the general subject of **character data** with a simple extension of our first Unit Pricing problem from Section 2.1.

### PROBLEM 11.1 Unit Pricing Revisited

Write a program that computes the unit price of several items. More precisely, write a program that computes the cost per ounce of an item, given its cost in cents and its weight in ounces. After each computation, ask if the user wishes to continue this series of computations. The program should then respond to a "Yes" or "No" typed by the user.

### Discussion of Problem 11.1

In this problem, the unit pricing computation can follow the same outline we used in Chapter 2, so here we focus on the exchange between the user and the computer about whether to continue.

This exchange may follow these steps:

**I.** The computer prints:
"Do you want to continue?"

**II.** The user responds appropriately.
(e.g., "Yes," "Yeah," "Yup," "No," "Nope.")

**III.** The computer repeats the unit pricing computation, until the user responds in the negative.

While the first of these steps can be implemented with a simple *Write* statement, we must consider Steps II and III with some care. Our sample responses above suggest that we should allow many possible answers from the user. In handling this variety, we might prepare a list of all reasonable user responses and then write our program to handle each anticipated answer, or we may identify a pattern in the various possible responses and then proceed on the basis of this pattern.

Here, we use the second approach. When we consider the possible responses, we see that negative responses normally start with the letter *N*. Similarly, the affirmative answers normally begin with *Y*. Thus, we write our program so that it responds to an initial *N* or *Y*. We will ignore all subsequent characters that the user may type on the response line.

From this discussion, we develop the following outline.

### Outline for Problem 11.1

**I.** Repeat until the user types the letter *N*.
   **A.** Compute unit price.
   **B.** Determine if user wants to continue.
      **1.** Print the question: "Do You Want To Continue?"
      **2.** Read the user's response, keeping the first character and discarding the rest.

This outline yields the following program.

```
Program UnitPricing {Revised} (Input, Output);

{This program computes the cost per ounce of an item,
 given cost and number of ounces.  The program continues processing
 data until the user tells the program to stop.}

Var Ounces, Cost, CostPerOunce: Real;
    Answer: Char;
```

```
Begin

    Repeat

        {Compute Unit Price}
        Write  ('Enter size of item in ounces and cost in dollars:');
        Readln (Ounces, Cost);
        CostPerOunce := Cost / Ounces;
        Writeln ('Cost per ounce = $ ', CostPerOunce:1:2);

        {Determine if user wants to continue}
        Write ('Do you want to continue?');
        Readln (Answer)

    Until (Answer = 'N') or (Answer = 'n')

End .
```

A sample run of this program might be:

```
Enter size of item in ounces and cost in dollars:12 3.60
Cost per ounce = $ 0.30
Do you want to continue?yes
Enter size of item in ounces and cost in dollars:5  1.10
Cost per ounce = $ 0.22
Do you want to continue?YUP
Enter size of item in ounces and cost in dollars:3 .99
Cost per ounce = $ 0.33
Do you want to continue?no
```

This program illustrates several important features of character data. When we want to process character information (rather than numbers), we can declare our variables to be type *Char.* For example,

Var Answer: Char;

specifies that the identifier *Answer* will be used to store *one character* of information, such as a letter, a digit, or a punctuation mark.

We can declare characters in just the same way that we declare reals, integers, and Booleans. Then, we can use character variables in much the same way as other variables.

1. We can input a character from the terminal using either *Read* or *Readln.*
2. We can specify one piece of character data by putting the character in quotes. For example, we can write 'N' and 'n'.

3. We can compare one character value against another. For example, we can test

```
(Answer = 'N') Or (Answer = 'n')
```

4. Similarly, we can use assignment statements, procedures, and functions with character data.
5. We can print character data using *Write* and *Writeln*, and we can specify formatting information. For example,

```
Writeln(Answer:5);
```

specifies that we should allow 5 spaces to print the character stored in *Answer*. (The character will be right-justified in the wide field.)

The last test in this Unit Pricing program also illustrates that the computer distinguishes between uppercase and lowercase letters. In fact, each individual character that we can type on our terminal is represented in a coded form inside the machine, and a different code is used for lowercase letters than for uppercase. Similarly, each punctuation mark and each digit has its own code. We will discuss some features of this coding in more detail in the next section.

Since character data are different from numeric data, some numeric operations do not apply to characters.

- The arithmetic operations +, −, *, /, *div*, *mod* cannot be used with character data.
- Numeric functions such as *abs*, *ln*, *exp*, and *sin* cannot be used with character data.
- Character data are stored differently from integer or real data, and the machine will not automatically convert from one to another (just as Pascal does not allow us to convert from reals to integers automatically).

To illustrate these distinctions, consider the statements:

```
Var Ch1, Ch2 : Char;
    I: Integer;
    R: Real;
Begin
      Ch1 := 'Q';
      Ch2 := 'Z';
      I := 7;
```

With this initialization, the following statements do not make sense and are illegal in Pascal.

| *Statement* | *Comment* |
|---|---|
| Ch1 := Ch1 + Ch2 | No single character could represent two letters. |

| | |
|---|---|
| R := Ch1 | No real number corresponds to a 'Q'. |
| Ch2 := I | The number 7 is distinct from the character '7'. |

This same distinction between character and numeric data make the following more subtle expressions invalid.

| | |
|---|---|
| I := '7' | Again, the number 7 and the |
| '7' = 7 | character '7' are distinct! |

In all cases, we can work with numeric data or with character data, but we cannot mix the two types. Pascal expects us to be precise in specifying what form of data we have and how we expect to use it.

To conclude this section, we apply these comments on character data to give a better, more complete solution to Problem 11.1.

## Further Discussion of Problem 11.1

Our first solution to Problem 11.1 continues as long as the user does not type the letter 'N' or 'n'. Any other response is considered to be an affirmative answer to the question.

In a more complete solution, we should check that the user types the 'Y' or 'N' expected, and we should ask the user to retype the answer if neither of these responses is given.

These details complicate our work considerably, and we can identify two special tasks that need to be done:

*Task 1.* We need to be able to determine if a character that we enter is 'Y', 'y', 'N', or 'n'.

*Task 2.* We need to continue asking for user input until an acceptable response is given.

In the following revised program, we separate these details by using functions and procedures, and we control our overall processing in another procedure.

```
Program UnitPricing {Revised Again} (Input, Output);

{This program computes the cost per ounce of an item,
 given cost and number of ounces.  The program continues processing
 data until the user tells the program to stop.}

Function YOrN (Ch: Char): Boolean;
{This function is True if the character Ch is a 'Y' or 'N'
 (upper or lower case) and False otherwise.}
    Begin
        YOrN := (Ch = 'Y') or (Ch = 'y') or (Ch = 'N') or (Ch = 'n')
    End {YOrN} ;
```

```
Procedure GetResponse (Var Ch: Char);
{This procedure asks if the user wants to continue,
 and the procedure continues to process responses
 until the user responds with a "Yes" or "No".}
    Begin

        Write ('Do you want to continue?');
        Repeat
            Readln (Ch);
            If Not YOrN(Ch)
                Then Write ('Please answer "Yes" or "No":')
        Until YOrN(Ch)

    End {GetResponse} ;

Procedure ControlProcessing;
{This procedure organizes our solution to the unit pricing problem.}
    Var Ounces, Cost, CostPerOunce: Real;
        Answer: Char;

    Begin
        Repeat

            {Compute Unit Price}
            Write  ('Enter size of item in ounces and cost in dollars:');
            Readln (Ounces, Cost);
            CostPerOunce := Cost / Ounces;
            Writeln ('Cost per ounce = $ ', CostPerOunce:1:2);

            {Determine if user wants to continue}
            GetResponse(Answer)

        Until (Answer = 'N') or (Answer = 'n')
    End {ControlProcessing} ;

Begin {Main}
    ControlProcessing
End {Main}
```

This program produces the same output as before, but it also allows for other user responses, as shown below.

```
Enter size of item in ounces and cost in dollars:7 14.49
Cost per ounce = $ 2.07
Do you want to continue?maybe
Please answer "Yes" or "No":who me?
Please answer "Yes" or "No":Yes
Enter size of item in ounces and cost in dollars:13 1.69
Cost per ounce = $ 0.13
Do you want to continue?No, Thank you!!
```

This program illustrates many aspects of character data that we have seen in this section. Character data can be used in functions and procedures, assignments and comparisons. Further, we can *Write* or *Read* character data to and from our terminal. This program shows how we can take advantage of functions and procedures when processing characters so that the details of our work can be separated from the program's main steps.

We expand our capabilities for processing characters in the next section, where we consider some special character functions.

## SECTION 11.2 SPECIAL FUNCTIONS

In the previous section, we saw some simple ways to process character data. Pascal allows us to declare character variables and to do the familiar operations of reading, writing, assigning, and comparing character data. We also noted that each character is stored in some coded form, and this code distinguishes between uppercase and lowercase letters. Thus, in our programs of the previous section, we read characters, and then we compared them with the letters 'Y', 'y', 'N', and 'n' to see if the user wanted to continue.

While our resulting program worked correctly, we did have to check our input against both uppercase and lowercase letters. When we give the user more choices in other applications, this distinction between uppercase and lowercase can become quite tedious. Thus, we may need to solve the following.

## PROBLEM 11.2 Capitalizing Letters

Write a function CAPITALIZE that capitalizes lowercase letters, while leaving punctuation and digit characters unchanged.

To solve this problem, we will take advantage of some special Pascal functions. These functions connect characters with their computer codes, and we will see how we can utilize these codes to solve our problem. We begin with a discussion of the codes themselves.

### Character Codes

When working with character data, the computer uses a specific coded value for each possible character. Thus, when we press a key at our terminal, the terminal translates our keystroke into the appropriate code, and this code is transmitted to the computer. Similarly, when the CPU wants some data printed at a terminal, the CPU translates this data into a sequence of **character codes.** These codes are sent to our terminal, and our terminal responds to these codes by displaying the characters that we recognize.

As a specific example, one commonly used code is the American Standard Code for Information Interchange, called the ASCII code. Part of this code is shown in Table 11–1. Here, we see that the number '2' is represented by the binary code 00110010 (code number 50), the letter 'A' is represented by the binary code 01000001 (code number 65), and the semicolon ';' is represented by 00111011 (code number 59). Other ASCII codes not included in Table 11–1 are the carriage return (code number 13), the tab (code number 9), and the letter 'a' (code number 97). In fact, each key or combination of keys on our terminal corresponds to a distinct code number in ASCII.

Table 11–1 also suggests another key consequence of machine codes, for the table provides an ordering for the various characters. For example, in the ASCII code, 'B' comes after 'A', ';' (code 59) comes before '<' (code

**TABLE 11–1 • A Portion of the ASCII 8-Bit Code**

| Binary Code | Decimal Code Number | Character or Comment |
|---|---|---|
| 00110000 | 48 | 0 |
| 00110001 | 49 | 1 |
| 00110010 | 50 | 2 |
| 00110011 | 51 | 3 |
| 00110100 | 52 | 4 |
| 00110101 | 53 | 5 |
| 00110110 | 54 | 6 |
| 00110111 | 55 | 7 |
| 00111000 | 56 | 8 |
| 00111001 | 57 | 9 |
| 00111010 | 58 | : |
| 00111011 | 59 | ; |
| 00111100 | 60 | < |
| 00111101 | 61 | = |
| 00111110 | 62 | > |
| 00111111 | 63 | ? |
| 01000000 | 64 | @ |
| 01000001 | 65 | A |
| 01000010 | 66 | B |
| 01000011 | 67 | C |
| 01000100 | 68 | D |
| 01000101 | 69 | E |
| 01000110 | 70 | F |
| 01000111 | 71 | G |
| 01001000 | 72 | H |
| 01001001 | 73 | I |

*Source:* United States of America Standards Institute, Standard X3.4-1968.

60), and '?' (code 63) comes before 'a' (code 97). Of course these relationships depend upon the particular code used on a specific machine, but the underlying ideas of coding and ordering apply to all computers.

Once we understand this idea of character coding and ordering, we find that Pascal allows us to utilize these ideas in several ways.

## Functions Ord and Chr

Two functions, *Ord* and *Chr*, allow us to translate easily between characters and the underlying code. In particular,

*Ord(Ch)* gives us the code number for the character *Ch* specified. For example, if we are using the ASCII code, then

Ord('A') = 65

and

Ord(';') = 59.

*Chr(N)* gives us the character with code *N*. For example, in the ASCII code,

Chr(65) = 'A'

and

Chr(59) = ';'.

## Functions Pred and Succ

Two functions, *Pred* and *Succ*, utilize the ordering of characters. In particular,

*Succ(Ch)* gives us the character that is the successor to *Ch* in our coding table.

*Pred(Ch)* gives us the character that is the predecessor to *Ch* in our coding table.

For example, if we use the ASCII code, we have

Pred('B') = 'A'
Succ('A') = 'B'

and

Succ(';') = '<'

## Inequalities

The ordering of characters also allows us to make **comparisons of characters within Boolean expressions.** For example, in the ASCII code, we find that all capital letters are between 'A' and 'Z.' Thus, the following function can be used to test if a given character is a capital letter (for the ASCII code).

```
Function CAP(Ch: Char): Boolean;
    Begin
        CAP := (Ch >= 'A') And (Ch <= 'Z')
    End
```

In the ASCII code, any capital letter has a code between 65 (code for 'A') and 90 (code for 'Z'), so any capital letter satisfies the test in the above function. Similarly, any other character is not in this range on the ASCII code, so other characters will not meet the above test.

## Notes on Various Codes and Some Cautions

Unfortunately, the exact ordering of characters depends upon the specific code used by a particular machine, so that we must be careful when comparing different characters in our programs. For example, in some codes, such as the ASCII, the capital letters come before the small letters so 'A' comes before 'a'. In other codes, such as the Extended Binary Coded Decimal Interchange Code or the EBCDIC code, the small letters come first.

On the other hand, in virtually all codes, the capital letters are in order, so

'A' < 'B' < 'C' . . . < 'Z'

Similarly, the small letters are in order, and the digits '0', '1', . . . , '9' are in order. Thus, regardless of the specific code used in a particular machine, we can use inequalities, such as '<' and '>', for alphabetizing letters and for ordering strings of digits. Beyond these general statements, however, we need to consult a manual for our specific machine to learn any details of the coding in a particular situation.

## Capitalization: An Application

With these capabilities for working with characters and their codes, we now can return to our Capitalization problem which began the section. Our problem requires a two-part solution:

**I.** Identify if a given character is a lowercase letter.
**II.** If the character is lowercase:
 **A.** Then capitalize it.
 **B.** Otherwise, leave it alone.

We consider each part separately:

**I.** We already have seen how to identify a capital letter in the ASCII code. A similar approach applies to lowercase letters.
**II.** Most codes (including both ASCII and EBCDIC) arrange their lowercase and uppercase letters in the same pattern. Thus, we can use the following approach to perform the actual capitalization.
 **A.** Given the letter *Ch*, determine how far it is from the start of the lowercase alphabet. This is done by

```
Distance := Ord(Ch) - Ord('a')
```

 **B.** Find the letter that is this prescribed distance from 'A'. This is given by

```
Chr ( Ord('A') + Distance )
```

For example, if we wish to capitalize 'c', we note:

**A.** 'c' is two letters beyond 'a' (Distance := 2)

**B.** Our desired letter is coded 2 letters beyond 'A'. Thus, we want the letter whose code is

Ord('A') + 2

that is, we want

Chr ( Ord ('A') + 2 )

These steps are coded in the following function, which produces correct results for virtually any coding system (including ASCII and EBCDIC).

```
Function CAPITALIZE(Ch: Char): Char;
{This function capitalizes a lower case character Ch,
 but the function leaves other characters unchanged}

    Begin
        If (Ch >= 'a') And (Ch <= 'z')
            Then CAPITALIZE := Chr( Ord(Ch) - Ord('a') + Ord('A') )
            Else CAPITALIZE := Ch
    End {CAPITALIZE} ;
```

In this function, we compare various characters, and we use character codes and Pascal functions to transform character data from one form to another. In the next section, we see how to apply these same ideas in the processing of several characters.

## SECTION 11.3 SEQUENCES OF CHARACTERS

The previous two sections have illustrated how we can process individual characters. In this section, we begin an investigation of techniques for processing several characters by considering two ways we can use arrays with character data. We will continue this study in the next two chapters.

Our first approach uses arrays of characters with integer subscripts.

### PROBLEM 11.3A Message Decoding

Decode a message by replacing each letter in the message by an appropriate alternate letter. More precisely, begin with a 'real' alphabet and a 'cipher' alphabet. Then decode a message by looking up each letter of the message in the cipher alphabet and replacing it by the corresponding letter in the real alphabet.

For example, suppose we are given

```
RealAlphabet   = ABCDEFGHIJKLMNOPQRSTUVWXYZ 0123456789
CipherAlphabet = 3456217089ACB QRSTUVWXYZDEFGHIJKLMNOP
```

Then the coded message

```
8 FHKPIF5QCWB4WUFU38C26FV02FQ523 F4CW2
```

becomes

```
IN 1492 COLUMBUS SAILED THE OCEAN BLUE
```

(To encipher a message, we just interchange the real and cipher alphabets.)

## Discussion of Problem 11.3A

In this problem, we need to work with several pieces of character information. In particular, we need a real alphabet, a cipher alphabet, and a coded message, and we must produce a decoded message. One natural way to store each of these is to use arrays, and we can declare

```
Const AlphabetLength = 37;
      MaxLen = 80; {Number of characters on a line of a terminal}
Type  Alphabet = Array [1..AlphabetLength] of Char;
      CharLine = Array [1..MaxLen] of Char;
Var   RealAlphabet: Alphabet;
      CipherAlphabet: Alphabet;
      Message: CharLine;
      CodedMess:CharLine;
```

Here, we store the first letter of our cipher alphabet as

*CipherAlphabet*[1]

and the corresponding letter in the real alphabet as

*RealAlphabet*[1].

Then, with this storage of our alphabets, we can decode each character of our message easily.

For each character in our coded message, we search through the cipher alphabet to find the position of the character in this cipher alphabet. Then we take the corresponding character from that position in the real alphabet to obtain the decoded letter.

With this deciphering process specified, we next examine how we can determine the two alphabets and the coded message. One simple approach for the alphabets is to ask the user to enter them. Since we know these alphabets will each contain exactly 37 characters, we can perform this task simply. For example,

```
For Index := 1 to 37
    Do Read (RealAlphabet [Index]);
```

However, in reading this character data, we must be a little careful when we come to the end of a line. After we read each alphabet, we want to start our next input on a new line. Thus, we need to be sure we move to the next line each time we finish a line. (When we read numbers, the computer automatically moves ahead to new lines when necessary, but this is not true in reading characters.) Therefore, after we read each alphabet, we need to insert a *Readln* in our program so we will be ready for the next line of data. The *Readln* clears the present line and moves to the next one.

Next, when we try to read our message, we note that we may not know the length of our input before we start. Thus, we will have to allocate some maximum amount of space in our program declaration and then count the actual number of characters as our coded message is entered.

These comments suggest the following solution to our problem.

## Outline for Problem 11.3A

**I.** Enter alphabets.
  - **A.** Enter *RealAlphabet* one character at a time.
  - **B.** Enter *CipherAlphabet* one character at a time.

**II.** Enter the coded message.
  - **A.** Start count of message length at 0.
  - **B.** Continue reading until we reach the end of line and as long as we still have room to store the coded message.
    - **1.** Increase the letter count by one.
    - **2.** Read the character.

**III.** Decipher the coded message. For each letter in the coded message:
  - **A.** Find the position of the letter in the *CipherAlphabet*.
  - **B.** Take the corresponding character in the *RealAlphabet* for our message.

**IV.** Print
  - **A.** The original message.
  - **B.** The decoded message.

This outline yields the following program. Here, for clarity, each step is written as a separate procedure.

Also, in this program, we must be able to test when we have read the last character on a line. To make this test, we use the function *EOLN* (End Of Line) from the Pascal library. This Boolean function is true when we have read the last character on a line, and false if more characters remain.

```
Program DecipherMessage (Input, Output);
{This program deciphers a message which has been coded
  according to a monoaphabetic substitution code.}

Const AlphabetLength = 37;
      MaxLen = 80;
```

```
Type Alphabet = Array [1..AlphabetLength] of Char;
     CharLine = Array [1..MaxLen] of Char;

Procedure EnterAlphabets (Var RealAl, CipherAl: Alphabet);
{Procedure asks user to enter the real and cipher alphabets
 for the deciphering.}
    Var Index: Integer;
    Begin
        Writeln ('Please enter the real alphabet');
        For Index := 1 To AlphabetLength
            Do Read (RealAl[Index]);
        Readln;     {Clear input line of any extra characters}
        Writeln ('Below each letter in the real alphabet, please enter');
        Writeln ('the corresponding letter of the cipher alphabet');
        For Index := 1 To AlphabetLength
            Do Write (RealAl[Index]);
        Writeln;
        For Index := 1 To AlphabetLength
            Do Read (CipherAl[Index]);
        Readln      {clear input line of any extra characters}
    End {EnterAlphabets} ;

Procedure EnterLine (Var CodedMess: CharLine; Var CodeLen: Integer);
{Procedure enters the coded message to be deciphered.}
    Var Index: Integer;

    Begin
        Writeln ('Please enter your coded message:');
        CodeLen := 0;
        While (Not Eoln) And (CodeLen < MaxLen)
          Do Begin
            CodeLen := CodeLen + 1;
            Read (CodedMess[CodeLen])
          End;
       If Not Eoln
           Then Writeln ('Your coded message was too long; ',
                         'message truncated to ', MaxLen:1, ' characters');
       Readln     {Clear input line}
    End {EnterLine} ;

Procedure Decipher (Code: CharLine; Var Plain: CharLine; Length: Integer;
                    RealAl, CipherAl: Alphabet);
{Procedure deciphers Coded message by looking up letters in the CipherAl,
 and using the corresponding letters in RealAl to get the Plain message}
    Var Index: Integer;
        Position: Integer;

    Procedure Find (Var Position: Integer; Letter: Char; Alpha: Alphabet);
    {Procedure finds the Position of the given Letter in the given Alpha.}
        Begin
            Position := 1;
            While (Letter <> Alpha[Position])
                Do Position := Position + 1
        End {Find} ;
```

```
    Begin {Decipher}
        For Index := 1 To Length
          Do Begin
            Find (Position, Code[Index], CipherAl);
            Plain[Index] := RealAl[Position]
          End
    End {Decipher} ;

Procedure PrintResults (Code, Message: CharLine; Length: Integer);
{This procedure prints the message and the resulting coded text.}
    Var Index: Integer;
    Begin
        Writeln ('When the coded message:');
        For Index := 1 To Length
            Do Write (Code[Index]);
        Writeln;
        Writeln ('is decoded with the above substitutions, the result is:');
        For Index := 1 To Length
            Do Write (Message[Index]);
        Writeln
    End {PrintResults} ;

Procedure ControlProcessing;
{This procedure controls the main steps of data entry and processing.}
    Var RealAlphabet: Alphabet;
        CipherAlphabet: Alphabet;
        Message: CharLine;
        CodedMess: CharLine;
        InputLen: Integer;

    Begin
        EnterAlphabets (RealAlphabet, CipherAlphabet);
        EnterLine (CodedMess, InputLen);
        Decipher (CodedMess, Message, InputLen, RealAlphabet, CipherAlphabet);
        PrintResults (CodedMess, Message, InputLen)
    End {ControlProcessing} ;

Begin {Main}
    Writeln ('Deciphering Program');
    ControlProcessing
End {Main} .
```

This program illustrates several general points. We can declare arrays of characters in the same way that we declare arrays of reals, integers, or Booleans. Then, we can use these arrays to process sequences of characters, by working with our input one character at a time. As we enter our characters, we may need to record the number of characters we have read. Then, in subsequent processing, we can refer to this length.

In working with character data, a space is treated in exactly the same manner as other characters; we cannot ignore spaces. (A space moves the printing element on our keyboard or the cursor at our terminal, so a space makes a difference in what we see.)

This example also shows that in reading from a terminal, we must be careful in processing the end of each line, and we need the *EOLN* function to tell us when we have read the last character on the line. *EOLN* is true when the last character has been read, so no more characters appear on the line. *EOLN* is false if more characters remain. Then, before we wish to enter character data from a new line, we need to use the *Readln* statement to move to the next line.

We now turn to a second problem, which illustrates other ways we can work with sequences of characters.

## PROBLEM 11.3B Distribution of Letters

Write a program that reads a line of input, counts the number of times each letter occurs, and displays the final frequency information.

### Discussion of Problem 11.3B

In this problem we can read our input line as before. (We will capitalize letters, so no distinction is made between upper- and lowercase.) The new features include counting letters and displaying the information.

In counting letters, we need a count for letter *A*, a count for letter *B*, a count for letter *C*, etc. Thus, we would like variables $Count_A$, $Count_B$, $Count_C$ . . . . This suggests the idea of subscripting we have seen before, but here we want our subscripts to be letters. Thus, in Pascal, we declare

```
Var Count: Array ['A'..'Z'] of Integer;
```

to record our frequency information.

Once we record this information, we want to print results for each letter which occurred in our line of input. Thus, we want to repeat an activity for the letters 'A', 'B', 'C', . . . , 'Z'. This suggests a *For* loop where the control variable is a character; that is, we want

```
For Letter := 'A' to 'Z'
```

Each of these capabilities is possible in Pascal, and we have the following outline.

### Outline for Problem 11.3B

**I.** Enter line of input.
  - **A.** Start with a line length of 0.
  - **B.** Continue reading until we reach the end of line or until we run out of storage space.
    - **1.** Increase the letter count by one.
    - **2.** Read the character.
    - **3.** Capitalize the letter if it was in lowercase.

**II.** Count letters. For each character entered:
  - **A.** Determine if the character is a letter.
  - **B.** If so, increase the letter count by 1.

**III.** Display the results. Repeat for each letter, 'A', . . . , 'Z'.
  **A.** Determine if the letter occurred in the line (i.e., if the count > 0).
  **B.** Print * for each occurrence of the letter.
  **C.** Print the number of occurrences.

This outline yields the following program.

---

```
Program LetterDistribution (Input, Output);
{This program reads a line of input, counts the number of times
 each letter appears in the line, and the displays these letter
 frequencies.  No distinction is made between upper case and
 lower case letters.}

Const MaxLen = 80;

Type  CharInput = Array[1..MaxLen] of Char;
      LetterCount = Array['A'..'Z'] of Integer;

Procedure EnterLine (Var Line: CharInput; Var Length: Integer);
{This procedure reads our line of input from the terminal.}

    Procedure CAPITALIZE (Var Ch: Char);
    {This procedure capitalizes lower case letters.}
        Begin
            If (Ch >= 'a') And (Ch <= 'z')
                Then Ch := Chr( Ord(Ch) - Ord('a') + Ord('A') )
        End {Capitalize} ;

    Begin {EnterLine}
        Writeln ('Please enter your input line:');

        Length := 0;
        While (Not Eoln) and (Length < MaxLen)
          Do Begin
            Length := Length + 1;
            Read (Line[Length]);
            Capitalize (Line[Length])
          End;
        If Not Eoln
            Then Writeln ('Your message was too long; ',
                          'message truncated to ', MaxLen:1, ' characters');
        Readln {clear any excess characters from the input line}
    End {EnterLine} ;

Procedure CountLetters (Line: CharInput; Length: Integer;
                        Var Count: LetterCount);

{This procedure counts the frequency of letters in the given line.}
    Var Letter: Char;     {Index variable}
        Index: Integer;   {Index variable for Line}
        Ch: Char;         {Character in the given Line}
```

```
    Begin
        {Initially all counts are 0}
        For Letter := 'A' to 'Z'
            Do Count[Letter] := 0;

        {For each letter in line, increment count by 1}
        For Index := 1 To Length
          Do Begin
            Ch := Line[Index];
            If (Ch >= 'A') and (Ch <= 'Z')
                Then Count[Ch] := Count[Ch] + 1
          End
    End {CountLetters} ;

Procedure DisplayResults (Count: LetterCount);
{Procedure displays the letter frequencies for the line.}
    Var Letter: Char;
        Index: Integer;  {Control variable to count *'s printed}
    Begin
        Writeln;
        Writeln ('Display of the letter frequencies in the input line.');
        Writeln;

        For Letter := 'A' to 'Z'
          Do Begin
            If (Count[Letter] > 0)
                Then Begin
                    Write (Letter, ' : ');
                    For Index := 1 To Count[Letter]
                        Do Write ('*');
                    Writeln (Count[Letter]:3)
                End
          End
    End {DisplayResults} ;

Procedure ControlPRocessing;
{This procedure controls the main processing steps of data entry,
 analysis, and printing.}
    Var Line: CharInput;
        Count: LetterCount;
        LineLen: Integer;

    Begin
        EnterLine (Line, LineLen);
        CountLetters (Line, LineLen, Count);
        DisplayResults (Count)
    End {ControlProcessing} ;

Begin {Main}
    Writeln ('This program computes the frequency of letters ',
                'in a line of input.');
    ControlProcessing
End {Main} .
```

When this program is run on a sample line of input, we get the following output. The graphic display of frequency information in this output is called a **histogram.**

```
This program computes the frequency of letters in a line of input.
Please enter your input line:
Pascal allows characters both as subscripts and as data.

Display of the letter frequencies in the input line.

A : **********
B : **
C : ****
D : **
E : *
H : **
I : *
L : ***
N : *
O : **
P : **
R : ***
S : ********
T : ****
U : *
W : *
```

As we can see, this program illustrates how we can combine many of the techniques involved in handling characters. We can declare arrays with characters as data or with character subscripts (or both). We can use character variables as control variables in our loops. In addition, to process characters, we can use internal codes to capitalize letters; we can compare characters with each other; we can work with one character at a time; and we can use characters as our subscripts in recording information.

## SECTION 11.4 THE CASE STATEMENT

While the previous section illustrates how we may write programs to analyze words of input, another type of application involves the use of character data in making choices. For example, we may have the computer print a list of options, and we may wish the user to enter a letter to choose the option desired. Here, we organize a program on the basis of the various options that the user can select, using a separate procedure to perform each option. The result is called a **menu-driven** program, and we illustrate this approach in the following problem. This problem also illustrates an alternate approach to the *If* statement, which is useful when we need to select from many cases.

## PROBLEM 11.4 A Menu-Driven Program

Write a statistics package that will allow us to enter data, modify data, and compute statistics, based on the following menu:

Statistics Package Menu
  E - Enter Data
  M - Modify Data
  S - Compute Statistics
  Q - Quit
Enter Option:

After this menu is printed, the user selects the appropriate option by typing the corresponding letter *E, M, S,* or *Q*, and an appropriate procedure is called.

In determining which choice a user selects, we could use a sequence of nested *If* statements, namely

```
If (Option = 'E')
   Then EnterData
   Else If (Option = 'M')
        Then ModifyData
        Else If—
```

Although this code works, it is hard to read, and it becomes particularly messy if we want to allow both lowercase and uppercase responses.

The following program demonstrates an alternative approach. Note that all procedures involving statistics contain only a stub that identifies the option. Here, the *ProcessMenu* procedure could be used to declare variables needed when we move from one processing step to another.

```
Program Menu (Input, Output);

Procedure PrintMenu;
    Begin
        Writeln ('Statistics Package Menu');
        Writeln ('E - Enter Data');
        Writeln ('M - Modify Data');
        Writeln ('S - Compute Statistics');
        Writeln ('Q - Quit')
    End {PrintMenu} ;

Procedure EnterOption (Var Option: Char);
    Begin
        Write ('Enter Option: ');
        Readln (Option)
    End {EnterOption} ;
```

```
Procedure EnterData;
    Begin
        Writeln ('Data entry option');
        Writeln ('      Option not yet available')
    End {Enter Data} ;

Procedure ModifyData;
    Begin
        Writeln ('Data modification option');
        Writeln ('      Option not yet available')
    End {ModifyData} ;

Procedure ComputeStatistics;
    Begin
        Writeln ('Computation of Statistics');
        Writeln ('      Option not yet available')
    End {ComputeStatistics} ;

Procedure ProcessMenu;
{This procedure handles menu printing and option selection,
 and then calls the appropriate processing procedures.}
    Var Option: Char;
    Begin
        Repeat
            PrintMenu;
            EnterOption (Option);
            Case Option Of
                'E', 'e':  EnterData;
                'M', 'm':  ModifyData;
                'S', 's':  ComputeStatistics;
                'Q', 'q':  ;
                End {Case}
        Until (Option = 'Q') Or (Option = 'q')
    End {ProcessMenu} ;

Begin {Main}
    ProcessMenu
End {Main} .
```

This program prints the desired menu, reads the user's option, and selects the appropriate procedure to do the processing. In this work, the key step is a *Case* statement which has the following syntax:

*Case* Index *Of*
    Constant(s) *:* Statement;
    Constant(s) *:* Statement;
    .
    .
    .
    Constant(s) *:* Statement;
    *End*

Here, the *Index* is an integer, Boolean, or character variable or expression. (Reals are not allowed.)

When this statement is executed, the value of the index is evaluated. The machine finds this value on the list below. The machine then performs the statement specified by the constant. In our example, if our *Option* is 'm', the machine finds the value and performs the procedure *ModifyData*.

Within the *Case* statement, each statement may be a simple one such as a *Read*, *Write*, assignment, or procedure call, or the statement may involve a *Begin–End* block. Further, as we see for cases 'Q' and 'q' in our example, this statement may be empty or null.

Further, the *Case* statement allows us to list as many cases together as we wish, as long as we separate these cases by commas. Thus, we could write a list

```
'Q', 'q', 'X', 'x' : —
```

However, only simple constants are allowed. We cannot use multiple characters such as 'QU' or 'Exit'. Further, our list of choices can involve only constants. Variables are not allowed.

In using *Case* statements, however, we must be careful that the value of our index is included in the list of constants. We may not be able to predict what the computer will do if this constant is not found. For example, if we typed 'B' as our option in this program, the computer might stop executing our program, or it might continue in some way.

On the other hand, some extensions of Pascal allow the inclusion of an *Otherwise* statement, placed before the *End*. When this is allowed, the *Otherwise* statement is executed if the *Index* value is not found. For example, we might write

```
Case Option of
     'E', 'e'    :  EnterData;
     'M', 'm'    :  ModifyData;
     'S', 's'    :  ComputeStatistics;
     'Q', 'q'    :  ;
     Otherwise   :  Writeln('Invalid Option')
  End
```

In this case, the computer would print

```
Invalid Option
```

if we entered a choice of 'B'.

As this example shows, the *Case* statement can be very useful whenever our work naturally splits into several cases. Once we identify these cases, the *Case* can help us organize our code accordingly.

This example also shows us a natural way to organize large programs that have many parts. We can divide our large task into small sections with a procedure for each task. Then we can tie the sections together with a general menu in a controlling menu-processing procedure. Further, when we use the technique of stubbing, this organization allows us to write and test a large program in pieces, so we do not have to write all of our code before we start the debugging process.

## SECTION 11.5 SUBRANGES

In many of our previous applications, we did not place any restrictions on our data; our numbers could take on any value, and our data could include any characters we could type. However, sometimes we may want to limit ourselves to a specific range of values. For example, in declaring subscripts we specify a range of allowable integers or characters; we do not allow all possible values for our subscripts. Such a limited range of values is called a **subrange.** In this section, we see how we can use these subranges in our programs.

In Pascal, we can define a subrange of values by specifying

```
Constant .. Constant
```

in our declarations. For example, we may write

```
Type Capital = 'A'..'Z';                {a subrange of letters}
     NonNegative = 1..MaxInt;           {a subrange of integers}
Var Letter: Capital;
    NaturalNum: NonNegative;            {values limited to a
    Little: -10..10;                     subrange of integers}
```

Here, we have defined two new types of data that involve a limited range of values. *Capital* includes only those letters between 'A' and 'Z', while *NonNegative* includes only those integers greater than zero.

These declarations also define three variables whose values are limited to the ranges specified. For example, *Letter* is a variable that can be used to store any character between 'A' and 'Z'; *NaturalNum* can be used to store positive numbers; and *Little* can be used to store integers between −10 and 10 (inclusive).

When we declare these new types, we still can use all of the operations available for the nonrestricted data, but we must be sure our final values stored are in the specified range. Thus, we may write

```
Letter := 'Q';
NaturalNum := ABS(-17);
Little := NaturalNum Mod 10;
```

In each case, we are performing operations on some data, and our final results are within the specified subranges for our variables. Thus, we can store the values computed in the given variables.

However, if we try to store values outside the specified range, our program will detect an error, and the computer may stop running our program. For example, suppose we have declared

```
Var A: Array [1..10] of Char;
```

and then we write

```
A[0] := 'Q';
```

From our experience with arrays, we realize that our subscript for *A* is not valid, and we expect the computer to stop with a statement such as

```
Subscript out of range
```

A similar result occurs if we try to work with values outside a declared subrange of a variable. For example, with the declarations earlier in this section, we expect the computer to report errors with any of the following:

```
Letter := Succ('Z');
NaturalNum := (15*7) Mod 5;
Little := MaxInt
```

To illustrate how subranges can be used effectively, we consider the following problem.

## PROBLEM 11.5 Computing a Time Interval

Write a program that reads two times (in hours and minutes), determines which time comes first, and computes the time interval (in hours and minutes) between these two times.

In this problem, base your computations on two times being entered for the same day, with values between 0 hours 0 minutes (midnight, start of day) and 24 hours and 0 minutes (midnight, end of day).

### Discussion of Problem 11.5

In this problem, we need to record times in hours and minutes, and we can expect that all hours will be between 0 and 24 and that minutes will be between 0 and 59.

Beyond this form for our data, our problem suggests three basic steps for our solution: recording data, determining which time comes first, and computing a time interval. When we expand these steps into an outline, we get the following.

### Outline for Problem 11.5

**I.** Enter data.

**A.** Read first time.

Check hour is between 0 and 24.
Check minute is between 0 and 59.
If hour = 24, check minute = 0.

**B.** Read second time.
Check hour is between 0 and 24.
Check minute is between 0 and 59.
If hour = 24, check minute = 0.

**II.** Determine which time comes first.
**A.** If hours are different,
check which hour comes first.
**B.** If hours are the same,
check which minute comes first.

**III.** Determine time interval.
**A.** If times are the same, time interval is zero.
**B.** If times are different, check if minutes of earlier time come before minutes of later time.
**1.** If so, compute
(late hour − early hour)
and (late minute − early minute)
**2.** If not, compute
(late hour − early hour − 1)
(late minute − early minute + 60)

### Further Discussion of Problem 11.5

In Step I of our outline, we allow the possibility that a user might enter an incorrect time, and we will ask the user to reenter the data in case of an error. However, after this step, all times should be in the range with

$$0 \le Hour \le 24 \text{ and } 0 \le Minute \le 59.$$

Thus, after data entry, we know we must have a programming error if our times lie outside this range. Therefore, in the following program, we limit our various *Hour* and *Minute* variables to a specific subrange for all work beyond Step I.

```
Program TimeInterval (Input, Output);
{This program reads two times (in hours and minutes),
 determines which time comes first, and computes the interval
 between them.}

Type HourRange = 0..24;
     MinuteRange = 0..59;

Procedure EnterData(Var FirstHr: HourRange; Var FirstMin: MinuteRange;
                 Var SecondHr: HourRange; Var SecondMin: MinuteRange);
{This procedure reads two times in hours and minutes, and checks these
 times are valid.}

    Procedure ReadTime (Var Hour: HourRange; Var Minute: MinuteRange);
    {This procedure reads a time in hours and minutes, and checks that
     the time is valid.}
        Var HourInput, MinuteInput: Integer;
            LegalTimes: Boolean;
```

```
        Begin
            {Read hour and minutes}
            Repeat
                Readln (HourInput, MinuteInput);
                If HourInput = 24
                    Then LegalTimes := (MinuteInput = 0)
                    Else LegalTimes := (HourInput >= 0) And
                             (HourInput < 24) And (MinuteInput >= 0)
                             And (MinuteInput <= 59);
                If Not LegalTimes
                    Then Begin
                        Writeln ('Hour must be between 0 and 24; ',
                                 'Minute must be between 0 and 59');
                        Write ('Please re-enter time: ')
                        End
            Until LegalTimes;

            {Return valid times}
            Hour := HourInput;
            Minute := MinuteInput
        End {ReadTime} ;
    Begin {EnterData}

        Writeln ('This program reads two times, determines which comes');
        Writeln ('first, and computes the time interval between them.');
        Writeln;
        Write ('Enter hours and minutes of first time: ');
        ReadTime (FirstHr, FirstMin);
        Writeln;
        Write ('Enter hours and minutes of second time: ');
        ReadTime (SecondHr, SecondMin)

    End {EnterData} ;

Function FirstTimeEarlier (FirstHr: HourRange; FirstMin: MinuteRange;
               SecondHr: HourRange; SecondMin: MinuteRange): Boolean;
{This function determines if the first time comes before the second time}
    Begin
        If FirstHr <> SecondHr
            Then FirstTimeEarlier := (FirstHr < SecondHr)
            Else FirstTimeEarlier := (FirstMin < SecondMin)
    End {FirstTimeEarlier} ;

Procedure DetermineInterval (EarlyHr: HourRange; EarlyMin: MinuteRange;
                              LateHr: HourRange; LateMin: MinuteRange);
{This procedure computes and prints the time interval between
 the two times specified}
    Var HourInt: HourRange;
        MinuteInt: MinuteRange;

    Begin
        If LateMin >= EarlyMin
            Then Begin
                HourInt := LateHr - EarlyHr;
                MinuteInt := LateMin - EarlyMin
                End
```

```
          Else Begin
              HourInt := LateHr - EarlyHr - 1;
              MinuteInt := LateMin - EarlyMin + 60
              End;
      If (HourInt = 0) And (MinuteInt = 0)
         Then Writeln ('The times specified are the same.')
         Else Writeln ('The time interval between these times is ',
                HourInt:1, ' hours and ', MinuteInt:1, ' minutes.')
    End {DetermineInterval} ;

Procedure ProcessTimes;
{This procedure guides the solution of the problem}
    Var FirstHr, SecondHr: HourRange;
        FirstMin,SecondMin: MinuteRange;

    Begin
        EnterData (FirstHr, FirstMin, SecondHr, SecondMin);
        If FirstTimeEarlier (FirstHr, FirstMin, SecondHr, SecondMin)
            Then DetermineInterval(FirstHr, FirstMin, SecondHr, SecondMin)
            Else DetermineInterval(SecondHr, SecondMin, FirstHr, FirstMin)
    End {ProcessTimes} ;

Begin {Main}
    ProcessTimes
End {Main} .
```

Two sample runs of this program follow.

```
First Trial Run

This program reads two times, determines which comes
first, and computes the time interval between them.

Enter hours and minutes of first time: 10 45

Enter hours and minutes of second time: 11 30
The time interval between these times is 0 hours and 45 minutes.


Second Trial Run

This program reads two times, determines which comes
first, and computes the time interval between them.

Enter hours and minutes of first time: 9 75
Hour must be between 0 and 24; Minute must be between 0 and 59
Please re-enter time: 9 10

Enter hours and minutes of second time: 7 00
The time interval between these times is 2 hours and 10 minutes.
```

As we can see from this example, subranges have several important features.

1. Subranges limit data values to a particular range (e.g., 0..24 or 0..59), and subranges allow the computer to continually monitor that values do not extend beyond the specified limits.
2. When variables have values limited to a subrange, those variables may still be used in computations with other values outside the subrange. For example, while *EarlyMinute* and *LateMinute* are both limited to the range 0 to 59, we still used them with the larger integer 60, in the statement

   ```
   LateMinute − EarlyMinute + 60
   ```

   Here, only the *Minute* variables are restricted, not the other parts of our expression.
3. Subranges are helpful when we want the computer to halt processing when invalid values are encountered. For example, in Steps II or III, an hour outside the interval 0..24 indicates a bug in the program, and we want the program to stop further processing if such a bug is detected.
4. On the other hand, subranges do not allow us to handle user input errors, as processing may halt if a user enters a value outside a subrange. Thus, for user input, it is better to allow for a wide range of values and then check for correctness. Once the values are verified as being acceptable, we can perform subsequent processing with values limited to the subrange.

## SECTION 11.6 ENUMERATED TYPES

Up to this point, our applications have been selected so we could use rather traditional types of data in our processing. Our data included numbers (real or integers) or Booleans or characters, and our processing involved either these types or subranges of these. However, in some applications we may wish to define a new data type in which we specify exactly which values are possible. Such a data type is called an **enumerated type,** and this section discusses how such types can be defined.

We begin with a problem which may remind us of our letter counting problem in Section 11.3.

## PROBLEM 11.6

Write a program that reads a line of input and counts the number of capital letters, small letters, spaces, digits, and punctuation marks.

### Discussion of Problem 11.6

In this problem, we need to read our line of input. Then, we need to decide which category each character falls into, and we need to update our category information appropriately.

We begin by defining these categories as a separate data type by declaring

Type Category = (Capital, Small, Space, Digit, Punc);
Var Item: Category;

Further, to record our frequency information, we can use these category values as subscripts. Thus, we declare

Type CounterType = Array [Category] of Integer;
Var Count: CounterType;

With this setup, we follow the same general approach we used in Section 11.3 to count letter frequencies. Our general plan includes the following outline.

### Outline for Problem 11.6

**I.** Enter line from terminal.
 **A.** Read until end of line or until we run out of space.
 **B.** Record the number of characters read.
**II.** Count letters in each category.
 **A.** Initialize all counts to 0.
 **B.** Repeat for each character in the input line.
  **1.** Determine which category the character is in.
  **2.** Increment the count for that category.
**III.** Display the results for each category.

This outline leads to the following program.

```
Program CountCharactersByCategories (Input, Output);
{This program counts the number of characters in a given line
 of input according to various categories.}

Const MaxLen = 80;

Type CharInput = Array [1..MaxLen] of Char;
     Category = (Capital, Small, Space, Digit, Punc);
     CounterType = Array [Category] of Integer;

Procedure EnterLine (Var Line: CharInput; Var Length: Integer);
{This procedure reads a line of input from the terminal.}

    Begin
        Writeln ('Please enter your line of input:');
        Length := 0;
        While (Not Eoln) And (Length < MaxLen)
          Do Begin
            Length := Length + 1;
            Read (Line[Length])
          End;
```

```
        If Not Eoln
            Then Writeln ('Your message was too long; ',
                          'message truncated to ', MaxLen:1, ' characters');
        Readln
    End {EnterLine} ;

Procedure CountCat (Line: CharInput; Length: Integer; Var Count: CounterType);
{This procedures counts the number of letters in each category.}
    Var Item: Category;
        Index: Integer;

    Procedure DetermineCat (Ch: Char; Var Item: Category);
    {This procedure determines which category a given character belongs to}
        Begin
            If (Ch >= 'A') And (Ch <= 'Z')
                Then Item := Capital
            Else If (Ch >= 'a') and (Ch <= 'z')
                Then Item := Small
            Else If (Ch >= '0') and (Ch <= '9')
                Then Item := Digit
            Else If (Ch = ' ')
                Then Item := Space
                Else Item := Punc
        End {DetermineCat} ;

    Begin {CountCat}
        {Initially, all counts are 0}
        For Item := Capital To Punc
            Do Count[Item] := 0;

        {For each character, find category and update count}
        For Index := 1 To Length
          Do Begin
              DetermineCat(Line[Index], Item);
              Count[Item] := Count[Item] + 1
          End
    End {CountCat} ;

Procedure DisplayResults (Count: CounterType);
{This procedure displays the frequencies for each category.}
    Var Item: Category;
        Index: Integer;

    Procedure PrintName (Item: Category);
    {This procedure prints the name of the specified category}
        Begin
            Case Item Of
                Capital:  Write ('Capital Letter: ');
                Small  :  Write ('Small Letter   : ');
                Space  :  Write ('Space          : ');
                Digit  :  Write ('Digit          : ');
                Punc   :  Write ('Punctuation    : ')
            End
        End {PrintName} ;
    Begin
        Writeln;
        Writeln ('Display of the frequencies in the input line by category');
        Writeln;
```

```
        For Item := Capital To Punc
          Do Begin
            PrintName(Item);
            For Index := 1 To Count[Item]
              Do Write ('*');
            Writeln (Count[Item]:3)
          End
    End {DisplayResults} ;

Procedure ControlProcess;
{This procedure controls the major steps of data entry,
 counting of character and printing of results}
    Var Line: CharInput;         {The line of input}
        LineLength: Integer;    {The length of the line of input}
        Count: CounterType;     {The frequency data for each category}

    Begin
        EnterLine (Line, LineLength);
        CountCat (Line, LineLength, Count);
        DisplayResults (Count)
    End {ControlProcess} ;

Begin {Main}
    Writeln ('This program computes the frequency of letters ');
    Writeln ('by category in a given input line.');
    ControlProcess
End {Main} .
```

When this program is run with some test data, we get the following output:

```
This program computes the frequency of letters
by category in a given input line.
Please enter your line of input:
>>>>>This line contains a variety of characters!!! 12345 <<<<<

Display of the frequencies in the input line by category

Captial Letter: *  1
Small Letter  : *********************************** 35
Space         : ********  8
Digit         : *****  5
Punctuation   : ************* 13
```

In this program, we have listed (or enumerated) all of the possible categories in our problem, namely *Capital, Small, Space, Digit,* and *Punc.* This program illustrates many features of using these enumerated types.

To begin, we declare our enumerated type, which we called *Category.* In this listing, we indicate what values are allowed; we separate these values by commas; and we put the entire list in parentheses. Some other examples of such declarations are shown below.

```
Type DayOfWeek = (Sunday, Monday, Tuesday,
                  Wednesday, Thursday, Friday, Saturday);
        SpeechPart = (Noun, Verb, Adjective, Adverb,
                      Conjunction, Preposition, Pronoun, Article);
Var Day:    DayOfWeek;
    Word:   SpeechPart;
    Month:     (January, February, March, April,
                May, June, July, August, September,
                October, November, December);
```

Once enumerated types are declared, they can be used in many familiar ways. For example, enumerated types can be used in assignment statements, as array subscripts, and for control variables in *For* loops. In addition, they can be compared in Boolean expressions and used as constants in *Case* statements.

Further, the application of enumerated types in *For* loops suggests another aspect of our declarations. When we declare

```
TypeCategory = (Capital, Small, Space, Digit, Punc);
```

we are specifying an ordering of these items and an internal coding value. In particular, the computer will consider

*Capital* as having a code number 0;

*Small* as having a code number 1;

*Space* as having a code number 2;

*Digit* as having a code number 3;

*Punc* as having a code number 4.

With this ordering, we can establish what happens in a *For* loop. When we write

```
For Item := Capital to Punc
```

or

```
For Item := Small to Digit
```

*Item* begins with the first value specified. Then *Item* takes on successive values until the final value is reached. Thus, the first of these examples covers all five values, while the second example continues the loop for *Small, Space,* and *Digit* only.

This coding also allows us to use the functions *Ord, Succ,* and *Pred* (which we discussed in Section 11.2) for characters. In particular, if

```
Item := Space
```

then

*Ord(Item)* is *3;*

*Succ(Item)* is *Digit;*

*Pred(Item)* is *Small.*

Finally, we note that we are limited in the use of enumerated types in that we cannot read or write these types directly. Thus, when we use enumerated types, we often need to write a procedure that translates from our input data to our special values (Procedure *DetermineCat* in our program). Also, we may need a special output procedure to print the values for these enumerated types. (In this output process, Procedure *PrintName* illustrates a particularly helpful use of the *Case* statement.)

With these comments, our sample program shows us that enumerated types can be quite helpful as we try to solve problems. In our example, we could write our program in the language of our problem, by giving special values for *Capital, Small,* etc. Then, we could record data and establish loops on the basis of these values.

Our program did require procedures to translate from our character input to these special values and from these values to our output. However, in the middle of our processing, our program could follow our solution outline quite naturally.

## SECTION 11.7 A SUMMARY OF SIMPLE DATA TYPES

At this point, we have seen all of the simple data types allowed in Pascal, and it is useful to look at these types to see some general patterns. In Pascal, we can organize our simple data types into two main classes: real type and ordinal type.

### Real Type

In our work with real numbers, we can perform arithmetic and make comparisons, but we do not think of reals as being isolated entities. For example, there is a vast range of reals between 1.0 and 2.0, and we do not try to work with the real number that comes just after 1.0. With this perspective that reals extend "continuously," we find that we cannot use reals in some contexts.

- We cannot use reals as subscripts, for there are just too many reals in an interval. For example, we would need too much storage for

```
Var A: Array [1.0..2.0] of Integer
```

- Pascal does not allow subranges of reals for a similar reason.
- Functions such as *Pred* and *Succ* do not apply to reals, for we do not know which real exactly precedes or succeeds another.

### Ordinal Type

On the other hand, all of the other simple data types do contain distinct, isolated values, and we call these other types **ordinal types.** Included in these are the standard integer, Boolean, and character types we have used in many of our applications. In addition, ordinal type includes enumerated types, where we define our own specific values, and subranges.

With any of these ordinal types, we can consider values in a given interval, and we can ask what precedes or succeeds a given value. This isolated or discrete quality of the data in ordinal types has the following consequences.

- We can define subranges for any ordinal type.
- We can use any ordinal type (including subranges) for array subscripts and for *Case* statements.
- We can use any ordinal type for control variables in *For* loops.
- We can apply *Ord*, *Pred*, and *Succ* functions to any ordinal type. However, in using *Pred* and *Succ*, we must be careful not to go beyond the limits of our type. For example, if

  ```
  Category = (Capital, Small, Space, Digit, Punc)
  ```

  we cannot try to obtain

  ```
  Pred(Capital)
  ```

  or

  ```
  Succ(Punc).
  ```

This discussion shows that we can view many of our data types as being similar in many ways. Each ordinal type represents a distinct set of values, but we can use these types in many similar ways. On the other hand, real data type is somewhat different from these ordinal types.

## SUMMARY

1. This chapter introduces three new data types: **characters, enumerated types,** and **subranges.**
2. With **character data type,** we can read, process, and print individual characters, and several characters can be stored in arrays.
3. With **enumerated types,** we can define new data types containing specific data values. Thus, we are not limited to using only integers, real, Boolean, or character values in processing.
4. When working with integers, Booleans, characters, or enumerated types, we can restrict the range of values being considered to a specific interval or **subrange.**
5. Integers, Booleans, characters, subranges, and enumerated types are all examples of **ordinal data types,** and they share many common features.

For example, any ordinal data type can be used as constants in *Case* statements.

6. Ordinal data are stored using an underlying code, and this code allows us to compare data in Boolean expressions and to use any of the ordinal data types for control variables in *For* loops. With this underlying ordering, the functions *Ord*, *Pred*, and *Succ* can be used in processing any of these ordinal types. (*Chr* is also available for processing characters.)
7. Finally, this ordinal data can be used in a variety of applications, including processing a *Yes* or *No* response, capitalizing letters in a line of input, enciphering and deciphering messages, counting letters or characters in various ways, writing menu-driven programs, and computing time intervals.

## EXERCISES

The following four problems all include some aspects of processing a line of input. With some care, the various tasks required can be organized into a few logical procedures that can be reused to solve several problems. Thus, readers are encouraged to spend some time designing procedures that fit together in various ways to meet the requirements of these problems.

Throughout, we will consider a *word* as a sequence of letters without punctuation.

**11.1** *Counting Words.* Write a program that reads a line of input and counts the number of words in the line.

**11.2** *Capitalizing Words.* Write a program that reads a line of input and then prints the line with the first letter of each word capitalized and subsequent letters in lowercase.

**11.3** *Formatting Words.* Write a program that reads a line of input, capitalizes all letters, and prints the words in the line with just one space between words. All punctuation should be omitted.

| KEY TERMS, PHRASES, AND CONCEPTS | | ELEMENTS OF PASCAL SYNTAX | |
|---|---|---|---|
| Case Statement | End of Line Processing | *Case* | *Ord* |
| Character Data Type | Enumerated Types | *Char* | *Pred* |
| Character Codes | Histogram | *Chr* | Subranges |
| Character Functions | Menu-Driven Programs | Enumerated Type | *Succ* |
| Comparison of Characters | Ordinal Data Types | *EOLN* | |
| | Subranges | | |

**11.4** *Average Number of Letters.* Write a program that reads a line of input, determines the number of words and the number of letters, and prints the average number of letters per word.

**11.5** *Caesar Cipher.* Suppose we are given the declarations

```
Const MaxLen = 80;
Type InputLine = Array [1..MaxLen] of Char;
```

With these declarations, we will store a line of input as an array of type *InputLine,* and we will record the length of the line.

**a.** Write a procedure of the form

```
Procedure Shift (Var Line: InputLine; Length: Integer);
```

which replaces each letter in the line by the letter following it in alphabetical order, except that 'A' will replace 'Z'. Thus, the word 'THE' is coded as 'UIF'. Spaces and punctuation are not to be changed.

HINT: Use the *Succ* function.

**b.** Write a program that reads a line of input and applies *Shift* three times, so that each letter is replaced by the third letter following in the alphabet. Print the resulting coded message.

HISTORICAL NOTE: This code was used effectively by Caesar in the Gallic Wars, and thus this type of enciphering algorithm is called a Caesar Cipher.

**11.6** *Deciphering a Caesar Cipher.* Write a program that will decipher the messages written using the Caesar Cipher of the previous problem.

**11.7** *Enciphering and Deciphering.* In Section 11.3, we used a procedure *Decipher* when we wanted to decode a message using the given real and cipher alphabets. Suppose we use this procedure with the following variable declarations.

```
Var RealAlphabet   : Alphabet;
    CipherAlphabet : Alphabet;
    Message        : CharLine;
    CodedMess      : CharLine;
    NewMess        : CharLine;
    InputLen       : Integer;
```

Then, after entering our message, suppose we have the following procedure calls.

```
Decipher (CodedMess, Message, InputLen, RealAlphabet,
          CipherAlphabet);
Decipher (Message, NewMess, InputLen, CipherAlphabet,
          RealAlphabet);
```

**a.** How does *NewMess* compare with our original *CodedMess?*

**b.** Use the answer in Part a. to write a procedure that can help check that the enciphering procedure works correctly.

**11.8** *Divisibility by 2 and 3.* Write a program that determines if an integer is divisible by either 2 or 3.

HINT: If we divide the number by 6, we can identify the following cases.

- If the remainder is 0, then the number is divisible by both 2 and 3.
- If the remainder is 1 or 5, then the number is divisible by neither.
- If the remainder is 2 or 4, then the number is divisible by 2 but not 3.
- If the remainder is 3, then the number is divisible by 3 but not 2.

**11.9** *Identifying Months.* Write a program that reads an integer between 1 and 12 and then prints the name of the corresponding month. For example, if the number 5 is typed, the computer should print

May is the fifth month.

HINT: Use a *Case* statement.

**11.10** *Common Error in Programming-1.* The following procedure for inputing characters contains an error that commonly occurs in using subranges. Find the error.

```
{This procedure assumes the following declarations:

Const MaxText = 80;

Type CharPosition = 1..MaxText;
     TextLine = Array[CharPosition] of Char; }

Procedure EnterText (Var Text: TextLine; Var Length: CharPosition);
{This procedure reads a line of text from a terminal.}
    Begin
        Length := 0;
        While (Not Eoln) and (Length < MaxText)
          Do Begin
            Length := Length + 1;
            Read(Text[Length])
          End;
        If Not Eoln
            Then Writeln ('Message Too Long;  Message Truncated To ',
                           MaxText:1, ' Characters.');
        Readln
    End {EnterText} ;
```

**11.11** *Common Error in Programming-2.* A more subtle problem with subranges is illustrated by the following example. Suppose we are searching an array

A: Array [1..Max] of Char

in order to locate a specific character Ch. One way to do this involves the use of a Boolean function *Done* to test the exit condition in a loop. For example, we might write

```
Function Done: Boolean;
     Begin
          If Index > Max
             Then Done := True
             Else Done := (A[Index] = Ch)
     End;
  .
  .
  .
Begin {Search Procedure}
    While Not Done
       Do Index := Index + 1;
  .
  .
  .
```

A second approach replaces the Boolean function *Done* with a condition in the *While* loop itself:

```
Begin {Search Procedure}
     While (Item <= Length) Or (Sequence [Item] = Ch)
          Do Index := Index + 1;
  .
  .
  .
```

Find a difficulty with this writing of the Boolean expression in the *While* loop that might motivate us to use the Boolean function *Done*.

# CHAPTER 12

# COLLECTIONS OF OBJECTS: SETS AND RECORDS

In past chapters, we have worked with individual pieces of data, such as numbers and characters, and we have been able to put these separate pieces together in arrays. This chapter examines the general concept of grouping pieces of data together more fully, and we will suggest an orientation that allows us to think of our data abstractly in terms of the problem we have at hand. We will not want to limit ourselves to thinking about specific values stored in a Pascal program.

In addition, this chapter introduces two specific ways we can work with collections of data. In particular, we consider **sets,** which allow us to store various values as a single entity, and **records,** which allow us to combine various types of data into logical units.

## SECTION 12.1 THE CONCEPTS OF GROUPING DATA AND ABSTRACTION

We can think of data on several distinct levels: we can consider each item of data individually; we can group items of data together in various ways; and we can group data items in complex ways, which include operations on data as well as the data themselves.

Up to this point, most of our work has involved the first of these levels, although the second level was introduced somewhat in Chapter 8 when we considered rows in a table as separate entities. In this section, we examine each of these levels more carefully.

## Level 1: Individual Data Items

Up to this point, we normally have considered each piece of data individually. We did not need to group our information in any way. This first level is most useful in problems that are simple enough to handle each piece of data separately. For example, in our unit pricing problems in Sections 2.1 and 11.1, we only needed three values (cost per ounce, price in dollars, and weight in ounces), and we could work with each value by itself. We might also choose to focus on individual pieces of information when we are starting to analyze a problem. For example, we might try to find patterns by working with many special cases.

## Level 2: Groups of Data

Once we master individual pieces of data, we often want to group the data in various ways. For example, we may form sequences from these pieces. Thus, when data are stored in an array, there is a first item, a second item, and so on.

Alternatively, we may put pieces of information together into groups in which order does not matter. For example, in considering a bridge hand, we care about the cards that we hold, not the order in which they were dealt. We might also want to group various types of information such as numbers and words. For example, an employer may include an employee's name, employee number, address, age, social security number, and telephone number in a single file. This information involves many individual pieces of data, but these pieces are grouped together in the records of the personnel office. At this level, we work with an entire collection of data at once.

In our programming, we have already seen that we can work at this level when we are dealing with arrays. In Chapter 8 we could refer to an entire array as a single entity. (For example, we wrote $A := B$.) Similarly, we could work with entire rows of tables. Later in this chapter, we will see that Pascal allows us to group data in other ways as well.

## Level 3: Abstract Data Structures

In more complex problems, we must consider not only the pieces of data that we need to store but also the ways we need to work with that data. For example, if we want to study traffic flow at a traffic light, our individual pieces of data may involve the vehicles turning left or right, the vehicles moving along straight, and the vehicles stopped for a red light. However, beyond these pieces, we also need to consider what happens when another car approaches the light or when a car finishes its turn. In this problem, we want to think in terms of cars entering and leaving the intersection, cars turning, and cars waiting. Our data involve cars, and we can specify various interactions among the cars.

For such complex problems, we need to free ourselves from specific programming details. We will be overwhelmed if we must translate each detail about traffic flow into specifics about numbers or Booleans or characters. Our programs must allow us to work on a more conceptual level.

This is the level of abstract data structures, where we group data items in complex ways and where we specify what operations we wish to perform on these data items. We will see one way we can include this level in our Pascal programs in Chapter 15.

## SECTION 12.2 PUTTING PIECES TOGETHER WITH SETS

This section discusses one way that pieces of data can be grouped together, following our second level for working with data. The particular approach uses the concept of a **set,** and we introduce this idea with an example.

### PROBLEM 12.2A Determining Letters and Counting Vowels

Write a program that determines which letters are present in a line that is entered at the keyboard and counts the number of vowels in the line. In this problem, lowercase and uppercase letters should be considered separately.

### Discussion of Problem 12.2A

In solving this problem, we can think in terms of three collections of objects: the letters in the alphabet (including both uppercase and lowercase); the letters in the line; and the vowels in the alphabet. Thus, we write our solution in terms of these collections, or **sets.** In our processing, we can describe the first and third of these collections immediately:

> The letters of the alphabet include the ranges:
> 'a'..'z' and 'A'..'Z'
>
> The vowels include the specific characters:
> 'a', 'e', 'i', 'o', 'u', 'A', 'E', 'I', 'O', 'U'

The second collection depends upon our input. Thus, we will start with this set of letters being **empty,** that is, containing no elements. Then, as we go through our input, we will add the letters.

Also, when we count vowels, we will go through each character in our input. If a character is a vowel, we will increment our vowel count.

This discussion suggests the following outline.

### Outline of Problem 12.2A

**I.** Enter line. (We proceed as in the examples in Sections 11.3 and 11.6.)
**II.** Process line.
  **A.** Define our collection of letters and vowels.
  **B.** At the start:
    **1.** We have not found any letters.
    **2.** Our count of vowels is 0.

**C.** For each character in the line:
  **1.** If the character is a vowel, we add 1 to our vowel count.
  **2.** If the character is a letter, we add it to our collection of letters.

**III.** Print results.
  **A.** Print letters in the line. For each lowercase and uppercase letter, if the letter was in our line of input, then we print the letter.
  **B.** Print the final vowel count.

This outline yields the following program. For clarity in processing, we have used a variable *Ch* for the characters in the line of input. We could use *Line*[*Index*] in procedure *ProcessLine* instead if we wished.

```
Program DetermineLettersAndCountVowels (Input, Output);
{This program determines what letters appear in a line of input
 and counts the number of vowels in the line.}

Const MaxLen = 80;

Type InputLine = Array [1..MaxLen] of Char;
     CharacterSet = Set Of Char;

Procedure EnterLine (Var Line: InputLine; Var Length: Integer);
{This procedure reads Line from the terminal.}

    Begin
        Writeln ('Please enter your line of input:');
        Length := 0;
        While (Not Eoln) And (Length < MaxLen)
          Do Begin
            Length := Length + 1;
            Read (Line[Length])
          End;
        If Not Eoln
            Then Writeln ('Your message was too long; ',
                          'message truncated to ', MaxLen:1, ' characters');
        Readln
    End {EnterLine} ;

Procedure ProcessLine (Line: InputLine; Length: Integer;
                    Var LetterSet: CharacterSet; Var VowelCount: Integer);
{This procedure forms a set of letters and counts the vowels}
    Var Letters: CharacterSet;
        Vowels: CharacterSet;
        Index: Integer;
        Ch: Char;

    Begin
        {Initialize sets and counter}
        Letters := ['a'..'z', 'A'..'Z'];
        Vowels := ['a','e','i','o','u','A','E','I','O','U'];
        LetterSet := [];
        VowelCount := 0;

        {Process each character in line of input}
        For Index := 1 To Length
```

```
            Do Begin
               Ch := Line[Index];
               If Ch In Vowels
                  Then VowelCount := VowelCount + 1;
               If Ch In Letters
                  Then LetterSet := LetterSet + [ Ch ]
            End
    End {ProcessLine} ;

Procedure DisplayResults (LetterSet: CharacterSet; VowelCount: Integer);
{This procedure prints the letters in the input and the count of the vowels}
    Var Ch: Char;
    Begin
        Writeln;
        Writeln ('The following letters were found in the line of input');
        For Ch := 'a' To 'z'
            Do If Ch In LetterSet
                 Then Write (Ch:2);
        For Ch := 'A' To 'Z'
            Do If Ch In LetterSet
                 Then Write (Ch:2);
        Writeln;
        Writeln;
        Writeln ('There were ',VowelCount:1, ' vowels in the line of input.')
    End {DisplayResults} ;

Procedure ControlProcessing;
{This procedure controls the major steps required to process the line}
    Var Line: InputLine;        {The line of input}
        LineLength: Integer;   {The length of the line of input}
        LetterSet: CharacterSet;{Set of letters from input line}
        VowelCount: Integer;   {Number of vowels in input line}
    Begin
        EnterLine (Line, LineLength);
        ProcessLine (Line, LineLength, LetterSet, VowelCount);
        DisplayResults (LetterSet, VowelCount)
    End {ControlProcessing} ;

Begin {Main}
    Writeln ('This programs processes letters and vowels ',
             'in a given line of input');
    ControlProcessing
End {Main} .
```

When this program is run with some sample data, we get the following output:

```
This programs processes letters and vowels in a given line of input
Please enter your line of input:
This program illustrates some simple ways that sets can help us group data.

The following letters were found in the line of input
 a c d e g h i l m n o p r s t u w y T

There were 21 vowels in the line of input.
```

## Sets in Pascal

In the program above, we illustrate several features of sets in Pascal, which allow us to handle groups of data. A **set** is a collection of data items in which duplicate values are not recorded and the order of items is ignored.

We work with groups of data by declaring them as sets. For example, we declare

```
Type CharacterSet = Set of Char;
Var  Letters: CharacterSet;
     Vowels: CharacterSet;
```

Alternatively, we could have declared

```
Var Letters, Vowels: Set of Char;
```

These declarations indicate that these variables will be collections or sets of characters. In this problem, all of our collections involved character data. More generally, sets may be constructed from any ordinal type.

Once a variable is declared, we can specify what data we wish to include in a group. Four ways of specifying the data in a group are illustrated in our example.

1. We can specifically list the items in a set. For example,

   ```
   Vowels := ['a', 'e', 'i', 'o', 'u', 'A', 'E', 'I', 'O', 'U'];
   ```

   lists the characters in the set of vowels. Here, each vowel is listed, the characters are separated by commas, and the entire list is placed in brackets [ ].
2. We can specify subranges of elements. For example,

   ```
   Letters := ['a'..'z', 'A'..'Z'];
   ```

   indicates that this set of letters is made up of the two subranges, 'a' to 'z' and 'A' to 'Z'.
3. A special case of this listing of elements is the specification of the **empty set.** For example, the statement

   ```
   LetterSet := [ ];
   ```

   specifies that the *LetterSet* begins with no elements, just as the statement

   ```
   VowelCount := 0;
   ```

   initializes this integer variable.
4. Once we have initialized a set, we can add elements to it. For example, our program contained the statement

   ```
   LetterSet := LetterSet + [Ch];
   ```

   Here, we use the "+" sign to add a character *Ch* to our *LetterSet*. Note

No duplicates

that the *Ch* is placed in brackets [ ] in this statement. (Later in this section, we will see that "+" can be used more generally.)

While sets do allow us to group data, we note that sets do not keep track of duplicates. Once an element is in a set, the set is not changed if that element is added again. Thus ['*a*', '*a*', '*a*'] is the same as ['*a*']. The multiple copies of '*a*' in the first set are ignored.

Next, we note that once a set is created, we can test if a particular element is in that set. For example, we wrote

```
If Ch In Vowels
```

to see if the character *Ch* under consideration was a vowel. In general, we may write the Boolean expression

boolean expression

**Element *In* SetVariable** ⟷ negation not( Element in SetVariable)

to test if the given *Element* is in the set specified by *SetVariable*. This expression is true if the *SetVariable* contains the *Element* and false otherwise.

From our example that analyzes a line of input, we see some ways we can declare sets, group elements together in those sets, and test if particular items are in those collections. Before considering a more extended example, we look at three important operations that we can use to manipulate sets, namely

- union
- intersection
- difference

## Unions of Sets

If we have two sets, we can put the elements of these two sets together to form a new set using the **union** or "+" operation. For example, suppose we have

```
UpperCase := ['A'..'Z'];
LowerCase := ['a'..'z'];
Vowels    := ['a', 'e', 'i', 'o', 'u', 'A', 'E', 'I', 'O', 'U'];
```

Then, we can put *UpperCase* and *LowerCase* together to get

```
Letters := UpperCase + LowerCase;
```

Here, *Letters* include both capital and small letters, so *Letters* has become ['*a*'..'z', 'A'..'Z'].

When we put sets together in this way, the union operation discards duplicates; sets only record that an element is present, not the number of times it occurs. In some cases, this means that the union operation does not change what elements we already have. For example, *Vowels* + *Letters* gives us *Letters* again, since all *Vowels* are already included in the *Letters*. Similarly, the union of any set with itself is just the same set.

With this background, we see that our previous statement

```
LetterSet := LetterSet + [Ch];
```

is just a special case of this union or "+" operation. Here, we start with the collection *LetterSet*. Then, we make a set out of our character *Ch* by putting *Ch* in brackets. At this point, we have two sets: *LetterSet* and [*Ch*]. Then, we take the union of these two sets, putting their elements together, to get our new *LetterSet*.

## Intersection

While the union operation puts elements from two sets together, the **intersection** or "*" operation identifies which elements are in both sets. For example, if we use our earlier declarations, then

```
Vowels * UpperCase
```

gives ['*A*', '*E*', '*I*', '*O*', '*U*']. Here, we find elements that are both vowels and capital letters.

As a second example,

```
UpperCase * LowerCase
```

is the empty set, [ ]. There are no characters that are both uppercase and lowercase.

## Difference

Our third operation, **difference** or "−", allows us to find all elements in one set that are not in a second. For example,

```
Vowels - UpperCase
```

gives ['*a*', '*e*', '*i*', '*o*', '*u*']. Here, we find all vowels that are not capitals; i.e., we obtain the lowercase vowels. On the other hand,

```
UpperCase - VowelSet
```

gives a different collection of characters, namely

```
['B', 'C', 'D', 'F', 'G', 'H', 'J', 'K', 'L', 'M', 'N',
     'P', 'Q', 'R', 'S', 'T', 'V', 'W', 'X', 'Y', 'Z']
```

Again, set differences may produce the empty set as a result. For example, both

```
UpperCase - Letters
```

and

```
Vowels - Vowels
```

give the empty set, as every element in the first set is also in the second.

## PROBLEM 12.2B Analyzing Categories of Letters

With the operations we just described, we can consider the following more complex problem involving an analysis of a line of characters.

Scan a line of input to determine

**a.** the letters (upper- and lowercase) used;
**b.** the uppercase letters used;
**c.** the lowercase letters used;
**d.** the vowels used; and
**e.** the consonants used.

### Discussion of Problem 12.2B

While the statement of our problem involves many categories of letters, our processing need not be complex if we group our letters conveniently.

From Problem 12.2A, we already have seen how to determine which letters are used in a line. Also, we can utilize the following relationships for sets:

```
Letters := UpperCase + LowerCase;
Consonants := Letters - Vowels;
```

Next, we can determine which letters in our line are in each category if we intersect *LetterSet* (letters in our input line) with the appropriate collections of upper- or lowercase letters, vowels, or consonants.

This suggests the following outline.

### Outline of Problem 12.2B

**I.** Enter line. (We proceed as in the examples in Sections 11.3 and 11.6.)
**II.** Determine letters used in line.
  **A.** At the start:
    **1.** We have not found any letters.
    **2.** We have not found any vowels.
  **B.** For each character in the input line:
    **1.** If the character is a vowel, then we add it to our list of vowels.
    **2.** If the character is a letter, then we add it to our collection of letters.
**III.** Print results. In each case, print a special note if no letters are present in the category.
  **A.** Print all letters in the line.
  **B.** Print letters both in line and uppercase.
  **C.** Print letters both in line and lowercase.
  **D.** Print letters both in line and vowels.
  **E.** Print letters both in line and consonants.

From this outline, we derive the following program.

```
Program GroupingLettersinCategories (Input, Output);
{This program determines what letters from a line of input
 occur in various categories.}

Const MaxLen = 80;

Type InputLine = Array [1..MaxLen] of Char;
     CharacterSet = Set Of Char;

Procedure InitializeSets(Var UpperCase, LowerCase, Vowels,
                             Consonants, Letters: CharacterSet);
{This procedure sets up our sets of upper and lower case letters,
 vowels, consonants, and all letters}
    Begin
        UpperCase := ['A'..'Z'];
        LowerCase := ['a'..'z'];
        Vowels := ['a','e','i','o','u','A','E','I','O','U'];
        Letters := UpperCase + LowerCase;
        Consonants := Letters - Vowels
    End {InitializeSets} ;

Procedure EnterLine (Var Line: InputLine; Var Length: Integer);
{This procedure reads Line from the terminal.}

    Begin
        Writeln ('Please enter your line:');
        Length := 0;
        While (Not Eoln) And (Length < MaxLen)
          Do Begin
            Length := Length + 1;
            Read (Line[Length])
          End;
        If Not Eoln
            Then Writeln ('Your message was too long; ',
                          'message truncated to ', MaxLen:1, ' characters');
        Readln
    End {EnterLine} ;

Procedure FindLetters (Line: InputLine; Length: Integer;
                       Var LetterSet: CharacterSet; Letters: CharacterSet);
{This procedure forms a set of letters from the input line}
    Var Index: Integer;

    Begin
        {Initialize set}
        LetterSet := [];

        {Process each character in line}
        For Index := 1 To Length
          Do Begin
            If Line[Index] In Letters
               Then LetterSet := LetterSet + [ Line[Index] ]
          End
    End {FindLetters};
```

```
Procedure DisplayResults (LetterSet, UpperCase, LowerCase, Vowels,
                          Consonants, Letters: CharacterSet);
{This procedure prints the letters in various categories}

    Procedure PrintIntersection (FirstSet, SecondSet: CharacterSet);
    {This procedure prints the letters in the intersection
     of the two given sets}
        Var Ch: Char;
            Intersection: CharacterSet;
        Begin
            Intersection := FirstSet * SecondSet;
            If Intersection = [] {test if intersection is empty}
                Then Writeln ('     No letters found')
                Else Begin
                    For Ch := 'a' To 'z'
                        Do If Ch In Intersection
                            Then Write (Ch:2);
                    For Ch := 'A' To 'Z'
                        Do If Ch In Intersection
                            Then Write (Ch:2);
                    Writeln
                    End;
            Writeln
        End {PrintIntersection} ;

    Begin {DisplayResults}

        Writeln;
        Writeln ('The following letters were found in the line');
        PrintIntersection (LetterSet, Letters);

        Writeln ('The following capital letters were found');
        PrintIntersection (LetterSet, UpperCase);

        Writeln ('The following lower case letters were found');
        PrintIntersection (LetterSet, LowerCase);

        Writeln ('The following vowels were found');
        PrintIntersection (LetterSet, Vowels);

        Writeln ('The following consonants were found');
        PrintIntersection (LetterSet, Consonants)

    End {DisplayResults} ;

Procedure ControlProcessing;
{This procedure controls the initialization, data entry, analysis, and
printing of the line of input.}
    Var Line: InputLine;        {The line of input}
        LineLength: Integer;    {The length of the line of input}
        LetterSet: CharacterSet;{Set of letters from line of input}
        UpperCase: CharacterSet;
        LowerCase: CharacterSet;
        Vowels: CharacterSet;
        Consonants: CharacterSet;
        Letters: CharacterSet;
```

```
    Begin
        InitializeSets(UpperCase, LowerCase, Vowels, Consonants, Letters);
        EnterLine (Line, LineLength);
        FindLetters (Line, LineLength, LetterSet, Letters);
        DisplayResults (LetterSet, UpperCase, LowerCase,
                        Vowels, Consonants, Letters)
    End {ControlProcessing} ;

  Begin {Main}
    Writeln ('This program processes letters and vowels ',
             'in a given line of input.');
    ControlProcessing
  End {Main} .
```

This program produces the following output:

```
This program processes letters and vowels in a given line of input.
Please enter your line:
pascal's set capabilities allow us to manipulate groups of data easily!!

The following letters were found in the line
 a b c d e f g i l m n o p r s t u w y

The following capital letters were found
     No letters found

The following lower case letters were found
 a b c d e f g i l m n o p r s t u w y

The following vowels were found
 a e i o u

The following consonants were found
 b c d f g l m n p r s t w y
```

This program combines many of the points we have made about sets. We see that we can work conceptually with groups of data by using sets. Once we declare and initialize our sets, then we can manipulate sets in various ways. Finally, we can test if particular elements are in our sets, and we can see if some sets are empty.

## SECTION 12.3 PUTTING PIECES TOGETHER WITH RECORDS

In the previous section, we combined various pieces of data of the same type into sets. In this section, we combine different types of data, such as numeric data and alphabetical characters.

We begin with a fairly straightforward problem.

## PROBLEM 12.3A Adjacent Concert Tickets

As part of a job selling tickets for a concert, we must sell pairs of seats. For each ticket, we store

Row: In this hall, rows go between 'A' and 'X'.

Seat Number: Within a row, seats are numbered between 1 and 30.

Cost: Ticket prices are $3.50, $5.00, and $7.35.

When we sell a pair of tickets, we follow these rules:

1. We assign the second seat next to the first. In this pairing, we normally group seats 1 and 2, 3 and 4, and so on, in the same row.
2. We sell the adjacent seat for 70% of the first seat's price.

Write a program that reads the row, seat number, and cost of the first ticket; assigns a seat for the second ticket; and computes the total cost.

### Discussion of Problem 12.3A

In this problem, we want to consider *Row*, *Seat*, and *Cost* as part of a single entity called *Ticket*. Then, we want to enter information for the *First* ticket, compute the appropriate information for a *Second* ticket, and print the results.

This suggests the following outline.

### Outline for Problem 12.3A

**I.** Enter data for first ticket.
- **A.** Row
- **B.** Seat
- **C.** Cost

**II.** Determine second ticket.
- **A.** Use same row.
- **B.** Pick the adjacent seat. With the pairing specified, we will add or subtract one from the first seat number, depending on whether the first seat is odd or even.
- **C.** Cost is 70% of first ticket.

**III.** Print the data for each ticket.

This outline suggests the following program, in which we first declare a ticket as a separate entity, and then we work with the first and second ticket.

```
Program AssignTicket (Input, Output);
{This program computes the cost and seat number for an adjacent seat}

Type Ticket = Record
        Row: 'A'..'X';
        Seat: 1..36;
        Cost: Real
        End;
```

```
Var First, Second: Ticket;

Begin {Main}

    {Enter Data for First Ticket}
    Writeln ('This program determines the Second Ticket of a pair');
    Writeln ('Please enter Row, Seat Number, and Cost of the First Ticket:');
    Readln (First.Row, First.Seat, First.Cost);

    {Determine Second Ticket}
    Second.Row := First.Row;
    If Odd(First.Seat)
        Then Second.Seat := First.Seat + 1
        Else Second.Seat := First.Seat - 1;
    Second.Cost := 0.70 * First.Cost;

    {Print Ticket Assignments}
    Writeln ('                 Row    Seat    Cost');
    Writeln (' First Ticket:', First.Row:2, First.Seat:8, First.Cost:9:2);
    Writeln ('Second Ticket:', Second.Row:2, Second.Seat:8, Second.Cost:9:2);
    Writeln;
    Writeln ('The total cost of the tickets is $',
             First.Cost + Second.Cost:1:2, ' .')

End {Main} .
```

Two trial runs of this program are shown below.

```
First Trial Run

This program determines the Second Ticket of a pair
Please enter Row, Seat Number, and Cost of the First Ticket:
C 1 7.35
              Row    Seat    Cost
 First Ticket: C       1     7.35
Second Ticket: C       2     5.14

The total cost of the tickets is $12.49 .


Second Trial Run

This program determines the Second Ticket of a pair
Please enter Row, Seat Number, and Cost of the First Ticket:
Q 36 5.00
              Row    Seat    Cost
 First Ticket: Q      36     5.00
Second Ticket: Q      35     3.50

The total cost of the tickets is $8.50 .
```

## Records in Pascal

The program above illustrates the concept of records in Pascal. A **record** is a collection of several pieces of data, and these pieces may be of different types. Within a record, data are divided into distinct sections, called **fields,** and names are given to each of these fields. When we wish to declare a record, we begin by specifying the word *Record*. Then, we list the various fields that make up the record, and we specify the type of each field. The list of fields concludes with the word *End*. In our example, we declared *Ticket* to be a type with three fields: *Row, Seat,* and *Cost;* and we specified the type of each of these fields. In this case, each field has a separate data type (character, integer, real). In other records, we may wish to have several fields with the same type. We may even want one field to be another record.

Once variables have been defined to be records, we may refer to one of the fields by specifying both the variable and the field, and we use a period to separate the variable identifier from the field. In our example, *First* is a record containing all three fields, and we can specify the seat number for the first ticket by writing

```
First.Seat
```

Here we add the field *Seat* to the variable *First*.

Then, once fields are specified, we can work with the individual fields just as we work with other types of variables. For example,

```
First.Row
```

is a character that enables us to read and write this datum. Similarly, *First.Seat* and *Second.Seat* are integers, so we can apply arithmetic functions, perform arithmetic operations, and assign values to these items.

With this example, we see that once we have defined a record type and declared variables of that type, we can work with each field just as we have previously with other variables.

In solving the following modified problem, we will see that we can work with records as a whole as well as with individual fields.

**PROBLEM 12.3B** Modify the previous problem to eliminate the discount for the second ticket. Seat assignment should be done as before.

### Outline for Problem 12.3B

In solving this revised problem, we follow the same general outline that we used for the original problem. However, here we place a greater emphasis on the ticket as a whole.

**I.** Enter data for first ticket.
- **A.** Row
- **B.** Seat
- **C.** Cost

**II.** Determine second ticket.
  **A.** Copy information from first ticket to second ticket.
  **B.** Modify the seat number.
**III.** Print the data for each ticket.
  **A.** Print a heading.
  **B.** For the first ticket, print row, seat, and cost.
  **C.** For the second ticket, print row, seat, and cost.
  **D.** Compute and print the total cost.

Our resulting program is organized into procedures with appropriate parameters.

```
Program AssignTicket {Revised Version} (Input, Output);
{This program computes the cost and seat number for an adjacent seat}

Type Ticket = Record
         Row: Char;
         Seat: 1..36;
         Cost: Real
         End;

Procedure DetermineTicket (Var Customer: Ticket);
{Enter Data for First Ticket}
    Begin {DetermineTicket}
        Writeln ('Please enter Row, Seat Number, and Cost ',
                 'of the First Ticket:');
        With Customer Do
            Readln (Row, Seat, Cost)
    End {DetermineTicket} ;

Procedure Assign (First: Ticket; Var Second: Ticket);
{Determine seat and compute cost for Second Ticket}
    Begin
        Second := First;
        If Odd(First.Seat)
            Then Second.Seat := First.Seat + 1
            Else Second.Seat := First.Seat - 1
    End {Assign} ;

Procedure PrintTickets (First, Second: Ticket);
{Print Ticket Assignments}
    Begin
        Writeln ('                 Row     Seat     Cost');
        With First
            Do Writeln (' First Ticket:',  Row:2,  Seat:8,  Cost:9:2);
        With Second
            Do Writeln ('Second Ticket:', Row:2, Seat:8, Cost:9:2);
        Writeln;
        Writeln ('The total cost of the tickets is $',
                 First.Cost + Second.Cost:1:2, ' .')
    End {PrintTickets} ;
```

```
Procedure ControlProcessing;
{This procedure controls the major steps in assigning tickets.}
    Var First, Second: Ticket;
    Begin
        DetermineTicket(First);
        Assign(First, Second);
        PrintTickets (First, Second)
    End {ControlProcessing} ;

Begin {Main}
    Writeln ('This program determines the Second Ticket of a pair');
    ControlProcessing
End {Main} .
```

record as a whole
– parameters
– assigning values

This program produces the same output as our previous one, except that the cost of the second ticket is the same as the first.

In this program, we have stressed each ticket as a whole in several ways. First, we have used tickets as parameters in our procedures. We can use both value and reference passage to transmit an entire record between procedures and functions. Next, as we saw with arrays, we can copy all parts of a record from one variable to another. The statement

Second := First;

in procedure *Assign* assigns each field of the record variable *First* to the corresponding field of *Second*.

As a final part of Pascal syntax, when we want to work with various fields of a record, we can use a *With* statement, which specifies the record variable. For example, in procedure *DetermineTicket*, we wrote

*With* Customer
    *Do* Readln(Row, Seat, Cost);

Here, *Customer* is a ticket record, and we wish to work with each field within that record. More generally, the *With* statement has the form

*With* RecordVariable
    *Do* Statement

As before, the *Statement* may be a simple Pascal statement, or it may be a *Begin–End* block. In this statement, we can refer to the fields of our *RecordVariable* directly. We do not need to write out the variable identifier each time. (Thus, we could write *Row* instead of the full name *Customer.Row*.)

In the second program, we see that records allow us to work with collections of data at two different levels. At the first level, we can work with individual pieces of data by specifying both the variable name and the field, as in *Customer.Row*. At the next level, we can consider the entire record as a single entity in parameters and assignments.

In the next chapter, we use both of these levels when we look more carefully at the processing of strings of characters.

## SUMMARY

1. In working with problems, we can consider data at any of **three levels,** namely:
   - individual data items;
   - groups of items; and
   - abstract data structures, in which we specify both the type of data and the operations to be performed on the data.
2. In earlier chapters, we considered individual data items as part of the introduction of real, integer, Boolean, and character data, and we grouped data using arrays. The current chapter also introduced two new ways to collect data, sets and records.
3. In Pascal, we can group unordered data of the same type together in **sets.** Sets are unordered collections of data that do not distinguish among duplicate values. In working with sets, we may specify individual elements or ranges of elements that will constitute a set, or we can specify no elements for an **empty set.** Then, once some sets are defined, we can put them together using various operations, including
   - + union
   - * intersection
   - − difference

   Also, we can check if a particular element is *in* a given set.
4. In addition, in Pascal, we can combine various pieces of data together

| KEY TERMS, PHRASES, AND CONCEPTS | | ELEMENTS OF PASCAL SYNTAX |
|---|---|---|
| Levels of Data | Sets | *Record* ____ End; |
| Abstraction | Difference | *Set Of* ____ |
| Individual Items | Elements in Sets | Set Operations |
| Groups of Data | Empty Set | [ ] |
| Abstract Data Structures | Intersection | +, −, * |
| Records | Union | *In* |
| Record Fields | | *With* ____ *Do* |

as **fields** within a **record.** Records allow us to work with each piece of data separately. Alternatively, we can consider an entire record as a single entity in assignment statements and in function and procedure parameters.

## EXERCISES

**12.1** *Letters in a Line of Input.* Write a program that reads a line of input and determines what letters appear in the line. (In this problem, you should not distinguish between upper- and lowercase letters.)

**12.2** Write a program that reads a line of input and determines which letters in the line occur both as capital letters and as lowercase letters.

**12.3** *Finding Letters.* Write a program that reads a line of input and then determines the first letter of the alphabet that appears in the line. In other words, the program determines if an 'A' occurs in the line; then, if no 'A' occurs, the program searches for a 'B', and so on. (Do not distinguish between upper- and lowercase letters in this problem.)

**12.4** *Analysis of Finding Letters.* Analyze the following two algorithms to solve the previous problem.

*Algorithm 1:*

Read the entire line into an array of characters.
Search the entire line for an 'A'.
    If an 'A' is found, stop.
If not, search the entire line for a 'B'.
    If a 'B' is found, stop.
If not, search the entire line for a 'C'.
Continue until either a letter is found or until all letters 'A' through 'Z' have been checked.

*Algorithm 2:*

Read the entire line and form a set of characters for these letters.
Check if 'A' is in the set.
    If so, stop.
If not, check if 'B' is in the set.
    If so, stop.
If not, check if 'C' is in the set.
Continue until either a letter is found or until all letters 'A' through 'Z' have been checked.

In your analysis of these algorithms, assume a full 80 character line of input has been entered. Then count the maximum number of steps that the program might have to make before reaching its conclusion.

In your analysis, count the comparison of one letter with one character of input as one step (Algorithm 1). Also, count each union operation and each test for the inclusion of an element in a set as one step (Algorithm 2).

NOTE: Sets can be implemented very efficiently inside computers, so a union or a test of inclusion can be done very efficiently.

**12.5** *Letters in Common.* Write a program that reads two lines of input and determines

- what letters appear in both of these lines;
- what letters appear in the first line, but not in the second; and
- what letters appear in the second line, but not in the first.

(Do not distinguish between upper- and lowercase letters in this exercise.)

**12.6** **a.** Name two syntactical constructions in Pascal where an *End* statement occurs without a *Begin.*

**b.** Can a *Begin* ever occur without an *End*?

**12.7** *Packaging.* In designing a package for a product, a small change in the dimensions of a packing case can make a significant change in the volume of the package. Write a program that reads initial dimensions (width, length, height) of a rectangular box and computes the volume. The program should then ask the user for changes in each dimension and compute the new value. The user should be allowed to continue typing new dimensions until he or she wishes to stop.

NOTES:

1. In this program, try reducing each dimension by 5 or 10% to see the change in volume. (Changes this small may be hard to see in a store.)
2. Try reducing just the depth by a small amount to see the change in volume. (The new box will look the same on the shelf if the front panel is facing the customer.)
3. In this program, store the width, length, height, and volume in a record called *Package.*

**12.8** *Nesting With Statements—A Caution.* When we put *With* statements together, we must be careful that there is no ambiguity about which fields we mean. Suppose we have the following declarations.

```
Type  Ticket = Record
          Row: Char;
          Seat: 1..36;
          Cost: Real
          End;
      BusinessExpense = Record
          Client: Array [1..30] of Char;
          Transportation: Real;
          Meals: Real;
          Cost: Real
          End;
```

```
Var  First, Second: Ticket;
     Evening: BusinessExpense;
```

Find the ambiguities in the following pieces of code:

a.
```
With First
   Do With Second
        Do Begin
           Row := Row;
           If Odd(Seat)
                    Then Seat := Seat + 1
                    Else Seat := Seat - 1;
           Cost := Cost
        End
   End;
```

b.
```
With Evening
   Do With First
       Do Begin
          Transportation := 100.00;
          Meals := 50.00;
          Cost := Transportation + Meals + Ticket.Cost
       End;
```

**12.9** *Employee Wages.* A program is to compute an employee's wages for a week. In particular, the program reads
- number of hours worked
- hourly rate
- tax withholding rate (entered as a percentage)

Then the program computes
- wages earned
  (The employee earns "time and a half" for any hours over 40 worked during the week.)
- tax withheld
- insurance premium (always $20.00 per week)
- take home pay

In writing this program, store all employee information in a single employee record. Further, perform the reading, computing, and printing tasks as separate procedures that have the employee record as a parameter.

**12.10** *Generating Dates.* We consider a *Date* as the following record:

```
Type Date = Record
              Month: 1..12;
              Day: 1..31;
              Year: 1..2000
              End;
```

Write

Procedure NextDate (OldDate: Date; Var NewDate: Date)

which takes *OldDate* as one date and computes *NewDate*, which is the following date on a calendar. For example,

- 2/3/1989 follows 2/2/1989
- 3/1/1987 follows 2/28/1987
- 3/1/1988 follows 2/29/1988
- 1/1/1986 follows 12/31/1985

Your procedure should include a check for leap years.

**12.11** *Common Error in Programming–2.* A more subtle problem with subranges is illustrated in the following code segment that counts the number of characters preceding the first blank (if any) in an array of characters.

```
{This procedure assumes the following declarations:

Const MaxText = 80;

Type TextLine = Array [1..MaxText] of Char; }

Procedure Count (Text: TextLine; Var Number: Integer);
{This procedure counts the characters preceeding the first
 space in an array.}
    Begin
        Number := 0;
        While (Number < MaxText) And (Text[Number+1] <> ' ')
            Do Number := Number + 1
    End {Count} ;
```

a. Find a difficulty with the Boolean expression in this code.
b. Correct this difficulty by revising the code.
   NOTE: Try moving the Boolean expression to a separate Boolean function *Done* where the tests are nested.

# CHAPTER 13

# STRINGS

In this chapter, we consider how we might store and process data that involve sequences of characters, such as letters that form words or characters that we type on a line at our terminal. Such sequences are called **character strings,** and we see how we can work with this data. In this work, we will apply many of the ideas introduced in earlier chapters, such as procedures and functions, arrays and records.

## SECTION 13.1 USING RECORDS TO STORE STRINGS

A **string** is a sequence of character information. In this section, we see how we can use records to store this character information.

To begin, we recall that in Chapter 11, when we stored strings in an array, we first declared a maximum length for our string. For example, in Section 11.3, we allocated space for up to 80 characters of input with the declarations

```
Const MaxLen = 80;
Type  CharLine = Array [1..MaxLen] of Char;
Var   Message: CharLine
```

Then, we declared

```
Var InputLen: Integer;
```

so we could keep track of the actual number of characters that were read. *InputLen* was initialized to 0, and each time we read a character, we increased *InputLen* by 1. We stopped reading either when we reached the end of a line or when we ran out of space in our array.

This program from Section 11.3 demonstrates that in handling strings of characters, we often need two types of information: the characters themselves, stored in an array, and the number of characters actually present.

With the concept of records from the previous chapter, we can combine these pieces into a single unit. For example, we might use the declarations

```
Const MaxLen = 80;
Type String = Record
        Line: Array [1..MaxLen] of Char;
        Length: 0..MaxLen
        End;
Var Message: String;
```

Here, *Message* involves all the information needed for our string information.

*Message.Line* is our array of characters, and

*Message.Length* gives the number of characters present.

With these declarations, a simple program to read and write a line of input might be as follows.

```
Program ReadAndPrint (Input, Output);
{This program reads and writes a line of input}

Const MaxLen = 80;

Type String = Record
        Data: Array [1..MaxLen] of Char;
        Length: 0..MaxLen
        End;

Procedure EnterLine (Var Message: String);
{This procedure reads a line of character information from a terminal.}
    Begin
        Writeln ('Please enter your line of input:');
        With Message
          Do Begin
            Length := 0;
            While (Not Eoln) and (Length < MaxLen)
              Do Begin
                Length := Length + 1;
                Read (Data[Length])
              End
          End;
```

```
        If Not Eoln
          Then Writeln ('Input is too long; line truncated to ',
                        MaxLen:1, ' characters.');
        Readln
    End {EnterLine} ;

Procedure PrintLine (Message: String);
{This procedure prints a line of character information.}
    Var Index: Integer;
    Begin
        Writeln ('Your input line is shown below:');
        For Index := 1 To Message.Length
            Do Write (Message.Data[Index]);
        Writeln
    End {PrintLine} ;

Procedure ControlProcessing;
{This procedure controls the reading and printing of character data}
    Var Line: String;
    Begin
        EnterLine (Line);
        PrintLine (Line)
    End {ControlProcessing} ;

Begin {Main}
    Writeln ('This program reads and prints a line of characters');
    ControlProcessing
End {Main} .
```

In subsequent processing, we can work with individual characters and the length of the input, or we can consider this string as a single entity. In this approach to strings, we have counted the exact number of characters in our input, and we have stored that information separately from the characters themselves.

## SECTION 13.2 PACKED AND UNPACKED ARRAYS

Now that we have seen that the processing of character information often involves arrays, perhaps in records it is useful to look at the way the machine actually allocates this storage. We identify two distinct forms of array storage.

In Section 8.2, we saw that arrays are stored in a block of main memory, and we noted that different types of data may require different amounts of storage. For example, an integer might take 1 unit of storage, whereas a real number might use 2 units of storage. Thus, an array of 100 integers might use 100 units of storage, and 100 reals might use 200 units of storage.

When we work with Booleans or character data, however, we find that each item may require only a fraction of a unit. For example, depending upon the computer, we may be able to store 16 or 32 Boolean values, or 2 or 4 characters in a unit of storage. Thus, to save space when storing arrays of Boolean or character data, we may want to pack as much information into a unit of storage as we can. This form of storage is called a **packed array.** We give an example to illustrate the difference between a packed array and the **unpacked arrays** we have used up to now.

*Example:* Suppose we wish to store the phrase *Pascal Programming* in an array, with one character for each array element. Suppose also that our computer is able to store 4 characters of information in each unit of its memory.

In Figure 13–1, we store these characters in an unpacked array, with one character for each unit of memory. Here, our data require 18 units of memory. Also, while each letter is stored in one unit of memory, this memory is only a quarter full. Much of the space in memory is wasted.

Figure 13–2 shows the same phrase in a packed array. Here we fill up each unit of storage with four characters, and we have no wasted space, except at the very end of our storage space. Here, our data require only 5 units of memory, and we have saved 13 units of memory from our previous approach. Thus, we see that packed arrays can save a great deal of space over unpacked arrays.

However, this savings of storage may be offset by increased processing

FIGURE 13–1 • **Storage of Pascal Programming in Array [1..18] of Char**

| Address | |
|---|---|
| 1 | P |
| 2 | a |
| 3 | s |
| 4 | c |
| 5 | a |
| 6 | l |
| 7 | |
| 8 | P |
| 9 | r |
| 10 | o |
| 11 | g |
| 12 | r |
| 13 | a |
| 14 | m |
| 15 | m |
| 16 | i |
| 17 | n |
| 18 | g |

FIGURE 13–2 • **Storage of Pascal Programming in Packed Array [1..5] of Char**

| Address | | | | |
|---|---|---|---|---|
| 1 | P | a | s | c |
| 2 | a | l | | P |
| 3 | r | o | g | r |
| 4 | a | m | m | i |
| 5 | n | g | | |

requirements. In particular, since each character in a packed array is embedded in a group, packed arrays may require some special work whenever we want to work with individual characters. In processing, we may need to extract the character from the unit of storage before we can proceed.

## Packed and Unpacked Arrays in Pascal

Pascal allows us to decide which type of storage we want to use for any particular array. Pascal interprets the declaration

```
Var Line: Array [1..Max] of Char;
```

as a specification for an unpacked array. If we add the word *Packed* to our declaration, then Pascal packs our data together. Thus,

```
Var Line: Packed Array [1..Max] of Char;
```

compresses our character data into a small space, but possibly increases processing time.

This flexibility of choosing between packed and unpacked arrays in Pascal extends to any type of data, although in practice we rarely specify packed arrays for data other than characters, Booleans, or enumerated types. With each of these types of data, we often can save a considerable amount of space by packing information in our arrays. With other types of data, packed arrays give little, if any, savings.

Beyond this initial declaration of packed and unpacked arrays, a Pascal program does not distinguish between these storage structures, and either form of storage allows us to write statements such as

```
Read(Line[7])

Line[8] := Chr(0)
```

Our use of array elements in Pascal does not depend on the form of declaration.

### String-Type

In Pascal, packed arrays of characters are considered to be a special type, called **string-type.** With these, we can work with individual characters or with entire arrays as before. However, packed arrays of characters may be used in three additional ways: with literal strings; in Boolean expressions; and in *Write* statements.

**Literal Strings.** Whenever we place characters in quotes within a program, those characters are considered to be a packed array of characters and are called a **literal string.** Thus, if we declare

```
Type String = Packed Array [1..26] of Char;
Var Alphabet: String;
```

we may assign

```
Alphabet := 'ABCDEFGHIJKLMNOPQRSTUVWXYZ'
```

Here, both sides have the same packed array type with the same number of characters, so we may assign the data in one array ('A'..'Z') to the other (Alphabet).

Similarly, if we declare

```
Procedure A(Letters: String);
```

we could have the call

```
A('ABCDEFGHIJKLMNOPQRSTUVWXYZ');
```

Here, parameter passage by reference is not allowed because the constant array cannot change; however, passage by value is allowed.

Next, string-type can be used in defining constants, so we could have

```
Const Capitals = 'ABCDEFGHIJKLMNOPQRSTUVWXYZ';
```

Here, the right-hand side of our declaration has 26 elements, so *Alphabet* is considered a constant array of 26 elements.

These capabilities for specifying character strings are particularly useful in setting up entire arrays of characters; we can work with the entire array rather than with individual elements. However, we must be careful that our declared arrays have exactly the same number of characters as the strings we specify. For example, with our previous declaration we could not write

```
Alphabet := 'ABCDE'
```

for the machine cannot match the 26 elements on the left with the five on the right. (Note, however, that some Pascal compilers *do* allow this type of assignment. In such a case, the letters 'ABCDE' may be placed at the beginning of the Alphabet array. Further details depend upon the particular compiler that is used.)

**Boolean Expressions.** Pascal also allows us to compare two string-type arrays of the same size. For example, given

```
Type String = Packed Array [1..10] of Char;
Var  Line1, Line2: String;
```

we can compare the arrays *Line1* and *Line2*. The expression *Line1* < *Line2* has the usual meaning of alphabetical order. In particular, the computer initially considers the first character of *Line1* and *Line2*. If they are different, then those first characters are compared according to the character codes (e.g., ASCII or EBCDIC). However, if the first characters are the same, the computer looks at the second characters, and the computer continues checking character-by-character until a difference is found or until the entire string is scanned.

Similarly, *Line1* = *Line2* is true if each character in *Line1* matches the corresponding character in *Line2*.

In this comparison of strings, it is important to note that all characters in the string may be checked, since strings are compared until a difference is found. Thus, when we take advantage of Pascal's special string-type, we must use an entire array to store our data. In particular, if we only read a few characters, we must fill the rest of our array with known values, so that we know what the entire array contains. For example, sometimes we might use "spaces" for this special purpose. However, more often, we use a character, called a *null*, which is Chr(O) in the standard codes. This special character takes up space in arrays, but it is ignored by most terminals. Thus, if we try to print this character, our terminal receives the character but does nothing, so our output is not affected by this extra character. (This is different from a "space" character, for a "space" causes the terminal to move its cursor or printing element over one space on the screen or paper.)

In addition, a null has the property that it comes before all other characters. In practice, this means that nulls allow us to alphabetize character strings correctly when we compare strings character by character. In short, a null (or *Chr*(O)) allows us to fill up extra space in arrays without creating special difficulties when we try to print or process character strings.

**Writing.** Finally, Pascal allows us to use string-type variables in *Write* statements. For example, with our earlier declaration, we could specify

```
Write (Alphabet)
```

Here, the entire packed array is printed; we do not have to write each character separately in a loop.

## SECTION 13.3 COMMON STRING PROCESSING FUNCTIONS OR PROCEDURES

The previous section illustrated how packed arrays allow us to perform some special operations on entire strings of characters. We often use packed arrays to take advantage of these capabilities. However, many applications require further string manipulations. Therefore, in this section, we look at several common functions and procedures that can help us perform more complex operations.

Throughout this section, we will find we need to know the length of the strings that we are processing, and we will assume the following declarations:

```
Const Max = ——;        {Some positive integer constant}
Type  String = Record
               Data: Packed Array [1..Max] of Char;
               Length: 0..Max
               End;
```

## String Concatenation

The first common procedure that we consider involves putting strings together. In this process, called **string concatenation,** we begin with two strings, *S1* and *S2*, and we want to form a new, longer string *NewS*, where the entire *S2* string is placed after the *S1* string.

In forming *NewS*, we follow several steps;

1. We copy the characters of *S1* to *NewS*.
2. We compute the length of *NewS* and the number of letters to be copied from *S2*.
3. We add the characters of *S2* to *NewS*.

Each of these steps is rather straightforward, except that we must be careful not to exceed the maximum number of characters allowed in the declaration of *NewS*. Our resulting procedure is as follows.

```
Procedure Concat (S1, S2: String; Var NewS: String);
{This procedure concatenates string S1 with S2 to yield NewS}
    Var Index: Integer;
        NumberFromS2: Integer;    {Number of characters copied from S2}

    Begin
        {Copy S1 to NewS}
        NewS := S1;

        {Compute number of letters to be copied from S2}
        If S1.Length + S2.Length <= Max
            Then Begin
                NumberFromS2 := S2.Length;
                NewS.Length := S1.Length + S2.Length
                End
            Else Begin
                NumberFromS2 := Max - S1.Length;
                Writeln ('Not enough storage space for string concatenation');
                Writeln (S2.Length-NumberFromS2:1, ' characters deleted');
                NewS.Length := Max
                End;
```

```
    {Add characters of S2 to NewS}
    For Index := 1 To NumberFromS2
        Do NewS.Data[Index+S1.Length] := S2.Data[Index]
End {Concat} ;
```

## Pattern Matching

The next task that we consider in this section is searching for one string that is contained in another. For example, if

*Alphabet* = 'ABCDEFGHIJKLMNOPQRSTUVWXYZ',

then

'ABC' is found in *Alphabet* beginning with the first character of *Alphabet;*

'HIJK' is found in *Alphabet,* beginning with character 8;

'YZ' is found in *Alphabet* beginning with character 25; and

'CBA' is not found in *Alphabet.*

In defining this task more carefully, we often find it convenient to specify this **pattern matching** as

Function Match(SubS, Str: String): Integer;

The function *Match* searches for the substring *SubS* in the string *Str*. If the substring is found, *Match* returns the starting position for the match. If the substring is not found, *Match* returns 0. Thus, in our previous matching examples, we have

| SubS Data | Str Data | Result Returned |
|---|---|---|
| 'ABC' | Alphabet | 1 |
| 'HIJK' | Alphabet | 8 |
| 'YZ' | Alphabet | 25 |
| 'CBA' | Alphabet | 0 |

In programming this matching function, we can identify several steps.

**I.** We begin trying to match the first letter of our substring *SubS* with a letter in the string *Str*.
  - **A.** If the first letter matches, we try subsequent letters.
    - **1.** If all subsequent letters match, we have found our substring. Thus, we record where the match started, and then we stop.
    - **2.** If some subsequent letter does not match, we look back at first letters again.
  - **B.** If the first letter does not match, we try the first letter of the substring against the next letters of our given string.

This general process can continue until we find a match or until we know a match is impossible. A match is impossible if there are not enough letters in our string to match the substring. More precisely, we can stop our search when

$$\text{Position} > \text{length of string} - \text{length of substring} + 1.$$

After this position in our string, we do not have enough characters to match our substring.

With this observation about when to stop our search, we are ready to code our procedure.

```
Function Match (SubS, Str: String): Integer;
{This function searches for the Substring SubS in the String Str
 and returns the first position where a match occurs
 or 0 if not match is found.}
    Var Found: Boolean;
        Position: Integer;  {location where match might begin}
        LastPosition: Integer; {last location where match could be}
        Index: Integer;
    Begin
        LastPosition := Str.Length - SubS.Length + 1;
        Found := False;
        Position := 0;
        While (Position < LastPosition) And Not Found
          Do Begin
            Position := Position + 1;
            Index := 1;
            While (Index < SubS.Length) And
                  (SubS.Data[Index] = Str.Data[Position+Index-1])
                Do Index := Index + 1;
            Found := (SubS.Data[Index] = Str.Data[Position+Index-1])
          End;
        If Found
            Then Match := Position
            Else Match := 0
    End {Match} ;
```

As an alternative to this procedure, we may want to require that we begin our search after a given position in the string *Str*. This is left to the reader as an exercise.

## Reading Words

The last common task that we consider in this section involves the breaking of a line of input into words. Variations of **reading words** appear in a very large number of applications; we look at one simple version here.

In the typical application, we proceed in several steps. To begin, we read the input character-by-character. Next, we combine characters into units (words), and we continue reading until we detect an end of the input (a sentinel).

Frequently, this work is done with two procedures:

```
Procedure GetChar(Var Ch: Char);
Procedure GetWord(Var Word: String);
```

With this structure, the *GetChar* procedure reads successive characters, processes ends of lines, and detects when all of the data have been read. The *GetWord* procedure uses *GetChar* to obtain characters of input and then divides those characters into words. (In this discussion, we will throw away punctuation.) Frequently, this processing also requires a global Boolean variable or function that is shared by *GetChar* and *GetWord* and that is set to true when the end of the data is reached.

More precisely, *GetChar* performs the following.

- returns the next character of input in a line
- returns a "space" at the end of a line (*GetChar* then gets ready for the next line).

Further, if we decide that a blank line will specify the end of our input, then *GetChar* does the following.

1. At the start of each line, *GetChar* sets a global Boolean variable *AllBlanks* to true.
2. During the reading of a line, *GetChar* changes *AllBlanks* to false if a nonblank character is found.
3. At the end of a line, *GetChar* sets a global Boolean variable *InputDone* to true if only blanks have been found on the line. (We assume *InputDone* is initialized to false by the program.)
4. Once *InputDone* is true, *GetChar* performs no more reading, and *GetChar* only returns blanks.

Similarly, we describe the formal specifications for *GetWord*.

1. *GetWord* initializes the length of the word returned to 0.
2. *GetWord* calls *GetChar* successively until either a letter is found or until *InputDone* is true.
3. If a letter is found, that letter is used to begin a word, and the word length is now 1.
4. When the first letter is found, *GetWord* calls *GetChar* successively and adds letters to the word until the maximum word length is found or until a nonletter is encountered.

With these detailed specifications, we are ready to write the code for these two procedures. This code is shown in complete detail as part of the program in Section 13.4.

As with the other string functions, *GetChar* and *GetWord* illustrate many tasks that we may wish to perform with strings. In each case, we identify a task, and we write a procedure or function to perform the details.

As the need arises, other tasks now can be specified in either of two ways. The individual procedures specified in this section can be put together to perform more complex operations. Or, new procedures can be defined similarly to the way we proceeded here.

## SECTION 13.4 EXAMPLE: DIVIDING CHARACTER INPUT INTO WORDS AND COUNTING

So far in this chapter, we have seen several ways to store and manipulate strings of characters. In this section, we use these various ideas to solve the following problem.

**PROBLEM 13.4**

Write a program that performs an elementary word analysis. In particular, the program should

- read multiple lines from the terminal until a blank line is entered;
- divide the input into words;
- count the number of times each word appears; and
- print the words and frequencies.

### Discussion of Problem 13.4

We will approach this problem by processing words as they are entered. For each word, we compare it with other words already entered.

Thus, we will store words as packed arrays of fixed length; we will fill any extra space in the array with nulls. We will also need a count of how many times the word has occurred in our input; and we will need to keep track of the number of words we have at any given moment in our list. These comments suggest that our major list of information should have the following declarations.

```
Const WordLength =  30;
      MaxList    = 100;
Type  String     = Packed Array [1. .WordLength] of Char;
      WordEntry  = Record
                     Word: String;
                     Count: Integer
                   End;
Var   List: Array [1. .MaxList] of WordEntry;
      NumberInList: Integer;
```

Here the main list can contain many word entries, where each entry contains a *Word* and a frequency *Count*.

Next, we consider how to structure our processing. As we read each word, we should look to see if it is already on our list of words. If so, we should add to our count. Otherwise, we need to add the word to our list with an initial count of 1. Throughout this step, we need to search our list of words, and we need to insert new words into our list. This searching and inserting of words is analogous to our work with numbers in Sections 8.5 and 8.6. Thus, here we will use the same efficient Binary Search that we used before, and we will maintain our words in alphabetical order using the same type of insertion procedure. Note, however, that whenever we want to move an item on our list, we must work with the entire record. The comparisons for insertion will depend only upon the letters of the words, but assignments must include the whole record.

binary search
insertion

Finally, once all data have been entered, we need to print our results. In this case, since the words have been stored alphabetically, we can get an alphabetical listing if we just proceed from the beginning of our word array to the end.

From this discussion, we can develop the following outline, which uses many concepts that we have discussed earlier in this text.

## Outline for Problem 13.4

**I.** Set up an array to begin.
- **A.** No characters have been read.
  Set *InputDone* to *False*.
  Set *AllBlanks* to *True*.
- **B.** No words have been found.
  Set *Number* in *List* to 0.

**II.** Read characters until no more data remains.
- **A.** Get a *Word*.
- **B.** If *Word* is not null:
  - **1.** Determine if word is on list using the Binary Search.
    - **a.** If so, add to word count.
    - **b.** If not, add word to list, maintaining words in alphabetical order.

**III.** Print list, from first word to last.

In the following program, we modify several of the procedures in this section to agree with the particular declarations we need for this problem. The ideas behind these procedures follow our earlier discussion.

```
Program WordCount (Input, Output);
{This program reads several lines of input, divides the input into words,
 counts the number of times each word appears, and prints the results}

Const WordLength = 25;
      MaxList = 50;
```

```
Type String = Packed Array [1..WordLength] of Char;

     WordEntry = Record
        Word: String;
        Count: Integer
        End;

     WordList = Array [1..MaxList] Of WordEntry;

Var InputDone: Boolean;     {Shared variables for reading data}
    AllBlanks: Boolean;     {used in GetChar and GetWord Procedures}
    NullWord: String;       {Used as constant string of nulls}

Procedure Initialize(Var NumberInList: Integer);
{This procedure prepares for processing of input}
    Var Index: Integer;
    Begin
        {No characters have been read}
        InputDone := False;
        AllBlanks := True;

        {No words have been found}
        NumberInList := 0;

        {Null word contains only nulls}
        For Index := 1 To WordLength
            Do NullWord[Index] := Chr(0)
    End {Initialize} ;

Procedure GetChar (Var Ch: Char);
{GetChar returns successive characters entered from the keyboard,
 processing ends of lines, and checking when a blank line occurs}
    Begin
      If InputDone
        Then Ch := ' '
      Else If Eoln
            Then {Processing end of line}
              Begin
                If AllBlanks
                    Then Begin {blank line}
                      InputDone := True;
                      Ch := ' '
                      End
                    Else Begin {not blank line}
                      Ch := ' ';
                      Readln;
                      AllBlanks := True
                      End
              End {Processing end of line}
            Else {Processing in middle of line}
              Begin
                Read (Ch);
                AllBlanks := AllBlanks And (Ch = ' ')
              End {Processing in middle of line}
    End {GetChar} ;
```

```
Procedure GetWord (Var Word: String);
{GetWord puts characters together to form words}
    Var Ch: Char;
        Length: Integer;

    Function Letter(Ch: Char): Boolean;
    {Function determines if Ch is a letter}
       Begin
          Letter := (Ch In ['a'..'z']) Or (Ch In ['A'..'Z'])
       End {Letter} ;

    Begin {GetWord}
        Length := 0;
        Word := NullWord;

        {Find first letter in input}
        GetChar(Ch);
        While (Not InputDone) And Not Letter(Ch)
            Do GetChar(Ch);

        {Put letters together to get a word}
        If Letter(Ch)
          Then Repeat
               Length := Length + 1;
               Word[Length] := Ch;
               GetChar(Ch)
             Until Not Letter(Ch) Or (Length >= WordLength)
    End {GetWord} ;

Procedure Find (Item: String; List: WordList;
                Top: Integer; Var Position: Integer);
{This Procedure uses a Binary Search to find where the given item
 should be found in the List}
    Var First, Last: Integer;   {Binary of List[First]
                                         to List[Last]}
        Middle: Integer;        {the middle of our array}
    Begin
        If Item > List[Top].Word
            Then Position := Top + 1
            Else Begin {Binary Search}
                {Initialize Search}
                First := 1;
                Last := Top;

                {Perform Search}
                Repeat
                    Middle := (First + Last) Div 2;
                    If Item < List[Middle].Word
                        Then Last := Middle - 1
                        Else First := Middle + 1
                Until (Item = List[Middle].Word) Or (Last < First) ;

                {Record where Item should be}
                If Item <= List[Middle].Word
                    Then Position := Middle
                    Else Position := Middle + 1
                End {Binary Search}
    End {Find} ;
```

```
Procedure Insert (Item: String; Var List: WordList;
                  Var Top: Integer; Position: Integer);
{This procedure inserts the given Item in the List}
    Var Index: Integer;
    Begin
        {Slide Subsequent Elements Down}
        For Index := Top DownTo Position
            Do List[Index+1] := List[Index];
        Top := Top + 1;

        {Insert Item}
        List[Position].Word := Item;
        List[Position].Count := 1
    End {Insert} ;


Procedure EnterData (Var List: WordList; Var NumberInList: Integer);
{This procedure processes words until no more input data remains}
    Var Item: String;
        Position: Integer;  {Location of Word in List}

    Begin {EnterData}
        Writeln ('Please enter your data.');
        Writeln ('Conclude by entering a blank line');

        {Process First Word}
        GetWord (Item);
        If Item <> NullWord
            Then Insert (Item, List, NumberInList, 1);

        {Process Subsequent Words}
        While Not InputDone
          Do Begin
            GetWord (Item);
            If Item <> NullWord
                Then Begin
                    Find (Item, List, NumberInList, Position);
                    If (Position <= NumberInList) And
                       (List[Position].Word = Item)
                        Then {Increase count by 1}
                            List[Position].Count := List[Position].Count + 1
                        Else {Add word to list}
                            Insert (Item, List, NumberInList, Position)
                    End

          End
    End {EnterData} ;
```

```
Procedure PrintAlphabetically (Var List: WordList; NumberInList: Integer);
{This procedure prints the elements of the array, which have been
 stored alphabetically}
    Var Index: Integer;
    Begin

        {Print words in order}
        Writeln;
        Writeln ('Printing of words in alphabetical order');
        Writeln;
        Writeln ('Count   Word');
        Writeln;
        For Index := 1 To NumberInList
          Do Writeln (List[Index].Count:3, '      ',
                      List[Index].Word)
    End {PrintAlphabetically} ;

Procedure ControlProcessing;
{This procedure controls the major steps of the word analysis}
    Var List: WordList;
        NumberInList: Integer;
    Begin
        Initialize(NumberInList);
        EnterData(List, NumberInList);
        PrintAlphabetically(List, NumberInList)
    End {ControlProcessing} ;

Begin {Main}
    Writeln ('This program counts words entered from the terminal.');
    ControlProcessing
End {Main} .
```

A sample run of this program appears below.

```
This program counts words entered from the terminal.
Please enter your data.
Conclude by entering a blank line
the program illustrates
    -- the procedure getchar and the procedure getword
    -- string comparisons and string output
    -- the binary search and the insertion procedure for string-type data


Printing of words in alphabetical order

Count   Word

  3     and
  1     binary
  1     comparisons
  1     data
  1     for
  1     getchar
```

```
1       getword
1       illustrates
1       insertion
1       output
3       procedure
1       program
1       search
3       string
5       the
1       type
```

From this program, we see how we can combine many of the string processing procedures and functions that we have discussed in this chapter, including processing characters and words with standard procedures and using packed arrays for comparing strings of characters. This program also illustrates that we can apply many of the techniques that we have seen earlier, such as insertion procedures and the Binary Search, to the processing of strings.

## SUMMARY

1. We can store **strings** of characters in several ways. For example, we often store strings in a record, which includes the length of the string as well as an array for the individual characters. In addition, the array data can be either packed or unpacked in a machine.
2. In **packed arrays,** data are packed together in main memory as tightly as possible, but processing may require extraction of particular characters.
3. In **unpacked arrays,** one piece of data is stored in an entire unit of main memory. Here, some space may be wasted, but processing is efficient.

| KEY TERMS, PHRASES, AND CONCEPTS | | ELEMENTS OF PASCAL SYNTAX | |
|---|---|---|---|
| Null | String-Type | *Pack* | *Unpack* |
| Packed Arrays | Strings | String-Type | |
| String Operations | Unpacked Arrays | Comparisons | |
| Concatenation | | in Boolean | |
| Pattern Matching | | Expressions | |
| Reading Words | | Constants | |
| | | Use in *Write* | |
| | | Statements | |

4. Pascal defines packed arrays of characters as a **string-type,** and we can perform some special operations with this, including
   - Constant declarations
   - Comparisons in Boolean expressions
   - Use in *Write* Statements

   In using string-type, we often need to fill up the end of the array with **nulls** or spaces.
5. Several common string functions or procedures include **concatenation, pattern matching,** and **reading words.**

## EXERCISES

**13.1** *Inserting Commas.* Write a program that reads an integer from a line of input and prints the integer with commas inserted every third digit from the right. Your program should allow both positive and negative integers up to 60 digits long, and it should not insert a comma before the first digit or just after a "+" or "−" sign.

For example, given the numbers 12345 or −123456789 or 123456, the program should print 12,345 or −123,456,789 or 123,456.

**13.2** *Pig Latin Translator.* Write a program that will input a word and translate the word into Pig Latin. Recall that to translate a word into Pig Latin, we

1. take the first letter of the word and place it at the end of the word;
2. add the letter *A* at the end of the word.

**13.3** *Compare Strings Stored as Records.* Suppose a string is stored in a record of the following type:

```
Type String = Record
  Data: Packed Array [1..Max] of Char;
  Length: 0..Max
  End;
```

as in Section 13.3. Write

```
Function First (String1, String2: String): Boolean;
```

which returns true if *String1* comes before *String2* in alphabetical order and is false otherwise.

**13.4** *InString Function.* Write

```
Function InString (SubS, Str: String; Start: Integer): Integer;
```

which extends the *Match* function by starting its search in character position *Start*. In other words, *InString* searches for the substring *SubS* within the string *Str*, starting with character position *Start* in

*Str*. If the substring is found, *InString* returns the position of string *Str* where the match begins. Otherwise, *InString* returns 0.

**13.5** *Replacing Letters*. Write a procedure to scan a string of characters and replace all vowels by '*'.

**13.6** *Replacing Substrings*. Write a program that replaces one substring by another in a line of input. For example, all occurrences of 'any' might be replaced by 'some' in the input. The program should ask the user to enter the substrings from the terminal as well as the line of input. (This type of program is very helpful in word processing, as typographical errors can be systematically corrected throughout a manuscript in a single operation.)

**13.7** *Name-Address Listing*. Write a program that reads a list of names, addresses, and zip codes and then prints this list in two ways: first ordered by name and then by zip code.

**13.8** *Grocery Checkout*. Write a program that simulates part of the grocery checkout process in which product codes are scanned by special sensors. In particular, your program should

- read a list of product information, including product name, product code, price;
- order the product data by code;
- ask the user for various product codes;
- use a Binary Search (Section 8.5) to locate the product; and
- print product name and price.

**13.9** *GetToken—An Extended GetWord*. Write

```
Procedure GetToken (Var TokenType: Integer;
                    Var Item: String);
```

which returns the next unit entered from the keyboard. Possible units are

| Token Type | Description |
|---|---|
| 1 | Punctuation |
| 2 | Real Number |
| 3 | Integer |
| 4 | Word |
| 5 | Separator (Tab, Space, Return) |

Each time *GetToken* is called, the procedure determines the type of object that appears next on the line. This type is returned as well as a string, stored as a record, which specifies the object itself. (All separators are translated to a space.)

For example, suppose we enter the line

```
In this line, we find 16 tokens!
```

Here, *GetToken* would return the following if it were called 16 times.

| Token Type | Length | Item Data |
|---|---|---|
| 4 | 2 | In |
| 5 | 1 | {space} |
| 4 | 4 | this |
| 5 | 1 | {space} |
| 4 | 4 | line |
| 1 | 1 | , |
| 5 | 1 | {space} |
| 4 | 2 | we |
| 5 | 1 | {space} |
| 4 | 4 | find |
| 5 | 1 | {space} |
| 3 | 2 | 16 |
| 5 | 1 | {space} |
| 4 | 6 | tokens |
| 1 | 1 | ! |
| 5 | 1 | {space for the return} |

NOTE: In writing this procedure, you will need a Boolean variable *ReRead* which tells *GetChar* to return the same character it read before. Also, the character read may need to be defined globally.

**13.10** *Double Words*. One common typographical error is the occurrence of the same word twice in a row. Write a program that reads multiple lines of character input (until a blank line) and determines if any word is repeated twice in a row.

NOTE: Your program should check that the last word on one line is not repeated as the first word on the next line.

**13.11** *Counting Words*. Write a program that reads multiple lines of character input (until a blank line), counts the number of words in each sentence, and computes the average number of words per sentence.

**a.** In the first version of this program, assume a sentence ends whenever one of the marks '.', '!', or '?' appears.

**b.** Revise your program in part (a) to check that the period is not following a person's initial. (If the period follows a word of length 1 which is capitalized, the program should assume the letter is an initial.)

# CHAPTER 14

# STORING DATA ON FILES

All of our programs up to this point have stored their data in the main memory of the CPU. This has the advantage that the computer can process data in main memory more quickly and efficiently than it can if data are stored elsewhere.

On the other hand, storing data in main memory also creates some difficulties. For example, all data must be read into the CPU each time a program is run, and the amount of data is limited by the size of main memory in the CPU. In addition, all data inside the computer itself are destroyed after each program is run, and no data are saved from one run to another.

In this chapter, we see how to overcome some of these disadvantages by studying some basic ways that disk files can be used for long-term, bulk storage, and we apply these files to solve some problems. In these applications, we may give up the efficiency of storing all data in fast memory, but we do overcome the disadvantages mentioned above.

## SECTION 14.1 STORING DATA ON A FILE—AN INTRODUCTION

When we analyze the flow of data through our programs up to now, we find that

- we use *Read* or *Readln* to move data from our keyboard or terminal into the program;
- we use *Write* or *Writeln* to move data back out.

This is shown on Figure 14–1.

This flow of data has several implications for our Pascal code. First, we must include *Input* and *Output* in our program header. Then, we use *Read* or *Readln* to enter data and *Write* and *Writeln* to print our data.

For data that involve a disk file rather than the terminal, our picture becomes somewhat more complex, as shown in Figure 14–2. Here we may

- bring data into our program either from a disk file (called "input file" in the figure) or from our terminal (or from both);
- move data out of our program either by putting the data on a disk file (called "output file" in the figure) or by printing at our terminal.

This more complex flow of information requires several additions to our Pascal program. First, we need to specify some file information in our program header, and we need to declare the type of data stored in our files.

Then, when we try to *Read*, we need to specify whether we expect to get data from the terminal or from the input file. When the computer is asked to get data, it must know what source to use. Similarly, when we *Write* results, we must specify where our results are to be sent. The computer must know whether the results should be printed at the terminal or in the output file.

We illustrate how these details are handled in Pascal by considering the following simple problem.

FIGURE 14–1 • **Flow of Data through a Program Using Only a Terminal**

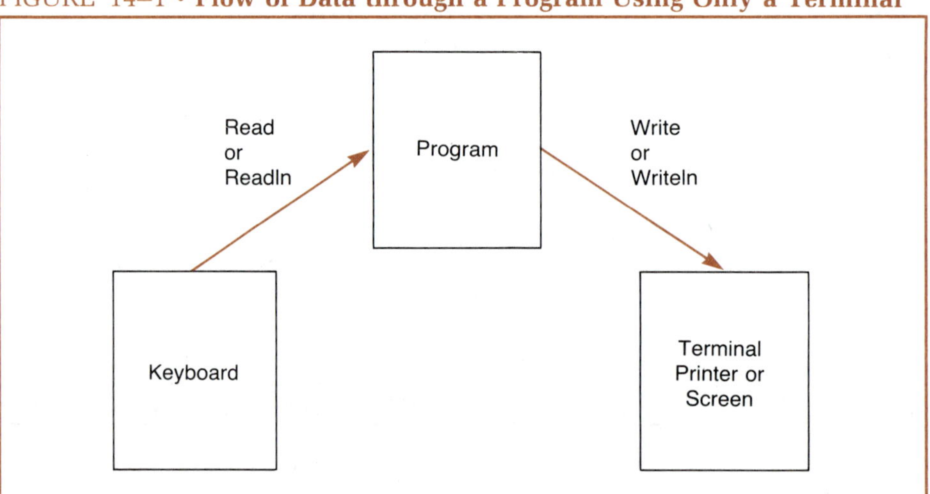

FIGURE 14–2 • **Flow of Data through a Program Using Both Terminal and File**

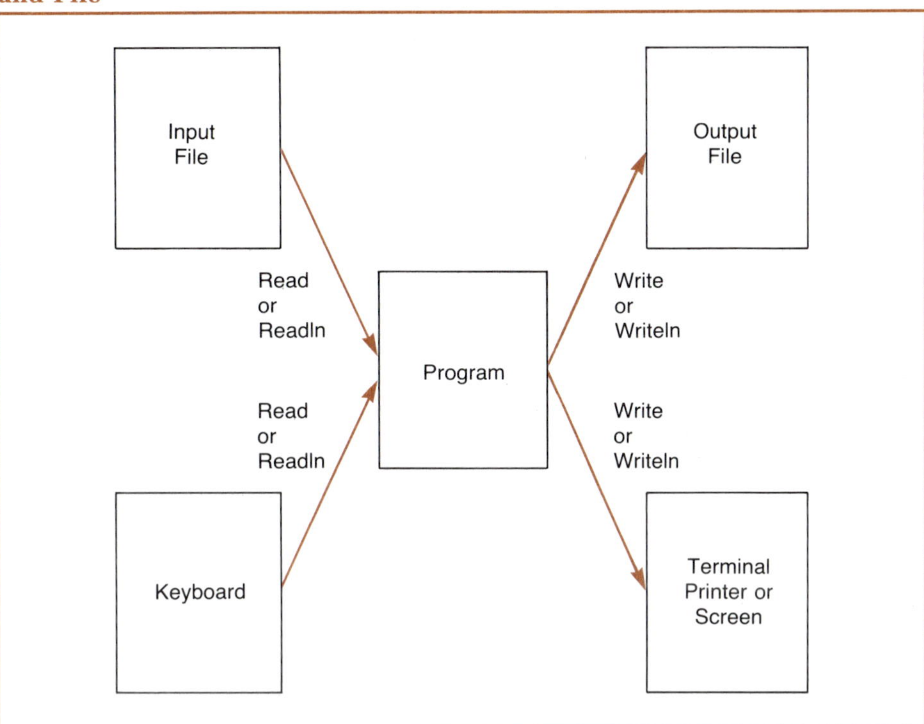


## PROBLEM 14.1 Creating and Printing Text Files

**A.** Write a program that reads some lines of input from a terminal and prints them on a file. Continue reading from the terminal until a blank line is entered.

**B.** Write a program that reads the lines from a file, copies them to another file, and prints the lines at the terminal.

This flow of data is shown in Figure 14–3.

To solve this problem, we write separate outlines for each part.

### Outline for Part A of Problem 14.1

Common Task: Read a line following the steps used in processing characters in the last chapter.

**A.** Read a line.
**B.** Record length of line.
**C.** Check if line is blank.

FIGURE 14–3 • **Flow of Data for Problem 14.1**

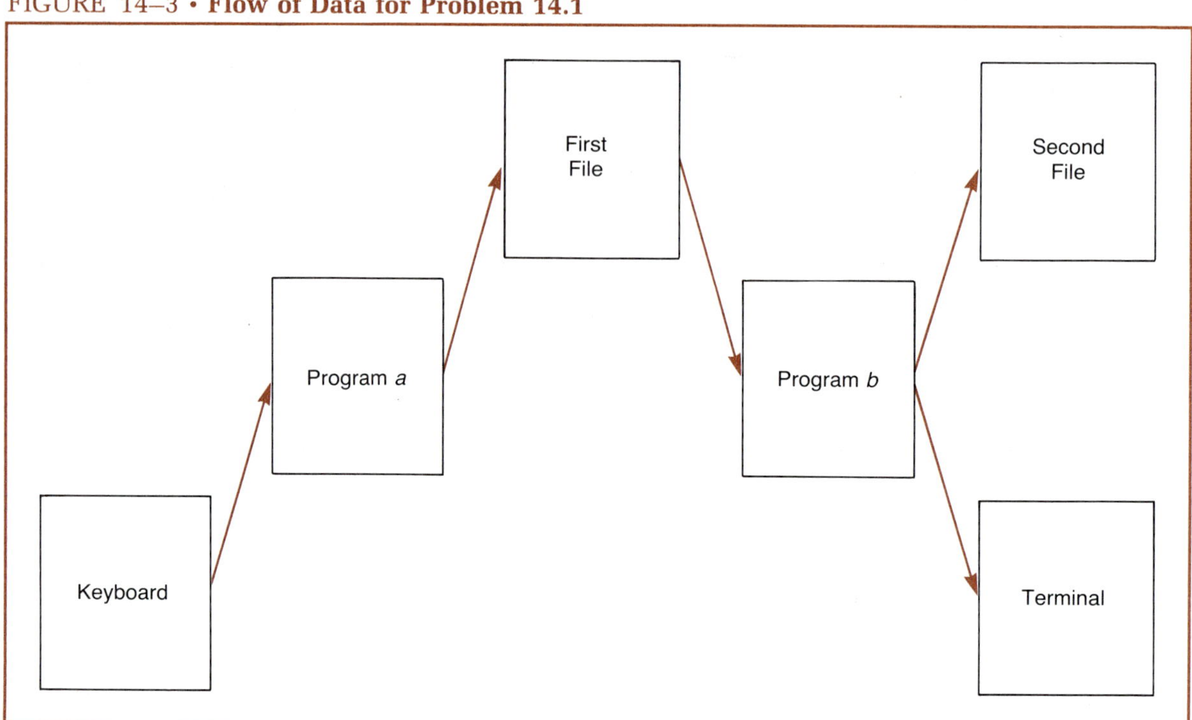


**I.** Specify file to be used for output.
**II.** Read a line.
**III.** While input line is not blank:
  **A.** Print line on output file.
  **B.** Read a line.

### Outline for Part B of Problem 14.1

**I.** Specify files for input and for copying.
**II.** Process successive lines until end of input file is reached. For each line:
  **A.** Continue processing characters until the end of a line is reached. For each character:
    **1.** Read a character from input file.
    **2.** Copy character to new file.
    **3.** Print character at terminal.
  **B.** At end of line of input:
    **1.** Go to new line of input.
    **2.** Move to new line in output file and at terminal.

These outlines yield the following two programs.

```
Program CreateTextFile (Input, Output, OutFile);
{This program transfers data from the terminal to a file;
 the program continues until a blank line is entered.}

Const MaxLength = 80;     {Length of line typed at terminal}

Type LineType = Array [1..MaxLength] of Char;

Var OutFile: Text;
    Line: LineType;
    Length: Integer;
    Index: Integer;
    BlankLine: Boolean;

Procedure ReadLine(Var Line: LineType; Var Length: Integer;
                   Var BlankLine: Boolean);
{This procedure reads a line of input from the terminal,
 determines its length, and records if the line is blank}
    Const Space = ' ';
    Begin
        Length := 0;
        If Eoln
            Then BlankLine := True
            Else Begin
                Repeat
                    Length := Length + 1;
                    Read (Line[Length]);
                    If Line[Length] <> Space
                        Then BlankLine := False
                Until Eoln Or (Length = MaxLength);
                Readln
                End
    End {ReadLine} ;

Begin {Main}
    {Specify output file}
    Rewrite (OutFile);

    {Read first line of input}
    Writeln ('Enter material to be transferred to a file.');
    Writeln ('Conclude by entering a blank line');
    ReadLine (Line, Length, BlankLine);

    {Transfer lines of data to output file}
    While Not BlankLine
      Do Begin
        {Print line on output file}
        For Index := 1 To Length
          Do Write (OutFile, Line[Index]);
        Writeln (OutFile);

        {Read a new line from the terminal}
        ReadLine  (Line, Length, BlankLine)
      End;

    Writeln ('Data Transferred')
End {Main} .
```

```
Program FileCopyAndPrint (InFile, CopyFile, Output);
{This program reads one file, copies it to another file,
 and writes the file to the terminal}

Var InFile: Text;     {The file which will be read}
    CopyFile: Text;   {The file for the next copy}
    Ch: Char;

Begin {Main}
    {Specify files for input and copying}
    Reset (InFile);
    Rewrite (CopyFile);

    {Process each line of input file until End Of File}
    While Not EOF(InFile)
      Do Begin

        {Process each character until End Of Line}
        While Not Eoln(InFile)
          Do Begin
            Read(InFile, Ch);
            Write(CopyFile, Ch);
            Write(Ch)
          End;

        {Move to new line}
        Readln (InFile);
        Writeln(CopyFile);
        Writeln
      End;

    Writeln ('-----File printed and copied-----')
End {Main} .
```

The following shows a typical run of the first program in which six lines are entered (including the blank line).

```
Enter material to be transferred to a file.
Conclude by entering a blank line
     This material will be transferred from the terminal to a disk file
by the first program run.  This first program continues until a blank line
is encountered.
     The second program then uses the disk file, creating a second file.
and printing out the data.

Data Transferred
```

In this program, we entered our data, but we did not print it out at the terminal. Instead, a new file has been created.

When we run the second program using this new file as input, we get the following.

```
     This material will be transferred from the terminal to a disk file
by the first program run.  This first program continues until a blank line
is encountered.
     The second program then uses the disk file, creating a second file,
and printing out the data.
-----File printed and copied-----
```

In addition, this second program creates a new copy of our original file.

### Using Files Like Terminals

The programs listed above illustrate several important points about using files like terminals in Pascal programs.

At the start, when we wish to use file storage in our programs, we declare identifiers to stand for our files. This is done in two steps.

*Step 1.* We include file identifiers in our program header. In the example, the identifiers *Outfile, InFile,* and *CopyFile* were added. Here, we used *Input* since our program expected us to type some data from the terminal. If we did not need to enter data from the terminal, we could omit *Input* from our header. Similarly, we could omit *Output* if we did not print any data at our terminal.

*Step 2.* In the main program declarations, we specify the type of file for each identifier. When we use a file like a terminal, for reading and writing lines of data, we are considering our file as a *Text* file. Thus, we declared

```
Var InFile: Text;
```

to indicate that the identifier *InFile* would represent a file of *Text*.

Once we have declared our file identifiers, we must tell the machine to prepare to read or write with our file. This is done in one of two ways. We use the *Reset* statement to prepare the file to be read. For example, once we write

```
Reset (InFile);
```

we can perform *Read* operations from this file. Alternatively, we use the *Rewrite* statement to prepare a new file for writing. For example, when we write

```
Rewrite (OutFile);
```

or

```
Rewrite (CopyFile);
```

we create a new file to write information out.

After we have declared file variables and prepared files for reading with the *Reset* statement, we can read from files just as we do from the terminal. Thus, we can consider a file as consisting of lines with characters or with numbers, and we can read individual characters or numeric values. Also, we can test for the end of a line and move to a new line in the file. For example,

```
Read (InFile, Ch);
```

allows us to get a new character *Ch* of data from a file called *InFile*. Similarly,

```
EOLN (InFile);
```

allows us to see if we are at the end of a line in the file. Also,

```
Readln (InFile);
```

moves us to a new line in the file. In fact, in reading from the terminal, *Read(Ch)*, *EOLN*, and *Readln* are just abbreviations that we can use in place of *Read(Input, Ch)*, *EOLN(Input)*, and *Readln(Input)*. In using files, we can specify a file identifier or *Input* as the first argument of our *Read*, *EOLN*, or *Readln*. However, if we omit this file identifier, Pascal assumes we are reading from *Input*. Otherwise, these statements work for files in just the same way that they do for the keyboard.

Next, in reading from a file, we can test if we have reached the End Of a File using the function *EOF*. The function

```
EOF (InFile)
```

is true when we have read the last character in the file *InFile* and false otherwise. Note that in reading our data in Part B of our solution, this function allowed us to determine very easily when we were done. In Part A, we spent much of our code testing for a blank line, but in Part B, we just test the *EOF* function. In fact, this same *EOF* function also can be applied to the keyboard. For example, *EOF* or *EOF (Input)* specifies when we reach the end of our data from the terminal. In typing, we may specify this end in various ways depending upon our terminal. However, once we indicate this end of file, we cannot read any more data from our terminal later in the program.

Similarly, once we declare file variables and prepare for writing with a *Rewrite* statement, we can write to files just as we write to our terminal. As with reading, we can imagine a file as being made up of a sequence of lines, and we can use

```
Write (OutFile, —)
```

and

```
Writeln (OutFile, —)
```

to print data on these lines in an appropriate format. Further, *Write(Ch)* and *Writeln* are just abbreviations for *Write(Output,Ch)* and *Writeln (Output)* and *Output* is assumed if a file identifier is not specified. In addition, in our printing, we may write numbers, Booleans, and string-type data on files just as we can at terminals.

In working with files, however, Pascal does not allow us to mix reading and writing with the same file. Thus, if we use

```
Reset (File1)
```

then we are only allowed to *Read* from this file. If we use

```
Rewrite (File2)
```

we can only *Write* to *File2*.

**Examples.** We illustrate these various capabilities further with two short examples.

**A.** Set up a text file containing the four lines:

```
1A  True
2B  False
3C  True
4D  False
```

**B.** Read the letters and numbers from this file, and print the results at the keyboard with the letter followed by the number. (Ignore the 'True' or 'False' at the end of each line for this processing.)

**Discussion of Examples.** In our processing, we consider two approaches.

*Approach 1.* We could use four *Writeln* statements to print our file, with one *Writeln* for each line. Then we could read the first two characters of each line, throw away the rest of the line, and then print these characters.

*Approach 2.* We could print three variables, *Number, Ch,* and *TOrF,* on each line. Our program would then have to initialize each of these variables and then recompute them in a loop. Similarly, in a loop, we could read a number and a letter from each line, throw away the rest of the line, and continue until we reach the end of the file.

Each approach to each part of our problem gives rise to a very simple outline, which is left for the reader.

In considering these different solutions, the first approach is quite concise and easy to use in situations where we need to store a very small amount of data in a file. In contrast, this second approach, which uses a loop, can be modified easily to store large amounts of data.

The resulting four programs illustrate many features of using files that we have already seen. First, we list the programs for Example A.

```
Program LoadFile (OutFile);
{This program prints four lines of data on OutFile}
Var OutFile: Text;
Begin
    Rewrite (OutFile);
    Writeln (OutFile, '1A  True');
    Writeln (OutFile, '2B False');
    Writeln (OutFile, '3C  True');
    Writeln (OutFile, '4D False')
End {Main} .
```

```
Program LoadFile {Version 2} (OutFile);
{This program prints four lines of data on OutFile}
Var OutFile: Text;
    Index: Integer;
    Ch: Char;
    TOrF: Boolean;
Begin
    Rewrite (OutFile);

    {Initialize Variables}
    Ch := 'A';
    TOrF := True;

    {Write each line in loop and prepare for next line}
    For Index := 1 To 4
      Do Begin
        Writeln (OutFile, Index:1, Ch, ' ', TOrF:5);
        Ch := Succ(Ch);
        TOrF := Not TOrF
      End
End {Main} .
```

When either of these programs are run, we will not see anything printed at the terminal. Instead, each program places data in a file as specified. The following programs then use this file to solve Example B.

```
Program FileRead (InFile, Output);
{This program reads a digit and a letter from InFile and prints
 these values in reverse order.}
Var InFile: Text;
    Ch1, Ch2: Char;
    Index: Integer;

Begin
    Reset (InFile);

    {Print title}
    Writeln ('This program prints the starting digit and letter ',
             'from four lines of a file');
    Writeln ('These characters are:');
```

```
    {Read write characters for each line}
    For Index := 1 To 4
      Do Begin
        Readln (InFile, Ch1, Ch2);
        Writeln (Ch2:1, Ch1:2)
      End
End {Main} .
```

---

```
Program FileRead {Version 2} (InFile, Output);
{This program reads a digit and a letter from InFile and prints
 these values in reverse order.}
Var InFile: Text;
    Number: Integer;
    Ch: Char;

Begin
    Reset (InFile);

    {Print title}
    Writeln ('This program prints the starting digit and letter ',
             'from four lines of a file');
    Writeln ('These characters are:');

    {Read write characters for each line until end of file}
    While Not EOF(InFile)
      Do Begin
        Readln (InFile, Number, Ch);
        Writeln (Ch:1, Number:2)
      End
End {Main} .
```

---

Either program for Example A can be run with either program for Example B. When either program for Example B runs, we get the following output.

```
This program prints the starting digit and letter from four lines of a file
These characters are:
A 1
B 2
C 3
D 4
```

These programs show that we can read and write with files using numbers, characters, and Booleans, just as we have before with the keyboard and terminal, using the *Read*, *Readln*, *Write*, and *Writeln* statements. Further, this example illustrates that when we work with files, we may not see any output at our terminal. For example, either program for Example A creates an output file, but we cannot tell this from our terminal. Thus, we often include lines such as

```
Writeln ('Printing Data On File');
```

at the beginning of our printing step, and we use

```
Writeln ('Printing on File Completed');
```

at the end. Then, we can monitor a program's progress from our terminal, and we know when the task is done. Without these lines, we may wonder if our program is doing anything at all.

## SECTION 14.2 MORE GENERAL DATA STORAGE

The previous section illustrated how we can use files just as we do our keyboard or terminal. This is particularly helpful in applications in which we can organize our data into a sequence of lines of input or output. In other applications, this organization of data into lines may be rather awkward, and we may want to organize our files in another way. For example, we may want to store

- the Dow Jones Industrial Average for the past five years;
- words, including letters and length;
- product information for a grocery store, including product name, product code, package size, and retail price.

This section discusses an alternative structure for storing data in files that is more natural in these applications.

Our approach is to define a file for a particular type of data. For example, if we have

```
Const MaxLength = 30;
      SizeLength = 10;
Type  Word = Record
              Letters: Array [1..MaxLength] of Char;
              Length:  0..MaxLength
              End;
      Item  = Record
              Name:    Array [1..MaxLength] of Char;
              Code:    Integer;
              Size:    Array [1..SizeLength] of Char;
              Price:   Real
              End
```

then we can declare

```
Var DowFile: File of Real;
    WordFile: File of Word;
    ProductFile: File of Item;
```

Here, we declare our files to contain a specified type of data rather than text. To illustrate how such files can be used, we consider the following example.

## PROBLEM 14.2 Dow Jones Averages

**A.** Write a program that reads past Dow Jones Industrial Averages and records these averages on a file. Continue reading data until a negative value is entered. Also, mark the end of the file with a negative value.

**B.** Write a program that reads the data on file and computes the high, low, and mean of the Dow Averages.

### Discussion of Problem 14.2

In Part A, we can continue reading and writing as we did in the last section. However, here our data consist only of real numbers, and these numbers are not naturally organized in lines. Thus, we will not use a text file, but rather a file of reals.

In Part B, we read this file, processing each number as it is read. In our reading, we could read until *EOF*. However, here, for variety, we have used a sentinel, a negative number, to mark the end of our file.

As with the previous problem, we need a separate outline for Part A and for Part B.

### Outline for Part A of Problem 14.2

**I.** Prepare for writing on a file.
**II.** Continue until a negative number is processed.
  **A.** Read a value from the keyboard.
  **B.** Print the value on the file.

### Outline for Part B of Problem 14.2

**I.** Prepare for reading a file.
**II.** Process first value.
  **A.** Read value from file.
  **B.** Record that one value has been read.
  **C.** This value is both the current minimum and the current maximum.
  **D.** This value is the current sum of the values read.
**III.** Prepare for loop to process remaining values.
  **A.** Read next value from file.
**IV.** Process remaining values. While value is not negative:
  **A.** Record that another value has been read.
  **B.** Check for a new minimum or maximum value.
  **C.** Add the value to the sum of values read earlier.
  **D.** Read a new value from file.
**V.** Compute mean.
**VI.** Print results.

These outlines yield the following programs.

```
Program CreateDowFile (Input, Output, DowFile);
{This program reads Dow Jones Industrial Averages from a terminal
 and prints them on a file.}
Var DowFile: File of Real;
    DowAvg: Real;
Begin
    Writeln ('This program stores Dow Jones Averages for later use');

    Rewrite (DowFile);

    Writeln ('Please enter the averages');
    Writeln ('Conclude by typing a negative value');
    Repeat
        Read (DowAvg);
        Write (DowFile, DowAvg)
    Until (DowAvg < 0.0);

    Writeln;
    Writeln ('Data have been recorded on file.')
End {Main} .
```

```
Program ProcessDow (DowFile, Output);
{This program reads Dow Jones Industrial Averages from a file
 and computes the low, high and mean values.}
Var DowFile: File of Real;
    DowAvg: Real;
    Minimum: Real;
    Maximum: Real;
    NumberAvg: Integer;
    Sum: Real;
    Mean: Real;

Begin
    Writeln ('This program computes low, high, and mean Dow Jones Averages.');

    Reset(DowFile);

    {Process first value}
    Read(DowFile, DowAvg);
    NumberAvg := 1;
    Minimum := DowAvg;
    Maximum := DowAvg;
    Sum := DowAvg;

    {Prepare to process remaining values}
    Read(DowFile, DowAvg);

    {Processing remaining values}
    While (DowAvg >= 0.0)
      Do Begin
        NumberAvg := NumberAvg + 1;
        If DowAvg < Minimum
            Then Minimum := DowAvg;
        If DowAvg > Maximum
            Then Maximum := DowAvg;
```

```
        Sum := Sum + DowAvg;
        Read(DowFile, DowAvg)
      End;

    {Compute Mean}
    Mean := Sum / NumberAvg;

    {Print Results}
    Writeln ('Given the Dow Jones Averages in the file,');
    Writeln ('     the minimum was ', Minimum:1:2);
    Writeln ('     the maximum was ', Maximum:1:2);
    Writeln ('     the mean value was ', Mean:1:2)

End {Main} .
```

When the first of these programs is run with some sample data, we get the following interaction:

```
This program stores Dow Jones Averages for later use
Please enter the averages
Conclude by typing a negative value
1066.0
1067.25
1080.5
1076.25
1093.75
1083.0
1103.5
1111.25
1120.75
1116.5
-3.0

Data have been recorded on file.
```

In this program, note how the addition of the last *Writeln* statement tells the user that the program has completed its work.

With this data, the second program gives the following results:

```
This program computes low, high, and mean Dow Jones Averages.
Given the Dow Jones Averages in the file,
     the minimum was 1066.00
     the maximum was 1120.75
     the mean value was 1091.88
```

These programs illustrate several points about files that are defined for particular types of data. First, we can specify that our files will store character data, numbers, or records by using a declaration:

```
Var FileName: File of DataType;
```

In this program, we indicated that the *FileName* will contain data of the given *DataType*. As before with text files, the *FileName* is also included in the program header. Next, we use *Reset* or *Rewrite* to prepare a file for reading or writing, respectively.

Once the file is declared and *Reset*, we use the *Read* statement to obtain data from the file. As with text files, our syntax is

```
Read (FileName, Value1, Value2, . . .)
```

We add the *FileName* to our *Read* statement to indicate where our data are stored. Here, however, each variable must have the type specified by our file declaration. In the previous problem, we used

```
Read (DowFile, DowAvg);
```

where *DowAvg* had type *Real*. We could not read values of other types from the *DowFile*.

Similarly, once we declare and *Rewrite* our file, we can use the *Write* statement to place values on our file. The syntax is

```
Write (FileName, Value1, Value2, . . .)
```

and *Value1*, *Value2*, . . . must have the same type as the *DataType* for the file. Unlike text files, we cannot mix data types on one of these files.

In these files, data are *not* organized into lines. Thus, we cannot use *Readln* or *Writeln* to read or write data with these files. The *Readln* and *Writeln* statements only apply to text files. The following section gives a more extended example using these files.

## SECTION 14.3 EXAMPLE: STORAGE OF LARGE DATA SETS

When we want to store large amounts of data on a file, we often find that we want to group pieces of data together in records; to correct or modify our data; and to retrieve particular data items.

These requirements are illustrated in the following problem.

## PROBLEM 14.3 Grocery Checkout

At a grocery store cash register, a clerk enters a product code (with a light pen). From this code, the cash register prints the product name, product code, package size, and price.

Write a program that will retrieve this information from a file given the code number. Also, write programs that allow this information to be stored on a file and modified.

### Discussion of Problem 14.3

We consider the pieces of information for a particular product to be part of a single entity. We want to keep product information together in the following record.

```
Const NameLength = 40;
      SizeLength = 10;
Type  Product = Record
                  Name:  Packed Array [1..NameLength] of Char;
                  Code:  Integer;
                  Size:  Packed Array [1..SizeLength] of Char;
                  Price: Real
                  End
```

With these declarations, we can use the same type of data entry we have seen before. Because product codes are positive, we will continue processing data until a negative code is entered. Since the outline is similar to what we used for data entry in the previous section, we proceed with the data entry program itself.

---

```
Program EnterGroceries (Input, Output, ProdFile);
{This program enters grocery information into a file}
Const NameLength = 40;
      SizeLength = 10;

Type Product = Record
        Name: Packed Array [1..NameLength] of Char;
        Code: Integer;
        Size: Packed Array [1..SizeLength] of Char;
        Price: Real
        End;
     GroceryFile = File of Product;

Var ProdFile: GroceryFile;

Procedure Enter (Var Item: Product);
{This procedure reads product name, size and price from the terminal.}
   Const BlankName = '                                        ';
         BlankSize = '          ';

   Var Index: Integer;

   Begin
      With Item
        Do Begin

          {Read product name}
          Name := BlankName;
```

```
            Write ('Product name: ');
            Index := 0;
            While Not Eoln and (Index < NameLength)
              Do Begin
                Index := Index + 1;
                Read (Name[Index])
              End;
            Readln;

            {Read size}
            Size := BlankSize;
            Write('Package size: ');
            Index := 0;
            While Not Eoln and (Index < SizeLength)
              Do Begin
                Index := Index + 1;
                Read (Size[Index])
              End;
            Readln;

            {Read price}
            Write ('Price: ');
            Readln (Price)
          End
    End {Enter} ;

Procedure LoadFileWithData (Var ProdFile: GroceryFile);
{This procedure controls the reading of grocery data and then
 stores this data on a file}
   Var Item: Product;

    Begin
        Rewrite (ProdFile);

        Writeln ('Please enter product information, ',
                 'ending with a negative product code');
        Write('Product code: ');
        Readln (Item.Code);
        While (Item.Code > 0)
          Do Begin
            Enter (Item);
            Write (Prodfile, Item);
            Write('Product code: ');
            Readln (Item.Code)
          End;
    End {LoadFileWithData} ;

Begin {Main}
    Writeln ('This program enters grocery information into a file');
    LoadFileWithData (ProdFile);
    Writeln ('Grocery information stored in file.')
End {Main} .
```

From this program, we see that we can store our product record on a file by declaring

```
Type GroceryFile = File of Product;
Var ProdFile: GroceryFile;
```

or, more simply

```
Var ProdFile: File of Product;
```

Then, we can use the *Rewrite* and *Write* statements as we did before. Note, however, that here we must print the data for the entire record at once. We cannot print the fields of the record separately, because the file contains entire records, not just separate pieces of these records.

### Discussion of Problem 14.3. (Continued)

Once the product file is created, we can use it to retrieve our product information. Here, for each product code, we start at the beginning of our file and continue reading the product information until we find the code or until we run out of data in the file.

### Outline for Returning Data in Problem 14.3

Repeat for each grocery item purchased (e.g., until the next product code is negative).

**I.** Prepare to read grocery file from the beginning.
**II.** Continue until code found or end of file.
  **A.** Read data for next product.
**III.** Print results.
  **A.** If code found, print product information.
  **B.** If code not found, indicate that product information is missing.

This outline yields the following program.

```
Program RetrieveGroceries (Input, Output, ProdFile);
{This program retrieves grocery information from a file}
Const NameLength = 40;
      SizeLength = 10;

Type Product = Record
        Name: Packed Array [1..NameLength] of Char;
        Code: Integer;
        Size: Packed Array [1..SizeLength] of Char;
        Price: Real
        End;

     ProdFileType = File of Product;

Var ProdFile: ProdFileType;

Procedure Enter (Var DesiredCode: Integer);
{This procedure reads a product code from the terminal}
```

```
    Begin
        Write ('Please enter product code ',
               '(enter a negative code to stop):');
        Readln (DesiredCode)
    End {Enter} ;

Procedure Search (Var DataFile: ProdFileType;
                  DesiredCode: Integer; Var Item: Product);
{This procedure searches the DataFile for an Item with the DesiredCode}
    Begin
        {Prepare to read file from the beginning}
        Reset (DataFile);

        {Read file record-by-record until code found
             or until end of file is found}
        {Program assumes at least one product item is stored in file}
        Repeat
            Read (DataFile, Item);
        Until EOF(DataFile) Or (Item.Code = DesiredCode)
    End {Search} ;

Procedure Print (Item: Product);
{This procedure prints the product information for the given item}
    Begin
        With Item
          Do Begin
            Writeln('Product Name','Code':36, 'Size':6, 'Price':13);
            Write (Name);
            Write (Code:8);
            Write ('  ', Size);
            Writeln(' $ ', Price:1:2)
          End;
       Writeln
    End {Print} ;

Procedure ControlProcessing (Var ProdFile: ProdFileType);
{This procedure controls the main steps in retrieving grocery data
 from the file}
    Var Item: Product;
        DesiredCode: Integer;
    Begin
        Enter (DesiredCode);
        While (DesiredCode > 0)
          Do Begin
            Search (ProdFile, DesiredCode, Item);
            If Item.Code = DesiredCode
                Then Print (Item)
                Else Writeln ('Product not listed on file');
            Enter (DesiredCode)
          End
    End {ControlProcessing} ;

Begin {Main}
    Writeln ('This program retrieves grocery information from a file');
    ControlProcessing (ProdFile)
End {Main} .
```

A sample interaction with this program appears below.

```
This program retrieves grocery information from a file
Please enter product code (enter a negative code to stop):2020
Product Name                                 Code  Size        Price
Soggy Cereal                                 2020  Large      $ 1.29

Please enter product code (enter a negative code to stop):1059
Product Name                                 Code  Size        Price
Cavaties Galore Candy                        1059  8 oz.      $ 1.25

Please enter product code (enter a negative code to stop):1789
Product not listed on file
Please enter product code (enter a negative code to stop):1081
Product Name                                 Code  Size        Price
Moo Juice                                    1081  1 Quart    $ 0.98

Please enter product code (enter a negative code to stop):1002
Product Name                                 Code  Size        Price
Tantalizing Toasties                         1002  24 oz.     $ 2.53

Please enter product code (enter a negative code to stop):-999
```

This program illustrates several additional features about data files. First, a *Reset* or a *Rewrite* statement prepares a file for reading or writing, respectively, and it places us at the beginning of the file. If we have read part of a file and then want to start over at the beginning of the file, we can use the *Reset* or *Rewrite* again. Each time we use these statements, we move back to the beginning of our file.

We also see that when we want to transfer data in a file from one program to another, the file variables in Pascal must be declared as global variables. Such files are called **external files.** In using these files, we cannot declare them inside a procedure, even if we only work with them in the procedure. All external files must be listed in the program header, so they are global identifiers, and they must be declared in the main program. On the other hand, Pascal does allow us to use file identifiers as reference parameters into procedures. In our example, we passed the parameter filename *ProdFile* into the *Search* procedure. However, Pascal does not permit the identifiers to be passed by value.

## Discussion of File Manipulations in Problem 14.3

Finally we look at how we might modify our files in Pascal. First, we observe that files in Standard Pascal are **sequential files.** With Standard Pascal files, we always must start at the beginning of a file and then proceed value-by-value or record-by-record to the end. We cannot back up in our processing, and we cannot skip records. These Pascal limitations mean that we cannot modify a file in one step.

In order to modify a file, we first must find the record where the change is to be made by using *Read* statements. Then, after we determine our revised data, we will need to *Write* the new data on a file. However, since we can use *Read* only with *Reset* and *Write* only with *Rewrite,* we cannot use the *Read* to find our data and then use *Write* on the same file to make the change. Instead, we will copy our file to a second file, making the change when we reach the desired record. After the file is copied to the new file, we can copy the entire file back. Our original file is now modified, and we can follow the same process again if further changes are needed.

### Outline for File Modification in Problem 14.3

For each change desired:

- **I.** Determine product code of item to be changed.
- **II.** Copy successive records from the product file to a temporary file until specified product code is found.
- **III.** Enter revised record for the item.
- **IV.** Write the revised product information on the temporary file.
- **V.** Copy the rest of the product file to the temporary file.
- **VI.** Copy the temporary file, with corrections, back to the product file.

In this outline, Steps III through VI only apply if we can find the appropriate record.

In the following program, this outline is implemented as a procedure that we call as needed from our main program. This program uses the same *Enter* procedure that we used in our data entry program earlier in this section. We omit the *Enter* procedure in the following listing.

```
Program ModifyGroceryFile (Input, Output, ProdFile);
{This program makes changes in the grocery information on a file}
Const NameLength = 40;
      SizeLength = 10;

Type Product = Record
        Name: Packed Array [1..NameLength] of Char;
        Code: Integer;
        Size: Packed Array [1..SizeLength] of Char;
        Price: Real
        End;

     ProdFileType = File of Product;

Var ProdFile: ProdFileType;
    TempFile: ProdFileType;
    Answer: Char;

{Procedure Enter (Var Item: Product)
     should be inserted here}

Procedure Modify;
{This procedure changes a specified item in the file}
    Var Item: Product;
        DesiredCode: Integer;
```

```
Begin
    {Determine product code of item to be changed}
    Write ('Enter code of product to be changed:');
    Readln (DesiredCode);

    {Copy successive records until specified record found}
    Reset (ProdFile);
    Rewrite (TempFile);
    Read (ProdFile, Item);
    While Not EOF(ProdFile) And (Item.Code <> DesiredCode)
      Do Begin
        Write (TempFile, Item);
        Read  (ProdFile, Item)
      End;

    If Item.Code <> DesiredCode
        Then Writeln ('Product not found')
        Else Begin
            {Make change}
            Enter (Item);
            Write (TempFile, Item);

            {Copy rest of file}
            While Not EOF(ProdFile)
              Do Begin
                Read  (ProdFile, Item);
                Write (TempFile, Item)
              End;

            {Copy back to original file}
            Rewrite (ProdFile);
            Reset   (TempFile);
                While Not EOF(TempFile)
                  Do Begin
                    Read  (TempFile, Item);
                    Write (ProdFile, Item)
                  End

              End
    End {Modify};

Begin {Main}

    Writeln ('This program makes changes in a product file');

    Repeat
        Modify;
        Write ('Do you wish to make another change? ');
        Readln (Answer)
    Until (Answer in ['n', 'N'] );

    Writeln ('Changes completed')
End {Main} .
```

A sample run is shown below:

```
This program makes changes in a product file
Enter code of product to be changed:2020
Product name: Improved Taltalizing Toasties
Package size: 23 oz.
Price: 2.53
Do you wish to make another change? y
Enter code of product to be changed:1059
Product name: More Cavaties
Package size: 9 oz.
Price: 1.40
Do you wish to make another change? n
Changes completed
```

This program shows how we can modify and copy files by working from the beginning of a file to the end.

In all our work with files, we first must specify the type of data that we will use, such as text, numbers, characters, or records. Then, we reset or rewrite a file before we use the file and when we want to return to the beginning of the file. Thereafter, we use *Read* or *Write*, specifying our file as we move data between our file and our program.

## SECTION 14.4 BUFFERS—AN OVERVIEW

The previous sections of this chapter have demonstrated that for many applications, we can work with data on files in much the same way that we work with data at our terminal. However, to use files effectively in many other applications, we first need to have some understanding of how this data transfer takes place. As we will see, there are differences between how data are accessed within main memory and how data are accessed from a disk file. These differences can affect not only where we store our data but also how we organize and process our data.

To appreciate the difference, we first consider data in main memory. Here, technical details of circuitry may vary from one machine to another, but in any machine all storage and retrieval is performed electronically, not mechanically. All parts of main memory are linked by some type of electrical path, and data can be moved using this circuitry alone. Here, the key point is that all processing can be done quite quickly. The computer never needs to wait for a mechanical operation to occur.

In contrast, disk storage does involve some mechanical processes. To begin, a simple disk looks like a flat, round platter, much like a phonograph record without grooves. This platter is coated with a magnetic substance, and data are stored on the platter by placing appropriate magnetic charges at various locations on the disk.

Next, the computer accesses this information in much the same way that we might play a phonograph record. The disk turns at a high rate of speed, and a read/write head (like a tone arm) moves back and forth to the appropriate spot on the disk. Thus, to obtain one piece of information from a disk, the computer must do three things:

1. move the read/write head to the appropriate position;
2. rotate the disk to the correct location;
3. read or write the desired data at the correction location.

See Figure 14–4.

This process clearly requires considerable mechanical activity, and mechanical work is much slower than electrical work. Thus, the disk access of a particular piece of data is much slower than the access of similar data stored in main memory.

With this inherent delay in working with data on disk, computers are designed to incorporate several features to speed up data transmission. The initial accessing of data never can be done quickly, but with care, subsequent data can be obtained somewhat more efficiently in several ways. First, instead of scattering individual pieces of data around the disk, some pieces are put close together. Then, once we move the read/write head to a particular location, we can let the disk continue to rotate, processing data as they go by. Thus, data on disks are organized onto **tracks** or **cylinders** just as phonograph records contain bands for separate pieces. With this structure, we still must move the read/write head, and we must wait for the disk to turn to the start of a track before we can begin processing data. However, once we start, we can process a whole track of data relatively quickly.

We can also increase efficiency by working with several items on a disk file at about the same time. For example, we may want to read or write

FIGURE 14–4 • **Organization of a Disk**

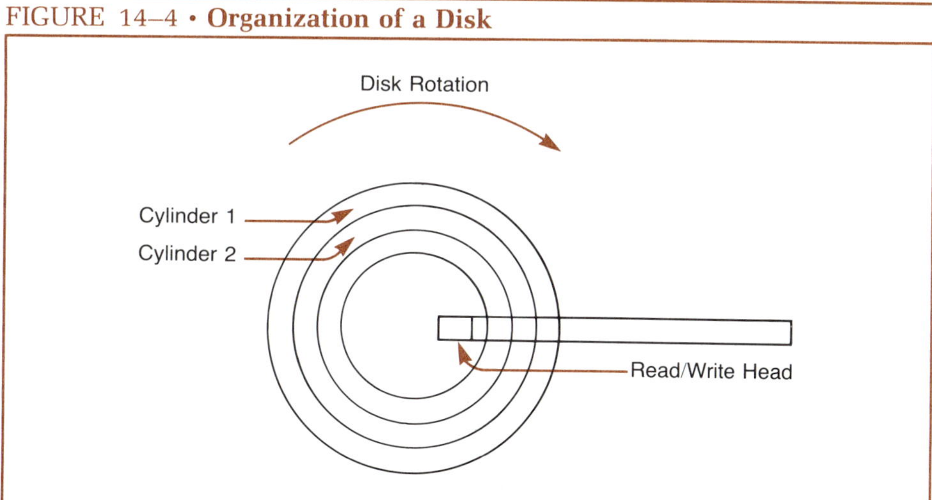

several characters of text, or we may want to work with a whole record of data. Combining this observation with our previous point, we find that processing disk data is often most effective if we can read or write several pieces of data at a time. We may not need all pieces of data in a record immediately, but we can save time if we read an entire record at once. Similarly, we may want to accumulate all fields of a record before transmitting it to disk.

### Buffers for Disk Files

With these considerations, we find that working with disk files involves several steps. First, the computer allocates some space, called a **buffer,** in main memory, so we can read or write several pieces of data at a time. In fact, a separate buffer is set up for each file that we use in a program. Then, transmission of data *into* a program proceeds in two steps.

1. Several pieces of data are moved from the disk to the appropriate input buffer.
2. Data are moved, as requested, from the buffer to the program itself.

Similarly, transmission of data *from* a program to disk involves two steps.

3. Data are moved piece by piece from the program to an output buffer.
4. The data are moved from the output buffer to the appropriate disk file.

This division of reading and writing into steps is shown in Figure 14–5, where Steps 1 and 2 are followed for reading data and where Steps 3 and 4 are used in writing.

### Buffers for Transmission to a Terminal

In practice, we also find that buffers are used with terminals and printers for much the same reason. In particular, typing at a terminal or printing on a printer is a slow, mechanical process. For example, while a printer is typing out data, the computer's CPU is fast enough to be doing other work.

FIGURE 14–5 • **Transmission of Data**

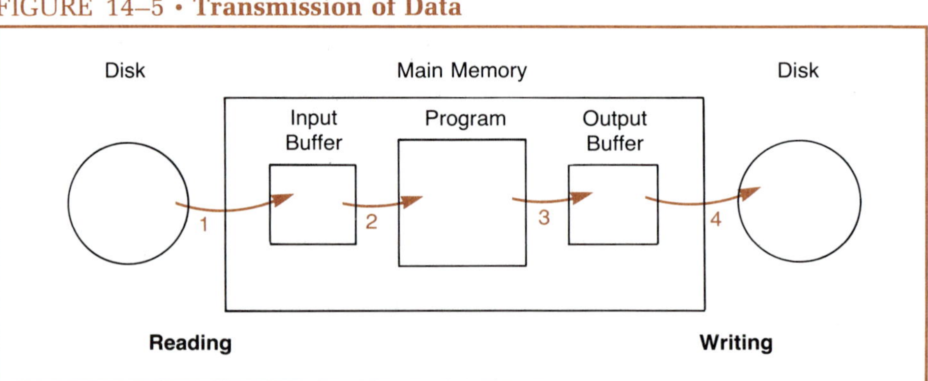

Thus, a buffer is reserved in main memory for a user's output, so the CPU does not have to wait for mechanical processes to be completed.

Similarly, when a buffer is used for input, a user can anticipate the data that will be needed next by a program, and this data can be entered ahead of time. The data are simply saved in an input buffer until the program actually needs them. Alternatively, if data are not already typed by a user, then the CPU may work on other jobs until the data for a particular job are entered.

### Buffers and Read or Write Statements

With this discussion of buffers, we need to make two final comments before we see how these buffers can be used effectively in our code.

While we have not explicitly used buffers in our coding up to this point, we should understand that these buffers have been present behind the scenes. Our input and output have always involved special buffer areas inside main memory. Similarly, our *Reset* or *Rewrite* statements of Section 14.1 cause the computer to allocate buffer space. The *Read* and *Write* statements offer a convenient way to do both steps of input and output. For example, the *Read* first moves data to a buffer and then into the program. With these *Read* or *Write* statements, we have not had to worry about the details of buffers, but internally, the computer still performed both steps.

## SECTION 14.5 STANDARD FUNCTIONS

Now that the concept of a buffer and its role in transmitting data have been introduced, we consider how we can control this transmission of data within a Pascal program.

As we saw in Section 14.1, we can use an identifier to refer to a specific file, and we declare this identifier in two steps.

1. We placed the identifier in parentheses, after the word *Program* in our program header.
2. We declared the identifier as a variable of the appropriate file type.

We then refer to our file by using the identifier. For example, we write

```
Reset(Infile)
```

when we want to prepare to read a file designated by the *Infile* variable. Then, we can read from this file using

```
Read(Infile, . . . )
```

and we can determine when we reach the end of the file by using the Boolean function

```
EOF(Infile)
```

buffers

GET : disk → buffer
PUT : buffer → disk

Now that we have expanded our understanding of file processing to include buffers, we find we must distinguish between two types of references: the reference to the file and its buffer, and the contents of the buffer. In Pascal, we will continue to use an identifier (e.g., *Infile*) to refer to the file and its associated buffer. Then, we add an up-arrow ↑ or caret ^ (e.g., *Infile*^) to refer to the contents of the buffer.

With these general conventions, we now outline the appropriate steps for using a file. Our work involves two new procedures: *Get* for moving data from the file to the buffer and *Put* for moving data back.

### Input from a File

**I.** Prepare to use the file. (These steps are accomplished by *Reset (Infile)*, which is the same statement we used in Section 14.1.)
  **A.** Set up buffer.
  **B.** Move first record from file to buffer.

**II.** Use the data within the buffer. (By adding the up-arrow or caret to the buffer/file identifier, we can refer to a buffer record the same way we refer to any record.)

**III.** Use a *Get* statement to move the next record in the file to the buffer. Thus, *Get (Infile)* updates the data in the buffer so that it refers to the next record on the file. (Note that a *Get* statement throws away any previous data in our buffer, although any data in our file is still present.)

### Output to a File

**I.** Prepare to use the file. (As in Section 14.1, these steps are accomplished by *Rewrite (Outfile)*.)
  **A.** Throw out any data that had been in the file, so the file starts fresh.
  **B.** Set up buffer.

**II.** Move data from the program to the buffer. (Again we refer to the contents of the output buffer by adding an up-arrow or caret to the buffer/file variable.)

**III.** Use a *Put* statement to add the contents in the buffer to the output file. Thus, *Put (Outfile)* causes the data in the buffer to be appended to any previous output.

To illustrate how these various steps are implemented in a Pascal program, we write the code for the following simple task.

## PROBLEM 14.5A Sequential Access, Reading and Writing Files

A file is to be created with the two records shown in Figure 14–6. Then, this file is to be read, and the data displayed at the terminal.

To solve this problem, we need two programs, one to create the initial file and the second to read it. In each program below, we demonstrate various ways to perform this work, following our outlines for input and output.

First, we write an appropriate output program.

FIGURE 14–6 • **A Very Simple File**

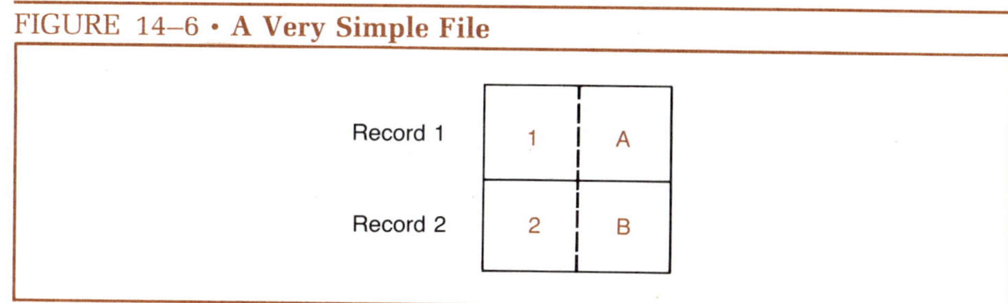


```
Program FileWrite (Outfile, Output);
{This program writes two records to a file.}

{Specify File Characteristics}
Type
     FileItem = Record
          Number: Integer;
          Letter: Char
          End;
Var
     Item: FileItem;
     Outfile: File of FileItem;

Begin {Main}

     Writeln ('Starting to create file');

     {Open File}
          Rewrite (Outfile);

     {Write First Record}
     {Move Data to Output File Buffer}
          Outfile^.Number := 1;
          Outfile^.Letter := 'A';

     {Move Data from Buffer to Disk File}
          Put(Outfile);

     {Write Second Record}
     {Move Data to Output File Buffer}
          Item.Number := 2;
          Item.Letter := 'B';
          Outfile^ := Item;

     {Move Data from Buffer to Disk File}
          Put(Outfile);

   Writeln ('File Created')

End {Main} .
```

In this program, we declare *Outfile* as our file identifier, and we begin by rewriting this file. At this point, we have a buffer available for data, but we still need to place data into that buffer.

In this example, the buffer is a record containing both a number and a letter, and our program illustrates two ways to place data into this buffer. In the first approach, we move data into the buffer one field at a time, using the following syntax.

| | |
|---|---|
| Outfile | is the buffer/file variable |
| Outfile^ | refers to the buffer record, containing a number and letter |
| Outfile^.Number | refers to the number field within the buffer record |

Thus,

```
Outfile^.Number := 1
```

places the integer 1 into the *Number* field within the buffer. Similarly,

```
Outfile^.Letter := 'A'
```

places a character in the buffer's *Letter* field. With these two statements, we now have placed data in each field of the buffer.

Our second method involves placing data in a record within our program, and then moving an entire record of data into the buffer at once. In our program, we first placed the number 2 and the letter 'B' into a record called *Item* with the statements

```
Item.Number := 2;
Item.Letter := 'B';
```

Then we copied this entire record into the buffer with the statement

```
Outfile^ := Item;
```

Here, *Outfile^* refers to the contents of the buffer, and we want to copy all data in the *Item* record into the buffer.

In either case, the program has placed appropriate data in the output buffer. Then, we write

```
Put (Outfile)
```

to move the data from the buffer to the file. If we omitted the first *Put* statement, then the data '1', 'A' would never get to the file. Instead that data would be lost, when the buffer data was superceded by '2', 'B'.

With this explanation of a file creation program, we now write a program to read this newly created file, following our outline for output.

```
Program FileRead (Output, Infile);
{This program reads two records from a file and prints them
 at the terminal.}
```

```
{Specify File Characteristics}
Type
     FileItem = Record
          Number: Integer;
          Letter: Char
          End;
Var
     Item: FileItem;
     Infile: File of FileItem;

Begin

     {Open File and Move First Record from Disk File to Buffer}
          Reset (Infile);

     {Move Data from Buffer}
          Item := Infile^;

     {Write Out Record}
          Writeln (Item.Number, Item.Letter);

     {Process Second Record}
     {Move Data From Disk File to Buffer}
          Get(Infile);

     {Move Data From Buffer to Terminal}
          Write(Infile^.Number);
          Writeln(Infile^.Letter)

End {Main} .
```

In tracing this program, we see that it involves the following elements.

1. The *Reset* statement sets up the buffer and then moves the first record of data (i.e., '1', 'A') into the buffer.
2. The entire contents of the buffer are moved to a record variable with a simple assignment *Item := Infile^*. Again, we use the up-arrow or caret to specify the contents of the buffer.
3. The next record in the file is read using *Get(Infile)*, which moves the next record of data into the buffer.
4. Individual fields within the buffer can be referenced separately instead of treating the buffer as a whole. For example, in our write statements, *Infile^.Number* refers to the *Number* field of the buffer record; while *Infile^.Letter* refers to the corresponding letter field.

These programs illustrate the mechanics of using buffers for input and output. The next example shows how to use buffers to streamline file processing tasks.

## PROBLEM 14.5B Copying Text Files

Write a program to copy text files. (Recall from Section 14.1 text files include character data organized into lines.)

### Discussion of Problem 14.5B

Following our work in Section 14.1, one approach to solving this problem would be to read the first file, character by character, until we reach the end of the file. In this process, we would write each character on the new file as soon as it was read. However, while this code is easy to write, the actual work would involve four steps.

1. Move character from initial file to input buffer.
2. Move character from input buffer to program.
3. Move character from program to output buffer.
4. Move character from output buffer to new file.

This flow of data was shown earlier, in Figure 14–5.

To make this code more efficient, we combine Steps 2 and 3 into a single step, which moves each character from the input buffer to the output buffer. Here, we do not bring the data into the program at all, since we never want to examine the data; we only want to copy it, as we see in the following program.

---

```
Program Copy (Output, Infile, Outfile);
{This program copies a file of text to another file.}

Var
     Infile, Outfile: Text;

Begin {Main}

     Writeln ('Starting to Copy File');

     {Open Files}
         Reset (Infile);
         Rewrite(Outfile);

     {Copy Files}

         While Not EOF(InFile)
           Do Begin

             {Transfer Data From Input Buffer to Output Buffer}
                 Outfile^ := Infile^;

             {Move Data From Output Buffer to Disk File}
                 Put(Outfile);

             {Move Data From Disk File to Input Buffer}
                 Get(Infile)

           End;
```

```
        {Transfer last character}
            Outfile^ := Infile^;
            Put(Outfile);

        Writeln ('File Copied')

End {Main} .
```

Here, the main loop has been streamlined to save the step we discussed. The loop simply

1. moves a character into the input buffer: *Get (Infile)*
2. copies the character to the output buffer: *Outfile^ := Infile^*
3. moves the character to the new file: *Put (Outfile)*

Thus, by using buffers, this program is more efficient than it would be using only *Read* and *Write* statements.

Finally, to explain the order of statements in our loop, we emphasize that the *Reset* statement already brings the first piece of data into the input buffer. Thus, at the start, we already have data that need processing, so we transfer data from input to output first in our loop. If we performed the *Get* operation at the start of the loop, this first data item would be thrown away before it was copied, and our new file would have lost some data.

This example shows that careful control of data in buffers can help us write code that uses files quite efficiently. This ability for handling file data is particularly important in some more complex applications.

## SUMMARY

1. Data can be stored and retrieved from two general types of files.
   a. **Text Files** allow the programmer to work with files in the same way as with a keyboard and terminal. Text files are organized into lines of data.
   b. **Files of data** enable the programmer to organize data in other ways. Such files can contain data of any declared type, including Booleans, characters, numeric data, and records.
2. In declaring files, we include a file identifier in our program header, and we declare the type of the file. (This is the only instance in Pascal where an identifer must be declared globally. Reference parameters are allowed, but file identifers may not be declared locally or as value parameters.)
3. Disk files require a mechanical process to store and retrieve data. In this process, the most time is spent in obtaining the first piece of data in a file. Thereafter, subsequent data in a file can be transmitted relatively

quickly. Thus, in practice, the computer reads or writes several pieces of data at a time to increase efficiency.

4. In the transmission process, a **buffer** is used to store these pieces of data.
   a. In reading, an entire record of data is read into a buffer. Then various fields of the record can be read into the program as needed.
   b. In writing, various fields of a record are gathered together in a buffer before being sent to the file in a single operation.
5. Within a Pascal program, buffers are created by a **Reset** or **Rewrite** statement. Thereafter, we can move data from disk to buffer or back using special procedures **Get** and **Put,** respectively. Then, adding an upward arrow or caret to a file's buffer variable allows us to access the contents of the buffer itself.
6. In using these files, we work with the file **sequentially;** we start at the beginning of the data in our file, and we work line-by-line or record-by-record to the end using *Read* or *Write* statements.

## EXERCISES

**14.1** *Grocery File Updating.*

a. Write a program that reads a product code from the keyboard and then deletes that product from the grocery file of Section 14.3.

   HINT: Copy the old grocery file to a new one, omitting the specified product. Then copy the new file back.

b. Write a program that adds new product information to the grocery file of Section 14.3.

   HINT: Copy the old file to a new one. Then copy the information back, adding data entered from the keyboard.

c. Combine parts (a) and (b) in a program that allows various modifications in a grocery file, including adding new products, modifying data, and deleting products. In this program, the user should be able to continue modifying the information stored until the user asks to quit.

| KEY TERMS, PHRASES, AND CONCEPTS | | ELEMENTS OF PASCAL SYNTAX | |
|---|---|---|---|
| Buffers | Reading | *EOF* | *Put* |
| Disk Cylinder | Writing | *File Of* | *Reset* |
| Disk Track | File Type and Declaration | *Get* | *Rewrite* |
| File Initialization | File of Data | Modified Statements | *Text* |
| Reset | Text | *EOLN* | |
| Rewrite | Sequential Files | Program Header | |
| File Manipulation | | *Read* | |
| Modifying | | *Write* | |

**14.2** *Grocery Checkout.*

**a.** Modify the grocery program of Section 14.3 so that the computer records all products purchased by customers and then prints a complete listing of items purchased and the total grocery bill for the customers.

**b.** Modify part (a) so that the product list is printed in order of ascending price.

**14.3** *EOLN not defined if EOF True.* The programs in Section 14.1 all assume that a text file ends with a complete line; we assume the file does not end in the middle of a line (before "Return" is encountered). Without this assumption, a programmer encounters the following difficulty.

- *EOF* always specifies *True* or *False*, depending upon whether the end of a file is reached.
- *EOLN* is defined only if *EOF* is false.

Thus, at the end of a file, we cannot test *EOLN.*

Write a revised *EndLine* function that will be true at the end of lines and at the end of files and false otherwise. We want to use *EndLine* to test for the end of a line of data anywhere in the program; *EndLine* works even if the file stops in the middle of a line.

**14.4** *Storage of Data on a File.* When performing experiments, it is often helpful to store the data obtained on a file for later processing.

**a.** Write a program that reads pairs of numbers from a terminal and stores them on a file. Thus, the file will consist of records, each containing two values.

**b.** Write a program that uses the data on file from part (a) to find the average first number of the pairs and the maximum second number.

**14.5** *Input and Output Buffers.* When we type at many terminals, material goes directly from the terminal to an input buffer. Then, for most processing, the CPU copies this information to an output buffer where it is transmitted back to the terminal to be displayed on a screen or printed. Use this flow of data to explain the following phenomena that are observed on many computing systems.

**a.** There may be a time delay between when a user types at the keyboard and when the data appears on the screen.

**b.** In entering a password, nothing appears on the screen at all. (Thus, people looking over one's shoulder during log-on cannot see one's password.)

**c.** When an instructor types on one keyboard, the same information can be displayed on many different terminals, even when others are logged on to other terminals.

**14.6** In the file copying program of Section 14.5, we observed that the transfer of data

```
Outfile^ := Infile^
```

had to come first in the loop so that we did not lose the first piece of data. Is it also necessary that

Put(Outfile)

comes before

Get(Infile)

Explain your conclusion, and write a Pascal program to check your answer.

**14.7** *Print End of File.* Write a program that prints out the last record in a file.

HINT: For efficiency, there is no reason to move most of the records into main memory beyond the buffer.

**14.8** **a.** Write a program that reads a list of grocery items, including product codes, names, and costs from the terminal and stores them on a disk file.

**b.** Write a second program that copies this disk record of codes, names, and costs to another file, decreasing all costs by 35%. (Such a program might be used to price all items during a storewide sale.)

**14.9** *Weekly Business Calendar.* Write a program that prints on a file an appointment calendar for a normal business week (Monday to Friday, 8:00 a.m. to 5:00 p.m.). The calendar should have the following form.

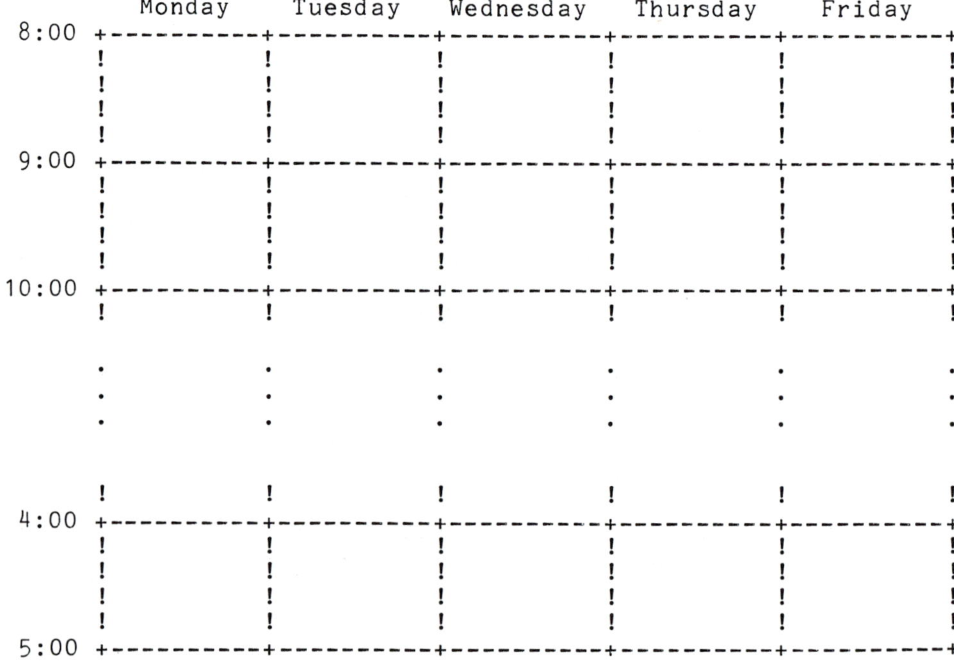

**14.10** *Address Book.* A popular application of microcomputers involves the storage of name, address, and telephone information to form an address book. In such an application, a user must be able to

- add entries (including name, address, and telephone number);
- change any part of an entry (which is useful not only when a person moves but also if the user makes a typographical error initially);
- delete entries;
- retrieve an entire entry from a name;
- print the entire name, address, and telephone information in the form of a directory.

Write a program for such an address book.

**14.11** *Season's Greetings Card List.* During the December holidays, we may send large numbers of cards to various friends and acquaintances. In this process, records may be kept about where each card is sent and when a card is received.

**a.** Modify the previous Address Book program, so that an entry stores information for which cards were sent this year, last year, and the year before, and whether a card was received from an individual for each of these years. The program should allow retrieval of these entries for

- a card sent this year;
- a card sent either of the past two years;
- a card received this year;
- a card received either of the past two years;
- a card sent this year, but one not received;
- a card received this year, but one not sent.

**b.** Write a second program that updates the file after the season is over. In preparation for the next year, records about cards sent or received become a year older, and we can discard the information for two years ago. Also, before the new season begins, no cards have been sent or received for the coming year.

**14.12** *Simple Calendar.* Write a program that prints on a file a calendar for a given month. The program should read the month and year from the keyboard and then print the appropriate calendar on a file.

# CHAPTER 15

# LINKED LIST DATA STRUCTURES: AN INTRODUCTION TO POINTERS

In previous chapters, we have stored data in arrays, records, and sets, and we have worked both with individual pieces of these data and with these collections of data as a whole. In this chapter, we consider another way to store data, called a *linked list,* and our work includes both a description of lists on a conceptual level and a consideration of how these structures can be implemented in Pascal. As part of this implementation of linked lists, we will need to introduce a new type of data called *pointers.*

In addition, we use this discussion of linked lists to see how we can work with data on a more conceptual level, and we introduce the notion of a *data structure,* which specifies both the type of data that we want to process and the ways we want to perform that processing.

## SECTION 15.1 LINKED LISTS AND THE CONCEPT OF POINTERS

To motivate what we mean by a linked list structure, we begin with an illustration involving lists that we might maintain for work we need to do. In preparing these lists, we initially might write down the tasks that we

FIGURE 15–1 • **List of Tasks Written on Paper**

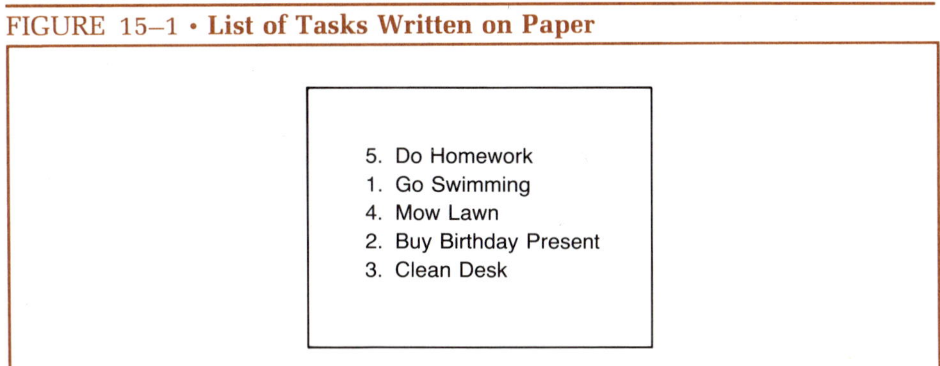


must do as we think of them. Then, we might number these tasks in the order in which we plan to do them. As we think of additional work to do, we would write down each new task (perhaps at the bottom of our paper) and then revise our numbering, which indicates our order for doing the work. Such a list is shown in Figure 15–1.

When we analyze the list in Figure 15–1, we can identify several important characteristics.

- One task, *Go swimming,* is designated as the first item.
- Another item, *Do homework,* will be done last.
- If we follow our numbering, each entry in our list (except the last) has exactly one item following it.
- In using this list, we do not attach any special significance to the order in which we wrote the tasks. For example, we thought of our homework first, and *Do Homework* appears as the first line of our figure. However, that task will be done last in our work schedule. On the other hand, *Go swimming* appears on the second line of our list, but that task is done first.

With these observations, we may write our list in a different form to better reflect what we have identified as being important. Such a representation of our list is shown on the following page in Figure 15–2.

In this figure, we have not tried to write separate tasks on different lines on paper. Rather, we represent each item on our list as a box that has two parts:

- the name of the task for our list entry, and
- a place to indicate which box is next. (In our diagrams, we indicate this next box with an arrow.)

| Task Name | Next |
|---|---|

FIGURE 15–2 • **List of Tasks Using Pointers**

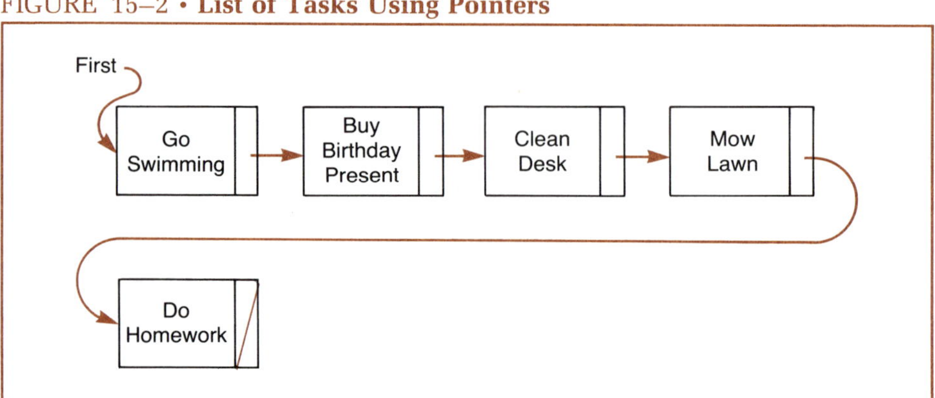


In this representation, the *Task Name* includes alphabetic characters which we have worked with before. However, the arrows for the *Next* part of the box are something new, called **pointers.** Pointers represent a new data type and indicate where other pieces of information are located. In our figure, a box contains both a task name and an arrow or pointer which points to another box. Arrows do not contain our task names; rather, arrows point to boxes, and the boxes contain the task names.

In using pointers to put our boxes of data together, Figure 15–2 also illustrates two other features that we must include in this representation of lists. First, we use a special pointer to specify the location of the initial item on our list. In addition, we need a special symbol to indicate the last element on our list, since the last box does not have an arrow pointing onward. In our diagram, we drew a diagonal line through the *Next* part of our box for the last item, *Do Homework*.

More generally, a **linked list** contains list items, which are made up of data (such as a task name) and a pointer to the next item. This list also contains a special pointer to indicate the first item on the list. With this structure, each item on the list can be reached starting with the first item and following the pointers from one item to the next. Here, we emphasize that the physical location of each item is unimportant; rather, we stress the linking of one item to the next by pointers. We illustrate this general form in Figure 15–3.

## Operations on Linked Lists

When we use linked lists to store our data, we often perform one of four types of operations on the list: finding and perhaps changing a data item, printing data, deleting an item, or inserting a new item. Conceptually, each of these operations is quite simple, but some details for item deletion and insertion require a bit of care. We now look closely at the specifics

FIGURE 15–3 • **A General Linked List**

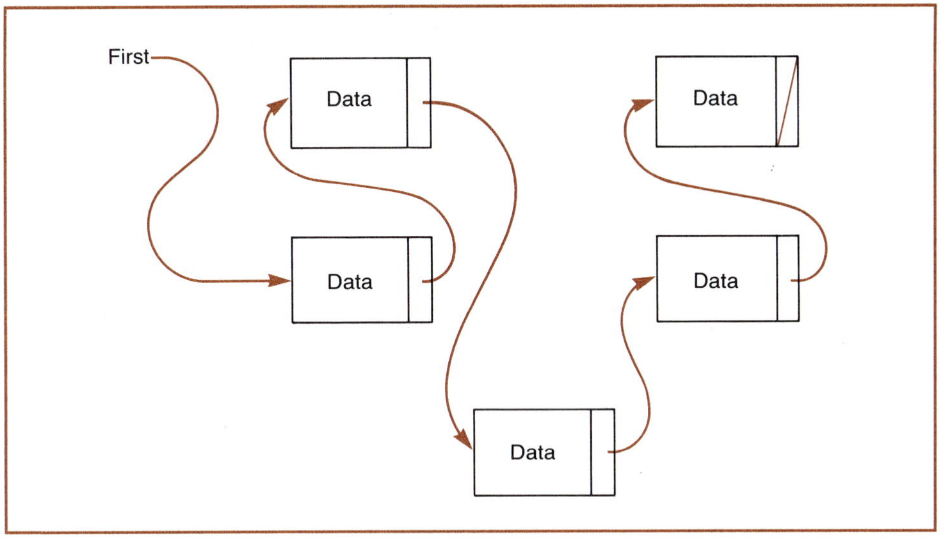

of these operations. In each case, we begin with the simple linked list shown in Figure 15–4, where our data consist of the numbers 2, 4, 6, and 8.

## Finding a Data Item

**Outline for Finding a Data Item.** In locating a particular data item in a linked list, we start with the first item on our list and then proceed from one item to the next until we find our desired piece of data or until we reach the end of the list.

**I.** Prepare to examine first item.
**II.** Continue until data found or no more items remain.
  **A.** Compare the data desired with the data stored in this item.
    **1.** If the data match, note data found.
    **2.** If the data do not match, prepare to examine the next item.

FIGURE 15–4 • **A Simple Linked List**

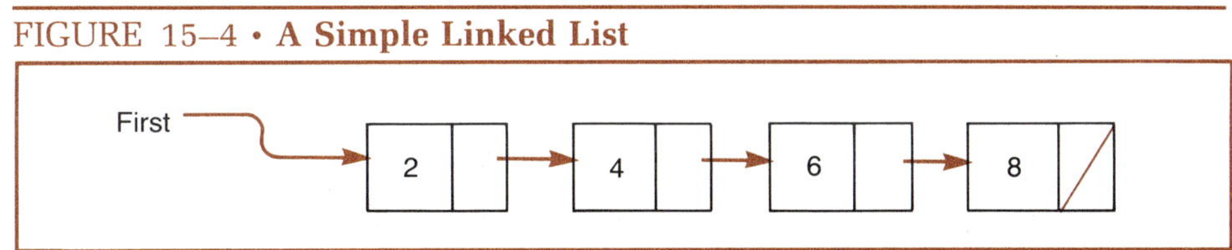

As an example, we try to find the number 6 on the list of Figure 15–4. We proceed in several steps. (See Figure 15–5.)

*Step 1.* We prepare to examine the first item.

*Step 2.* The 2 of the first item does not match the 6 we want, so we move to the next item on the list.

*Step 3.* The 4 of this item does not match the 6 we want, so we again move to the next item on the list.

*Step 4.* The 6 of this item does match our desired number, and we are done.

This process illustrates the distinction between list items and pointers. Throughout our work, we first use a pointer to identify the item that we want to check. Then, we consider the data within that item. Further, in this process, we maintain a pointer that tells us what item we wish to examine next. That pointer begins at the first item. Then we move that pointer along from item to item as we check data in subsequent items.

FIGURE 15–5 • **Locating a Data Item on a List**
**Locating "6" on the List of Figure 15–4**

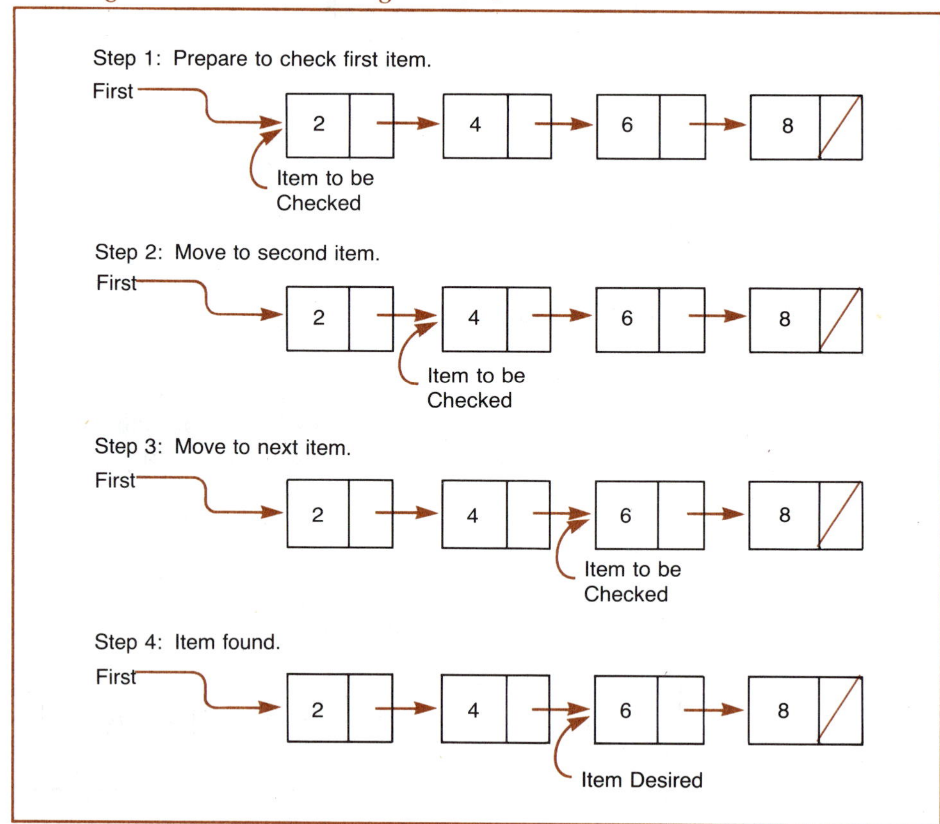

## Printing the Data on a List

We can print the data on a list following much the same process as for finding a particular item, except that we keep printing successive items until no more items are present. We do not stop partway through.

**Outline for Printing List Data.** The following outline for printing follows the same general form as our previous outline.

**I.** Prepare to print data in first item.
**II.** Continue until no more items remain.
  **A.** Print the data at the current item.
  **B.** Prepare to examine the next item.

## Deleting a Data Item

The deletion of an item from a list is illustrated in Figure 15–6, where we delete the third item. In the new list, the "4" box no longer specifies that the "6" box comes next. Rather, the pointer for the "4" box indicates that the "8" box comes next. Thus, within a linked list structure, we can delete an item by changing pointers; the "6" box is no longer on our list, because we cannot reach that box by starting at the beginning of our list and moving from one item to the next. Even if the box is physically present somewhere, it is lost for all future work, since we cannot find this box by searching, starting from the beginning of the list. Beyond this changing of pointers, we also may decide to throw away the old item that we deleted, so we can use that space again.

This example illustrates the main steps involved in deleting an item from a linked list.

*Step 1.* Find the item to be deleted.
*Step 2.* Change the pointer of the previous item to specify the next item (This deletes the item from the list itself.)
*Step 3.* Free the space occupied by the deleted item, if desired.

These steps are shown more carefully in Figure 15–7.

FIGURE 15–6 • **List Deletion**

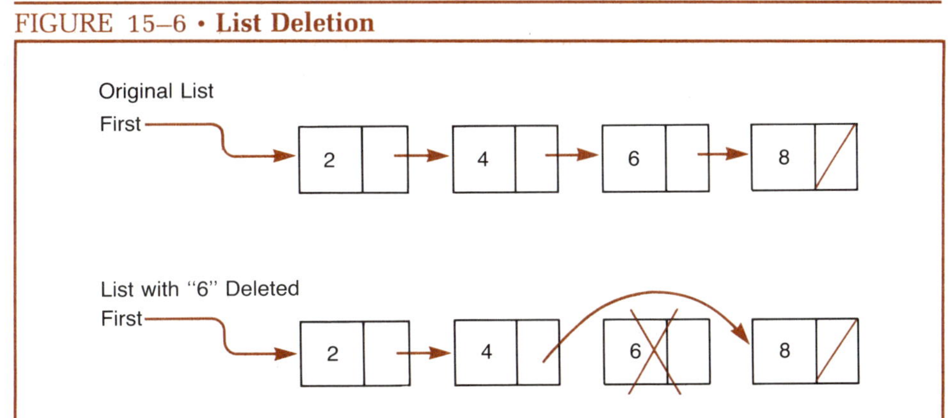

As the figure shows, the ideas behind this deletion are fairly simple. However, in actually writing an outline to perform this task, we find two complications. First, the deletion of the first item in a list requires a special case. Specifically, we must now designate a new "first" item. Secondly, when we find the item we wish to delete, we still must keep track of the previous item. For example, in Figure 15–7, when we locate the "6" box, we must also be able to locate the "4" box.

This second point illustrates an important characteristic of linked lists that requires explicit mention. When we consider a particular item on a list, it is easy to find items that come later in the list; we can just follow the arrows. However, a linked list does not allow us to back up toward the front. At each list item, we have information about the next item, but we do not have information about previous ones, so we cannot follow our arrows backward. Thus, when we delete an item from a list, we must explicitly keep track of previous items as we perform our search. More specifically, when we write a search procedure, we might return a pointer to the

FIGURE 15–7 • **Steps in Deleting an Item**

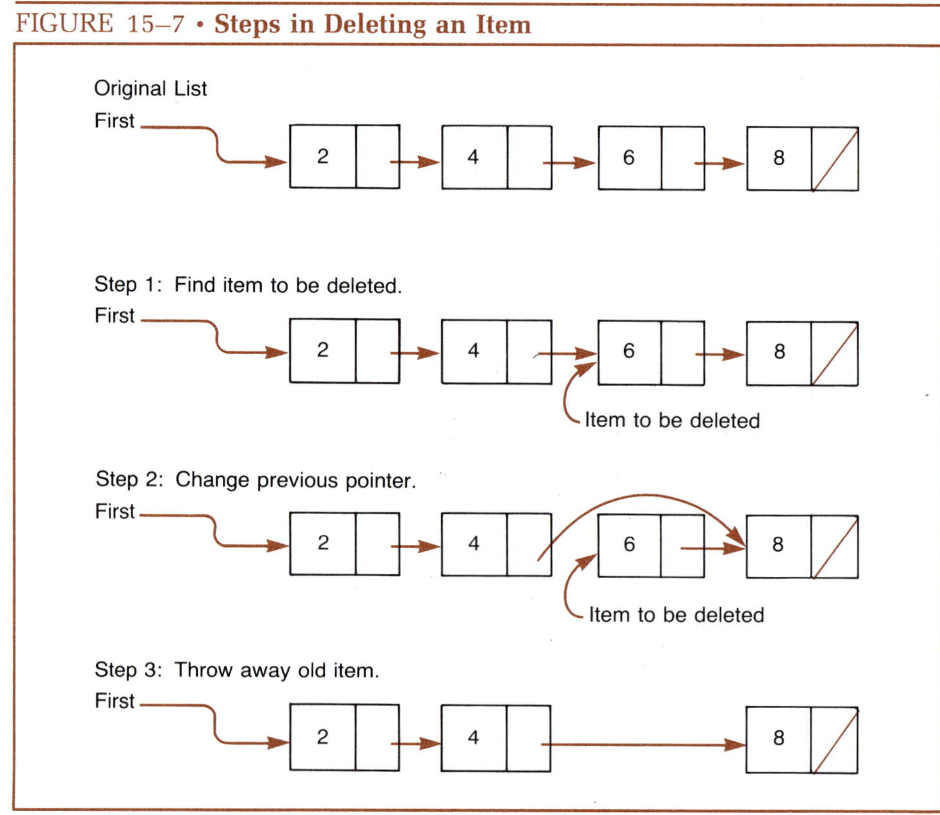

previous item on the list. From this previous item, we can move ahead easily to the item we will actually delete.

With this observation, we now outline the operation to delete an item from a list.

**Outline for Deleting an Item.** Determine if the item to be deleted appears first on the list.

**I.** If so:
  **A.** Move the first pointer to the new "first" item on the list.
  **B.** Throw away the old item.

**II.** If not:
  **A.** Find the item to be deleted on the list, keeping track of the previous item as the search continues.
  **B.** Change the pointer of the previous item to specify the next item.
  **C.** Throw away the old item.

### Inserting a Data Item

The insertion of an item into a list is illustrated in Figure 15–8, where we insert a "5" into a new third box in our list. In the new list, we have created a new box, placed the "5" as the data for this box, made the pointer of the "5" box indicate that the "6" box comes next, and changed the pointer of the "4" box to this new list item. In this insertion process, we can build our "5" box at any convenient place; then we can add this box to our list by changing pointers appropriately.

This example illustrates the main steps involved in inserting an item into a linked list.

FIGURE 15–8 • **List Insertion**

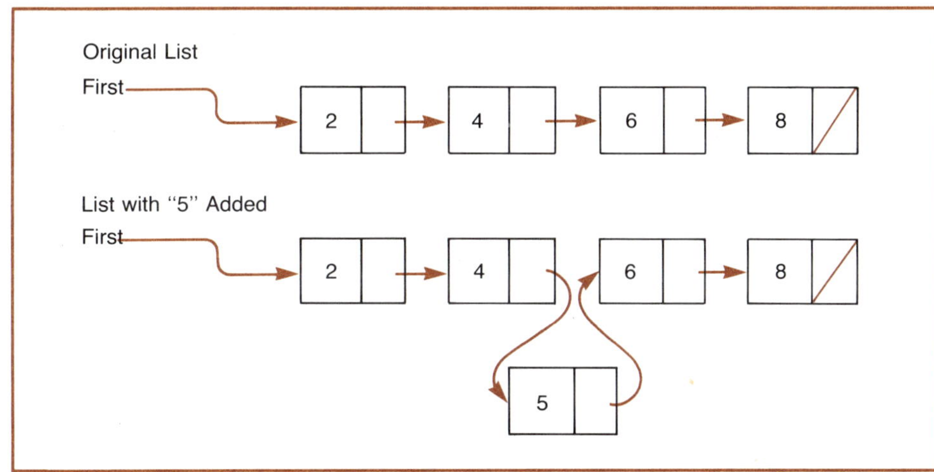

*Step 1.* Determine where item will be inserted.
*Step 2.* Create a new box.
*Step 3.* Place data in the new box.
*Step 4.* Make pointer of new box specify the appropriate next element.
*Step 5.* Update the pointer in the previous box to specify the newly created box.

complications in list insertion

As with list deletion, the details of list insertion include two complications. If we wish to insert an item at the beginning of a list, then we must update the "first" pointer rather than the pointer in the previous list item. Secondly, when we are finding the place to insert the new item, we must be able to identify the item that will precede our new item. In our example, we must know that the "4" box will precede the "5" box. When we keep these details in mind, we can expand the above steps for list insertion into a complete outline.

## Formal Definition of a Data Structure

In this description of a linked list, we have worked with a particular type of information, and we have organized those data in a particular way. Our discussion has involved the type of data we wish to store and the operations we use to manipulate this information (e.g., inserting, deleting, or printing data on a list). In this discussion, we have not considered how this data might be stored in actual computer programs.

This description of pieces of information together with the operations required to manipulate the information make up an abstract data structure that we mentioned in Section 12.1. A **data structure** consists of two parts: A description of the type of data to be stored, and a description of the operations that can be performed on the data. In programming terms, we may consider these parts as the declaration of a data type and a complete specification of procedures and functions for the data type.

An abstract data structure specifies what data we will store and how we will work with that data on a conceptual level. The structure does not specify how we will perform the details of the operations within our programs.

In our actual programs, we work with a data structure at two levels.

1. We write the code to perform each prescribed operation, and we may wish to write some additional procedures to perform the specified operations. Also, we may find we can perform the required work in several ways, so we must pick one particular approach for an actual program.
2. Once the procedures are defined, we use them on a conceptual level without worrying about the programming details. In fact, we could even change the approach we used to implement the procedures without changing our application code at all.

In the next section, we see how we can use the concept of a linked list data structure in a Pascal program.

## SECTION 15.2 IMPLEMENTATION OF LINKED LISTS WITH POINTERS

In the previous section, we saw how to represent linked lists in picture form, where arrows or pointers allowed us to move from one list item to the next. In this section, we translate this representation of lists into Pascal code. In this translation, we will meet a new Pascal data type called **pointers.** Then, with these Pascal pointers, we will find that the pictures of our list operations carry over in a rather straightforward way into corresponding procedures.

As with our conceptualization of pointers and lists in the previous sections, we must be careful in programming to distinguish between the pointers themselves and the item which the pointers specify. In Pascal, the upward arrow ↑ is used in conjunction with pointers, and this symbol helps us make this distinction. On some terminals, the upward arrow is printed as a caret ^. Alternatively the "at sign," @, may be used instead of the upward arrow or caret. In using pointers and this upward arrow or caret in programming, we must consider several important topics:

- pointer type and type declarations;
- variable declaration and initialization;
- manipulation of pointers and items; and
- storage of list items.

To illustrate our discussion, we consider the following problem.

### PROBLEM 15.2

Write a program that will maintain a list of tasks. In particular, the program should allow us to

- insert a new task after a specified task;
- delete a task; and
- print the list of tasks.

To solve this problem, we need to address each programming topic mentioned above.

### Declarations

In our declarations, we must specify two types of objects: list items and pointers to list items. Following our discussion of list items in the first section, the list items themselves will contain two parts, data and a pointer to another item.

The following declarations define these objects.

```
Const Max = 20;
Type ListData = Packed Array [1..Max] of Char;
     ListPointer = ^Item;
     Item = Record
          Data: ListData;
          Next: ListPointer
          End;
```

In this declaration,

```
^Item
```

designates a pointer to an *Item*. In declarations, we use the ^ to declare a new **pointer data type,** which is a pointer or arrow to a specified type of item. You will also note that this declaration of *ListPointer* illustrates the one exception to the general Pascal rule that identifiers must be declared before they are referenced. Here, the pointer to Item, *^Item,* is declared before *Item* itself.

This declaration specifies our list items as having two parts by defining an *Item* to be a record. Here, the *Data* field is a packed array of characters holding our task names, and the *Next* field points to another *Item*. Thus, this declaration exactly parallels our concept of a list item as a box with two parts.

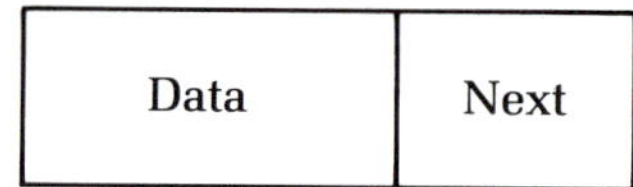


After we declare these new types that involve pointers, we also need to declare a variable that will indicate the first item on our list. Thus, we write

```
Var First: ListPointer;
```

Alternatively, we could write

```
Var First: ^Item;
```

In either case, our variable declaration specifies a new variable that we will be able to use to find the beginning of our list.

## Initialization

In the previous section, we noted that in reading through a list, we need to know when we come to the end of our list. We must know when an arrow does not point to a new box, and we notated this end by placing a line through the *Next* part of a box.

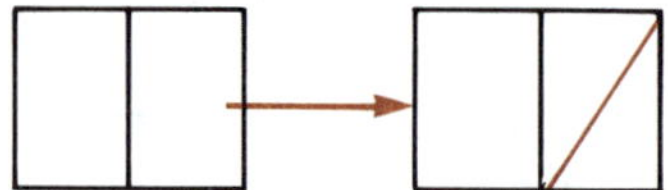

In Pascal, the value **Nil** is used to indicate that a pointer does not specify a new item.

Using this value, we normally initialize our first pointer to *nil*

```
First := Nil;
```

at the beginning of our program, since we start our program with no items on our list. Then as we add items to our list, *First* is updated to point to these new items. Also, we can use this *nil* value to check when we reach the end of our list. When a *Next* field is *nil*, we know we have found the last list item.

## Manipulation of Pointers and Items

Suppose we have built a list of tasks, such as that shown in Figure 15–2. We now consider how to manipulate pointers and items to print our list.

From our discussion of printing in the previous section, we need to declare another variable that we can move along our list as we print. Thus, we begin

```
Var ListElt: ListPointer;
```

Then, our processing starts by examining the first element on our list. At first, *ListElt* points to the same item as the *First* pointer, and we use the assignment

```
ListElt := First;
```

The assignment statement makes the two pointers indicate the same item. At this point, *First* and *ListElt* are arrows that point to our first list item. (See Figure 15–9.)

Next, we want to work with the box at the end of our arrow. In Pascal,

FIGURE 15–9 • **Distinguishing Pointers and Items**

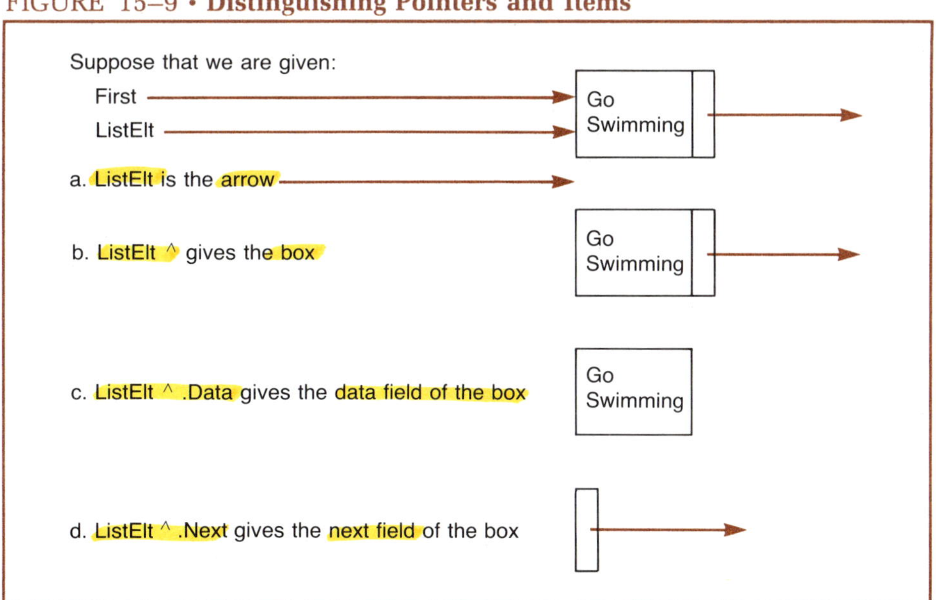

this is the second use of the upward arrow ↑ or caret ^. When we want the information that an arrow points to, we follow our pointer with the ^. Here,

- *ListElt* is the arrow, and
- *ListElt^* is the item specified by the arrow.

(See Figure 15–9.) Thus, by using the upward arrow, we can distinguish between a pointer and an item itself.

Once we have our item *ListElt^*, we work with it just as with any of the variables we have encountered before. In this case, *ListElt^* specifies an item which is a record. In printing, we want to write the data in the record. As in the past, we precede a field by a period, so

```
.Data
```

specifies the task name within our box. Putting this field together with the box specification, we find

```
ListElt^.Data
```

allows us to work with the data field inside the box pointed to by the pointer *ListElt*. Then, to print out this field in our program, we state

```
Writeln(ListElt^.Data);
```

When we want to move from one box to the next, a similar sequence allows us to update our *ListElt*. In particular,

- ListElt — points to the box in the list we are currently considering;
- ListElt^ — is the current box itself; and
- ListElt^.Next — is the next pointer in the current box.

Then, in moving from one list item to the next, we need to update *ListElt* to the next pointer, *ListElt^.Next*. Again, this involves the assignment:

```
ListElt := ListElt^.Next
```

With this discussion, we now can write out the entire code for printing our list.

```
Procedure Print (First: ListPointer);
      Var   ListElt: ListPointer;
      Begin
            ListElt := First;
            While  (ListElt <> Nil)
                Do Begin
                    Writeln(ListElt^.Data);
                    ListElt := ListElt^.Next
                End
      End {Print} ;
```

This procedure illustrates several important features about using pointers in Pascal. We can use assignment statements to change what a pointer is pointing to. In addition, a *nil* value allows us to determine when we come to the end of a list. Finally, we can move from a pointer to the item pointed to by adding an upward arrow ↑ or caret ^ to our variable. Here, we say we are **dereferencing** the pointer. The pointer itself gives a reference to an item. Adding the arrow ↑ or caret ^ gives us the item itself.

## Storage Allocation

Now that we have seen how to move from one list item to another when we print our list data, we turn to the creation and elimination of list items. Here, we find that list items are stored differently than other information. Up to now, storage for variables was created each time functions and procedures were called, and this space was freed when the functions and procedures finished. Such storage represents **static storage allocation;** within a function or procedure, this storage does not change.

In contrast, items that are specified by pointers can be created and destroyed within a function or procedure. Such storage is called **dynamic storage allocation.** For example, when we want to add an item to a list, we will need to explicitly create some space for the new data; when we want to delete an item, we will explicitly dispose of the old item.

This dynamic creation and deallocation of storage space are performed with two new procedures, *New* and *Dispose.* To see how these procedures work, suppose we have the declaration:

```
Var Elt:^ Item;
```

Then

*New(Elt)* allocates a new box for an item, and the variable *Elt* points to that new space.

*Dispose(Elt)* deallocates the box pointed to by the variable *Elt.*

## Special Cases for Insertion and Deletion

To illustrate how these procedures are used, we consider two special cases that occur in our task problem.

**Case 1: Insertion of New Task at Start of List.** To add an item to the start of our list, we declare a pointer variable.

```
Var NewItem: ListPointer;
```

After this declaration, we start our insertion by allocating the space for *NewItem* with the statement

```
New(NewItem); {Create Box for NewItem}
```

Next, we read the name of the task as data for the item. If we do this reading in a procedure *ReadData*, we might write

```
ReadData (NewItem^.Data);
```

Then, we need to change arrows, so that *NewItem* appears at the start of our list. In particular, the previous head of the list should come after *NewItem:*

```
NewItem^.Next := First;
```

Then, the *NewItem* should be put first:

```
First := NewItem;
```

These steps are shown in Figure 15–10.

**Case 2: Deletion of an Item from Middle of List.** To delete an item from a list, we follow our steps from Figure 15–7 (Section 15.1) carefully. Recall that in this process we need to keep track of the item to be deleted and the previous item on the list. Thus, our declarations include

```
Var PrevElt, ListElt: ListPointer;
```

Then, we search our list to find the item that we wish to delete. Such a search may be performed by a procedure call

```
FindPrevious (Name, PrevElt, First);
```

which locates *PrevElt*, the item that precedes the *Name* on the list given by the *First* pointer. Then

```
ListElt := PrevElt^.Next;
```

gives the item actually deleted. Next, we remove our element from the list by changing the previous list item. Again, following Step 2 of Figure 15–7, we write

```
PrevElt^.Next := List Elt^.Next;
```

Finally, we can throw away the old item with

```
Dispose (ListElt);
```

With these cases, we see that our insertion and deletion steps follow our discussions and figures from the previous section. We just translate the pictures into Pascal. We also have to be careful about those possibilities where our list does not contain any elements or when we need to work with the first item on our list.

FIGURE 15–10 • **Insertion of New Task at Start of List**

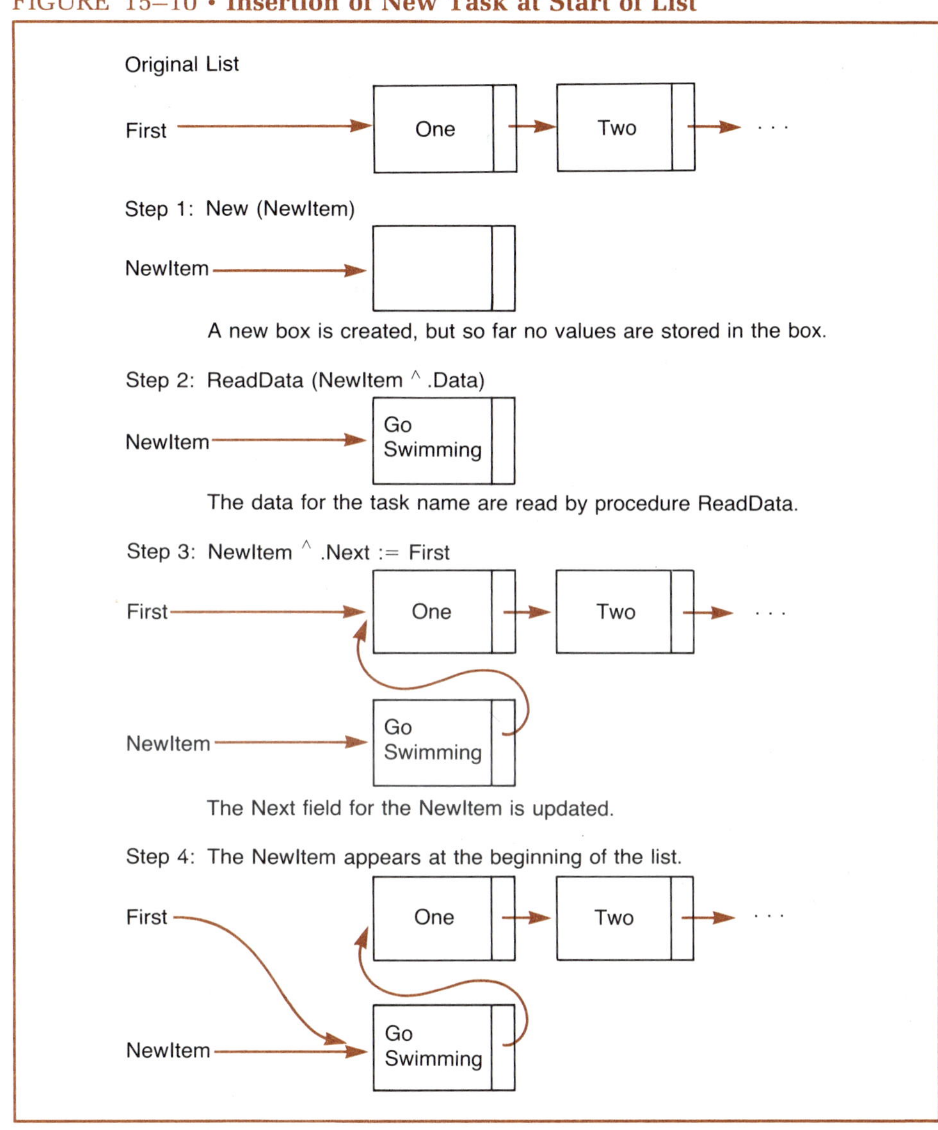


The final program to perform these operations for Problem 15.2 is given below. Here, we will define two separate procedures, *ReadData* and *FindPrevious*, to read names from the terminal and to find names on our list. We will also write the program as a series of procedures which are driven by a single menu. This program illustrates most of the features of pointers and list items that we have discussed in this section.

```
Program TaskList (Input, Output);
{This program maintains a list of tasks}

Const Max = 20;     {Length of task names}

Type ListData = Packed Array [1..Max] of Char;
     ListPointer = ^Item;
     Item = Record
          Data: ListData;
          Next: ListPointer
          End;
Var NullChar: Char;        {the null character, Chr(0)}

Procedure Initialization(Var First: ListPointer);
{This procedure initializes all appropriate variables}
    Begin
        First := Nil;
        NullChar := Chr(0)
    End {Initialization} ;

Procedure ReadData (Var Name: ListData);
{This procedure reads a name from the terminal}
    Var Index: Integer;
    Begin
        Index := 1;
        While (Index <= Max) and Not Eoln
          Do Begin
            Read (Name[Index]);
            Index := Index + 1
          End;
        Readln;
        While (Index <= Max)
          Do Begin
            Name[Index] := NullChar;
            Index := Index + 1
          End
    End {ReadData} ;

Procedure FindPrevious (Name: ListData; Var PrevElt: ListPointer;
                        First: ListPointer);
{This procedure locates the task that comes before given name on the list.
 If the name is not found, PrevElt^.Next will be Nil.
 The procedure assumes the Name is not the first list element.}

    Var ListElt: ListPointer;  {This pointer gives the list item
                                where the Name is checked}

    Function Done: Boolean;
    {This function determines if more items must be searched on the list}
        Begin
            If ListElt = Nil
                Then Done := True
                Else Done := (Name = ListElt^.Data)
        End {Done} ;
```

```
    Begin {FindPrevious}
        PrevElt := First;
        ListElt := PrevElt^.Next;
        While Not Done
          Do Begin
            PrevElt := ListElt;
            ListElt := PrevElt^.Next
          End
    End {FindPrevious} ;

Procedure AddName( Var First: ListPointer);
{This procedure reads a task name and inserts it into the list}

    Var NewItem: ListPointer;
        OldName: ListData;

    Procedure InsertFirst (NewItem: ListPointer; Var First: ListPointer);
    {This procedure inserts the new item at the beginning of the list}
        Begin
            NewItem^.Next := First;
            First := NewItem
        End;

    Procedure InsertAfterFirst (NewItem, First: ListPointer);
    {The procedure inserts the new item after the start of the list}
        Var PrevElt: ListPointer;

        Begin
            FindPrevious (OldName, PrevElt, First);
            NewItem^.Next := PrevElt^.Next;
            PrevElt^.Next := NewItem
        End {InsertAfterFirst} ;

    Begin {AddName}
        New(NewItem);
        Write ('Enter new task: ');
        ReadData (NewItem^.Data);
        If First = Nil
            Then InsertFirst (NewItem, First)
            Else Begin
                Writeln ('Enter old task which new task should preceed, ');
                Write ('or enter a blank if new task should be ',
                        'placed "last": ');
                ReadData(OldName);
                If OldName = First^.Data
                    Then InsertFirst (NewItem, First)
                    Else InsertAfterFirst(NewItem, First)
            End
    End {AddName} ;

Procedure DeletionName(Var First: ListPointer);
{This procedure reads a task name and deletes the name from the list}
    Var Name: ListData;

    Procedure DeleteName (Name: ListData; Var First: ListPointer);
    {This procedure deletes the name from the specified list}
        Var PrevElt, ListElt: ListPointer;
```

```
    Begin
        If First^.Data = Name
            Then Begin {delete first element on list}
                ListElt := First;
                First := ListElt^.Next;
                Dispose(ListElt)
                End
            Else Begin
                FindPrevious (Name, PrevElt, First);
                ListElt := PrevElt^.Next;
                If ListElt = Nil
                      Then Writeln ('Task not found on list')
                      Else Begin
                          PrevElt^.Next := ListElt^.Next;
                          Dispose(ListElt)
                          End
                End
    End {DeleteName} ;
    Begin
        If First = Nil
            Then Writeln ('List is empty - no deletions are possible')
            Else Begin
                Write ('Enter task name to be deleted: ');
                ReadData(Name);
                DeleteName (Name, First)
                End
    End {DeletionStep} ;

Procedure Print(First: ListPointer);
{This procedure prints the current data items on the list}
    Var ListElt: ListPointer;
    Begin
        Writeln ('The list of tasks are:');
        Writeln;
        ListElt := First;
        While (ListElt <> Nil)
          Do Begin
            Writeln (ListElt^.Data);
            ListElt := ListElt^.Next
          End;
        Writeln;
        Writeln ('End of List');
        Writeln
    End {Print} ;

Procedure ProcessFromMenu;
{This procedure presents the menu options and calls the requested task}
    Var First: ListPointer;     {pointer to the first list item}
        Option: Char;           {user response to menu selection}
    Begin
        Initialization(First);
        Repeat
            Writeln ('Options available');
            Writeln ('I - Insert a task into the list');
            Writeln ('D - Delete a task from the list');
            Writeln ('P - Print the tasks on the list');
            Writeln ('Q - Quit');
```

```
            Write   ('Enter desired option: ');
            Readln (Option);
            If Option in ['i','I','d','D','p','P','q','Q']
                Then Case Option of
                    'I', 'i': AddName(First);
                    'D', 'd': DeletionName(First);
                    'P', 'p': Print(First);
                    'Q', 'q':
                    End
                Else Writeln ('Invalid Option - Try Again!')
        Until (Option = 'Q') Or (Option = 'q')
    End {ProcessFromMenu} ;

Begin {Main}
    Writeln ('Program to Maintain a List of Tasks');
    ProcessFromMenu
End {Main} .
```

A sample run of this program follows.

```
Program to Maintain a List of Tasks
Options available
I - Insert a task into the list
D - Delete a task from the list
P - Print the tasks on the list
Q - Quit
Enter desired option: I
Enter new task: do homework
Options available
I - Insert a task into the list
D - Delete a task from the list
P - Print the tasks on the list
Q - Quit
Enter desired option: i
Enter new task: go swimming
Enter old task which new task should preceed,
or enter a blank if new task should be "last": do homework
Options available
I - Insert a task into the list
D - Delete a task from the list
P - Print the tasks on the list
Q - Quit
Enter desired option: p
The list of tasks are:

go swimming
do homework

End of List

Options available
I - Insert a task into the list
D - Delete a task from the list
```

```
P - Print the tasks on the list
Q - Quit
Enter desired option: i
Enter new task: mow lawn
Enter old task which new task should preceed,
or enter a blank if new task should be "last": do homework
Options available
I - Insert a task into the list
D - Delete a task from the list
P - Print the tasks on the list
Q - Quit
Enter desired option: p
The list of tasks are:

go swimming
mow lawn
do homework

End of List

Options available
I - Insert a task into the list
D - Delete a task from the list
P - Print the tasks on the list
Q - Quit
Enter desired option: d
Enter task name to be deleted: do homework
Options available
I - Insert a task into the list
D - Delete a task from the list
P - Print the tasks on the list
Q - Quit
Enter desired option: p
The list of tasks are:

go swimming
mow lawn

End of List

Options available
I - Insert a task into the list
D - Delete a task from the list
P - Print the tasks on the list
Q - Quit
Enter desired option: q
```

## SECTION 15.3 DOUBLY LINKED LISTS

Up to this point, our lists have been structured so we can start at the front and move efficiently item by item to the end. However, in many applications, we need more flexibility than this. For example, consider the following:

## PROBLEM 15.3 Recording and Retrieving Golf Scores

In recording scores for a golf tournament, we enter the name and score of the player as the player finishes. This information is to be retrieved in each of the following ways.

- Scores and names can be printed in order by ascending or by descending scores.
- Given the name of a player, other players with the same score can be printed.

### Discussion of Problem 15.3.

This problem requires the frequent updating of names and scores and the ordering of the information. Such requirements naturally suggest a linked list structure. However, here a simple linked list is difficult to use efficiently because all of the pointers move in one logical direction from the start to the end. This structure makes it hard to print the list in reverse order or to move backward from a given name.

To resolve these difficulties we consider a new type of structure, called a **doubly linked list,** where each item contains a pointer to the previous item as well as to the next one. A doubly linked list for this problem is shown in Figure 15–11.

This figure illustrates several important features of a doubly linked list. Each item on the list contains two pointers as well as some data. Thus, this doubly linked list might use either of the following declarations.

```
Const Length = 30;
Type  ListPtr = ^Item;
      Name = Packed Array [1..Length] of Char;
      Item =   Record
               Score: Integer;
               Player: Name;
               Previous: ListPtr;
               Next: ListPtr
               End;
Var   First:  ListPtr;
      Last:   ListPtr;
```

FIGURE 15–11 • **A Doubly Linked List with Golf Data**

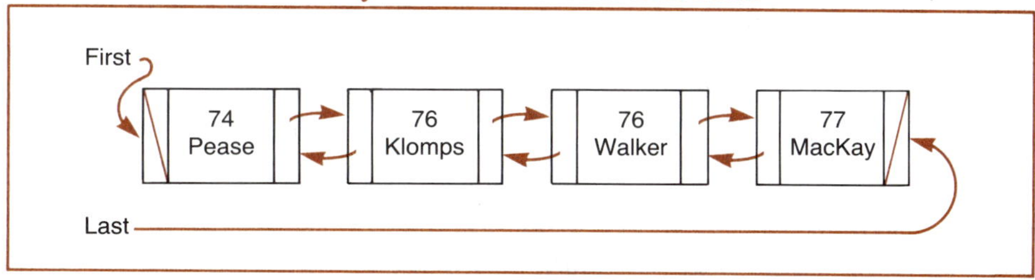

In this declaration, we list *Score* and *Name* as two separate data fields. In the next declaration, these fields are combined as parts of a single data field.

```
Const Length = 30;
Type ListPtr = ^Item;
     Name = Packed Array [1..Length] of Char;
     Item = Record
              Data = Record
                 Score: Integer;
                 Player: Name
                 End;
              Previous: ListPtr;
              Next: ListPtr
              End;
Var  First:  ListPtr;
     Last:   ListPtr;
```

With these declarations, the *Data* fields store appropriate scores and names, the *Previous* field points to the previous item on the list, and the *Next* field specifies the next item on the list. The *First* and *Last* pointers give the ends of the list, and we use *nil* to specify an end of our list.

With this structure, we can perform the same general operations we discussed for simple lists, namely

- printing the data on the list;
- inserting or deleting an item; and
- finding and perhaps modifying an item.

However, here the pointers going backward as well as forward simplify some of these operations and expand our capabilities.

**Printing.** We now can print the list in reverse order just as easily as in the normal order. To print from the first to last item, we start with the item specified by the *First* pointer, and we then proceed item by item using the *Next* field of each item. To print in reverse order, we start with the item specified by the *Last* pointer. Then we proceed item by item using the *Previous* field of each item.

**Insertion and Deletion.** In these operations, we can follow the same general steps that we discussed for simple lists in Section 15.1. However, now we must take care of backward pointers as well as forward ones. This suggests the following main steps for insertion into a doubly linked list.

*Step 1.* Determine where item will be inserted.
*Step 2.* Create a new box or record.
*Step 3.* Place data in new record.
*Step 4.* Make *Previous* and *Next* pointers of new record specify the appropriate list elements.

FIGURE 15–12 • **Insertion into a Doubly Linked List**

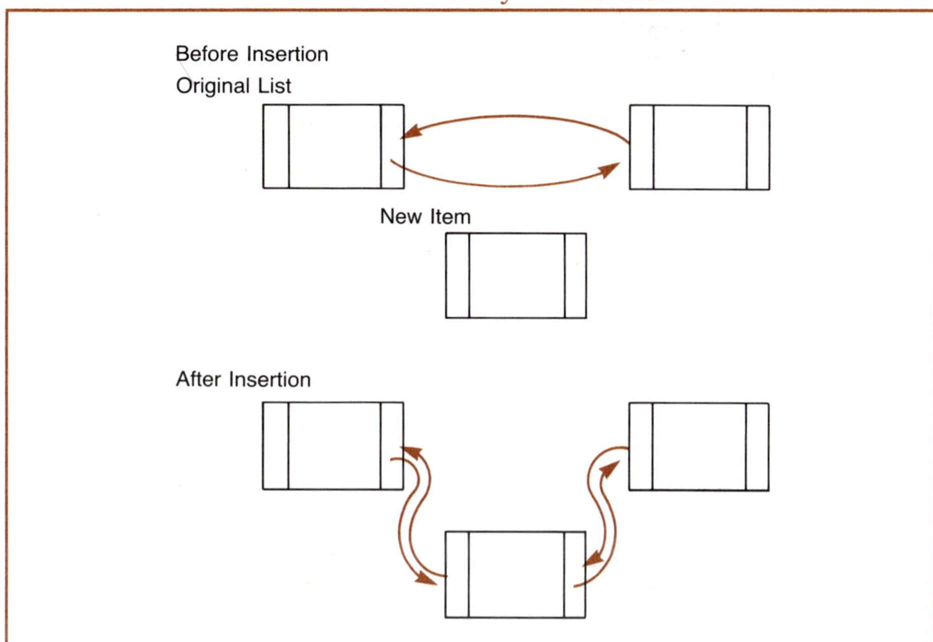


*Step 5.* Update the *Next* pointer in the previous record to specify the newly created record.

*Step 6.* Update the *Previous* pointer in the next record to specify the newly created record.

The final pointers are shown in Figure 15–12.

With this outline, the programming details for doubly linked lists now proceed in much the same way as singly linked lists. However, in this process, we must remember to modify the *Previous* pointers as well as the *Next* ones. In addition, we organize our list of scores in ascending order, and we insert a new score on the basis of this ordering. The necessary details are seen in the following revised *Find* and *Insert* procedures for doubly linked lists.

```
Procedure Insert (Var First, Last: ListPtr);
{This procedure inserts a new element into an ordered, doubly linked list}
    Var Element: ListPtr;

    Procedure Enter (Var Element: ListPtr);
    {This procedure reads a name and score from the terminal
     and creates a new record for this data}
```

```
    Var Index: Integer;
    Begin
        New (Element);
        With Element^
          Do Begin
            Write ('Enter player''s name: ');
            {Read Name From Terminal}
            Index := 0;
            While (Index < Length) And Not Eoln
              Do Begin
                Index := Index + 1;
                Read (Player[Index])
              End;
            Readln;

            {Fill rest of string with nulls}
            While (Index < Length)
              Do Begin
                Index := Index + 1;
                Player[Index] := Chr(0)
              End;

            Write ('Enter player''s score: ');
            Readln (Score);

            Previous := Nil;
            Next := Nil
          End;
    End {Enter} ;

Procedure InsertInOrder (Element: ListPtr; Var First, Last: ListPtr);
{This procedure inserts the given Element on the List}

    Var PrevElt: ListPtr;

    Procedure Find (Var PrevElt: ListPtr; Element, First: ListPtr);
    {This procedure returns the record on the list that preceeds the
     specified element}

        Function MoveNeeded: Boolean;
        {This function determines if the specified element must be
         inserted further in the list}
            Begin
                If PrevElt^.Next = Nil
                    Then MoveNeeded := False
                    Else MoveNeeded :=
                            (PrevElt^.Next^.Score <= Element^.Score)
            End {MoveNeeded} ;

        Begin {Find}
            PrevElt := First;
            While MoveNeeded
                Do PrevElt := PrevElt^.Next
        End {Find} ;
```

```
    Procedure InsertAfter (PrevElt, Element: ListPtr; Var Last: ListPtr);
    {This procedure inserts the Element after the PrevElt on the list}
        Begin
            Element^.Next := PrevElt^.Next;
            Element^.Previous := PrevElt;
            If (PrevElt^.Next = Nil)
                Then Last := Element
                Else PrevElt^.Next^.Previous := Element;
            PrevElt^.Next := Element
        End {InsertAfter} ;

    Begin {InsertInOrder}

        If First = Nil
            Then Begin {List is empty}
                Element^.Next := First;
                First := Element;
                Last := Element
                End
            Else If (Element^.Score < First^.Score)
                Then Begin {Insert before head of list}
                    Element^.Next := First;
                    First^.Previous := Element;
                    First := Element
                    End
                Else Begin {Insert after head}
                    Find (PrevElt, Element, First);
                    InsertAfter (PrevElt, Element, Last)
                    End;

    End {InsertInOrder} ;

Begin {Insert}
    Enter (Element);
    InsertInOrder (Element, First, Last)

End {Insert} ;
```

These procedures are quite similar to the corresponding ones for singly linked lists; the major changes involve the updating of *Previous* pointers as well as *Next* ones and some modification of our search operation. The deletion operation for doubly linked lists requires similar modifications; we leave the details as an exercise.

### Discussion of Problem 15.3 (continued)

Now that we have introduced this doubly linked structure, we return to Problem 15.3. In storing scores and names, we will maintain a doubly linked list, ordered by name. With our comments on printing, we can print our data in ascending and descending order quite easily. Our remaining task involves printing the names of all people who shot the same score as a given person. This task illustrates further the considerable flexibility that we can obtain by adding the *Previous* pointers to our list elements.

One natural way to print these names involves the following general steps.

**I.** Determine name.
**II.** Find name on list.
If name not found, stop.
**III.** Look up score for given name.
**IV.** Move backward along list to find first item with the given score.
  **A.** If a previous field is *nil*, we have the first entry.
  **B.** If previous field is not *nil*, look at previous record.
    **1.** If previous record's score is same, move to previous item and repeat this step.
    **2.** If previous record's score is different, stop.
**V.** Move forward along list. Continue until end of list or until score changes.
  **A.** Print name and score.
  **B.** Move to next item.

This outline gives rise to the following procedure.

```
Procedure PrintSameScore (First: ListPtr);
{This procedure prints the names of those players that scored the same
 as a given player.}

    Var Element: ListPtr;
        Person: Name;

    Procedure Determine (Var Person: Name);
    {This procedure reads a name from the terminal}
        Var Index: Integer;
        Begin
            Write ('Enter Player''s Name: ');
            {Read Name From Terminal}
            Index := 0;
            While (Index < Length) And Not Eoln
              Do Begin
                Index := Index + 1;
                Read (Person[Index])
              End;
            Readln;

            {Fill rest of string with nulls}
            While (Index < Length)
              Do Begin
                Index := Index + 1;
                Person[Index] := Chr(0)
              End
        End {Determine} ;

    Procedure Find (Person: Name; Var Element: ListPtr; First: ListPtr);
    {This procedure finds the Element on the List where the
     player's name is the given Person}
```

```
    Function Done: Boolean;
    {This Function determines when the search of the list is done}
        Begin
            If Element = Nil
                Then Done := True
                Else Done := (Person = Element^.Player)
        End {Done} ;

    Begin {Find}
        Element := First;
        While Not Done
          Do Element := Element^.Next
    End {Find} ;

Procedure FindFirstScore (Var Element: ListPtr);
{This procedure moves backward along the list to find the first
 element with the given score}

    Function BackUp: Boolean;
    {This function determines if we should move to the previous
     element in the list}
        Begin
            If (Element^.Previous = Nil)
                Then BackUp := False
                Else BackUp :=
                        (Element^.Score = Element^.Previous^.Score)
        End {BackUp} ;

    Begin {FindFirstScore}
        While Backup
            Do Element := Element^.Previous
    End {FindFirstScore} ;

Procedure PrintPlayers (Element: ListPtr);
{This procedure prints the names of the players with the same score as
 found in the given element}

    Function Continue: Boolean;
    {This Function determines if printing should continue
     with the next element}
        Begin
            If Element^.Next = Nil
                Then Continue := False
                Else Continue :=
                        Element^.Score = Element^.Next^.Score
        End {Continue} ;

    Begin {PrintPlayers}
        Writeln ('The following players shot a score of ',
                  Element^.Score:1);
        Writeln (Element^.Player);
        While Continue
          Do Begin
            Element := Element^.Next;
            Writeln (Element^.Player)
            End
    End {PrintPlayers} ;
```

```
Begin {PrintSameScore}
    Determine (Person);
    Find (Person, Element, First);
    If (Element = Nil)
        Then Writeln ('Player not found on list')
        Else Begin
            FindFirstScore (Element);
            PrintPlayers (Element)
            End
End {PrintSameScore} ;
```

With this procedure, we see that doubly linked lists allow us to move both backward and forward along our lists very easily. The backward pointers have added considerable flexibility to our capabilities for processing.

In the next section, we see how the addition of other pointers can increase this flexibility and capacity even further.

## SECTION 15.4 MORE GENERAL LINKED STRUCTURES

In the previous section, we used pointers to previous list items as well as pointers to later ones to permit more flexibility in our retrieval of data. In this section, we further expand our retrieval capabilities by adding more pointers to form more general structures.

First, we consider a problem where we need to maintain our data records in several lists. Here, we will need to store several different types of information, and pointers will be needed to organize records of different types. Further, we will find that some records will need several pointers, with one set of pointers for one type of data and a second set of pointers for another type of data.

## PROBLEM 15.4 A Very Simple Date Book

A date book contains information on special events, scheduled meetings, and important commitments for various days throughout the year. For this date book, we need the following capabilities:

adding appointments for any specified day;

printing appointments for a given day; and

printing all appointments.

Develop a data structure for this date book.

### Discussion of Problem 15.4

In this problem, we must deal with two types of information:

1. dates (month, day, year)
2. appointments for a given date

In considering this data and the requirements we have for processing, we can make several observations and conclusions. First, we can expect many additions to our list as our schedule fills up. Thus, we will want the flexibility of a linked structure to store our data. Second, there will be some days on which no appointments are scheduled, while other days are heavily scheduled. Overall, we must be prepared to handle a large number of commitments, which may not be evenly distributed through the year. Finally, once we have scheduled many appointments, we do not want to take the time to search through all of them when we add new ones or print our schedule for a given day. A list of all our appointments is likely to be too long for a linear search to be adequate.

With these observations, we conclude that a simple linear list of appointments is unlikely to meet our processing demands. However, we do need the flexibility that a list structure gives us. To meet these needs, we use a structure that separates the dates and the appointments for the day. In particular, we form one linked list for the dates that have appointments. Then, for each date, we have a list of appointments for that day. Such a structure is shown in Figure 15–13.

FIGURE 15–13 • **A Data Structure for a Simple Date Book**

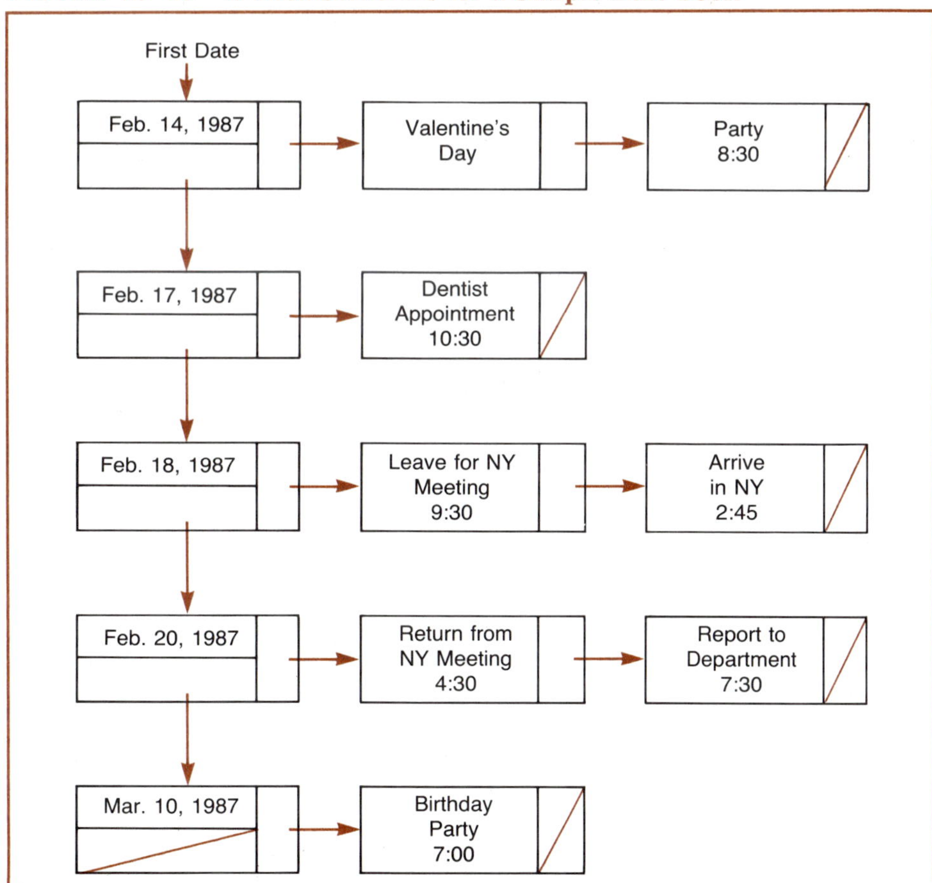

Such a structure requires two separate types of records. Dates must include month, day, and year information, a pointer to the first appointment on that date, and a pointer to the next date. Appointments must contain character data and a pointer to the next appointment. The appropriate declarations follow.

```
Const Length = 60;
Type  DatePtr = ^Date;
      ApptPtr = ^Appointment;
      Date = Record
             Month: 1..12;
             Day: 1..31;
             Year: Integer;
             FirstAppt: ApptPtr;
             NextDate: DatePtr
             End;
      Appointment = Record
             Data: Packed Array [1..Length] of Char;
             Next: ApptPtr
             End;
Var   FirstDate: DatePtr;
```

With these declarations, we consider the dates as a simple linked list, with *FirstDate* specifying the initial item on our list and the *NextDate* field indicating how to proceed from one date to the next.

Then, for a given date, we have another simple list. Here the *FirstAppt* field for our date specifies the initial item on our list and the *Next* field for each appointment indicates how we can proceed from one appointment to the next.

**Outline for Insertion of a New Appointment.** Next, we consider the operations we will need to solve our problem. In outlining the insertion operations we find we need to proceed in two steps (plus data entry), following the organization of our data.

**I.** Enter date and appointment information.
**II.** Starting with date specified by *FirstDate*, search the date list for the specified date.
  **A.** If the date is found, work with the existing date record.
  **B.** If the date is not found:
    **1.** Create a new record for this date.
    **2.** Store day, month, year data in the record.
    **3.** Set *FirstAppt* field to *nil*.
    **4.** Insert new date record into date list.
    **5.** Work with this new date record.

**III.** With the given date record, insert appointment.
  **A.** Create new appointment record.
  **B.** Store new appointment data.
  **C.** Insert new appointment into appointment list for the given date.

In this work, both Steps II and III follow the same procedures that we used before in singly linked lists. The new feature here is the combining of these lists as part of a more complex structure.

**Outline for Printing Appointments for a Given Date.** Similarly, our printing requires two steps (beyond data entry).

**I.** Enter date.
**II.** Search list of dates to find the one specified.
  **A.** Start with date specified by first date.
  **B.** Use *NextDate* field to find successive dates.
**III.** When date record is found, print list for that date.
  **A.** Start with appointment specified by the date's *FirstAppt* field.
  **B.** Continue while appointment pointer is not *nil*.
    **1.** Print appointment information.
    **2.** Use next field to find next appointment.

The printing of all appointments combines Steps II and III in a loop.

In analyzing this structure, we can identify several important features. By using list structures, we maintain the flexibility that we need for easy insertion and deletion of items. In addition, by separating dates from appointments, we can reduce our search time considerably, since we only have to search one record for each date. We may have several appointments on certain dates, but our data structure does not require us to look at all of these appointments as we go from one date to another. Thus, we are able to ignore many appointments that occur on dates that do not interest us in a particular processing request. Finally, if we want to reduce searching time further, we could break down this data into more pieces. For example, we could consider

months,

days within a month, and

appointments for a given day.

Here, we could search a month list until we found the correct month, then we could search a day list for that month to find the correct date. Finally, the day record would specify our desired list of appointments.

More generally, the list structures in this example illustrate that pointers allow us to organize our data in many ways that allow easy storage and retrieval. We can order the same data records in several ways by using distinct pointers for separate lists. We also can separate our data into different types of records and then use distinct lists to tie these pieces together. In these data structures, the details of data organization may vary from one application to another. However, the basic ideas behind the list operations for insertion, deletion, and searching all depend on the simple cases for singly and doubly linked lists that we saw in the previous sections.

## SUMMARY

1. **Linked list data structures** allow us to store individual data elements, and these list elements are interconnected by **pointers.**
2. In a **singly linked list,** we declare a **pointer variable** that specifies the location of the first element on the list. Then, each subsequent list element includes a pointer to the next element until a *Nil* pointer marks the end of the list. With this structure, we include the operations *insert, delete, search,* and *print.*
3. These lists also motivate a discussion of storage allocation in computers.
   a. **Static storage** depends upon declarations in a Pascal program. This space is allocated when a function or procedure is called. In this allocation, all space requirements depend upon the variables declared, and the amount of this space does not change during procedure execution.
   b. With **dynamic storage,** a program can allocate and deallocate space as the program is running. The total amount of space used is not fixed by the variable declarations.
4. Beyond the singly linked structure, we find several variations of list structures.
   a. We can add pointers to previous data elements as well as to the next ones, and we can specify last items on lists as well as first ones. These additions introduce **doubly linked lists.**

### KEY TERMS, PHRASES, AND CONCEPTS

- Data Structure
- Doubly Linked Lists
- General Linked Structures
- List Data Structure
  - Operations
  - Delete
  - Find
  - Insert
  - Print
- Nil Pointers
- Pointers
  - Dereferencing
- Singly Linked Lists
- Storage Allocation
  - Dynamic
    - New
    - Dispose
  - Static

### ELEMENTS OF PASCAL SYNTAX

- *Dispose*
- Pointer, ↑ , ^ , or @
- *New*
- *Nil*

**b.** We can organize our data into several types of records, using pointers to move from one type of record to another. These **general linked structures** allow us great flexibility in organizing our information.

## EXERCISES

**15.1** *Outline for List Insertion.* Section 15.1 gives the basic steps required to insert a new piece of data into a list. The section also notes some complications that arise when insertion is actually attempted. Write an outline for list insertion that takes these complications into account.

**15.2** *Changing List Items.* Section 15.2 includes a program that inserts, deletes, and prints items on a list. Modify this program so that a user can change a task. In particular, write

```
Procedure ChangeListItem (Var First: ListPointer);
```

where ChangeListItem
- reads the name of a current task;
- finds the task on the list;
- asks for a revised task name; and
- changes the task name on the list.

**15.3** Write a complete outline for the solution of the problem in Section 15.2.

**15.4** *Insertion and Deletion for Ordered Lists.* Suppose that we want to maintain a simple linked list of names, so that the data are stored in alphabetical order.

**a.** Modify the Searching, Insertion, and Deletion outlines from Section 15.1 to reflect this alphabetical ordering of data. (When we insert data in this revised list, we will not have to enter where new data are to be inserted, since we can infer the location by checking alphabetical order.)

**b.** Write the Pascal procedures that follow these outlines.

**15.5** *Deletion of Duplicates.* Write a procedure that deletes duplicate records from a list.

**a.** Assume the list is ordered.

**b.** Assume the list is unordered.

After writing your procedures for parts (a) and (b), compare the number of steps required for each case.

**15.6** *Deletion and Modification of Doubly Linked Lists.* Section 15.3 introduces the concept of doubly linked lists and also presents the details required to insert new elements into such lists.

**a.** Write similar detailed outlines and procedures for deleting and for modifying elements in doubly linked lists.

**b.** Put these procedures together in a program that expands the golf scoring problem from Section 15.3.

**15.7** *Two-Round Golf Tournament.* A local golf tournament consists of two rounds of golf, played on different days. On the first day, names and scores in the first round are entered into the computer as the players finish their rounds. On the second day, the second-round scores will be added. This information is to be retrieved in each of the following ways.

- Scores and names can be printed in ascending order of scores for either round.
- Total scores, with names, can be printed in either ascending or descending order of scores.
- Given the name of a player, other players with the same total score can be printed.

**a.** Write a detailed outline to solve this two-round golf tournament scoring.

**b.** Write a program for this problem based on your outline.

**15.8** *Player Withdrawing from a Tournament.* Expand the program for the Two-Round Golf Tournament to allow a person to withdraw from the tournament. This operation will require a procedure that deletes the person's name from the first-round list and sometimes from the second-round list and total list.

**15.9** *Improving Average Search Time.* One way to improve the average time required for the linear search of a list is to group the frequently accessed items near the head of the list. A practical way to approximate this grouping involves the modification of the list after every search. In particular, whenever an item is found on the list, that item is moved to the front of the list. (Thus, if an item is found often, that item will stay close to the start. If an item is not used often, that item will gradually move back.) Write a search procedure that implements this list modification as a side effect.

**15.10** *Telephone Directory.* This problem applies the search improvement of the previous problem to the storage and retrieval of records for a telephone answering service that keeps track of commonly used names and telephone numbers. In particular, a program for a telephone answering service must perform the following tasks.

**I.** The user specifies a name, which is searched in an abbreviated telephone directory.

**II.** If the name is found:

  **A.** The person's name and telephone number are printed.

  **B.** The entry printed for that person is moved to the beginning of the list of names and numbers.

**III.** If the person is not found:

  **A.** The user is asked to verify that the name was typed correctly. (If the name was incorrect, the processing goes back to Step I.)

  **B.** The user is asked to look up the person's telephone number in a more complete directory (or call directory assistance, etc.) and enter the number from the terminal.

**C.** A new entry, with the new name and telephone number, is added to the beginning of the list.

Write a program to perform these tasks.

**15.11** *Expanded Directory.* Modify the program in the previous exercise so that retrieval by individual names uses this efficient list organization but also so that an alphabetical listing of names, with telephone numbers, is possible.

**15.12** *Recording Prescriptions.* A doctor keeps records on all her patients, including their names and all medicines prescribed.

**a.** Design a data structure to store each patient's name and all medicines prescribed for each patient. The structure must allow the doctor to obtain a complete list of her patients' names and a complete list of medicines for any specific patient. Your design should describe

1. the format in which data will be stored (e.g., include fields for all records); and
2. how data can be added, modified, and searched.

**b.** Write a program to implement your design.

CAUTION: In this problem, it should not be necessary to scan the entire data structure to obtain the desired results.

**15.13** Modify your work in the previous problem so that the doctor will also be able to obtain a list of all patients who have used a specified medicine.

# CHAPTER 16

# TREE DATA STRUCTURES AND RECURSION

This chapter ties together many of the programming topics that we have seen throughout this book by applying them in two basic ways. First, this chapter discusses *trees,* which constitute a second type of formal data structure. As with our discussion of linked lists, we consider trees both on a conceptual level and on the detailed level of programming in Pascal using records and pointers. Second, we will find that many needed tree operations are best performed by procedures and functions that call themselves, and this introduces the subject of *recursion*, where tasks call themselves. These subjects of trees and recursion will provide us with powerful tools to solve a wide variety of problems.

## SECTION 16.1 INTRODUCTION TO TREES

To introduce the concept of tree data structures, we first consider an organizational chart for a company. (See Figure 16–1.) This chart organizes personnel in a hierarchical structure and has the following characteristics.

1. Exactly one person, the president, appears at the top of the structure.
2. Under the president, several people, called vice presidents, are in positions that report directly to the president.

FIGURE 16–1 • **A Simple Hierarchical Structure Illustrating the Organization of a Corporation**

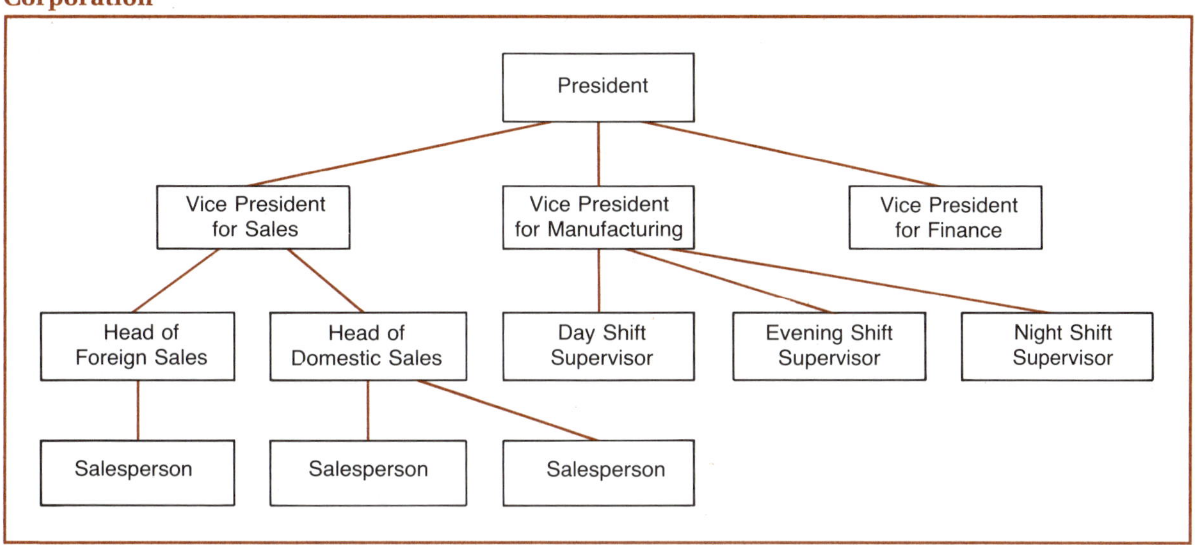


**3.** Moving down the structure, each person reports directly to exactly one person, and each person may supervise zero, one, or more others.

In the tree data structure, we generalize these characteristics. (See Figure 16–2.) In this structure, we store data in positions called **nodes.** In Figure 16–2, these nodes are shown as circles, and we have stored the letters 'a' through 'o' as our data. In Figure 16–1, the nodes contained the positions in the company as data. Further, these nodes are organized in a hierarchy. We now look at these nodes in more detail.

First, we introduce some terminology. Throughout this terminology, we might think of the structure as a family tree starting with one ancestor as the "root." The single node containing 'a' at the top of the tree structure is called the **root** of the tree. Further, each node, except the root, has exactly one other node above it. For example, the node containing 'e' has the 'b' node above it. In this situation, we say that the 'e' node has the 'b' node as its **parent,** and the 'e' node is the **child** of the 'b' node. We note that several nodes may have the same parent and one node may have several children. For example, the nodes containing 'g', 'h', and 'i' all have the 'c' node as parent. Further, it is not necessary for two nodes to have the same number of children. For example, the 'c' node and the 'l' nodes have three children each, but the 'b' and 'h' nodes have only two children. We say that two nodes with the same parent are **siblings.** Also, some nodes may not have any children. In a mixing of metaphors, such nodes are called **leaves.** In our example, the nodes containing 'j', 'f', 'g', 'k', 'm', 'n', 'o', 'i', and 'd' are leaves.

FIGURE 16–2 • **A Typical Tree Structure**

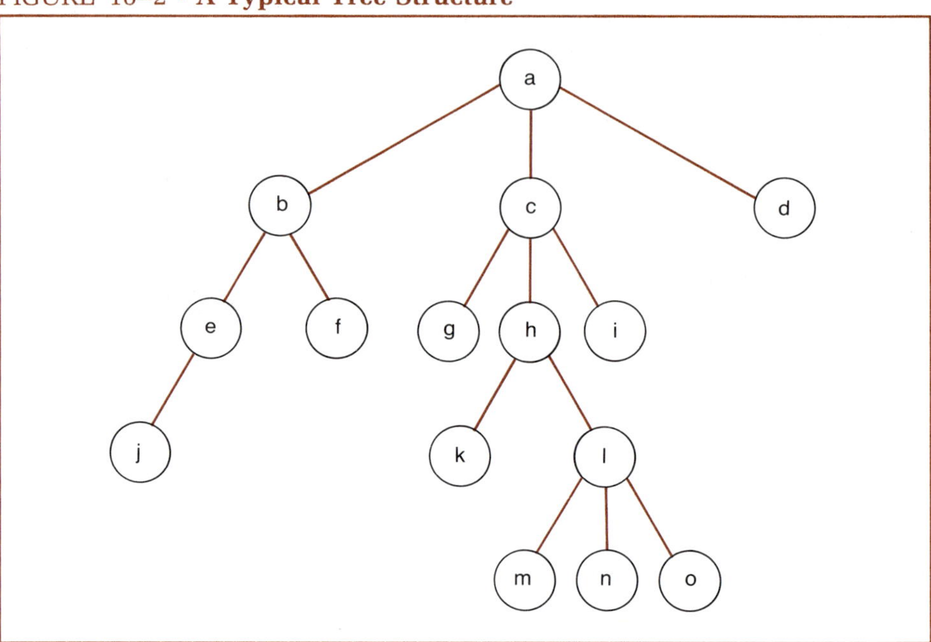


For any node, we may proceed upward from parent to parent. This line upward gives us the **ancestors** of the given node. For example, the ancestors of the 'k' node are the nodes containing 'h', 'c' and 'a'. As a special case, the root is an ancestor of every node in the tree (except itself). Similarly, starting at any node, we may move away from the root by selecting one child at each subsequent node until we reach a leaf. For example, starting with the 'c' node, we may pick the nodes containing 'h', 'l', and 'm'. Such a collection of nodes is called a **branch** of the tree, and the branch has the same general structure as a linked list. For any branch, there is a first element. Each element (except the final leaf) has a single successor.

This last observation that a branch of a tree forms a linked list also suggests another observation. We can view any singly linked list as a tree if we consider the first element of the list as the root and if we think of each successive item in the list as a child of the previous item. In this special tree, all list items or tree nodes lie on a single branch that starts with the root.

Finally, in any tree, we may get another tree by starting at any node and including all its descendants. For example, starting with the 'b' node, we include the nodes containing 'e', 'f' and 'j'. This small collection of nodes fit together in a hierarchical structure called a **subtree** of the original tree.

## Tree Operations

Now that we have identified the basic structure of a tree, we need to consider which operations we might want to apply to trees. As in our work with lists, the most common tree operations include

- finding and perhaps modifying a piece of data in a tree;
- printing the data in a tree;
- inserting a piece of data; and
- deleting data.

For insertion, we might place data in the middle of trees and at the end of trees to form new leaves. In this text, we will consider insertion of new data items only in the form of new leaves. Insertion within a tree can be more complex and is best left to more advanced texts.

Next, in considering the deletion operation, we can delete individual nodes and entire subtrees. In practice, deleting individual nodes can be more complex than deleting an entire subtree. This is because the children of a deleted node must be attached to a new parent node, for instance, the parent of the deleted node. Such an operation may require considerable care so that no nodes are lost by mistake.

## Binary Trees

Finally, within this general discussion of trees, we identify one special type of tree structure that arises frequently in applications. In this type of tree, each node may have only zero, one, or two children, as illustrated in Figure 16–3. Here, below each node, we think of children on the left and the right sides of the parent. In this situation, we also can add operations *Left* and

FIGURE 16–3 • **A Typical Binary Tree**

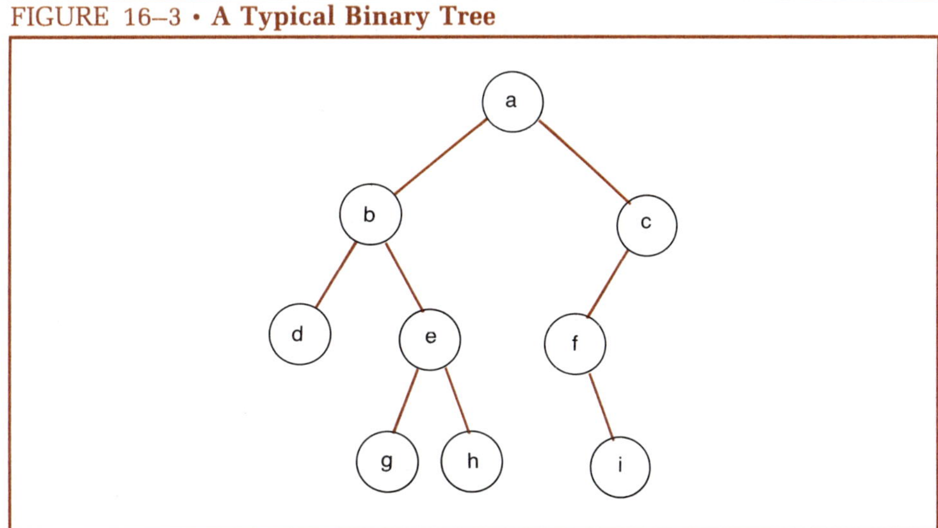

*Right*, which move us from one node to the appropriate child of that node. Trees with this special structure are called **binary trees,** and we will see several applications of them in the next section.

## SECTION 16.2 EXAMPLES

The last section considered the general structure of a tree, and it described some typical operations that we might want to perform on such a structure. In this section, we consider three applications that illustrate many of the common uses for these tree structures. In particular, we discuss

- tree representations of arithmetic structures;
- game trees; and
- ordering data in trees for efficient searching.

In each case, we will be able to utilize the hierarchical structure of trees to organize data efficiently.

### Tree Representations of Arithmetic Expressions

In our first example, we use trees to clarify the structure of arithmetic expressions. Specifically, we store both arithmetic operations (+, −, *, /) and numbers as the data in our nodes, and we use the connections between nodes to specify which operations are applied to which numbers and expressions. Several typical representations are illustrated in Figure 16–4.

The tree representation of the number 2 (Figure 16–4a) contains only one piece of data, and the tree contains only one node.

In the expression 2*3, the operation * is applied to the numbers 2 and 3. In this situation, we place * in the root node, and this node has two children containing the numbers 2 and 3. (See Figure 16–4b.) As our expressions become more complex, these individual pieces are linked in the tree. For example, when we represent 2*3 + 4, we first need to apply the * operation to the numbers 2 and 3. Then, we apply the + operation to the 4 and the result of the * operation. This process of evaluation is seen in the tree of Figure 16–4c, where the + has children (* and 4) and where the * in turn is applied to its children (2 and 3).

When we evaluate the operations in a different order, the corresponding changes are seen in the tree structure. For example, if we perform the addition before multiplication by adding parentheses in the expression 2 * (3 + 4), the root of the tree changes as do various relationships. (See Figure 16–4d.)

These examples illustrate several important properties of tree representation of arithmetic expressions.

1. The structure of a tree provides us with an unambiguous way of determining which operations should be applied to which objects.

FIGURE 16–4 • **Tree Representations of Arithmetic Expressions**

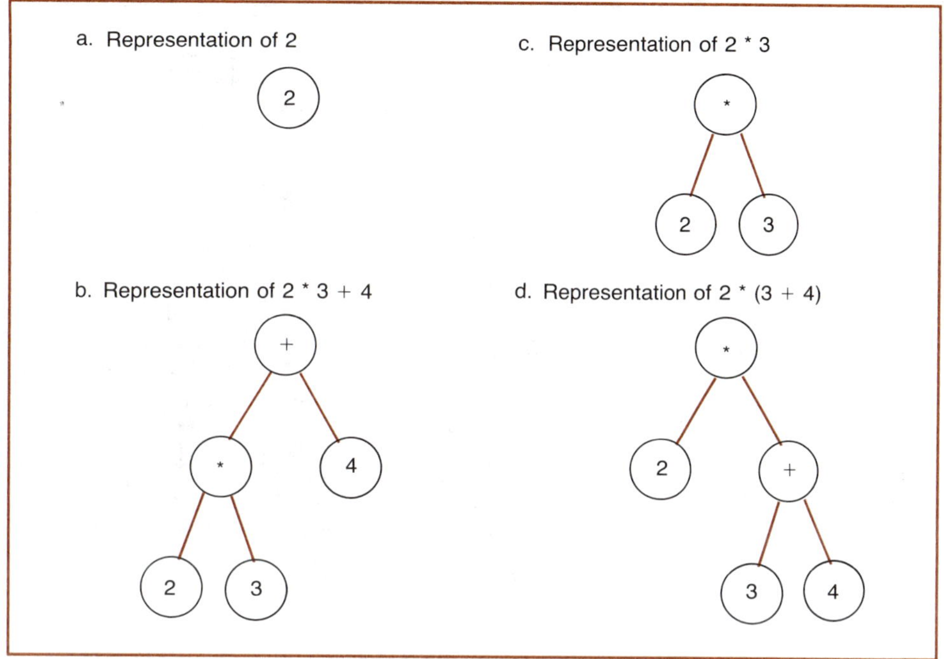


2. In structuring the tree, we do not have to store parentheses; the tree structure defines the appropriate relationships without parentheses.
3. In this application, the leaf nodes always contain numbers as data, and the nonleaves always contain operations.

## Game Trees

A second major application of trees involves the recording and analyzing of various possible moves in games. In this application, each node contains data for a particular situation that can arise in a game, and a connection from one node to its child represents a move in the game. This structure is seen more clearly if we look at two examples from Tic-Tac-Toe.

*Example 1:* In playing Tic-Tac-Toe, we can consider the current board position as the root of a tree, as shown in Figure 16–5. Then, from this root, we can consider all possible moves starting with a given board position, assuming *X* is to move next. Thus, in Figure 16–5, four squares are filled, and *X* could be placed on any of the remaining five squares. Then for each move by *X*, *O* could move into any of the remaining squares.

This game tree also illustrates one way that these structures are used in programming games in computers and in analyzing different potential moves. In particular, if *X* first moves into the lower right square, then any

FIGURE 16–5 • **A Complete Game Tree for a Specified Position**

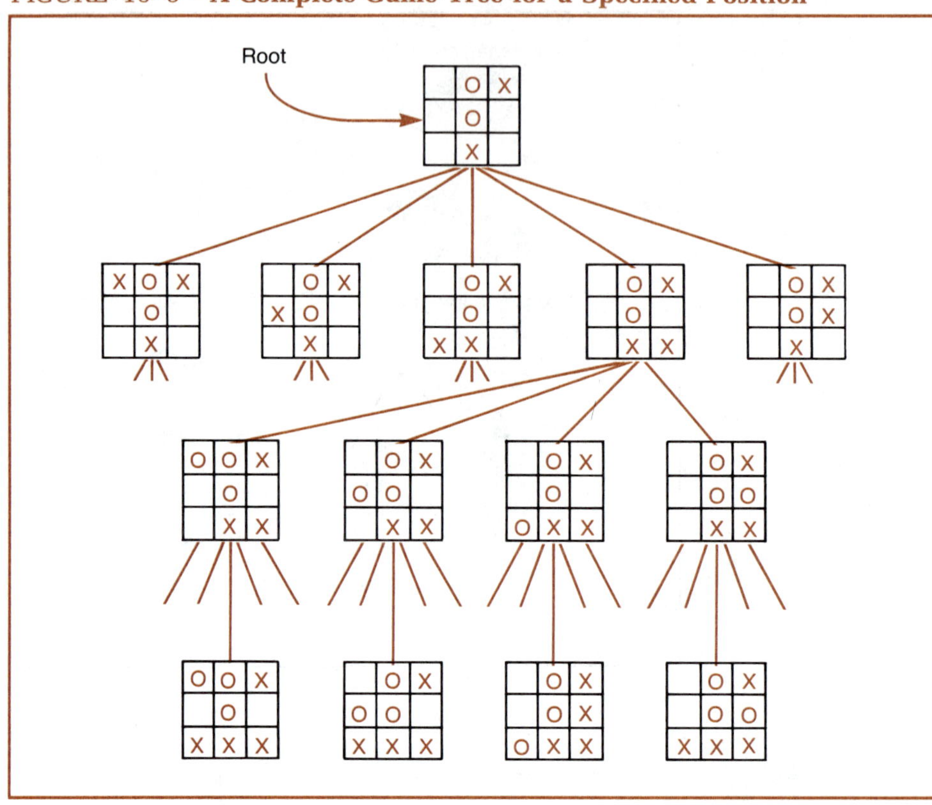


move for *O* can be followed by a win for *X*. Thus, from this position, our analysis of the tree shows that by a proper selection of moves, *X* can be assured of a win.

This observation is the basis for many of the game-playing programs now in existence. For a given position, a computer can build a game tree to determine what might happen after every possible move it could make. Then, by analyzing these possible consequences, the computer can select a move which is best.

*Example 2:* The previous example also shows one potential difficulty with the use of game trees in analyzing possible moves. In particular, starting with all possible first moves, the full game tree for Tic-Tac-Toe contains something like 900,000 nodes. Thus, even for a simple game, complete game trees can become very large, and the creation and analysis of such trees can take an unacceptably long length of time. For this reason, game trees that are used in game programs are abbreviated, or "pruned," in a variety of ways.

One way this may be done is to consider only a certain number of moves in the future in the tree. In this situation, we call the move by each player a "ply," and we may record only a specific number of "plies." A two-ply tree is shown in Figure 16–6. Such limited trees do not allow us to see all possible consequences of our moves, so in some cases we may not be able to be sure which of several moves is best. On the other hand, Figure 16–6 shows that even a two-ply tree can be enough in some cases. In that figure, all but one move for *O* results in an immediate win for *X*. Thus, the only hope *O* has is to move into the upper right box.

A second method tries to eliminate some branches by clever analysis. Once one branch can be identified to include a sure loss or a sure win, then no further analysis along that branch is needed.

In practice, sophisticated game programs use a variety of methods to prune trees in careful ways.

### Ordering Data in Trees for Efficient Searching

As our final application of this section, we consider an important way that data can be arranged in a tree so that searching can be done very efficiently.

A basic approach to arranging data is shown in Figure 16–7. In the figure, we start with a binary tree, with names entered as the data in each node. Then these nodes are arranged in a special way so that for any node the descendants along the left branch precede their ancestor in alphabetical order, and all descendants along a right branch follow their ancestor.

For example, in the figure if we start with the root, we obtain the name *MacKay*, and we find that the descendants along the left branch *(Bliven, Colpitts,* and *Klomps)* all come before *MacKay* in alphabetical order. Simi-

FIGURE 16–6 • **A Two-Ply Tree for a Specific Tic-Tac-Toe Position**

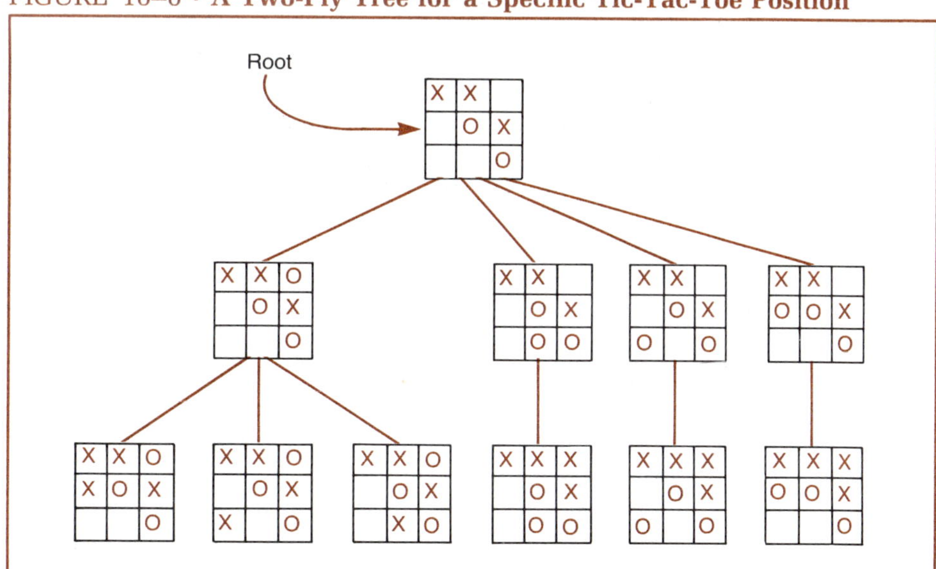

FIGURE 16–7 • **A Binary Tree with Data Arranged for Efficient Searching**

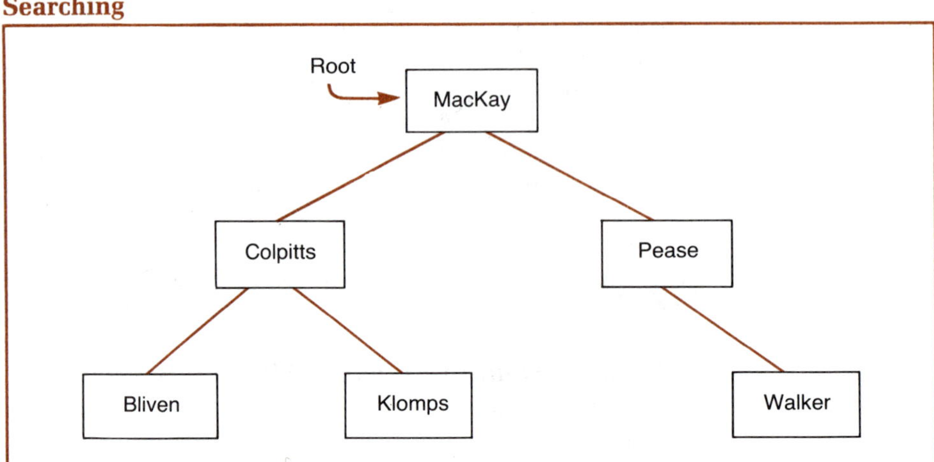


larly, if we look at the *Colpitts* node, we find that *Bliven* appears along the left branch and *Klomps* along the right branch. With this placement of the *Klomps* node, we note that *Klomps* comes after *Colpitts* but before *MacKay* in alphabetical order.

Once we have ordered data in this way, we can search a binary tree very quickly. In particular, we start at the root of the tree, and if this is our desired item, we stop. Otherwise, we check if our desired name comes before the name at this node. If the desired name comes before, we move to the child on the left and repeat the process. If the desired name comes after, we move to the child on the right and repeat this step.

This search strategy is very efficient, just as was the Binary Search from Section 8.5, because after working with one node we can rule out half of the remaining nodes. For example, if our desired name comes after *MacKay*, then we know all nodes along the left branch from *MacKay* can be ignored in our search.

Of course, such a search strategy requires that the names are split up evenly, so the number of nodes to the left is about the same as the number to the right. However, if a tree is arranged properly, it can be a particularly effective way to store and retrieve data. Thus, this structuring of data is seen in a great number of applications, where quick retrieval of data is needed.

More generally, the examples in this section have illustrated several important ways that trees can be of considerable value in applications. In each case, we stored relevant data in the nodes of a tree, and we used the tree structure to organize this data in a conceptually clear and effective way. In the next section, we see how to translate this conceptual structure into Pascal code.

## SECTION 16.3 IMPLEMENTATION OF BINARY TREES WITH POINTERS

Now that we have seen several applications that use trees, we turn to various techniques for implementing these trees. In this section, we look at the special case of binary trees, and we see how such trees could be built. Then in Section 16.6, we look at ways to implement more general trees.

In considering a binary tree, a typical node must contain the three pieces of information:

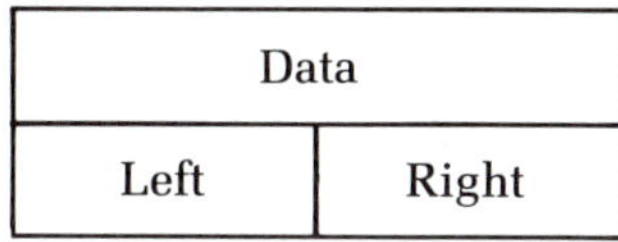


First, the node must contain the appropriate data, such as arithmetic operations or numbers, game board positions, or names. Next, the node must contain information about the child on the left (if any) and about the child on the right (if any). We might also want to record information about the parent of the node, but in practice we often can omit this information. This description of a node suggests the following declaration.

```
Type Data  = . . .     ;
     Ptr   = ^Node;
     Node  = Record
             Info: Data;
             Left: Ptr;
             Right: Ptr
             End;
Var Root: Ptr;
```

This node information is analogous to our list item declaration. In each case, we store our appropriate information in a cell. Then we use pointer fields (*Next* for lists, *Left* and *Right* for binary trees) to specify the next objects in the list or tree.

To see how these declarations can be used to form a tree, we consider the following problem.

## PROBLEM 16.3 Building an Ordered Binary Tree

We wish to build an ordered tree of names, such as shown in Figure 16–7, so that we can locate specific names efficiently as discussed earlier. To this end, we include the following declarations:

```
Const Max = 20;
Type  Data = Packed Array [1..Max] of Char;
```

Write a procedure that adds a name, in an appropriate node, to an ordered binary tree. More precisely, write

```
Procedure Insert (Name: Data; Var Root: Ptr);
```

which places the given *Name* into a new node and then inserts that node into the ordered tree with the given *Root*.

### Discussion of Problem 16.3

Procedure *Insert* must perform two operations: create an appropriate new node; and insert the new node into the tree. The creation process is similar to our creation of new list items. The insertion process is a bit more complex. In particular, we must start at the root of the tree, and we must see if the new name comes before the name stored in the root. If so, we move left; otherwise, we move right.

This process continues from node to node as we work down the tree. Finally, when the appropriate left or right pointer is *nil*, we insert the new node as a new leaf of the tree.

This suggests the following outline which also includes the special case where the tree is *nil*.

### Outline for Problem 16.3

**I.** Create a new node.
  - **A.** Allocate space for the node.
  - **B.** Place the name in the data field.
  - **C.** Initialize left and right pointers to *nil*.

**II.** Insert new node.
  - **A.** If root is *nil*, insert new node as root and stop.
  - **B.** If root is not *nil*, then start with root node.
  - **C.** With the given tree node
    - **1.** If new name comes before name in the tree node, then move left.
      - **a.** If left pointer is *nil*, insert new node and stop.
      - **b.** If left pointer is not *nil*, move on to the left tree node and repeat step C.
    - **2.** If new name comes after name in the tree node, then move right.
      - **a.** If the right pointer is *nil*, insert new node and stop.
      - **b.** If the right pointer is not *nil*, move on to the right tree node and repeat step C.

Throughout Step II, we move steadily down the tree from the root, going left or right as needed to maintain our ordering. Then, when we finally reach the bottom of the tree, we insert our new node. This outline gives rise to the following code.

```
Procedure Insert (Name: Data; Var Root: Ptr);
{This procedure creates a new node for the name and inserts the
new node in the tree with the specified root.}

  Var NewNode: Ptr;

  Procedure InsertNode (NewNode: Ptr; Var Root: Ptr);
  {This procedure inserts the new node on the tree with a simple loop.}
     Var Done: Boolean;
         TreeNode: Ptr;

     Begin
        If Root = Nil
           Then Root := NewNode
           Else Begin
              Done := False;
              TreeNode := Root;
              While Not Done
                Do Begin {Move down tree}
                  If NewNode^.Info < TreeNode^.Info
                      Then Begin {Move Left}
                          If TreeNode^.Left = Nil
                              Then Begin
                                  TreeNode^.Left := NewNode;
                                  Done := True
                                  End
                              Else TreeNode := TreeNode^.Left
                          End {Move Left}
                      Else Begin {Move Right}
                          If TreeNode^.Right = Nil
                              Then Begin
                                  TreeNode^.Right := NewNode;
                                  Done := True
                                  End
                              Else TreeNode := TreeNode^.Right
                          End {Move Right}
                End {Move down tree}
              End
      End {InsertNode};

   Begin {Insert}
      {Create and initialize new node}
      New (NewNode);
      NewNode^.Info := Name;
      NewNode^.Left := Nil;
      NewNode^.Right := Nil;

      {Insert new node into tree}
      InsertNode (NewNode, Root)
   End {Insert} ;
```

This processing with Pascal pointers follows many of the same ideas that we saw in writing our procedures for lists. If we were to follow this procedure when it is called six times for the names *MacKay, Pease, Colpitts, Bliven, Walker,* and *Klomps,* we should find that the resulting tree agrees with the structure shown in Figure 16–7. From this code, we see that much of our work with pointers for lists carries over to our manipulation of binary trees. Our initial declaration of a node is new, but the techniques of pointers for building trees are similar.

In the next section, however, we encounter a new type of algorithm that prints a listing of data stored in a tree.

## SECTION 16.4 PRINTING DATA (TREE TRANSVERSALS)

In much of our work with data up to now, we have started at one end of our data and moved to the other end. When we try to print out all of the data stored in a binary tree, however, we cannot proceed linearly from one end to another. Rather, from any particular node, we may have to move left for some data and then right for more data. Thus, if we use our previous printing techniques, we may become overwhelmed with the complexity of our task. We must keep track of what we have printed at a node and on its left and right, and our code can become quite messy.

Instead of trying to keep track of all details of printing, we consider an alternative approach that turns out to be extremely powerful. We begin by focusing on a typical node in an ordered tree. If we want to print names in alphabetical order, we identify three steps.

1. Print names (if any) on the left of the node.
2. Print the name at the given node.
3. Print names (if any) on the right of the node.

Further, we observe that we want to repeat this process at each node.

In implementing this simple outline, we write procedure *Print* so that it will process a single node. Then, as part of our work, we have *Print* call itself to process its left and right children. After we look at this code itself, we analyze in some detail why the procedure works.

```
Procedure Print (Base: Ptr);
{This procedure prints all node on the tree with the given base,
 focusing on the printing for the given node}

    Begin
        If Base <> Nil
        Then Begin
            Print (Base^.Left);
            Writeln (Base^.Info);
            Print (Base^.Right)
            End;
    End {Print} ;
```

### Details of Processing with a Recursive Print Procedure

To understand why procedure *Print* works, we follow the execution of statements for the data in Figure 16–8. In this analysis, we need to refer to each arrow from parent to child and to consider *nil* pointers at the leaf nodes. Thus, for reference, we have numbered all of the pointers in Figure 16–8. We now follow the steps involved when procedure *Print* is called. These steps are shown pictorially in Figure 16–9.

To begin, procedure *Print* is called with *Root* (or pointer(1)) as the actual parameter, and formal parameter *Base* becomes pointer(1).

The first part of *Print* involves a test. Here pointer(1) is not *nil*, so we continue with the *Then* clause of the procedure. Within this *Then* clause, *Print* is called again, with *Base^.Left* (or pointer(2)) as actual parameter. Here, when *Print* is called, we know a new storage location is created for the new parameter *Base*, and we know pointer(2) is used for this new *Base* parameter.

Again, *Base* (now pointer(2)) is not *nil*, so *Print* is called another time, with *Base^.Left* (or pointer(4)) as actual parameter. At this point, *Print* has been called three times, each with a different value parameter for *Base*. These three calls are shown as nested boxes in Figure 16–9. Once again, the new *Base* (pointer(4)) is not *nil*, and *Print* is called with actual parameter *Base^.Left* (or pointer(8)). This gives the first inside box in our figure. Finally, pointer(8) is *nil*, so this last procedure call can finish.

We return to the next box, where *Base* is pointer(4). Now

```
Print (Base^.Left)
```

with *Base* = (4) is complete, so we continue with

```
Writeln (Base^.Info)
```

This prints our first name, *Bliven*. Next, the procedure states

```
Print (Base^.Right)
```

FIGURE 16–8 • **An Ordered Binary Tree with All Pointers Numbered**

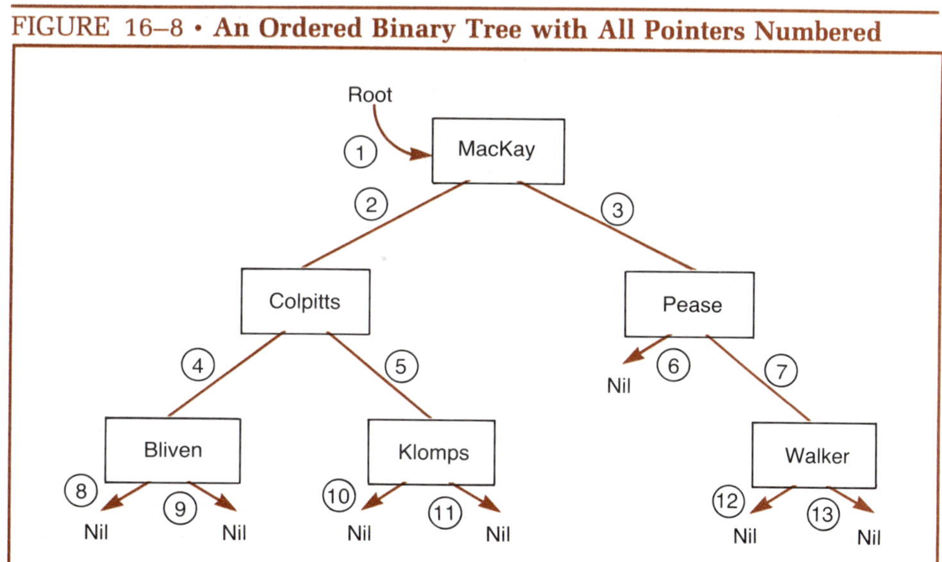

FIGURE 16–9 • **Steps Involved When Procedure Print Acts on the Tree of Figure 16–8**

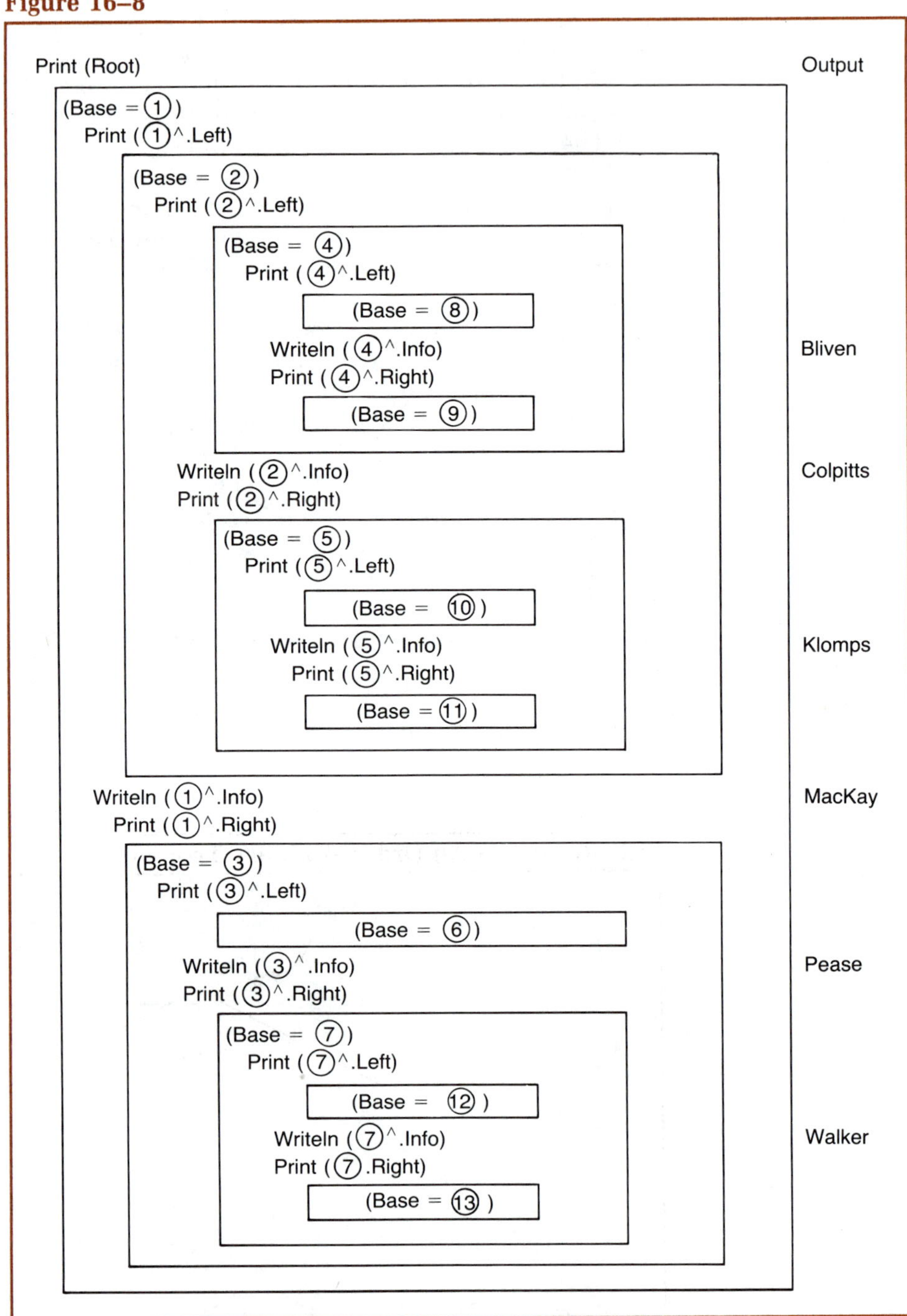

with *Base* = (4) so we call *Print* again, this time with actual parameter pointer (9).

This new *Base* (pointer (9)) is *nil*, so *Print* returns, and *Base* = (4) as before. However, now we have completed all steps for this *Print* procedure as well; our processing with *Base* = (4) is done, and we return to our previous work. In the figure, we have left the box where *Base* = (4), and we continue in the box where *Base* = (2).

The next step with *Base* = (2) involves

```
Writeln (Base^.Info)
```

and the name *Colpitts* is printed.

Moving along, *Print* is again called with *Base^.Right* (pointer (5)) as actual parameter. This procedure call allows the program to process the *Klomps* node in much the same way we have already seen for the *Bliven* node. When the *Klomps* node is done, the machine returns to the *Colpitts* node where *Base* is pointer (2). This completes the processing of this node, and the machine returns to the first call of *Print* where *Base* = (1).

Next, *MacKay* is printed, and the machine calls *Print* with actual parameter pointer (3). This leads to the printing of the right hand part of the tree.

## Overview of Processing with the Print Procedure

Now that we have followed the details of what happens when we call procedure *Print,* we need to organize these details on a more conceptual level, and we focus on the work required at each node.

1. We process the left child node.
2. We print the name at the node itself.
3. We process the child node on the right.

When we repeat these steps at one node, the first step processes the left child which in turn handles all nodes on the left. The computer repeats these steps at each node in turn by a sequence of procedure calls, and the entire data eventually are printed. In this example, we have reduced the details of all nodes to the specific steps for a single node by having the procedure *Print* call itself.

## Recursive Programming

This example illustrates a more general technique that is very useful in programming. In a more general setting, we may proceed in two steps. In the first step, we identify a small part of the task or some simple cases that are easy to handle. In our problem, we focused on the work required at a node. Then, in the second step, we reduce more complex situations to these easier ones. In our example, we instructed the computer to repeat the same process for each child.

In applying this approach to solving problems, we often want a procedure or function to call itself. In such cases, we write out the details for one situation and have the computer repeat these steps by having the function or procedure refer to itself.

For example, in printing the data in a tree, we identified what we needed to do at a particular node. Then we reduced our general printing task to a single node problem by telling the computer to repeat this process with both the left and the right children.

In general, **recursion** is a technique in which a function or procedure calls itself, and a **recursive algorithm** is one in which a process refers to itself. Such algorithms often can yield very clean solutions to problems that otherwise could be quite complex. Our example of printing data in a tree structure is a good illustration of this technique, and we will find that many other tasks involving trees also can be solved rather simply by recursive algorithms. Later in this chapter, we will see other examples where recursion is useful when no trees are being considered.

Before turning to a second example using trees, we need to make two practical points about recursion in our programming. To start a recursive algorithm, we need a procedure call outside of our recursive procedure. For example, in our printing procedure, we assume that the printing process begins with a procedure call:

```
Print (Root)
```

In addition, in a recursive algorithm, we expect procedure calls to move us from one case to another. However, if this process is to stop eventually, we must include some condition in our code so that further procedures are not called. For example, in our printing procedure, we started with a test to see if a pointer was *nil*, and work on a node continued only if a non-*nil* was encountered. With this condition, we could be sure our printing would stop eventually whenever we reached the leaves of our tree.

## Insertion by Recursion

With these comments about recursion, we now turn to a second example, and we reconsider the insertion of a new node into an ordered binary tree from Section 16.3.

In reviewing the insertion process, we can identify one particularly simple case: when we reach a *nil* pointer, we know we need to insert our new node. Further, we can work our way down the tree with the simple observation: if our new name comes before the name at a tree node, then we should move left. Otherwise, we should move right.

**Outline for Tree Insertion.** Putting these ideas together, we obtain the following outline.

**I.** Start at root of tree.
**II.** General step.
  **A.** If we are at the end of the tree (i.e. if our pointer is *nil*), then insert the new node.

**B.** If we are not at the end, then compare the new name to the name in the tree node.
   **1.** If the new name comes first, repeat this Step II, moving left.
   **2.** If the new name comes later, repeat this Step II, moving right.

In this outline, the details in Step IIB tell us to repeat the entire Step II with a new node. This suggests that our procedure for node insertion should call itself with a new, revised parameter for the repetition step. Thus, this outline suggests the following recursive procedure for insertion.

```
Procedure Insert (Name: Data; Var Root: Ptr);
{This procedure creates a new node for the name and inserts the
new node in the tree with the specified root.}
{The insertion process itself is done recursively}

    Var NewNode: Ptr;

    Procedure InsertNode (NewNode: Ptr; Var Base: Ptr);
    {This procedure inserts the new node on the tree recursively.}
        Begin
            If Base = Nil
                Then Base := NewNode
                Else Begin
                    If NewNode^.Info < Base^.Info
                        Then InsertNode (NewNode, Base^.Left)
                        Else InsertNode (NewNode, Base^.Right)
                    End
        End {InsertNode};

    Begin {Insert}
        {Create and initialize new node}
        New (NewNode);
        NewNode^.Info := Name;
        NewNode^.Left := Nil;
        NewNode^.Right := Nil;

        {Insert new node into tree}
        InsertNode (NewNode, Root)
    End {Insert} ;
```

In this code, the recursive *InsertNode* procedure is much simpler than the nonrecursive version in the previous section. Here, we have been able to focus on a single node where the work is quite easy, and we can move from one node to another by appropriate procedure calls. In tracing through this code, we can see how recursion has allowed us to handle each node simply and to move easily from node to node down the tree. In the next section, we describe another application of recursion: solving a puzzle.

## SECTION 16.5 APPLICATIONS OF RECURSION TO SIMPLE PUZZLES

In the previous section, we were able to insert nodes into ordered trees and to print all nodes in a tree by focusing on a single node and then telling the computer to repeat this work at the children of a node. In this section, we see an example of recursion that arises in a rather different context. As in the previous section, our approach will be to solve a simple case and then to have the computer repeat this case as often as necessary.

First, we state a problem that is the basis for several commercially available puzzles.

## PROBLEM 16.5 The Towers of Hanoi

One classic puzzle is often called "The Towers of Hanoi." It contains three rods and several rings of different sizes that can fit over the rods.

At the start, the rings are placed over one rod, so that each ring rests on the next larger one. This initial configuration is shown in Figure 16–10, where all rings are positioned around Rod 1.

With this starting point, the goal of the puzzle is to move all rings from Rod 1 to Rod 2 so that at the end the rings again are in order.

The challenge of the puzzle arises from the following rules for moving these rings.

1. Only one ring may be moved at a time.
2. Only a ring on the top of a rod may be moved to the top position on another rod.
3. A ring may never be placed on top of a smaller ring.

FIGURE 16–10 • **Initial Position for the Towers of Hanoi**

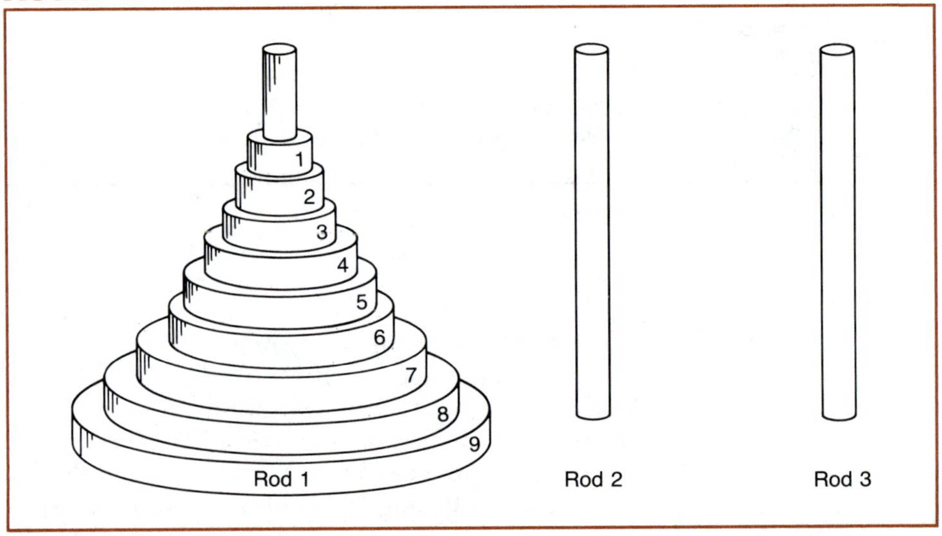

For example, looking at Figure 16–10, initially we may move the smallest ring (Ring 1) to either Rod 2 or Rod 3. So suppose we move Ring 1 to Rod 2. Then, on our next turn, we may move Ring 2 to Rod 3, but we may not move Ring 2 to Rod 2, because the smaller Ring 1 is already there.

## Discussion of Problem 16.5

In attacking this puzzle, our first approach might be to describe the motion of each ring in detail, establishing a pattern for each move. However, if the number of rings is large, this level of detail can become quite complex and hard to program. Instead, we take a broader view of the problem. We begin our analysis by identifying the three rods as follows.

| | |
|---|---|
| Original Rod: | Where all rings start (e.g., Rod 1) |
| Final Rod: | Where all rings are to end (e.g., Rod 2) |
| Spare Rod: | Neither the starting nor ending rod—the rod we can use for intermediate steps (e.g., Rod 3) |

Further, if we have $N$ rings that we want to move, we can imagine performing our task by

```
Procedure Move (Original, Final, Spare: Rod; Number: Ring);
```

With this procedure, we solve our puzzle with the initial procedure call

```
Move (1, 2, 3, N)
```

This moves $N$ rings from Rod 1 to Rod 2, using Rod 3 as a spare.

Now that we have set up this general framework, we consider the work we need for the moving of Ring $N$. In our analysis, our major breakthrough is to identify the following general steps:

1. Move the top $N-1$ rings from the original rod to the spare rod.
2. Move the Nth rod from the original rod to the final rod.
3. Move the $N-1$ rings from the spare rod to the final rod.

With these steps, we can perform Step 2 as one move of a single ring from one rod to another. Thus, this step can be done directly. Further, Steps 1 and 3 can be done with the same *Move* procedure, applied to a pile of one fewer rings.

This discussion suggests the following program which depends upon recursion to repeat Steps 1 and 3.

```
Program TowersOfHanoi (Output);
{This program prints solution of the Towers Of Hanoi problem.}
    Const Total = 4;  {Number of rings given in the problem}

    Type Rod = Integer;
         Ring = Integer;

Procedure Move (Original, Final, Spare: Rod; Number: Ring);
{This procedure moves the ring with the given Number from the original
 rod to the Final rod, using the Spare rod as necessary}
    Begin
        If Number > 1
            Then Move (Original, Spare, Final, Number-1);

        {Move ring with given Number}
        Writeln (Number:8, Original:11 ,Final:9);

        If Number > 1
            Then Move (Spare, Final, Original, Number-1)
    End {Move} ;

Begin {Main}
    Writeln ('This program prints a solution ',
             'to the Towers of Hanoi puzzle,');
    Writeln ('where ', Total:1, ' rings are move from Rod 1 to Rod 2.');
    Writeln;
    Writeln ('List of turns');
    Writeln ('Move Ring:  from Rod:  To Rod:');
    Move (1, 2, 3, Total)
End {Main} .
```

When this program is run for 4 rings, we get the following output:

```
This program prints a solution to the Towers of Hanoi puzzle,
where 4 rings are move from Rod 1 to Rod 2.

List of turns
Move Ring:  from Rod:  To Rod:
       1          1        3
       2          1        2
       1          3        2
       3          1        3
       1          2        1
       2          2        3
       1          1        3
       4          1        2
       1          3        2
       2          3        1
       1          2        1
       3          3        2
       1          1        3
       2          1        2
       1          3        2
```

As with our recursive tree procedures, this program illustrates several major features of recursion. First, we concentrate on a simple part of the puzzle that we want to solve, and we reduce the general problem to this simple case. Then, we solve the simple case (Step 2 in our current solution). Next, if our problem is more complex, we apply the same process to the rest of the problem after solving the simple case. Finally, our procedure involves a Boolean condition, and the procedure is called again only in some cases. When we put the various cases together, we must be sure that our work will stop eventually.

## The Forward Statement

Our solution to this problem also can illustrate what we must do if we have several functions or procedures that call each other. For example, we might consider one procedure that processes the top rings, if any, in our problem in addition to the *Move* procedure that we have already used. Thus, we might use procedure *ProcessTop* to perform Steps 1 and 3 in the outline, while we continue to use a *Writeln* statement for Step 2. When we write out our program, we will need *ProcessTop* to refer to our *Move* procedure and *Move* will need to refer to *ProcessTop*. However, in writing our program, we can only declare one of these two procedures first. (We might declare *ProcessTop* first and *Move* second.) Thus, the first procedure will need to refer a procedure that is not declared until later. In Pascal, this situation requires us to use a ***Forward*** statement, so we can tell the compiler that procedure *Move* is coming. Then, the compiler will know how to handle the reference to *Move* in procedure *ProcessTop*.

In Pascal, we handle this situation in two parts. First, early in the program, we specify the procedure *Move* and its formal parameters in a *Forward* statement. For example,

```
Procedure Move (Original, Final, Spare: Rod; Number: Ring);
Forward;
```

Second, later in the program we give the rest of the information about our procedure. (Note, we do not repeat the parameters this second time.) For example,

```
Procedure Move;
    Begin
        ProcessTop (Original, Spare, Final, Number-1);
        Writeln (Number:8, Original: 11, Final:9);
        ProcessTop (Spare, Final, Original, Number-1)
    End Move;
```

The first statement tells the computer what *Move* will look like, with its parameters and resulting type; the second part fills in the details. The revised program has the following form:

```
Program TowersOfHanoi {Version 2} (Output);
{This program prints solution of the Towers Of Hanoi problem.}
{In this program two procedures call each other}

    Const Total = 4;  {Number of rings given in the problem}

    Type Rod = Integer;
         Ring = Integer;

Procedure Move (Original, Final, Spare: Rod; Number: Ring); Forward;
{The details of this procedure are given below;
 only the parameters and the procedure name are declared here}

Procedure ProcessTop (First, Second, Third: Rod; Number: Ring);
{This procedure processes the top Number of rings, if any}
    Begin
        If Number >= 1
            Then Move (First, Second, Third, Number)
    End {ProcessTop} ;

Procedure Move;
{This procedure moves the ring with the given Number from the original
 rod to the Final rod, using the Spare rod as necessary}
    Begin
        ProcessTop (Original, Spare, Final, Number-1);

        {Move ring with given Number}
        Writeln (Number:8, Original:11 ,Final:9);

        ProcessTop (Spare, Final, Original, Number-1)
    End {Move} ;

Begin {Main}
    Writeln ('This program prints a solution ',
             'to the Towers of Hanoi puzzle,');
    Writeln ('where ', Total:1, ' rings are move from Rod 1 to Rod 2.');
    Writeln;
    Writeln ('List of turns');
    Writeln ('Move Ring:  from Rod:  To Rod:');
    Move (1, 2, 3, Total)
End {Main} .
```

This program produces the same output as our previous problem. However, in this version, we used two procedures that called each other, and we needed to tell the computer that the second one was coming. To do this, we use a *Forward* statement. More generally, we can use this *Forward* statement anytime we want to refer to a procedure in our program before the declaration of that procedure appears in our listing.

## SECTION 16.6 IMPLEMENTATION OF GENERAL TREES

Whereas in the past sections we implemented binary trees, in this section we return to our study of other types of tree structures. In fact, we find three alternative approaches for defining various types of trees.

To illustrate the various ways we might implement more general trees, consider the following problem.

## PROBLEM 16.6 Department Store Organizational Chart

Write the appropriate Pascal declarations necessary for creating the tree of Figure 16–11, which shows a simple organizational chart for a small department store.

### Discussion of Problem 16.6

While the tree of Figure 16–11 is not a binary tree, we can observe that no node has more than three children. Thus, this tree is a special structure called a **ternary tree.** In developing the declarations for this tree, we will find some approaches that make use of this ternary tree structure, and we will find another approach that will work more generally.

*Approach 1.* Since Figure 16–11 pictures a ternary tree, our first approach might involve modifying our binary tree declarations to include three possible children at each node. In particular, each node might have

1. a child node on the left
2. a child node underneath (in the middle)
3. a child node on the right

FIGURE 16–11 • **Personnel Organization in a Small Department Store**

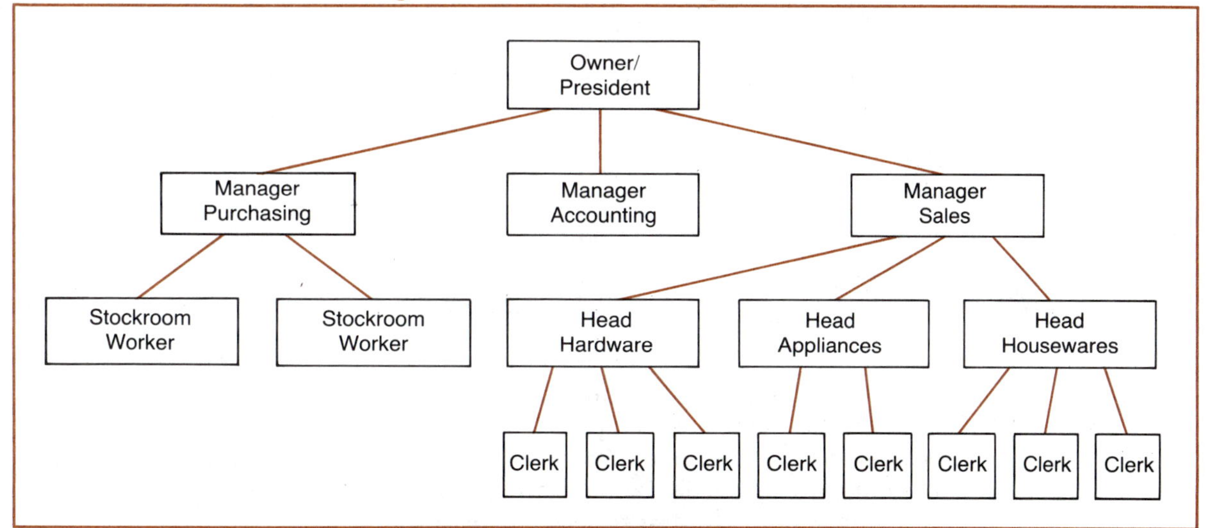

With this structure we use the following declarations:

```
Const Max = 20;
Type  Data = Packed Array [1..Max] of Char;
      Ptr = ^Node;
      Node = Record
               Name : Data;
               Left : Ptr;
               Middle : Ptr;
               Right : Ptr
               End;
Var   Root : Ptr;
```

With these declarations, the root variable can specify the root node of the tree. Then, at each node, we have pointers available to specify the left, middle and right children.

More generally, if we knew that each node in our tree would contain no more than N children, we could declare:

```
Const Max = 20;
Type  Data = Packed Array [1..Max] of Char;
      Ptr = ^Node;
      Node = Record
               Name : Data;
               Child1 : Ptr:
               Child2 : Ptr;
                   .
                   .
                   .
               ChildN : Ptr
               End;
Var   Root : Ptr;
```

In this first approach, we simply write out a pointer field for each possible child of a node. Then, in processing, we explicitly refer to the appropriate child whenever necessary. In practice, we have already seen that this approach can work very well for binary trees, when a node has no more than two children. Similarly, this approach can work well for ternary trees, where we need only three pointer fields for the three possible children of a node.

However, this approach is cumbersome if each node can have many children. With even four or five possible children, we need four or five pointer fields, and working with these different specific fields requires writing special code for each field. Thus, in more general trees, we may want another, less cumbersome approach.

*Approach 2.* Our second approach for declaring nodes in trees uses arrays for pointers. In particular, we use the following declarations, where we store our pointers to descendants in an array *Child*.

```
Const Max = 20;
      MaxChildren = 3;
Type  Data = Packed Array [1..Max] of Char;
      Ptr = ^Node;
      Node = Record
                 Name : Data;
                 Child : Array [1..MaxChildren] of Ptr
                 End;
Var   Root : Ptr;
```

In this structure, our node pointers have the form

```
Child[Index]
```

Thus, if we want to create and initialize a node using a specific name for data, we might write the following code:

```
Procedure Create (Item : Data; Var NewNode : Ptr);
      Var   Index : Integer;
      Begin
            New (NewNode);
            NewNode^.Name := Item;
            For Index := 1 to MaxChildren
               Do NewNode^.Child[Index] := Nil
End;
```

Here, we create the node, insert the appropriate name in this node, and set all pointers in the node to *nil*.

This approach has two advantages over the previous approach. First, we can refer to each child easily, using the child field and a subscript. Secondly, this form works well whenever we know the limit on the number of children that a node might have; we just need to choose the constant *MaxChildren* to reflect this limit.

Thus, this approach allows us to work with general trees whenever we know a reasonable limit for the number of children at each node. However, this approach is still inadequate if we cannot anticipate this limit. Hence, in working with general trees, we must consider one more approach as well.

*Approach 3*. Another alternative is suggested by Figure 16–12, which shows the same personnel structure for the small department store from Figure 16–11, but the lines connecting the positions are drawn differently. For example, in this revised figure, the purchasing manager, the accountant, and the sales manager are all shown as being under the owner/president, but we have arranged these three positions in a row. Similarly, the clerks are shown in a row under their department head.

This organization of children in a row suggests the third implementation of trees, and this implementation places no restrictions on the number of children a node may have. Rather, in our declarations, we consider all children of a node as forming a linked list of children; and we use the parent node to specify the head of this list of children.

FIGURE 16–12 • **Alternate Description of Personnel Organization in a Small Department Store**

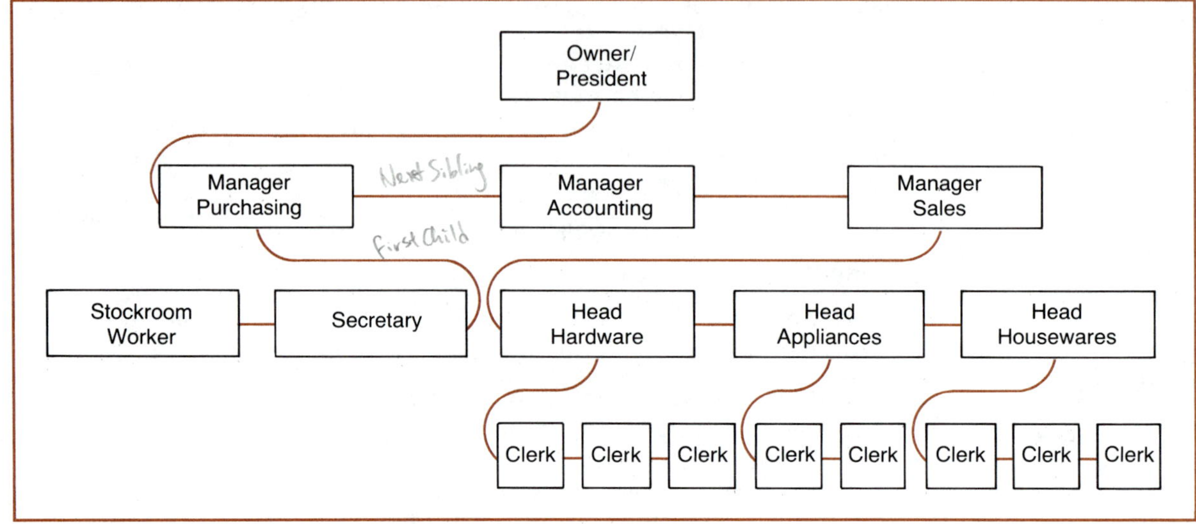


This discussion suggests the following declarations:

```
Const Max = 20;
Type  Data = Packed Array [1..Max] of Char;
      Ptr = ^Node;
      Node = Record
                Name : Data;
                NextSibling : Ptr;
                FirstChild : Ptr
             End;
```

With these declarations, we use the *NextSibling* field to form a linked list of children of a given node, and the *FirstChild* pointer of the parent specifies the first of these siblings. Such a structure is shown in Figure 16–13.

This approach to trees has the disadvantage that we must use lists to record our tree information, and we may have to perform a Linear Search if we want to find a particular child. On the other hand, this approach has the advantage that all children are handled by the same list structure. We do not have to distinguish here between left and right children or among *Child*[1], *Child*[2], etc.

As a final note, with the linked structure, we sometimes find it appropriate to record explicitly the parent of each node. In this case, we may add a parent field to our declarations of a node. With this field added, we include the dotted lines of Figure 16–13 as well.

FIGURE 16–13 • **Children of a Parent Node**

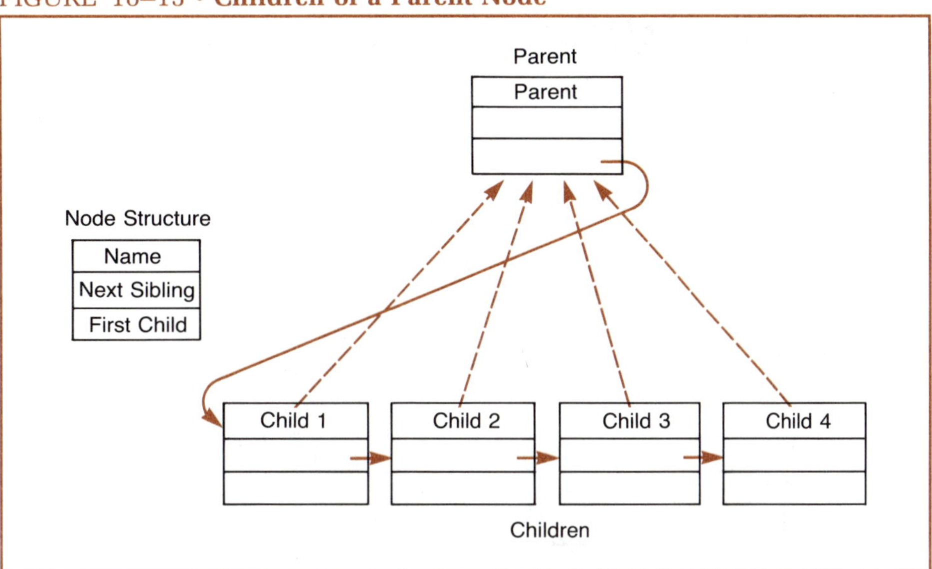


## SECTION 16.7 SORTING WITH TREES OR RECURSION

Earlier in this chapter, we applied trees and recursion to solving puzzles. In this section, we use these same ideas in developing two excellent sorting algorithms.

### Correspondence Between Binary Trees and Arrays

To begin, we need to impose a binary tree structure on an array. In order to see how this can be done, we look at a full binary tree in Figure 16–14. In this figure, we have created nodes for ten pieces of data. To condense this tree as much as possible, we started at the root. Then, we worked down the tree, one row at a time; within a row, we worked left to right. At each stage, we established two children for each node until we had created all ten desired nodes.

In Figure 16–14, we also have numbered all ten nodes, again starting from the root and then moving downward row by row. As before, within a row, we have numbered the nodes from left to right. With this numbering of nodes, we can establish a natural correspondence between binary trees and elements in arrays. In particular, in the tree, we see that for any node $I$, its left child, if any, is numbered $2*I$; and its right child, if any, is numbered $2*I + 1$. This pattern suggests that whenever we have an array $A[1]$, . . . , $A[N]$, we can think of the array elements as being in a tree if we consider

$A[2*I]$ as the left child of $A[I]$

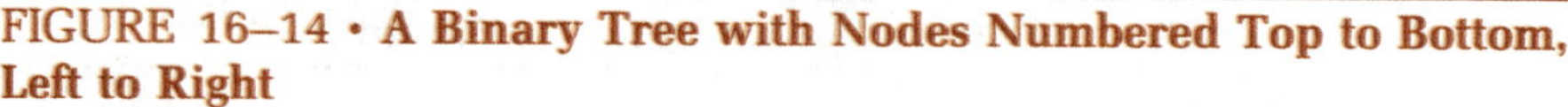
**FIGURE 16–14 • A Binary Tree with Nodes Numbered Top to Bottom, Left to Right**

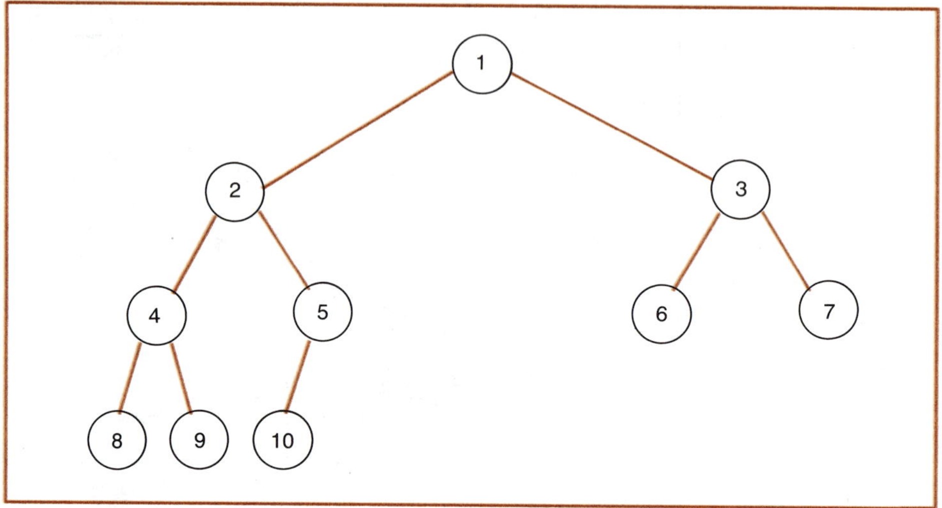


$A[2*I + 1]$ as the right child of $A[I]$

$A[I \text{ Div } 2]$ as the parent of $A[I]$

In this way, we can work with an array as if its elements were arranged in a tree.

## Heap Sort

Our first new sorting algorithm, called a **heap sort,**[1] illustrates a use of trees that does not involve recursion. With this connection between binary trees and arrays, we can describe the heap sort. To begin, we suppose the binary tree is partially ordered, so each parent is greater than or equal to each of its children. (See Figure 16–15a).

Once our tree is partially ordered, the elements can be completely ordered fairly easily as follows.

*Step 1A.* (See Figure 16–15b.) The first (and largest) element on the tree is interchanged with the last element, and the last element is then ignored.

*Step 1B.* (See Figures 16–15c and d.) We now put the resulting tree back into a partially ordered state. Since only the (1) node has been moved in the present tree, that is the only node that we must work with. When we compare (1) with its two children, we observe that if the (15) and (1) are swapped, the left half of the tree will be partially ordered (as 15 > 12 and 15 > 1).

[1]The Heap Sort was devised by J. W. J. Williams. For more details, see *Communication of the Association for Computing Machinery*, Vol. 7 (1964), pages 347–348.

**FIGURE 16–15 • Ordering Data Given a Partially Ordered Array**

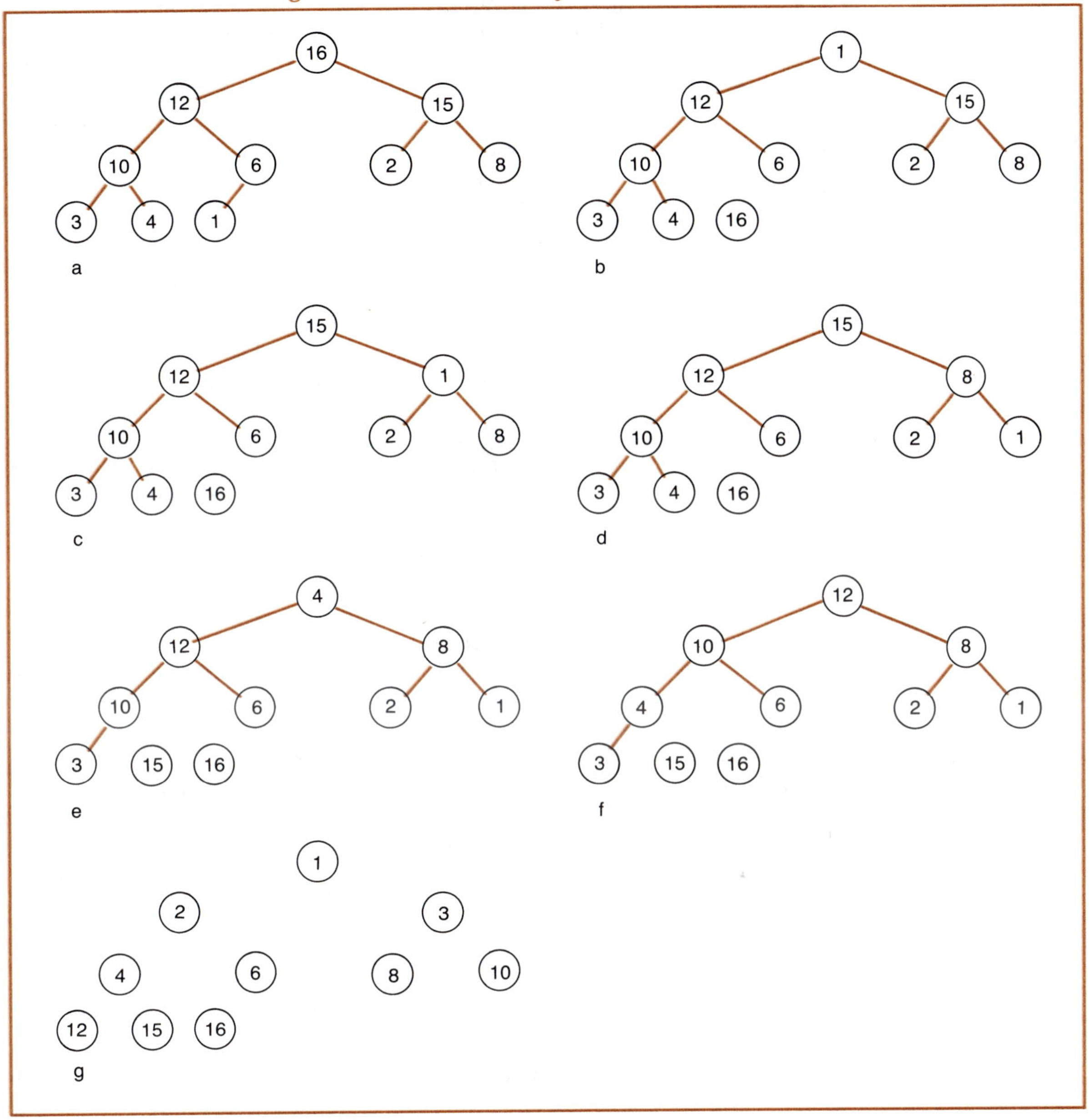

After this swap is made (Figure 16–15c), we again look at the (1) node and its offspring. By interchanging the (1) and (8), the tree again becomes partially ordered (Figure 16–15d).

*Step 2.* We repeat this process again. We interchange the first and last elements in the tree and the last element is ignored (Figure 16–15e). We move the (4) node down the resulting tree to obtain another partially ordered tree. In particular, we compare the (4) node with each of its offspring and swap the (4) with the larger of its two children as necessary. In this case, the (4) node moves along the leftmost edge of the tree until it reaches the present (10) node. The result is shown in Figure 16–15f.

*General Step*. We continue the above process. We interchange the root with the last element in the tree, and we ignore the last element. We move the new root down the tree as necessary to obtain a new, partially ordered tree. This process continues until there are no more elements remaining on the tree. (See Figure 16–15g.) The ordered elements can now be read off, one row at a time, from top to bottom. In other words, our initial array is now ordered.

To complete our description of the heap sort, we must consider how we might obtain our first partially ordered array. For example, we must determine how we can transform Figure 16–16a into Figure 16–15a.

For this work, we proceed from the bottom of the tree toward the root.

*Step 1*. We consider the last node that has an offspring (Figure 16–16b). This small subtree is already partially ordered, so we do nothing.

*Step 2*. We consider the next small subtree at the end of the big tree (Figure 16–16c). Here, we can interchange nodes (4) and (12) to obtain a partial ordering.

*Step 3*. We consider the next small subtree (Figure 16–16d). Here the (2) and (15) nodes must be swapped.

*Step 4*. Again, moving up from the bottom of the tree, we consider the next subtree (Figure 16–16e). As before, in this structure only the root is out of order, and we can move the root into place by interchanging the (6) and (16) nodes.

*Step 5*. We now can consider the entire tree (Figure 16–16f). As in the previous step, only the root remains out of order in this tree, and we can move it down into an appropriate place as we have several times earlier in our discussion. In particular, we interchange nodes (10) and (16) to obtain the partially ordered tree with which we began this discussion.

## Programming the Heap Sort

When we try to program the heap sort, we first observe that the major step involves the consideration of a part of a tree, where the root of the tree may be out of order but where the rest of the tree is partially ordered. Thus, the key step in programming is to develop Procedure *SearchDown*, which moves the root data down to the appropriate place in the tree.

Further, in specifying this procedure, we need to indicate what part of the tree we wish to consider at a particular step. Since the tree in a heap sort is represented by an array, this specification corresponds to indicating which part of an array is to be used in this *SearchDown* procedure. Hence,

FIGURE 16–16 • **Moving Data to Obtain a Partially Ordered Array**

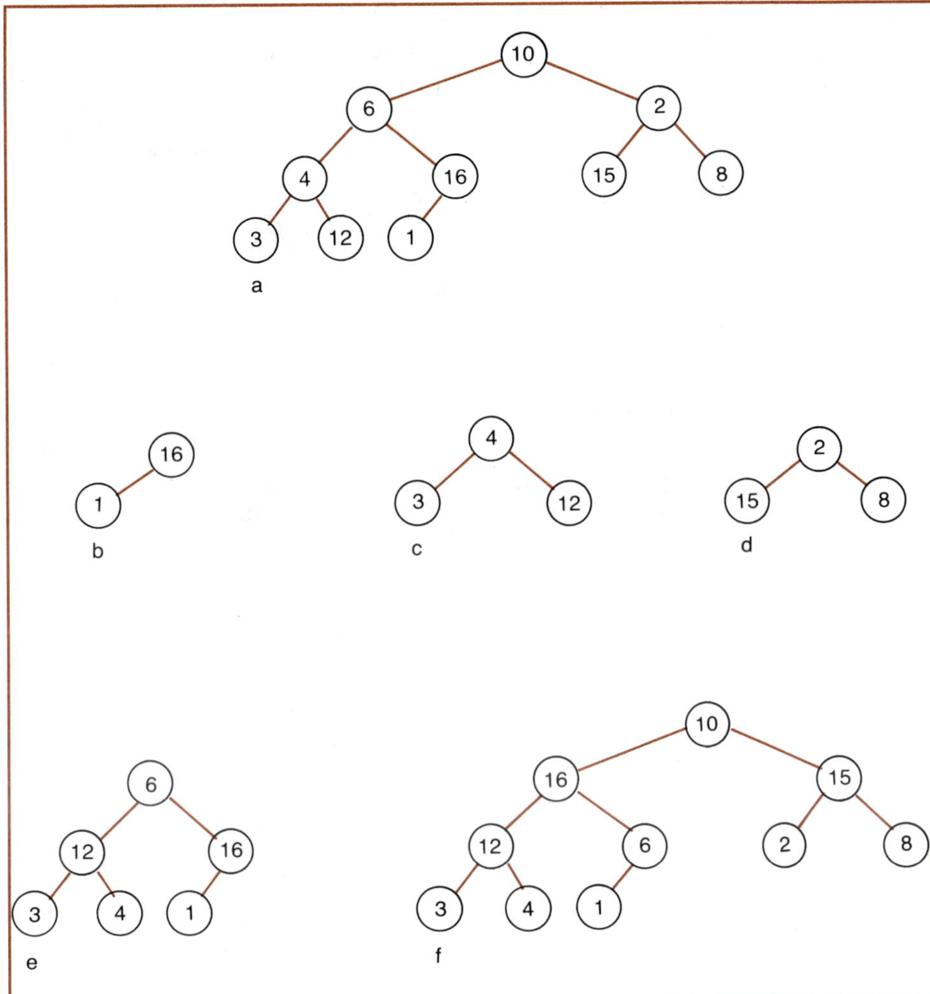


in declaring the *SearchDown* procedure, we include two parameters, *First* and *Last*, which give the appropriate bounds on the array elements. Next, once *SearchDown* is defined, we need to use it in two ways.

1. To set up the partially ordered array at the beginning, we need a sequence of calls:

```
For Index := (ArraySize Div 2) DownTo 1
    Do SearchDown (Index, ArraySize)
```

2. Then, once the initial tree is partially ordered, we need to finish the ordering by another sequence of procedure calls:

```
For Index := ArraySize DownTo 3
    Do Begin
            Swap (Data[Index], Data [1]);
            SearchDown (1, Index − 1)
        End
Swap (Data[1], Data[2])
```

In this code, the *Swap* procedure just interchanges the two data elements specified in the array.

With these notes, we leave the remaining programming details as an exercise, and we turn to our final sorting algorithm.

## Quicksort[2]

Quicksort is a recursive approach to sorting, and we begin by outlining the principal recursive step. In this step, we make a guess at the value that should end up in the middle of the array. In particular, given the array

$$A[1], \ldots, A[N]$$

of data, arranged at random, then we might guess that the first data item $A[1]$ often should end up in about the middle of the array when the array is finally ordered. ($A[1]$ is easy to locate, and it is as good a guess at the median value as another.) This suggests the following steps.

I. Rearrange the data in the $A$ array, so that $A[1]$ is moved to its proper position. In other words, move $A[1]$ to $A[Mid]$ and rearrange the other elements so that

$$A[1], A[2], \ldots, A[Mid - 1] < A[Mid]$$

and

$$A[Mid] < A[Mid + 1], \ldots, A[N].$$

II. Repeat this process on the smaller lists

$$A[1], \ldots, A[Mid - 1]$$

and

$$A[Mid + 1], \ldots, A[N].$$

A specific example is shown in Figure 16–17.

**Outline to Move the First Array Element to the Appropriate Middle.** With this outline, we now need to consider how we might move the first

---

[2]The Quicksort was originally devised by C. A. R. Hoare. For more details, see the *Computing Journal*, Volume 5 (1962), pages 10–15.

FIGURE 16–17 • **Main Steps in a Sample Quicksort**

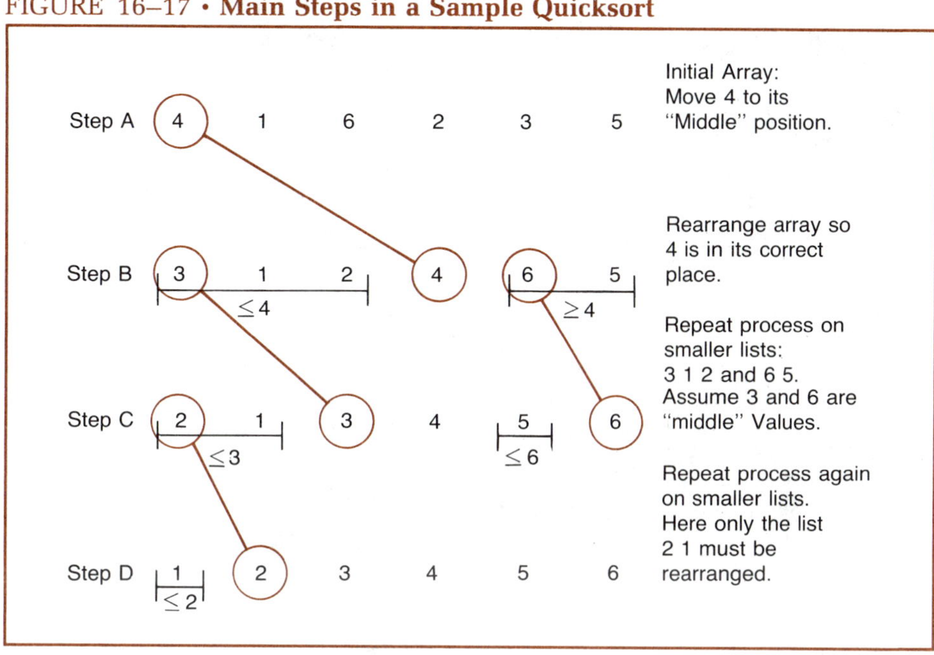


element to its appropriate location in the array. Here the basic approach is to work from the ends of the array toward the middle, comparing data elements to the first element and rearranging the array as necessary. The outline details are given below.

**I.** Compare $A[First]$ to $A[Last]$, $A[Last - 1]$, etc. until an element $A[U]$ is found where $A[U] < A[First]$. Then $A[U]$ and $A[First]$ are swapped. At this point:
 **A.** the first element has moved to $A[U]$
 **B.** $A[U] < A[U + 1], \ldots, A[Last]$
 **C.** $A[First] < A[U]$.

**II.** Compare $A[U]$ with $A[First + 1]$, $A[First + 2]$, etc. to find an element $A[L]$ where $A[L] > A[U]$. Then $A[L]$ and $A[U]$ are swapped. At this point:
 **A.** the original first element has moved to $A[L]$
 **B.** $A[L] < A[U], A[U + 1], \ldots, A[Last]$
 **C.** $A[First], \ldots, A[L - 1] < A[L]$.

**III.** We continue Steps I and II, comparing the original first element against the ends of the array until the "first" element is placed into $A[Mid]$ where
 **A.** $A[Mid] < A[Mid + 1], \ldots, A[Last]$
 **B.** $A[First], \ldots, A[Mid - 1] < A[Mid]$.

FIGURE 16–18 • **Putting the First Array Element in Its Place**

| | | | | | | |
|---|---|---|---|---|---|---|
| 4 | 1 | 6 | 2 | 3 | 5 | Original Array |
| 4 | 1 | 6 | 2 | 3 | 5 | Search Up |
| 3 | 1 | 6 | 2 | 4 | 5 | Swap |
| 3 | 1 | 6 | 2 | 4 | 5 | Search Down |
| 3 | 1 | 4 | 2 | 6 | 5 | Swap |
| 3 | 1 | 4 | 2 | 6 | 5 | Search Up |
| 3 | 1 | 2 | 4 | 6 | 5 | Swap<br>4 is in its correct position. |

This process is illustrated in Figure 16–18, where *A*[1] is put in its appropriate place. The circled numbers in the figure follow the movement of this element. The elements in color show which parts of the array have already been checked.

## Programming the Search Up and Down Steps

In programming this process, it is convenient to use several variables to record what we have done at each point.

We use *First* and *Last* to indicate that we want to work with the list

*A*[*First*], . . . , *A*[*Last*].

We use *Mid* to indicate where our "first" element is located on its way to the middle. (Initially, *Mid* = *First*. Then *Mid* changes as this element is moved.)

Finally, we use *LowerCheck* and *UpperCheck* to note how far we have checked the list. The use of these variables is illustrated in Figure 16–19, which follows the work in Figure 16–18.

With these comments, we now can write the code for a quicksort. In this code, the parameter *Data* is an array to be sorted. In addition, we assume we have declared *Bigger* as a Boolean function that indicates if the

FIGURE 16–19 • **Use of Variables in the Quicksort Searching Process**

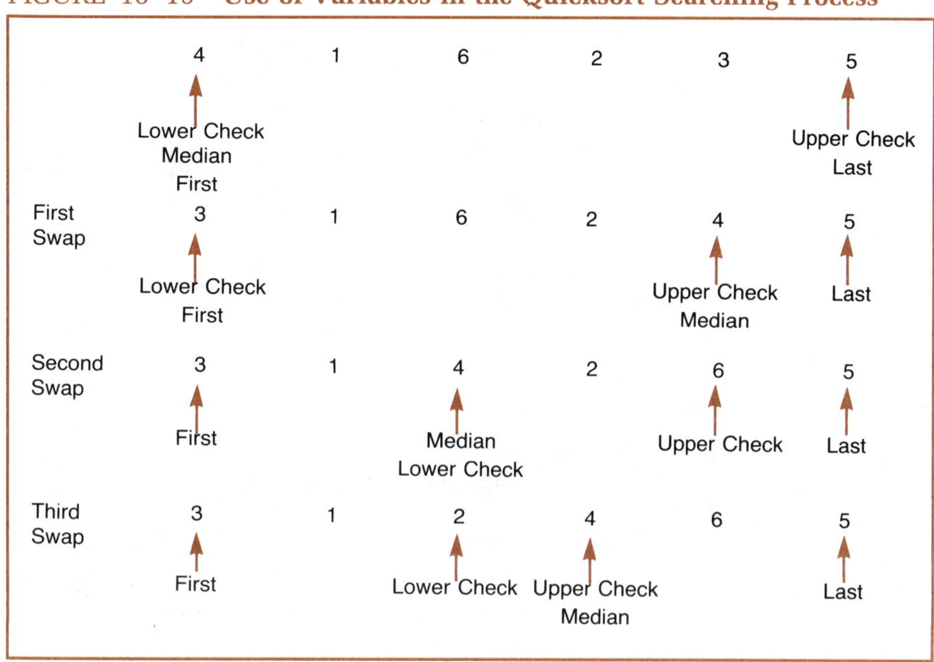


first data element is bigger than the second. Also, we assume *Swap* is a procedure that interchanges the elements specified. Finally, to start this quicksort procedure, we use the call

Quicksort (Data, 1, N)

which indicates that we are to sort elements 1 through *N* of the *Data* array.

```
{This procedure assumes the following declarations}

Const ArraySize = ... ;  {Number of items to be sorted}


Type  ArrayData = Array [1..ArraySize] of Integer;

Procedure QuickSort (Var Data: ArrayData;
                    LowerArrayBound, UpperArrayBound: Integer);
   {Procedure performs a QuickSort on the array Data}
   Var
      Median, LowerCheck, UpperCheck: Integer;
      ExitLoop, Quit: Boolean;
```

```
Procedure CheckUp;
    Begin
        Quit := False;
    While (Median < UpperCheck) And Not Quit
            Do Begin
                If Bigger(Data[Median], Data[UpperCheck])
                Then Begin {Swap Variables}
                        Swap(Data[Median], Data[UpperCheck]);
                        LowerCheck := Median + 1;
                        Median := UpperCheck;
                    Quit := True
                    End;
                UpperCheck := UpperCheck - 1
                End
    End {CheckUp};

Procedure CheckDown;
    Begin
        Quit := False;
        While (LowerCheck < Median) And Not Quit
        Do Begin
                If Bigger(Data[LowerCheck], Data[Median])
                    Then Begin {Swap Variables}
                        Swap(Data[Median], Data[LowerCheck]);
                        UpperCheck := Median - 1;
                        Median := LowerCheck;
                        Quit := True
                    End;
            LowerCheck := LowerCheck + 1;
            End
End {CheckDown};

Begin {Main Part of QuickSort}

     {Set Up Procedure Variables}
     LowerCheck := LowerArrayBound;
     UpperCheck := UpperArrayBound;
     Median := LowerArrayBound;

     {Put "Median" value in its proper place}
     ExitLoop := False;
     Repeat
     CheckUp;
         If (LowerCheck < Median)
         Then CheckDown
             Else ExitLoop := True
     Until (Median >= UpperCheck) or ExitLoop ;

     {Repeat Process on Smaller Lists}
     If LowerArrayBound < Median - 1
     Then QuickSort (Data, LowerArrayBound, Median - 1);
     If Median + 1 < UpperArrayBound
     Then QuickSort (Data, Median + 1, UpperArrayBound)
 End {QuickSort} ;
```

## Evaluation of Efficiency

With these descriptions of the heap sort and the quicksort, we now need to consider how efficient each of these algorithms is, and we need to compare these methods with the Insertion Sort of Section 8.6. One approach to evaluating efficiency uses a mathematical analysis that involves two basic aparts.

1. Determine how many basic steps are needed to perform the algorithm.
2. Determine the number of comparisons and interchanges required within each step.

When we apply this approach to either of the new algorithms in this chapter to data in random order, we find that the number of comparisons and interchanges is proportional to $n\log_2 n$. (In contrast, the number of interchanges in an insertion sort is proportional to $n^2$ for random data.) We say the insertion sort is an **order ($n^2$) algorithm,** while the heap sort and quicksort are **order ($n\log_2 n$) algorithms.**

A second method for evaluating the efficiency of these algorithms is to run each algorithm on some data and count the number of comparisons and interchanges required. Here, rather than perform the sophisticated mathematical analysis required for each algorithm, we can try these algorithms with different types of data and compare our results. For example, Table 16–1 shows what happens when these sorting algorithms are applied to three data sets containing 100 elements. In particular, we consider the work done when the data are already ordered in ascending or descending order and when the data are quite random. The results illustrate several points.

1. The work required for $n^2$ algorithms, such as the insertion sort, normally is very high.
2. The work required for $n\log_2 n$ algorithms, such as the heap sorts, is much less.
3. Some algorithms can be very efficient at processing some types of data but very poor on other data sets. For example, the insertion sort is outstanding if the data are already in ascending order, but it is very poor otherwise. In contrast, the quicksort, which we developed for random data, is outstanding for that random data, but it is less efficient on data that are already ordered.

**TABLE 16–1 • Comparison of Insertion Sort, Quicksort, and Heap Sort Used on Data Sets of 100 Elements.**

| | Ascending Data | | Descending Data | | Random Data | |
|---|---|---|---|---|---|---|
| Sorting Algorithm | Compare | Assign | Compare | Assign | Compare | Assign |
| Insertion | 99 | 198 | 4950 | 5148 | 2860 | 2964 |
| Quicksort | 4950 | 0 | 4950 | 150 | 712 | 657 |
| Heap Sort | 1081 | 1920 | 944 | 1548 | 1026 | 1740 |

4. Some algorithms are very stable for all types of data. For example, the heap sort may not be the most efficient algorithm for one type of data, but its performance is always quite good. The heap sort always can be counted on to work fairly well, even though other algorithms may work better in certain cases.

These observations demonstrate that in solving a problem our choice of algorithm often must take into account the type of data we expect to encounter. Some algorithms may work particularly well in certain cases, but quite poorly in other circumstances. Other algorithms may be quite consistent in their performance under many circumstances.

These heap sort and quicksort algorithms also demonstrate that the concepts of trees and recursion can be applied effectively in many different situations. Initially, we considered trees as a data structure that helped us organize data in a certain way, and we introduced recursion as a useful technique in working with these trees. These sorting techniques show that both subjects can be useful in other contexts as well.

## SUMMARY

1. The **tree data structure** allows us to organize data in a hierarchical structure, and this structure is helpful in many applications such as
   a. Representing arithmetic expressions graphically.
   b. Illustrating the moves that can be made in a given situation in a game, and allowing us to analyze various possible moves in a game.
   c. Organizing data for fast retrieval.
2. Conceptually, we can consider three basic types of trees.
   a. In **binary trees,** each node has at most two children, a right child and a left child.
   b. In **ternary trees,** each node has at most three children.
   c. In **general trees,** nodes can have arbitrarily large numbers of children.
3. Beyond the conceptual structure of trees, we can implement trees:

| KEY TERMS, PHRASES, AND CONCEPTS | | ELEMENTS OF PASCAL SYNTAX |
|---|---|---|
| Ancestor | Sibling | *Forward* |
| Branch | Sorting Algorithms | |
| Child | Heap Sort | |
| Efficiency | Quicksort | |
| Leaf | Subtree | |
| Node | Trees | |
| Parent | Binary | |
| Recursion | General | |
| Root | Ternary | |

a. by explicitly declaring a pointer field for each possible child. (For example, binary tree nodes might have left and right pointer fields.)
b. by declaring an array of pointers to specify the children of each node.
c. by organizing the children of each node into a linked list.
d. by placing the elements of a binary tree into an array structure.

4. **Recursion** is a technique in which a function or procedure may call itself. In developing recursive algorithms, we typically
   a. identify and solve simple cases;
   b. reduce harder cases to these simple ones by appropriate function or procedure calls.
5. Recursive algorithms are particularly helpful in working with trees, where we can focus our attention on individual nodes and then ask the computer to repeat the processing for all descendant nodes. Recursion also is useful in solving some puzzles such as the Towers of Hanoi.
6. Both trees and recursion are helpful in developing some new, efficient sorting algorithms.

## EXERCISES

**16.1** a. In the Tree Insertion procedure of Section 16.4, suppose procedure *Insert* is called with the tree shown in Figure 16–7 and with the name Ellen. Describe the sequence of events that results, including all procedure calls and the results of these calls.
b. In the same Tree Insertion procedure, why is the parameter *Base* passed by reference and not by value?

**16.2** *Ordered Binary Tree.* Write a program that performs each of the following tasks.
1. Names can be entered from the keyboard and stored in an ordered binary tree.
2. A specific name, entered by the user, can be searched for on the tree.
3. Names can be printed in alphabetical order.

Include each of these tasks as part of a main menu that drives your program.

**16.3** *Tree Searching.* A tree is defined with the following declarations:

```
Const Length = 3;
Type String = Packed Array [1..Length] of Char;
     NodePtr = ^Node;
     Node = Record
            ChData: String;
            Number: Integer;
            Left: NodePtr;
            Right: NodePtr
            End;
Var Root: NodePtr;
```

Here, *Root* specifies the root node of the tree, and the *Left* and *Right* fields specify the children of each node. (A pointer of *Nil* specifies no offspring.) Write

```
Function Value (Item: String; Base: NodePtr): Integer;
```

which considers a tree, starting at the node specified by *Base*. The function searches this tree for a node where *ChData* matches the given *Item*. When a match is found, the function returns the *Number* at the node. If no match is found, then 0 is returned. For example, consider the tree

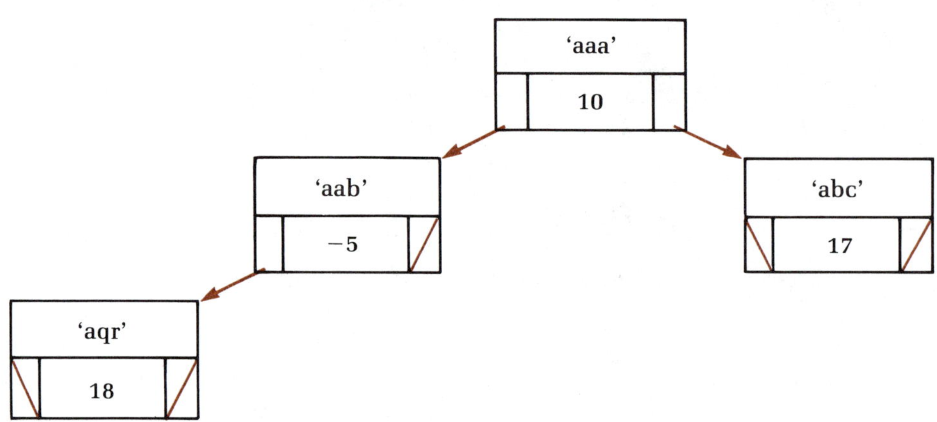


Here, Value ('abc', Root) returns 17, while Value ('cba', Root) returns 0.

HINT: Use recursion.

**16.4** *Printing Leaves.* Using the tree declaration of the previous problem, write

```
Procedure PrintLeaf (Base: NodePtr)
```

which prints out all data at all leaves of the tree with the given *Base*.

**16.5** *Erase a Tree.* Using the declarations for Exercise 16.5, write

```
Procedure Erase (Base: NodePtr)
```

which erases (disposes of) all nodes in the tree with the given *Base*.

HINT: For any node, erase all descendants and then erase the node itself.

**16.6** Consider the following:

```
Program One (Input, Output);
Const Length = 10;
Type NodePtr = ^Node;
     Node = Record
          Text: Packed Array[1..Length] of Char;
          Size: Integer;
          Left, Right: NodePtr
          End;
Var Root: NodePtr;
Procedure Enter;
    Var NewNode: NodePtr;
        Entry: Integer;
  Procedure ReadText (Var Ptr: NodePtr);
      Var Index: Integer;
      Begin
          New(Ptr);
          Index := 0;
          While (Index < Length) and (Not EOLN)
            Do Begin
              Index := Index + 1;
              Read(Ptr^.Text[Index])
            End;
          Readln;
          Ptr^.Size := Index;
          While (Index < Length)
            Do Begin
              Index := Index + 1;
              Ptr^.Text[Index] := Chr(0)
            End;
          Ptr^.Left := Nil;
          Ptr^.Right := Nil
      End {ReadText} ;
  Function First(Node1, Node2: NodePtr): Boolean;
      Begin
          If Node1^.Size <> Node2^.Size
              Then First := (Node1^.Size < Node2^.Size)
              Else First := (Node1^.Text < Node2^.Text)
      End {First} ;
  Procedure EnterNode(Var Base: NodePtr);
      Begin
          If Base = Nil
              Then Base := NewNode
              Else If First (NewNode, Base)
                      Then EnterNode (Base^.Right)
                      Else EnterNode (Base^.Left)
      End {EnterNode} ;
   Begin {Enter}
       Root := Nil;
       Writeln ('Enter Data');
       For Entry := 1 To 10
           Do Begin
               ReadText(NewNode);
               EnterNode(Root)
           End
   End {Enter} ;
```

```
Procedure Print (Base: NodePtr);
    Begin
        If Base^.Left = Nil
            Then Writeln (Base^.Text)
            Else Print (Base^.Left);
        If Base^.Right <> Nil
            Then Print (Base^.Right)
    End {Print} ;

Begin {Main}
    Enter;
    Print (Root)
End {Main} .
```

Suppose this program is run with the following data: ONE, TWO, THREE, FOUR, FIVE, SIX, SEVEN, EIGHT, NINE, and TEN.

**a.** After the entire procedure is completed, describe the data structure pointed to by the variable *Root*. (For instance, draw a picture of the appropriate nodes created with their data, left pointers, and right pointers.)

**b.** What is printed by this program?

**16.7** *Heap Sort Procedure.* Write a procedure which sorts an array using the heap sort algorithm.

**16.8** A list is defined with the following declarations

```
Const Length = 3;
Type String = Packed Array [1..Length] of Char;
     Ptr = ^Item;
     Item = Record
               Data: String;
               Next: Ptr
               End;
Var FirstItem: Ptr;
```

Write

```
Procedure PrintReverse (First: Ptr)
```

which prints out the data in the list of items, from the last item in the list to the *First*.

HINT: Use recursion.

**16.9** *Computing Powers.* In computing $x^n$, where x is any real number and $n$ is a non-negative integer, we can proceed by noting

$$x^0 = 1,$$
$$x^1 = x, \text{ and}$$
$$x^n = x(x^{n-1}), \text{ for } n > 1.$$

**a.** Use this observation to write

```
Function Power (x: Real; n: Integer): Real;
```

which computes $x^n$ using recursion.

**b.** What happens in your function if $N$ is negative? How might you correct this problem for negative values of $N$?

**16.10** *The Fibonacci Sequence.* In the thirteenth century, Leonardo of Pisa, nicknamed Fibonacci, used a simple model to study the breeding of rabbits. In this model, the number of rabbits in one generation is thought to be equal to the number of rabbits in the previous two generations combined. Thus, if $Fib(n)$ is the number of rabbits in the $n$th generation, then Fibonacci's model says that

$$Fib(n) = Fib(n-1) + Fib(n-2).$$

In practice, this same formula turns out to apply in many other situations as well.

Today, we usually start with

$$Fib(1) = Fib(2) = 1$$

(although we might argue that only 1 rabbit in an entire generation would be unlikely to produce offspring). With this start, the first few generations are

1, 1, 2, 3, 5, 8, 13, . . .

**a.** Write

```
Function Fib(N: Integer): Integer
```

which uses the formula (recursively) to compute the $N$th number in the Fibonacci sequence.

**b.** Use your function in part (a) to compute and print all terms of the Fibonacci sequence that do not exceed 1000.

**c.** Let $R$ be the ratio of successive terms in the series, so

$$R = Fib(N)/Fib(N - 1).$$

Modify part (b) so that the ratio $R$ and the expression $(2R - 1)^2$ are also printed for each term.

NOTE: It can be shown that $R$ approaches

$$(1 + \sqrt{5})/2.$$

Thus $(2R - 1)^2$ should approach 5.

**16.11** *Combinations.* In dealing cards, we may ask how many different possible hands we could get. In poker, this is a question of how many ways we can get 5 cards from a 52 card deck. More generally, we can ask how many ways we can select $m$ things from a collection of $n$ objects. In mathematics, this is called the number of combinations of $n$ things, taken $m$ at a time, and we sometimes say "$n$ choose $m$," and write

$$\binom{n}{m}.$$

One can show that

$$\binom{n}{m} = \frac{n!}{m!\,(n - m)!}$$

where $n!$ (or $n$ factorial) is the product

$$n*(n - 1)*(n - 2)* \ldots *3* 2*1$$

In practice, $n!$ can be very large, and this number may be larger than a computer can store. Thus, the computation of these computations is often done following the formulas

$$\binom{n}{0} = \binom{n}{n} = 1$$

$$\binom{n}{m} = \frac{n}{m}\binom{n-1}{m-1} \qquad \text{for } n > 1,\ n > m > 1$$

Write

**Function Comb (M, N: Integer): Integer**

that uses these formulas (with recursion) to compute

$$\binom{n}{m}$$

Apply your function to compute the number of possible poker hands and the number of possible bridge hands.

**16.12** One can show that the number of combinations (mentioned in the previous problem) also satisfies the formulas

$$\binom{n}{0} = \binom{n}{n} = 1$$

$$\binom{n}{m} = \binom{n-1}{m} + \binom{n-1}{m-1} \qquad \text{for } n > 1,\ n > m > 1$$

Revise your function in part (a) to reflect these new formulas.

**16.13** Sometimes, in longer programs, we might want to organize our procedures by placing them in alphabetical order, and in such cases, we may find that we will need to use a procedure before it would normally be declared. In such cases, we must use *Forward* statements, so that procedure headings can be given early in the program, while the main body of the procedure is declared later.

Rewrite the *TaskList* program of Section 15.2 so that the procedures are declared in alphabetical order.

**16.14** Rewrite the recursive *InsertNode* procedure of Section 16.4, by dividing the procedure into two pieces, each of which has one *If–*

*Then–Else* statement. In this revised code, the resulting two procedures will need to call each other.

**16.15** *Tic-Tac-Toe Playing Program.* (A particularly challenging exercise.) Write a program that plays Tic-Tac-Toe. In your program, you may decide to look ahead only a prescribed number of moves in determining the "best" next move.

# APPENDIX A: PASCAL LANGUAGE SUMMARY

This Appendix concisely outlines significant elements of Pascal syntax in pictorial form. The interpretation of this form follows a few simple rules.

For each syntax element, we start at the top left of a picture and follow the arrows. Then, when arrows divide, we may follow any of the possible paths. For example, Section 2.2 stated that an identifier is any sequence of letters and digits starting with a letter. On page 517, the corresponding pictorial specification begins with a LETTER. Then, we can follow the arrows to the end or in a loop for additional DIGITs or LETTERs.

Next, definitions of one syntax element may include references to other elements. For example, on page 516, a PROGRAM starts with the reserved word **program,** followed by the IDENTIFIER just discussed, and possibly a list in parentheses (for Input and Output). Various declarations may follow in a specified order. In this work, each of these separate PARTs are defined as separate syntax elements elsewhere in the Appendix. The PROGRAM concludes with some ACTION elements enclosed within the keywords **begin** and **end**.

Throughout, reserved words are printed in boldface, pre-defined identifiers are in regular lowercase letters without underlining, and syntactical elements are in capital letters and underlined.

Finally, note that this Appendix does not include a few relatively minor Standard Pascal elements, such as the *GoTo* statement of Appendix B and *Variant Records* of Appendix D.

## SECTION A.1 SYNTAX DIAGRAMS FOR REFERENCE

PROGRAM

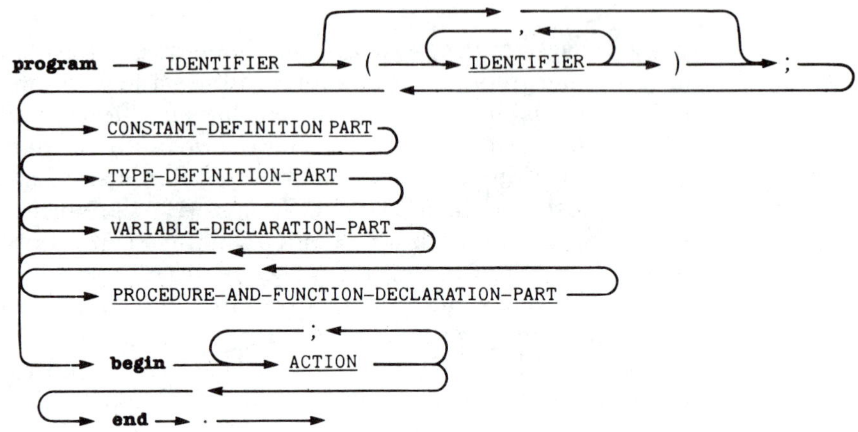


CONSTANT-DEFINITION-PART

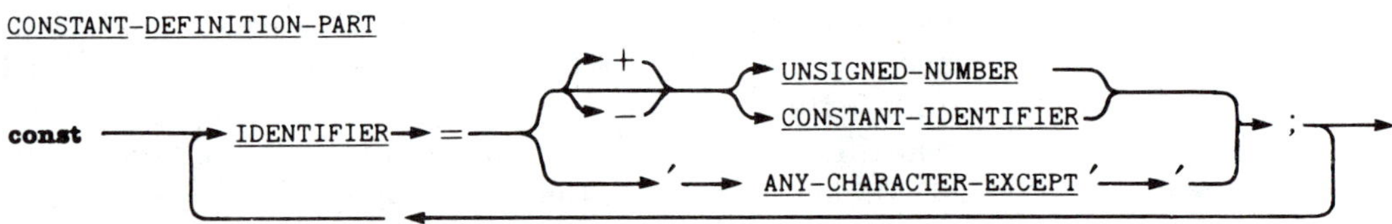


TYPE-DEFINITION-PART

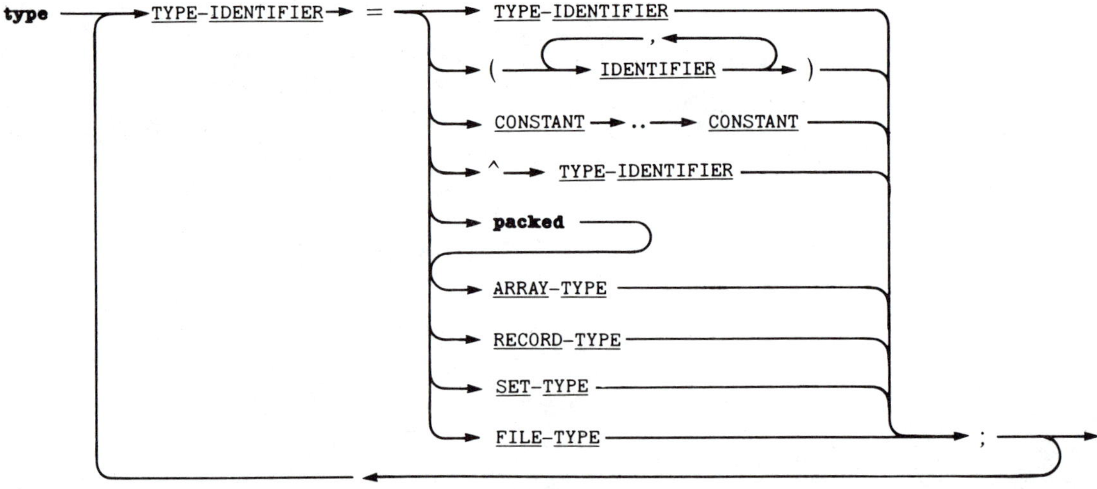

VARIABLE-DECLARATION-PART

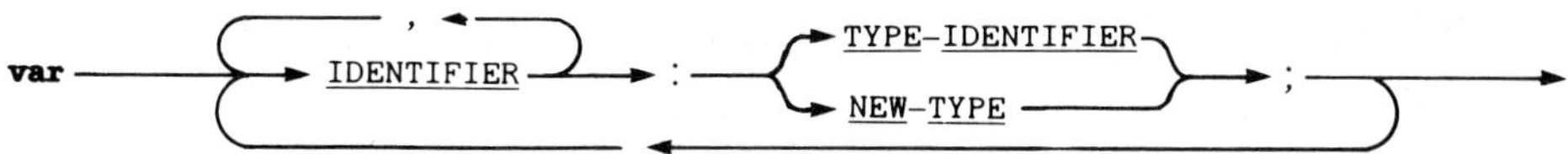


IDENTIFIER

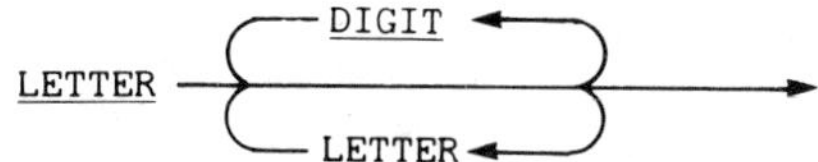


ARRAY-TYPE

array → [ ORDINAL-TYPE , ] → of TYPE-IDENTIFIER NEW-TYPE

RECORD-TYPE

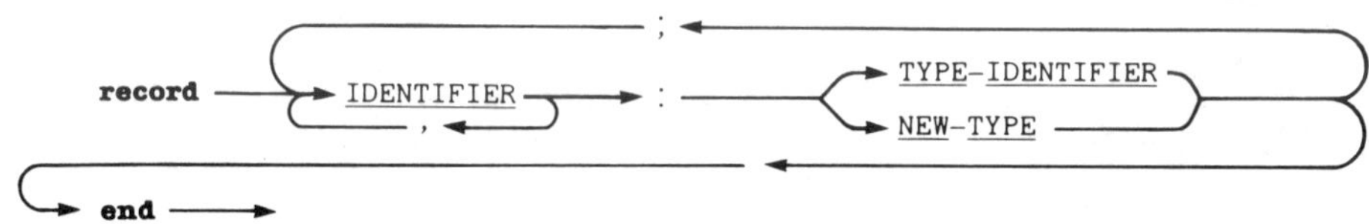


SET-TYPE

set → of ORDINAL-TYPE-IDENTIFIER NEW-ORDINAL-TYPE

NEW-ORDINAL-TYPE

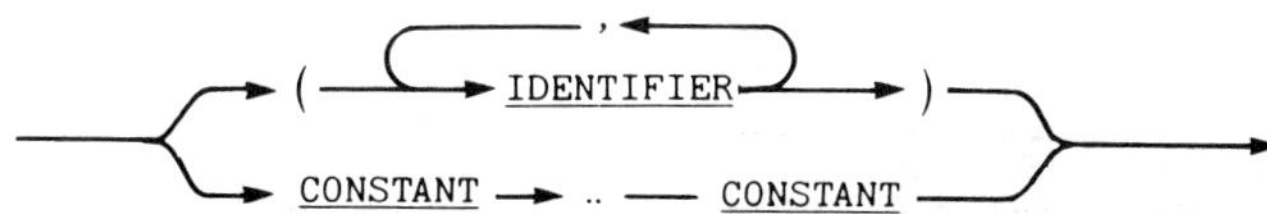

FILE-TYPE

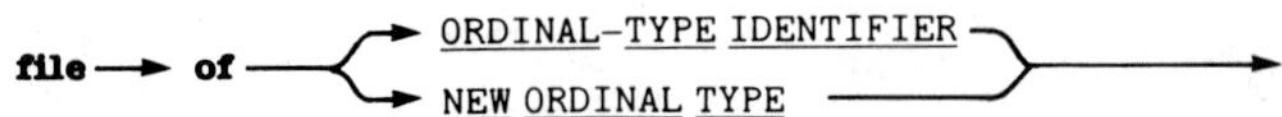


ACTION

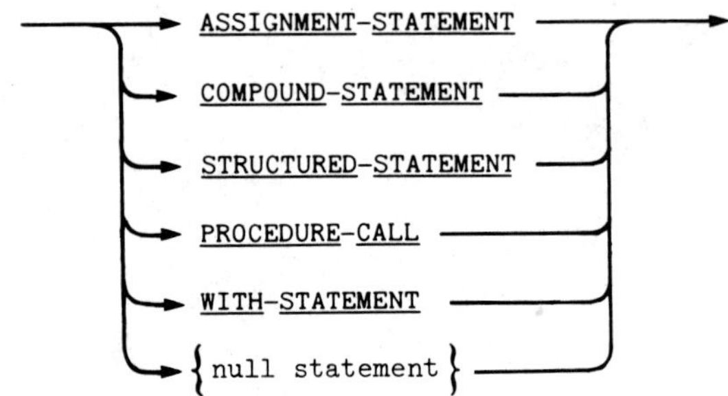


STRUCTURED-STATEMENT

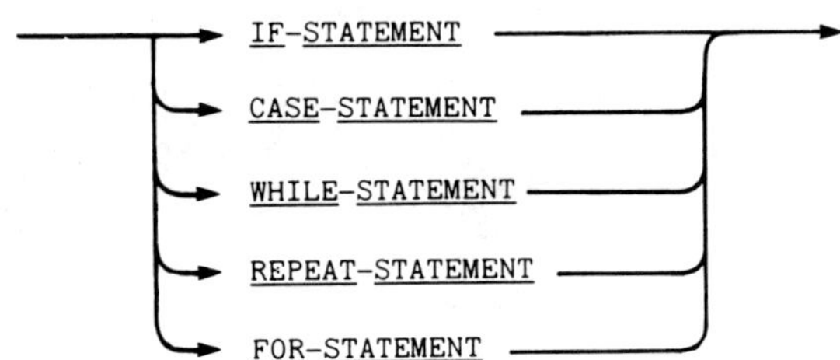


ASSIGNMENT-STATEMENT

IDENTIFIER → := → EXPRESSION →

EXPRESSION

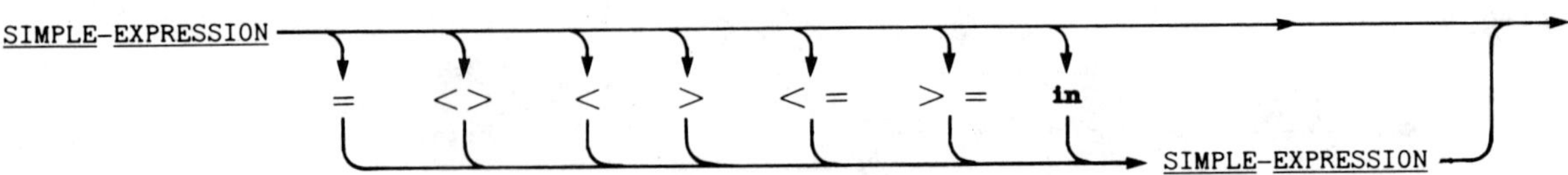

SIMPLE-EXPRESSION

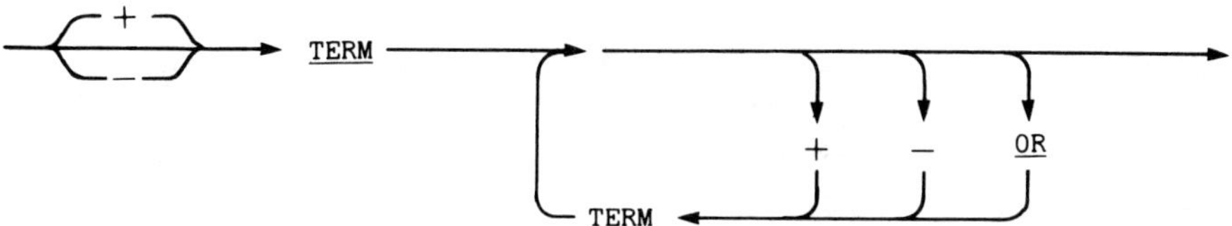


TERM

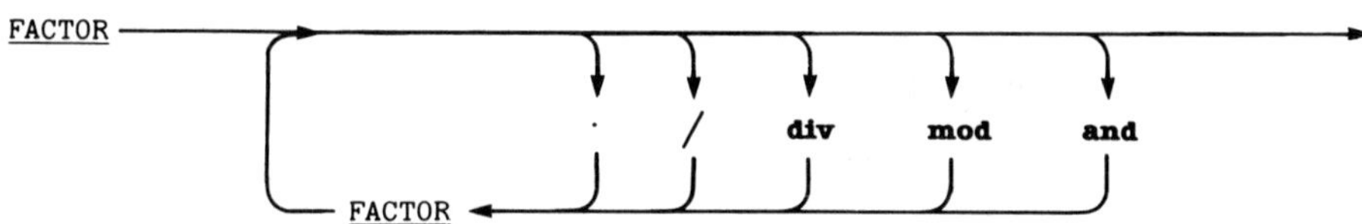


FACTOR

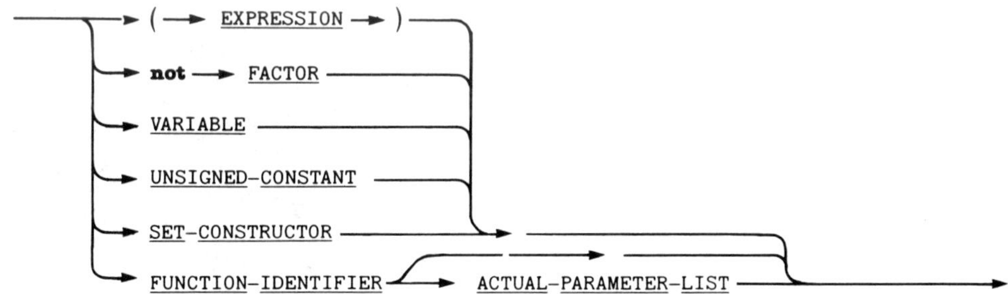


COMPOUND STATEMENT

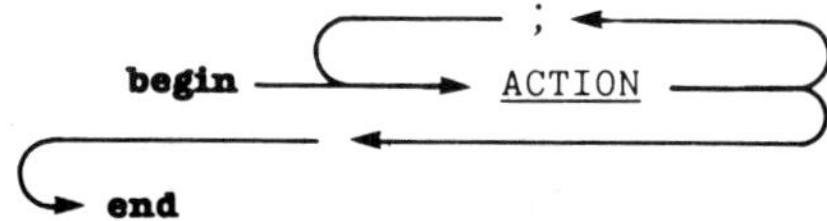

IF STATEMENT

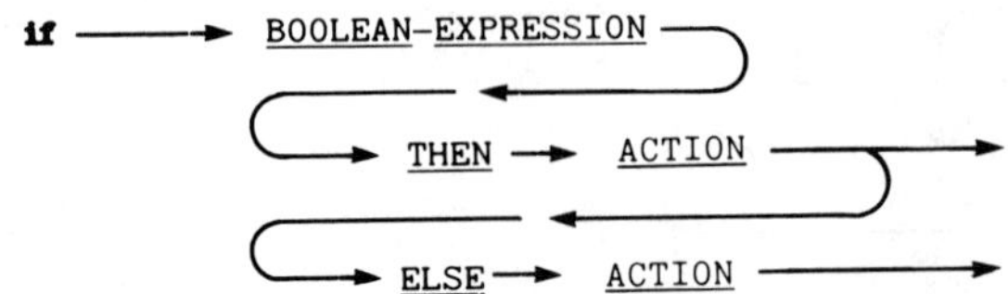


CASE STATEMENT

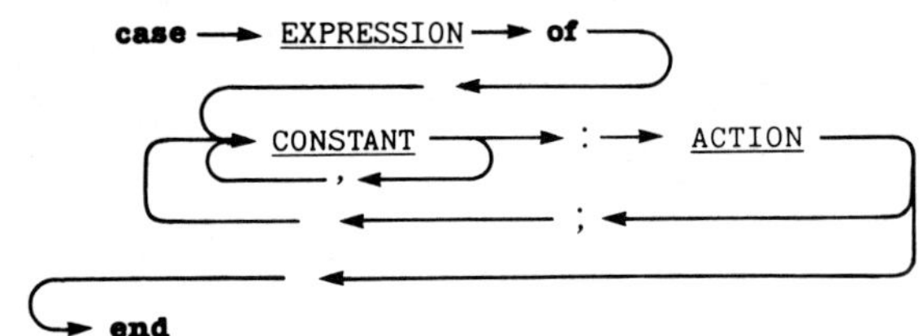


WHILE STATEMENT

while → BOOLEAN-EXPRESSION

do → ACTION

REPEAT STATEMENT

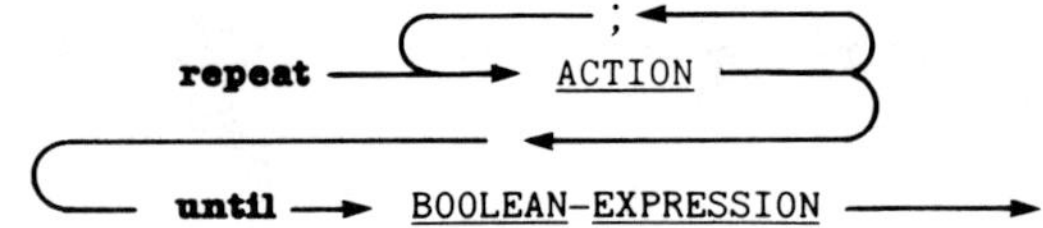


WITH STATEMENT

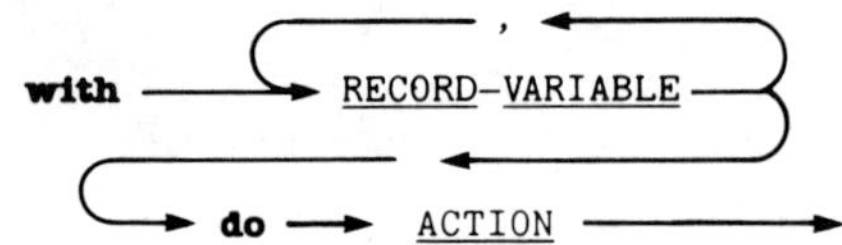

FOR STATEMENT

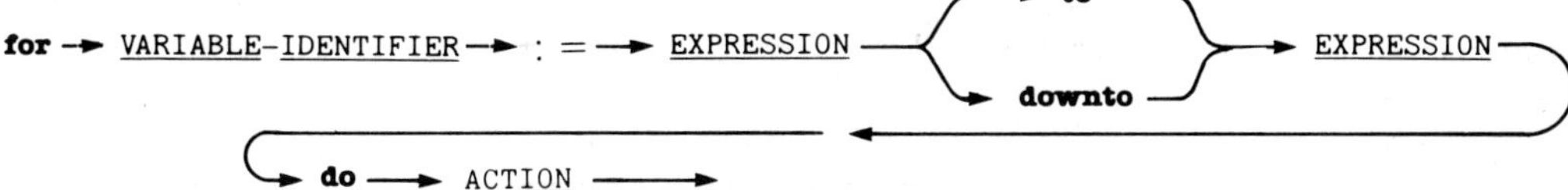


PROCEDURE-CALL

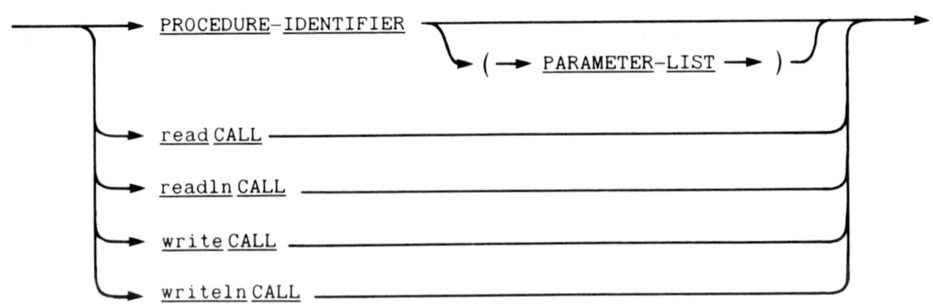


*read* CALL

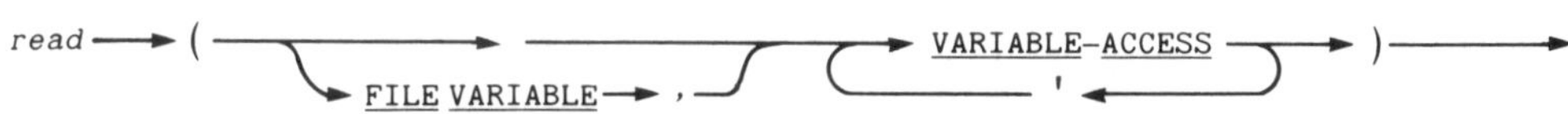


*readln* CALL

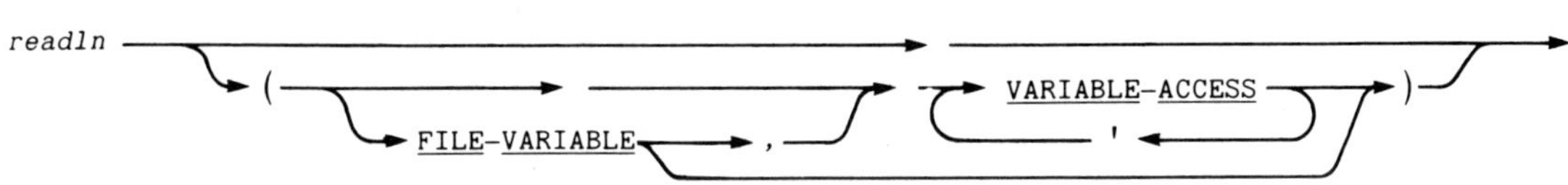


*write*-CALL

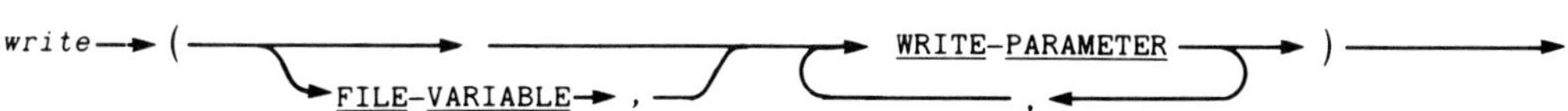

*writeln* CALL

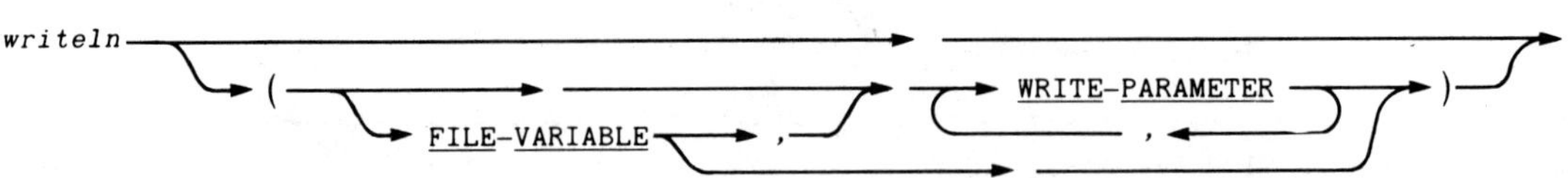


WRITE-PARAMETER

# APPENDIX B: UNCONDITIONAL BRANCHING

In most problem solving, we organize a program in one of several ways, depending on what we wish to do. For example, we may want to perform a sequence of steps, proceeding one step at a time (sequential execution). Alternatively, we may want to repeat certain steps several times (repetitive execution), or we may want to execute some steps only under certain circumstances (conditional execution). For each choice, we use a different structure to organize our program. We organize sequential execution into blocks using procedures and functions; we use *For*, *Repeat*, or *While* loops for repetition; and we use *If* or *Case* statements for conditional execution.

Occasionally, however, our work requires an additional capability. For example, we may need to jump out of the middle of a loop, or we may want to leave the middle of a procedure. Here, we do not intend to return to our current processing at a later time; instead, we want to move directly to a new section of code. Thus, this jump is not the same as a normal procedure or function call where we perform a task and return. Rather, this **unconditional branch** moves us out of our current code, and we will not return later. Unconditional branching breaks the normal flow of program execution.

## Pascal Syntax

When we need to make a jump within our program, we logically must specify where the machine should jump and when the jump should occur. In Pascal, the first of these parts is addressed by labeling a particular statement. Then, we perform the second part with a *GoTo* statement. These points are illustrated in the following program.

```
Program GotoExample (Output);
{This syntactically correct program demonstrates the use
 of the Goto statement}

Label 1;      {"1" will be the label of a statement}

Procedure P;
{We will use a Goto statement to jump out of the middle of this procedure}
    Begin
        Writeln ('Start of Procedure P');

        { . . .  First part of procedure P }

        Goto 1;  {Jump directly from here back to the main program}

        { . . .  Second part of procedure P}

        Writeln ('Normal end of Procedure P');
    End {P} ;
```

```
Begin {Main}
    Writeln ('Start of Program');
    P;
    Writeln ('Line after call to P');
    1: Writeln ('Main Continues');
    Writeln ('End of Program')
End {Main} .
```

When this program is run, we get

```
Start of Program
Start of Procedure P
Main Continues
End of Program
```

This program illustrates the syntax for **unconditional branches,** which consists of three elements: a label declaration, a label within a statement, and a *GoTo* statement. A statement in a Pascal program can be labeled following two steps.

1. We use a *Label* statement in our declarations to indicate that a particular integer will be used as a label. For example,

   ```
   Label 1;
   ```

   indicates that we will use "1" to label a statement within our main program.

   More generally, we can declare any integer in the range 0 . . 9999 as a label in the program. Note that the *Label* statement, if present, is always the first declaration, coming before any constants, types, etc.
2. We label a specific statement by placing the declared number before the statement, followed by a colon. For example, we labeled a *Write* statement by specifying

   ```
   1: Writeln ('Main Continues');
   ```

When a statement is labeled, we can instruct the computer to jump directly from one point in our program to another by writing *GoTo* and the appropriate label. For example, in our sample program,

```
GoTo 1;
```

told the computer to jump out of procedure *P*, back to the designated point in the main program. When a *GoTo* is executed, the machine skips any intervening statements in our code. In our example, the last *Write* statement in procedure *P* was skipped. Similarly, the *Write* statement

```
Writeln ('Line after call to P');
```

was not executed. Rather, the machine returned directly from the procedure to the spot designated by the *GoTo* statement.

With this example, we see that the *GoTo* causes the computer to interrupt its normal flow of execution. Such a jump allows us to skip steps in our program, and occasionally this is very helpful. However, such jumps also can introduce difficulties if the *GoTo* is not carefully controlled.

## Constraints on GoTo Statements

Some of the possible abuses of the *GoTo* are reduced in Pascal by specific restrictions imposed by the Pascal language itself. To illustrate these limitations, we consider several cases where the *GoTo* could yield ambiguous code. We then state the rules in Pascal that address the problem.

The first case where code becomes ambiguous involves variables within loops, since jumping into a loop can cause variables to be undefined. For example, consider the following:

```
Label 2;
   .
   .
   .
Sum := 0.0;
GoTo 2;
For Index := 1 to Max
    Do Begin
       2: Sum := Sum + A[Index]
       End;
```

In this code, the statement

```
For Index := 1 to Max
```

gives *Index* a specific initial value. However, a jump into the middle of such a loop would skip this initialization, so *Index* would not be defined correctly. Thus, our first rule in Pascal becomes:

*Branches into loops (or into any block) are prohibited.*

Pascal allows us to jump out of loops prematurely, but it does not allow us to jump into a loop or a *Begin-End* block.

Another problem occurs when we jump into a procedure or function without allowing the computer to allocate needed space. In addition, needed return addresses cannot be stored. Thus, the second rule in Pascal is:

*Branches into a procedure or function are prohibited.*

Pascal does allow jumps out of procedures, and in such cases, the computer must deallocate any space used for these procedures. For example, in our program *GoTo*, space for procedure *P* is freed when the machine jumps from the middle of *P* back to the main program. However, jumps into a procedure or function are not allowed. (This prohibition also resolves initialization difficulties that might arise if we jumped into a procedure without specifying needed parameters.)

Finally, in coding, we want to avoid "global labels" wherever possible, just as we want to avoid global variables. Instead, labels should be used to designate a point in a particular task; they should not be embedded in the details of the task. Thus, the third rule in Pascal is:

*Labels must be declared at the same level that they are used.*

For example, labels cannot be declared globally and then used to designate a statement in a procedure.

This is the same restriction that we have already discussed in Section 5.4 for control variables. We can declare and use labels or loop control variables within procedures and functions, but our top-down methodology prevents us from declaring them at one level and then using them to specify statements or index loops at a lower level.

# APPENDIX C: THE PACK AND UNPACK PROCEDURES

Chapter 13 introduces the concepts of packed and unpacked arrays, and we find that array declarations can specify how data are to be placed in main memory. When we apply this concept to the actual processing of data, we may want to store data in a packed array most of the time to save space. However, during a brief time during processing, we may need to work with the data in the array a great deal, so we want the data in an unpacked array for efficiency. In this situation, we might move our data from the packed array to the unpacked one first and then move the data back later. We can do this with the *Unpack* and *Pack* procedures.

To illustrate the *Unpack* procedure, suppose we have the unpacked array *U* and the packed array *P* declared as in Figure C–1. Then we may move the data from array *P* to the array *U* with the *Unpack* procedure. Further, since the array *U* has more data elements, we need to specify where to place the first elements of the array *P*. If we want *P*[1] moved to *U*[3], *P*[2] moved to *U*[4], etc., as shown in the figure, then we write

```
Unpack(P, U, 3)
```

More generally, we write

```
Unpack(P, U, S)
```

FIGURE C–1 • **The Unpack Procedure**

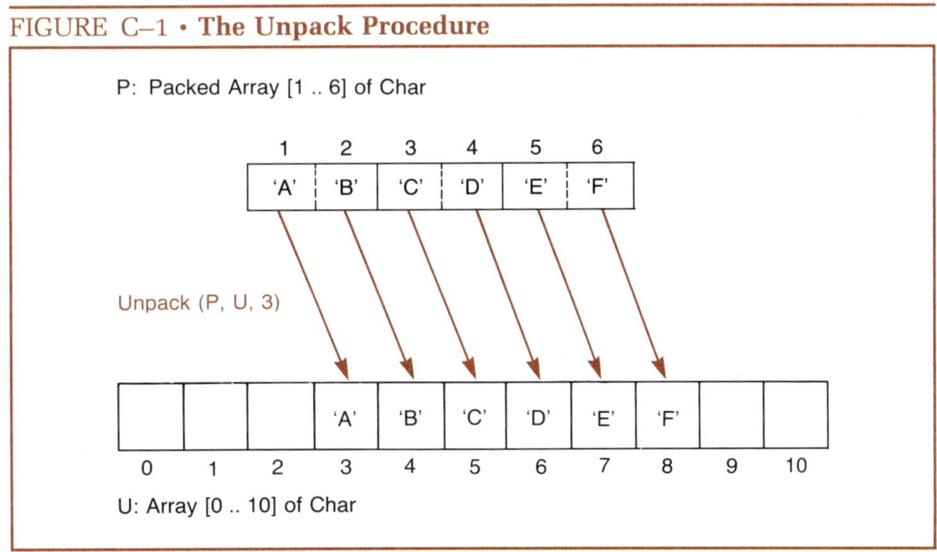

to transfer the data elements in *P* to *U*, where the first element in *P* moves to *U*[S]. Of course, in this case, array *U* must be able to hold at least as many data elements as array *P*.

Similarly, we can move data from the unpacked array *U* to the packed array *P*, although again, we need to specify where the first element of *U* will be placed. If we want this first element moved to *P*[S], then we use the *Pack* procedure with the syntax

```
Pack (U, S, P)
```

In contrast to the *Pack* procedure, when we use *Unpack*, the packed array must contain at least as many data elements as the unpacked array.

# APPENDIX D: VARIANT RECORDS

Chapter 12 introduces the concept of a record that allows us to store several types of information as a single entity. For example, in baseball, we might want to record the following information for a fielder:

```
Type Fielder = Record
           Plays:   Integer;   {Number of fielding plays}
           Errors:  Integer;
           AB:      Integer;   {Number of times at bat}
           Hits:    Integer;
           RBI:     Integer;   {Runs Batted In}
           End;
```

Similarly, for a pitcher, we might want to record:

```
Type Pitcher = Record
           Throws:    Integer;   {Pitches thrown}
           Innings:   Real;      {Innings worked;
                                  can be ⅓ inning}
           Walks:     Integer;
           HitsGiven: Integer;   {Hits given up}
           Runs:      Integer;   {Earned runs given up}
           ERA:       Real       {Earned run average}
           End;
```

However, when we consider the roster of an entire team, we will need to keep track of one type of information for some players and the second type of information for other players. In Pascal, such flexibility is allowed by incorporating a *Case* statement within a declaration using records. For example, in declaring variables for an individual baseball player, we might write the following declarations, which include the fields listed above for fielders and pitchers.

```
Const Max = 15;                 {Maximum length of player's name}
Type Player = Record
           Name: Packed Array [1..Max] of Char;
           Case Pitcher: Boolean of
                True: ( Throws:Integer;
                     Innings:   Real;
                     Walks:     Integer;
                     HitsGiven: Integer;
                     Runs:      Integer;
                     ERA:       Real      );
```

```
        False:   (Plays:Integer;
                 Errors:   Integer;
                 AB:       Integer;
                 Hits:     Integer;
                 RBI:      Integer  )
        End;
Var Individual: Player;
```

In this declaration, an *Individual* may hold different types of data depending upon the value of the *Pitcher* field. Every player has a name, and the name field is part of every player record. Also, for every player, we have a Boolean field *Pitcher* that we will make *True* for pitchers and *False* for fielders. This field is called a ***Tag Field,*** and several names are used for this new type of record, including ***variant records, record variants,*** and ***records with variants.*** Then, the other fields depend upon the value of this Pitcher field. For example, if *Individual.Pitcher* = *True,* then the *Player* record has several fields for pitchers, and we can refer to

```
Individual.Innings
Individual.Walks
```

or

```
Individual.ERA
```

In contrast, if *Individual.Pitcher* = *False,* then these fields are not defined, and instead we can refer to various fielder fields, including

```
Individual.Plays
Individual.AB
```

or

```
Individual.Hits
```

With such variant records, we can use the same variable in different contexts to store different types of data, and we can shift from one type of data to another if we are careful.

For example, the following program contains procedures to read and print data for an individual baseball player.

```
Program ReadAndPrintPlayer (Input, Output);
{This program illustrates the use of variant records by reading
 and printing information about a baseball player.}

Const Max = 15;          {Maximum length of players's name}
```

```
Type Player = Record
     Name: Packed Array [1..Max] of Char;
     Case Pitcher: Boolean of
          True: ( Throws:   Integer;
                  Innings:  Real;
                  Walks:    Integer;
                  HitsGiven:Integer;
                  Runs:     Integer;
                  ERA:      Real     );
          False: (Plays:    Integer;
                  Errors:   Integer;
                  AB:       Integer;
                  Hits:     Integer;
                  RBI:      Integer )
          End;

Function YesAnswer: Boolean;
{This function is true if a user enters 'yes'
 and false if the user types 'no'.}
    Var Ch: Char;
        YOrN: Boolean;
    Begin
        Repeat
            Readln (Ch);
            YOrN := (Ch In ['y', 'Y', 'n', 'N']);
            If Not YOrN
                Then Write ('Please answer "Yes" or "No": ')
        Until YOrN;
        YesAnswer := (Ch In ['y', 'Y'])
    End {YesAnswer} ;

Procedure EnterData (Var Ind: Player);
{This procedure reads data for an individual player}
    Var Index: Integer;
    Begin
        Writeln ('Please enter the data on an individual player:');

        {Enter player's name}
        Index := 0;
        Write ('Enter player''s name: ');
        While (Not Eoln) And (Index < Max)
          Do Begin
            Index := Index + 1;
            Read (Ind.Name[Index])
          End;
        While (Index < Max)
          Do Begin
            Index := Index + 1;
            Ind.Name[Index] := Chr(0)
          End;
        Readln;

        {Determine if Player is a Pitcher}
        Write ('Is this player a pitcher? ');
        Ind.Pitcher := YesAnswer;
```

```
        If Ind.Pitcher
            Then Begin {Enter Pitcher Data}
                Write ('Enter number of pitches thrown: ');
                Readln (Ind.Throws);
                Write ('Enter number of innings pitched: ');
                Readln (Ind.Innings);
                Write ('Enter number of walks given up: ');
                Readln (Ind.Walks);
                Write ('Enter number of hits allowed: ');
                Readln (Ind.HitsGiven);
                Write ('Enter number of runs given up: ');
                Readln (Ind.Runs);
                Write ('Enter earned run average: ');
                Readln (Ind.ERA)
                End {Pitcher Data}
            Else Begin {Enter Fielder Data}
                Write ('Enter number of fielding plays: ');
                Readln (Ind.Plays);
                Write ('Enter number of errors committed: ');
                Readln (Ind.Errors);
                Write ('Enter number of times at bat: ');
                Readln (Ind.AB);
                Write ('Enter number of hits made: ');
                Readln (Ind.Hits);
                Write ('Enter number of runs batted in: ');
                Readln (Ind.RBI)
                End {Fielder Data}

    End {EnterData} ;


Procedure PrintData (Var Ind: Player);
{This procedure prints data for an individual player}
    Begin
        Writeln;
        Writeln ('Player:  ', Ind.Name);
        If Ind.Pitcher
            Then Begin
                Writeln ('       Position   Pitches   Innings     Walks ',
                         '    Hits      Runs');
                Writeln ('         Played     Thrown    Worked    Allowed',
                         '   Allowed   Allowed    ERA');
                Writeln ('         Pitcher', Ind.Throws:8, Ind.Innings:10:2,
                          Ind.Walks:10, Ind.HitsGiven:10, Ind.Runs:10,
                          Ind.ERA:10:2)
                End
            Else Begin
                Writeln ('       Position     Plays    Errors    At Bats',
                         '      Hits     RBI''s');
                Writeln ('         Fielder', Ind.Plays:8, Ind.Errors:10,
                         Ind.AB:10, Ind.Hits:10, Ind.RBI:10)
                End;
        Writeln

    End {PrintData} ;
```

```
Procedure ControlProcessing;
{This procedure organizes the reading and writing of player information}
    Var Individual: Player;
    Begin
        Repeat
            EnterData (Individual);
            PrintData (Individual);
            Write ('Do you want to continue with another player? ')
        Until Not YesAnswer
    End {ControlProcessing} ;
Begin {Main}
    Writeln ('This program reads and prints information ',
             'on baseball players.');
    ControlProcessing
End {Main} .
```

When this program is run on some sample data, we get the following output.

```
This program reads and prints information on baseball players.
Please enter the data on an individual player:
Enter player's name: Al L. Wright
Is this player a pitcher? Yes
Enter number of pitches thrown: 67
Enter number of innings pitched: 4.33
Enter number of walks given up: 3
Enter number of hits allowed: 15
Enter number of runs given up: 6
Enter earned run average: 1.04

Player:  Al L. Wright
       Position   Pitches   Innings     Walks     Hits      Runs
        Played     Thrown    Worked    Allowed   Allowed   Allowed   ERA
        Pitcher     67       4.33        3        15         6      1.04

Do you want to continue with another player? yes
Please enter the data on an individual player:
Enter player's name: I. Ron Smith
Is this player a pitcher? no
Enter number of fielding plays: 8
Enter number of errors committed: 2
Enter number of times at bat: 12
Enter number of hits made: 2
Enter number of runs batted in: 1

Player:  I. Ron Smith
       Position      Plays    Errors    At Bats     Hits     RBI's
        Fielder        8         2        12          2        1

Do you want to continue with another player? No
```

In this program, we see that the tag field allows us to work with different types of data in different contexts, and we can organize our program to take advantage of whichever type of data is needed at a particular time. More generally, a tag field may contain any ordinal type of data; we just need to specify the possible tag field values within record's *Case* statement. Then for each tag field value, we need to list the desired record fields for our data.

# APPENDIX E: STYLE SUMMARY AND CHECKLIST

## SECTION E.1 PROGRAM FORMAT, STYLE, AND READABILITY

| Never 1 | Sometimes 2 | Almost Always 3 | Always 4 | |
|---|---|---|---|---|
| | | | | **Structure** |
| ___ | ___ | ___ | ___ | Program divided into appropriate functions and procedures. |
| ___ | ___ | ___ | ___ | Procedures and functions of appropriate length and complexity. |
| | | | | **Comments** |
| ___ | ___ | ___ | ___ | Program and each function and procedure begin with appropriate comments describing purpose. |
| ___ | ___ | ___ | ___ | Other comments added as needed to interpret program. |
| ___ | ___ | ___ | ___ | Comments aid program readability. |
| | | | | **Variables and Parameters** |
| ___ | ___ | ___ | ___ | Descriptive identifiers used. |
| ___ | ___ | ___ | ___ | Variables initialized. |
| ___ | ___ | ___ | ___ | Use of global variables minimized. |
| ___ | ___ | ___ | ___ | Parameters used effectively to control passage of data in and out of procedures and functions. |
| | | | | **Format and Statement Use** |
| ___ | ___ | ___ | ___ | Program easy to read and understand. |
| ___ | ___ | ___ | ___ | Indenting helps clarify program logic and readability. |
| ___ | ___ | ___ | ___ | Appropriate selection of repetitive statements (For, Repeat, While). |
| ___ | ___ | ___ | ___ | Appropriate use of conditionals (If, Case, Boolean expressions). |
| | | | | **Input and Output Format** |
| ___ | ___ | ___ | ___ | User reminded what input is required. |

| Never 1 | Sometimes 2 | Almost Always 3 | Always 4 | |
|---|---|---|---|---|
| ___ | ___ | ___ | ___ | Output labeled clearly. |
| ___ | ___ | ___ | ___ | Output put in columns when appropriate. |
| ___ | ___ | ___ | ___ | Input and output neat; not cluttered. |
| | | | | **Testing** |
| ___ | ___ | ___ | ___ | Test cases appropriate to the problem. |
| ___ | ___ | ___ | ___ | A sufficient number of test cases considered. |
| ___ | ___ | ___ | ___ | Hand calculations provided when appropriate. |
| | | | | **Algorithm Design and Correctness** |
| ___ | ___ | ___ | ___ | Program meets specifications of problem. |
| ___ | ___ | ___ | ___ | Algorithms used correctly solve problem. |
| ___ | ___ | ___ | ___ | Algorithms used are sufficiently efficient. |

## SECTION E.2 OVERALL STYLE AND FORMAT

| Bad 1 | 2 | 3 | 4 | Good 5 | |
|---|---|---|---|---|---|
| ___ | ___ | ___ | ___ | ___ | Program |
| ___ | ___ | ___ | ___ | ___ | Input and Output |
| ___ | ___ | ___ | ___ | ___ | Testing |
| ___ | ___ | ___ | ___ | ___ | Algorithms |

# INDEX

## OPERATIONS AND PRECEDENCE RULES

Operations are arranged in groups according to precedence. Within each group, operations have the same precedence, and evaluation proceeds from left to right.

| Operation | Type of Arguments | Type of Result | Description |
|---|---|---|---|
| *Highest Precedence* | | | |
| Not | Boolean | Boolean | Logical Negation |
| *Second Highest Precedence* | | | |
| * | Integer or real | (1) | Multiplication |
| * | Set (2) | Set | Intersection |
| / | Integer or real | Real | Real division |
| Div | Integer | Integer | Integer quotient |
| Mod | Integer | Integer | Integer remainder |
| And | Boolean | Boolean | Logical "and" |

*Notes:*

1. Result is integer if both arguments are integer; Result is Real otherwise.
2. Arguments are sets of the same type; Result also has the same set type.